To All the World

FARMS Publications

Teachings of the Book of Mormon

The Geography of Book of Mormon Events: A Source Book

The Book of Mormon Text Reformatted according to Parallelistic Patterns

Eldin Ricks's Thorough Concordance of the LDS Standard Works

A Guide to Publications on the Book of Mormon: A Selected Annotated Bibliography

Book of Mormon Authorship Revisited: The Evidence for Ancient Origins

Ancient Scrolls from the Dead Sea: Photographs and Commentary on a Unique Collection of Scrolls

LDS Perspectives on the Dead Sea Scrolls

Isaiah in the Book of Mormon

King Benjamin's Speech: "That Ye May Learn Wisdom"

Mormons, Scripture, and the Ancient World: Studies in Honor of John L. Sorenson

Latter-day Christianity: Ten Basic Issues

Illuminating the Sermon at the Temple and Sermon on the Mount

Scripture Study: Tools and Suggestions

Finding Biblical Hebrew and Other Ancient Literary Forms in the Book of Mormon

Charting the Book of Mormon: Visual Aids for Personal Study and Teaching

Pressing Forward with the Book of Mormon: The FARMS Updates of the 1990s

King Benjamin's Speech Made Simple

Periodicals

Insights: A Window on the Ancient World

FARMS Review of Books

Journal of Book of Mormon Studies

Reprint Series

Book of Mormon Authorship: New Light on Ancient Origins

The Doctrine and Covenants by Themes

Offenders for a Word

Ancient Texts and Mormon Studies

Romans 1: Notes and Reflections

Temples through the Ages

Temples of the Ancient World

The Temple in Time and Eternity

Copublished with Deseret Book Company

An Ancient American Setting for the Book of Mormon

Warfare in the Book of Mormon

By Study and Also by Faith: Essays in Honor of Hugh W. Nibley

The Sermon at the Temple and the Sermon on the Mount

Rediscovering the Book of Mormon

Reexploring the Book of Mormon

Of All Things! Classic Quotations from Hugh Nibley

The Allegory of the Olive Tree

Expressions of Faith: Testimonies from LDS Scholars

Feasting on the Word: The Literary Testimony of the Book of Mormon

The Collected Works of Hugh Nibley

Old Testament and Related Studies

Enoch the Prophet

The World and the Prophets

Mormonism and Early Christianity

Lehi in the Desert; The World of the Jaredites; There Were Jaredites

An Approach to the Book of Mormon

Since Cumorah

The Prophetic Book of Mormon

Approaching Zion

The Ancient State

Tinkling Cymbals and Sounding Brass

Temple and Cosmos

Brother Brigham Challenges the Saints

Published through Research Press

Pre-Columbian Contact with the Americas across the Oceans: An Annotated Bibliography

A Comprehensive Annotated Book of Mormon Bibliography

New World Figurine Project, vol. 1

Images of Ancient America: Visualizing Book of Mormon Life

Chiasmus in Antiquity (reprint)

Chiasmus Bibliography

Publications of the FARMS Center for the Preservation of Ancient Religious Texts (CPART)

Islamic Translation Series

The Incoherence of the Philosophers

The Niche of Lights

The Philosophy of Illumination

Dead Sea Scrolls Electronic Reference Library

To All the World

The Book of Mormon Articles
from the *Encyclopedia of Mormonism*

Selected by
Daniel H. Ludlow, S. Kent Brown, and John W. Welch

The Foundation for Ancient Research
and Mormon Studies (FARMS)
at Brigham Young University
Provo, Utah

The Foundation for Ancient Research and Mormon Studies (FARMS)
at Brigham Young University
Provo, Utah 84602

Library of Congress Cataloging-in-Publication Data

Encyclopedia of Mormonism. Selections.
    To all the world : the Book of Mormon articles from the Encyclopedia of Mormonism /
selected by Daniel H. Ludlow, S. Kent Brown, and John W. Welch.
        p. cm.
    Includes bibliographical references and index.
    ISBN 0-934893-47-0 (alk. paper)
    1. Book of Mormon—Encyclopedias. I. Ludlow, Daniel H. II. Brown, S. Kent. III.
Welch, John W. (John Woodland) IV. Title.

BX8627.A1 E532 2000
289.3′22′03—dc21
                                                            99-058964

CONTENTS

1992 Editorial Board

Preface

According to standard definition, an encyclopedia is a work designed to "treat comprehensively all the various branches of knowledge" pertaining to a particular subject. The subject of this collection of reprints from Macmillan's *Encyclopedia of Mormonism* (1992) is the Book of Mormon, a key scripture of The Church of Jesus Christ of Latter-day Saints. The *Encyclopedia*, as well as this new spin-off volume, is intended for all kinds of readers, young and old, novices and experts, Latter-day Saints and those of other faiths. Readers will find concise articles about the contents, peoples, teachings, and coming forth of the Book of Mormon, although no article is exhaustive because of space limitations. Most articles include a BIBLIOGRAPHY; some of these have been expanded to include ADDITIONAL SOURCES on the Book of Mormon since the *Encyclopedia's* bibliography was compiled. Where a few inconsistencies and inaccuracies occurred in the original, we have silently corrected these. Otherwise the text remains untouched. Cross-references to other articles in the *Encyclopedia* are indicated when relevant by small capital letters.

For further study on many topics, please see the original four volumes of the *Encyclopedia*. The first of those volumes contains a list of contributors and their institutional affiliations, as well as a helpful synoptic outline. Additionally, volume four includes thirteen appendixes ranging from a chronology of church history to letters from the First Presidency. Beyond those acknowledged in the full edition of the *Encyclopedia,* we wish to thank Wendy H. Christian for her extensive help in the production of this volume.

Lest the role of this reprint of the *Encyclopedia* be given more weight than it deserves, the current editors make it clear that those who have written and edited these materials have tried only to explain their understanding of church history, doctrines, and procedures; their statements and opinions remain their own. The contents of this reprint do not necessarily represent the official position of The Church of Jesus Christ of Latter-day Saints, Brigham Young University, or the Foundation for Ancient Research and Mormon Studies. It is hoped that these materials, conveniently gathered under one cover, will serve as a valuable introduction to the Book of Mormon, leading readers into its pages and especially into its covenantal testament of and with the Savior Jesus Christ.

LIST OF ARTICLES

ENTRIES BY CATEGORY

II. Books of the Book of Mormon

III. Studies of the Book of Mormon

IV. TEACHINGS FROM THE BOOK OF MORMON

V. Coming Forth of the Book of Mormon

Key to Abbreviations

AF	Talmage, James E. *Articles of Faith*. Salt Lake City, 1890. (All references are to pagination in printings before 1960).
CHC	*Comprehensive History of the Church*, 6 vols., ed. B. H. Roberts. Salt Lake City, 1930.
CR	*Conference Reports*. Salt Lake City, 1898–.
CWHN	Collected Works of Hugh Nibley, ed. S. Ricks, J. Welch, et al. Salt Lake City, 1985–.
Dialogue	*Dialogue: A Journal of Mormon Thought*, 1965–.
DS	Smith, Joseph Fielding. *Doctrines of Salvation*, 3 vols. Salt Lake City, 1954–1956.
FARMS	Foundation for Ancient Research and Mormon Studies. Provo, Utah.
HC	*History of the Church*, 7 vols., ed. B. H. Roberts. Salt Lake City, 1st ed., 1902; 2nd ed., 1950. (All references are to pagination in the 2nd edition.)
HDC	Historical Department of the Church, Salt Lake City.
IE	*Improvement Era*, 1897–1970.
JC	Talmage, James E. *Jesus the Christ*. Salt Lake City, 1915.
JD	*Journal of Discourses*, 26 vols., ed. J. Watt. Liverpool, 1854–1886.
MD	McConkie, Bruce R. *Mormon Doctrine*, 2nd ed. Salt Lake City, 1966.
MFP	*Messages of the First Presidency*, 5 vols., ed. J. Clark. Salt Lake City, 1965–1975.
PJS	*Papers of Joseph Smith*, ed. D. Jessee. Salt Lake City, 1989.
PWJS	*The Personal Writings of Joseph Smith*, ed. D. Jessee. Salt Lake City, 1984.
T&S	*Times and Seasons*, 1839–1846.
TPJS	*Teachings of the Prophet Joseph Smith*, comp. Joseph Fielding Smith. Salt Lake City, 1938.
WJS	*Words of Joseph Smith*, ed. A. Ehat and L. Cook. Provo, Utah, 1980.

KEY TO SCRIPTURES

Book of Mormon

1 Ne.	1 Nephi
2 Ne.	2 Nephi
Jacob	Jacob
Enos	Enos
Jarom	Jarom
Omni	Omni
W of M	Words of Mormon
Mosiah	Mosiah
Alma	Alma
Hel.	Helaman
3 Ne.	3 Nephi
4 Ne.	4 Nephi
Morm.	Mormon
Ether	Ether
Moro.	Moroni

Doctrine and Covenants

D&C	Doctrine and Covenants

Pearl of Great Price

Moses	Moses
Abr.	Abraham
JS—M	Joseph Smith—Matthew
JS—H	Joseph Smith—History
A of F	Articles of Faith

ABINADI

Abinadi was a courageous prophet (150 B.C.), and the best known martyr in the Book of Mormon. His ministry and execution recounted at the heart of the Book of Mosiah sharpen the contrast between righteous King BENJAMIN and wicked King Noah. ALMA₁, a converted eyewitness, recorded Abinadi's main words shortly after they were spoken (Mosiah 17:4).

Abinadi belonged to a small group of reactionary NEPHITES who had returned from Zarahemla a generation earlier to repossess from the LAMANITES the city of Nephi, the traditional Nephite capital, and its temple. When the excesses of the apostate Nephite king and priests grew intolerable, Abinadi was commanded of the Lord to denounce publicly their abominations; he prophesied their coming captivity and affliction. Abinadi was condemned to death by Noah for this, but escaped.

Where he lived in exile is unknown. Similarities between his and Benjamin's words (cf. Mosiah 16:1; 3:20; 16:5; 2:38; 16:10–11; 3:24–25) could mean that he spent some time in Zara-hemla with King Benjamin and his people (W of M 1:16–17), or received similar revelation during this period.

After two years, having been commanded again by the Lord to prophesy, Abinadi reentered the city of Nephi in disguise. Before a crowd, he pronounced a curse in the name of the Lord upon the unrepentant people, their land, and their grain, with forthright predictions of destruction and humiliating bondage, reminiscent of Israel's suffering in Egypt. In a potent curse, like those used in the ancient Near East to condemn covenant breakers, he testified that Noah's life would "be valued even as a garment in a hot furnace" (Mosiah 12:3).

Abinadi was apprehended by the people, bound, delivered to Noah, and accused of lying about the king and prophesying falsely. Both accusations were violations under their law, the LAW OF MOSES (Mosiah 13:23; Ex. 20:16; Deut. 18:20–22). The dual nature of the charges appears to have complicated the ensuing trial, the king typically having jurisdiction over political charges and the priests over religious matters.

The trial first focused on the charge of

false prophecy. The priests challenged Abinadi to interpret Isaiah 52:7–10. They presumably thought this text showed that God had spoken "comfort" to their own people, who had seen the land "redeemed." They contended that whereas Isaiah extolled those who brought "good tidings," Abinadi spoke ill. Under such interpretation, Abinadi's curses conflicted with Isaiah and were held by the priests to be false and unlawful (Mosiah 12:20–24).

Abinadi rebutted the priests in several ways. He accused them of misunderstanding and disobeying the law. He extracted from them an admission that salvation requires obedience to the law and then rehearsed to them the Ten Commandments, the basic law of the covenant that they had not kept. He miraculously withstood the king's attempt to silence him, "and his face shone with exceeding luster, even as Moses' did while in the mount of Sinai" (Mosiah 13:5). He then quoted Isaiah 53 and explained its relation to the coming Messiah.

Abinadi's prophetic words are among the most powerful in the Book of Mormon. He explained the "form" and coming of God mentioned in Isaiah 52:14 and 53:2 (Mosiah 13:34; 14:2) as the coming of a son in the flesh, thus "being the Father and the Son" (Mosiah 15:1–5). He also taught that God would suffer as the "sheep before her shearers" (Isa. 53:7; Mosiah 14:7). Abinadi was then in a position to answer the priests' question about Isaiah 52:7–10. He proclaimed that those "who shall declare his generation" (cf. Mosiah 15:10) and "[publish] peace" (Mosiah 15:14) are God's prophets and that they and all who hearken unto their words are his "seed" (Mosiah 15:11, 13). They are the ones who truly bring "good tidings" of salvation, redemption, comfort through Christ, and the reign of God at the Judgment Day.

Using Isaiah's text, Abinadi showed that God could not redeem Noah's people who had willfully rebelled against deity, and that true redemption comes only through repentance and acceptance of Christ. He also showed that his prophecies did not contradict the Isaiah text quoted by the priests.

Noah desired that Abinadi should be put to death, evidently on the charge of bearing false witness against him as the king. A young priest named Alma valiantly attested to the truthfulness of Abinadi's testimony, whereupon he was expelled and the trial recessed for three days while Abinadi was held in prison.

When the trial reconvened, Abinadi was presumably accused of blasphemy (Mosiah 17:8), another capital offense under the law of Moses (Lev. 24:10–16). Noah gave him the opportunity to recant, but Abinadi refused to change God's message, even on threats of death.

Noah was intimidated and desired to release Abinadi. The priests, however, accused Abinadi of a fourth crime, that of reviling against the king (Mosiah 17:12; Ex. 22:28). On this ground Noah condemned Abinadi, and his priestly accusers scourged and burned him. It was normal under Mosaic law for the accusers to inflict the punishment, but burning was an extraordinary form of execution. It mirrored Abinadi's alleged crime: he was burned just as he had said Noah's life would be valued as a garment in a furnace. As Abinadi died, he prophesied that the same fate would befall his accusers. This prophecy was soon fulfilled (Mosiah 17:15–18; 19:20; Alma 25:7–12).

Abinadi was remembered by the Nephites in at least three roles:

1. To Alma, his main convert, Abinadi was a prophet of Christ. Alma taught Abinadi's words concerning the death and resur-

rection of Christ, the RESURRECTION of the dead, the redemption of God's people (Mosiah 18:1–2), and the mighty change of heart through their conversion (Alma 5:12). Through Alma's descendants, Abinadi influenced the Nephites for centuries.

2. To Ammon, who beheld the martyrdom of 1,005 of his own converts (Alma 24:22), Abinadi was recalled as the prime martyr "because of his belief in God" (Alma 25:11; cf. Mosiah 17:20; see also Mosiah 7:26–28). This was recognized as the real reason for Abinadi's death, since the priests' charge of reviling proved to be a false pretext.

3. To MORMON, who witnessed the decadence and destruction of the Nephites 500 years later, Abinadi was remembered for prophesying that because of wickedness evil would come upon the land and that the wicked would be utterly destroyed (Morm. 1:19; cf. Mosiah 12:7–8).

BIBLIOGRAPHY

Welch, John W. "Judicial Process in the Trial of Abinadi." Provo, Utah: FARMS, 1981.

ADDITIONAL SOURCE

Matthews, Robert J. "Abinadi: Prophet and Martyr." *Ensign*, April 1992, 25–30.

LEW W. CRAMER

ALLEGORY OF ZENOS

The Allegory of Zenos (Jacob 5) is a lengthy, prophetic declaration made by ZENOS, a Hebrew prophet, about the destiny of the house of Israel. Evidently copied directly from the plates of brass into the Book of Mormon record by JACOB, it was intended (1) to reinforce Jacob's own teachings both about Jesus Christ ("We knew of Christ, and we had a hope of his glory many hundred years be-

fore his coming"—Jacob 4:4) and about the house of Israel's anticipated unresponsiveness toward the coming Redeemer ("I perceive . . . they will reject the stone upon which they might build and have safe foundation"—Jacob 4:15); and (2) to instruct his people about the promised future regathering of Israel, to which Jacob's people belonged.

Framed in the tradition of parables, the allegory "likens" the house of Israel to an olive tree whose owner struggles to keep it from dying. The comparison figuratively illustrates God's bond with his chosen people and with the Gentiles and underscores the lesson that through patience and compassion God will save and preserve the compliant and obedient.

The narrative contains seventy-six verses, divisible into five parts, all tied together by an overarching theme of good winning over bad, of life triumphing over death. In the first part, an alarmed owner, recognizing threatening signs of death (age and decay) in a beloved tree of superior quality, immediately tries to nurse it back to health (verses 3–5). Even though new growth appears, his ministering does not fully heal the tree; and so, with a servant's help, he removes and destroys waning parts and in their place grafts limbs from a "wild" tree. At the same time, he detaches the old tree's "young and tender" new growth for planting in secluded areas of his property. Though disappointed, he resolves to save his beloved tree (verses 6–14).

Second, following a lengthy interval of conscientious care, the owner's labor is rewarded with a generous harvest of choice fruit, not only from the newly grafted limbs on his old tree but also from the new growth that he planted around the property. These latter trees, however, have produced unequally: the two trees with the least natural advantages have the highest, positive yield;

while the most advantaged tree's production is only half good, compelling removal of its unprofitable parts. Even so, the owner continues an all-out effort on every tree, even this last one (verses 15–28).

In the third part, a long time passes. The owner and the servant return again to measure and evaluate the fruit, only to learn the worst: the old tree, though healthy, has produced a completely worthless crop; and it is the same for the other trees. Distressed, the owner orders all the trees destroyed. His assistant pleads for him to forbear a little longer. In the fourth segment, the "grieved" owner, accompanied by the servant and other workers, carefully tries again in one last effort. Together they reverse the previous implantation (the "young and tender" plants are returned to the old tree) and splice other old tree limbs into the previously selected trees, appropriately pruning, cultivating, and nurturing each tree as required (verses 29–73). This particular operation of mixing and blending, mingling and merging all the trees together, meets with success in replicating the superior quality crop of "natural fruit" everywhere on his property. Elated, he promises his helpers a share ("joy") in the harvest for as long as it lasts. But he also pledges destruction of all the trees if and when their capacity for a positive yield wanes again (verses 73–77).

In the subsequent chapter Jacob renders a brief interpretation (6:1–4). Conscious that his people, the Nephites, branched from the house of Israel, he is particularly anxious to redirect their increasingly errant behavior, and therefore reads into the allegory a sober caution of repentance for these impenitent New World Israelites: "How merciful is our God unto us, for he remembereth the house of Israel, both roots and branches; and he

stretches forth his hands unto them all the day long; . . . but as many as will not harden their hearts shall be saved in the kingdom of God" (6:4).

Modern interpretations of the allegory have emphasized its universality. Accordingly, readers have explored its application to the house of Israel and the stretch of covenant time, that is, beginning with God's pact with Abraham and finishing with the Millennium and the ending of the earth; its doctrinal connection to the ages of spiritual apostasy, the latter-day Restoration, Church membership, present global proselytizing, the return of the Jews, and the final judgment. Other studies have begun to explore its literary and textual correspondences with ancient documents (Hymns from Qumran) and with the Old (Genesis, Isaiah, Jeremiah) and New Testaments (Romans 11:16–24), and even its association with the known laws of botany. Some scholars have declared it one of the most demanding and engaging of all scriptural allegories, if not the most important one.

BIBLIOGRAPHY

Hess, Wilford M. "Botanical Comparisons in the Allegory of the Olive Tree." In *The Book of Mormon: Jacob through Words of Mormon, To Learn with Joy,* ed. M. Nyman and C. Tate, pp. 87–102. Provo, Utah, 1990.

McConkie, Joseph Fielding, and Robert L. Millet. *Doctrinal Commentary on the Book of Mormon,* Vol. 2, pp. 46–77. Salt Lake City, 1988.

Nibley, Hugh W. *Since Cumorah,* pp. 283–85. In CWHN 7.

Nyman, Monte S. *An Ensign to All People,* pp. 21–36. Salt Lake City, 1987.

ADDITIONAL SOURCES

Hoskisson, Paul Y. "Explicating the Mystery of the Rejected Foundation Stone: The Allegory of the Olive Tree." *BYU Studies* 30/3 (1990): 77–87.

Ricks, Stephen D., and John W. Welch, eds. *The Allegory of the Olive Tree: The Olive, the Bible, and Jacob 5*. Salt Lake City and Provo, Utah: Deseret Book and FARMS, 1994.

L. GARY LAMBERT

ALMA₁

Alma₁ (c. 174–92 B.C.) was the first of two Almas in the Book of Mormon. He was a descendant of NEPHI₁, son of LEHI, and was the young priest in the court of king Noah who attempted a peaceful release of the prophet ABINADI. For that action, Alma incurred royal vengeance, banishment, and threats upon his life. He had been impressed by Abinadi's accusations of immorality and abuses within the government and society and by his testimony of the gospel of Jesus Christ (Mosiah 17:2). Subsequently forced underground, Alma wrote out Abinadi's teachings, then shared them with others, attracting sufficient adherents—450—to organize a society of believers, or a church. The believers assembled in a remote, undeveloped area called Mormon. Participants in the church pledged to "bear one another's burdens," "mourn with those that mourn," "comfort those that stand in need of comfort," and "stand as witnesses of God at all times and in all things" (Mosiah 18:8–9). This pledge was then sealed by BAPTISM, which was considered "a testimony that ye have entered into a covenant to serve him [Almighty God] until you are dead as to the mortal body" (verse 13). Believers called themselves "the church of God, or the church of Christ, from that time forward" (verse 17).

Alma's leadership included ordaining lay priests—one for every fifty members—whom he instructed to labor for their own support, and to limit their sermons to his teachings and the doctrine "spoken by the mouth of the holy prophets . . . nothing save it were repentance and faith on the Lord" (Mosiah 18:19–20). Alma also required that there be faithful observance of the Sabbath, daily expressions of gratitude to God, and no contention, "having their hearts knit together in unity and in love" (18:21–23). The priests assembled with and taught the people in a worship meeting at least once weekly (18:25). Through generous donations, everyone cared for one another "according to that which he had" (18:27–28).

Eventually the believers were discovered and king Noah accused Alma of sedition, ordering his army to crush him and his followers. Forced into exile, Alma led the people deeper into the wilderness, where they thrived for twenty years in a region they named Helam (Mosiah 18:32–35; 23:1–5, 20). Alma ardently declined well-intended efforts to make him king, and successfully dissuaded his people from adopting a monarchical government, urging them to enjoy the new "liberty wherewith ye have been made free" and to "trust no man to be a king" (Mosiah 23:13). He did not oppose monarchies as such but, rather, acknowledged their fundamental limitation: "If it were possible that ye could always have just men to be your kings it would be well for you to have a king" (23:8).

Alma and his people afterward suffered oppression at the hands of Amulon, also an ex-priest and deserter from king Noah's court, who, along with the remnant of a LAMANITE army, discovered Alma's people in their wilderness refuge. During their suffering the voice of the Lord promised relief and deliverance because of their covenant with him: "I, the Lord God, do visit my people in their afflictions" (Mosiah 24:14). Once again, in Moses-like fashion, Alma guided his people out of bondage, and led them during a twelve-day journey to a new land—the Land of Zarahemla—where they joined with the people of Zarahemla and exiled NEPHITES to form a new and stronger Nephite nation (Mosiah 24:24–25).

The king of Zarahemla, Mosiah₂, also a descendant of transplanted God-fearing Nephites, sanctioned and even authorized expansion of Alma's church in his kingdom; the church, however, operated separately and independently of the state. The king also assigned the reins of leadership to Alma (Mosiah 25:19; 26:8), who successfully directed the church during twenty years characterized largely by tribulations, with many confrontations between nonbelievers and church members resulting in ordeals for both him and the church (Mosiah 26:1–39). Eventually, widespread antagonism necessitated a royal injunction to lessen the tension (27:1–6). Even one of Alma's sons was among the ranks of the enemies of the church, his agitation and criticism inviting yet worse persecution for church members (27:8–10).

During his lifetime Alma watched king Mosiah dismantle the monarchy and transform it into a system of judges elected by the people (Mosiah 29:11); he also saw his own son, Alma₂—the one who earlier had brought grief to him and the church—become the first chief judge (Mosiah 29:1–44). This political transformation proved pivotal in the history of the Land of Zarahemla. Directly and indirectly Alma had a hand in bringing it about; the record of his and his people's pain under oppressive rulers was widely known throughout the kingdom (25:5–6) and remained distinct in king Mosiah's mind (29:18). Alma's influence, then, can be seen as

transcending the immediate spiritual boundaries of his stewardship over the church. Indeed, because of this influence the entire Nephite nation came to know unprecedented changes in almost every dimension of daily living—political, social, and economic, as well as religious. These changes—and all their connected ramifications for the social order and the populace—prepared the backdrop against which the resurrected Christ's visit to the Americas was staged. Loved by his followers for his devotion and faith, and held in esteem by his peers for his effective leadership, Alma will probably always be best known as the founder of the church in Zarahemla. His posterity became the leading Nephite family for over 400 years, down to Ammaron in A.D. 321 (4 Ne. 1:48). Alma died at age eighty-two, less than a hundred years before the birth of Jesus Christ.

L. GARY LAMBERT

Alma₂

Few individuals have had greater influence upon a civilization than Alma₂, son of Alma₁. He was a key figure in the rise of the Nephite church and republic, serving as the first chief judge in Zarahemla, commander-in-chief of the Nephite army, and high priest (c. 90–73 B.C.). His efforts to protect his people from war, dissension, and wickedness were exceeded only by his single-minded dedication to the Savior, whom he came to know through revelation.

This crusader for righteousness first appears in the Book of Mormon as a rebellious young man. He and four of the sons of King Mosiah₂, described as "the very vilest of sinners" (Mosiah 28:4), rebelled against the teachings of their parents and sought to over-

Alma the Younger Called to Repentance, by James C. Christensen (1980, leaded stained glass). The angel of the Lord rebukes the young and rebellious Alma: "If thou wilt of thyself be destroyed, seek no more to destroy the church of God" (Alma 36:9).

throw the church. As they went about that work (c. 100–92 B.C.), the angel of the Lord appeared to them, spoke with a voice of thunder, calling these wayward young men to repentance, and explaining that he did so because of the prayers of the people and of Alma's father. For three days and three nights Alma lay in a physically comatose state, during which time he spiritually confronted all his sins, "for which," he later said, "I was tormented with the pains of hell" (Alma 36:12–14).

In the depth of his anguish of soul, Alma remembered his father's words concerning the coming of Jesus Christ to atone for the sins of the world. As Alma cried out in his heart to Christ, pleading for mercy and deliverance from "the gall of bitterness" and "the everlasting chains of death," he stated: "I could remember my pains no more; yea, I was harrowed up by the memory of my sins no more" (Alma 36:17–19). After their conversion, Alma and the sons of Mosiah devoted their lives to preaching repentance and the joyous gospel (Alma 36:24).

For about nine years Alma served as both the high priest over the church and the chief judge or governor over a new political system of judges among the Nephites. He was well educated, the keeper of sacred and civil records, an inspiring orator, and a skillful writer. As a young civil and religious leader, he faced a number of challenges. Several religio-political factions were emerging in Nephite society, notably the Zoramites, Mulekites, members of the church, and an anti-church group, the followers of Nehor (*see* PEOPLES OF THE BOOK OF MORMON). Maintaining Nephite leadership over all these groups proved impossible. In a landmark case in his first year as chief judge, Alma held the popular Nehor guilty of enforcing priestcraft with the sword, which resulted in his execution (Alma 1:2–15). This soon led to civil war with Alma himself slaying the new rebel leader, one of Nehor's protégés, in battle (Alma 2–3). There followed a serious epidemic of pride and inequality among many in the church (Alma 4) and the secession of the arrogant Zoramites. "Seeing no way that he might reclaim [the people] save it were in bearing down in pure testimony against them" (Alma 4:19), Alma resigned his position as chief judge and devoted himself completely to the work of the ministry (Alma 4:16–19; 31:5). His religious work, especially in the Nephite cities of Zarahemla (Alma 5, 30) and Gideon (Alma 7), the Nehorite stronghold of Ammonihah (Alma 8–16), and the Zoramite center in Antionum (Alma 31–35), revitalized the church and set the pattern of administration for the next century down to the coming of Christ.

Alma's most enduring contributions are to be found in his sermons and his blessings upon the heads of his children. No doubt as a result of his own conversion (Mosiah 27), Alma's words frequently center on the atoning sacrifice of the Redeemer and on the necessity for men and women to be BORN OF GOD, changed, and renewed through Christ. To the people of Gideon, Alma delivered a profound prophetic oracle regarding the birth of Jesus and the atonement he would make, "suffering pains and afflictions and temptations of every kind . . . that he may loose the bands of death which bind his people; and he will take upon him their infirmities, that his bowels may be filled with mercy . . . that he may know according to the flesh how to succor his people according to their infirmities" (Alma 7:11–12). In Zarahemla, Alma stressed the need for the new birth and for acquiring the image and attributes of the Master; in doing so, he provided a series of over forty questions that assess one's depth of conversion and readiness to meet one's Maker (see Alma 5).

In Ammonihah, Alma and his convert Amulek were accused of a crime, taunted, and imprisoned for several weeks without clothing or adequate food. After being forced to witness the burning of several faithful women and children, Alma and Amulek were miraculously delivered and their persecutors annihilated. The discourses of Alma and Amulek on the Creation, the Fall, and the Atonement are among the clearest and most fundamental theological statements on these subjects in scripture (see Alma 11–12, 34, 42). In explaining humility, faith, and prayer to the poor in Antionum (Alma 32–34), Alma and Amulek set forth a pattern whereby those without faith in Christ (or those within the fold who desire to strengthen their belief) would plant the seed of the word of Christ in their hearts and eventually receive the confirming impressions of testimony that come by the power of the Holy Ghost.

Some of the most penetrating doctrinal information in the Book of Mormon comes through words that Alma spoke to his sons. To HELAMAN₁, his eldest son and successor, Alma eloquently recounted the story of his own conversion, gave him loving fatherly counsel, and entrusted him with custody of the plates of brass, the plates of Nephi, the plates of Ether, and the LIAHONA (Alma 36–37). To Shiblon, he gave wise practical advice (Alma 38). To his errant youngest son, Corianton, who eventually went on to serve valiantly in the church, Alma explained the seriousness of sexual sin, that wickedness never was happiness (Alma 39, 41:10), that all spirits will be judged after death and will eventually stand before God after a perfect resurrection (Alma 40), and that the word "restoration" does not mean that God will restore a sinner to some former state of happiness (Alma 41), for divine mercy cannot rob justice when the law of God has been violated (Alma 42).

A relatively young man at the time of his conversion, Alma lived fewer than twenty years thereafter. Yet in those two decades he almost single-handedly invigorated and established the cause of truth and liberty in the Nephite church and society. Never forgetting the thunderous voice of the angel at the time of his conversion, Alma always carried with him this unchanging desire: "O that I were an angel, and could have the wish of mine heart, that I might go forth and speak with the trump of God, with a voice to shake the earth, and cry repentance unto every people! . . . that there might not be more sorrow upon all the face of the earth" (Alma 29:1–2). When he left one day and was never seen or heard again, his sons and the church supposed "that [the Lord] received Alma in the spirit, unto himself," even as Moses (Alma 45:19), drawing an apt comparison between these two great lawgivers, judges, commanders, spiritual leaders, and prophets.

For Latter-day Saints, Alma's life and lessons are rich and timeless. He serves as a hope to parents who have wandering children, and as a beacon to those who stray. He stands as a model public servant, a sterling illustration of the new life in Christ, a fearless preacher, missionary, and gifted theologian. Alma was a prophet who received a prophet's reward.

BIBLIOGRAPHY

Holland, Jeffrey R. "Alma, Son of Alma." *Ensign* 7 (March 1977): 79–84.

Perry, L. Tom. "Alma the Younger." *CR* (April 1979): 16–17.

ROBERT L. MILLET

AMULEK

Amulek (fl. c. 82–74 B.C.), a Nephite inhabitant of the city Ammonihah (Alma 8:20), was a wealthy man in his community (Alma 10:4). Formerly rebellious toward God, he heeded an angel of the Lord and became a missionary companion to ALMA₂ (Alma 10:6–10). An articulate defender of gospel principles, he displayed virtues of long-suffering and faith, gave up his wealth to teach the gospel, and became a special witness for Christ (see Alma 8–16; 32–34).

Amulek bore powerful testimony to his own city, which earlier had rejected Alma. He confounded opposing lawyers and called upon them to repent—particularly Zeezrom, who had plotted to tempt and destroy him (Alma 11:25). He taught about the nature of the Godhead and the role of Christ, emphasizing the resurrection and final judgment (Alma 11:28–45). Touched by the words of Amulek and Alma, Zeezrom recognized the truth, repented, and defended the two missionaries (Alma 14:6–7).

When nonbelievers forced Alma and Amulek to witness the burning of women and children, Amulek desired to save them from the flames. He was restrained, however, by Alma (Alma 14:10–11). They themselves were bound, were smitten, and endured hunger as they lay naked in prison (Alma 14:14–22). At last, receiving strength according to their faith, they miraculously broke their bonds and walked out of the collapsing prison, while those who had smitten them died in its ruins (Alma 14:26–28).

Because of his faith in Christ, Amulek was rejected by his family and friends (Alma 15:16). When peace was restored after the Lamanite destruction of Ammonihah, Alma, Amulek, and others built up the church among the Nephites (Alma 16:15).

As a special witness for Christ and filled with the Holy Spirit, Amulek testified to the poor of the Zoramites that only in Christ was salvation possible (Alma 34:5–13). He stated that Christ would come into the world and make an infinite atonement for the sins of the people. "Not any man" could accomplish this

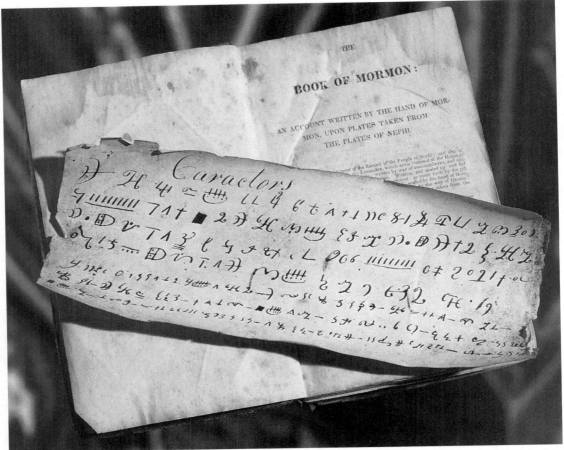

Facsimile of the Anthon Transcript on a copy of the first printing of the Book of Mormon. © by Intellectual Reserve, Inc. Used by permission.

act, which would be the great and last sacrifice, bringing mercy to satisfy the demands of justice and saving those who believe on his name (Alma 34:8–16). In return, Amulek said, Christ asked for faith unto repentance, charitable deeds, acceptance of the name of Christ, no contending against the Holy Ghost, no reviling of enemies, and bearing one's afflictions patiently (Alma 34:17–41).

BIBLIOGRAPHY

Dahl, Larry E. "The Plan of Redemption—Taught and Rejected." In *Studies in Scripture,* ed. Kent P. Jackson, Vol. 8, pp. 307–20. Salt Lake City, 1987.

NORBERT H. O. DUCKWITZ

ANTHON TRANSCRIPT

The Anthon Transcript was a sheet of paper, thought to be lost, upon which Joseph SMITH copied sample "reformed Egyptian" characters from the plates of the Book of Mormon. In the winter of 1828, Martin HARRIS showed these characters to Dr. Charles Anthon of Columbia College (now Columbia University), and hence the name.

In February 1828, Martin Harris, a farmer from Palmyra, New York, visited the Prophet Joseph Smith, who was then residing in Harmony, Pennsylvania, where he had just begun to translate the Book of Mormon (*see* TRANSLATION OF THE BOOK OF MORMON BY JOSEPH SMITH). Smith had earlier turned to

Harris for financial backing for the translation; now Harris came to Harmony to take samples of the reformed Egyptian characters from the GOLD PLATES (cf. Morm. 9:32), thereafter to obtain scholarly opinion about their authenticity. Smith gave Harris a copy of some of the characters, along with a translation, which Harris then presented to at least three scholars in the eastern United States. The most important of these, given the nature of the inquiry, was Charles Anthon, an acclaimed classicist at Columbia College.

The two men's accounts of the meeting differ. Harris said that Professor Anthon gave him a certificate verifying the authenticity of the characters but that when Anthon learned that Joseph Smith claimed to have received the plates from an angel, he took the certificate back and destroyed it. Anthon, for his part, left written accounts in 1834 and 1841 in which he contradicted himself on whether he had given Harris a written opinion about the document. In both accounts, apparently to dissociate himself from appearing to promote the book, he maintained that he told Harris that he (Harris) was a victim of a fraud. Modern research suggests that, given the state of knowledge of Egyptian in 1828, Anthon's views would have been little more than opinion. Whatever the case may be about a written statement from Anthon, Harris returned to Harmony ready to assist Joseph Smith with the translation.

The Reorganized Church of Jesus Christ of Latter Day Saints possesses a handwritten text known as the Anthon Transcript that contains seven horizontal lines of characters apparently copied from the plates. David WHITMER, who once owned the document, said it was this text that Martin Harris showed to Charles Anthon. However, this claim remains uncertain because the transcript does not correspond with Anthon's assertion that the manuscript he saw was arranged in vertical columns. Even if the document is not the original, it almost certainly represents characters either copied from the plates in Joseph Smith's possession or copied from the document carried by Harris. Twice in late 1844, after the Prophet's martyrdom, portions of these symbols were published as characters that Joseph Smith had copied from the gold plates—once as a broadside and once in the December 21 issue of the Mormon newspaper *The Prophet*. In 1980 a document surfaced that seemed to match Anthon's description and appeared to be the original Anthon Transcript. But in 1987, Mark W. Hofmann admitted that he had forged it.

Harris's visit with scholars was more than just an interesting sidelight in the history of Mormonism. By his own report,

Charles Anthon (1787–1867), a professor of classical languages at Columbia College (now Columbia University) in New York from 1820 to 1867. His library in 1828 included recent works on hieroglyphic and demotic Egyptian. © by Intellectual Reserve, Inc. Used by permission.

Harris returned to Harmony convinced that the characters were genuine. Thereafter, he willingly invested his time and resources to see the Book of Mormon published. Moreover, the Prophet, Harris himself, and later generations of Latter-day Saints have viewed his visit as a fulfillment of Isaiah 29:11–12, which speaks of "a book that is sealed" being delivered to "one that is learned" who could not read it (*PJS* 1:9; cf. 2 Ne. 27:6–24; *see also* BIBLICAL PROPHECIES ABOUT THE BOOK OF MORMON). His efforts apparently encouraged Joseph Smith in the initial stages of the translation. The Anthon Transcript is also important to subsequent generations as an authentic sample of characters that were inscribed on the gold plates and thus one of the few tangible evidences of their existence.

[*See also* Language.]

BIBLIOGRAPHY

FARMS Staff. "Martin Harris' Visit to Charles Anthon: Collected Documents on Short-hand Egyptian." *FARMS Preliminary Report*. Provo, Utah, 1985.

Kimball, Stanley B. "I Cannot Read a Sealed Book." *IE* 60 (Feb. 1957): 80–82, 104, 106.

——. "The Anthon Transcript: People, Primary Sources, and Problems." *BYU Studies* 10 (Spring 1970): 325–52.

DANEL W. BACHMAN

ANTICHRISTS

Antichrists are those who deny the divinity of JESUS CHRIST or essential parts of his gospel and actively oppose the followers of Christ or seek to destroy their faith.

The epistles of John explicitly condemn as antichrists those with a lying spirit who deny that Jesus is the Christ and deny the physical resurrection. Antichrists are to be notably active in the last days (1 Jn. 2:18, 22; 4:3; 2 Jn. 1:7).

The Book of Mormon profiles many subtle and sophisticated aspects of antichrist characters, though the text explicitly refers to only one of them as antichrist.

Sherem (c. 540 B.C.) rejected the prophetic Christian teachings of the Nephite prophets, arguing that belief in the coming Christ perverted the law of Moses. He employed several archetypical arguments and methods, claiming that no one could know of things to come, including the coming of Christ. When confronted, Sherem asserted that if there were a Christ he would not deny him, but he knew "there is no Christ, neither has been, nor ever will be," thus contradicting his own argument that no one could "tell of things to come." Demanding a sign of divine power, Sherem was stricken by God, and then confessed that he had been deceived by the devil in denying the Christ (Jacob 7:1–23).

Nehor (c. 91 B.C.), a practitioner of priestcraft, preached and established a church to obtain riches and worldly honor and to satisfy his pride. He taught that God had created everyone, had redeemed everyone, and that people need not "fear and tremble" because everyone would be saved. Furthermore, he said priests should be supported by the people. Nehor attacked and killed a defender of the true doctrine of Christ, and was tried before Alma$_2$ and executed (Alma 1:2–16). He was not executed for being an antichrist, but for having enforced his beliefs "by the sword."

Korihor (c. 74 B.C.) was an extremist, rejecting all religious teachings, even to the point of not posturing either as a defender of traditions or as a reformer of corrupted religious practices. He was labeled "Anti-Christ" because he taught that there was no need for a Christ and that none would come. He described the religious teachings of the church as foolish traditions designed to subject the people to corrupt and lazy priests. In a dramatic confrontation with the Nephite chief judge, and with the prophet Alma$_2$, Korihor claimed that one cannot know anything that cannot be seen, making knowledge or prophecy of future events impossible. He ridiculed all talk of visions, dreams, and the mysteries of God. He called belief in sin, the atonement of Christ, and the remission of sins a derangement of the mind caused by foolish religious traditions. He denied the existence of God and, after demanding a sign as proof of his existence, was struck dumb. After Alma accused him of possessing a lying spirit, Korihor confessed that he had been deceived by Satan, had taught words and doctrines pleasing to the carnal mind, and had even begun to believe them himself (Alma 30:6–60).

BIBLIOGRAPHY

Riddle, Chauncey C. "Korihor: The Arguments of Apostasy." *Ensign* 7 (Sept. 1977): 18–21.

RUSSELL M. FRANDSEN

ARCHAEOLOGY

Archaeology is the study and interpretation of past human cultures based on known material remains. Biblical and Mesoamerican archaeological research is of special interest to Latter-day Saints.

Archaeological data from the ancient Near East and the Americas have been used both to support and to discredit the Book of Mormon. Many scholars see no support for the Book of Mormon in the archaeological records, since no one has found any inscriptional evidence for, or material remains that can be tied directly to, any of the persons, places, or things mentioned in the book (Smithsonian Institution).

Several types of indirect archaeological evidence, however, have been used in support of the Book of Mormon. For example, John L. Sorenson and M. Wells Jakeman tentatively identified the Olmec (2000–600 B.C.) and Late Pre-Classic Maya (300 B.C.–A.D. 250) cultures in Central America with the JAREDITE and NEPHITE cultures, based on correspondences between periods of cultural development in these areas and the pattern of cultural change in the Book of Mormon.

Likewise, parallels between cultural traits of the ancient Near East and Mesoamerica perhaps indicate transoceanic contacts between the two regions. Among these are such minor secondary traits as horned incense burners, models of house types, wheel-made pottery, cement, the true arch, and the use of stone boxes. All of these may, however, represent independent inventions. Stronger evidence for contacts may be found in the TREE OF LIFE motif, a common religious theme, on Stela 5 from Izapa in Chiapas, Mexico. Jakeman, in 1959, studied Stela 5 in detail and concluded that it represented the sons of a legendary ancestral couple absorbing and perhaps recording their knowledge of a munificent Tree of Life. This can be compared favorably to the account of Lehi's vision in the Book of Mormon (1 Ne. 8).

The presence of a bearded white deity, Quetzalcoatl or Kukulcan, in the pantheon of the Aztec, Toltec, and Maya has also been advanced as indirect evidence of Christ's visit to the New World. The deity is represented as a feathered serpent, and elements of his worship may have similarities to those associated with Christ's atonement.

Recent work by LDS professional archaeologists such as Ray Matheny at El Mirador and by the New World Archaeological Foundation in Chiapas has been directed toward an understanding of the factors that led to the development of complex societies in Mesoamerica in general. Under C. Wilfred Griggs, a team of Brigham Young University scholars has sponsored excavations in Egypt, and other LDS archaeologists have been involved in projects in Israel and Jordan.

Another area of archaeological investigation is in LDS history. Dale Berge's excavations at Nauvoo; the Whitmer farm in New York; the early Mormon settlement of Goshen (Utah); the Utah mining town of Mercur; and, most recently, Camp Floyd, the headquarters of Johnston's army in Utah, have provided information about the economic and social interactions between early Mormon and non-Mormon communities.

BIBLIOGRAPHY

Griggs, C. Wilfred, ed. *Excavations at Seila, Egypt.* Provo, Utah, 1988.

Jakeman, M. Wells. "The Main Challenge of the Book of Mormon to Archaeology; and a Summary of Archaeological Research to Date Giving a Preliminary Test of Book-of-Mormon Claims." In *Progress in Archaeology, An Anthology,* ed. R. Christensen, pp. 99–103. Provo, Utah, 1963.

———. "Stela 5, Izapa, as 'The Lehi Tree-of-Life Stone.'" In *The Tree of Life in Ancient America,* ed. R. Christensen. Provo, Utah, 1968.

Matheny, Ray T. "An Early Maya Metropolis Uncovered, Elmirador." *National Geographic* 172, no. 3 (1987): 316–39.

Smithsonian Institution. "Statement regarding the Book of Mormon." Department of Anthropology, National Museum of Natural History, SIL–76, 1982.

Sorenson, John L. "An Evaluation of the Smithsonian Institution's 'Statement regarding the Book of Mormon'" *FARMS Paper.* Provo, Utah, 1982.

———. *An Ancient American Setting for the Book of Mormon.* Salt Lake City, 1985.

DAVID J. JOHNSON

AUTHORSHIP OF THE BOOK OF MORMON

Many studies have investigated Book of Mormon authorship because the book presents itself as a composite work of many ancient authors. Those who reject Joseph SMITH's claim that he translated the book through divine power assume that he or one of his contemporaries wrote the book. Various claims or arguments have been advanced to support or discount these competing positions.

Disputes about the book's authorship arose as soon as its existence became public knowledge. The first general reaction was ridicule. Modern minds do not easily accept the idea that an angel can deliver ancient records to be translated by an untrained young man. Moreover, most Christians in 1830 viewed the canon of scripture as complete with the Bible; hence, the possibility of additional scripture violated a basic assumption of their faith. Opponents of Joseph Smith, such as Alexander Campbell, also argued that the Book of Mormon was heavily plagiarized from the Bible and that it reflected themes and phraseology current in New York in the 1820s. Many critics have speculated that Sidney Rigdon or Solomon Spaulding played a role in writing the book (*see* SPAULDING MANUSCRIPT). It has also been suggested that Joseph Smith borrowed ideas from another book (*see* VIEW OF THE HEBREWS). Though these varieties of objections and theories are still defended in many quarters, they are not supported by modern authorship studies and continue to raise as many questions as they try to answer (e.g., CWHN 8:54–206).

Some have suggested that Joseph Smith admitted that he was the author of the Book of Mormon because the title page of the first edition lists him as "Author and Proprietor." This language, however, comes from the federal copyright statutes and legal forms in use in 1829 (1 *Stat.* 125 [1790], amended 2 *Stat.* 171 [1802]). In the preface to the same 1830 edition, Joseph Smith stated that he translated Mormon's handwriting "by the gift and power of God" (*see* TRANSLATIONS OF THE BOOK OF MORMON). The position of The Church of Jesus Christ of Latter-day Saints has invariably been that the truth of Joseph Smith's testimony can be validated through the witness of the Holy Ghost.

Scholarly work has produced a variety of evidence in support of the claim that the texts of the Book of Mormon were written by multiple ancient authors. These studies significantly increase the plausibility of Joseph Smith's account of the origin of the book.

The internal complexity of the Book of Mormon is often cited as a strong indication of multiple authorship. The many writings reportedly abridged by MORMON are intricately interwoven and often expressly identified (*see* PLATES AND RECORDS IN THE BOOK OF MORMON). The various books within the Book of Mormon differ from each other in historical background, style, and distinctive characteristics, yet are accurate and consistent in numerous minute details.

Historical studies have demonstrated that many things either not known or not readily knowable in 1829 about the ancient Near East are accurately reflected in the Book of Mormon. This body of historical research was expanded by the work of Hugh W. Nibley (*see*

STUDIES OF THE BOOK OF MORMON), who has recently discovered that ancient communities, such as Qumran, have many characteristics parallel to those of Book of Mormon peoples (CWHN 5–8). The Jews at Qumran were "sectaries," purists who left Jerusalem to avoid corruption of their covenants; they practiced ablutions (a type of baptism) before the time of Christ and wrote one of their records on a copper scroll that they sealed and hid up to come forth at a future time. One of Nibley's analyses demonstrates that King BENJAMIN's farewell speech to his people (Mosiah 2–5) is a good example of the ancient year-rite festival (CWHN 6:295–310). Subsequent studies have suggested that King Benjamin's people might have been celebrating the Israelite festival of Sukkoth and doing things required by Jewish laws not translated into English until after the Book of Mormon was published (Tvedtnes, 1990).

Structural studies have identified an artistic literary form, chiasmus, that appears in rich diversity in both the Bible and the Book of Mormon (*see* LITERATURE, BOOK OF MORMON AS). The most significant structural studies of the Book of Mormon derive from John W. Welch's analysis (Reynolds, pp. 33–52). Little known in 1829, this literary form creates inverted parallelism such as is found in this biblical passage in Leviticus 24:17–21:

> He that killeth any man . . .
> > He that killeth a beast . . .
> > > If a man cause a blemish . . .
> > > > Breach for breach,
> > > > Eye for eye
> > > > Tooth for tooth.
> > > As he hath caused a blemish . . .
> > He that killeth a beast . . .
> He that killeth a man. . . .

And from the Book of Mormon, in Alma 41:13–14 (cf. Welch, pp. 5–22):

Good for that which is good
  Righteous for that which is righteous
    Just for that which is just
      Merciful for that which is merciful
        Therefore, my son
        See that you are merciful
      Deal justly
    Judge righteously
  And do good continually.

Although chiasmus can appear in almost any language or literature, it was prevalent in the biblical period around the early seventh century B.C., the time of the Book of Mormon prophets LEHI and NEPHI₁. The especially precise and beautiful crafting of several Book of Mormon texts further supports the idea that their authors deliberately and painstakingly followed ancient literary conventions, which is inconsistent with seeing the New England born Joseph Smith as the author of these passages.

Other stylistic studies have examined the frequency of Hebrew root words, idioms, and syntax in the Book of Mormon (Tvedtnes, 1970). Some Book of Mormon names that have no English equivalents have Hebrew cognates (Hoskisson; CWHN 6:281–94). There are also discernible differences between the vocabularies and abridging techniques of Mormon and his son Moroni (see Keller).

Extensive statistical studies, including stylometry (or wordprinting), have been conducted on the Book of Mormon (Reynolds, pp. 157–88; cf. Hilton). Blocks of writing were analyzed to identify the writers' near-subconscious tendencies to use noncontextual word patterns in peculiar ratios and combinations. Wordprinting has been used to ascertain the authorship of such works as twelve disputed *Federalist Papers* and a posthumously published novel by Jane Austen. When applied to the Book of Mormon, wordprinting reveals that the word patterns of the Book of Mormon differ significantly from the personal writings of Joseph Smith, Solomon Spaulding, Sidney Rigdon, and Oliver COWDERY, who served as Joseph Smith's scribe. Furthermore, patterns of Nephi₁ are consistent among themselves but different from those of ALMA₂. The results of objectively measuring these phenomena indicate an extremely low statistical probability that the Book of Mormon could have been written by one author. The introduction of new vocabulary into the text is at a low rate, which is consistent with the uniform role of Joseph Smith as translator.

BIBLIOGRAPHY

Hilton, John L. "On Verifying Wordprint Studies: Book of Mormon Authorship." *BYU Studies* 30 (Summer 1990): 89–108.

Hoskisson, Paul. "An Introduction to the Relevance of and a Methodology for a Study of the Proper Names of the Book of Mormon." In *By Study and Also by Faith*, ed. J. Lundquist and S. Ricks, Vol. 2, pp. 126–35. Salt Lake City, 1990.

Keller, Roger R. "Mormon and Moroni as Authors and Abridgers." *FARMS Update*, Apr. 1988.

Reynolds, Noel B., ed. *Book of Mormon Authorship: New Light on Ancient Origins*. Provo, Utah, 1982.

Tvedtnes, John A. "Hebraisms in the Book of Mormon: A Preliminary Survey." *BYU Studies* 2 (Autumn 1970): 50–60.

———. "King Benjamin and the Feast of Tabernacles." In *By Study and Also by Faith*, ed. J. Lundquist and S. Ricks, Vol. 2, pp. 197–237. Salt Lake City, 1990.

Welch, John W. "Chiasmus in Biblical Law." In *Jewish Law Association Studies IV*, ed. B. Jackson, pp. 5–22. Atlanta, 1990.

Wirth, Diane E. *A Challenge to the Critics: Scholarly Evidences of the Book of Mormon.* Bountiful, Utah, 1986.

ADDITIONAL SOURCES

Keller, Roger R. *Book of Mormon Authors: Their Words and Messages.* Provo, Utah: BYU Religious Studies Center, 1996.

Reynolds, Noel B., ed. *Book of Mormon Authorship Revisited: The Evidence for Ancient Origins.* Provo, Utah: FARMS, 1997.

Welch, John W. "The Power of Evidence in the Nurturing of Faith." In *Nurturing Faith through the Book of Mormon*, 149–86. Salt Lake City: Deseret Book, 1995.

D. BRENT ANDERSON

DIANE E. WIRTH

B

Baptism

The fourth Article of Faith of The Church of Jesus Christ of Latter-day Saints declares that "baptism by immersion for the remission of sins" is one of the "first principles and ordinances of the Gospel." Latter-day Saints believe, as do many Christians, that baptism is an essential initiatory ordinance for all persons who are joining the Church, as it admits them to Christ's church on earth (John 3:3–5; D&C 20:37, 68–74). It is a primary step in the process, which includes faith, repentance, baptism of fire and of the Holy Ghost, and enduring to the end, whereby members may receive remission of their sins and gain access to the celestial kingdom and eternal life (e.g., Mark 16:15–16; 2 Ne. 31:13–21; D&C 22:1–4; 84:64, 74; *MD*, pp. 69–72).

Latter-day Saint baptisms are performed for converts who have been properly instructed, and are at least eight years of age (the age of accountability). Baptism must be performed by one who has proper priesthood authority. The major features of the ordinance include the raising of the right hand, the reciting of the prescribed BAPTISMAL PRAYER by the one performing the baptism, and the complete immersion of the candidate (3 Ne. 11:23–26; D&C 20:71–74; 68:27). Baptism symbolizes the covenant by which people promise to come into the fold of God, to take upon themselves the name of Christ, to stand as a witness for God, to keep his commandments, and to bear one another's burdens, manifesting a determination to serve him to the end, and to prepare to receive the spirit of Christ for the remission of sins. The Lord, as his part of the covenant, is to pour out his spirit upon them, redeem them from their sins, raise them in the first resurrection, and give them eternal life (Mosiah 18:7–10; D&C 20:37).

The rich symbolism of the ordinance invites candidates and observers to reflect on its meanings. Burial in the water and arising out of the water symbolize the candidate's faith in the death, burial, and resurrection of Jesus Christ, as well as the future resurrection of all people. It also represents the candidate's new birth to a life in Christ, being BORN OF GOD, thus born again of the water and of the spirit (Rom. 6:3–6; Mosiah 18:13–14; Moses 6:59–60; D&C 128:12–13).

Latter-day Saint scriptures indicate that

People are baptized by immersion to become a member of The Church of Jesus Christ of Latter-day Saints. Jesus said, "Ye shall go down and stand in the water, and in my name shall ye baptize them" (3 Ne. 11:23); "and he commandeth all men that they must repent, and be baptized in his name" (2 Ne. 9:23). A person who is baptized covenants with God to serve him and keep his commandments.

the history of this ordinance predates the ministry of John the Baptist. Beginning with Adam (Moses 6:64–66), baptism by immersion in water was introduced as standard practice, and has been observed in all subsequent dispensations of the gospel when priesthood authority was on the earth (D&C 20:25–27; 84:27–28). For variants of such precedents, Latter-day Saints trace the baptismal initiations in many pre-Christian religions (see Meslin, 1987). As recorded in the Book of Mormon, LEHI and NEPHI₁ foresaw the baptism of Jesus Christ in vision and taught their people to follow his righteous example (1 Ne. 10:7–10; 11:27; 2 Ne. 31:4–9). Moreover, before the time of Jesus Christ, ALMA₁ initiated converts into the church of God by baptism as a sign of their covenant (Mosiah 18:8–17; Alma 4:4–5).

According to the account of his appearance to the Nephites, Jesus taught the necessity of faith, repentance, baptism, and the gift of the Holy Ghost, and he authorized twelve disciples to baptize (3 Ne. 11:18–41; 19:11–13; 26:17–21). The Book of Mormon provides adequate instructions for baptism and proper words for the baptismal prayer (3 Ne. 11:23–28; Moro. 6:1–4; cf. D&C 20:73).

In addition to relying on information in the Book of Mormon, Latter-day Saints follow the New Testament teachings on baptism. Jesus taught that baptism is necessary for salvation. He told Nicodemus, "Except a man be born of water and of the Spirit, he cannot enter into the kingdom of God" (John 3:1–5). He required baptism of those who professed to become his disciples (John 4:1–2). His farewell commission to his apostles was that they should go to all nations, teaching and baptizing (Matt. 28:19), and he declared, "He that believeth *and is baptized* shall be saved; but he that believeth not shall be damned" (Mark 16:16; emphasis added). Paul, after his miraculous vision on the road to Damascus, was taught the gospel by Ananias who told him to "arise, and be baptized, and wash away thy sins" (Acts 22:16). To the penitent multitude on the day of Pentecost, Peter proclaimed, "Repent, and be baptized every one of you in the name of Jesus Christ for the remission of sins" (Acts 2:38).

Latter-day Saints do not accept baptismal practices and teachings that arose among some Christian groups in the centuries after the death of the apostles, including INFANT BAPTISM, baptism by means other than immersion, and the idea that baptism is not necessary for salvation. The Nephite prophet MORMON denounced the practice of infant baptism, which had apparently crept in among his people, and declared that anyone who supposed that little children need baptism would deny the mercies of Christ, setting at naught the value of his atonement and the power of his redemption (Moro. 8:4–20).

The authority to baptize was restored by

John the Baptist to Joseph Smith and Oliver COWDERY on May 15, 1829 (JS—H 1:68–72). From the early days of the restored Church, missionaries have been sent to "declare repentance and faith on the Savior, and remission of sins by baptism" (D&C 19:31; 55:2; 84:27, 74). "He that believeth and is baptized shall be saved, and he that believeth not, and is not baptized, shall be damned" (D&C 112:29). This is the central teaching of the GOSPEL OF JESUS CHRIST (3 Ne. 11:31–40).

Consequently, persons coming into The Church of Jesus Christ of Latter-day Saints at age eight or older are required to submit to baptism, even though they may have been previously baptized in other churches (D&C 22). Likewise, excommunicants undergo baptism again once they have qualified for readmission into the Church.

The form of the ordinance is prescribed in latter-day revelation, which makes clear that the baptism must be performed by a person who has priesthood authority and that it requires completely immersing the penitent candidate below the water and then bringing the person out of the water (3 Ne. 11:25–26; D&C 20:72–74). Baptism is followed by the laying on of hands for the gift of the Holy Ghost.

Contemporary Church practice provides for the candidate to be interviewed and approved by an authorized priesthood official (usually the bishop or other officer presiding over the congregation or a mission official), who determines whether the applicant meets the qualifying conditions of repentance, faith in the Lord Jesus Christ, and an understanding of and willingness to obey the laws and ordinances of the gospel. It is also necessary that an official record of each baptism be kept by the Church.

Baptism may be performed in the font provided in many meetinghouses or in any body of water that is suitable for the sacred occasion and deep enough for complete immersion. The candidate and the person performing the ordinance will be dressed in plain and modest white clothing. The ceremony is unpretentious, typically attended by the candidate's family, close friends, and interested members of the congregation. A speaker or two may offer a few words of instruction and joyous welcome to the candidate.

The earlier practice of rebaptism to manifest repentance and recommitment, or for a restoration of health in time of sickness, is no longer practiced in the Church.

Belief that baptism is necessary for the salvation of all persons who reach the age of accountability (D&C 84:64, 74) does not condemn persons who have died without the opportunity to hear the true gospel of Jesus Christ or to receive baptism from proper priesthood authority. Latter-day Saints believe that proxy baptism for the dead should be performed vicariously (1 Cor. 15:29; D&C 124:28–35, 127–28), and that it becomes effective if the deceased beneficiary accepts the gospel while in the spirit world awaiting resurrection (see 1 Pet. 3:18–20; 4:6; cf. D&C 45:54). This vicarious work for the benefit of previous generations, binding the hearts of the children to their fathers (Mal. 4:5–6), is one of the sacred ordinances performed in Latter-day Saint temples (D&C 128:12–13).

BIBLIOGRAPHY

Meslin, Michel. "Baptism." In *Encyclopedia of Religion*, Mircea Eliade, ed. Vol. 2, pp. 59–63. New York, 1987.

Smith, Joseph Fielding. *Doctrines of Salvation*, Vol. 2, pp. 323–37. Salt Lake City, 1955.

Talmage, James E. *AF*, pp. 109–42. Salt Lake City, 1984.

CARL S. HAWKINS

Baptismal Covenant

When a person enters into a Latter-day Saint baptism, he or she makes a covenant with God. Baptism is a "sign . . . that we will do the will of God, and there is no other way beneath the heavens whereby God hath ordained for man to come to Him to be saved" (*TPJS*, p. 198).

Candidates promise to "come into the fold of God, and to be called his people, . . . to bear one another's burdens, . . . to mourn with those that mourn, . . . and to stand as witnesses of God . . . even until death" (Mosiah 18:8–9). A person must enter this covenant with the proper attitudes of humility, REPENTANCE, and determination to keep the Lord's commandments, and serve God to the end (2 Ne. 31:6–17; Moro. 6:2–4; D&C 20:37). In turn, God promises remission of sins, redemption, and cleansing by the Holy Ghost (Acts 22:16; 3 Ne. 30:2). This covenant is made in the name of the Father, the Son, and the Holy Ghost.

The baptized can renew this covenant at each sacrament meeting by partaking of the SACRAMENT. This continual willingness to remember Christ and to keep his commandments brings the Lord's promise of his Spirit and produces the "fruits" (Gal. 5:22) and "gifts" (D&C 46) that lead to eternal life.

BIBLIOGRAPHY

Tripp, Robert M. *Oaths, Covenants, and Promises*, pp. 11–19. Salt Lake City, 1973.

JERRY A. WILSON

Baptismal Prayer

The wording of the baptismal prayer used in The Church of Jesus Christ of Latter-day Saints is prescribed in the earliest compilation of instructions for Church operations (D&C 20). When an individual is baptized, the person with the proper priesthood authority goes down into the water with the candidate, raises his right arm to the square, calls the individual by the full legal name, and says, "Having been commissioned of Jesus Christ, I baptize you in the name of the Father, and of the Son, and of the Holy Ghost. Amen," and then immerses the candidate (D&C 20:73). A version of the prayer that differs only slightly from this was given by Jesus Christ to the NEPHITES and is recorded in the Book of Mormon (3 Ne. 11:25).

Earlier in the Book of Mormon there is a somewhat different account of the baptismal prayer that was spoken. When ALMA₁ in the second century B.C. established the Church among the Nephites, he prayed: "O Lord, pour out thy Spirit upon thy servant, that he may do this work with holiness of heart" (Mosiah 18:12). The baptismal prayer that followed emphasized the covenant represented in BAPTISM and the need for a subsequent baptism of the Spirit: "I baptize thee, having authority from the Almighty God, as a testimony that ye have entered into a covenant to serve him until you are dead as to the mortal body; and may the Spirit of the Lord be poured out upon you; and may he grant unto you eternal life, through the redemption of Christ, whom he has prepared from the foundation of the world" (Mosiah 18:13).

BIBLIOGRAPHY

It is informative to compare LDS practice and scriptural accounts with the Christian tradition as reported in E. C. Whitaker, *Documents of the Baptismal Liturgy*, London, 1970.

JERRY A. WILSON

BEATITUDES

The Beatitudes, or promises of blessings in Jesus' SERMON ON THE MOUNT (Matt. 5:3–12), hold a particular significance for Latter-day Saints because the resurrected Lord gave essentially that same sermon to the Nephites and the Lamanites in the Western Hemisphere, as recorded in 3 Nephi 12–14. The words in the Beatitudes echo Isaiah 61:1–2 and Psalm 107:4–7, 9. Church members cite the setting of the Book of Mormon sermon as well as a few notable verbal differences (such as "Blessed are the poor in spirit *who come unto me,*" and the phrase "for they shall be filled *with the Holy Ghost*") as examples of how the Book of Mormon complements the Bible, attesting to its message while clarifying and expanding it (cf. 1 Ne. 13 [esp. verses 39–42]; 2 Ne. 27, 29).

In the Book of Mormon, most of the sermon is addressed to baptized members of the Church (cf. 3 Ne. 11 and 12:1–2). Thus, the expectations in the sermon concern those living the law of the gospel as taught by Christ. Other parts of the sermon are directed specifically to leaders.

Some significant differences appear in the wording of the biblical and Book of Mormon versions of the Beatitudes. In the Book of Mormon, two new "beatitudes" precede those in Matthew: baptized members are blessed if they give heed to their leaders and have faith in Christ (3 Ne. 12:1), and "more blessed" are those who receive the testimony of emissaries whom Christ has called (3 Ne. 12:2). These two additional beatitudes are incorporated into the biblical sermon in the Joseph Smith Translation of the Bible (JST). Matthew 5:3 is elaborated as noted above (cf. D&C 84:49–53). Matthew 5:4 is virtually unchanged at 3 Nephi 12:4 but is somewhat developed at 3 Nephi 12:19 (cf. Morm.

2:11–13). The words "shall be filled with the Holy Ghost" (3 Ne. 12:6) express on a spiritual level (cf. Ps. 17:15, Septuagint) the implicit meaning of cattle feeding upon grass (Matt. 5:6; Greek, *chortasthêsontai*; cf. the grass [*chortos*] where the disciples are miraculously fed at Matt. 14:19 and the verb "filled" at Matt. 15:33, 37). Matthew 5:5 is unchanged, as are Matthew 5:7–9; but Matthew 5:10 reads "which are persecuted for righteousness' sake," while 3 Nephi 12:10 has "who are persecuted for my name's sake," reflecting the Christ-centered theme throughout the Nephite version of the sermon. For the first two verbs of Matthew 5:12, which the KJV takes as imperatives, 3 Nephi 12:12 has "For ye shall have great joy and be exceedingly glad."

Church leaders often refer to the Beatitudes as the Lord's promises of blessings and happiness to those who follow him and as the result of obedience or the "fruit of the Spirit" (Gal. 5:22–23). Those who would be obedient have the individual responsibilities of turning to the Lord and of implementing the principles inherent in the qualities described in the Beatitudes (cf. D&C 88:63–65 and 97:16, which adapt the sixth beatitude to temple worship).

BIBLIOGRAPHY

Thomas, Catherine. "The Sermon on the Mount: The Sacrifice of the Human Heart (Matthew 5–7; Luke 6:17–49)." In *Studies in Scripture,* ed. R. Millet, Vol. 5, pp. 236–50. Salt Lake City, 1986.

Welch, John W. *The Sermon at the Temple and the Sermon on the Mount.* Salt Lake City, 1990.

Wilcox, S. Michael. "The Beatitudes—Pathway to the Savior." *Ensign* 21 (Jan. 1991): 19–23.

THOMAS W. MACKAY

BENJAMIN

Benjamin, son of MOSIAH₁, was an important king in Nephite history (d. c. 121 B.C.). His reign came at a crucial juncture in the history of the NEPHITES and was important both culturally and politically. His father, Mosiah₁, "being warned of the Lord," had led the Nephites out of the land of Nephi to the land of Zarahemla (Omni 1:12, 19). Thereafter, during his own reign, Benjamin fought, as was customary for kings in the ancient world (cf. Mosiah 10:10), with his "own arm" against invading LAMANITES (W of M 1:13), keeping his people "from falling into the hands of [their] enemies" (Mosiah 2:31). He succeeded in consolidating Nephite rule over the land of Zarahemla (Omni 1:19) and reigned there "in righteousness" over his people (W of M 1:17).

Benjamin, described as a "holy man" (W of M 1:17) and "a just man before the Lord," also led his people as a prophet (Omni 1:25) and was, with the assistance of other prophets and holy men, able to overcome the contentions among his people and to "once more establish peace in the land" (W of M 1:18). Accordingly, Amaleki, who was himself without seed, entrusted Benjamin with the record on the small plates (Omni 1:25). Keenly interested in the preservation of sacred records, Benjamin taught his sons "in all the language of his fathers" and "concerning the records . . . on the plates of brass" (Mosiah 1:2–3).

Mosiah 2–6 records Benjamin's farewell address, designed primarily to effect a "change in heart" in his people and to bring them to Jesus Christ. He deals with man's obligations to his fellow men and to God, punishment for rebellion against God, gratitude, faith, and service. This address is as relevant now as it was when first presented. In addition, reporting the words spoken to him by an angel,

Benjamin prophesied that "the Lord Omnipotent . . . shall come down from heaven among the children of men" as the Messiah, "working mighty miracles" (Mosiah 3:5). Further, Benjamin declared that the Messiah would "be called Jesus Christ, the Son of God, . . . and his mother shall be called Mary" (3:8)—the earliest mention of her name in the Book of Mormon. Moreover, Jesus would "suffer temptations, and pain of body, hunger, thirst, and fatigue, even more than man can suffer" (3:7). After being crucified, Jesus would "rise the third day from the dead; and behold, he standeth to judge the world" (3:10). Significantly, Benjamin taught that the power of the atonement of Jesus Christ was in effect for him and his people, "as though he had already come" to earth (3:13).

The impact of Benjamin's address on subsequent Nephite generations can be gauged by how much it is mentioned later in the Book of Mormon. Following Benjamin's death, his son and successor, MOSIAH₂, sent Ammon and fifteen other representatives from Zarahemla to the land of Nephi (Mosiah 7:1–6), where they found the Nephite king Limhi and his people in bondage to the Lamanites. After the representatives had identified themselves, Limhi caused his people to gather at the local temple, where he addressed them. Thereafter, Ammon "rehearsed unto them the last words which king Benjamin had taught them, and explained them to the people of king Limhi, so that they might understand all the words which he spake" (Mosiah 8:3). Similarly, HELAMAN₂ (c. 30 B.C.) admonished his sons Lehi₄ and NEPHI₂ to "remember . . . the words which king Benjamin spake unto his people; yea, remember that there is no other way nor means whereby man can be saved, only through the atoning blood of Jesus Christ" (Hel. 5:9). These words mirror one of the central themes of Benjamin's address: "Salvation was, and is, and is to come, in and through the atoning blood of Christ" (Mosiah 3:18–19; cf. Hel. 14:12).

After a long and prosperous reign, Benjamin died about 121 B.C. No higher tribute was paid to his greatness than that given by his son Mosiah₂. In a discourse given at the end of his own reign, in which he considers the advantages and pitfalls of various forms of government, Mosiah says, "If ye could have men for your kings who would do even as my father Benjamin did for this people, . . . then it would be expedient that ye should always have kings to rule over you" (Mosiah 29:13).

BIBLIOGRAPHY

Nibley, Hugh W. *An Approach to the Book of Mormon*. In CWHN 4:295–310.

ADDITIONAL SOURCE

Welch, John W., and Stephen D. Ricks, eds. *King Benjamin's Speech: "That Ye May Learn Wisdom."* Provo, Utah: FARMS, 1998.

STEPHEN D. RICKS

BIBLE

[The entry on the Bible is designed as an overview of the positive LDS appraisal and extensive use of this scriptural collection. Articles under this entry here are:

> Bible
> LDS Belief in the Bible

The first article explains the importance of the Bible among the standard works of the Church. The second article explores the depth of belief in the Bible. For discussions of the range of matters associated with the LDS view of scripture in general, see the set of articles under the general heading Scripture: Interpretation within Scripture.*]*

Bible

The Bible stands at the foundation of The Church of Jesus Christ of Latter-day Saints, constitutes one of its standard works, and is accepted as the word of God. In 1820 a New Testament passage in the epistle of James prompted the young Joseph Smith to ask God about the religions of his time, and thereupon he received his first vision, in which he saw God the Father and Jesus Christ (James 1:5; JS—H 1:11–12, 17–18). Three years later, Old Testament and New Testament passages provided the principal scriptural foundation of Joseph's second major spiritual experience when the angel MORONI appeared to him and taught him from Malachi, Isaiah, Joel, Daniel, and other scriptures (JS—H 1:36–41; *JD* 24:241; *Messenger and Advocate* 1 [Apr. 1835]: 109). After completing the Book of Mormon translation and organizing the restored Church of Jesus Christ in 1830, the Prophet Joseph Smith thoroughly studied the Bible as instructed by the Lord and prepared the Joseph Smith Translation of the Bible (JST).

From childhood, Latter-day Saints are introduced to the teachings of the Bible. Certain passages are emphasized in teaching children. Most children in Primary—and particularly those in families who hold family home evening and follow scripture reading programs—become familiar with the events recorded in Genesis, including stories of Adam and Eve, Noah, Abraham, Jacob, and Joseph. Later episodes of the prophets, judges, and kings (such as Moses, Samson, Samuel, David, Solomon, Jonah, and Daniel), as well as those of New Testament personalities (e.g., Peter, Paul, and Stephen), are also favorites. The stories of Deborah, Ruth, Esther, and Mary are especially loved by girls. However, the life and teachings of Jesus Christ are the most studied and appreciated.

Richer gospel teachings come into focus in repeated study of the Bible by Latter-day

Saints. In addition to Sunday School instruction, teenagers attending seminary classes spend two years of their four-year curriculum on the Bible. A similar emphasis is found in college-level religion classes in the universities and colleges of the Church educational system and in institute of religion classes at other universities and colleges. LDS missionaries often refer to Bible passages as they teach investigators of the Church. One of the strongest demonstrations of the importance of Bible study to the Latter-day Saints is found in the adult Sunday School program. In the Gospel Doctrine classes, two of every four years are devoted to reading, studying, and discussing the Bible. Another strong evidence of LDS commitment to the Bible is the effort and expense incurred to produce the LDS publication of the Bible in 1979. The General Authorities of the Church frequently quote from the Bible in their writings and general and stake conference addresses. Thus, the Bible forms an important gospel foundation for all Church members, from the newly baptized to the presiding leaders.

PREVALENT BIBLICAL TEACHINGS AND PRACTICES. Among the teachings found in the Bible, some concepts receive special emphasis. For example, Latter-day Saints readily identify with the Old Testament pattern of God speaking through living prophets (Amos 3:7), a pattern visible in the Church today. They also relate to the house of Israel through their individual patriarchal blessings, which usually identify a genealogical line back to one of the tribes of Israel. The concept of a covenant people, as taught in Genesis, Exodus, and Deuteronomy, conforms to LDS beliefs about being a covenant people today. Many laws and commandments, in particular a health code, distinguish both ancient Israel and its modern spiritual counterpart in the Church (Lev. 11; D&C 89). The wanderings of

ancient Israel and the challenges in settling the promised land also parallel early LDS history, so much so that Brigham Young has been called a modern Moses (e.g., Arrington, 1985).

New Testament teachings that are emphasized among Latter-day Saints include the teachings of the Savior and the apostles on basic gospel principles, especially faith and repentance, and covenant ordinances, particularly baptism and the gift of the Holy Ghost. Latter-day parallels to the New Testament Church organization, priesthood offices, and missionary work have their counterparts in contemporary LDS beliefs, practices, and Church organization.

BIBLICAL EMPHASIS WITHIN THE BOOK OF MORMON. Among Old Testament writings, those of Moses, Isaiah, and Malachi receive special attention from Latter-day Saints because of their prominence within the Book of Mormon. The teachings of Moses as found in the Pentateuch (an expanded portion of Genesis 1–6 being available also in the Pearl of Great Price) provide the foundation for understanding the Mosaic dispensation of the house of Israel. The Book of Mormon record, which originated with LEHI and with the people of Zarahemla (see MULEK), came mostly out of this Israelite setting. The record includes Adam and Eve and events in the Garden of Eden (e.g., 2 Ne. 2:15–25), and references to the flood at the time of Noah (e.g., Alma 10:22), to people divinely led to the Americas at the time of the Tower of Babel (Ether 1:3–5, 33), to events in the lives of the patriarchs (e.g., 2 Ne. 3:4–16), and to the calling, works, and words of Moses (e.g., 1 Ne. 17:23–31; 2 Ne. 3:16–17; see also LAW OF MOSES). The fifth chapter of 1 Nephi reviews the biblical records that Lehi's family brought out of Jerusalem (see PLATES AND RECORDS IN THE BOOK OF MORMON) and, along with 1 Nephi

17, highlights key biblical events, particularly the Israelite exodus from Egypt, although without the details found in the Pentateuch. The examples and teachings of Old Testament prophets, judges, and kings were also part of the biblical records of the community of Lehi. Because this group lived under the law of Moses (2 Ne. 25:24), Old Testament religious practices are continued in the Book of Mormon.

Fully one-third of the writings of Isaiah are found in the Book of Mormon, making Isaiah the most frequently quoted biblical book there. Twenty-two of the sixty-six chapters of Isaiah are quoted in whole or in part in the Book of Mormon (a total of 433 of Isaiah's 1,292 verses). Book of Mormon prophets and writers typically selected those chapters highlighting God's covenant relationships and his promises to Israel, the role and calling of the Messiah, and prophecies concerning the last days. These themes are prevalent in contemporary LDS theology as well (A of F 3, 4, 9, 10).

Malachi's teachings in the Book of Mormon are important because the resurrected Jesus quoted them and thus emphasized them (cf. 3 Ne. 24–25; Mal. 3–4; D&C 2:1–3). Malachi's words concerning a messenger sent to prepare the way for Christ's second coming, the payment of tithes and offerings, and the latter-day mission of Elijah thus form another important nucleus of Old Testament teachings within LDS society.

Because the main Book of Mormon colony left Jerusalem approximately six hundred years before the beginning of the New Testament period, Book of Mormon writers did not have access to New Testament records. However, they had access to two important sources of doctrines paralleling some of the New Testament: the resurrected Christ and divine revelation. The resurrected Christ de-livered to his hearers in the Americas a sermon essentially the same as the one he had delivered near the Sea of Galilee. He also gave important additions and clarifications that focus on him as the Redeemer and Lord, on the fulfillment of the law of Moses, and on the latter days (3 Ne. 11–18). In addition, he amplified teachings recorded in John 10, especially verse 16, about his role as the Good Shepherd of the scattered sheep of Israel (3 Ne. 15:12–24). Mormon's important teachings about baptism and about faith, hope, and charity parallel New Testament teachings, especially those of Paul in 1 Corinthians 13.

Is the Bible Complete? Latter-day Saints revere the Bible as the word of God revealed to humankind. However, Joseph Smith recognized that translations do not reflect totally and exactly the original words and intentions of the ancient prophets and other biblical writers. Thus, in the Wentworth letter he wrote, "We believe the Bible to be the word of God as far as it is translated correctly" (A of F 8). Joseph Smith observed that "our latitude and longitude can be determined in the original Hebrew with far greater accuracy than in the English version. There is a grand distinction between the actual meaning of the prophets and the present translation" (TPJS, pp. 290–91). While Latter-day Saints accept rather explicitly what the Bible now says, they realize that more is to be accounted for than is available in the extant biblical record.

In addition to difficulties associated with translating from ancient to modern languages, other scriptures also declare that some parts of the original biblical text have been lost or corrupted (e.g., 1 Ne. 13:28–29; D&C 6:26–27; 93:6–18). Joseph Smith commented on the Bible's incompleteness: "It was apparent that many important points touching the salvation of men, had been taken from the Bible, or lost before it was compiled"

(*TPJS*, pp. 10–11). He later said, "Much instruction has been given to man since the beginning which we do not possess now. . . . We have what we have, and the Bible contains what it does contain" (*TPJS*, p. 61). The Prophet Joseph further stated, "I believe the Bible as it read when it came from the pen of the original writers. Ignorant translators, careless transcribers, or designing and corrupt priests have committed many errors" (*TPJS*, p. 327). Thus, the elements of mistranslation, incompleteness, and other errors weaken the Bible; but the spirit of its messages still reveals enough of God's word to fulfill his appointed purposes. Joseph Smith summarized thus: "Through the kind providence of our Father a portion of His word which He delivered to His ancient saints, has fallen into our hands [and] is presented to us with a promise of a reward if obeyed, and with a penalty if disobeyed" (*TPJS*, p. 61). Latter-day Saints have continued to trust in the general accuracy of the biblical texts even though they know that that text may not always be correct. Thus, they study and revere the Bible, especially in the context of other scriptures and modern revelation, which have much to say about the Bible and how it is to be interpreted, and as they study they ponder and pray that they may receive inspiration from God and come to understand the Bible's messages as they need to be applied in their lives (cf. Moro. 10:3–5).

FIRST PRESIDENCY'S ENDORSEMENT OF BIBLE READING. Each of the Presidents of the Church has encouraged Latter-day Saints to read the scriptures and to apply scriptural teachings in their lives, as the scriptures also admonish (cf. 2 Tim. 3:16; 1 Ne. 19:23). As a demonstration of this emphasis, in 1983, a year proclaimed as the "Year of the Bible" in the United States, the members of the First Presidency of the Church issued a strong statement in support of Bible reading and application: "We commend to all people everywhere the daily reading, pondering and heeding of the divine truths of the Holy Bible." They also declared the Church's attitude toward the Bible by saying that "the Church of Jesus Christ of Latter-day Saints accepts the Holy Bible as essential to faith and doctrine" and that the Church is committed to Bible reading and scholarship as demonstrated by the publishing of an enhanced edition of the King James Version. "Moreover," they continued, "the Holy Bible is the textbook for adult, youth and children's classes throughout the Church each year."

In the same statement, the First Presidency highlighted the role and value of the Bible in the lives of individuals. They observed that when "read reverently and prayerfully, the Holy Bible becomes a priceless volume, converting the soul to righteousness. Principal among its virtues is the declaration that Jesus is the Christ, the Son of God, through whom eternal salvation may come to all." They continued with the promise that "as we read the scripture, we avail ourselves of the better part of this world's literature," and they encouraged all to "go to the fountain of truth, searching the scriptures, reading them in our homes, and teaching our families what the Lord has said through the inspired and inspiring passages of the Holy Bible" ("Statement of the First Presidency," p. 3).

The Latter-day Saint use of the Bible differs from the Judeo-Christian norm because it is not the sole LDS source of authority. The Bible is interpreted and understood by Latter-day Saints through four important means: (1) other LDS scriptures, which enrich and give perspective to an understanding of biblical teachings; (2) statements of modern prophets and apostles on the meaning of some biblical passages; (3) the Joseph Smith Translation of the Bible; and (4) personal revelation through the gift of the Holy Ghost enhancing the comprehension of the scriptures. Consequently, Latter-day Saints are not left without information about the meaning of many difficult passages that have divided the entire Christian world for two millennia.

The LDS perspective on the Bible is summarized well in the statement of the seventh Church president, Heber J. Grant, who said, "All my life I have been finding additional evidences that the Bible is the Book of books, and that the Book of Mormon is the greatest witness for the truth of the Bible that has ever been published" (*IE* 39 [Nov. 1936]: 660).

BIBLIOGRAPHY

Anderson, Richard L. *Understanding Paul.* Salt Lake City, 1983.

Arrington, Leonard. *Brigham Young: American Moses.* New York, 1985.

Barlow, Philip L. *Mormons and the Bible.* New York, 1990.

Harrison, Roland Kenneth. *Introduction to the Old Testament.* Grand Rapids, Mich., 1969.

Ludlow, Daniel H. *A Companion to Your Study of the Old Testament.* Salt Lake City, 1981.

Ludlow, Victor L. *Unlocking the Old Testament.* Salt Lake City, 1981.

———. *Isaiah: Prophet, Seer, and Poet.* Salt Lake City, 1982.

Matthews, Robert J. *A Bible! A Bible!* Salt Lake City, Utah, 1990.

McConkie, Bruce R. *The Mortal Messiah.* Salt Lake City, 1979.

Nyman, Monte S., ed. *Isaiah and the Prophets.* Provo, Utah, 1984.

Reynolds, Noel B. "The Brass Plates Version of Genesis." In *By Study and Also by Faith*, ed. J.

Lundquist and S. Ricks, Vol. 2, pp. 136–73. Salt Lake City, 1990.

Sperry, Sidney B. *Paul's Life and Letters.* Salt Lake City, 1955.

———. *The Voice of Israel's Prophets.* Salt Lake City, 1965.

———. *The Spirit of the Old Testament.* Salt Lake City, 1970.

"Statement of the First Presidency." *Church News*, Mar. 20, 1983, p. 3.

Talmage, James E. *Jesus the Christ.* Salt Lake City, 1915.

Welch, John W. *The Sermon at the Temple and the Sermon on the Mount.* Salt Lake City, 1990.

ADDITIONAL SOURCE

Matthews, Robert J. "What the Book of Mormon Tells Us about the Bible." In *Doctrines of the Book of Mormon: The 1991 Sperry Symposium*, edited by Bruce A. Van Orden and Brent L. Top, 93–113. Salt Lake City: Deseret Book, 1992.

VICTOR L. LUDLOW

LDS Belief in the Bible

The Church believes the word of God contained in the Bible. It accepts the Bible "as the foremost of [the Church's] standard works, first among the books which have been proclaimed as . . . written guides in faith and doctrine. In the respect and sanctity with which the Latter-day Saints regard the Bible they are of like profession with Christian denominations in general" (*AF*, 1966 ed., p. 236).

Latter-day Saints value the Bible for many reasons. The Bible presents the revelations of God in several dispensations or eras, each headed by prophets. They also read and follow the Bible for the instructional and spiritual value of the events it describes. While some of the Old Testament describes the law of Moses that Latter-day Saints believe was fulfilled with the atonement of Christ (3 Ne. 9:17), nevertheless the Old Testament stories, commandments, ordinances, proverbs, and prophetic writings still express the basic patterns of God's will toward his children and how they should act toward him.

Latter-day Saints revere the New Testament for its account of the birth, ministry, atonement, and resurrection of the Savior, Jesus Christ. The teachings of Jesus in the New Testament comprise the core of LDS doctrine, and their preeminence is evidenced by their frequent appearance in other LDS standard works accepted as scripture and in LDS speaking and writing.

The writings of the New Testament apostles are accepted and appreciated for their doctrine and wise and inspired counsel and for documenting the apostolic challenge of proclaiming the gospel, adhering to the original teachings of Christ, establishing the unity of the faith, and promoting the righteousness of believers in a rapidly growing Church. Latter-day Saints also find references in several letters of the early apostles of the falling away that necessitated the restoration, alerting the faithful to remain fervent and active in the faith and to stay true to the love of Jesus Christ.

While Latter-day Saints devoutly regard the Bible, they do not consider it the sole authoritative source of religious instruction and personal guidance. They also study accounts of God's dealings with other ancient peoples such as those found in the Book of Mormon along with the teachings of the Prophet Joseph SMITH and the latter-day prophets and apostles. Latter-day Saints consider personal revelation the individual's ultimate source for understanding scripture and knowing God's will.

Viewed as being harmonious with each other, all these sources enhance and clarify one another, and aid modern readers in correctly comprehending and translating these texts.

Latter-day Saints believe all that God has revealed. They seek to know and do the word of God wherever it has been made known in truth and authority. They believe that salvation is in Jesus Christ and not in any combination of words or books. They believe in God and in his son Jesus Christ, whose words and ways can be known through a lifetime of scripture study, service, and prayer, and by personal revelation through the power of the Holy Ghost.

BIBLIOGRAPHY

Matthews, Robert J. *A Bible! A Bible!* Salt Lake City, 1990.

PAUL C. HEDENGREN

BIBLICAL PROPHECIES ABOUT THE BOOK OF MORMON

Latter-day Saints believe that the coming forth of the Book of Mormon as an instrument in God's hand for bringing his latter-day work to fruition was revealed to biblical prophets such as ISAIAH and Ezekiel (cf. 1 Ne. 19:21). Their prophecies about these matters, like those about the coming of Jesus Christ, are better understood when some of the historical events that surround them are known.

JOSEPH'S PROPHECY. Allusions are made to a branch that would be broken off in Jacob's blessing to Joseph, promising that he would become a fruitful bough whose "branches" would run "over the wall" and that his posterity would be heir to divine blessings (Gen. 49:22–26; 1 Ne. 19:24; cf. Deut. 33:13–17). A further prophecy in the Book of Mormon aids in interpreting Genesis 49.

According to a prophecy of Joseph in

Egypt, preserved in the Book of Mormon (2 Ne. 3:4–21), two sets of records would be kept by two tribes of Israel—one (the Bible) written by the tribe of Judah and the other (Book of Mormon) kept by the tribe of Joseph (2 Ne. 3:12; cf. Ezek. 37:15–19). Those kept by the tribe of Joseph were written on PLATES of brass and largely parallel the biblical records (1 Ne. 5:10–16; 13:23). They were carried to a promised land in the Western Hemisphere by LEHI, a prophet and descendant of Joseph, who fled Jerusalem about 600 B.C. Lehi exclaimed, "Joseph truly saw our day. And he obtained a promise of the Lord, that out of the fruit of his loins the Lord God would raise up a righteous branch unto the house of Israel; not the Messiah, but a branch which was to be broken off" (2 Ne. 3:5).

VISIT OF RESURRECTED JESUS. A succession of prophets taught the gospel of Jesus Christ to Lehi's "branch" of Joseph's descendants and prophesied that after Jesus was resurrected, he would visit them (e.g., 2 Ne. 26:1). Regarding this circumstance, Jesus told his hearers in Palestine that he had "other sheep . . . which are not of this fold: them also I must bring, and they shall hear my voice; and there shall be one fold, and one shepherd" (John 10:16). When he appeared in the Western Hemisphere (c. A.D. 34), he allowed the multitude to touch the wounds in his hands and side and feet so that they would understand the reality of his resurrection (3 Ne. 11:10–15). Later, he specifically referred to his words recorded in John's gospel (3 Ne. 15:16–24; John 10:16), saying, "Ye are they of whom I said: Other sheep I have which are not of this fold" (3 Ne. 15:21). Further, he taught them his gospel, called twelve disciples, announced the fulfillment of the LAW OF MOSES, instituted the SACRAMENT, and organized his church— causing them to become of one fold with his disciples in Palestine, having him as their common shepherd (3 Ne. 11–29).

RECORD FROM THE GROUND. Latter-day Saints teach that Isaiah foresaw that part of this branch of Joseph's family would eventually be destroyed. He likened it to David's city Ariel, that would also be destroyed when hostile forces "camp[ed] against" or laid siege to it (Isa. 29:3). But despite the fact that many of the people of this branch would be slain, both Isaiah and Nephi explained that the voice of Joseph's descendants would be heard again as a voice "out of the ground"; their speech would "whisper out of the dust" (Isa. 29:4; 2 Ne. 26:16). For "the words of the faithful should speak as if it were from the dead" (2 Ne. 27:13; cf. 26:15–16; *see* "VOICE FROM THE DUST").

Perceiving how this would take place, NEPHI₁, the first writer in the Book of Mormon, wrote about 570 B.C. to unborn generations: "My beloved brethren, all those who are of the house of Israel, and all ye ends of the earth, I speak unto you as the voice of one crying from the dust" (2 Ne. 33:13). Similarly, the last writer in the Book of Mormon, MORONI₂, wrote about A.D. 400: "I speak unto you as though I spake from the dead; for I know that ye shall have my words" (Morm. 9:30; cf. Moro. 10:27). As he was about to bury the records, he wrote: "No one need say [the records] shall not come, for they surely shall, for the Lord hath spoken it; for out of the earth shall they come, by the hand of the Lord, and none can stay it" (Morm. 8:26; cf. *TPJS*, p. 98).

The phrase "out of the ground" is thus a metaphor for the voice of those who have died, but it also refers to records being buried in the earth until they come forth. The overall connection between Isaiah, chapter 29, and the Book of Mormon people is discussed in 2 Nephi, chapters 26–29 (cf. Morm. 8:23–26).

THE RECORD APPEARS. Parts of the GOLD PLATES were sealed when Joseph Smith received them. Isaiah spoke of "the words of a book that is sealed" that would be delivered to a "learned" person (Isa. 29:11). Latter-day Saints see the role of the "learned" person fulfilled by Professor Charles Anthon of Columbia College (New York), and these "words of a book" constitute the ANTHON TRANSCRIPT. The book itself, however, would be delivered to another (Joseph Smith) who would simply acknowledge, "I am not learned" (Isa. 29:12), but would be divinely empowered to translate it.

Isaiah foresaw that when the book would appear, people would be contending over God's word (Isa. 29:13). This circumstance would provide the context wherein God could perform his "marvelous work and a wonder," causing the "wisdom of their wise men" to perish and the "understanding of their prudent men [to] be hid" while the meek would "increase their joy in the Lord" and the "poor among men shall rejoice in the Holy One of Israel" (Isa. 29:14, 19). Meanwhile, those who had "erred in spirit shall come to understanding, and they that murmured shall learn doctrine" (Isa. 29:22–24; cf. 2 Ne. 27:6–26).

TWO RECORDS. Ezekiel also prophesied concerning the two records—that of Joseph or Ephraim (i.e., the Book of Mormon) and that of Judah (i.e., the Bible)—that would be joined in the last days as an instrument provided by the Lord to gather his people back to himself (Ezek. 37:15–22; cf. 2 Ne. 3:11–12).

For Latter-day Saints, when Ezekiel spoke of "sticks" (probably waxed writing boards), he was illustrating the instruments by which God would bring peoples together in the latter days, just as he used the concept of the Resurrection to illustrate the gathering of God's people, which is the theme of chapters 34–37. Just as bodies are reconstituted in the Resurrection, so will Israel be reconstituted in

the gathering; and the formerly divided nations will become one (Ezek. 37:1–14). Thus, the publication of the Book of Mormon in 1830 was a sign that the divided tribes of Israel were to become one under God and that God's latter-day work was beginning to be implemented (Ezek. 37:21–28; cf. 1 Ne. 13:34–41; 3 Ne. 20:46–21:11).

BIBLIOGRAPHY

McConkie, Bruce R. *A New Witness for the Articles of Faith*, pp. 422–58. Salt Lake City, 1985.

Meservy, Keith H. "Ezekiel's Sticks and the Gathering of Israel." *Ensign* 17 (Feb. 1987): 4–13.

Robison, Parley Parker, comp. *Orson Pratt's Works on the Doctrines of the Gospel*, pp. 269–84. Salt Lake City, 1945.

KEITH H. MESERVY

BOOK OF MORMON

[*This entry introduces the Book of Mormon, with the* Overview *describing its basic nature, contents, and purposes; a brief article follows on the* Title Page from the Book of Mormon; *and the remaining articles are devoted to a brief explanation of each book in the Book of Mormon.*

Book of Helaman

Third Nephi

Fourth Nephi

Book of Mormon

Book of Ether

Book of Moroni

The teachings of the Book of Mormon are discussed in doctrinal articles throughout the Encyclopedia; see Gospel of Jesus Christ. *See also* Religious Teachings and Practices in the Book of Mormon; Jesus Christ in the Scriptures: Jesus Christ in the Book of Mormon; Prophecy in the Book of Mormon.

Concerning its essential relationship with the Bible and other scripture, see Bible; Biblical Prophecies about the Book of Mormon; Book of Mormon in a Biblical Culture; Isaiah; Scripture: Interpretation within Scripture.

On the writing and composition of the Book of Mormon, see Authorship of the Book of Mormon; Language; Literature, Book of Mormon as; Plates and Records in the Book of Mormon.

For information about its origin and publication, see Editions; Manuscripts of the Book of Mormon; Translation of the Book of Mormon by Joseph Smith; Translations of the Book of Mormon; Witnesses of the Book of Mormon; Manuscript, Lost 116 Pages; Moroni, Visitations of. *See, generally,* Studies of the Book of Mormon.

Separate articles can be found on Peoples of the Book of Mormon; Jaredites; Lamanites; Nephites; Women in the Book of Mormon; *articles on the main individuals in this scripture are listed under* Book of Mormon Personalities.

Internal aspects of Book of Mormon culture and civilization are discussed in such entries as Chronology; Economy and Technology; Geography; Government and Legal History in the Book of Mormon; Warfare in the Book of Mormon; Jesus Christ: Forty-Day Ministry and Other Post-Resurrection Appearances of; Liahona; Secret Combinations; Sword of Laban; Three Nephites; Tree of Life.]

Overview

The Prophet Joseph SMITH called the Book of Mormon "the most correct of any book on earth, and the keystone of our religion" and said that a person "would get nearer to God by abiding by its precepts, than by any other book" (*TPJS*, p. 194), for it contains the fulness of the GOSPEL OF JESUS CHRIST (D&C 20:8–9). To members of The Church of Jesus Christ of Latter-day Saints, the Book of Mormon forms the doctrinal foundation of the Church and speaks the word of God to all the world.

The Book of Mormon both confirms and supplements the Bible: "Behold, this [the Book of Mormon] is written for the intent that ye may believe that [the Bible]; and if ye believe [the Bible] ye will believe [the Book of Mormon] also" (Morm. 7:9). The Bible is primarily a record of God's dealings with the forebears and descendants of Jacob or Israel in the ancient Near East. Latter-day Saints believe the Book of Mormon to be a record of God's dealings principally with another group of Israelites he brought to the Western Hemisphere from Jerusalem about 600 B.C. (*see* LEHI). They anticipated the birth and coming of Jesus Christ and believed in his atonement and gospel. Their complex, lengthy records were abridged by a prophet named MORMON, inscribed on plates of gold, and buried by his son, MORONI₂, after internecine wars destroyed all of the believers in Christ in the New World except Moroni (A.D. 385).

JOSEPH SMITH AND THE BOOK OF MORMON. In his short lifetime, Joseph Smith brought forth many scriptures. His first prophetic calling was to bring forth the Book of Mormon. In 1823, at age seventeen, he was

In this wooden box, Joseph kept the Book of Mormon plates. The inside of the box measures 14¼" x 16¼". The depth is 6¼" sloping to 4". The lid and bottom are walnut, and the sides are made from boxwood. The box was originally Samuel Smith's lap desk. In the possession of Emeritus Church Patriarch Eldred G. Smith.

shown the hidden record by Moroni, then a resurrected angelic messenger from God (JS—H 1:27–54). After several visitations during the next four years, Joseph was allowed to remove the sacred record from its resting place in the hill CUMORAH, near Palmyra, New York. Despite many interruptions and persistent persecutions (JS—H 1:57–60), Joseph Smith translated the lengthy record in about sixty working days. Latter-day Saints bear testimony that he did this "through the mercy of God, by the power of God" (D&C 1:29), "by the inspiration of heaven" (*Messenger and Advocate* [Oct. 1834]: 14–16; JS—H 1:71, n.). He had the assistance of several scribes, chiefly Oliver COWDERY, who wrote what Joseph Smith dictated. The book was published in Palmyra in 1830. At least eleven witnesses, in addition to Joseph Smith, saw and/or hefted the Book of Mormon plates before he returned them to Moroni (*see* WITNESSES OF THE BOOK OF MORMON).

PURPOSES AND CONTENTS. The Book of Mormon, as its modern subtitle states, stands with the Bible as "Another Testament of Jesus Christ." Its main purposes are summarized

on its title page: to show the remnants of the Book of Mormon people what great things God did for their forefathers, to make known the covenants of the Lord, and to convince "Jew and Gentile that Jesus is the Christ, the Eternal God, manifesting himself unto all nations." The central event in the Book of Mormon is the appearance of the resurrected Christ to righteous inhabitants of the Western Hemisphere after his ascension into heaven at Jerusalem. During his visit, Christ delivered a sermon that is similar to the SERMON ON THE MOUNT recorded in the New Testament, but with certain vital clarifications and additions. He declared his doctrine, the fulness of his gospel necessary to enter the kingdom of God; and he established his Church with its essential ordinances, and ordained disciples to preside over the Church. At this time, Christ also explained the promises of God to Israel; healed the sick and disabled; blessed the children and their parents; and expressed his great love, allowing each individual to come forward and touch the wounds he had received during his crucifixion (see 3 Ne. 11–26). The record of Jesus' visit and many other passages in the Book of Mormon verify the divine sonship, ministry, atonement, resurrection, and eternal status of the Lord Jesus Christ and show that the fulness of his gospel is the same for all people, whenever and wherever they have lived.

The ancestors of these people to whom Jesus appeared had been in the Western Hemisphere for about 600 years. The Book of Mormon opens with the family of Lehi in Jerusalem at the time of the biblical prophet Jeremiah. Lehi was warned by God about 600 B.C. to take his family and flee Jerusalem before it was destroyed by Babylon (1 Ne. 1:1–2). The account, written by Lehi's son NEPHI₁, first tells of his family's departure from Jerusalem and of his dangerous return to the city with his brothers to obtain sacred records that contained their lineage, the five books of Moses, and a history of the Jews and writings of prophets down to Jeremiah's time (1 Ne. 3–5).

The group traveled in the wilderness until they reached a pleasant land by the sea where Nephi, with God's instruction, built a ship that took them to the New World (1 Ne. 17–18). Nephi's older brothers, LAMAN and Lemuel, expressed resentment at Nephi's closeness to the Lord and did not want him to rule over them (1 Ne. 16:37–39; 18:10). When the family reached the New World, this antagonism led to a schism between the NEPHITES and LAMANITES that pervades the Book of Mormon.

As the Nephite sermons, prophecies, and historical records were compiled and handed down, the writers emphasized that those who keep God's commandments prosper. Unfortunately, many who prospered became proud and persecuted others, with war as the eventual result. The desolation of war humbled the people, who began again to call upon God.

Ancient American prophets, like biblical prophets such as Moses, Isaiah, and Daniel, were shown visions of the future of various nations. For example, Nephi foresaw Christopher COLUMBUS' discovery of America, the influx of Gentiles into the New World, and the American Revolution (1 Ne. 13:12–15, 18–19), as well as the birth and earthly ministry of Jesus Christ. Christ's birth, ministry, and death were prophesied by Lehi, Nephi, BENJAMIN, SAMUEL THE LAMANITE, and other prophets. When MOSIAH₁ discovered a people who had left Jerusalem with MULEK, a son of Zedekiah (see Jer. 52:10; Omni 1:12–15; Hel. 8:21), and King Limhi's messengers found a record of the extinct JAREDITES, the Nephites learned that they were not the only people God had brought to the Western Hemisphere.

After the appearance of Jesus Christ, the

Jesus Christ Is the God of That Land, by Minerva K. Teichert (1949, oil on board, 36" x 48"). Superimposed on the Western Hemisphere and flanked by Quetzal birds, Native American symbols of liberty and freedom, this painting conveys the central message of the Book of Mormon "that Jesus is the Christ, the Eternal God, manifesting himself unto all nations" (Book of Mormon title page). Courtesy Harriet Arrington.

Nephites and Lamanites enjoyed peace for more than 160 years (4 Ne. 1:18–24). Then, many who had been righteous broke their covenants with God, and the Church and their civilization began to collapse. At last, in A.D. 385, the few remaining Nephites were hunted and killed by Lamanites. The book ends with Moroni, the last Nephite, writing to the people of modern times, admonishing them to "come unto Christ, and be perfected in him" (Moro. 10:32).

MODERN APPLICATIONS. Latter-day Saints embrace the Book of Mormon as a record for all people. In addition to instructing their contemporaries and descendants, the prophets who wrote these ancient records foresaw modern conditions and selected lessons needed to meet the challenges of this world (Morm. 8:34–35). Their book is a record of a fallen people, urging all people to live righteously and prevent a similar fall today.

The Book of Mormon has had a profound effect on the Church and its members. It is so fundamental that Joseph Smith said, "Take away the Book of Mormon and the revelations and where is our religion? We have none" (*TPJS*, p. 71).

The Book of Mormon teaches that the living God has spoken to several peoples throughout the earth who have written sacred records as he has commanded (2 Ne. 29:11–12). The Book of Mormon is one such record.

It also stands as evidence to Latter-day Saints that God restored his true and living Church through Joseph Smith. The importance of this belief for Latter-day Saints cannot be overestimated, for they are confident that God watches over the people of the earth and loves them, and that he continues to speak to them through contemporary prophets who apply unchanging gospel principles to today's challenges.

The Book of Mormon also is important to Latter-day Saints as an aid in understanding the Bible and the will of God. Nephi prophesied that many "plain and . . . precious" truths and covenants would be taken from the gospel and the Bible after the deaths of the apostles (1 Ne. 13:26–27). Many questions that have arisen from the Bible are answered for Latter-day Saints by the Book of Mormon, such as the mode of and reasons for baptism (2 Ne. 31; 3 Ne. 11:23–26); the proper way to administer the sacrament of the Lord's Supper (Moro. 4–5); the nature of the Resurrection (Alma 40); the effects of the FALL OF ADAM; and the reasons for evil and suffering in the world (2 Ne. 2). The Book of Mormon reinforces the LDS doctrine that the gospel of Jesus Christ existed before the Creation and has been revealed to prophets and believers throughout time.

Also sacred to Latter-day Saints is the Book of Mormon as a tutor in discerning the promptings of the Holy Ghost. Many Latter-day Saints, including those born into LDS families, trace their conversion to Jesus Christ and their commitment toward the Church to prayerful study of the Book of Mormon, and through it they learn to recognize the Holy Spirit. Thus, the book becomes a continuing symbol of personal revelation and of God's love for and attention to the needs of each person. It also declares that all mankind will be judged by its precepts and commandments (Mosiah 3:24; Moro. 10:27; *see* JUDGMENT). It is evidence that God remembers every creature he has created (Mosiah 27:30) and every covenant he has made (1 Ne. 19:15; 3 Ne. 16:11). The Book of Mormon is the base from which millions have begun a personal journey of spiritual growth and of service to others.

For LDS children, the Book of Mormon is a source of stories and heroes to equal those of the Bible—Joseph in Egypt, Daniel in the lions' den, the faithful Ruth, and brave Queen Esther. They tell and sing with enthusiasm about the army of faithful young men led by HELAMAN$_1$ (Alma 56:41–50); of the prophet ABINADI's courage before wicked King Noah (Mosiah 11–17); of Nephi and his unwavering faithfulness (1 Ne. 3–18); of Abish, a Lamanite woman who for many years appears to be the lone believer in Christ in King Lamoni's court until the missionary Ammon taught the gospel to the king and queen (Alma 19); and of Jesus' appearances to the Nephites (3 Ne. 11–28). There are many favorites. The book is used to teach children doctrines, provide examples of the Christlike life, and remind them of God's great love and hope for all his children.

The book is central to missionary work. It is the Church's most important missionary tool and is destined to go to every nation, kindred, tongue, and people (Rev. 14:6–7). All LDS missionaries encourage those they contact to read and pray about the book as a means of receiving their own testimony from God about the truthfulness of the Book of Mormon, a witness of Jesus Christ.

Latter-day Saints are regularly admonished to make fuller use of the Book of Mormon. In 1832, two and one-half years after the book was published, the word of the Lord warned the Saints that they had treated the revelations too lightly and had neglected to "remember the new covenant, even the Book of Mormon" (D&C 84:57). Church leaders repeatedly encourage members to make the Book of Mormon a greater part of their lives. President Ezra Taft Benson has counseled Latter-day Saints to read the book daily and to share it and the gospel message with all the world.

READING THE BOOK OF MORMON. This sacred record asks the reader to approach its words with faith and prayer. One of its teachings is that readers will "receive no witness until after the trial of [their] faith" (Ether 12:6). Therefore, although aspects of the book may seem unusual or improbable at first, it invites its readers to entertain them as possibilities until the whole picture becomes clear and other feelings are experienced and thoughts considered. Moreover, the final inscription of Moroni$_2$ on the title page asks readers to look beyond human weaknesses in the book: "If there are faults they are the mistakes of men; wherefore, condemn not the things of God." He closed his own book within the Book of Mormon by exhorting all who receive these things to ask God, with a sincere heart and with real intent, having faith in Christ, if they are not true, and promises that God will manifest the truth of it (Moro. 10:4).

Latter-day Saints of all ages and interests find rewards in reading the Book of Mormon. At first, people tend to focus attention on its main messages and story lines. With further

reading and pondering, they discover numerous themes, meaningful nuances, interesting details, and profound spiritual expressions.

The first-time reader may find the Book of Mormon difficult at times. Its style, as translated into English, is somewhat similar to that of the King James Version of the Bible, and the reader who is not familiar with the Bible will encounter some unfamiliar word usages. The 1981 edition of the Book of Mormon is annotated with many Bible references and aids to facilitate a more detailed comparison.

Book of Mormon prophets Nephi, JACOB, and Abinadi quote extensively from Isaiah (see, e.g., 2 Ne. 6–8 [Isa. 49–51]; 2 Ne. 12–24 [Isa. 2–14]; Mosiah 14 [Isa. 53]), an Old Testament prophet whose poetic style and allusions have challenged readers of the Bible and also have proved difficult to many who study the Book of Mormon. Initially, some Church leaders encourage first-time readers to move through these chapters, understanding what is accessible and saving the rest for later study. In Isaiah's writings, Latter-day Saints find an important testimony of Christ and of the fulfillment of God's covenants with the house of Israel. Christ admonished his followers to "search these things diligently; for great are the words of Isaiah" (3 Ne. 23:1).

Another possible hurdle for readers is the book's nonchronological insertions. Nephi and Jacob and Jacob's descendants wrote first-person accounts from about 590 B.C. until about 150 B.C., and then Mormon (about A.D. 385) inserted a shorter chapter to explain his role as abridger of another record. Then the reader is returned via Mormon's abridgment to the history of Nephi's successors and of the descendants of ALMA$_1$. As groups of people break away from and return to the main body, parts of their records are incorporated into the book, causing the reader to jump back to earlier events. Likewise, Moroni's abridgment of the very ancient book of Ether appears out of chronological order near the end. In addition, the Book of Mormon, like the Old Testament, describes events from widely separated intervals. As an abridgment, it contains only a small part of the proceedings of these ancient peoples.

Approaching the Text. The arrangement of the Book of Mormon lends itself to many approaches. Three mutually supportive avenues are most often followed. First, the book serves as a source of guidance and doctrine, yielding lessons and wisdom applicable to contemporary life. This approach is recommended in the writings of Nephi, who wrote that he "did liken the scriptures unto [his people], that it might be for [their] profit and learning" (1 Ne. 19:23). Latter-day Saints find its pages rich with ennobling narratives, clear doctrines, eternal truths, memorable sayings, and principles. Knowing the conditions of the latter days, the ancient prophets periodically address the individual reader directly. Latter-day Saints emphasize the need to read the Book of Mormon prayerfully, with faith in God, to benefit personally from its teachings and to come unto Christ.

A second approach to the Book of Mormon, adding historical dimension to the first approach, is to study the book as an ancient text. The reader who accepts the Book of Mormon as an ancient Hebrew lineage history written by prophets in the New World will find the book consistent with that description and setting. The book is a repository of ancient cultures that are as far removed from modern readers as are those of the Old and New Testaments. Continuing research has found Hebrew poetic forms, rhetorical patterns, and idioms, together with many Mesoamerican symbols, traditions, and artifacts, to be implicit in the book or consistent with it.

Finally, one may enjoy the Book of Mormon as a work of literature. Although the style may seem tedious or repetitive at times, there are order, purpose, and clarity in its language. Its words are often as beautiful and as memorable as passages in the Psalms, the Gospel of John, and other notable religious works of prose and poetry.

Most faithful readers of the Book of Mormon, however, do not define or limit themselves to any single approach or methodology, for these approaches are all transcended by the overriding implications of the book's divine origins and eternal purposes. Study and faith, reflection and application, all help a person know and comprehend the messages of the Book of Mormon. But for millions of Latter-day Saints, their most important experience with the Book of Mormon has been the spiritual knowledge that they have received of its truth. It has changed and enriched their lives and has brought Jesus Christ and his teachings closer to them.

BIBLIOGRAPHY

Benson, Ezra Taft. *A Witness and a Warning*. Salt Lake City, 1988.

Downs, Robert B. *Books That Changed America*. London, 1970.

Faust, James E. "The Keystone of Our Religion." *Ensign* 13 (Nov. 1983): 9.

Nibley, Hugh W. "The Mormon View of the Book of Mormon." *Concilium* 10 (Dec. 1967): 82–83; reprinted, CWHN 8:259–64.

MONTE S. NYMAN

LISA BOLIN HAWKINS

Title Page from the Book of Mormon

Joseph Smith once wrote, "I wish to mention here that the title-page of the Book of Mormon is a literal translation, taken from the very last leaf, on the left hand side of the collection or book of plates, which contained the record which has been translated; . . . and that said title-page is not . . . a modern composition, either of mine or of any other man who has lived or does live in this generation" (*HC* 1:71).

The title page is therefore the translation of an ancient document, at least partially written by MORONI₂, son of Mormon, in the fifth century A.D. It describes the volume as an "abridgment of the record of the people of Nephi, and also of the Lamanites" and "an abridgment taken from the Book of Ether also, which is a record of the people of Jared" (*see* PLATES AND RECORDS IN THE BOOK OF MORMON).

According to the title page, the Book of Mormon is addressed to LAMANITES, Jews, and gentiles and is designed to inform Lamanites of promises made to their forebears and to convince "Jew and Gentile that Jesus is the Christ, the Eternal God, manifesting himself unto all nations."

The title page was used as the description of the Book of Mormon on the federal copyright application filed June 11, 1829, with R. R. Lansing, Clerk of the District Court of the United States for the Northern District of New York, at Albany.

BIBLIOGRAPHY

Ludlow, Daniel H. "The Title Page." In *The Book of Mormon: First Nephi, The Doctrinal Foundation*, ed. Monte S. Nyman and Charles D. Tate, Jr., pp. 19–33. Provo, Utah, 1988.

ADDITIONAL SOURCE

Sperry, Sidney B. "Moroni the Lonely: The Story of the Writing of the Title Page to the Book of Mormon." *Journal of Book of Mormon Studies* 4 (Spring 1995): 255–59.

ELDIN RICKS

First Book of Nephi

Written by NEPHI₁, an ancient prophet who fled Jerusalem with his father, LEHI, and Lehi's family shortly after 600 B.C., this book tells of their travels under divine guidance to the Western Hemisphere. With its detailed testimony of the mission of Jesus Christ and its panoramic view of sacred history, 1 Nephi is the doctrinal and historical foundation for all of the Book of Mormon. Its stated intent is to testify that the God of Israel can save all who repent and exercise faith in him (1 Ne. 1:20; 6:4).

Composed several years after Nephi arrived in the "promised land," the record, of which the First Book of Nephi was a part, contained prophesying and sacred preaching "for Christ's sake, and for the sake of [his] people" (Jacob 1:4). Its fundamental message is that the God of Israel is merciful and has the power to save those who obey him (1 Ne. 1:20; 6:4; 22:30–31). Nephi supports this thesis with historical and prophetic evidence. He cites Israel's exodus from Egypt twice as evidence of God's redeeming power, and saw the same power at work in his family's exodus from a doomed Jerusalem. A seer of remarkable spiritual stature, Nephi testified that greater acts of redemption lay in the future: God himself would come to earth to ransom man from death and sin (1 Ne. 11:33; 19:10), and before the end of the world, Israel would be redeemed.

The narrative of 1 Nephi is vivid and dramatic; acts of divine intervention dominate this account. It begins in the first year of the Judean King Zedekiah (1 Ne. 1:4; cf. 2 Kgs. 24:8–18; dated by Babylonian documents at 597 B.C.). Jerusalem had just capitulated after a brief Babylonian siege, and King Jehoiachin, together with many of Judah's prominent citizens, had been deported. When Jerusalem persisted in its arrogance, a host of prophets, including Jeremiah and Lehi, warned of destruction. As people conspired to kill Lehi, he was warned by the Lord and escaped with his family south into the desert. Twice his four sons returned to the region, once to obtain a copy of the scriptures written on plates of brass and again to convince Ishmael and his family to flee with them (chaps. 3–7). Guided by a miraculous brass compass (*see* LIAHONA), Lehi's group then completed a grueling odyssey that covered eight years in the wilderness, arriving at a verdant spot on the southern coast of the Arabian Peninsula. There, Nephi was summoned by the Lord to a mountain where he was instructed to build a ship to carry the group to a land of promise. Through God's frequent inspiration and protection, the ship was finished and the treacherous voyage completed (chaps. 16–18).

Through all these events, Lehi and Nephi were opposed by the oldest sons in the family, LAMAN and Lemuel, who were not only skeptical but sometimes violent in their opposition. The record vindicates Nephi in many ways. An angel once intervened to protect Nephi from his brothers; twice he escaped from them, being filled with the power of God. Several times, by his faith, he succeeded where they failed.

Records of powerful visions are interspersed throughout the narrative. Lehi received his prophetic commission in a vision as he prayed on Jerusalem's behalf: He saw a pillar of fire dwelling upon a rock and God seated upon his throne and was given a book to read that decreed judgment upon the city (chap. 1). Soon after, Nephi heard the voice of the Lord, saying that Nephi would teach and rule over his elder brothers (chap. 2); and Lehi had a dream that centered around a magnificent tree, a river, an iron rod, and a great and spacious building (chap. 8; *see also* TREE OF LIFE). The family's escape from a proud and materialistic Jerusalem and their

Wadi Sayq, near the border between Yemen and Oman on the Gulf of Aden (1989). Areas with vegetation such as this along the southern coast of the Arabian peninsula match the description of the place where Lehi and his group built their ship (1 Ne. 17:5), but they were unknown to Westerners until after the Book of Mormon was published. Courtesy Warren Aston.

subsequent quest for salvation in the wilderness are vividly reflected in the imagery of this dream. Lehi also prophesied about the Babylonian captivity of the Jews, their eventual return to Palestine, and the coming of a Messiah who would redeem mankind from its lost and fallen state (chap. 10).

Inspired by Lehi's spiritual experiences and wanting to know the meaning of his father's dream, Nephi sought and received the same vision, together with its interpretation. This revelation puts the experiences of Lehi and his posterity into the context of God's redemptive plan and provides much of the historical and doctrinal framework for subsequent Book of Mormon prophecy: (1) Nephi saw the birth, ministry, and atoning sacrifice of the Son of God, and the rejection of his apostles by Israel; (2) he witnessed the division of Lehi's family, followed by the rise, decline, and destruction of his own posterity by the descendants of his brothers, and saw that the Lamb of God would visit various branches of Israel, including Nephi's posterity; (3) he saw a GREAT AND ABOMINABLE CHURCH among the Gentiles, as well as a dispensation of the gospel to the Gentiles and their crucial role in gathering Israel and a remnant of Nephi's seed; and (4) he was shown the final victory of God over the powers of evil at the end of the world (chaps. 11–14).

Citing other corroborating prophecies, 1 Nephi 19–22 reinforces those four themes, the mainstays of the Nephite outlook on world history. Nephi first gives a detailed testimony of the atoning sacrifice of the God of Israel, his rejection, and the scattering of God's covenant people, quoting ZENOS, ZENOCK, and NEUM (chap. 19); he then quotes ISAIAH to show that God will defer his anger and will eventually gather his people through the assistance of gentile kings and queens (chaps. 20–21); and, finally, he exhorts all to obey God's commandments and be saved, for in the last days the wicked shall burn and the Holy One of Israel shall reign (chap. 22).

BIBLIOGRAPHY

Axelgard, Frederick W. "1 and 2 Nephi: An Inspiring Whole." *BYU Studies* 26 (Fall 1986): 53–65.

Nibley, Hugh W. *Lehi in the Desert*. In CWHN 5.

Nyman, Monte S., and Charles D. Tate, Jr., eds. *The Book of Mormon: First Nephi, the Doctrinal Foundation*. Provo, Utah, 1988.

ADDITIONAL SOURCES

Aston, Warren P., and Michaela Knoth Aston. *In the Footsteps of Lehi: New Evidence for Lehi's Journey across Arabia to Bountiful*. Salt Lake City: Deseret Book, 1994.

Brown, S. Kent. "The Exodus Pattern in the Book of Mormon." In *From Jerusalem to Zarahemla*: *Literary and Historical Studies of the Book of Mormon*, 75–98. Provo, Utah: BYU Religious Studies Center, 1998.

———. "Recovering the Missing Record of Lehi." In *From Jerusalem to Zarahemla*: *Literary and Historical Studies of the Book of Mormon*, 28–54. Provo, Utah: BYU Religious Studies Center, 1998.

RULON D. EAMES

Second Book of Nephi

The Second Book of Nephi (2 Nephi) is a work written about 550 B.C. by the same author who wrote 1 Nephi and included it on his small PLATES. The second book contains four prophetic discourses and treatises from three Book of Mormon prophets, LEHI, JACOB, and Nephi₁, as well as substantial excerpts of the prophecies of Isaiah from the brass plates. Additionally, 2 Nephi briefly records the difficult transition from the founding generation of Lehi's colony to the succeeding generation in their new homeland.

The first segment of the book consists of Lehi's admonitions and testament to his posterity before his death (1:1–4:11). He directed his opening words to his older sons, Laman, Lemuel, and Sam, as well as to the sons of Ishmael. He reminded them of God's mercy in leading them to a promised land, taught them concerning the covenant of righteousness that belongs to the land, warned of the loss of liberty and prosperity that will follow disobedience to God, and urged them to become reconciled to their brother Nephi as their leader (1:1–27).

Following this admonition, Lehi pronounced specific blessings on all of his descendants, either as individuals or as family groups. His blessings contain prophecies and promises concerning the future of each individual or group in the covenant land and are followed by counsel "according to the workings of the Spirit" (1:6). His instructions to his youngest sons, Jacob and Joseph, are doctrinally significant. He spoke to Jacob concerning God's plan of salvation for his children, teaching principles that are fundamental to understanding the gospel of Jesus Christ, including the doctrine of redemption through the Messiah, the necessity of opposition and agency, the role of Satan, and the importance of the fall of Adam and Eve (2:1–30). Lehi taught his son Joseph concerning the prophecies of his ancestor Joseph of Egypt, who foretold the latter-day mission of another Joseph (the Prophet Joseph SMITH) and of the coming forth of the Book of Mormon (3:1–25).

Nephi₁, son of Lehi, is author of the next section, the only historical segment in the record (4:12–5:34). After recounting the death of Lehi and the subsequent rebellion of Laman, Lemuel, and the sons of Ishmael (4:12–13), Nephi noted that he was keeping two records: the large plates on which he wrote his people's secular history and the small plates on which he recorded "that which is pleasing unto God," including many excerpts from the plates of brass (4:14–15; 5:29–33).

As Nephi wrote of his delight in pondering the scriptures and "the things of the Lord," he was moved to compose a beautiful psalm (4:16–35). In these verses, much like the biblical psalmist, Nephi used inspiring imagery and poetic parallelism to praise God for his goodness, to lament his own weaknesses, and to declare his devotion to the Lord.

Nephi closed this segment by telling of the partitioning of Lehi's posterity into two distinct peoples, the NEPHITES (the believers) and the LAMANITES (the unbelievers). He described the theological, cultural, and geographical divisions that developed between the brother nations, lamenting that within forty years of separating they were at war one with another (5:1–34).

A sermon by Jacob constitutes the third entry in 2 Nephi (chaps. 6–10), followed by the fourth and final part, a long written discourse from Nephi (chaps. 11–33). Quoting substantial portions of Isaiah, both Nephi and Jacob emphasized two major themes: the history and future of God's covenant people and the mission of the Messiah. For his discourse on these topics, Nephi first quoted the text of Isaiah 2–14 in 2 Nephi 12–24 and then commented on them in chapters 25–30, incorporating portions of Isaiah 29 in his discussion. Jacob quoted Isaiah 50:1–52:2 in chapters 7–8. Apparently, Joseph Smith put these quotations from Isaiah in King James English, but with many variant readings reflecting the Nephite source.

Citing and reflecting on Isaiah, Jacob and Nephi focused on such events as the Babylonian captivity and return (6:8–9; 25:10–11); the apostasy, scattering, and oppression of the house of Israel; and the latter-day gathering of their descendants, their restoration by conversion to the gospel of Christ, and the establishment of Zion—themes that concerned them because of their own Israelite ancestry (6:6–18; 8:1–25; 10:1–25; 25:14–17; 26:14–30:18). They further prophesied the destruction of the wicked before the second coming of the Savior followed by the subsequent era of peace (12:1–22; 21:1–24:3).

In their discourses, Jacob and Nephi taught of the Messiah's earthly ministry, rejection, and crucifixion (6:9; 7:1–11; 9:1–54; 10:3–5; 17–19) and his gospel fundamentals of faith, repentance, baptism, and obedience (9:23–24; 31:1–21; *see* GOSPEL OF JESUS CHRIST); they then prophesied his baptism, atoning sacrifice, and resurrection, followed by his ministry among the Nephites, his ultimate second coming, and the final judgment (9:5–27; 26:1–9; 31:4–12).

In chapter 29, Nephi made special mention of the Lord's desire that the Book of Mormon be used as "a standard" by his people, along with the Bible (29:2), noting that other books will come forth. In closing the record, Nephi testified that the words therein are the words of Christ, the words by which readers shall be judged (33:10–15).

BIBLIOGRAPHY

Jackson, Kent P., ed. *Studies in Scripture*, Vol. 7, pp. 86–174. Salt Lake City, 1987.

McConkie, Joseph Fielding, and Robert L. Millet. *Doctrinal Commentary on the Book of Mormon*, Vol. 1, pp. 182–376. Salt Lake City, 1987.

Nyman, Monte S., and Charles D. Tate, Jr., eds. *The Book of Mormon: Second Nephi, The Doctrinal Structure*. Provo, Utah, 1989.

TERRY B. BALL

Book of Jacob

Written by JACOB, fifth son of LEHI, sometime after 545 B.C., the work follows the pattern outlined by NEPHI₁ for making entries on the small PLATES by including sacred sermons, significant revelations, prophecies, and some historical information. Jacob, a Nephite prophet, wrote to persuade all men to "come unto Christ" (Jacob 1:7).

The book appears to have been written in three stages. The first constitutes an important discourse by Jacob at the temple, in which he called his people to repent from immorality, materialism, and pride (chaps. 2–3). He counseled men and women to be generous with their possessions, promising that, if they sought the kingdom of God before seeking riches, they would be blessed with sufficient wealth to assist others (2:17–19). Jacob

strongly warned his people against sins of immorality because many had transgressed the law of chastity, including practicing polygamy not authorized by the Lord (2:30). He reminded his hearers that the Lord "delight[s] in the chastity of women" and that the sins of the men had broken the hearts of their wives and children (2:22–35).

The second part contains prophecies concerning the atonement of Christ, the rejection of Jesus of Nazareth by many Jews, and the scattering and gathering of Israel (chaps. 4–6). Jacob desired that later generations would "know that we knew of Christ, and we had a hope of his glory many hundred years before his coming" (4:4). The major component of this section is Jacob's quoting of the allegory of the tame and wild olive trees (chap. 5). Written by ZENOS, an Israelite prophet whose writings were preserved on the brass plates, this allegory outlines in symbolic narrative the prophetic story of the scattering and gathering of Israel, including Lehi's descendants, from the establishment of Israel to the end of the earth.

The third segment recounts Jacob's experience with an ANTICHRIST named Sherem, who with skill and power of language endeavored to flatter and deceive people away from belief in Christ (7:1–4). Sherem had accused Jacob of blasphemy and false prophecy and had tried to convince people that there would be no Christ. In the end, Sherem was confounded by Jacob and, after seeking for a sign, was smitten by God and died shortly thereafter (7:7–8, 13–20). Recovering from Sherem's divisive teachings through searching the scriptures, Jacob's people were able to experience anew the peace and love of God (7:23).

BIBLIOGRAPHY

Matthews, Robert J. "Jacob: Prophet, Theologian, Historian." In *The Book of Mormon: Jacob through Words of Mormon*, ed. M. Nyman and C. Tate, Jr. Provo, Utah, 1990.

ADDITIONAL SOURCES

Tanner, John S. "Jacob and His Descendants as Authors." In *Rediscovering the Book of Mormon*, edited by John L. Sorenson and Melvin J. Thorne, 52–66. Salt Lake City and Provo, Utah: Deseret Book and FARMS, 1991.

Nyman, Monte S., and Charles D. Tate, Jr., eds. *The Book of Mormon: Jacob through Words of Mormon, To Learn with Joy*. Provo, Utah: BYU Religious Studies Center, 1990.

CLYDE J. WILLIAMS

Book of Enos

Following the pattern set by his father and predecessors (Jacob 1:2–4; cf. Enos 1:13–16), Enos, son of JACOB, personally recorded the testimony and prophetic promises granted to him. Enos (c. 515–417 B.C.) is a figure who touches the heart. He typifies conversion, compassion, and confidence before the Lord. While he was hunting beasts, the words of his father "concerning eternal life, and the joy of the saints, sunk deep into [his] heart," and his "soul hungered" (1:3–4). All day and into the night he "wrestle[d] . . . before God" in "mighty prayer" until he received a remission of his sins. He successively prayed for his own welfare, for the welfare of his brethren the NEPHITES, who strayed too easily from righteousness, and then for his brethren the LAMANITES, who had become increasingly ferocious and wild. Enos received a covenant declaration from the Lord that the Nephite records would be brought forth to the Lamanites. He knew with a surety that he would see his Redeemer's face with pleasure and would receive a place in the mansions of the Father (1:27).

MARILYN ARNOLD

Book of Jarom

Jarom, son of Enos, recorded a brief summary of the fortunes of the NEPHITES during his lifetime (c. 440–355 B.C.). Twice he justified the brevity of his account, pleading limited space and little new doctrine to add to the words of his predecessors. Reflecting an era of strict conservatism in the flourishing colony, Jarom recounted great Nephite efforts to observe the LAW OF MOSES and to anticipate the coming Messiah. Despite their larger numbers, the LAMANITES were unsuccessful in their frequent attacks on the prospering Nephites, and Jarom attributed the Nephite successes to the prophets, priests, and teachers who stirred them continually to repentance.

MARILYN ARNOLD

Book of Omni

This book concluded and filled the small PLATES of Nephi. It contains brief statements by a succession of record keepers who were descendants of JACOB but apparently not spiritual leaders: Omni, Amaron, Chemish, Abinadom, and Amaleki (fourth–second centuries B.C.). Amaleki, whose account is the longest of the five, described the important transition that occurred in Book of Mormon history when MOSIAH$_1$ led the escape of a band of faithful NEPHITES from the land of Nephi to Zarahemla (c. 200 B.C.). Here they discovered descendants of a group that had left Jerusalem with MULEK but had lost their religion and language. Amaleki connected the corruption of their language with the absence of written records, establishing the importance of record preservation. Mosiah brought with him the plates of brass containing "the record of the Jews" (Omni 1:14), including the laws that kings were required to have under the LAW OF MOSES (see Deut. 17:18–19). He was accepted as king over both these peoples and ruled for a generation. Amaleki survived

Mosiah but had no heirs, so he transmitted his records to Mosiah's son, King BENJAMIN.

MARILYN ARNOLD

The Words of Mormon

MORMON was at work on his abridgment of the large PLATES of NEPHI₁ when he discovered the small plates of Nephi, a prophetic record from early NEPHITE history (W of M 1:3). Because he was deeply impressed with the messianic prophecies that he read on the small plates, and in response to "the workings of the Spirit," Mormon included that set of plates with his digest (W of M 1:4–7). But because that record ended a few years before the book of Mosiah began (c. A.D. 130), Mormon assumed the prerogative of an editor and appended this historical postscript to the small plates to bring its conclusion into correlation with the opening of the book of Mosiah. This appendage, called the Words of Mormon, was composed about A.D. 385.

ELDIN RICKS

Book of Mosiah

The book of Mosiah is religiously rich, symbolically meaningful, chronologically complex, and politically significant. Although its disparate events range from 200 to 91 B.C., they are unified particularly by the theme of deliverance and by the reign of the Nephite king MOSIAH₂.

Several groups figure prominently in this history: (1) the main body of Nephites under King BENJAMIN and his son Mosiah₂, together with the people of Zarahemla (Mulekites), who outnumbered their Nephite rulers and neighbors; (2) the people of Zeniff, who failed in their attempt to reoccupy the Nephites' homeland, the land of Nephi; and (3) the people of ALMA₁, who broke away from the people of Zeniff and became the people of Alma,

believers in the martyred prophet ABINADI. The last two groups returned to Zarahemla shortly after Mosiah became king.

The book of Mosiah is drawn from several underlying textual sources: Benjamin's speech (124 B.C.); the record of Zeniff (c. 200–120 B.C.), including Alma's record of Abinadi's trial (c. 150 B.C.) and of his people (c. 150–118 B.C.); and the annals of Mosiah (124–91 B.C.).

BENJAMIN'S SPEECH (CHAPS. 1–6). The coronation of Mosiah occurred in a setting similar to the traditional Israelite assembly at the temple, together with sacrifices, covenant renewal, confessions, pronouncements regarding Christ's atoning blood, and admonitions to serve God and help the poor. Benjamin died, and Mosiah reigned. He sponsored Ammon's expedition to find the people of Zeniff (7:1–8:21).

RECORD OF ZENIFF (CHAPS. 9–22). About seventy-five years earlier, Zeniff had established his colony; he fought two wars, and his wicked son Noah succeeded him. Twice, the prophet Abinadi delivered a condemnation of Noah; Abinadi rehearsed the Ten Commandments, quoted Isaiah 53, and discoursed on the atonement of Jesus Christ and the resurrection. As he was suffering death by fire, Abinadi prophesied that his death would prefigure Noah's. One of Noah's priests, Alma₁, believed Abinadi's preaching, fled into the wilderness, and assembled a group of converts who escaped together from Noah's soldiers. Meanwhile, a military officer named Gideon opposed Noah, the Lamanites attacked, and Noah fled and was subsequently executed by his own people in the manner that Abinadi had predicted. Noah's son, Limhi, was left to reign for many years as a vassal king in servitude to the Lamanites. At length, Limhi and his people were delivered and escaped to Zarahemla.

ALMA'S RECORD (CHAPS. 23–24). The followers of Alma₁ practiced baptism and placed strong emphasis on unity, loving one another, and avoiding contention. In a speech that presaged Mosiah's final words establishing the reign of the judges, $Alma_1$ refused to become a king, wanting his people to be in bondage to no person. Nevertheless, they came under cruel bondage to the Lamanites, now led by some of Alma's former associates, the evil priests of Noah. Several years later, the people of Alma were miraculously delivered.

THE ANNALS OF MOSIAH (CHAPS. 25–29). The Nephites, the people of Zarahemla (Mulekites), the people of Limhi, and the people of $Alma_1$ were unified under Mosiah as king, with Alma as high priest. Alma was given authority to organize and regulate churches, but many members apostatized and persecuted the righteous. Among the wicked were his son $ALMA_2$ and the four sons of Mosiah. When they were confronted by an angel of the Lord, they repented and were converted. Mosiah translated the Jaredite record, passed the Nephite records and sacred artifacts to $Alma_2$, and installed $Alma_2$ as the first chief judge according to the voice of the people.

The narratives in the book of Mosiah emphasize the theme of deliverance from bondage, whether physical or spiritual. In his address, Benjamin speaks of spiritual deliverance through the atoning blood of Christ, emphasizing mankind's dependence on God and its responsibility to the poor (both themes or typologies are similarly shaped in the Bible by the Exodus tradition). The account of the conversion of $Alma_2$ is a notable case of deliverance from spiritual bondage by calling upon the name of Jesus Christ (Mosiah 27; Alma 36). Two groups are delivered from physical bondage and oppression: Limhi's people and the converts of Alma after their enslavement by the Lamanites. As in the Exo-

dus pattern, they "cried" to the Lord, who heard and delivered them from bondage. An emissary named Ammon expressly compared the deliverance of the people of Zeniff to the exodus of Israel from Egypt and of Lehi from Jerusalem (Mosiah 7:19–22, 33).

The book of Mosiah establishes several pairs of comparisons in a manner similar to a literary technique often used in the Bible: $Alma_1$ and Amulon are examples of good and bad priests; Benjamin and Noah are contrasting exemplars of noble and corrupt kingship. The extreme contrast between these kings is cited by Mosiah at the end of his reign to explain the wisdom in shifting the government of the Nephites from kingship to a reign of judges (Mosiah 29).

The Jaredite record is mentioned three times (Mosiah 8:9; 21:27; 28:11–19). In an attempt to get help from Mosiah's settlement, Limhi dispatched a search party; it did not find Mosiah, but found human remains, weapons of war, and twenty-four gold plates. The party returned this record to Limhi, who gave it to Mosiah, who translated it using two stones called "interpreters" (see URIM AND THUMMIM). The record told of the rise and fall of the Jaredites (see BOOK OF MORMON: BOOK OF ETHER).

BIBLIOGRAPHY

Tate, George S. "The Typology of the Exodus Pattern in the Book of Mormon." In *Literature of Belief*, ed. N. Lambert, pp. 245–66. Provo, Utah, 1981.

Thomasson, Gordon C. "Mosiah: The Complex Symbolism and the Symbolic Complex of Kingship in the Book of Mormon." *FARMS Paper*. Provo, Utah, 1982.

Tvedtnes, John A. "King Benjamin and the Feast of Tabernacles." In *By Study and Also by Faith*, ed. J. Lundquist and S. Ricks, Vol. 2, pp. 197–237. Salt Lake City, 1990.

ADDITIONAL SOURCE

Nyman, Monte S. and Charles D. Tate, Jr, eds. *The Book of Mormon: Mosiah, Salvation Only through Christ.* Provo, Utah: BYU Religious Studies Center, 1989.

ALAN GOFF

Book of Alma

The book of Alma is the longest book in the Book of Mormon. It was abridged by MOR-MON, principally from the records of three men, ALMA₂ (chaps. 1–16, 27–44), Ammon (chaps. 17–26), and Alma's son HELAMAN₁ (chaps. 45–62), and concludes with remarks by Mormon (chap. 63). Its broad theme is that the preaching of the word of God in pure testimony is mightier than politics or the sword in establishing peace, justice, equality, and goodness (Alma 4:19; 31:5). The book demonstrates this theme through repeated examples of individuals who were converted to faith in the anticipated Savior, Jesus Christ, and examples of people who were given victory by God over their wicked and ambitious enemies.

The book of Alma covers thirty-nine years (91–52 B.C.). The first fourteen years are covered by two concurrent accounts—one encompassing the teachings and activities of Alma₂, who resigned his judgeship in order to engage in missionary work in the land of Zarahemla (chaps. 1–16), and the other containing the words and deeds of the sons of King MOSIAH₂ and their companions as they made considerable personal sacrifice in their efforts to preach the gospel among the LAMANITES (chaps. 17–26).

The first section begins with the trial of Nehor before the chief judge Alma; Nehor was convicted and executed for the crime of enforcing priestcraft with the sword (chap. 1). Alma then fought a civil war against Nehor's followers and prevailed (chaps. 2–4), but he soon relinquished the judgeship to devote full time to the ministry. He preached powerful sermons at the cities of Zarahemla (chaps. 5–6), Gideon (chap. 7), and Melek (chap. 8), and went to the wicked city of Ammonihah, where he was cast out, but ordered by an angel to return. In Ammonihah the second time, he met and was assisted by Amulek, who was instructed by an angel to find Alma (chap. 8). Although they were opposed by a skilled lawyer named Zeezrom, eventually they converted many, including Zeezrom. However, their male converts were expelled from the city, and Alma and Amulek were imprisoned and forced to watch the wives and children of their converts being burned to death. Eventually, Alma and Amulek were delivered when an earthquake destroyed the prison and killed their captors (chaps. 9–14). Shortly thereafter, this apostate city was annihilated by invading Lamanites (chap. 16).

During the same fourteen years, the sons of Mosiah and their companions were in the land southward. Ammon went to the land of Ishmael, and through his service to, and love of, King Lamoni, he converted the king and many of his people (chaps. 17–19), whom he taught to live the LAW OF MOSES in anticipation of the coming of Christ (Alma 25:15). Ammon and Lamoni then went to the land of Middoni to free his fellow missionaries from prison. En route they were confronted by Lamoni's father, the king of all the Lamanites, who took to the sword. Ammon withstood his blows, gained control over the king, and made him promise freedom for his brothers and autonomy for Lamoni and his people (chap. 20). Once Ammon's brother, Aaron, and his companions were free, they went to

Lamoni's father and taught and converted him, his household, and many of his people. These converted Lamanites, concerned about the return of prior blood guilt, made an oath never to shed blood again (chap. 23). Other Lamanites and dissident Nephites attacked these converts and killed 1,005, who would not defend themselves because of that oath. Many of the attacking Lamanites (but not the Nephite dissenters) felt remorse for their actions and laid down their arms and also became converted (chaps. 24–25). Eventually, Ammon led these converts, called Anti-Nephi-Lehies, to Nephite territory, where they settled in the land of Jershon (chap. 27). The Lamanites who were left behind became angry at the Nephites and then attacked and destroyed Ammonihah (Alma 25:1–2; described more fully in Alma 16:1–11).

After these developments, Korihor, an ANTICHRIST and advocate of blasphemous doctrines, confronted Alma as high priest in the court of the chief judge, where he asked for a sign from God, was struck dumb, and died shortly thereafter (chap. 30). Next, Alma led a delegation to preach to the Zoramites, a group that had defected from the Nephites. Many poverty-stricken Zoramites were reconverted and cast out by the other Zoramites. The unconverted promptly allied with the Lamanites, attacked the Nephites, and were defeated (chaps. 31–35, 43–44).

The chapters focusing on Alma also contain his blessings and instructions to his three sons (chaps. 36–42) and an account of his disappearance (being taken to heaven; chap. 45). The book of Alma ends with the detailed accounts by HELAMAN₁ of further wars between the Nephites and Lamanites (chaps. 43–62; see WARFARE IN THE BOOK OF MORMON). The final chapter (chap. 63) notes the deaths of Pahoran, Moroni, Helaman, and his brother Shi-

blon, marking the end of this era of righteous Nephite control of Zarahemla. It also tells of Hagoth, a shipbuilder who transported people to the north, but he was never heard from again after a second departure.

The book of Alma covers a critical period in Nephite history, the opening years of the Nephite judgeship (see GOVERNMENT AND LEGAL HISTORY IN THE BOOK OF MORMON). The survival of this popularly based form of government was threatened several times in the course of the book, starting when Nehor's follower Amlici sought to become king. It was threatened again when the Zoramites (described above) defected. Further trouble arose when Amalickiah, a Zoramite, persuaded many of the lower judges to support him as king. A general named Moroni₁ rallied the Nephite troops by raising a banner that he called the Title of Liberty; it proclaimed the need to remember and defend their God, their religion, their freedom, their peace, their wives, and their children. Amalickiah and a few of his men fled to the Lamanites, where he, through treachery and murder, established himself as king and led the Lamanites in a prolonged war against the Nephites. Amalickiah was killed after seven years of war, but the wars continued under his brother Ammoron for six more years. Those years became particularly perilous for the Nephites when "kingmen" arose in Zarahemla and expelled the Nephite government from the capital (discussed in CWHN 8:328–79). Moroni was forced to leave the battlefront to regain control of the capital before he could turn his full attention to defeating the Lamanites. In each case, the Nephites ultimately prevailed and gave thanks and praise to God.

In the book of Alma, the delineation of the Nephite and Lamanite nations along ancestral lines becomes blurred. Several groups of

Nephites—Amlicites (chaps. 2–3), Zoramites (chaps. 31–35, 43), Amalickiahites (chaps. 46–62), and kingmen (chaps. 51, 61)—rejected Nephite religious principles and joined the Lamanites in an attempt to overthrow the Nephite government. Several groups of Lamanites—Anti-Nephi-Lehies (chaps. 17–27), converts from the army that marched against the Anti-Nephi-Lehies (chap. 25), and some Lamanite soldiers captured by Moroni (chap. 62)—embraced the gospel and Nephite way of life and went to live among the Nephites. By the end of the book, these populations are distinguished more by ideology than by lineage. Those who desired government by the "voice of the people" and embraced the teachings of the gospel are numbered among the Nephites, while those who opposed them are called Lamanites.

Many important religious teachings are found in the book of Alma. Alma 5 is a speech given by Alma calling the people of the city of Zarahemla to repent and teaching all followers of Christ to judge the state of their former spiritual rebirth and present well-being. Alma 7, delivered to the righteous city of Gideon, teaches believers to make the atonement of Christ a reality in their lives. Chapters 12 and 13 elucidate the mysteries of redemption, RESURRECTION, and the priesthood after the order of the Son of God. Alma 32 and 33 are a sermon given by Alma to the Zoramite poor, explaining the correct manner of prayer, the relationship between humility and faith in Jesus Christ, and the process of increasing faith. Alma 34 is Amulek's talk on the need for the "infinite and eternal sacrifice" made by the Son of God. In it Amulek also teaches the people how to pray and tells them how to live so that their prayers will not be vain.

Alma teaches his sons trust in God by telling of his personal conversion (chap. 36).

He also gives instructions about the keeping of sacred records and explains how God's purposes are accomplished through small means (chap. 37). He teaches the evil of sexual sin (chap. 39), the nature of resurrection and restoration (chaps. 40–41), the purpose and consequences of the FALL OF ADAM, including spiritual and temporal death, and the relationship between JUSTICE AND MERCY (see chap. 42).

The war chapters include instances of, and statements about, justifiable reasons for war (chap. 48), along with the example of the protective power of faith exercised by the young warriors who fought under Helaman, none of whom died in battle, for they believed their mothers' teachings that "God would deliver them" (Alma 56:47–48).

Overall, the book of Alma teaches through vivid, detailed narratives how personal ambition can lead to apostasy and war, and shows how the Lord gathers his people through the preaching of the gospel of Christ and delivers them in righteousness against aggression.

BIBLIOGRAPHY

For essays on Alma the Younger, Ammon, King Lamoni, Ammonihah, Korihor's sophistry, Amlici, several dissenters, Captain Moroni, the Nephite chief judges, and other figures in the book of Alma, see Jeffrey R. Holland, *The Book of Mormon: It Begins with a Family*, pp. 79–170. Salt Lake City, 1983.

ADDITIONAL SOURCE

Nyman, Monte S., and Charles D. Tate, Jr. eds. *The Book of Mormon: Alma, the Testimony of the Word*. Provo, Utah: BYU Religious Studies Center, 1992.

CHERYL BROWN

Book of Helaman

The book of Helaman chronicles one of the most tumultuous periods in the history of the NEPHITES and LAMANITES (52–1 B.C.). The narrative focuses on the unexpected difficulties (e.g., the Lamanites' invasion and unprecedented occupation of the land of Zarahemla narrated in chaps. 4 and 5) and unexpected resolutions that came from God (e.g., the withdrawal of the Lamanite occupation forces as the direct result of the missionary work of two sons of Helaman, NEPHI₂ and Lehi, in 5:49–52).

This book takes its name from its first author, HELAMAN₂, son of HELAMAN₁. Other contributors to the record were Nephi and Lehi, sons of Helaman₂ (16:25), and MORMON, the principal editor of the Book of Mormon, who added political and religious commentary.

The account opens after Helaman had received custody of the Nephite records from his uncle Shiblon (Alma 63:11) in the fortieth year of the reign of the judges (c. 52 B.C.; Hel. 1:1). The narrative falls into six major segments: the record of Helaman (chaps. 1–3); the record of Nephi (chaps. 4–6); the prophecy of Nephi (chaps. 7–11); Mormon's editorial observations on God's power (chap. 12); the prophecy of SAMUEL THE LAMANITE (chaps. 13–15); and a brief statement about the five-year period before Jesus' birth (chap. 16). Several religious discourses are woven into the narrative, including Helaman's admonition to his sons (5:6–12), Nephi₁'s psalm (7:7–9), Nephi's sermon from the tower in his garden (7:13–29; 8:11–28), Nephi's prayer (11:10–16), and Samuel's long speech atop the walls of Zarahemla (13:5–39; 14:2–15:17).

Perhaps the most prominent person mentioned in the book is Nephi₂. After Nephi resigned from the office of chief judge, he and his brother Lehi devoted themselves fully to preaching the message of the gospel (5:1–4). His defense of God's providence affirmed the power of prophecy (8:11–28) and, on a practical level, led to the conviction of the murderer of the chief judge (9:21–38). The Lord entrusted him with the power to seal the heavens so that no rain would fall (10:4–11), a power that Nephi used to bring about the cessation of civil strife and wickedness (11:1–18).

The rise of the gadianton robbers (1:9–12; 2:3–11), a hostile and secret society within the Nephite and Lamanite polities, was perhaps the most disheartening and ominous occurrence during those fifty-one years. Mormon informs readers of both the organization's character (6:17–30) and its debilitating impact on society (2:13–14; 6:38–39; 11:24–34).

In contrast to these despairing observations is one of the book's central themes: the surprising ascendancy of the Lamanites in spiritual matters. After the Nephites were overrun by a Lamanite army led by Nephite dissidents in 35 B.C. and failed to regain lost territories (4:5–10), Nephi and Lehi went among the Lamanites to preach the gospel (5:16–20). Their remarkable success in converting listeners to Christ led to their imprisonment (5:21). But in an extraordinary outpouring of the Spirit of God, all in the prison were converted, an event that led to a spiritual reversal among the Lamanites and the eventual withdrawal of Lamanite military forces from Nephite lands (5:22–52). Thereafter, Lamanites carried out the work of the Church, preaching to both their own people and the Nephites (6:1–8, 34–36).

Almost thirty years later (c. 6 B.C.), a Lamanite prophet named Samuel prophesied at Zarahemla. He condemned the decadence of Nephite society, warning of destruction of both individuals and society (13:5–39, esp. 38; 14:20–15:3). He also prophesied that signs to be seen in the Western Hemisphere would accompany both the birth and death of Jesus (14:2–25). He declared the power of the Atonement in redeeming mankind from the fall of Adam and in bringing about the Resurrection. Finally, he spoke of the Lamanites' righteousness and the promises of God to them in the latter days (15:4–16).

BIBLIOGRAPHY

Jackson, Kent P., ed. *Studies in Scripture*, Vol. 8, pp. 92–124. Salt Lake City, 1988.

PAUL R. CHEESMAN

Third Nephi

The book of 3 Nephi is the dramatic and spiritual climax of the Book of Mormon. It focuses on three advents of Jesus: first, as the child born in Bethlehem; second, as the resurrected Lord visiting the Nephites; and third, at his second coming as the final judge at the end of the world. Within a year of the devastating destructions at the time of his crucifixion, the resurrected Jesus descended among a group of righteous people in the Nephite city of Bountiful. He revealed himself unmistakably as the Lord and Savior of the world, expounded his gospel, and established his Church.

The book's author, NEPHI₃, was the religious leader of an ethnically mixed group of Nephites and Lamanites at the time of Christ's birth. His book covers events from that time to A.D. 34. It appears Mormon copied much of Nephi's text verbatim into his abridgment.

Nephi's record begins at the time when the fulfillment of the messianic prophecies of SAMUEL THE LAMANITE miraculously saved believers from a threatened antimessianic persecution. The signs of Jesus' birth appeared—a night of daylight and a new star—vindicating the faith of those who believed the prophecies that Jesus would be born into the world (chap. 1).

After these signs, many were converted to the Church led by Nephi. On the other hand, greed, pleasure-seeking, and pride increased drastically, and the government was soon infiltrated with organized corruption that caused complete anarchy and a breakdown of the people into family tribes and robber bands. Prolonged attacks by these bands plagued the Nephites, who finally abandoned their own properties and formed a single body with enough provisions to subsist for seven years. The Nephites eventually prevailed, but these disruptions and wickedness brought on the collapse of the central government. Although most rejected Nephi₃'s warnings and miracles, he baptized and ordained those who would believe and follow (chaps. 2–7).

The believers began looking for the calamitous signs of Christ's death, also prophesied by Samuel. A violent storm arose and massive earthquakes occurred demolishing many cities, killing thousands of the wicked, and leaving the more righteous survivors in a thick vapor of darkness for three days of mourning. After the tumult settled, the voice of Jesus Christ spoke out of the darkness, expressing his sadness over the unrepentant dead and his hope that those who were spared would receive him and his redemption. He announced that his sacrifice had ended the need for blood sacrifice as practiced under the law of Moses (chaps. 8–10).

Later, in radiant white, the resurrected Christ descended to show his wounds, to heal, to teach, and to ordain leaders for his Church. On the first day of several such visits,

Jesus Christ Visits the Americas, by John Scott (1969, oil on canvas, 47" x 121"). The resurrected Jesus Christ appears to 2,500 men, women, and children who had gathered at their temple in Bountiful. He instructed them for three days (see 3 Ne. 11–28). © by Intellectual Reserve, Inc. Used by permission.

Jesus appeared to a group of 2,500 men, women, and children assembled at the temple in Bountiful. He ordained twelve disciples and gave them the power to baptize and bestow the gift of the Holy Ghost; he instructed the people in the principles, ordinances, and commandments of his gospel (*see* SERMON ON THE MOUNT); he explained that he had fulfilled the law of Moses; he healed the sick and blessed their families. He announced his plan to show himself to still other people not then known by the Jews or the Nephites. Finally, he entered into a covenant with them. The people promised to keep the commandments he had given them, and he administered to them the sacrament of bread and wine, in remembrance of his resurrected body that he had shown to them and of the blood through which he had wrought the Atonement (chaps. 11–18).

On the morning of the second day, the disciples baptized the faithful and gave them the gift of the Holy Ghost, and they were encircled by angels and fire from heaven. Jesus appeared again and offered three marvelous prayers, explained God's covenant with Israel and its promised fulfillment, reviewed and corrected some items in the Nephite scriptures, and foretold events of the future world, quoting prophesies from Isaiah, Micah, and Malachi. He inspired even babes to reveal "marvelous things" (3 Ne. 26:16). Then he explained the past and future history of the world, emphasizing that salvation will extend to all who follow him (chaps. 19–26).

A third time, Jesus appeared to the twelve Nephite disciples alone. He named his Church and explained the principles of the final judgment. Three of the disciples were transfigured and beheld heavenly visions. Jesus granted these three disciples their wish to remain on earth as special servants until the end of the world (chaps. 27–28; *see also* THREE NEPHITES).

Christ revisited the Nephites over an extended period, and told them that he would also visit the lost tribes of Israel.

His Church grew having all things common, with neither rich nor poor. This peaceful condition lasted nearly 180 years, and "surely there could not be a happier people" (4 Ne. 1:16).

Mormon wrote his abridgment of 3 Nephi more than three hundred years after the actual events. By then, the descendants of the Nephites who had been so blessed had degenerated into terminal warfare. Mormon's final, sober testimony to his future readers speaks of the Lord's coming in the last days, which, like his coming to the land Bountiful, would be disastrous for the ungodly but glorious for the righteous (chaps. 29–30).

The text of 3 Nephi fits several categories. First, it is a Christian testament, a Christian gospel. It contains many direct quotations from Jesus and establishes his new covenant. Recorded in a touching personal tone by a participating eyewitness of awesomely tragic and beautiful events, the account convincingly invites the reader to believe the gospel of Jesus Christ and to feel the love he has for all people.

The text also has been compared to the pseudepigraphic forty-day literature that describes Christ's ministry to the faithful in the Holy Land after his resurrection (see JESUS CHRIST, FORTY-DAY MINISTRY AND OTHER POST-RESURRECTION APPEARANCES OF; CWHN 8:407–34). Others have seen in chapters 11–18 a covenant ritual that profoundly expands the meaning of the Sermon on the Mount in the Gospel of Matthew (Welch, pp. 34–83). The account also resembles the apocalyptic message of the books of Enoch: From the type and purpose of the initial cataclysm, to the sublimity of its revelations to the faithful, to the creation of a righteous society, 3 Nephi is a story of theodicy, theophany, and theocracy.

The text yields practical instructions for sainthood. It is not a wishful utopian piece but a practical handbook of commandments to be accepted in covenantal ordinances and obeyed strictly, with devotion and pure dedication to God. This is not the genre of wisdom literature, not merely a book of moral suggestions for the good life. It explains Christ's gospel plainly, and makes the lofty ideals of the Sermon on the Mount livable by all who receive the Holy Ghost. Empowered by true Christian ordinances and the gifts of the Holy Spirit, the Nephites established a paradise surpassed in righteousness only by Enoch's Zion.

This Zion welcomes everyone, from every place and every time. It promises blessings to "*all* the pure in heart" who come unto Christ (3 Ne. 12:3–9; emphasis added). Thus, 3 Nephi urges all to accept and live Christ's gospel, to perfect earthly society, and to join with the Zion of all the former and future righteous peoples so that, as Malachi states, the earth will not be "utterly wasted" at Christ's second coming (JS—H 1:39). This was Enoch's ancient achievement and Joseph SMITH's modern hope. The text does not discuss God's millennial kingdom; nor does Christ here pray, "Thy kingdom come." For among those happy Nephites, it had come already.

[See also Jesus Christ in the Scriptures: Jesus Christ in the Book of Mormon.]

BIBLIOGRAPHY

Anderson, Richard L. "Religious Validity: The Sacrament Covenant in Third Nephi." In *By Study and Also by Faith*, ed. J. Lunquist and S. Ricks, Vol. 2, pp. 1–51. Salt Lake City, 1990.

Ludlow, Victor L. *Jesus' "Covenant People Discourse" in 3 Nephi*. Religious Education Lecture Series. Provo, Utah, 1988.

Stendahl, Krister. "The Sermon on the Mount and Third Nephi." In *Reflections on Mormonism*, ed. Truman G. Madsen. Provo, Utah, 1978.

Welch, John W. *The Sermon at the Temple and the Sermon on the Mount*. Salt Lake City, 1990.

ADDITIONAL SOURCES

Nyman, Monte S., and Charles D. Tate, Jr., eds. *The Book of Mormon: 3 Nephi 9–30, This Is My Gospel: Papers from the Eighth Annual Book of*

Mormon Symposium, 1993. Provo, Utah: BYU Religious Studies Center, 1993.

Welch, John W. *Illuminating the Sermon at the Temple and Sermon on the Mount: An Approach to 3 Nephi 11–18 and Matthew 5–7.* Provo, Utah: FARMS, 1999.

CHARLES RANDALL PAUL

Fourth Nephi

Abridged by MORMON, this brief work contains the writings of four Nephite prophets (A.D. 34–320): NEPHI₄, son of NEPHI₃, who was a disciple of the risen Jesus; Amos, son of Nephi₄; and Amos and Ammaron, two sons of Amos. The first section of 4 Nephi briefly summarizes four generations of peace, righteousness, and equality that resulted from the conversion of the people to the GOSPEL OF JESUS CHRIST after the visit of the resurrected Savior. In contrast, the last section foreshadows the later destruction of the Nephite nation that followed a gradual and conscious rejection of the gospel message.

Fourth Nephi narrates an unparalleled epoch in human society when all the people followed the teachings of Christ for nearly two centuries. The book is best known for its account of the social and religious power of the love of God that overcame contention and other social and political ills (4 Ne. 1:15–16). The people experienced urban renewal, stable family life, unity in the Church, and social and economic equality, as well as divine miracles (1:3–13, 15–17). "Surely there could not [have been] a happier people . . . created by the hand of God" (1:16).

The book also previews the ensuing apostasy of most of the population from the teachings of Christ, introducing a state of wickedness and chaos that eventually led to total destruction. According to the account the individual and collective decline was gradual and sequential, with the loss of social and religious order manifested in contention, PRIDE in prosperity, class distinctions with widening social divisions, rejection of Christ and his gospel, and persecution of the Church (1:24–46).

BIBLIOGRAPHY

Skinner, Andrew C. "The Course of Peace and Apostasy." In *Studies in Scripture,* ed. K. Jackson, Vol. 8. Salt Lake City, 1988.

ADDITIONAL SOURCE

Skinner, Andrew C. "Zion Gained and Lost: Fourth Nephi as the Quintessential Model." In *The Book of Mormon: Fourth Nephi through Moroni, From Zion to Destruction,* edited by Monte S. Nyman and Charles D. Tate, Jr., 289–302. Provo, Utah: BYU Religious Studies Center, 1995.

REX C. REEVE, JR.

Book of Mormon

The short book of Mormon (A.D. 320–400/421), within the Book of Mormon, documents the extraordinary collapse of Nephite civilization, as had been foretold (1 Ne. 12:19–20; Alma 45:10–14). It consists of MORMON's abridgment of his larger and more complete history (Morm. 1–6), his final admonition both to future LAMANITES and to other remnants of the house of Israel (chap. 7), and the prophetic warnings of Mormon's son MORONI₂ to future readers of the record (chaps. 8–9). Because Nephites of Mormon's day had rejected JESUS CHRIST and his gospel, superstition and magic replaced divine revelation (Morm. 1:13–19). A border skirmish (1:10) escalated into a major war, driving the Nephites from their traditional lands (2:3–7, 16, 20–21). Following a ten-year negotiated peace, they repulsed a Lamanite attack, which Mormon, former commander of the Nephite army, refused to lead. As conditions worsened, Mormon reluctantly agreed to command the Nephite army at CUMORAH, where they were destroyed (chaps. 3–6). With poignant anguish, Mormon lamented over his slain people: "O ye fair ones, how could ye have rejected that Jesus, who stood with open arms to receive you!" (6:17–22).

Mormon concluded his record by inviting Lamanites and other remnants of the house of Israel to learn of their forefathers, to lay down their weapons of war, and to repent of their sins and believe that Jesus Christ is the Son of God. His final words were, "If it so be that ye believe in Christ, and are baptized, first with water, then with fire and with the Holy Ghost, . . . it shall be well with you in the day of judgment. Amen" (7:10).

After the final battle (A.D. 385), Moroni₂—alone and unsure of his own survival—noted his father's death and concluded his father's record (8:1–5). Fifteen years later (A.D. 400), Moroni recorded that survivors of his people had been hunted from place to place until they were no more except for himself. He also observed that the Lamanites were at war with one another and that the whole country witnessed continual bloodshed. For a second time he closed the work, promising that those who would receive this record in the future and not condemn it would learn of greater spiritual matters (8:6–13).

Moroni apparently returned to the record a third time (between A.D. 400 and 421). Having seen a vision of the future (8:35), he testified that the PLATES of the Book of Mormon would come forth by the power of God in a day when people would not believe in miracles. SECRET COMBINATIONS would abound, churches be defiled, and wars, rumors of wars, earthquakes, and pollutions be upon the earth. Moroni also spoke warnings to those in the latter days who do not believe in

Christ and who deny the revelations of God, thus standing against the works of the Lord (8:14–9:27). He mentioned the difficulty of keeping records, written as they were in "reformed Egyptian" (9:31–33; cf. Ether 12:23–25). Moroni closed his father's volume with a testimony of the truth of his words (9:35–37).

BIBLIOGRAPHY

Mackay, Thomas W. "Mormon and the Destruction of Nephite Civilization." In *Studies in Scripture*, ed. K. Jackson, Vol. 8. Salt Lake City, 1988.

REX C. REEVE, JR.

Book of Ether
The book of Ether is MORONI₂'s abbreviated account of the history of the JAREDITES, who came to the Western Hemisphere at the time of the "great tower" of Babel and lived in the area later known as the Nephite "land northward," much earlier than Lehi's colony. Moroni retold their account, recorded on twenty-four plates of gold found by the people of Limhi and translated by MOSIAH₂ (Mosiah 28:11–19). Ether, the last prophet of the Jaredites and a survivor of their annihilation, inscribed those plates soon after the final destruction of his people. It is not known whether Moroni relied on Mosiah's translation or retranslated the Jaredite record in whole or in part. Moroni humbly claims not to have written "the hundredth part" of the record by Ether (Ether 15:33).

The structure of the book of Ether is much like the rest of the Book of Mormon. It tells of the emigration of people by land and sea from the Near East, the Lord's prophetic guidance of these people, and their rise, prosperity, and fall, all in direct relation to their obedience to the Lord's commandments in their promised land. Moroni included the book of Ether because his father MORMON had planned to do so (Mosiah 28:19) but for some reason did not complete the project. Both knew the value of this record and could see that the Jaredite history closely paralleled certain Nephite events.

Moroni appended this history to the Nephite account as a second witness against the evils and SECRET COMBINATIONS that led to the annihilation of both the Jaredites and the Nephites. Several of its themes reinforce the messages in the Nephite section of the Book of Mormon: the necessity to follow the prophets away from persistent and pernicious wickedness, the power of faith in the Lord demonstrated by Jared and the BROTHER OF JARED, the testimony that Jesus Christ is the eternal saving God, and the collapse of a nation when its people determinedly choose wickedness. Nevertheless, there are notable cultural differences between the Jaredite and the Nephite civilizations; for example, the Jaredites were ruled solely by kings, and they lacked Israelite law and customs, since they were pre-Mosaic.

Although condensed, the book reflects an epic style (see CWHN 5:153–449; 6:329–58). It begins with the emigration of the Jaredites from "the great tower" (Ether 1:33, cf. Gen. 11:9) and the valley of "Nimrod" (Ether 2:1; cf. Gen. 10:8) to a new land of promise in the Western Hemisphere. It then abridges a history of the Jaredite kings and wars, and concludes with the destruction of the Jaredite civilization. A brief outline of the book follows: Ether's royal lineage is given (chap. 1); the premortal Jesus appears to the brother of Jared in response to his prayers and touches sixteen small stones, causing them to shine to provide light as the Jaredite barges cross the sea (chaps. 2–6); the generations of Jaredite kings live, hunt, quarrel, enter into secret combinations, and Jaredite prophets warn of impending destruction (chaps. 7–11); Moroni

attests that Ether was a prophet of great faith and knowledge (chaps. 12–13); Ether witnesses and records the annihilation of the Jaredite armies (chaps. 14–15).

The main figures and doctrinal statements appear mostly at the beginning and end of the book of Ether. Moroni's editing is of key importance, for he infuses the story with major insights, admonitions, and comparisons. Jared is mentioned at the outset as the founder of the Jaredite people. The revelations and faith of the brother of Jared are given special significance at the beginning and end of the book. Shiz and Coriantumr are crucial historical and symbolic figures because they become the instruments of annihilation. Ether, the author of the underlying text, was an eyewitness to the final battles, and Moroni esteemed his prophecies as "great and marvelous" (Ether 13:13). The middle of the book recounts the more mundane events associated with the reigns of the Jaredite kings.

Several doctrines taught within the book of Ether are greatly valued among Latter-day Saints, namely, that prosperity in the promised land (the Americas) is conditioned on serving "the God of the land, who is Jesus Christ" (Ether 2:12), that the premortal Christ had a spirit body "like unto flesh and blood" (3:6), that God is a God of power and truth (3:4, 12), that three witnesses would verify the truth of the Book of Mormon (5:3), that the corruption and downfall of society can come because of secret combinations (8:22), that the Lord will show mankind its weakness so that through humility weak things may become strengths (12:27), and that a New Jerusalem will eventually be built in the Western Hemisphere (13:3–12).

BIBLIOGRAPHY

Sperry, Sidney B. *Book of Mormon Compendium*, pp. 460–81. Salt Lake City, 1968.

Welch, John W. "Sources behind the Book of Ether." *FARMS Paper*. Provo, Utah, 1986.

MORGAN W. TANNER

Book of Moroni

Between A.D. 400 and 421, MORONI₂, the last custodian of the GOLD PLATES, compiled the final book in the Book of Mormon record. He wrote: "I had supposed not to have written any more; but I write a few more things, that perhaps they may be of worth unto my brethren" (Moro. 1:4). He then brought together loosely related but important items, including ordinances performed both in the church of his day and in The Church of Jesus Christ of Latter-day Saints today (chaps. 2–6), one of his father's sermons (chap. 7), and two of his father's letters (chap. 9). He concluded with his own testimony and exhortations to readers (chap. 10).

ORDINANCES (CHAPS. 2–6). Chapter 2 contains instructions given by the resurrected Jesus Christ to his twelve disciples in the Western Hemisphere at the time when he bestowed upon them the gift of the Holy Ghost. This gift is conferred in the name of Jesus Christ and by the laying on of hands from one who has received authority. Chapter 3 explains that priests and teachers were ordained in the name of Jesus Christ by the laying-on of hands by one holding proper authority. The main function of priests and teachers was to teach repentance and faith in Jesus Christ. Chapters 4 and 5 contain the set prayers for blessing the SACRAMENT of the Lord's Supper, prayers currently used in the Church. Chapter 6 outlines the requirements for BAPTISM, which include a "broken heart," contrite spirit, and true repentance. Moroni then detailed how Church members recorded the names of all members, taught one another, met together in fasting and prayer, and partook of the sacrament often.

MORMON'S SERMON AND LETTERS (CHAPS.

7–9). Mormon's sermon (chap. 7) deals with faith, hope, and charity and includes teachings on how to distinguish between good and evil, the necessity of spiritual gifts, the nature of miracles, and instruction on how to obtain charity, "the pure love of Christ" (7:47).

The first letter (chap. 8) condemns INFANT BAPTISM. Mormon taught that children are made pure through the atonement of Christ and do not need the cleansing power of baptism until they are old enough to be accountable for their actions and can repent of their sins.

The second letter (chap. 9) recites the level of depravity to which the Nephites and LAMANITES had fallen (before A.D. 385), offering reasons for their prophesied destruction ("they are without principle, and past feeling"—verse 20), along with Mormon's charge to his son to remain faithful to Christ in spite of their society's wickedness.

EXHORTATION AND FAREWELL (CHAP. 10). Moroni exhorts all who read the Book of Mormon to ponder and pray for a divine witness of its truthfulness (verses 3–5) and urges his readers not to deny the gifts of the Holy Ghost, which he enumerates (verses 8–19). He bears his personal testimony of Jesus Christ and urges all to "come unto Christ, and be perfected in him, and deny yourselves of all ungodliness" (verse 32). He bids his readers farewell until he meets them on the final Judgment Day at "the pleasing bar of the great Jehovah" (verse 34).

BIBLIOGRAPHY

Jackson, Kent P., ed. *Studies in Scripture*, Vol. 8, pp. 282–312. Salt Lake City, 1988.

ADDITIONAL SOURCE

Miner, Alan C. "A Chronological Setting for the Epistles of Mormon to Moroni." *Journal of Book of Mormon Studies* 3 (Fall 1994): 94–113.

S. MICHAEL WILCOX

BOOK OF MORMON IN A BIBLICAL CULTURE

One does not need to look beyond the prevailing revivalist sects in America to discover why the earliest Mormon elders won an immediate hearing for their sacred book. Firm calls for personal righteousness and obedience to the moral requirements of the Judeo-Christian scriptures were by 1830 the dominant motifs in all Protestant communions. Moreover, each of the American sects shared speculations about the ancient and future history of Indians and Jews.

These interests and beliefs were also predominant among Methodist, Congregational, and Baptist ministers serving congregations in and around Cheshire, in northern England. Heber C. Kimball's *Journal*, giving an account of his mission to Great Britain, shows how the flowering of biblical study and of millennial speculation prepared the soil for early Mormon evangelization there. He reported that even clergymen in the Church of England told their congregations that the teachings of the Latter-day Saints reveal the same principles taught by the apostles of old.

The Book of Mormon also gives clear direction on several matters that the Christian scriptures seem to have left unclear, including baptism by immersion and the promises that all believers, and not just the apostles, might be "filled with the Holy Ghost"; that Christian believers can be made pure in heart (as John Wesley had insisted in the previous century); that the experience of salvation received by a free response to free grace is available to all persons, and not simply to the "elect"; and that obedience and works of righteousness are the fruit of that experience. The book also affirms the veracity of the biblical accounts of the scattering of Israel by affirming that Native Americans originated from descendants of Joseph and Judah.

The persuasive power of the new scriptures and of the missionaries who expounded them, therefore, lay in their testimony to beliefs that were central to evangelical Protestant sects in both Jacksonian America and early Victorian England. An early LDS missionary, Parley P. Pratt, told his English hearers that two errors in interpretation of the Bible had produced widespread uncertainty. One was the belief that direct inspiration by the Holy Ghost was not intended for all ages of the Church; and the other was that the Jewish and Christian scriptures contained all truth necessary to salvation and comprised a sufficient rule of faith and practice.

Some nineteenth-century deacons and elders and a few evangelical pastors struggled with grave temptations to doubt the truth and relevance of large portions of the book upon which they had been taught to stake their eternal destiny. True, the details of the histories recounted in the two sacred books were radically different. But they fit together wondrously. And their moral structure, the story they told of Jesus, their promise of salvation, and their description of humankind's last days were remarkably similar. Though the new scriptures had similarities with evangelical Arminianism, at the expense of the Calvinist views long dominant in colonial America, the same was true of the early nineteenth-century teachings of many Protestants, even Presbyterians, to say nothing of Methodists and Disciples of Christ. In the voice of two witnesses, the Bible and the Book of Mormon, Latter-day Saints declared the truth confirmed, just as the prophet NEPHI₁ had predicted (cf. 2 Ne. 29:8).

In five important ways, the Book of Mormon seems to some who are not members of the Church to strengthen the authority of Holy Scripture. First in importance is the volume's affirmation that the Christian religion is grounded upon both the Old and New Testaments. The book affirms what recent biblical scholarship is now making plain: the continuity of the theology, ethics, and spirituality that the two Testaments proclaimed. In the Book of Mormon, Jesus is the Lord who gave the law to Moses, and the risen Christ is identical to the prophet Isaiah's Messiah. He delivers exactly the same message of redemption, faith, and a new life of righteousness through the Holy Spirit that the New Testament attributes to him.

Second, the Book of Mormon reinforces the unifying vision of biblical religion, grounding it in the conviction of a common humanity that the stories of creation declared, God's promise to Abraham implied, and Jesus affirmed. Puritan millenarianism may have inspired an ethnocentric view of Anglo-Saxon destiny, but the image of the future in the Book of Mormon is a wholly opposite one. It envisions a worldwide conversion of believers and their final gathering into the kingdom of God. This begins where John Wesley's "world parish" leaves off.

Third, the biblical bond linking holiness to hope for salvation, both individual and social, also finds confirmation in the Book of Mormon. Certainly, Methodists had no corner on that linkage, for Baptist preachers, Charles G. Finney's Congregationalists, Alexander Campbell's Disciples of Christ, and Unitarians like William E. Channing affirmed it. Ancient Nephites heeded the word of their prophets and looked forward to the second coming of Jesus Christ, the Son of Righteousness. When he appeared to their descendants in the New World, Jesus repeated even more understandably the words of the SERMON ON THE MOUNT that he had proclaimed in the Old.

Fourth, Joseph Smith's translation of an ancient sacred book helped bring to fruition another movement, long growing among Puritans, Pietists, Quakers, and Methodists, to restore to Christian doctrine the idea of the presence of the Holy Spirit in the lives of believers. Charles G. Finney came eventually to believe, for example, that the baptism of the Holy Spirit, or the experience of entire sanctification, would remedy the inadequacies of righteousness and love that he saw in his converts. So, of course, did almost all Methodists. Observers from both inside and outside the restored Church testified that in the early years something akin to modern pentecostal phenomena took place among at least the inner circle of the Saints. By the 1830s, evangelicals in several traditions were greatly expanding their use of the example of the Day of Pentecost to declare that God's power is at work in the world.

Fifth, the Book of Mormon shared in the restoration of some Christian expectations that in the last days biblical prophecies will be literally fulfilled. Those who by faith and baptism become Saints will be included among God's people, chosen in "the eleventh hour." They, too, should gather in Zion, a New Jerusalem for the New World, and a restored Jerusalem in the Old; and Christ will indeed return.

Whatever LDS interpretations of the King James Version of the Holy Scriptures developed later, the mutually supportive role of the Bible and the Book of Mormon was central to the thinking of Joseph Smith, the early missionaries, and their converts.

BIBLIOGRAPHY

Kimball, Heber C. *Journal*. Nauvoo, Ill., 1840.

Smith, Timothy L. "The Book of Mormon in a Biblical Culture." *Journal of Mormon History* 7 (1980): 3–21.

TIMOTHY L. SMITH

BOOK OF MORMON PERSONALITIES

[*The experiences, thoughts, feelings, and personalities of several individuals are brought to light in the Book of Mormon. Jesus Christ is central in the book; see* Jesus Christ in the Book of Mormon.

The founding prophet was Lehi. For articles concerning him and members of his family, see Lehi; Laman; Nephi₁; Jacob; *and* Ishmael. *Concerning Lehi's wife, Sariah, and the other women of the Book of Mormon, see* Women in the Book of Mormon.

The last Nephite king (153–90 B.C.*) was* Mosiah₂. *For articles on his grandfather, father, and brother, see* Mosiah₁, Benjamin, Helaman₁. *From 90* B.C. *to* A.D. *321 the Nephite records were kept by descendants of Alma₁; see* Alma₁; Alma₂; Helaman₂; Helaman₃; Nephi₂; Nephi₃; Nephi₄. *The last Nephite prophets, military leaders, and historians were* Mormon *and his son,* Moroni₂, *named after an earlier chief captain* Moroni₁.

Four other prophets figure prominently in the Book of Mormon; see Abinadi; Amulek; Samuel the Lamanite; *and* Brother of Jared. *Prophets from the Old World quoted in the Book of Mormon include* Ezias; Isaiah; Joseph; Moses; Neum; Zenock; *and* Zenos. *Regarding the various groups of people in the Book of Mormon, see* Peoples of the Book of Mormon; Jaredites; Lamanites; Mulek; *and* Nephites. *See also* Names in the Book of Mormon.]

BORN OF GOD

Born of God or "born again" refers to the personal spiritual experience in which repentant individuals receive a forgiveness of sins and a witness from God that if they continue to live the commandments and endure to the end, they will inherit eternal life. The scriptures teach that just as each individual is "born into the world by water, and blood, and the spirit," so must one be "born again" of water and the Spirit and be cleansed by the blood of Christ (John 3:5; Moses 6:59). To be born of God implies a sanctifying process by which the old or natural man is supplanted by the new spiritual man who enjoys the companionship of the Holy Ghost and hence is no longer disposed to commit sin (Col. 3:9–10; Mosiah 3:19; *TPJS*, p. 51). When individuals are born again they are spiritually begotten sons and daughters of God and more specifically of Jesus Christ (Mosiah 5:7; 27:25). The Book of Mormon prophet ALMA₁ calls this inner transformation a "mighty change in your hearts" (Alma 5:14).

LDS scripture and literature contain numerous examples of individuals who have undergone this process of spiritual rebirth. Enos relates that after "mighty prayer and supplication" the Lord declared that his sins had been forgiven (Enos 1:1–8). After King Benjamin's discourse, the people said that the Spirit had "wrought a mighty change in us, or in our hearts," and that they had "no more disposition to do evil, but to do good continually" (Mosiah 5:2). Of his conversion experience, Alma₂ says, "Nevertheless, after wading through much tribulation, repenting nigh unto death, the Lord in mercy hath seen fit to snatch me out of an everlasting burning, and I am born of God" (Mosiah 27:28). Similar experiences are recounted about King Lamoni and his father (Alma 19, 22). In an account written in 1832, the Prophet Joseph Smith describes his first vision as being significant not only for opening a new dispensation of the gospel, but also for his personal conversion. He writes, "The Lord opened the heavens upon me and I saw the Lord and he spake unto me saying Joseph my son thy sins are forgiven thee. [A]nd my soul was filled with love and for many days I could rejoice with great joy and the Lord was with me" (*PJS* 1:6–7).

MORMON explains the "mighty change" that must occur if one is to be born of God.

The first fruit of repentance is the BAPTISM of water and fire, which baptism "cometh by faith unto the fulfilling of the commandments." Then comes a REMISSION OF SINS that brings a meekness and lowliness of heart. Such a transformation results in one's becoming worthy of the companionship of the Holy Ghost, who "filleth with hope and perfect love, which love endureth by diligence unto prayer" (Moro. 8:25–26).

LDS scriptures teach that spiritual rebirth comes by the GRACE of God to those who adhere to the principles and ordinances of the gospel of Jesus Christ, namely, faith, repentance, baptism, and reception of the gift of the Holy Ghost. For the process to be genuine, however, one must be diligently engaged in good works, for as James says, "faith without works is dead; . . . by works [is] faith made perfect" (James 2:20, 22). A mere confession of change, or receiving baptism or another ordinance, does not necessarily mean that one has been born of God.

Other Christian faiths also emphasize the importance of being "born again." Unlike many of these, Latter-day Saints do not believe this experience alone is sufficient for salvation. Instead, the process of spiritual rebirth signals to Latter-day Saints the beginning of a new life abounding with faith, grace, and good works. Only by enduring to the end may the individual return to the presence of God. Those who receive the ordinance of baptism and are faithful in keeping the commandments may enjoy the constant presence of the Holy Ghost who, like fire, will act as a sanctifier, and will witness to the hearts of the righteous that their sins are forgiven, imparting hope for eternal life.

Persons who have experienced this mighty change manifest attitudinal and behavioral changes. Feeling their hearts riveted to the Lord, their obedience extends beyond performance of duty. President Harold B. Lee

taught, "Conversion must mean more than just being a 'card-carrying' member of the Church with a tithing receipt, a membership card, a temple recommend, etc. It means to overcome the tendencies to criticize and to strive continually to improve inward weaknesses and not merely the outward appearances" (*Ensign*, June 1971, p. 8). Latter-day Saints believe that individuals who are truly born of God gladly give a life of service to their fellow beings—they share the gospel message, sacrifice their own time, energy, and resources for the benefit of others, and in general hold high the light of Christ, being faithful to all the commandments.

BIBLIOGRAPHY

Cannon, Elaine, and Ed J. Pinegar. *The Mighty Change*. Salt Lake City, 1978.

ED J. PINEGAR

BROTHER OF JARED

The brother of Jared (c. 2200 B.C.) was the first JAREDITE prophet (*see* BOOK OF MORMON: BOOK OF ETHER). He led his people from "the great tower" in Mesopotamia to the Western Hemisphere. "A large and mighty man, and a man highly favored of the Lord" (Ether 1:34), he is remembered most for his very great faith that allowed him to see and converse face to face with the premortal Jesus Christ (Ether 3:13; 12:19–21) and to be shown in vision all the inhabitants and events of the earth from beginning to end (Ether 3:25).

Only a few details are known about the life and revelations of this ancient prophet. In response to his prayer of faith, the Lord did not confound his language or that of his family and friends at the time of the Tower of Babel. Instead, the Lord instructed him to lead those people to a land "choice above all the lands of the earth" (Ether 1:42), and he was promised that his descendants would become a great and righteous nation. They were called the Jaredites. The Lord came in a cloud to tell the brother of Jared where they should travel, but he did not see him (Ether 2:4). They gathered flocks and seeds, and journeyed to a place on the sea that they called Moriancumer (Ether 2:13). Although the Book of Mormon does not give this prophet's name, Joseph Smith later identified it as Mahonri Moriancumer (*T&S* 2 [1841]: 362; *Juvenile Instructor*, Vol. 27 [May 1, 1892]: 282).

For four years the Jaredites dwelt in tents on the seashore. During those years, the brother of Jared apparently ceased praying for guidance, and when the Lord appeared again in a cloud, he talked with him for three hours and chastened him, which caused him to repent and return to favor with God. Latter-day Saints see this as evidence of God's concern for his children, of the importance of daily prayer, and of the fact that the Spirit of the Lord will not always strive with man, even with a great prophet, unless he continues to petition the Lord in righteousness (Ether 2:15).

The brother of Jared built eight unique barges (Ether 2:16–25) in which to cross the ocean. Then he prepared sixteen clear molten stones and asked the Lord to make them shine to illuminate the inside of the barges (Ether 3:1–5). As the Lord touched the stones, the brother of Jared saw the finger of the Lord and was "struck with fear" (Ether 3:6). Never before, the record states, had man come before God with such exceeding faith; as a result, he was brought into the presence of the Lord Jesus Christ and saw the premortal spirit body of Christ (Ether 3:9–13).

In this vision, the brother of Jared learned many things: he was told that he had been redeemed from the Fall; he saw that human beings were physically created in the image of God and that the spirit body of Jesus looked the same as would his future physical body; he beheld all the inhabitants of the earth from the beginning to the end; and he learned many other sacred things, which he was commanded to record in a cryptic language, sealed up to come forth in the "due time" of the Lord (Ether 3:24; 4:1–3). With that record he included two stones that had been prepared by the Lord to aid future prophets in interpreting the record. For all these reasons, Latter-day Saints esteem the brother of Jared as one of the mightiest prophets who ever lived.

The brother of Jared and his people crossed the sea to the promised land. His great faith, as noted by Moroni, once caused a mountain, Zerin, to be removed (Ether 12:30). He had twenty-two sons and daughters. He lived to see his people begin to prosper and his nephew, Orihah, anointed as their king.

BIBLIOGRAPHY

Eyring, Henry B. "The Brother of Jared." *Ensign* 8 (July 1978): 62–65.

ADDITIONAL SOURCE

Holland, Jeffrey R. "Rending the Veil of Unbelief." In *Nurturing Faith through the Book of Mormon*, 1–24. Salt Lake City: Deseret Book, 1995.

REX C. REEVE, JR.

C

CHARITY

Charity is a concept found in many cultures, its meaning ranging from a general selfless love of humanity to the specific alms-giving that is often its focus in modern times. Latter-day Saints take their understanding of charity from the Book of Mormon: "Charity is the pure love of Christ, and it endureth forever; and whoso is found possessed of it at the last day, it shall be well with him" (Moro. 7:47; cf. Ether 12:34; 2 Ne. 26:30).

As the love of Christ, charity is characterized as selfless and self-sacrificing (1 Cor. 13:5), emanating from a pure heart, a good conscience, and faith unfeigned (1 Tim. 1:5). Thus, more than an act, charity is an attitude, a state of heart and mind (1 Cor. 13:4–7) that accompanies one's works and is proffered unconditionally (D&C 121:45). It follows, but surpasses in importance, faith and hope (1 Cor. 13:13).

This may have been what Jesus was trying to teach Peter in John 21:15–17, wherein he asks Peter three times if he "loves" him, and, to Peter's affirmative answers, responds, "Feed my sheep" and "Feed my lambs," teaching that the true love of Christ always goes out to others. Loving all of God's children and being willing to sacrifice for them are the depth and breadth of the pure love of Christ. This "bond of . . . perfectness and peace" (D&C 88:125; Col. 3:14) becomes the foundation of all human relationships (cf. 1 Cor. 13). The everlasting love of charity is intended to be an integral part of one's nature: one is to cleave unto it (Moro. 7:46) and be clothed in it (D&C 88:125). In fact, *all* things are to be done in charity. Charity is everlasting; it covers sins (1 Pet. 4:8), it casts out all fears (Moro. 8:16), and it is a prerequisite for entering the kingdom of Heaven (Ether 12:34; Moro. 10:21).

Throughout its history, the law of the LDS Church has been that its members are to do all things with charity. Since its inception in 1842, the LDS Relief Society has had the motto Charity Never Faileth (1 Cor. 13:8; Moro. 7:46). The concept of charity is fundamental to the teachings and the procedures of the Church, being the very core of all it does, including missionary work, welfare services,

temple work, tithes and offerings, and home and visiting teaching. As the spiritual welfare of the individual member of the Church is contingent upon charity, so is the welfare of Zion dependent upon the charity in the hearts of Latter-day Saints (2 Ne. 26:28–31).

BIBLIOGRAPHY

Benson, Ezra Taft. "To the Elderly in the Church." *Ensign* 19 (Nov. 1989): 4–8.

Hansen, W. Eugene. "Love." *Ensign* 19 (Nov. 1989): 23–24.

Holland, Jeffrey R. "He Loved Them unto the End." *Ensign* 19 (Nov. 1989): 25–26.

ADDITIONAL SOURCE

Millet, Robert L. "The Love of God and of All Men: The Doctrine of Charity in the Book of Mormon." In *Doctrines of the Book of Mormon: The 1991 Sperry Symposium*, edited by Bruce A. Van Orden and Brent L. Top, 127–44. Salt Lake City: Deseret Book, 1992.

ADDIE FUHRIMAN

CHILDREN

[*This entry consists of one article here:*

Salvation of Children

This article discusses the innocence of children until they reach the age of accountability; that their salvation is assured until that time.]

Salvation of Children
In Latter-day Saint doctrine children are to be instructed in the principles of the gospel and baptized when eight years of age (D&C 68:25–27). They are then responsible to adhere to the teachings of the Church relative to obtaining salvation. Before that time they are considered "infants" or "little children" and are not required to be baptized. They are considered "alive in Christ" and are "whole" (Moro. 8:8–12; JST, Matt. 18:10–11).

Although children, with all the rest of mankind, feel the mortal "effects" of Adam's transgression, they (and all others) do not have any mystical stain of original sin upon them. Adults must have their own personal sins remitted by repentance and baptism (John 3:5; Acts 2:38; Moses 6:57–62), but "the Son of God hath atoned for original guilt, wherein the sins of the parents [both Adam's and their mortal parents'] cannot be answered upon the heads of the children, for they are whole from the foundation of the world" (Moses 6:54).

The prophet MORMON taught: "Listen to the words of Christ; . . . the curse of Adam is taken from them in me, that it hath no power over them. . . . It is solemn mockery before God, that ye should baptize little children" (Moro. 8:8–9). The Lord instructed Joseph SMITH that "little children are redeemed from the foundation of the world through mine Only Begotten; wherefore, they cannot sin, for power is not given unto Satan to tempt little children, until they begin to become accountable before me" (D&C 29:46–47).

This unconditional benefit of Christ's atonement saves all little children regardless of race, color, or nationality, for "all children are alike unto me" (Moro. 8:17). They all begin their mortal lives pure and innocent (D&C 93:38), and "little children also have eternal life" (Mosiah 15:25).

If they die while in this state of innocence and purity, they return to that God who gave them life, saved, and fit for his company. They are in a "blessed" condition, for God's "judgment is just; and the infant perisheth not that dieth in his infancy" (Mosiah 3:16, 18). The Prophet Joseph Smith saw in vision "that all children who die before they arrive at the years of accountability are saved in the celestial kingdom of heaven" (D&C 137:10; *TPJS*, p. 200).

All that is said of infants and little children applies also to those who may be adults in physical body but are not accountable mentally (D&C 29:49–50).

Concepts outlined in scripture and by the prophets clearly demonstrate the marvelous uniting of the laws of justice and mercy because of the Atonement: none are eternally disadvantaged by noncompliance to gospel laws or ordinances they do not know or are not capable of understanding and thus cannot comply.

CALVIN P. RUDD

CHRONOLOGY

The Book of Mormon contains a chronology that is internally consistent over the thousand-year NEPHITE history, with precise Nephite dates for several events, including the crucifixion of Jesus Christ. However, its chronology has not been unequivocally tied to other calendars because of uncertainties in biblical dates and lack of details about the Nephite calendars. Even less information exists about JAREDITE chronology (Sorenson, 1969).

INTERNAL NEPHITE CHRONOLOGY. Nephites kept careful track of time from at least three reference points:

1. Years were counted from the time LEHI left Jerusalem (Enos 1:25; Mosiah 6:4); not only was this an important date of origin, but also an angel had said that the Savior would come "in six hundred years" from that time (1 Ne. 19:8).

2. Time was also measured from the commencement of the reign of the judges (c. 91 B.C.; cf. 3 Ne. 1:1), which marked a major political reform ending five centuries of Nephite kingship (Jacob 1:9–11; Alma 1:1), during which the years of each king's reign were probably counted according to typical ancient practices (1 Ne. 1:4; Mosiah 29:46).

3. The Nephites later reckoned time from the sign of the birth of Christ (3 Ne. 2:8).

The Book of Mormon links all three systems in several passages that are apparently consistent. Table 1 lists several events using the Nephite systems.

Most of the Nephite record pertains to three historical periods: the time of Lehi and his sons (c. 600–500 B.C.), the events preceding and following the coming of Christ (c. 150 B.C.–A.D. 34), and the destruction of the Nephites (c. A.D. 300–420). Thus, the relatively large book of Alma covers only thirty-nine years, while the much smaller books of Omni and 4 Nephi each cover more than two hundred years.

LDS editions of the Book of Mormon show dates in Nephite years, deduced from the text, at the bottom of the pages. The exact nature of the Nephite year, however, is not described. The Nephite year began with the "first day" of the "first month" (Alma 51:37–52:1; 56:1), and it probably had twelve months because the eleventh month was at "the latter end" of the year (Alma 48:2, 21; 49:1), but the lengths of the months and of the year itself are not mentioned.

Until the coming of Christ, the Nephites observed the LAW OF MOSES (2 Ne. 25:24; Alma 25:15), which generally used lunar months (new moon to new moon). The Savior was crucified on the *fourteenth* day of the first lunar month of the Jewish calendar (John 19:14; Lev. 23:5), but on the *fourth* day of the first Nephite month (3 Ne. 8:5). This may imply that Nephite months at that time were not lunar and that their civil calendar may have differed from their religious calendar.

John L. Sorenson (1990) has observed that during the reign of the judges warfare was mostly limited to four consecutive Nephite months. These months can be approximately correlated with our calendar because even today warfare in Mesoamerica (the probable

Table 1: Selected Events in Nephite History

Nephite Years				
Lehi	Judges	Christ	Event	Reference
1		(−600)	Lehi departs from Jerusalem	1 Ne. 10:4; 19:8
9		(−592)	Lehi's group arrives in Bountiful	1 Ne. 17:4–5
56		(−545)	Jacob receives plates from Nephi	Jacob 1:1
200		(−401)	Law of Moses strictly observed	Jarom 1:5
477		(−124)	King Benjamin's Speech	Mosiah 6:3–4
510	1	(−91)	Alma$_1$, Mosiah die; Alma$_2$ first judge	Mosiah 29:44–46
	9	(−83)	Nephihah becomes judge	Alma 4:20–8:2
	15	(−77)	The return of the sons of Mosiah	Alma 17:1–6
	18	(−74)	Korihor refuted	Alma 30
			Alma's Mission to the Zoramites	Alma 31:6–35:12
	18	(−74)	War because of Zoramites	Alma 35:13; 43:3–4
			Moroni leads army	Alma 43:17
	37	(−55)	Nephites begin migrating northward	Alma 63:4–6
	42	(−50)	Helaman$_2$ becomes judge; Gadianton	Hel. 2:1–5
	53	(−39)	Helaman$_2$ dies; Nephi$_2$ chief judge	Hel. 3:37
	58	(−34)	Zarahemla captured	Hel. 4:5
	67	(−25)	Most Nephites join Gadianton	Hel. 6:16, 21
	73	(−19)	Nephi invokes a famine	Hel. 11:2–5
	75	(−17)	Gadianton robbers expelled	Hel. 11:6–17
	77	(−15)	Most Nephites reconverted	Hel. 11:21
	80	(−12)	Robbers return	Hel. 11:24–29
	86	(−6)	Samuel the Lamanite prophesies	Hel. 13:1–16:9
601	92	(1)	Sign of the birth of Christ	3 Ne. 1:1, 4, 19
609	100	9	Begin to reckon time from Christ	3 Ne. 2:5–8
		13	Severe war with robbers begins	3 Ne. 2:11–13
		19	Major Nephite victory	3 Ne. 4:5, 11–15
		26	Nephites prosper	3 Ne. 6:1–4
		30	Nephite society disintegrates	3 Ne. 6:14–7:13
		34	Destruction; Christ appears	3 Ne. 8:2–28:12
		36	All converted; property held in common	4 Ne. 1:2–3
		201	Private ownership reinstituted	4 Ne. 1:24–25
		231	Tribalization reemerges	4 Ne. 1:35–38
		245	The wicked outnumber righteous	4 Ne. 1:40
		300	Nephites as wicked as Lamanites	4 Ne. 1:45
		326	Mormon leads army	Morm. 2:2
		350	Treaty with Lamanites and Robbers	Morm. 2:28
		362	Mormon refuses to lead Nephites	Morm. 3:8–11
		385	Nephites destroyed; Mormon dies	Morm. 6:5–8:3
		421	Moroni seals up the record	Moro. 10:1–2

NOTE: Years in parentheses are calculated, with the year −600 beginning just over 600 Nephite years before the birth of Christ.

area of Book of Mormon GEOGRAPHY for most of Nephite history) is conducted mostly during the dry season after the fall harvest. This correlation implies that the Nephite year at that time began in December (*see* WARFARE IN THE BOOK OF MORMON). This would mean that because the crucifixion of Christ (presumably in early April) occurred in the first Nephite month, the Nephites probably shifted their calendar to begin the first month in April at the same time they began reckoning time from the birth of Christ. This conclusion is consistent with the Nephite record that Christ was born some time after the end of the Nephite year (3 Ne. 1:1–9).

EXTERNAL CHRONOLOGY. Evidence supports two possible lengths for Nephite years: 365 days and 360 days. Each can be correlated to external history. The internal chronology is consistent, so that if the exact nature of the Nephite calendar were known, only one reference point in external history would be needed to fix the entire Nephite chronology. However, at least two such dates would be required to determine the length of the Nephite year. Three principal events are common to both Nephite and Old World sources: (1) the first year of the reign of Zedekiah, King of Judah; (2) the birth of Christ; and (3) the death of Christ. Because there are varying degrees of uncertainty about these three reference points, alternative correlation methods have been proposed, each using two of these dates.

First, Orson Pratt proposed that the Nephites used a 365-day year, as had the Egyptians previously and as did the Mesoamericans afterward (*Millennial Star* 28 [Dec. 22, 1866]: 810). It has been noted (Lefgren) that such a year agrees, to the very day, with one choice for the birth and death dates of Christ—namely, Thursday, April 6, 1 B.C., and Friday, April 1, A.D. 33, respectively (Gregorian calendar). Both of these dates are sup-

ported by other arguments (J. Pratt, 1985 and 1990). This theory assumes that the third system of Nephite reckoning began on the very day of the birth of Christ, which is not explicitly stated in the Book of Mormon but is consistent with Sorenson's conclusions above.

Second, most historians believe that the first year of King Zedekiah began in 598–596 B.C. Lehi left Jerusalem shortly afterward (1 Ne. 1:4; 2:4). The date of the birth of Christ is not known directly from historical sources, but it is believed that King Herod died in 5–4 B.C., implying that Christ was born shortly before (Matt. 2:1). Using these two events as reference points, Huber has proposed a 360-day Nephite year because 600 such years fit the interval from Lehi to Christ (3 Ne. 1:1); such a system has historical precedent, and apparently underlies certain prophecies in which the word "time" may equal 360 days (e.g., Rev. 12:6, 14).

BIBLIOGRAPHY

Brown, S. Kent; C. Wilfred Griggs; and H. Kimball Hansen. "Review of *April Sixth* by John C. Lefgren." *BYU Studies* 22 (Summer 1982): 375–83. See rebuttal and response in *BYU Studies* 23 (Spring 1983): 252–55.

Huber, Jay H. "Lehi's 600 Year Prophecy and the Birth of Christ." *FARMS Paper.* Provo, Utah, 1982.

Lefgren, John C. *April Sixth.* Salt Lake City, 1980.

Pratt, John P. "The Restoration of Priesthood Keys on Easter 1836. Part 1: Dating the First Easter." *Ensign* 15 (June 1985): 59–68.

———. "Yet Another Eclipse for Herod." *The Planetarian* 19 (Dec. 1990): 8–14.

Sorenson, John L. "The Years of the Jaredites." *FARMS Paper.* Provo, Utah, 1969.

———. "Seasonality of Warfare in the Book of Mormon and in Mesoamerica." In *Warfare in the Book of Mormon*, ed. S. Ricks and W. Hamblin, pp. 445–77. Salt Lake City, 1990.

JOHN P. PRATT

COLUMBUS, CHRISTOPHER

Latter-day Saints generally regard Columbus as having fulfilled a prophecy contained early in the Book of Mormon. NEPHI$_1$ recorded a vision of the future of his father's descendants. After foreseeing the destruction of his own seed, Nephi beheld a gentile "separated from the seed of my brethren by the many waters," and saw that the Spirit of God "came down and wrought upon the man; and he went forth upon the many waters, even unto the seed of my brethren, who were in the promised land" (1 Ne. 13:12).

Nephi appears to give an accurate account of Columbus's motives. Even though he was well-acquainted with the sciences of his day and his voyages have been viewed by some historians as primarily an economic triumph of Spain over Portugal, Columbus apparently had bigger motives for his voyage and felt himself spiritually driven to discover new lands. Newly acknowledged documents show that medieval eschatology, the scriptures, and divine inspiration were the main forces compelling him to sail. His notes in the works of Pierre d'Ailly and his own unfinished *Book of Prophecies* substantiate his apocalyptic view of the world and his feelings about his own prophetic role.

Among the themes of this book was the conversion of the heathen. Columbus quoted Seneca, "The years will come . . . when the Ocean will loose the bonds by which we have been confined, when an immense land shall lie revealed" (Watts, p. 94). He believed himself chosen by God to find that land and deliver the light of Christianity to the natives there. He was called *Christoferens* (the Christ-bearer). A map contemporaneous with his voyages depicts him bearing the Christ child on his shoulders across the waters. He believed that he was to help usher in the age of "one fold, and one shepherd," citing John 10:16 (cf. 3 Ne. 15:21), and spoke of finding "the new heaven and new earth."

Writing to King Ferdinand and Queen Isabella to gain financial support, Columbus testified that a voice had told him he had been watched over from infancy to prepare him for discovering the Indies. He felt that he was given divine keys to ocean barriers that only he could unlock (Merrill, p. 135). In a second letter, he emphasized his prophetic role: "Reason, mathematics, and maps of the world were of no use to me in the execution of the enterprise of the Indies. What Isaiah said [e.g., Isa. 24:15] was completely fulfilled" (Watts, p. 96). Unknowingly, Columbus also fulfilled Nephi's prophecy.

BIBLIOGRAPHY

Merrill, Hyde M. "Christopher Columbus and the Book of Mormon." *IE* 69 (1966): 97–98, 135–36.

Nibley, Hugh W. "Columbus and Revelation." *Instructor* 88 (1953): 319–20; reprinted in CWHN 8:49–53.

Watts, Pauline Moffitt. "Prophecy and Discovery: On the Spiritual Origins of Christopher Columbus's 'Enterprise of the Indies.'" *American Historical Review* 90 (1985): 73–102.

LOUISE G. HANSON

COMMENTARIES ON THE BOOK OF MORMON

Because the Book of Mormon is the best known and most widely circulated LDS book, many commentaries on and reference books about it have been written to assist readers. Inasmuch as its historical timeline spans from

c. 2200 B.C. to A.D. 421 and its doctrinal content is extensive, it is difficult for a one-volume work to meet the many needs and interests. The references cited herein contain bibliographies that will provide readers with additional sources.

George Reynolds and Janne M. Sjodahl coauthored a *Commentary on the Book of Mormon* (1955–1961), a seven-volume work (published posthumously to both authors) that has been widely circulated. Hugh Nibley's *Lehi in the Desert and the World of the Jaredites* (1952; rev. 1988) provides insightful historical material on the travels of Lehi's party from Jerusalem, which occurred about 600 B.C., through the Arabian Peninsula, to the Western Hemisphere, and also on the journey of the Jaredite colony at about 2200 B.C. from the Near East to the Western Hemisphere. Francis W. Kirkham wrote a two-volume work entitled *A New Witness for Christ in America* (rev. ed. 1959–1960) that discusses the coming forth and the translation and printing of the Book of Mormon and non–LDS explanations of the same topics. B. H. Roberts authored a three-volume work titled *New Witnesses for God* (1909). Volumes 2 and 3 addressed four topics: the Book of Mormon as a witness of the Bible; the discovery, translation, and people of the Book of Mormon; evidence of its truth; and Roberts's responses to various objections to the book. Sidney B. Sperry authored *Our Book of Mormon* (1947); *The Book of Mormon Testifies* (1952); and *Book of Mormon Compendium* (1968). Daniel H. Ludlow wrote a popular one-volume work, *A Companion to Your Study of the Book of Mormon* (1976).

The Religious Studies Center at Brigham Young University sponsors an annual symposium on the Book of Mormon. Beginning in 1985, it has published a volume of selected lectures for each symposium. Both doctrinal and historical materials are included. Other volumes are planned as additional symposia

are held. A volume entitled *A Book of Mormon Treasury* (1959), taken from the pages of the *Improvement Era*, contains thirty-six articles by General Authorities and other respected students of the Book of Mormon on historical, geographical, and doctrinal matters, as well as biblical relationships. Following a similar format, Kent P. Jackson compiled a two-volume work, *Studies in Scripture Volume Seven— 1st Nephi–Alma 29* (1987) and *Studies in Scripture Volume Eight—Alma 30–Moroni* (1988). Jackson also edited a special Book of Mormon issue of *BYU Studies* 30 (Summer 1990): 1–140. Other scholarly materials related to Book of Mormon topics are available through FARMS (Foundation for Ancient Research and Mormon Studies).

Others who have contributed to the literature about the Book of Mormon are Paul R. Cheesman, whose works include *The World of the Book of Mormon* (1984), and Monte S. Nyman, whose publications include *An Ensign to All People: The Sacred Message and Mission of the Book of Mormon* (1987).

Church headquarters publishes materials for use in weekly priesthood quorum meetings, Relief Society meetings, Sunday School classes, and Institute and Seminary classes to assist members in better understanding the Book of Mormon.

Several authors have written on Book of Mormon archaeology and geology. Two popular books with an archaeological approach are Dewey and Edith Farnsworth, *The Americas Before Columbus* (1947), and Milton R. Hunter and Thomas Stuart Ferguson, *Ancient America and the Book of Mormon* (1950). More recent studies on Book of Mormon geography include John L. Sorenson, *An Ancient American Setting for the Book of Mormon* (1985); F. Richard Hauck, *Deciphering the Geography of the Book of Mormon* (1988); and Joseph L. Allen, *Exploring the Lands of the Book of Mormon* (1989). The Nephites, Lamanites,

Mulekites, and Jaredites were historical cultures that occupied time and space; however, Church leaders have declared no official position as to where the Book of Mormon civilizations were situated other than that they were in the Western Hemisphere.

[*See also* other Book of Mormon entries.]

ADDITIONAL SOURCES

Matthews, Robert J. "The Power and the Purpose of the Written Record." In *Nurturing Faith through the Book of Mormon*, 89–118. Salt Lake City: Deseret Book, 1995.

McConkie, Joseph Fielding, Robert L. Millet, and Brent L. Top. *Doctrinal Commentary on the Book of Mormon*. 4 vols. Salt Lake City: Bookcraft, 1987–1992.

Nyman, Monte S. and Charles D. Tate, Jr., eds. *The Book of Mormon: Papers from the Annual Book of Mormon Symposia*. Book of Mormon Symposium Series. Salt Lake City and Provo, Utah: Bookcraft and BYU Religious Studies Center, 1988–94.

H. DONL PETERSON

CONDESCENSION OF GOD

The Book of Mormon prophet Nephi₁ (c. 600 B.C.) was asked by an angel, "Knowest thou the condescension of God?" (1 Ne. 11:16). Nephi was then shown in a vision a virgin who was to become "the mother of the Son of God, after the manner of the flesh" (verse 18). He next beheld the virgin with a child whom the angel identified as "the Lamb of God, yea, even the Son of the Eternal Father" (11:21). Then Nephi understood that the condescension of God is the ultimate manifestation of God's love through Jesus Christ (11:20–22). Such condescension denotes, first, the love of God the Father, who deigned to sire a son, born of a mortal woman, and then allow this

Son to suffer temptations and pain (Mosiah 3:5–7), be "judged of the world," and be "slain for the sins of the world" (1 Ne. 11:32–33). Second, it signifies the love and willingness of God the Son (Jesus Christ) to die for mankind.

The word "condescension" implies "voluntary descent," "submission," and "performing acts which strict justice does not require." This definition is particularly applicable to Jesus in the portrayal of him by prophets who lived before his birth and who affirmed: "God himself shall come down" to make an atonement (Mosiah 15:1); "the God of Abraham, and of Isaac, and the God of Jacob, yieldeth himself . . . into the hands of wicked men" (1 Ne. 19:10); "the great Creator . . . suffereth himself to become subject unto man in the flesh" (2 Ne. 9:5); and "he offereth himself a sacrifice for sin" (2 Ne. 2:7). "The Lord Omnipotent," said King Benjamin, "shall come down from heaven among the children of men, and shall dwell in a tabernacle of clay" (Mosiah 3:5).

In fulfillment of these prophecies, Jesus descended from the realms of glory for the purposes of experiencing mortal infirmities that he might have mercy and compassion according to the flesh and of taking upon himself the sins, transgressions, pains, and sicknesses of men in order to satisfy the demands of justice and gain victory over death, thereby redeeming his people (Mosiah 15:8–9; Alma 7:11–13). Christ's selfless sacrifice merits profound gratitude and endearing love from all who are recipients of his supernal offering.

BIBLIOGRAPHY

Bruce R. McConkie. "Behold the Condescension of God." *New Era* 14 (Dec. 1984): 34–39.

BYRON R. MERRILL

CONVERSION

From its beginnings to the present day, the Church has had a strong missionary orientation. It teaches that conversion is essentially a process of REPENTANCE and personal spiritual experience.

THE NATURE OF CONVERSION. A number of theories have been advanced by sociologists to explain why people are likely to convert to another religious denomination. Glenn M. Vernon indicated that conversion involves several subprocesses, which must be accounted for, including (1) the manner in which the convert becomes aware of the group possessing the ideology; (2) the acceptance of new religious definitions; and (3) the integration of the new convert into the group. John Lofland and Rodney Stark proposed that conversion is a problem-solving process in which the individual uses organizational facilities, programs, and ideologies to resolve various life problems. More recently, David A. Snow, Louis A. Zurcher, and Sheldon Ekland-Olson have emphasized structural proximity, availability, and affective interaction with members of the new denomination as the most powerful influences in determining who will join. Roger A. Straus has proposed that religious conversion is an active accomplishment by the person who converts. Straus thinks that previous theories focus too heavily on the idea that conversion is something which happens to a person as a result of circumstances external to himself. Similarly, C. David Gartrell and Zane K. Shannon propose that conversion should be characterized as a rational choice based on the recruit's evaluation of the social and cognitive outcomes of converting or not converting.

Recovery from crisis, social proximity to members of the Church, and personal problem solving are certainly involved to some extent in at least some conversions. However, research about people who have converted to many churches, (Snow and Phillips; Heirich) including The Church of Jesus Christ of Latter-day Saints (Seggar and Kunz), has failed to provide much support for the problem-solving theory of Lofland and Stark. Research by David A. Snow and Cynthia L. Phillips and by Max Heirich provides more evidence of the influence of social networks in conversion.

Most scientific theories, however, lack any significant reference to the influence of the Holy Spirit in conversion, which is the dominant element in the Latter-day Saint understanding of conversion. The visitation of Jesus Christ to Paul on the road to Damascus (Acts 9:1–9) does not fit into any secular theoretical categories. Paul was not seeking a new faith to solve problems in his life. He did not begin to serve Christ in order to be accepted by his friends. He persecuted Christians because he thought they had fallen away from the true faith. As a religious man, he recognized the voice of God when it spoke to him.

Similar conversion stories are told in the Book of Mormon. For example, as Alma$_2$ and the sons of King Mosiah$_2$ were going about teaching that the religion of their fathers was not true, they were stopped by the angel of the Lord, who asked why they persecuted the believers. Alma$_2$ was struck dumb and fell to the ground unable to move. While his father and others fasted and prayed in his behalf for two days and two nights, Alma$_2$ suffered excruciating pains and torment and finally called upon Jesus Christ for mercy to take away his sins. Immediately, the pain left and his soul was filled with exquisite joy (Alma 36:6–22). Alma arose and proclaimed that he had been reborn through the spirit of the Lord. Alma and the sons of Mosiah spent the rest of their lives preaching of Christ and do-ing many good works (Mosiah 27:8–31; cf. the spiritual rebirth of the people of Zarahemla at the time of King BENJAMIN in Mosiah 4–5).

Most conversions are not as dramatic as those of Paul and Alma₂ and the sons of Mosiah. The conversion of Alma₁ is closer to the kind experienced by most people who join the Church (Mosiah 17:2–4; 18:1). When Abinadi called him and the other priests of the wicked king Noah to repentance, Alma₁ knew in his heart that Abinadi spoke the truth. He repented of his sins and began to keep the commandments, with which he was already basically familiar. This wrought a sig-nificant change in his life.

From these and other scriptural accounts of the conversion process, it is evident that conversion "implies not merely mental ac-ceptance of Jesus and his teaching but also a motivating faith in him and his gospel—a faith which works a transformation, an actual *change* in one's understanding of life's mean-ing and in his allegiance to God—in interest, in thought, and in conduct" (Romney, p. 1065). Conversion involves a newness of life, which is effected by receiving divine forgive-ness that remits sins (*see* BORN OF GOD). It is characterized by a determination to do good continually, forsaking all sins, and by the healing of the soul by the power of the Holy Spirit, being filled with peace and joy (cf. Romney, p. 1066).

THE PROCESS OF CONVERSION TO THE CHURCH OF JESUS CHRIST OF LATTER-DAY SAINTS. The three subprocesses proposed by Vernon fit quite well the three most obvious aspects of conversion to the Church. The first is "the manner in which the convert becomes aware of the group possessing the ideology." This corresponds to what is referred to in LDS missionary circles as "finding." People come into contact with missionaries in many ways.

The most effective source is referral by cur-rent Church members who invite friends or family relatives to meet with the missionaries to be taught about the gospel. A second way is for missionaries to knock on doors to invite people to learn about the Church. They also may talk with people they meet on the street or in any other form of normal social contact. Missionaries occasionally set up booths at fairs or expositions. The Church has adver-tised through the broadcast and print media, offering Church literature. It also operates several visitors centers, usually associated with a Church temple or historical site. Two of the best known are Temple Square in Salt Lake City, Utah, and at historic Nauvoo, Illi-nois. All these visitors centers offer interested people the opportunity to accept teaching vis-its by missionaries.

The second of Vernon's subprocesses—ac-ceptance of new religious definitions—corre-sponds to the second major missionary activ-ity, teaching. Missionaries teach the basic principles of God's plan of salvation. They in-vite those they teach to learn more by study-ing the Bible and the Book of Mormon on their own. They encourage, inform, teach, and testify. Study is an important part of the conversion process, for the mind plays a role as the investigator learns to understand and ponder the wisdom, logic, and ethic of gospel principles. As B. H. Roberts once stated, "It is frequently the case that a proper setting-forth of a subject makes its truth self-evident. . . . To be known, the truth must be stated and the clearer and more complete the statement is, the better opportunity will the Holy Spirit have for testifying to the souls of men that the work is true" (Vol. 2, pp. vi–vii).

Prospective converts are invited to seek through prayer a spiritual witness from the Holy Ghost to let them know the truth. As Roberts stated regarding the Book of Mormon, "[The Holy Ghost] must ever be the chief source of evidence for the truth of the Book of Mormon. All other evidence is secondary to this, the primary and infallible. No arrangement of evidence, however skillfully ordered; no argument, however adroitly made, can ever take its place" (pp. vi–vii). A quotation from the Book of Mormon is generally used to invite the prospective convert to seek this spiritual manifestation of the truthfulness of the Book of Mormon and of the gospel message: "And when ye shall receive these things, I would exhort you that ye would ask God, the Eternal Father, in the name of Christ, if these things are not true; and if ye shall ask with a sincere heart, with real intent, having faith in Christ, he will manifest the truth of it unto you, by the power of the Holy Ghost" (Moro. 10:4).

Most converts to the Church do not seem to have personal characteristics that predispose them to conversion. While those who begin looking into the Church tend to be younger than the average population and tend somewhat more often to be women, these factors do not predict who will ultimately accept BAPTISM. Those who seek baptism do not tend to have more personal problems than those who do not, nor do they differ significantly from others in personality traits or personal dispositions.

Conversion to the Church is usually not precipitous. The process begins with the first signs of interest, and may continue for many years, even after baptism. It is not simply a matter of accepting and believing the teachings of the Church. Many who do accept baptism indicate that they do not fully understand the teachings, but that they have come to feel that accepting baptism is the right thing to do. Most of them achieve a more complete understanding and acceptance of Church doctrine as they become integrated

into membership. Such integration is the third process mentioned by Vernon.

Becoming a member of the Church has broader implications than simply adopting a new set of religious beliefs. For many new members it means adopting a new lifestyle quite different from the one to which they were accustomed. For nearly all new members, it also means that they become part of a new social network of friends and acquaintances. In some cases, the new Church member is rejected and ostracized by family and former friends. This social transition is made easier if the new convert has previously developed friends and acquaintances among members of the Church.

MISSIONARY WORK IN THE CHURCH. Those who have been converted usually want to share their newfound understanding with others (cf. Perry, pp. 16–18). Paul, Alma$_1$, and Alma$_2$ passionately taught the truth of Christ's saving mission throughout the remainder of their lives following their conversions. To the convert who loves people, there is a balance to be achieved between having genuine tolerance for the beliefs of others and fulfilling the desire and obligation to share with them the joy of conversion. The major Jewish and Christian religions have gone through phases when the proselytizing spirit was dominant and other periods when the desire to proselytize was restrained (Marty and Greenspahn).

The Church of Jesus Christ of Latter-day Saints has actively proselytized from its beginnings. Its leaders and members have accepted a mandate to proclaim the restored gospel to "every nation, and kindred, and tongue, and people" (Rev. 14:6; D&C 133:37), to all who will listen. Soon after the formal organization of the Church, Samuel Smith, a brother of Joseph Smith, traveled from place to place offering the Book of Mormon to any who would receive it. Missionaries were soon bringing in converts from the United States, Canada, England, Scandinavia, and Western Europe.

After the main body of members moved to the Intermountain West, the missionary work continued. Increasingly the missionary responsibility was given to young men who had not yet married. Their converts continued to migrate to the American West until well into the twentieth century, in spite of the fact that around the turn of the century Church leaders began to encourage converts to remain where they were and to build up the Church in their homelands.

The Church growth rate since 1860 has never been less than 30 percent for any ten-year period. Since 1950, Church growth has accelerated, advancing to more than 50 percent in each ten-year period from 1950 to 1980 (Cowan).

In recent years the Church has become less and less a church confined to the western United States. As late as 1960, more than half of Church members were located in the intermountain West, with only 10 percent outside the United States. In 1980, nearly one-third of Church members lived outside the United States, with only about 40 percent in the intermountain West. In 1989 less than one convert in four was an American citizen.

By far the greatest convert growth outside the United States has been in Latin America, particularly in Mexico, Brazil, Chile, Peru, and Argentina. There has also been considerable increase in the number of baptisms in Asia and the Philippines. In 1979 there were three missions in the Philippines; this increased to twelve by 1990, and the number of convert baptisms per year tripled in that same period. New missions were opened in eastern Europe in 1989 and 1990. In 1990 the Church had more than 40,000 full-time missionaries in 257 missions around the world.

Latter-day Saints believe, as stated by President Marion G. Romney: it may be that "relatively few among the billions of earth's inhabitants will be converted. Nevertheless . . . there is no other means by which the sin-sick souls of men can be healed or for a troubled world to find peace" (p. 1067).

BIBLIOGRAPHY

Burton, Theodore M. "Convince or Convert?" In *BYU Speeches of the Year*. Provo, Utah, 1964.

Cowan, Richard O. *The Church in the Twentieth Century*. Salt Lake City, 1985.

Gartrell, C. David, and Zane K. Shannon. "Contacts, Cognitions, and Conversion: A Rational Choice Approach." *Review of Religious Research* 27 (Sept. 1985): 32–48.

Heirich, Max. "Change of Heart: A Test of Some Widely Held Theories about Religious Conversion." *American Journal of Sociology* 83 (Nov. 1977): 653–80.

Lofland, John, and Rodney Stark. "Becoming a World-Saver: A Theory of Conversion to a Deviant Perspective." *American Sociological Review* 30 (1965): 862–75.

Marty, Martin E., and Frederick E. Greenspahn, eds. *Pushing the Faith: Proselytism and Civility in a Pluralistic World*. New York, 1988.

Perry, L. Tom. "When Thou Art Converted, Strengthen Thy Brethren," *Ensign* 4 (Nov. 1974): 16–18.

Roberts, B. H. *New Witnesses for God*. Vol. 2, pp. vi–vii. Salt Lake City, 1926.

Romney, Marion G. "Conversion." *IE* 66 (1963): 1065–67.

Seggar, John, and Phillip Kunz. "Conversion: Evaluation of a Step-Like Process for Problem-Solving." *Review of Religious Research* 13 (Spring, 1972): 178–84.

Snow, David A., and Cynthia L. Phillips. "The Lofland-Stark Conversion Model: A Critical

Reassessment." *Social Problems* 27 (Apr. 1980): 430–47.

Snow, David A.; Louis A. Zurcher, Jr.; and Sheldon Ekland-Olson. "Social Networks and Social Movements: A Microstructural Approach to Differential Recruitment." *American Sociological Review* 45 (Oct. 1980): 787–801.

Straus, Roger A. "Religious Conversion as a Personal and Collective Accomplishment." *Sociological Analysis* 40 (Summer, 1979): 158–65.

Vernon, Glenn M. *Sociology of Religion*, pp. 101–2. New York, 1962.

KAY H. SMITH

COWDERY, OLIVER

Oliver Cowdery (1806–1850) was next in authority to Joseph Smith in 1830 (D&C 21:10–12), and was a second witness of many critical events in the restoration of the gospel. As one of the three Book of Mormon witnesses, Oliver Cowdery testified that an angel displayed the GOLD PLATES and that the voice of God proclaimed them correctly translated. He was with Joseph Smith when John the Baptist restored to them the Aaronic Priesthood and when Peter, James, and John ordained them to the Melchizedek Priesthood and the apostleship, and again during the momentous Kirtland Temple visions (D&C 110).

Oliver came from a New England family with strong traditions of patriotism, individuality, learning, and religion. He was born at Wells, Vermont, on October 3, 1806. His younger sister gave the only reliable information about his youth: "Oliver was brought up in Poultney, Rutland County, Vermont, and when he arrived at the age of twenty, he went to the state of New York, where his older brothers were married and settled. . . . Oliver's occupation was clerking in a store

Oliver Cowdery (1806–1850), scribe to Joseph Smith and witness of the Book of Mormon (1829), Second Elder of the Church (1830), Assistant President of the Church (1834), editor, and lawyer. Cowdery was with Joseph Smith when the Aaronic and Melchizedek priesthoods and keys were restored. After ten years of separation from the Church, he was rebaptized. He died at age forty-three, faithful to his testimony. Photograph c. 1848. © by Intellectual Reserve, Inc. Used by permission.

until 1829, when he taught the district school in the town of Manchester" (Lucy Cowdery Young to Andrew Jenson, March 7, 1887, Church Archives).

While boarding with Joseph Smith's parents, he learned of their convictions about the ancient record that their son was again translating after Martin HARRIS had lost the manuscript in 1828. The young teacher prayed and received answers that Joseph Smith mentioned in a revelation (D&C 6:14–24). The Prophet's first history states the "Lord appeared unto . . . Oliver Cowdery and shewed unto him the plates in a vision and . . . what the Lord was about to do through me, his unworthy

OLIVER COWDERY'S MAIN JOURNEYS

		Oct	1834	Kirtland to Pontiac, Michigan, and return
		Nov	1835	Kirtland to New York City, and return
		Sum	1836	Kirtland to New York City, Boston, Salem, and return
		Nov	1836	Kirtland to Philadelphia, and return
		Fall	1837	Kirtland to Far West, Missouri
			1838	Far West to Richmond, and Kirtland, Ohio
			1840	To Tiffin, Ohio
		Sum	1847	To Elkhorn, Wisconsin
		Oct	1848	To Kanesville, Iowa
		Jan	1849	To Richmond, Missouri

Apr	1828	To Manchester, New York
Jun	1829	Manchester to Harmony, Pennsylvania
Jun	1829	Harmony to Fayette, New York
Fall	1830	Fayette to Harmony, and to Colesville, New York, and return
Fall	1830	Fayette to Mentor and Kirtland, Ohio, and into the unorganized territory west of Independence, Missouri, and return
Nov	1831	Kirtland to Independence
Jul	1833	Independence to Kirtland
Oct	1833	Kirtland to Buffalo, New York, and return

BYU Geography Department

servant. Therefore he was desirous to come and write for me to translate" (*PJS* 1:10).

From April 7 through the end of June 1829, when they finished the translation, Joseph dictated while Oliver wrote, with "utmost gratitude" for the privilege (*Messenger and Advocate* 1:14). Oliver penned a letter then, expressing deep love for Christ, a lifetime theme. He later told how he and Joseph interrupted their work as they were translating the record of the Savior's post-resurrection American ministry, and how, as they prayed about baptism, they heard the "voice of the Redeemer" and were ministered to by John the Baptist, who gave them authority to baptize (JS—H 1:71, note).

In 1835 Oliver helped Joseph Smith correct and publish the revelations for the Doctrine and Covenants. Section 27 lists the major priesthood messengers of the restoration: John the Baptist, whom "I have sent unto you, my servants, Joseph Smith, Jun., and Oliver Cowdery, to ordain you unto the first priesthood" (D&C 27:8); and "Peter, and James, and John, whom I have sent unto you, by whom I have ordained you and confirmed you to be apostles, and especial witnesses of my name, and bear the keys of your ministry" (D&C 27:12).

The lesser priesthood was restored on May 15, 1829, two weeks before the Prophet and Cowdery moved to the Whitmers' in New York to complete the translation of the Book of Mormon (*HC* 1:39–41, 48–49). The higher priesthood also came before this move; David Whitmer remembered he was ordained as an elder only weeks after their first arrival at his upstate farm (Whitmer, p. 32). The ancient apostles appeared with priesthood keys as Joseph and Oliver traveled between their Pennsylvania home and Colesville, New York (D&C 128:20), where Joseph Knight, Sr., lived. Knight remembered

their seeking help to sustain them while translating in April or May (Jessee, p. 36).

After the move to the Whitmer farm, the angel showed the plates to Joseph Smith and the Three Witnesses in June 1829. Oliver supervised the printing of the Book of Mormon that fall and winter. After the publication of the book on March 26, the Church was organized on April 6, 1830. Oliver spoke in a meeting the next Sunday, which was "the first public discourse that was delivered by any of our number" (*HC* 1:81).

Few exceeded Cowdery in logical argument and elevated style. Moreover, his speeches and writings carry the tone of personal knowledge. Generally serving as editor or associate editor in the first publications of the Church, Oliver wrote with unusual consistency through two decades of published writings and personal letters. He insisted that a relationship with God required constant contact: "Whenever [God] has had a people on earth, he always has revealed himself to them by the Holy Ghost, the ministering of angels, or his own voice" (*Messenger and Advocate* 1:2). Oliver Cowdery led the Lamanite mission, the first major mission of the Church (D&C 28:8; 30:5), which doubled Church membership and took the Book of Mormon to Native Americans. After the temple site was designated in Jackson County in 1831, he traveled there with copies of the revelations for their first printing. Because publishing was vital for spreading the gospel and instructing members, Oliver was called to work with William W. Phelps, an experienced editor (D&C 55:4; 57:11–13). After Missouri ruffians destroyed the press, Cowdery returned to Ohio to counsel with Church leaders, who assigned him to relocate Church publications there. Because of the importance of accurate information, he and Sidney Rigdon remained in Ohio in 1834 when many faithful men marched to Missouri with Zion's Camp to assist the Saints in returning to their homes and land in Jackson County.

In 1830–1831, Oliver Cowdery served as the first Church Recorder, a calling he again resumed between 1835 and 1837. Even in other years, he often kept the official minutes of meetings, and was often editor and contributor for the first Church newspapers. He wrote articles for the *Messenger and Advocate* that help document early LDS history. From June to October 1830, Oliver served as scribe while the Prophet completed important portions of the Joseph Smith Translation of the Bible.

An 1830 revelation named Oliver Cowdery next only to Joseph Smith in priesthood leadership (D&C 20:2–3), a status formalized in December 1834, when he was ranked above Sidney Rigdon, who had long served as Joseph's first counselor. Each would "officiate in the absence of the President, according to his rank and appointment, viz.: President Cowdery first; President Rigdon second, and President Williams third" (*PJS* 1:21). Cowdery wrote that this calling was foretold in the first heavenly ordination, though Missouri printing duties had intervened: "This promise was made by the angel while in company with President Smith, at the time they received the office of the lesser priesthood" (*PJS* 1:21; cf. *HC* 1:40–41). His office next to the Prophet—sometimes called "associate president"—was given to Hyrum SMITH in 1841 (D&C 124:94–96), after Cowdery's excommunication.

Oliver's Church career peaked from 1834 to 1836. Minutes and letters picture him as a highly effective preacher, writer, and administrator. His 1836 journal survives, showing his devotion to religion and family, his political activities, his study of Hebrew, and the spiritual power he shared at the completion of the Kirtland Temple. Cowdery's last entry in this journal, penned the day of the temple dedication, says of the evening meeting: "I saw the glory of God, like a great cloud, come down and rest upon the house. . . . I also saw cloven tongues like as of fire rest upon many . . . while they spake with other tongues and prophesied" (Arrington, p. 426).

Oliver also alluded to more. A year later he penned an editorial "Valedictory." After mentioning "my mission from the holy messenger" prior to the organization of the Church, he wrote that such manifestations were to be expected, since the Old Testament promised that God would "reveal his glorious arm" in the latter days "and talk with his people *face to face*" (*Messenger and Advocate* 3:548). The words he italicized match his recent temple vision of Christ on April 3, 1836, which he experienced in company with the Prophet (D&C 110:1–10). This was also the time that these first priesthood leaders received special priesthood keys from Moses, Elias, and Elijah, completing restoration of the "keys of [the] kingdom" (D&C 27:6–13) and completing Cowdery's mission as "second witness" to such restoration. Oliver had deep confidence in divine appearances. In 1835 he charged the newly appointed Twelve: "Never cease striving until you have seen God face to face" (*HC* 2:195).

Despite these profound spiritual experiences, Oliver's letters reveal a crisis of personal and family estrangement from Joseph Smith by early 1838. The Three Witnesses had seen an angel with Joseph Smith, but later they tended to compete rather than cooperate with his leadership. Cowdery disagreed with the Prophet's economic and political program and sought a personal financial independence that ran counter to the cooperative economics essential to the Zion society that Joseph Smith envisioned. Nonetheless, when

Oliver was tried for his membership, he sent a resignation letter in which he insisted that the truth of modern revelation was not at issue: "Take no view of the foregoing remarks, other than my belief on the outward government of this Church" (*Far West Record*, pp. 165–66).

This trial was related to the excommunications of Oliver's brothers-in-law John Whitmer and David Whitmer, also at this time; this paralleled Oliver's earlier support of the Whitmer family in the matter of Hiram Page's competing revelations (D&C 28:11–13). The Church court considered five charges against Cowdery: inactivity, accusing the Prophet of adultery, and three charges of beginning law practice and seeking to collect debts after the Kirtland bank failure.

Oliver's charge of adultery against the Prophet was simplistic, for Oliver already knew about the principle of plural marriage. Rather than deny the charge, the Prophet testified that because Oliver had been his "bosom friend," he had "intrusted him with many things" (*Far West Record*, 168). Brigham Young later said that the doctrine was revealed to Joseph and Oliver during the Book of Mormon translation (cf. Jacob 2:30); clearly a fuller understanding of the principle of plural marriage came by 1832, in connection with Joseph Smith's translation of Genesis (cf. D&C 132:1–2). Brigham Young added that Oliver impetuously proceeded without Joseph's permission, not knowing "the order and pattern and the results" (Charles Walker Journal, July 26, 1872, Church Archives). Oliver married Elizabeth Ann Whitmer in 1832, and problems with polygamy apparently influenced him and the Whitmer family to oppose the principle later.

In 1838, following his excommunication, Oliver returned to Ohio, though he did not, as a fictitious deed states, then pay Bishop Ed-ward Partridge $1,000 for the temple lot in Independence on behalf of his children, John, Jane, and Joseph Cowdery. Such children never existed; Oliver had no such money and showed no interest in Jackson County then or later. In fact, he continued law study and practiced in Kirtland, but in 1840 he moved to Tiffin, Ohio, where he became a prominent civic leader as an ardent Democrat. His law notices and public service regularly appeared in local newspapers, and he was personally sketched in the warm recollections of the prominent Ohio lawyer William Lang, who apprenticed under Cowdery and described him as being of slight build, about five and a half feet tall, clean, and courteous. Professionally, Cowdery was characterized as "an able lawyer," well informed, with "brilliant" speaking ability; yet "he was modest and reserved, never spoke ill of anyone, never complained" (Anderson, 1981, p. 41).

In 1847 Oliver moved to Wisconsin, where he continued his law practice and was almost elected to the first state legislature, in spite of newspaper accounts ridiculing his published declaration of seeing the angel and the plates. In his ten years outside the Church, Cowdery never succumbed to the considerable pressure to deny his Book of Mormon testimony. Indeed, letters to his LDS relatives show that he was hurt at the Church's rejection but remained a deep believer. Feeling that his character had been slandered, he asked for public exoneration, explaining that anyone would be sensitive about reputation "had you stood in the presence of John with our departed Brother Joseph, to receive the Lesser Priesthood, and in the presence of Peter, to receive the Greater" (Gunn, pp. 250–51).

These statements contradict a pamphlet that Oliver was alleged to have published in 1839 as a "Defense" for leaving the Church.

Surfacing in 1906, it portrays Oliver as confused about seeing John the Baptist. But no original exists, nor does any reference to it in Cowdery's century. Its style borrows published Cowdery phrases but rearranges his conclusions. A clumsier forgery is the "Confession of Oliver Overstreet," which claims that the author was bribed to impersonate Cowdery and return to the Church. Abundant documents show that Oliver returned to Council Bluffs, Iowa, in 1848 with his wife and young daughter.

Diaries and official minutes record Oliver Cowdery's words in rejoining the Church. He sought only rebaptism and fellowship, not office. He publicly declared that he had seen and handled the Book of Mormon plates, and that he was present with Joseph Smith on the occasions when "holy angels" restored the two priesthoods (Anderson, *BYU Studies*, 1968, p. 278). The High Council questioned him closely about his published letter (to David Whitmer) in which Oliver claimed that he retained the keys of priesthood leadership after Joseph Smith's death. That was his opinion, Oliver said, before seeing the Nauvoo revelation giving all powers to Hyrum Smith "that once were put upon him that was my servant Oliver Cowdery" (D&C 124:95). "It was that revelation which changed my views on this subject" (Anderson, *IE*, Nov. 1968, p. 19).

Because they had started for Council Bluffs late in the season, the Cowdery family were forced to winter in Richmond, Missouri, where most of the Whitmer family lived. Letters throughout 1849 repeat Oliver's hope to move west and also disclose his lack of means. They speak of his coughing up blood, a long-term respiratory condition that finally took his life March 3, 1850. The circuit court recorded a resolution of fellow lawyers that in the death of "Oliver Cowdery, his profes-

sion has lost an accomplished member, and the community a valuable and worthy citizen" (Anderson, 1981, p. 46).

David Whitmer and other relatives living near Oliver Cowdery in his final year later claimed that he disagreed with many Kirtland and Nauvoo doctrines, but Oliver's documented criticisms at this time concern only intolerance and a continuing concern about polygamy. Although David Whitmer considered Joseph a fallen prophet, in 1848 Cowdery said publicly and privately "that Joseph Smith had fulfilled his mission faithfully before God until death" (Geo. A. Smith to Orson Pratt, *MS* 11 [Oct. 20, 1848]: 14), and "that the priesthood was with this people, and the 'Twelve' were the only men that could lead the Church after the death of Joseph" (Anderson, *IE*, Nov. 1968, p. 18). In his last known letter, Oliver accepted an assignment from the Twelve to lobby in Washington, and acknowledged the leadership of the "good brethren of the [Salt Lake] valley" (Gunn, p. 261).

Oliver's wife, Elizabeth Ann Whitmer Cowdery (1815–1892), had known him when he was taking dictation during the translation of the Book of Mormon, before their marriage. Said she of his lifelong commitment: "He always without one doubt . . . affirmed the divinity and truth of the Book of Mormon" (Anderson, 1981, p. 63). This confidence stood the test of persecution, poverty, loss of status, failing health, and the tragic deaths of five of his six children. Dying at forty-three, Oliver was surrounded by family members who told how he reaffirmed the divinity of the Book of Mormon and the restored priesthood—and voiced total trust in Christ. Just before rejoining the Church, he penned his inner hopes to fellow witness David Whitmer: "Let the Lord vindicate our characters, and cause our testimony to shine, and then will men be saved in his kingdom" (Oliver Cowdery to David Whitmer, July 28, 1847, *Ensign of Liberty*, 1:92).

BIBLIOGRAPHY

Anderson, Richard L. "Reuben Miller, Recorder of Oliver Cowdery's Reaffirmations." *BYU Studies* 8 (Spring 1968): 277–93.

———. "The Second Witness of Priesthood Restoration." *IE* 71 (Sept. 1968): 15–24; and 71 (Nov. 1968): 14–20.

———. *Investigating the Book of Mormon Witnesses.* Salt Lake City, 1981.

Arrington, Leonard J. "Oliver Cowdery's Kirtland, Ohio, 'Sketch Book.'" *BYU Studies* 12 (Summer 1972): 410–26.

Cannon, Donald Q., and Lyndon W. Cook. *Far West Record.* Salt Lake City, 1983.

Gunn, Stanley R. *Oliver Cowdery, Second Elder and Scribe.* Salt Lake City, 1962.

Jessee, Dean C. "Joseph Knight's Recollection of Early Mormon History." *BYU Studies* 17 (1976): 36.

Porter, Larry C. "Dating the Restoration of the Melchizedek Priesthood." *Ensign* 9 (June 1979): 5–10.

Whitmer, David. *Address to All Believers in Christ.* Richmond, Mo., 1887.

RICHARD LLOYD ANDERSON

CUMORAH

Cumorah in the Book of Mormon refers to a hill and surrounding area where the final battle between the NEPHITES and LAMANITES took place, resulting in the annihilation of the Nephite people (*see* PEOPLES OF THE BOOK OF MORMON). Sensing the impending destruction of his people, Mormon records that he

The north end of the hill Cumorah, near Palmyra, New York, as it appeared in 1904 in this single view from an Underwood and Underwood stereo view. More than thirty years after the final Nephite battle in A.D. 385, Moroni deposited the gold plates on the west side of this hill not far from the top. In 1827, the angel Moroni here entrusted those Book of Mormon plates to Joseph Smith, who translated them into English. The hill is a drumlin, a long hill with steep sides and a sloping end formed under an advancing continental ice sheet. Courtesy Rare Books and Manuscripts, Brigham Young University.

concealed the plates of Nephi$_1$ and all the other records entrusted to him in a hill called Cumorah to prevent them from falling into the hands of the Lamanites (*see* PLATES AND RECORDS IN THE BOOK OF MORMON). He delivered his own abridgment of these records, called the plates of Mormon, and the small plates of Nephi, which he placed with them, to his son MORONI$_2$ (W of M 1:5; Morm. 6:6), who continued writing on them before burying them in an unmentioned site more than thirty-six years later (Moro. 10:1–2).

The Book of Mormon mentions a number of separate records that would have been part of Mormon's final record repository in the hill Cumorah. Though the contents of these can be known to us only to the extent that they are summarized or mentioned in the

Book of Mormon, Latter-day Saints expect them someday to become available. Alma$_2$ prophesied to his son Helaman that the brass plates of Laban (the NEPHITES' version of the Old Testament) would be "kept and preserved by the hand of the Lord until they should go forth unto every nation" (Alma 37:4; cf. 1 Ne. 5:17–19). He further explained that "all the plates" containing scripture are the "small and simple" means by which "great things [are] brought to pass" and by which the Lord will "show forth his power . . . unto future generations" (Alma 37:5–6, 19).

Cumorah had also been the site of the destruction of the JAREDITES roughly 900 years earlier. Moroni states in the book of Ether that the Jaredites gathered for battle near "the hill Ramah," the same hill where his father, Mormon, hid up "the records unto the Lord, which were sacred" (Ether 15:11). It was near the first landing site of the people of Mulek (Alma 22:30), just north of the land Bountiful and a narrow neck of land (Alma 22:32).

The more common reference to Cumorah among Latter-day Saints is to the hill near present-day Palmyra and Manchester, New York, where the plates from which the Prophet Joseph SMITH translated the Book of Mormon were found. During the night of September 21, 1823, Moroni$_2$ appeared to Joseph Smith as an angel sent from God to show him where these plates were deposited (JS—H 1:29–47).

In 1928 the Church purchased the western New York hill and in 1935 erected a monument recognizing the visit of the angel Moroni. A visitors' center was later built at the base of the hill. Each summer since 1937, the Church has staged the Cumorah pageant at this site. Entitled *America's Witness for Christ,* it depicts important events from Book of Mormon history. This annual pageant has re-inforced the common assumption that Moroni buried the plates of Mormon in the same hill where his father had buried the other plates, thus equating this New York hill with the Book of Mormon Cumorah. Because the New York site does not readily fit the Book of Mormon description of Book of Mormon GEOGRAPHY, some Latter-day Saints have looked for other possible explanations and locations, including Mesoamerica. Although some have identified possible sites that may seem to fit better (Palmer), there are no conclusive connections between the Book of Mormon text and any specific site that has been suggested.

BIBLIOGRAPHY

Clark, John. "A Key for Evaluating Nephite Geographies." *Review of Books on the Book of Mormon* 1 (1989): 20–70.

Palmer, David A. *In Search of Cumorah: New Evidences for the Book of Mormon from Ancient Mexico.* Bountiful, Utah, 1981.

Sorenson, John L. "Digging into the Book of Mormon: Part One." *Ensign* 14 (1984): 26–37.

DAVID A. PALMER

CURSINGS

Cursings are the opposite of blessings and may be expressed as (1) the use of vulgar or profane language by people; (2) words or actions by God or his representatives expressing divine displeasure with or warning against wickedness; or (3) God's chastisement of mankind.

Cursing in the form of profane language employing names of deity literally "in vain" has been present in most societies. Since thought is expressed in language, vulgar and blasphemous language corrupts its user by establishing vulgar or profane thought patterns. The statement "Among the wicked, men shall lift up their voices and curse God and die" (D&C 45:32) illustrates both a cause and a consequence regarding profane language, with its effect on and relationship to spiritual life. Cursing that invokes the name of deity is a form of blasphemy and, in biblical times, was punishable by stoning (Lev. 24:16). Cursing of parents was also cause for offenders to be put to death in ancient Israel (Ex. 21:17; Matt. 15:4).

Cursing may be the expression of divine displeasure, warning, or exclusion from God's blessing. Just as blessings are obtained by RIGHTEOUSNESS, cursings result from breaking God's law and failing to keep his commandments (Deut. 11:26–28; D&C 104:1–8; 124:48). Intelligent human beings are largely responsible for their own circumstances, and President Brigham Young said the most severe cursings come upon "those who know their Master's will, and do it not" (JD 1:248). Sinning against light and knowledge has more serious consequences than sinning in ignorance (see Mosiah 2:36–37; cf. Alma 32:19–20; 39:6). ALMA₂ gives an example wherein the same land was simultaneously blessed for those who acted righteously and cursed for those who did not (Alma 45:16).

Curses may be pronounced by God, or they may be invoked by his authorized servants, as was the case with Moses (Deut. 27–30); Elijah (1 Kgs. 17:1; 21:20–24); Peter (Acts 5:1–10); Paul (Acts 13:9–12); and Joseph Smith (D&C 103:25; cf. 124:93). However, the Lord's earthly agents are sent forth primarily to bless and not to curse (Matt. 5:44; Rom. 12:14).

Not all curses have totally negative consequences. As God only does good, his cursings are for "[the] sake" of improving the person cursed (Gen. 3:17; Deut. 23:5), even though the immediate consequence may be extremely unpleasant. When there is need for correction, the Lord has instructed his servants to reprove "with sharpness," but afterward to show forth an "increase of love" (D&C 121:43).

Some cursings are given first as warnings rather than a more severe immediate chastisement (2 Ne. 1:21, 22); and, like blessings, they sometimes require a long time for their full consequences to be realized. After being invoked, cursings may often be lessened or lifted entirely by subsequent righteousness. Mormon describes an experience of the LAMANITES: "And they began to be a very industrious people; yea, and they were friendly with the NEPHITES; therefore, they did open a correspondence with them, and the curse of God did no more follow them" (Alma 23:18).

Cursings may affect all temporal and spiritual aspects of our lives because all things are governed by law. Lands, crops, handiwork, employment, children, missionary endeavors, interpersonal relationships, and relationships with God are all subject to both cursing and blessing—depending upon individual and collective righteousness or lack of it.

SHERWIN W. HOWARD

E

ECONOMY AND TECHNOLOGY

The Book of Mormon reports information about three pre-Hispanic American peoples. Although its writers do not offer a detailed picture of the economic and material culture of their societies, numerous incidental details are preserved in the account. In many cases, though not in every instance, archaeology confirms the general details. The problems that remain in matching the Book of Mormon to its presumed ancient setting are no doubt due both to the scant information given in the book itself and to incompleteness in the archaeological record.

Testing what the Book of Mormon says about pre-Columbian material culture is more difficult than it might at first appear to be. For instance, it is a historically well-established fact that craft techniques can be lost; thus one cannot confidently assume that technologies mentioned for limited Book of Mormon populations survived after the destruction of the Nephites. Nor can one assume what Old World technologies were successfully transferred to the New. Many crafts would not have been known to the small colonist parties, and even among the skills that were transported across the sea, many may not have proved useful or adaptable in the new environment. For that matter, items attested in early portions of the Book of Mormon may not safely be assumed to have survived into subsequent history within the record itself.

The economy of Book of Mormon peoples seems, on the whole, to have been relatively simple. Although many Nephites and Jaredites lived in cities of modest size (a point whose plausibility has been enhanced by recent research), their societies were agriculturally based. Trade was mentioned for some periods, but was constrained by frequent wars. In the infrequently mentioned times of free travel, trade barriers fell, and Lamanites and Nephites predictably prospered (e.g., Hel. 6:7–9).

Despite the economy's agrarian base, wealth was manifested in terms of movable flocks, herds, costly clothing, gold, silver, and "precious things" rather than land (Jacob 2:12–13; Enos 1:21; Jarom 1:8; Mosiah 9:12;

The use of cement appears extensively in Mesoamerican archaeology around the first century A.D., as, for example, in these cement buildings at Teotihuacan in the Valley of Mexico. The Book of Mormon states that some Nephite dissenters who moved into a land northward "became exceeding expert in the working of cement" and built "cities both of wood and of cement" beginning in 46 B.C. (Hel. 3:7, 11). Courtesy John W. Welch.

Alma 1:6, 29; 17:25; 32:2; Ether 10:12). The ideology of the leading Book of Mormon peoples undoubtedly contributed to this phenomenon: They referred to themselves as a righteous remnant obliged to abandon their comfortable dwellings and depart into the wilderness because of their religious convictions. Since entire populations seem to have moved often, land may not have been a stable source of wealth (2 Ne. 5:5–11; Omni 1:12–13, 27–30; Mosiah 9; 18:34–35; 22; 24:16–25; Alma 27; 35:6–14; 63:4–10; Hel. 2:11; 3:3–12; 4:5–6, 19; 3 Ne. 3:21–4:1; 7:1–2). Ideally, wealth was to be shared with the poor and for the common good, but strong contrasts between rich and poor are evident more often than not.

Agriculture in the Book of Mormon in-volved livestock and sown crops. For example, in the fifth century B.C., the Nephites "did till the land, and raise all manner of grain, and of fruit, and flocks of herds, and flocks of all manner of cattle of every kind, and goats, and wild goats, and also many horses" (Enos 1:21). In the second century B.C., the people of Zeniff cultivated corn, wheat, barley, "neas," and "sheum" (Mosiah 9:9; cf. Alma 11:7). Early nineteenth-century American language usage suggests that Book of Mormon "corn" may denote maize or "Indian corn," which was and is a staple in diets in most parts of native America. Some of the other listed items remain less certain. Only in 1982 was evidence published demonstrating the presence of cultivated pre-Columbian barley in the

New World (Sorenson, 1985, p. 184). "Neas" is not identifiable; but the word "sheum" appears to be cognate with early Akkadian *she-um*, a grain probably of the barley type (*see* FARMS Staff, "Weights and Measures").

Book of Mormon mention of horses in pre-Columbian America has drawn much criticism, and no definitive answer to this question is at present available. Linguistic data suggest that Book of Mormon "horse" need not refer to *equus*, but could indicate some other quadruped suitable for human riding, as Mesoamerican art suggests (Sorenson, 1985, p. 295). Moreover, some little-noticed archaeological evidence indicates that in certain areas the American Pleistocene horse could have survived into Book of Mormon times (*Update*, June 1984).

Most transportation was evidently on human backs; in the two contexts that the Book of Mormon mentions "chariots," it appears that their use was quite limited (Alma 18:9–12; 20:6; 3 Ne. 3:22). Chariots are never mentioned in military settings. Wheels are nowhere mentioned in the Book of Mormon (except in a quote from Isaiah). Thus, it is unknown what Nephite "chariots" may have been. "Highways" and "roads" are mentioned as used by the Nephites (3 Ne. 6:8). Some Latter-day Saints consider these to be reflected in the extensively documented road systems of ancient Mexico. "Ships" of unknown form were used during the middle of the first century B.C. for travel on the "west sea" coast (Alma 63:5–6) and for shipping timber to the north (Hel. 3:10), and at times maritime travel was evidently extensive (Hel. 3:14). Fine pearls are also mentioned as costly items (4 Ne. 1:24).

"Silk and fine-twined linen" are mentioned (e.g., Alma 1:29; Ether 10:24) along with common (cotton?) cloth. The "silk" is unlikely to have been produced from silk-worms as in China, but similar fabrics were known, at least in Mesoamerica. For example, in Guatemala fiber from the wild pineapple plant, and among the Aztecs rabbit hair, served to make silklike fabrics. Although flax apparently was not known in America prior to the arrival of the Spaniards (linen was made from flax in the Old World), several vegetable-based fabrics with similar characteristics are well attested in ancient America (*Update*, Nov. 1988).

Care must be exercised when reading the Book of Mormon, or any other text originating in a foreign or ancient culture, to avoid misunderstanding unfamiliar things in light of what is familiar. For instance, the Nephites are said to have used "money," but since the Israelites in Lehi's day lacked minted coinage, Nephite "money" was probably noncoined.

A well-integrated system of dry measures and metal-weight units is outlined in Alma 11; some analysts have pointed out that the system sketched is strikingly simple, efficient, and rational (Smith). In its binary mathematical configuration and its use of barley and silver as basic media of exchange, the Nephite system recalls similar systems known in Egypt and in the Babylonian laws of Eshnunna (FARMS Staff, "Weights and Measures"; *Update*, March 1987).

Making weapons of "steel" and "iron" is mentioned by the Nephites only during their first few generations (2 Ne. 5:15; Jarom 1:8; iron is mentioned only as a "precious" ornamental metal during the time of Mosiah 11:8). Just what these terms originally meant may not be clear. Jaredite "steel" and "iron" and other metals are mentioned twice but are not described (Ether 7:9; 10:23). The weapons of the common soldier were distinctly simpler: stones, clubs, spears, and the bow and arrow (e.g., Alma 49:18–22).

The relative simplicity of Book of Mormon society does not imply lack of sophistication by ancient standards. For example, it would seem that literacy was not uncommon among either Nephites or Jaredites. The founding leaders of the migrations were definitely literate, and the Nephites in their middle era are said to have produced "many books and many records of every kind" (Hel. 3:15). The Lamanites and Mulekites, on the other hand, were less consistent record keepers (Omni 1:17–18; Mosiah 24:4–6; Hel. 3:15). The Jaredites and Nephites kept their most sacred records on almost imperishable metal PLATES, although some of their books were on flammable material (Alma 14:8). The plates that Joseph Smith had in his possession, and that he and other contemporary eyewitnesses described, seem well within the skill of pre-Hispanic metallurgists (Putnam; Sorenson, 1985, pp. 278–88), and the manner of their burial has rich precedent in the Eastern Hemisphere (Wright).

BIBLIOGRAPHY

Cheesman, Paul R. *Ancient Writing on Metal Plates.* Bountiful, Utah, 1985.

FARMS *Updates* (Provo, Utah), contain useful discussions, including bibliographies, of pre-Columbian horses (June 1984), metallurgy of gold plates (Oct. 1984), pre-Hispanic domesticated barley (Dec. 1984), the loss of technologies (July 1985), the legal implementation of the Nephite system of weights and measures (Mar. 1987), and possible silks and linens (Nov. 1988).

FARMS Staff. "Weights and Measures in the Time of Mosiah II." Provo, Utah, 1983.

Nibley, Hugh W. *The Prophetic Book of Mormon*, in CWHN 8:245–46, 385–86, and *Since Cumorah*, in CWHN 7:220–27. Discusses metallic plates, steel, cement, money, and fauna.

Putnam, Reed. "Were the Golden Plates Made of Tumbaga?" *IE* (Sept. 1966): 788–89, 828–31.

Smith, R. P. "The Nephite Monetary System." *IE* 57 (May 1954): 316–17.

Sorenson, John L. "A Reconsideration of Early Metal in Mesoamerica." *Katunob* 9 (Mar. 1976): 1–18.

———. *An Ancient American Setting for the Book of Mormon.* Salt Lake City, 1985.

Wright, H. Curtis. "Ancient Burials of Metallic Foundation Documents in Stone Boxes." In *Occasional Papers, University of Illinois Graduate School of Library and Information Science* 157 (1982): 1–42.

ADDITIONAL SOURCE

Sorenson, John L. "Metals and Metallurgy Relating to the Book of Mormon Text." Provo, Utah: FARMS, 1992.

DANIEL C. PETERSON

EDITIONS (1830–1981)

Two major goals of each published edition of the Book of Mormon have been (1) to faithfully reproduce the text; and (2) to make the text accessible to the reader. The goal of textual accuracy has led later editors to earlier editions and, when available, to the original and printer's manuscripts (*see* MANUSCRIPTS OF THE BOOK OF MORMON). The goal of accessibility has led to some modernization and standardization of the text itself and the addition of reader's helps (introductory material, versification, footnotes, chapter summaries, dates, pronunciation guides, and indexes).

Four editions were published during Joseph SMITH's lifetime:

1. 1830: 5,000 copies; published by E. B. Grandin in Palmyra, New York. In general, the first edition is a faithful copy of the

printer's manuscript (although on one occasion the original manuscript rather than the printer's was used for typesetting). For the most part, this edition reproduces what the compositor, John H. Gilbert, considered grammatical "errors." Gilbert added punctuation and determined the paragraphing for the first edition. In the Preface, Joseph Smith explains the loss of the Book of Lehi—116 pages of manuscript (*see* MANUSCRIPT, LOST 116 PAGES). The testimonies of the Three and the Eight Witnesses were placed at the end of the book. In this and all other early editions, there is no versification.

2. 1837: Either 3,000 or 5,000 copies; published by Parley P. Pratt and John Goodson, Kirtland, Ohio. For this edition, hundreds of grammatical changes and a few emendations were made in the text. The 1830 edition and the printer's manuscript were used as the basis for this edition.

3. 1840: 2,000 copies; published for Ebenezer Robinson and Don Carlos Smith (by Shepard and Stearns, Cincinnati, Ohio), Nauvoo, Illinois. Joseph Smith compared the printed text with the original manuscript and discovered a number of errors made in copying the printer's manuscript from the original. Thus the 1840 edition restores some of the readings of the original manuscript.

4. 1841: 4,050 copies (5,000 contracted); published for Brigham Young, Heber C. Kimball, and Parley P. Pratt (by J. Tompkins, Liverpool, England). This first European edition was printed with the permission of Joseph Smith; it is essentially a reprinting of the 1837 edition with British spellings.

Two additional British editions, one in 1849 (edited by Orson Pratt) and the other in 1852 (edited by Franklin D. Richards), show minor editing of the text. In the 1852 edition, Richards added numbers to the paragraphs to aid in finding passages, thereby creating the

first—although primitive—versification for the Book of Mormon.

Three other important LDS editions have involved major changes in format as well as minor editing:

1. 1879: Edited by Orson Pratt. Major changes in the format of the text included division of the long chapters in the original text, a true versification system (which has been followed in all subsequent LDS editions), and footnotes (mostly scriptural references).

2. 1920: Edited by James E. Talmage. Further changes in format included introductory material, double columns, chapter summaries, and new footnotes. Some of the minor editing found in this edition appeared earlier in the 1905 and 1911 editions, also under the editorship of Talmage.

3. 1981: Edited by a committee headed by members of the Quorum of the Twelve. This edition is a major reworking of the 1920 edition: The text appears again in double columns, but new introductory material, chapter summaries, and footnotes are provided. About twenty significant textual errors that had entered the printer's manuscript are corrected by reference to the original manuscript. Other corrections were made from comparison with the printer's manuscript and the 1840 Nauvoo edition.

The Reorganized Church of Jesus Christ of Latter Day Saints (RLDS) also has its own textual tradition. Prior to 1874, the RLDS used an edition of the Book of Mormon published by James O. Wright (1858, New York), basically a reprinting of the 1840 Nauvoo edition. The first and second RLDS editions (1874, Plano, Illinois; and 1892, Lamoni, Iowa) followed the 1840 text and had their own system of versification. Unlike the later LDS editions, all RLDS editions have retained the original longer chapters.

In 1903 the RLDS obtained the printer's

manuscript and used it to produce their third edition (1908, Lamoni, Iowa). The text of the 1908 edition restored many of the readings found in that manuscript, but generally did not alter the grammatical changes made in the 1837 Kirtland edition. This edition also included a new versification, which has remained unchanged in all subsequent RLDS editions. In 1966 the RLDS published a thoroughly modernized Book of Mormon text. Both the 1908 (with minor editing) and the 1966 texts are available, but only the 1908 edition is authorized for use in the RLDS Church.

A critical text of the Book of Mormon was published in 1984–1987 by the Foundation for Ancient Research and Mormon Studies. This is the first published text of the Book of Mormon to show the precise history of many textual variants. Although this textual study of the editions and manuscripts of the Book of Mormon is incomplete and preliminary, it is helpful for a general overview of the textual history of the Book of Mormon.

BIBLIOGRAPHY

Anderson, Richard L. "Gold Plates and Printer's Ink." *Ensign* 6 (Sept. 1976): 71–76.

Heater, Shirley R. "Gold Plates, Foolscap, & Printer's Ink; Part II: Editions of the Book of Mormon." *Zarahemla Record* 37–38 (1987): 2–15.

Larson, Stanley R. "A Study of Some Textual Variations in the Book of Mormon Comparing the Original and the Printer's Manuscripts and the 1830, the 1837, and the 1840 Editions." Master's thesis, Brigham Young University, 1974.

Matthews, Robert J. "The New Publication of the Standard Works 1979, 1981." *BYU Studies* 22 (1982): 387–424.

Skousen, Royal. "Towards a Critical Edition of the Book of Mormon." *BYU Studies* 30 (1990): 41–69.

Stocks, Hugh G. "The Book of Mormon, 1830–1879: A Publishing History." Master's thesis, UCLA, 1979.

———. "The Book of Mormon in English, 1870–1920: A Publishing History and Analytical Bibliography." Ph.D. diss., UCLA, 1986.

ROYAL SKOUSEN

EZIAS

Ezias was a prophet of Old Testament times whose prophecies were apparently recorded on the PLATES of brass, a record brought to the Western Hemisphere by the Book of Mormon prophet LEHI. Ezias was mentioned by NEPHI$_2$ (c. 22 B.C.) in a list of prophets who testified of the coming ministry and redemption of Christ (Hel. 8:13–20).

MELVIN J. THORNE

F

Faith in Jesus Christ

Faith in Jesus Christ is the first principle of the GOSPEL OF JESUS CHRIST (A of F 4). One who has this faith believes him to be the living Son of God, trusts in his goodness and power, repents of one's sins, and follows his guidance. Faith in the Lord Jesus Christ is awakened as individuals hear his gospel (Rom. 10:17). By faith they enter the gate of REPENTANCE and BAPTISM, and receive the gift of the Holy Ghost, which leads to the way of life ordained by Christ (2 Ne. 31:9, 17–18). Those who respond are "alive in Christ because of [their] faith" (2 Ne. 25:25). Because God's way is the only way that leads to salvation, "it is impossible to please him" without faith (Heb. 11:6). Faith must precede miracles, signs, gifts of the Spirit, and righteousness, for "if there be no faith . . . God can do no miracle" (Ether 12:12). The Book of Mormon prophet MORONI₂ summarized these points:

> The Lord God prepareth the way that the residue of men may have faith in Christ, that the Holy Ghost may have place in their hearts, according to the power thereof; and after this manner bringeth to pass the Father, the covenants which he hath made unto the children of men. And Christ hath said: If ye will have faith in me ye shall have power to do whatsoever thing is expedient in me. And he hath said: Repent all ye ends of the earth, and come unto me, and be baptized in my name, and have faith in me, that ye may be saved. (Moro. 7:32–34)

Although in common speech people speak of having faith in people, principles, or things, faith in its eternal sense is faith in, and only in, Jesus Christ. It is not sufficient to have faith in just anything; it must be focused on "the only true God, and Jesus Christ" whom he has sent (John 17:3). Having faith means having complete confidence in Jesus Christ alone to save humankind from sin and the finality of death. By his grace "are ye saved through faith" (Eph. 2:8). If "Christ be not risen," then "your faith is also vain" and "ye are yet in your sins" (1 Cor. 15:14, 17). To trust in the powers of this world is to "trust in the arm of flesh" and, in effect, to reject Christ and his gospel (2 Ne. 4:34).

Paul explained, "Now faith is the substance [or assurance] of things hoped for, the evidence [the demonstration or proof] of things not seen" (Heb. 11:1). Mortals must live by faith, since divine realities are veiled from their physical senses. The invisible truths of the gospel are made manifest by the Holy Spirit and are seen in the lives of people who live by faith, following the daily directions of that Spirit. Though most mortals have not seen the spiritual realities beyond this physical world, they can accept such premises in faith, based on personal spiritual witness(es) and the scriptural record of former and latter-day special witnesses whom God has called and who have experienced these realities firsthand.

True faith is belief plus action. Faith implies not only the mental assent or cognition of belief but also its implementation. Beliefs in things both spiritual and secular impel people to act. Failure to act on the teachings and commandments of Christ implies absence of faith in him. Faith in Jesus Christ impels people to act in behalf of Christ, to follow his example, to do his works. Jesus said, "Not every one that saith unto me, Lord, Lord, shall enter into the kingdom of heaven; but he that *doeth* the will of my Father which is in heaven" (Matt. 7:21; italics added). James further emphasized that "faith, if it hath not works, is dead, being alone. Yea, a man may say, Thou hast faith, and I have works: shew me thy faith without thy works, and I will shew thee my faith by my works" (James 2:17–18; *see also* GRACE).

Righteousness leads to greater faith, while sin and wickedness diminish faith. "The just [man] shall live by his faith" (Hab. 2:4). Violating the commandments of God brings a loss of the Spirit of the Lord and a loss of faith, for faith in Jesus Christ is incompatible with disobedience. The Book of Mormon prophet ALMA₂ characterized the words of Christ as a seed that is tested as people plant it in their hearts and nourish it. If they desire to see the seed grow, they must give it room and nourish it with their faith. If it is a good seed, it will swell and grow, and they will know that it is good. However, if they neglect the seed, it will wither away. But if they will "nourish the word . . . by [their] faith with great diligence," it will grow into a tree of life, and they will taste its fruit, which is eternal life (Alma 32:26–43).

Faith may be nurtured and renewed through scripture study, prayer, and works consistent with the commandments of the gospel. Because those who act on faith, repent, and are baptized receive a remission of sins, they have reason to hope for eternal life (Moro. 7:41). With this hope, their faith in Jesus Christ further inspires individuals to minister to each other in CHARITY, even as Christ would have done (Moro. 7:44), for the "end of the commandment is charity out of . . . faith unfeigned" (1 Tim. 1:5). "Charity is the pure love of Christ, and it endureth forever" (Moro. 7:47). Thus, faith, or "steadfastness in Christ," enables people to endure to the end, continuing in faith and charity (2 Ne. 31:20; 1 Tim. 2:15; D&C 20:29). True faith is enduring and leads to an assurance that one's efforts have not gone unnoticed and that God is pleased with one's attitude and effort to implement the principles of the gospel of Jesus Christ in one's personal life.

While Alma explained how faith leads to knowledge, modern LDS commentary also points out how certain kinds of knowledge strengthen faith (*MD*, pp. 261–67). The knowledge that God exists, a correct understanding of his character, and a reassurance that he approves of one's conduct can help one's faith "become perfect and fruitful, abounding in righteousness" ("Lectures on Faith," pp. 65–66).

The restoration of the gospel in modern times was initiated by an act of faith by the youthful Joseph Smith. Reading the Bible, he was struck by the encouragement of James to all who lack wisdom that they should "ask in faith, nothing wavering" (James 1:6). The visions that came to Joseph Smith in answer to his prayers (see VISIONS OF JOSEPH SMITH) are evidence that prayers are "answered according to [one's] faith" (Mosiah 27:14). Though God delights to bless his children, he "first, [tries] their faith, . . . then shall the greater things be made manifest" (3 Ne. 26:9). But there will be "no witness until after the trial of your faith" (Ether 12:6), and "without faith you can do nothing" (D&C 8:10). "Signs come by faith, not by the will of men" (D&C 63:10).

Because faith involves the guidance of the Holy Ghost to individuals, it leads them by an invisible hand to "the unity of the faith" (Eph. 4:13). Through the strength of others and increased confidence in the Lord's way, faith provides a shield against the adversary (Eph. 6:16). Similarly, faith has been described as part of one's armor, serving as a "breastplate of faith and love" (1 Thes. 5:8) in protecting the faithful from evil.

BIBLIOGRAPHY

Benson, Ezra Taft. *The Teachings of Ezra Taft Benson*, pp. 65–69. Salt Lake City, 1988.

Kimball, Spencer W. *Faith Precedes the Miracle*. Salt Lake City, 1973.

"Lectures on Faith." In *The Lectures on Faith in Historical Perspective*, ed. L. Dahl and C. Tate, Jr., pp. 29–104. Provo, Utah, 1990.

DOUGLAS E. BRINLEY

FALL OF ADAM

Latter-day Saints recognize the fall of Adam and Eve as an actual event that occurred in the Garden of Eden and has affected the entire earth and everyone in the human family. The Fall was a necessary step in the eternal progress of mankind and introduced the conditions that made the mission of Jesus Christ absolutely necessary for salvation. The four standard works and the teachings of many prominent leaders of the Church are the sources for the LDS doctrine of the Fall. These sources dwell at length on the beneficial effects of the Fall as part of God's "great plan of happiness" (Alma 42:8) for his children and testify that Adam and Eve are to be honored for their actions (see PLAN OF SALVATION).

The creation of the earth was a multistep process in which the fall of Adam and Eve and their expulsion from the Garden of Eden were the final necessary steps in bringing about the mortal condition. Without the Fall, Adam and Eve would have had no children (2 Ne. 2:23); hence, the human family would not have come into existence upon this earth under the conditions and circumstances in the garden. The prophet LEHI explained, "Adam fell that men might be" (2 Ne. 2:25), and Enoch declared, "Because that Adam fell, we are" (Moses 6:48).

After the Fall, Adam and Eve were taught the gospel of Jesus Christ and rejoiced in their situation. Adam blessed God, saying, "Because of my transgression my eyes are opened, and in this life I shall have joy, and again in the flesh I shall see God" (Moses 5:10). And Eve was glad, saying, "Were it not for our transgression we never should have had seed, and never should have known good and evil, and the joy of our redemption, and the eternal life which God giveth unto all the obedient" (Moses 5:11).

The Fall was not an accident, not an obstruction to God's plan, and not a wrong turn in the course of humanity. "The Lord . . . created the earth that it should be inhabited" by his children (1 Ne. 17:36), and since Adam and Eve would have had no children in their Edenic condition, the Fall was a benefit to mankind. It was part of the Father's plan, being both foreknown to him and essential to the human family. All these things were "done in the wisdom of him who knoweth all things" (2 Ne. 2:24).

The Fall brought two kinds of death upon Adam, Eve, and their posterity: the separation of the spirit and the physical body, which the scriptures call the "temporal death" (Alma 11:42–43); and being shut out of God's presence, which is called spiritual death (2 Ne. 9:6; D&C 29:41). Jesus Christ redeems all mankind unconditionally from the two deaths brought by the fall of Adam, raises all mankind from the grave, and restores them to God's presence for a judgment (Hel. 14:16–17). The Atonement also redeems individuals from the consequences of their own sins on conditions of repentance.

The Book of Mormon explains, "The natural man is an enemy to God, and has been from the fall of Adam, and will be, forever and ever, unless he yields to the enticings of the Holy Spirit, and putteth off the natural man and becometh a saint through the atonement of Christ the Lord" (Mosiah 3:19; cf. Alma 22:14; 42:9–15). God "created Adam, and by Adam came the fall of man. And because of the fall of man came Jesus Christ, . . . and because of Jesus Christ came the redemption of man" (Morm. 9:12; cf. 2 Ne. 9:6).

The Doctrine and Covenants states that the Fall occurred as a result of transgression: "The devil tempted Adam, and he partook of the forbidden fruit and transgressed the commandment. . . . Wherefore, I, the Lord God, caused that he should be cast out from the Garden of Eden, from my presence, because of his transgression, wherein he became spiritually dead" (D&C 29:40–41). Thereafter, God sent angels to teach Adam and his seed "repentance and redemption, through faith on the name of mine Only Begotten Son" (D&C 29:42; cf. Moses 5:6–8).

The Fall was not a sin against chastity. Adam and Eve were "man and wife" and were commanded by God to multiply (Gen. 1:27–28; Moses 3:21–25; Abr. 5:14–19). Joseph Fielding Smith, an apostle, explained, "The transgression of Adam did *not* involve sex sin as some falsely believe and teach. Adam and Eve were married by the Lord while they were yet immortal beings in the Garden of Eden and before death entered the world" (*DS* 1:114–15; cf. *JC*, pp. 29–31).

An inseparable relationship between the fall of Adam and the atonement of Jesus Christ is established in ancient and modern scripture. Paul's summation is, "For as in Adam all die, even so in Christ shall all be made alive" (1 Cor. 15:22). Latter-day revelation further emphasizes that Christ will redeem all things from death and the effects of the Fall.

The Prophet Joseph SMITH taught that Adam's role was "to open the way of the world" (*TPJS*, p. 12); thus, he was the first man to enter mortality, and the fall of Adam has a mortal effect upon the entire earth. The earth shall die (D&C 88:25–26), but through the atoning power of Jesus Christ "the earth will be renewed and receive its paradisiacal glory" (A of F 10). "All things shall become new, even the heaven and the earth, and all the fulness thereof, both men and beasts, the fowls of the air, and the fishes of the sea; and not one hair, neither mote, shall be lost, for it is the workmanship of mine hand" (D&C 29:24–25; cf. 101:24–26; Isa. 51:6).

As Lehi declared, "If Adam had not transgressed he would not have fallen, but he would have remained in the Garden of Eden. And all things which were created must have remained in the same state in which they were after they were created; and they must have remained forever, and had no end" (2 Ne. 2:22; cf. Moses 3:9). Various interpretations have been suggested concerning the nature of life on the earth before the Fall and how the Fall physically affected the world, but these go beyond the clearly stated doctrine of the Church. The Church and the scriptures are emphatic, however, that the Fall brought the two kinds of death to Adam and his posterity.

BIBLIOGRAPHY

McConkie, Joseph Fielding, and Robert L. Millet, eds. *The Man Adam.* Salt Lake City, 1990.

Packer, Boyd K. "The Law and the Light." In *The Book of Mormon: Jacob through Words of Mormon, to Learn With Joy*, pp. 1–31. Provo, Utah, 1990.

Smith, Joseph Fielding. *Man, His Origin and Destiny.* Salt Lake City, 1954.

ROBERT J. MATTHEWS

G

Geography

Although the Book of Mormon is primarily a religious record of the NEPHITES, LAMANITES, and JAREDITES, enough geographic details are embedded in the narrative to allow reconstruction of at least a rudimentary geography of Book of Mormon lands. In the technical usage of the term "geography" (e.g., physical, economic, cultural, or political), no Book of Mormon geography has yet been written. Most Latter-day Saints who write geographies have in mind one or both of two activities: first, internal reconstruction of the relative size and configuration of Book of Mormon lands based upon textual statements and allusions; second, speculative attempts to match an internal geography to a location within North or South America. Three questions relating to Book of Mormon geography are discussed here: (1) How can one reconstruct a Book of Mormon geography? (2) What does a Book of Mormon geography look like? (3) What hypothetical locations have been suggested for Book of Mormon lands?

RECONSTRUCTING INTERNAL BOOK OF MORMON GEOGRAPHY. Although Church leadership officially and consistently distances itself from issues regarding Book of Mormon geography in order to focus attention on the spiritual message of the book, private speculation and scholarship in this area have been abundant. Using textual clues, laymen and scholars have formulated over sixty possible geographies. Dissimilarities among them stem from differences in (1) the interpretation of scriptural passages and statements of General Authorities; (2) procedures for reconciling scriptural information; (3) initial assumptions concerning the text and traditional LDS identification of certain features mentioned (especially the hill CUMORAH and the "narrow neck of land," which figure prominently in the text); and (4) personal penchants and disciplinary training.

Those who believe that reconstructing a Book of Mormon geography is possible must first deal with the usual problems of interpreting historical texts. Different weights must be given to various passages, depending upon the amount and precision of the information conveyed. Many Book of Mormon cities cannot be situated because of insufficient textual information; this is especially true for Lamanite and Jaredite cities. The Book of Mormon is essentially a Nephite record, and most geographic elements mentioned are in Nephite territory.

From textual evidence, one can approximate some spatial relationships of various natural features and cities. Distances in the Book of Mormon are recorded in terms of the time required to travel from place to place. The best information for reconstructing internal geography comes from the accounts of wars between Nephites and Lamanites during the first century B.C., with more limited information from Nephite missionary journeys. Travel distance can be standardized to a degree by controlling, where possible, for the nature of the terrain (e.g., mountains versus plains) and the relative velocity (e.g., an army's march versus travel with children or animals). The elementary internal geography presented below is based on an interpretation of distances thus standardized and directions based on the text.

AN INTERNAL BOOK OF MORMON GEOGRAPHY. Numerous attempts have been made to diagram physical and political geographies depicting features mentioned in the text, but this requires many additional assumptions and is difficult to accomplish without making approximate relationships appear precise (Sorenson, 1991). The description presented below of the size and configuration of Book of Mormon lands and the locations of settlements within it summarizes the least ambiguous evidence.

Book of Mormon lands were longer from north to south than from east to west. They consisted of two land masses connected by an isthmus ("a narrow neck of land") flanked by a "sea east" and a "sea west" (Alma 22:27, 32). The land north of the narrow neck was known as the "land northward" and that to the south as the "land southward" (Alma 22:32). The Jaredite narrative took place entirely in the land northward (Omni 1:22; Ether 10:21), but details are insufficient to place their cities relative to one another. Most of the Nephite narrative, on the other hand, took place in the land southward. Travel accounts for the land southward indicate that the Nephites and Lamanites occupied an area that could be traversed north to south by normal travel in perhaps thirty days.

The land southward was divided by a "narrow strip of wilderness" that ran from the "sea east" to the "sea west" (Alma 22:27). Nephites occupied the land to the north of this wilderness, and the Lamanites, that to the south. Sidon, the only river mentioned by name, ran northward between eastern and western wildernesses from headwaters in the narrow strip of wilderness (Alma 22:29). The Sidon probably emptied into the east sea— based on the description of the east wilderness as a rather wide, coastal zone—but its mouth is nowhere specified.

The relative locations of some important Nephite cities can be inferred from the text. Zarahemla was the Nephite capital in the first century B.C. That portion of the land southward occupied by the Nephites was known as the "land of Zarahemla" (Hel. 1:18). The city of Nephi, the original Nephite colony, by this time had been occupied by Lamanites and served at times as one of their capitals for the land south of the narrow wilderness divide (Alma 47:20). Based upon the migration account of Alma$_1$, the distance between the cities of Zarahemla and Nephi can be estimated to be about twenty-two days' travel by a company that includes children and flocks, mostly through mountainous terrain (cf. Mosiah 23:3; 24:20, 25).

The distance from Zarahemla to the narrow neck was probably less than that between Zarahemla and Nephi. The principal settlement near the narrow neck was the city of Bountiful, located near the east sea (Alma 52:17–23). This lowland city was of key military importance in controlling access to the land northward from the east-sea side.

The relative location of the hill Cumorah is most tenuous, since travel time from Bountiful, or the narrow neck, to Cumorah is nowhere specified. Cumorah was near the east sea in the land northward, and the limited evidence suggests that it was probably not many days' travel from the narrow neck of land (Mosiah 8:8; Ether 9:3). It is also probable that the portion of the land northward occupied by the Jaredites was smaller than the Nephite-Lamanite land southward.

Book of Mormon lands encompassed mountainous wildernesses, coastal plains, valleys, a large river, a highland lake, and lowland wetlands. The land also apparently experienced occasional volcanic eruptions and earthquakes (3 Ne. 8:5–18). Culturally, the Book of Mormon describes an urbanized, agrarian people having metallurgy (Hel. 6:11), writing (1 Ne. 1:1–3), lunar and solar calendars (2 Ne. 5:28; Omni 1:21), domestic animals (2 Ne. 5:11), various grains (1 Ne. 8:1), gold, silver, pearls, and "costly apparel" (Alma 1:29; 4 Ne. 1:24). Based upon these criteria, many scholars currently see northern Central America and southern Mexico (Mesoamerica) as the most likely location of Book of Mormon lands. However, such views are private and do not represent an official position of the Church.

HYPOTHESIZED LOCATIONS OF BOOK OF MORMON LANDS. Two issues merit consideration in relation to possible external correlations of Book of Mormon geography. What is the official position of the Church, and what are the pervading opinions of its members?

In early Church history, the most common opinion among members and Church leaders was that Book of Mormon lands encompassed all of North and South America, although at least one more limited alternative view was also held for a time by some. The official position of the Church is that the events narrated in the Book of Mormon occurred somewhere in the Americas, but that the specific location has not been revealed. This position applies both to internal geographies and to external correlations. No internal geography has yet been proposed or approved by the Church, and none of the internal or external geographies proposed by individual members (including that proposed above) has received approval. Efforts in that direction by members are neither encouraged nor discouraged. In the words of John A. Widtsoe, an apostle, "All such studies are legitimate, but the conclusions drawn from them, though they may be correct, must at the best be held as intelligent conjectures" (Vol. 3, p. 93).

Three statements sometimes attributed to the Prophet Joseph Smith are often cited as evidence of an official Church position. An 1836 statement asserts that "Lehi and his company . . . landed on the continent of South America, in Chili [sic], thirty degrees, south latitude" (Richards, Little, p. 272). This view was accepted by Orson Pratt and printed in the footnotes to the 1879 edition of the Book of Mormon, but insufficient evidence exists to clearly attribute it to Joseph Smith ("Did Lehi Land in Chili [sic]?"; cf. Roberts, Vol. 3, pp. 501–3, and Widtsoe, Vol. 3, pp. 93–98).

In 1842 an editorial in the Church newspaper claimed that "Lehi . . . landed a little south of the Isthmus of Darien [Panama]" (T&S 3 [Sept. 15, 1842]: 921–22). This would move the location of Lehi's landing some 3,000 miles north of the proposed site in Chile. Although Joseph Smith had assumed editorial responsibility for the paper by this time, it is not known whether this statement originated with him or even represented his views. Two weeks later, another editorial appeared in the Times and Seasons that, in effect, constituted a book review of *Incidents of Travel in Central America, Chiapas and Yucatan*, by John Lloyd Stephens. This was the first accessible book in English containing detailed descriptions and drawings of ancient Mayan ruins. Excerpts from it were included in the *Times and Seasons*, along with the comment that "it will not be a bad plan to compare Mr. Stephens' ruined cities with those in the Book of Mormon: light cleaves to light, and facts are supported by facts. The truth injures no one" (*T&S* 3 [Oct. 1, 1842]: 927).

In statements since then, Church leaders have generally declined to give any opinion on issues of Book of Mormon geography. When asked to review a map showing the supposed landing place of Lehi's company, President Joseph F. Smith declared that the "Lord had not yet revealed it" (Cannon, p. 160 n.). In 1929, Anthony W. Ivins, counselor in the First Presidency, added, "There has never been anything yet set forth that definitely settles that question [of Book of Mormon geography]. . . . We are just waiting until we discover the truth" (*CR*, Apr. 1929, p. 16). While the Church has not taken an official position with regard to location of geographical places, the authorities do not discourage private efforts to deal with the subject (Cannon).

The unidentified *Times and Seasons* editorialist seems to have favored modern Central America as the setting for Book of Mormon events. As noted, recent geographies by some Church members promote this identification, but others consider upstate New York or South America the correct setting. Considerable diversity of opinion remains among Church members regarding Book of Mormon geography; however, most students of the problem agree that the hundreds of geographical references in the Book of Mormon are remarkably consistent—even if the students cannot always agree upon precise locations.

Of the numerous proposed external Book of Mormon geographies, none has been positively and unambiguously confirmed by archaeology. More fundamentally, there is no agreement on whether such positive identification could be made or, if so, what form a "proof" would take; nor is it clear what would constitute "falsification" or "disproof" of various proposed geographies. Until these methodological issues have been resolved, all internal and external geographies—including supposed archaeological tests of them—should, at best, be considered only intelligent conjectures.

BIBLIOGRAPHY

Allen, Joseph L. *Exploring the Lands of the Book of Mormon*. Orem, Utah, 1989.

Cannon, George Q. "Book of Mormon Geography." *Juvenile Instructor* 25 (Jan. 1, 1890): 18–19; repr., *Instructor* 73 (Apr. 1938): 159–60.

Clark, John E. "A Key for Evaluating Nephite Geographies." *Review of Books on the Book of Mormon* 1 (1989): 20–70.

Hauck, F. Richard. *Deciphering the Geography of the Book of Mormon*. Salt Lake City, 1988.

Palmer, David A. *In Search of Cumorah: New Evidences for the Book of Mormon from Ancient Mexico*. Bountiful, Utah, 1981.

Richards, F., and J. Little, eds. *Compendium of the Doctrines of the Gospel*, rev. ed. Salt Lake City, 1925.

Roberts, B. H. *New Witnesses for God*, 3 vols. Salt Lake City, 1909.

Sorenson, John L. *An Ancient American Setting for the Book of Mormon*. Salt Lake City, 1985.

———. *A Hundred and Fifty Years of Book of Mormon Geographies: A History of the Ideas*. Salt Lake City, 1991.

Warren, Bruce W., and Thomas Stuart Ferguson. *The Messiah in Ancient America*. Provo, Utah, 1987.

Washburn, J. Nile. *Book of Mormon Lands and Times.* Salt Lake City, 1974.

Widtsoe, John A. *Evidences and Reconciliations,* 3 vols. Salt Lake City, 1951.

ADDITIONAL SOURCES

Aston, Warren P., and Michaela Knoth Aston. *In the Footsteps of Lehi: New Evidence for Lehi's Journey across Arabia to Bountiful.* Salt Lake City: Deseret Book, 1994.

Hilton, John L., and Janet F. Hilton. "A Correlation of the Sidon River and the Lands of Manti and Zarahemla with the Southern End of the Rio Grijalva (San Miguel)." *Journal of Book of Mormon Studies* 1 (Fall 1992): 142–62.

Sorenson, John L. *Images of Ancient America: Visualizing Book of Mormon Life.* Provo, Utah: Research Press, 1998.

———. *Mormon's Map.* Provo, Utah: FARMS, 2000.

JOHN E. CLARK

GOLD PLATES

On September 21, 1823, the angel Moroni appeared to Joseph SMITH and instructed him about a record engraved on thin goldlike sheets. The record, written by MORONI[2], his father MORMON, and other ancient inhabitants of the Americas, was buried in a stone box in a hill not far from the Smith residence. Moroni eventually delivered these plates to Joseph, who translated and published them as the Book of Mormon and returned them to Moroni. While the plates were in Joseph's keeping, others saw them, including eleven witnesses whose testimonies appear in all editions of the book. Various descriptions provided by eyewitnesses suggest that the plates may have been made of a gold alloy, measured about 6 inches by 8 inches (15.2 cm by 20.3 cm), were 6 inches (15.2 cm) thick, and weighed about 50 pounds (22.7 kg).

[*See also* Plates and Records in the Book of Mormon; Translation of the Book of Mormon by Joseph Smith; Witnesses of the Book of Mormon; Plates, Metal.]

GRANT R. HARDY

GOSPEL OF JESUS CHRIST

[*This entry is discussed here under the heading:*

The Gospel in LDS Teaching

This article outlines the Latter-day Saint conception of the gospel of Jesus Christ, the fundamental teaching of the Church, as it is presented in scripture and in the teachings of the modern prophets.]

The Gospel in LDS Teaching

JESUS CHRIST and his apostles and prophets have repeatedly announced the "good news" or "gospel" that by coming to Christ, a person may be saved. The Father is the author of the gospel, but it is called the gospel of Jesus Christ because, in agreement with the Father's plan, Christ's atonement makes the GOSPEL operative in human lives. Christ's gospel is the only true gospel, and "there shall be no other name given nor any other way nor means whereby salvation can come unto the children of men, only in and through the name of Christ, the Lord Omnipotent" (Mosiah 3:17; cf. Acts 4:12).

Even though Latter-day Saints use the term "gospel" in several ways, including traditional Christian usages, the Book of Mormon and other latter-day scriptures define it precisely as the way or means by which an individual can come to Christ. In all these scriptural passages, the gospel or doctrine of Christ teaches that salvation is available through his authorized servants to all who will (1) believe in Christ; (2) repent of their sins; (3) be baptized in water as a witness of their willingness to take his name upon them and keep his commandments; (4) receive the Holy Ghost by the laying on of hands; and (5) endure to the end. All who obey these commandments and receive the baptism of fire and of the Holy Ghost and endure in faith, hope, and charity will be found guiltless at the last day and will enter into the kingdom of heaven (Alma 7:14–16, 24–25; Heb. 6:1–2).

THE PLAN OF SALVATION. President Brigham Young taught that the "Gospel of the Son of God that has been revealed is a plan or system of laws and ordinances, by strict obedience to which the people who inhabit this earth are assured that they may return again into the presence of the Father and the Son" (*JD* 13:233). The gospel of Jesus Christ is a key part of the PLAN OF SALVATION (or plan of redemption), which provides an opportunity for all people to obtain eternal life. Because of the FALL OF ADAM, which has passed upon all individuals by inheritance, all are subject to a physical death and a spiritual death (2 Ne. 9:4–12; D&C 29:39–45; 1 Cor. 15:12–22) and cannot save themselves. God, the loving Father of all spirits, has declared that it is his work and glory "to bring to pass the immortality and eternal life of man" (Moses 1:39). For this purpose he provided a savior, Jesus Christ, who, because of his perfect love, his sinlessness, and his being the Only Begotten of the Father in the flesh, was both willing and able to offer himself as a sacrifice for the sins of the world (John 3:16). Through his atonement, Christ redeemed all men, women, and children unconditionally from the two deaths occasioned by the transgression of Adam and Eve, and will also redeem them from their own sins, if they accept and obey his gospel (Moses 6:62; D&C 20:17–25; 76:40–53).

BASIC ELEMENTS. Modern revelations state that the Book of Mormon contains "the fulness of the gospel" (D&C 20:9; 27:5; 42:12). Of all the standard works, the Book of Mormon contains the most detailed exposition of the gospel. In three separate passages the basic elements of the gospel are explained by a prophet or by Jesus himself (2 Ne. 31:2–32:6; 3 Ne. 11:31–41; 27:13–21). Each of these passages is framed by the affirmation that "this is my doctrine" or "this is my gospel." The revelations to the Prophet Joseph SMITH confirm these Book of Mormon statements of the gospel in every detail (see D&C 18:17–23; 19:29–31; 20:25–29).

These core texts repeat the basic elements of the gospel message several times in slightly varied ways. Joseph Smith referred to them in abbreviated form as "the first principles and ordinances of the Gospel" (A of F 4).

1. Faith. LDS teaching emphasizes FAITH IN JESUS CHRIST as the first principle of the gospel. The priority of faith is twofold. The individual who accepts the gospel must start with faith in Jesus Christ, believing in him and his power to save people from their sins. Without faith, no one would be strongly motivated to repent and to live the rest of the gospel principles. Faith is also fundamental to the other elements of the gospel in that each of them is dependent on acts of faith in important ways. In this sense, NEPHI₁ compares living the gospel to entering a strait and narrow path that leads to eternal life. The gate by which one can enter this path is repentance and baptism. With the guidance of the Holy Ghost, one can follow the path, exercising faith and enduring to the end. Thus, faith in Jesus Christ is a link between what one does to enter the gate and what must be done thereafter. One cannot have entered the gate by repenting and making baptismal covenants "save it were by the word of Christ with unshaken faith in him, relying wholly

upon the merits of him who is mighty to save" (2 Ne. 31:19). After starting on this strait and narrow path, one cannot reach salvation except by "press[ing] forward with a steadfastness [faith] in Christ . . . feasting upon the word of Christ" (2 Ne. 31:20), which includes those things that the Holy Ghost tells one to do (2 Ne. 32:3, 5).

2. Repentance. The centrality of faith is emphasized by the way the gospel is presented in the Book of Mormon, with faith usually mentioned in the center and the call to REPENTANCE at the first. Individuals must forsake their sins and offer up "a sacrifice . . . [of] a broken heart and a contrite spirit." This requires that the sinner come down into the depths of humility and become "as a little child" (3 Ne. 9:20–22).

3. Baptism. The gospel emphasizes the absolute need for baptism for those accountable and capable of sin. Like repentance, baptism is also a commandment, and candidates for salvation must be baptized in order to obey the commandment (see 2 Ne. 31:6–7).

This essential ordinance is a witness to the Father that the repentant individual has covenanted with God to keep his commandments and has taken upon himself or herself the name of Christ. Faith in Jesus Christ, repentance, and baptism are the gate by which one enters into the way that leads to eternal life (2 Ne. 31:13–15). Because infants are incapable of sin or of making such covenants, parents are instructed to prepare them for baptism by the time they reach eight years of age, the age of accountability established in revelation (D&C 68:25–28; *see* INFANT BAPTISM).

4. The Holy Ghost. While water baptism symbolizes purification and rising from death to life, the actual cleansing or REMISSION OF SINS comes by obedience, and as a gift from God "by fire and by the Holy Ghost" (2 Ne.

31:17; Matt. 3:11), by which the individual is BORN OF GOD, having become a "new creature" (Mosiah 27:24–26; 1 Pet. 1:23). This spiritual experience is a witness from the Father and the Son that the sacrifice of the penitent has been accepted. After Jesus had taught the NEPHITES and they were baptized, "the Holy Ghost did fall upon them, and they were filled with the Holy Ghost and with fire" (3 Ne. 19:13; cf. Acts 2:4).

The gift of the Holy Ghost, administered by the laying on of hands by one having authority, includes the promise "If ye will enter in by the way, and receive the Holy Ghost, it will show unto you all things what ye should do" (2 Ne. 32:5). This gift is a constant companion by which the individual receives "the words of Christ" directly for guidance in his or her own life, in addition to inspired instruction from Church leaders (2 Ne. 32:3; see also John 14:26; 16:13).

5. Endure to the End. "Enduring to the end" is the scriptural phrase describing the subsequent life of a member of Christ's church who has embraced the first principles of the gospel and has entered the gate that leads to eternal life. Once on this strait and narrow path, the member must press forward in faith, and continue in obedience to all the commandments of God.

Faith is linked with hope and charity. Receiving a remission of sins generates a hope of salvation. This is more than a desire, and gives a feeling of assurance. Such hope grows continually brighter through the workings of the Holy Ghost if one is consistently obedient (Ether 12:4). Charity, the "pure love of Christ," is characteristic of those who obey the commandments (Moro. 7:3–4, 47). Such persons reflect to others the same kind of pure love that they experience from the Lord.

6. Salvation. In addition to receiving

daily blessings, Jesus Christ promises that those who comply with all of the principles and ordinances will receive eternal life. As revealed to the Prophet Joseph Smith, salvation entails becoming an heir to the fulness of the celestial kingdom (D&C 76:50–70).

All LDS standard works contain clear statements of the gospel of Jesus Christ (see D&C 10:63–70; 11:9–24; 19:29–32; 20:37; 33:10–13; 39:6; 68:25; Moses 5:14–15, 58; 6:50–53). Latter-day Saints find the same concept in many New Testament passages (Matt. 3:11; 24:13–14; Acts 2:38; 19:4–6; Rom. 1:16), although frequently only a few of the six key elements are specifically mentioned in any one passage. This is also true of the Book of Mormon. For example, the promise "They that believe in him shall be saved" (2 Ne. 2:9) may be understood as a merism (an abbreviation of a formula retaining only the first and last elements) that implicitly invokes all six components even though they are not mentioned individually. Another merism states that believing in Jesus and enduring to the end is life eternal (2 Ne. 33:4; cf. v. 9).

OTHER MEANINGS. Although emphasis is placed on truths necessary for salvation, LDS usage of the term "gospel" is not confined to the scriptural definition. Latter-day Saints commonly refer to the entire body of their religious beliefs as "the gospel." By the broadest interpretation, all truth originating with God may be included within the gospel. President Joseph F. Smith said:

> In the theological sense, the gospel means more than just the tidings of good news, with accompanying joy to the souls of men, for it embraces every principle of eternal truth. There is no fundamental principle, or truth anywhere in the universe, that is not embraced in the gospel of Jesus Christ, and it is not confined to the simple first principles, such as faith in

God, repentance from sin, baptism for the remission of sins, and the laying on of hands for the gift of the Holy Ghost, although these are absolutely essential to salvation and exaltation in the kingdom of God. (pp. 85–86)

Notwithstanding this wide range of meanings associated with the gospel, as President Smith explained, the saving truths encompassed by the first principles are indispensable and must be followed to obtain salvation. They are the central focus of the Church's teachings and practices. Latter-day Saints are under strict command to share the fundamental, first principles of the gospel with others so that all may have an equal chance to obtain salvation. Proselytizing efforts of individual members and full-time missionaries are intended to invite others to come to Christ through obedience to gospel principles and ordinances.

President Ezra Taft Benson has similarly explained that "the gospel can be viewed from two perspectives. In the broadest sense, the gospel embraces all truth, all light, all revealed knowledge to mankind. In a more restrictive sense the gospel means the doctrine of the Fall . . . [and] atonement." Clarifying the restrictive sense, he explained:

> When the Savior referred to his gospel, He meant the . . . laws, covenants, and ordinances that men must comply with to work out their salvation. He meant faith in the Lord Jesus Christ, repentance from all sin, baptism by immersion by a legal administrator for the remission of our sins, and the receipt of the gift of the Holy Ghost, and finally he meant that one should be valiant in his testimony of Jesus until the end of his days. This is the gospel Jesus preached. (p. 30)

Those who die without hearing the gospel while in mortality will receive this opportunity in the spirit world. The necessary ordinances of baptism and the laying on of hands for the gift of the Holy Ghost will be performed on behalf of the dead by living members in Latter-day Saint temples. The deceased will decide for themselves whether to accept or reject the ordinances performed in their behalf.

ETERNAL NATURE OF THE GOSPEL. Latter-day Saints believe that the gospel has always existed and will continue to exist throughout the eternities. The Prophet Joseph Smith said, "The great Jehovah contemplated the whole of the events connected with the earth, pertaining to the plan of salvation, before it rolled into existence, or ever 'the morning stars sang together' for joy" (*TPJS*, p. 220). The eternal nature of the gospel was also emphasized by President John Taylor, who declared that 'the gospel is a living, abiding, eternal, and unchangeable principle that has existed co-equal with God, and always will exist, while time and eternity endure, wherever it is developed and made manifest" (p. 88).

LDS scriptures explain that after the Lord had taught Adam and Eve the plan of salvation and the gospel (Moses 5:4–11), Adam was "caught away by the Spirit of the Lord" into the water where he was baptized. Following his baptism, the "Spirit of God descended upon him, and thus he was born of the Spirit" (Moses 6:48–68). In describing this experience, Enoch explained that God called upon Adam with his own voice, teaching him the same gospel set out in other scriptures:

> If thou wilt turn unto me, and hearken unto my voice, and believe, and repent of all thy transgressions, and be baptized, even in water, in the name of mine Only Begotten Son, who is full of grace and truth, which is Jesus Christ, the only name which shall be given under heaven, whereby salvation shall come unto the children of men, ye shall receive the gift of the Holy Ghost. (Moses 6:52)

Latter-day scripture records that Adam and Eve taught their children the gospel, but that Satan came among them and persuaded some to love him more than God (Moses 5:13). Thus it has been with the descendants of Adam and Eve, and in this situation, the Lord called upon people everywhere to believe in the Son and to repent of their sins that they might be saved. This gospel message was a "firm decree" sent forth "in the world, until the end thereof," and was preached from the beginning by angels, by the voice of God, and by the Holy Ghost (Moses 5:12–15, 58–59).

Latter-day Saints understand the history of the world in terms of periods of faithfulness and of apostasy. Although there have been many times when the gospel of Jesus Christ has been lost from the earth, it has repeatedly been restored through prophets sent to declare new dispensations of the gospel. The gospel has been given to successive generations and will maintain its efficacy forever. The restoration of the fulness of the gospel to Joseph Smith initiated the "last dispensation," or the dispensation of the fulness of times, and he was promised that the gospel will never again be taken from the earth. The gospel of Jesus Christ continues to be the only means given under heaven whereby men and women can come to their Savior and be saved, and is the standard against which all people will be judged.

BIBLIOGRAPHY

Benson, Ezra Taft. *Teachings of Ezra Taft Benson*. Salt Lake City, 1988.

Smith, Joseph F. *Gospel Doctrine*, pp. 85–86.

Talmage, James E. *AF*, pp. 52–170.

Taylor, John. *Gospel Kingdom*. Salt Lake City, 1964.

Yarn, David H., Jr. *The Gospel: God, Man, and Truth*. Salt Lake City, 1965.

ADDITIONAL SOURCE

Reynolds, Noel. B. "The Gospel of Jesus Christ as Taught by the Nephite Prophets." *BYU Studies* 31 (Summer 1991): 31–50.

NOEL B. REYNOLDS

GOVERNMENT AND LEGAL HISTORY IN THE BOOK OF MORMON

Because the Book of Mormon focuses on religious themes, information about political and legal institutions appears only as background for the religious account. Even so, it is apparent that several different political institutions characterized NEPHITE, LAMANITE, and JAREDITE society.

The Nephites were ruled by hereditary kings from c. 550 to 91 B.C., when the rule changed to a reign of judges. After the coming of Christ, two centuries of peace under the government of his Church were followed by a breakdown of society into tribal units and finally by the destruction of the Nephites.

From the beginning, the Nephite legal system was based on the LAW OF MOSES as it was written in the scriptures, as it was possibly practiced by Israel in the seventh century B.C., and as it was modified (slightly) over the years until the coming of Jesus Christ. As the Nephite prophets had long predicted (2 Ne. 25:24), Jesus fulfilled the law of Moses. After his coming, Nephite law consisted of the commandments of Christ.

GOVERNMENT. After leading his family and a few others out of Jerusalem, Lehi established his colony in the Western Hemisphere as a branch of Israel in a new promised land,

but its organization was inherently unstable, for it seems to have given no clear principle for resolving political disputes. The seven lineage groups established at Lehi's death and mentioned consistently in the Book of Mormon were Nephites, Jacobites, Josephites, Zoramites, Lamanites, Lemuelites, and Ishmaelites (Jacob 1:13; 4 Ne. 1:36–38; Morm. 1:8; Welch, 1989, p. 69). When this system proved unable to keep the peace, NEPHI₁ led away the first four of these family groups, who believed the revelations of God; established a new city; and accepted the position of Nephite king by popular acclamation. The other three groups eventually developed a monarchical system, with a Lamanite king receiving tribute from other Ishmaelite, Lamanite, and Lemuelite vassal kings.

This original split provides the basic political theme for much of Nephite and Lamanite history. Laman and Lemuel were Lehi's oldest sons, and they naturally claimed a right to rule. But a younger brother, Nephi, was chosen by the Lord to be their ruler and teacher (1 Ne. 2:22), and Nephi's account of this early history was written in part to document his calling as ruler (Reynolds). The conflict over the right to rule continued, providing much of the rhetorical base for the recurring wars between Lamanites and Nephites hundreds of years later.

Possibly because of the controversial circumstances in which Nephite kingship was established, its ideology was clear from earliest times. Nephite kings were popularly acclaimed (2 Ne. 5:18). They had a temple as their religious center (2 Ne. 5:16) and were careful to maintain venerable symbols of divinely appointed kingship in the sword of Laban, the Liahona, and ancient records (2 Ne. 5:12–14; cf. Ricks).

Only the first Nephite king (Nephi₁) and the last three kings (MOSIAH₁, BENJAMIN, and MOSIAH₂) are named in the Book of Mormon.

These four kings served as military leaders and prophets, and worked closely with other prophets in reminding people of their obligations to God and to one another. For example, in his final address to his people, King Benjamin reported to the people a revelation from God and put them under covenant to take the name of Christ upon them and to keep God's and the king's commandments.

Some Nephite kings were unrighteous. Noah, a king of one Nephite subgroup (the people of Zeniff), exploited the weaknesses of the Nephite system, sustaining himself and his council of corrupt priests in riotous living from the labors of the people. Doubts about the institution of kingship became acute when the oppressions of Noah were reported to the main body of Nephites. King Mosiah$_2$, when his sons declined the monarchy, resolved the succession crisis by proposing to change the kingship into a system of lower and higher judges. This form of government was accepted by the people in 91 B.C. (Mosiah 29) and lasted, in spite of several crises and corruptions, for approximately a hundred years. Though the position of chief judge continued to have military and religious preeminence and was frequently passed from father to son, it differed from the kingship pattern in that the higher judges could be judged by lower judges if they broke the law or oppressed the people (Mosiah 29:29).

ALMA$_2$ became the first chief judge and served simultaneously as high priest, governor, and military chief captain. Because these offices required the approval of the people, who had rejected monarchy, critics have tended to confuse the Nephite system with the democracy of the United States. However, there was no representative legislature, the essential institution in American republican ideology. Also, the major offices were typically passed from father to son, without elections (Bushman, pp. 14–17); "the voice of the

people" is reported many times as authorizing or confirming leadership appointments and other civic or political actions.

It appears that during the first two centuries after the coming of Christ, the Nephites operated under an ecclesiastical system without judges or kings, with courts constituted only of the church elders (4 Ne. 1:1–23; Moro. 6:7). With the eventual apostasy and collapse of the Nephite church, no civil institutions were in place to preserve law and order. Attempts to organize and conduct public affairs by reversion to a tribal system and, later, to military rule did not prevent the final destruction of the civilization.

The Book of Mormon also gives a brief account of the Jaredites, a much earlier civilization that began at the time of the great tower and was monarchical from beginning to end. Jaredite kings seem to have been autocrats, and succession was more often determined through political and military adventurism than through legal procedures.

LAW. Until the coming of Christ, the Nephites and converted Lamanites strictly observed the law of Moses as they knew and understood it (2 Ne. 5:10; 25:24–26; Jarom 1:5; Jacob 4:4–5; Alma 25:15; 30:3; Hel. 13:1; 3 Ne. 1:24–25). Preserved on the brass plates, the law of Moses was the basis of their criminal and civil law, as well as of the rules of purity, temple sacrifice, and festival observances of the Nephites; they knew, however, that the law of Moses would be superseded in the future messianic age (2 Ne. 25:24–27).

Recent publications (Welch, 1984, 1987, 1988, 1989, 1990) have identified a rich array of legal information in the text of the Book of Mormon. Procedural and administrative aspects of Nephite law developed from one century to another, while the substance of the customary law changed very little. Nephite leaders seem to have viewed new legislation as presumptuous and generally evil (Mosiah

29:23) and any change of God's law without authority as blasphemous (Jacob 7:7). Their religious laws included many humanitarian provisions and protections for persons and their religious freedom and property. These rules were grounded in a strong principle of legal equality (Alma 1:32; 16:18; Hel. 4:12).

In two early incidents, Jacob, the brother of Nephi$_1$, was involved in controversies concerning the law. The first involved the claimed right of some Nephites to have concubines (Jacob 2:23–3:11), and the second arose when Sherem accused Jacob of desecrating the law of Moses (Jacob 7:7).

The trial of ABINADI (Mosiah 11–17) indicates that, at least in the case of Noah, the king had jurisdiction over political issues but took counsel on religious matters from a body of priests: Causes of action were brought against Abinadi for cursing the ruler, testifying falsely, giving a false prophecy, and committing blasphemy (Mosiah 12:9–10, 14; 17:7–8, 12). Legal punishments in the Book of Mormon were often fashioned so as to match the nature of the crime; thus, Abinadi was burned for reviling the king, whose life he had said would be valued as a garment in a furnace (Mosiah 12:3; 17:3).

At the time the Nephites abandoned monarchy, Mosiah$_2$ instituted a major reform of Nephite procedural law. A system of judges and other officers was instituted; lower judges were judged by a higher judge (Mosiah 29:28); judges were paid for the time spent in public service (Alma 11:3); a standardized system of weights and measures was instituted (Alma 11:4–19); slavery was formally prohibited (Alma 27:9); and defaulting debtors faced banishment (Alma 11:2). There were officers (Alma 11:2) and lawyers who assisted, but their official functions are not clear. It appears that ordinary citizens had sole power to initiate lawsuits (otherwise, the

judges would have brought the action against Nephi$_2$ in Helaman 8:1).

The trial of Nehor was an important precedent, establishing the plenary and original jurisdiction of the chief judge (Alma 1:1–15). It appears that under the terms of Mosiah 29, the higher judges were intended only to judge if the lower judges judged falsely. But in the trial of Nehor, Alma$_2$ took the case directly, enhancing the power of the chief judge.

The reform also protected freedom of belief, but certain overt conduct was punished (Alma 1:17–18; 30:9–11). The case of Korihor established the rule that certain forms of speech (blasphemy, inciting people to sin) were punishable under the Nephite law even after the reform of Mosiah.

All this time, the underlying Nephite law remained the law of Moses as interpreted in light of a knowledge of the gospel. Public decrees regularly prohibited murder, plunder, theft, adultery, and all iniquity (Mosiah 2:13; Alma 23:3). Murder was defined as "deliberately kill[ing]" (2 Ne. 9:35), which excluded cases where one did not lie in wait (on Nephi's slaying of Laban, cf. Ex. 21:13–14 and 1 Ne. 4:6–18). Theft was typically a minor offense, but robbery was a capital crime (Hel. 11:28), usually committed by organized outsiders and violent and politically motivated brigands, who were dealt with by military force (as they were typically in the ancient Near East).

Evidently, technical principles of the law of Moses were consistently observed in Nephite civilization. For example, the legal resolution of an unobserved murder in the case of Seantum in Helaman 9 shows that a technical exception to the rule against self-incrimination was recognized by the Nephites in the same way that it was by later Jewish jurists, as when divination detected a corpus delicti (Welch, Feb. 1990). The execution of Zemnarihah by the Nephites adumbrated an obscure point attested in later Jewish law that required the tree from which a criminal was hanged to be chopped down (3 Ne. 4:28; Welch, 1984). The case of the Ammonite exemption from military duty suggests that the rabbinic understanding of Deuteronomy 20 in this regard was probably the same as the Nephites' (Welch, 1990, pp. 63–65).

One may also infer from circumstantial evidence that the Nephites observed the traditional ritual laws of Israelite festivals. One example might be the assembly of Benjamin's people in tents around the temple and tower from which he spoke. There are things in the account that are similar to the New Year festivals surrounding the Feast of Tabernacles and the Day of Atonement (Tvedtnes, in Lundquist and Ricks, *By Study and Also by Faith*, Salt Lake City, 1990, 2:197–237).

With the coming of the resurrected Christ, recorded in 3 Nephi, the law of Moses was fulfilled and was given new meaning. The Ten Commandments still applied in a new form (3 Ne. 12); the "performances and ordinances" of the law became obsolete (4 Ne. 1:12), but not the "law" or the "commandments" as Jesus had reformulated them in 3 Nephi 12–14.

BIBLIOGRAPHY

Bushman, Richard L. "The Book of Mormon and the American Revolution." *BYU Studies* 17 (Autumn 1976): 3–20.

Reynolds, Noel B. "The Political Dimension in Nephi's Small Plates." *BYU Studies* 27 (Fall 1987): 15–37.

Ricks, Stephen D. "The Ideology of Kingship in Mosiah 1–6." *FARMS Update*, Aug. 1987.

Welch, John W. "The Execution of Zemnarihah." *FARMS Update*, Nov. 1984.

———. "The Law of Mosiah." *FARMS Update*, Mar. 1987.

———. "Statutes, Judgments, Ordinances and Commandments." *FARMS Update*, June 1988.

———. "Lehi's Last Will and Testament: A Legal Approach." In *The Book of Mormon: Second Nephi, the Doctrinal Structure*, ed. M. Nyman and C. Tate, Jr., pp. 61–82. Provo, Utah, 1989.

———. "The Case of an Unobserved Murder." *FARMS Update*, Feb. 1990.

———. "Law and War in the Book of Mormon." In *Warfare in the Book of Mormon*, ed. S. Ricks and W. Hamblin, pp. 46–102. Salt Lake City, 1990.

ADDITIONAL SOURCE

Welch, John W. "The Law of Mosiah." In *Reexploring the Book of Mormon*, edited by John W. Welch, 158–61. Salt Lake City and Provo, Utah: Deseret Book and FARMS, 1992.

NOEL B. REYNOLDS

GRACE

One of the most controversial issues in Christian theology is whether salvation is the free gift of unmerited grace or is earned through good works. Paul's statement that "a man is justified by faith without the deeds of the law" (Rom. 3:28) is frequently cited to support the former view, while James's statement that "faith without works is dead" (James 2:20) is often quoted in favor of the latter view. The LDS doctrine that salvation requires *both* grace and works is a revealed yet commonsense reconciliation of these contradictory positions.

C. S. Lewis wrote that this dispute "does seem to me like asking which blade in a pair of scissors is most necessary" (p. 129). And in one way or another almost all Christian denominations ultimately accept the need for both grace and works, but the differences in meaning and emphasis among the various doctrinal traditions remain substantial.

LDS doctrine contains an affirmative sense of interaction between grace and works that is unique not only as to these concepts but also reflects the uniqueness of the restored gospel's view of man's nature, the FALL OF ADAM, the atonement, and the process of salvation. At the same time, the LDS view contains features that are similar to basic elements of some other traditions. For example, the LDS insistence that such works as ordinances be performed with proper priesthood authority resembles the Catholic teaching that its sacraments are the requisite channels of grace. Also the LDS emphasis on the indispensability of personal faith and REPENTANCE in a direct relationship with God echoes traditional Protestant teachings. The LDS position "is not a convenient eclecticism, but a repossession [through the Restoration] of a New Testament understanding that reconciles Paul and James" (Madsen, p. 175).

The Church's emphasis on personal responsibility and the need for self-disciplined obedience may seem to de-emphasize the role of Christ's grace; however, for Latter-day Saints, obedience is but one blade of the scissors. All of LDS theology also reflects the major premise of the Book of Mormon that without grace there is no salvation: "For we know that it is by grace that we are saved, after all we can do" (2 Ne. 25:23). The source of this grace is the atoning sacrifice of Jesus Christ: "Mercy cometh because of the atonement" (Alma 42:23).

The teachings of Christian theology since the Middle Ages are rooted in the belief that, primarily because of the effects of the Fall and original sin, humankind has an inherently evil nature. In both the Catholic and the Protestant traditions, only the grace of God can overcome this natural evil. Various Chris-

tian writers have disputed the extent to which the bestowal of grace completely overcomes man's dark nature. In the fifth century, reflecting his personal struggle with what he believed to be his own inherent evil nature, Augustine saw grace as the only escape from the evil of earthly pleasures and the influence of the worldly "city of man." In the thirteenth century Thomas Aquinas was more sanguine, recognizing the serious wounding caused by original sin, but also defending man's natural potential for good.

In the early sixteenth century, Martin Luther, through his reading of Paul and reacting against the sale of indulgences, concluded that faith, God's unilateral gift to chosen individuals, is the true source of grace and, therefore, of justification before God. Luther thus (perhaps unintentionally) broke the medieval church's control over grace, thereby unleashing the political force of the Protestant reformation. For Luther, man's individual effort can in no way "earn" or otherwise be part in the righteousness infused by grace. Even the good works demonstrated in a life of obedience to God are but the visible *effects* of grace. This idea later influenced the development of the Puritan ethic in America. John Calvin, Luther's contemporary, developed a complete doctrine of predestination based on Luther's idea that God unilaterally chooses those on whom he bestows the gifts of faith and grace.

The Catholic response to Luther's challenge rejected predestination and reaffirmed both that grace is mediated by church sacraments and that grace cannot totally displace human agency. At the same time, Catholic thought underscored the primacy of God's initiative. "Prevenient grace" operates upon the human will before one turns to God; yet, once touched by grace, one is still free to cooperate or not. The interaction between divine grace and human freedom is not totally clear; however, grace is increased as one obeys God's commandments, and grace raises one's natural good works to actions of supernatural value in a process of spiritual regeneration.

In recent years, some Protestant theologians have questioned the way an exclusive emphasis on unmerited grace negates a sense of personal responsibility. Dietrich Bonhoeffer, for example, condemned the idea of "cheap grace," which falsely supposes that because "the account has been paid in advance . . . everything can be had for nothing" (*The Cost of Discipleship*, 1963, p. 45). John MacArthur was concerned that contemporary evangelism promises sinners that they "can have eternal life yet continue to live in rebellion against God" (*The Gospel according to Jesus*, 1988, pp. 15–16). And Paul Holmer wrote that stressing the dangers of works is "inappropriate if the listeners are not even trying! Most Church listeners are not in much danger of working their way into heaven" ("Law and Gospel Re-examined," *Theology Today* 10 [1953–54]: 474).

Some Latter-day Saints have shared similar concerns about the limitations of a one-sided view of the grace-works controversy, just as they have shared the Catholic concern about a doctrine of grace that undercuts the fundamental nature of free will. Latter-day Saints see Paul's writing about the inadequacy of works and "the deeds of the law" (Rom. 3:27–28) as referring mainly to the inadequacy of the ritual works of the law of Moses, "which had been superseded by the higher requirements of the Gospel [of Jesus Christ]"; thus, Paul correctly regarded many of "the outward forms and ceremonies" of the law of Moses as "unessential works" (*AF*, p. 480). As the prophet ABINADI declared in the Book of Mormon (c. 150 B.C.), "Salvation doth not come by the law alone; and were it not for the atonement, which God himself shall make

for the sins and iniquities of his people, . . . they must unavoidably perish, notwithstanding the law of Moses" (Mosiah 13:28).

In a broader sense, LDS devotion to the primary role of grace while concurrently emphasizing self-reliance stems from a unique doctrinal view of man's nature and destiny. As noted by Reformation scholar John Dillenberger, "In stressing human possibilities, Mormonism brought things into line, not by abandoning the centrality of grace but by insisting that the [real] powers of humanity . . . reflected the actual state of humanity as such. . . . Mormonism brought understanding to what had become an untenable problem within evangelicalism: how to reconcile the new power of humanity with the negative inherited views of humanity, without abandoning the necessity of grace." In this way, Dillenberger concluded, "perhaps Mormonism . . . is the authentic American theology, for the self-reliance of revivalist fundamentalist groups stood in marked contrast to their inherited conception of the misery of humanity" (p. 179).

In LDS teachings, the fall of Adam made Christ's redemption necessary, but not because the Fall by itself made man evil. Because of transgression, Adam and Eve were expelled from Eden into a world that was subject to death and evil influences. However, the Lord revealed to Adam upon his entry into mortality that "the Son of God hath atoned for original guilt"; therefore, Adam's children were not evil, but were "*whole* from the foundation of the world" (Moses 6:54). Thus, "every spirit of man was *innocent* in the beginning; and God having redeemed man from the fall, men became again, in their infant state, *innocent* before God" (D&C 93:38).

As the descendants of Adam and Eve then become accountable for their own sins at age eight, all of them taste sin as the result of their own free choice. "All have sinned, and come short of the glory of God" (Rom. 3:23). One whose cumulative experience leads her or him to love "Satan more than God" (Moses 5:28) will eventually become "carnal, sensual, and devilish" (Moses 5:13; 6:49) by nature. On the other hand, one who consciously accepts Christ's grace through the Atonement by faith, repentance, and baptism yields to "the enticings of the Holy Spirit, and putteth off the natural man and becometh a saint through the atonement of Christ the Lord" (Mosiah 3:19). In this way, the individual takes the initiative to accept the grace made available by the Atonement, exercising faith through a willing "desire to believe" (Alma 32:27). That desire is often kindled by hearing others bear testimony of Christ. When this word of Christ is planted and then nourished through obedience interacting with grace, as summarized below, the individual may "become a saint" by nature, thereby enjoying eternal (meaning godlike) life.

Grace is thus the source of three categories of blessings related to mankind's salvation. First, many blessings of grace are *unconditional*—free and unmerited gifts requiring no individual action. God's grace in this sense is a factor in the Creation, the Fall, the Atonement, and the plan of salvation. Specifically regarding the Fall, and despite death and other conditions resulting from Adam's transgression, Christ's grace has atoned for original sin and has assured the resurrection of all humankind: "We believe that men will be punished for their own sins, and not for Adam's transgression" (A of F 2).

Second, the Savior has also atoned *conditionally* for personal sins. The application of grace to personal sins is conditional because it is available only when an individual repents, which can be a demanding form of works. Because of this condition, mercy is able to satisfy the demands of justice with neither mercy nor justice robbing the other. Personal repentance is therefore a *necessary* condition of salvation, but it is not by itself *sufficient* to assure salvation. In addition, one must accept the ordinances of BAPTISM and the laying on of hands to receive the gift of the Holy Ghost, by which one is born again as the spirit child of Christ and may eventually become sanctified (cf. D&C 76:51–52; *see also* GOSPEL OF JESUS CHRIST).

Third, after one has received Christ's gospel of faith, repentance, and baptism unto forgiveness of sin, relying "wholly upon the merits of him who is mighty to save," one has only "entered in by the gate" to the "strait and narrow path which leads to eternal life" (2 Ne. 31:17–20). In this postbaptism stage of spiritual development, one's best efforts—further works—are required to "endure to the end" (2 Ne. 31:20). These efforts include obeying the Lord's commandments and receiving the higher ordinances performed in the temples, and continuing a repentance process as needed to "retain a remission of your sins" (Mosiah 4:12).

In the teachings of Martin Luther, such works of righteousness are not the result of personal initiative but are the spontaneous effects of the internal grace one has received, wholly the fruits of the gracious tree. In LDS doctrine by contrast, "men should . . . do many things of their own free will, and bring to pass much righteousness; For the power is in them, wherein they are agents unto themselves" (D&C 58:27–28). At the same time, individuals lack the capacity to develop a Christlike nature by their own effort. The perfecting attributes such as hope and charity are ultimately "bestowed upon all who are true followers of . . . Jesus Christ" (Moro. 7:48) by grace through his atonement. This interactive relationship between human and divine powers in LDS theology derives both from the significance it attaches to free will and from its optimism about the "fruit of the Spirit" (Gal. 5:22–25) among the truly converted, "those who love me and keep all my commandments, *and* him that seeketh so to do" (D&C 46:9; emphasis added).

God bestows these additional, perfecting expressions of grace conditionally, as he does the grace that allows forgiveness of sin. They are given "after all we can do" (2 Ne. 25:23)—that is, in addition to our best efforts. In general, this condition is related less to obeying particular commandments than it is to one's fundamental spiritual character, such as "meekness, and lowliness of heart" (Moro. 8:26) and possessing "a broken heart and a contrite spirit" (Ps. 51:17; 3 Ne. 9:20; Hafen, chap. 9). Or, as Moroni wrote at the end of the Book of Mormon, "If ye shall deny yourselves of all ungodliness, and love God with all your might, mind and strength, then is his grace sufficient for you, that by his grace ye may be perfect in Christ; . . . then are ye sanctified in Christ by the grace of God, through the shedding of the blood of Christ" (Moro. 10:32–33).

BIBLIOGRAPHY

Dillenberger, John. "Grace and Works in Martin Luther and Joseph Smith." In *Reflections on Mormonism: Judaeo-Christian Parallels,* ed. Truman G. Madsen. Provo, Utah, 1978.

Hafen, Bruce C. *The Broken Heart: Applying the Atonement to Life's Experiences.* Salt Lake City, 1989.

Holmer, Paul L. "Law and Gospel Re-examined." *Theology Today* 10 (1953–1954): 474.

Keller, Roger R. *Reformed Christians and Mormon Christians: Let's Talk!* Urbana, Ill., 1986.

Lewis, C. S. *Mere Christianity.* New York, 1943.

Madsen, Truman G. *Reflections on Mormonism,* p. 175. Provo, Utah, 1978.

McDonald, William, ed. "Grace." In *New Catholic Encyclopedia,* Vol. 6. New York, 1967.

Millet, Robert L. *By Grace Are We Saved.* Salt Lake City, 1989.

Rahner, Karl, ed. *The Teaching of the Catholic Church.* Regensburg, Germany, 1965.

BRUCE C. HAFEN

GREAT AND ABOMINABLE CHURCH

The phrase "great and abominable church," which appears in an apocalyptic vision received by the Book of Mormon prophet NEPHI₁ in the sixth century B.C. (1 Ne. 13:6), refers to the church of the devil and is understood by Latter-day Saints to be equivalent to the "great whore that sitteth upon many waters" described in Revelation 17:1. This "whore of all the earth" is identified by Nephi's brother JACOB as all those who are against God and who fight against Zion, in all periods of time (2 Ne. 10:16). Nephi did not write a detailed account of everything he saw in the vision, as this responsibility was reserved for John the apostle, who was to receive the same vision; however, Nephi repeatedly refers to its content and teachings, using various images and phrases (1 Ne. 13:4–9, 26–27, 34; 14:1–4, 9–17).

Like John, Nephi and Jacob describe persecutions that evil people will inflict on God's people, particularly in the last days. The angel who explained the vision to Nephi emphasized that this great and abominable church would take away from the Bible and "the gospel of the Lamb many parts which are plain and most precious; and also many covenants of the Lord" (1 Ne. 13:26), causing men to "stumble" and giving Satan "great power" over them (1 Ne. 13:29; D&C 86:3; Robinson, "Early Christianity," p. 188). Though many Protestants, following the lead of Martin Luther, have linked this evil force described in Revelation 17 with the Roman Catholic church, the particular focus of these LDS and New Testament scriptures seems rather to be on earlier agents of apostasy in the Jewish and Christian traditions (see A. Clarke, *Clarke's Commentary*, Vol. 6, pp. 1036–38, Nashville, Tenn., 1977).

When Nephi speaks typologically rather than historically, he identifies all the enemies of the Saints with the church of the devil (1 Ne. 14:9–10; 2 Ne. 10:16). They are those from all nations and all time periods who desire "to get gain, and . . . power over the flesh, and . . . to become popular in the eyes of the world, . . . who seek the lusts of the flesh and the things of the world, and to do all manner of iniquity" (1 Ne. 22:23). Other scriptural terms related to the great and abominable church include "Babylon" and the "mother of harlots" (Rev. 17:5; 1 Ne. 22:13; D&C 1:16). Images of pride, greed, and covenant abandonment are associated with these terms, in sharp contrast to the church of God. The scriptures are consistent in warning people to flee from the church of evil and find refuge in the church of God (Jer. 51:6; Rev. 18:4; 1 Ne. 20:20; D&C 133:14; see also P. Minear, "Babylon," in *Interpreter's Dictionary of the Bible*, 1:338, Nashville, Tenn., 1962). The Book of Mormon image of a great and abominable church complements the biblical images of Babylon and the harlot.

The fate of the great and abominable church is described in both ancient and modern scriptures (Jer. 51:37; Rev. 18:21; 1 Ne. 14:15–16; 22:14; D&C 1:16): Though the nations of the earth will gather together against them, "the covenant people of the Lord, who were scattered upon all the face of the earth" are promised redemption even if it requires power sent down from heaven, as if by fire (1 Ne. 14:14; 22:17). When Jesus Christ returns, he will claim his own and reject those who have opposed him (Mal. 4:1–3; 2 Thes. 2:6–10; 1 Ne. 22:23–26). As the Savior institutes his millennial reign, great will be the fall of Babylon, the harlot, and the great and abominable church (Rev. 18; 2 Ne. 28:18), for every knee will bow and every tongue confess, with thankfulness, that Jesus is the Christ (Isa. 45:23; Mosiah 27:31).

BIBLIOGRAPHY

Nibley, Hugh W. "The Passing of the Primitive Church: Forty Variations on an Unpopular Theme." In CWHN 4:168–208.

———. "Prophecy in the Book of Mormon: The Three Periods." In CWHN 7:410–35.

Robinson, Stephen E. "Warring against the Saints of God." *Ensign* 18 (Jan. 1988): 34–39.

———. "Early Christianity and 1 Nephi 13–14." In *The Book of Mormon: First Nephi, The Doctrinal Foundation*, ed. M. Nyman and C. Tate, Jr., pp. 177–91. Provo, Utah, 1988.

DENNIS A. WRIGHT

H

HARRIS, MARTIN

Martin Harris (1783–1875), a New York farmer, was one of the Three Witnesses to the divine origin of the Book of Mormon. He also financed the first publication of the Book of Mormon in 1830 at a cost of $3,000 and later helped finance publication of the Book of Commandments.

Martin Harris was born May 18, 1783, in Easton (now Saratoga), Washington County, New York, and died July 10, 1875, in Clarkston, Cache County, Utah. On March 27, 1808, he married his first cousin, Lucy Harris. At least six children were born to the couple. In the War of 1812, Private Harris was a teamster in the Battle of Buffalo. By May 1814, at the Battle of Puttneyville, he was first sergeant in the Thirty-ninth New York Militia. He returned home an honored war veteran. He inherited 150 acres and by 1828 owned a total of 320 acres. His wife characterized him as industrious, attentive to domestic concerns, and an excellent provider and father.

Harris stood about five feet, eight inches tall; had a light complexion, blue eyes, and brown hair; and wore a Greek-style beard off the edge of his jaw and chin. When formally dressed, he wore a favorite gray suit and a large, stiff hat. Non-Mormon contemporaries extolled Harris's sincerity, honesty, memory, generosity, neighborliness, shrewd business practices, and civic spirit.

Harris promoted construction of the Erie Canal through Palmyra along a route that passed not far from his house. Palmyra's citizens elected him road overseer for seven years, and he was a member of Palmyra's vigilance committee. A Jeffersonian-Jacksonian Democrat, he was a believer in the value of homespun common sense. He favored gold and silver money and rejected paper currency. He distrusted banks, Federalists, and authoritarians. A Christian democratic activist, he admired ancient Greek culture and raised money for Greek Christians to fight the Turks.

Looking on himself as an unchurched Christian, Harris chose to follow God on his own. As a "restorationist," he looked for the return of biblical Christianity. He stated that "in the year 1818 . . . I was inspired of the

Martin Harris (1783–1875) at about age eighty-seven. Harris gave financial support to Joseph Smith and for the publication of the Book of Mormon. He served as one of Joseph's scribes, became one of the Three Witnesses of the Book of Mormon, and testified of its truthfulness throughout his life. Used by permission, Utah State Historical Society. Photo no. 12477.

Lord and taught of the Spirit that I should not join any church" (interview by Edward Stevenson, Sept. 4, 1870, Stevenson Microfilm Collection, Vol. 32, HDC).

Martin Harris met Joseph SMITH some time after 1816, when the Smith family moved to Palmyra. By 1824, Joseph Smith, Sr., had told him about the angel Moroni's appearances and the golden plates, and in the fall of 1827, Martin consented to help publish the translation. He helped Joseph Smith protect the plates from thieves and financed the Prophet's move from Manchester to Harmony, Pennsylvania, when persecution intensified.

In February 1828, Harris visited Joseph Smith in Harmony and obtained a transcrip-

tion and translation of characters from the plates. He took the two documents to "learned men" in Utica, Albany, and New York City, where Samuel Latham Mitchill and Charles Anthon examined the texts. Harris and Smith believed that these visits fulfilled a prophecy in Isaiah 29:11–14 concerning a book to be translated by an unlearned man. Harris hoped that the scholars' comments would help win financial and religious support for the Book of Mormon in the comunity (*see* ANTHON TRANSCRIPT).

From April 12 to June 14, 1828, Martin Harris served as Joseph Smith's scribe, producing 116 manuscript pages. To gain family support, he persuaded Joseph to let him take the pages to Palmyra to show his family, and during a three-week period when he visited relatives, attended to business, and served jury duty, the 116 pages were stolen. It is reported that Lucy Harris said that she burned them. Ill and suffering the insecurity of progressive deafness, she reportedly feared that Palmyra's boycott of the Book of Mormon would lead to her and her husband's financial ruin. After the loss of the manuscript, Harris ceased his work as scribe.

In June 1829, Martin Harris, along with Joseph Smith, Oliver COWDERY, and David Whitmer, prayed and received no answer. Harris blamed himself for the failure and withdrew. The Prophet, Cowdery, and Whitmer prayed again and were shown the gold plates of the Book of Mormon by the angel Moroni. Subsequently, the angel appeared to Harris and Joseph Smith. In this vision, Harris heard the voice of God say that Joseph's translation was correct, and Jesus Christ commanded Harris to testify of what he had seen and heard. The testimony of the Three Witnesses is printed in the Book of Mormon (*see* WITNESSES OF THE BOOK OF MORMON).

When translation of the book was completed, Joseph Smith had trouble finding a printer who would undertake publication. The printers feared that local opposition would hurt sales. A Palmyra printer, Egbert B. Grandin, finally agreed to print the Book of Mormon after Harris agreed to mortgage some of his farm for $3,000 as security. On April 7, 1831, Harris sold part of his farm to pay the printing bill, though he may have had other reasons to part with this acreage than just to satisfy Grandin.

Martin Harris was present at the organization of the Church on April 6, 1830, and was baptized that day by Oliver Cowdery. In May 1831 he led fifty converts from Palmyra to Kirtland, Ohio. Lucy and their children remained in Palmyra, resulting in two households and periodic trips for Harris between the two locations.

In the summer of 1831, Harris accompanied Joseph Smith and others to Missouri to purchase property and designate the site for Zion, where the Saints were to gather. He was one of the first to be asked to live the "law of consecration," a divinely revealed plan for equalizing the distribution of property and providing for the poor. That year, he also helped supervise and finance Church publications.

Returning east in 1832, Harris and his brother Emer served a mission together, baptizing one hundred persons at Chenango Point (now Binghamton), New York. In January 1833, Martin Harris was imprisoned briefly in Springville, Pennsylvania, in an attempt to stop him from preaching.

Returning to Kirtland in January 1834, Harris became a member of the first high council of the Church. Later that year, he volunteered to go to Jackson County, Missouri, with Zion's Camp to assist persecuted Mormons. On February 14, 1835, in accord with an earlier revelation (D&C 18:37–38), "the

E. B. Grandin Press, on which pages of the first edition of the Book of Mormon were printed, August 1829 to March 1830, in Palmyra, New York. © by Intellectual Reserve, Inc. Used by permission.

three witnesses" selected the first Quorum of Twelve Apostles.

In 1836, Harris attended the dedication of the Kirtland Temple. Later that summer Lucy Harris died. Harris married Caroline Young, Brigham Young's niece, on November 1, 1836. The couple had seven children.

During 1837, a time of intense conflict within the Church, Harris clashed with Sidney Rigdon and refused to join the Church-sponsored Kirtland Safety Society, which was issuing paper money. Harris was released from the high council on September 3, 1837, and was excommunicated during the last week of December 1837. Although evidence exists that Harris's excommunication was never official, he accepted the action and subsequently applied for and was baptized on November 7, 1842.

When Brigham Young led the body of Latter-day Saints west, Harris went to England to bear witness of the Book of Mormon. The Strangites, a splinter group formed after Joseph Smith's death, paid his expenses, though he did not believe or preach Strangite doctrine. In 1829, Harris had prophesied that the Book of Mormon would be preached in England, and he was eager to preach there himself. Returning to Kirtland, he prospered and acted as a self-appointed guide-caretaker of the deserted Kirtland Temple, listing himself in the 1860 census as "Mormon preacher."

Prior to 1856, LDS missionaries, some of whom had already gone to Utah, the Harris family, and Brigham Young invited Martin and Caroline Harris to join the Saints in Utah. In the spring of 1856, Caroline and the children journeyed to Utah, but Harris remained in Kirtland until 1870. In 1860 he lived with George Harris, his son by Lucy. From 1865 to 1870, he supported himself by leasing ninety acres of land in Kirtland.

In 1869, efforts were renewed to bring Martin Harris to Utah. William H. Homer, Edward Stevenson, Brigham Young, and many other Latter-day Saints helped him financially to make the journey. Still active and vigorous at age eighty-seven, Martin Harris, accompanied by Edward Stevenson, arrived by train in Salt Lake City on August 30, 1870. He accepted rebaptism as evidence of his reaffirmation of faith on September 17, 1870, and, at Brigham Young's invitation, publicly testified of the Book of Mormon. He moved to Harrisville, then to Smithfield, Utah (where he saw Caroline and their son Martin Harris, Jr.), and in 1874 to Clarkston, Utah, where he died on July 10, 1875, after once more bearing testimony of the Book of Mormon.

Martin Harris inspired a folk-hero tradition that has lasted down to the present. In 1983 the Church's musical play *Martin Harris: The Man Who Knew* was produced in Clarkston. The play marked a fourth generation's rehearsal of Martin Harris's witness: "Yes, I did see the plates on which the Book of Mormon was written. I did see the angel, I did hear the voice of God, and I do know that Joseph Smith is a true Prophet of God, holding the keys of the Holy Priesthood" ("The Last Testimony of Martin Harris," recorded by William H. Homer in a statement sworn before J. W. Robinson, Apr. 9, 1927, HDC).

BIBLIOGRAPHY

Anderson, Richard Lloyd. *Investigating the Book of Mormon Witnesses.* Salt Lake City, 1981.

Gunnell, Wayne Cutler. "Martin Harris—Witness and Benefactor to the Book of Mormon." Master's thesis, Brigham Young University, 1955.

James, Rhett Stephens. *The Man Who Knew: The Early Years—A Play about Martin Harris, 1824–1830, and Annotated History of Martin Harris.* Salt Lake City, 1983.

Shelton, Scott R. "Martin Harris in Cache Valley—Events and Influences." Master's thesis, Utah State University, 1986.

Tuckett, Madge Harris, and Belle Harris Wilson. *The Martin Harris Story.* Provo, Utah, 1983.

RHETT STEPHENS JAMES

HELAMAN₁

The first Helaman noted in the Book of Mormon (c. 130 B.C.) was one of the three sons of BENJAMIN, king of the NEPHITES and the people of Zarahemla. He is mentioned only once in connection with his father's efforts to educate him and his brothers, MOSIAH₂ and Helorum. Benjamin taught them both the language of their fathers and the prophecies spoken by their fathers, "that thereby they might become men of understanding" (Mosiah 1:2).

MELVIN J. THORNE

HELAMAN₂

Helaman₂ (c. 100–57 B.C.) was a noted BOOK OF MORMON military commander and prophet. The eldest son of ALMA₂, he was brother to Shiblon and Corianton (Alma 31:7) and father to HELAMAN₃. He became a high priest (Alma 46:38) and was known for teaching REPENTANCE to his people.

While a young man, he remained behind during the mission of his father and brothers to the Zoramites (Alma 31:7), apparently to manage domestic and ecclesiastic affairs in Alma's absence. Later, his father gave him a special blessing, which is often quoted among Latter-day Saints, admonishing him to keep the commandments of God and promising that, if he did so, he would prosper in the land (Alma 36:30; 37:13). Helaman's father also instructed him to continue the record of his people and charged him with the sacred custody of the NEPHITE records, the plates of brass, the twenty-four plates of the JAREDITES, the interpreters, and the LIAHONA, that is, the divine compass that led LEHI's family to the new promised land in the western hemisphere (Alma 37:1–47). Before his father's death, Helaman recorded his father's prophecy concerning the final destruction of the Nephite people (45:9–14).

Although Helaman was known simply as one of the "high priests over the church" (Alma 46:6), apparently he was the chief priest because "Helaman and his brethren" (45:22–23; 46:1, 6; 62:45) or "Helaman and the high priests" (46:38) always performed the ecclesiastical functions; no other presiding high priest is named. When Helaman and his brothers attempted "to establish the church again in all the land" (45:22) after a protracted war with the LAMANITES (43–44), their action triggered civil unrest led by Amalickiah, which in turn embroiled the NEPHITES in one of their most devastating wars.

During Helaman's youth, a large number of Lamanite converts, called Ammonites (see PEOPLES OF THE BOOK OF MORMON), moved to the Nephite territory of Jershon (Alma 27). They swore an oath that they would never again take anyone's life (Alma 24:17–18). Later, when other Lamanites attacked their Nephite protectors, the Ammonites offered to break their oath in order to help the Nephite army defend their families and land. It was "Helaman and his brethren" who persuaded them not to break their covenant. They did welcome 2,060 Ammonite young men, who were not under their parents' oath, who volunteered to fight in the Nephite cause and chose Helaman to lead them (53:10–22; 57:25). Accepting their invitation, he became both military leader and spiritual father, an observation found in Helaman's long letter to his commander MORONI₁ (Alma 56–58). While Helaman led these "stripling soldiers" (53:22) into many battles, none was killed, although all received wounds (56:56; 57:25; 58:39). These young men credited God with their protection and paid solemn tribute to their mothers who had trained them in faith (56:47). During Helaman's military campaign as leader of these young men, he won victory after victory, often capturing enemies without shedding blood. Exhibiting extraordinary ingenuity and character, he always acknowledged God's blessings in his successes (56:19; 57:35; 58:33).

After the war, Helaman returned home and spent his remaining years regulating the affairs of the Church, convincing "many people of their wickedness, which did cause them to repent of their sins and to be baptized unto the Lord their God" (Alma 62:45). An era of peace resulted from his final efforts. He died in 57 B.C.

PAUL R. CHEESMAN

HELAMAN₃

Helaman₃, son of HELAMAN₂, was the record keeper and chief judge in the land of Zarahemla for the fourteen years prior to his death in 39 B.C. Little is known of his personal affairs. He was given charge of NEPHITE historical records by his uncle, Shiblon, in 53 B.C. (Alma 63:11–13), and the book of Helaman in the BOOK OF MORMON takes its name from him.

After the assassination of the chief judge Pacumeni in 50 B.C., Helaman was elected by the people to this highest national office. A murder plot against him was subsequently uncovered, and the would-be assassin, Kishkumen, was mortally wounded. The murderous band, led by Gadianton, escaped into the wilderness. Of Gadianton, MORMON wrote "In the end of this book [Book of Mormon] ye shall see that this Gadianton did prove the overthrow . . . of the people of Nephi" (Hel. 2:13; *see also* SECRET COMBINATIONS).

During the three-year period 48–46 B.C., a substantial number of people left Zarahemla—because of unspecified dissensions—and "went forth unto the land northward" (Hel. 3:3). So extensive was the migration that only a fraction of its impact could be discussed in Mormon's record (Hel. 3:14). Despite dissension, emigration, and war, "Helaman did fill the judgment-seat with justice and equity; yea, he did observe to keep the statutes, and the judgments, and the commandments of God; and he did do that which was right in the sight of God continually; and he did walk after the ways of his father, insomuch that he did prosper in the land" (3:20). During his tenure, tens of thousands of people were baptized into the church, even to the astonishment of the high priests and teachers (3:24–25). Through the force of his personality, Helaman maintained peace throughout two-thirds of his political career.

When Helaman died, he left the spiritual responsibilities and the sacred records in the hands of his son, NEPHI₂ (Hel. 3:37; 5:5–14; 16:25).

BIBLIOGRAPHY

Moss, James R. "Six Nephite Judges." *Ensign* 7 (Sept. 1977): 61–65.

CHRISTINE PURVES BAKER

I

Infant Baptism

LDS Perspective

Children are baptized as members of The Church of Jesus Christ of Latter-day Saints when they reach age eight and receive a bishop's interview to assess their understanding and commitment. This age for baptism was identified by revelation (D&C 68:25, 28). The Church does not baptize infants.

The practice of baptizing infants emerged among Christians in the third century A.D. and was controversial for some time. According to the Book of Mormon, it similarly became an issue and was denounced among the Nephites in the fourth century A.D. When MORMON, a Nephite prophet, inquired of the Lord concerning baptism of little children, he was told that they are incapable of committing sin and that the curse of Adam is removed from them through the atonement of Christ. Hence little children need neither repentance nor baptism (Moro. 8:8–22). They are to be taught "to pray and walk uprightly" so that by the age of accountability their baptism will be meaningful and effective for their lives.

BIBLIOGRAPHY

McConkie, Bruce R. "The Salvation of Little Children." *Ensign* 7 (Apr. 1977): 3–7.

ROBERT E. PARSONS

Isaiah

[*It is the emphasis on Isaiah's words in LDS scripture that necessitates a treatment of his writings under two titles here:*

    Authorship
    Texts in the Book of Mormon

The article Authorship *deals with the issue of the single authorship of the book of Isaiah in light of the existence of an Isaiah text possessed by Book of Mormon peoples as early as 600* B.C. *The article* Texts in the Book of Mormon *focuses on the question of what can be learned about the history of the text of Isaiah's book from the portions preserved in the Book of Mormon.*]

Authorship

Of the writings in the Old Testament, the message of Isaiah enjoys high priority among Latter-day Saints. The attraction derives primarily from the extensive use of Isaiah in the Book of Mormon. Secondarily, chapter 11 of Isaiah was quoted to Joseph Smith in a vision in his earliest days as a prophet (JS—H 1:40) and became the subject of a section in the Doctrine and Covenants (D&C 113). In addition, Jesus Christ has given revelations about, and prophets and apostles of the latter days have frequently quoted from and commented upon Isaiah's words when instructing the Saints.

Traditionally, the book of Isaiah has been ascribed to a prophet living in the kingdom of Judah between 740 and 690 B.C. In Germany during the late 1700s, several scholars challenged this view, claiming that chapters 40–66 were written by one or more other individuals as late as 400 B.C. because of the specific references to events that occurred after Isaiah's death. This outlook now permeates many Bible commentaries and has led to the postulation of a second prophetic writer who is commonly called in scholarly literature "Deutero-Isaiah." Indeed, a wide variety of theories regarding the date and authorship of Isaiah now exist. However, LDS belief in revelation and the seership of prophets, along with the quotations from Isaiah in the Book of Mormon and its admonitions to study his writings, have reinforced Latter-day Saints in the traditional view concerning the date and authorship of Isaiah, in the following ways.

First, while some scholars argue that prophets could not see the future and that, therefore, the later chapters of Isaiah must have been written after Isaiah's time (e.g., Isa. 45 concerning Cyrus), Latter-day Saints recognize that prophets can see and prophesy about the future. In chapters 40–66, Isaiah prophesies of the future, just as the apostle John does in Revelation 4–22, and the prophet Nephi₁ in 2 Nephi 25–30.

Second, the Book of Mormon prophet

Lehi and his family left Jerusalem about 600 B.C. and took with them scriptural writings on plates of brass that contained much of the Old Testament, including Isaiah (1 Ne. 5:13; 19:22–23). Book of Mormon prophets taught from the brass plate records, not only from chapters 1–39, which are usually assigned by scholars to the prophet Isaiah of the eighth century B.C., but also from the later chapters, the so-called Deutero-Isaiah. For example, Isaiah chapters 48–54 are all quoted in the Book of Mormon, with some passages mentioned a number of times (1 Ne. 20–21; 2 Ne. 6:16–8:25; Mosiah 12:21–24; 14; 15:29–31; 3 Ne. 16:18–20; 20:32–45; 22). Hence, the existence of a virtually complete Isaiah text in the late seventh century B.C., as witnessed by the Book of Mormon, negates arguments for later multiple authorship, whether those arguments be historical, theological, or literary.

Finally, other significant witnesses exist for the single authorship of Isaiah, including Jesus Christ in particular (cf. Matt. 13:14–15; 15:7–9; Luke 4:17–19; 3 Ne. 16, 20–22). Indeed, after quoting much from Isaiah 52 (3 Ne. 16:18–20; 20:32–45) and repeating Isaiah 54 in its entirety (3 Ne. 22), the resurrected Jesus Christ admonished his Book of Mormon disciples to study Isaiah's words and then said, "A commandment I give unto you that ye search these things diligently; for great are the words of Isaiah. For surely he spake as touching all things concerning my people which are of the house of Israel" (3 Ne. 23:1–2).

Jewish and Christian traditions from the earliest times have supported the single authorship of Isaiah. The Septuagint, the Dead Sea Scrolls, and other ancient texts also give no hint of multiple authorship. Latter-day Saints accept the words of the risen Jesus that Isaiah was a seer and revelator whose prophecies, as recorded throughout his book, will eventually all be fulfilled (3 Ne. 23:1–3). Particularly from Jesus' attribution of Isaiah 52 and 54 to the ancient prophet have Latter-day Saints concluded that the book of Isaiah is the inspired work of the eighth-century prophet Isaiah, son of Amoz.

BIBLIOGRAPHY

Adams, Larry L., and Alvin C. Rencher. "A Computer Analysis of the Isaiah Authorship Problem." *BYU Studies* 15 (Autumn 1974): 95–102.

Anderson, Francis I. "Style and Authorship." *The Tyndale Paper* 21 (June 1976): 2.

Gileadi, Avraham. *A Holistic Structure of the Book of Isaiah*. Ph.D. diss., Brigham Young University, 1981.

Kissane, E. J. *The Book of Isaiah*, 2 vols. Dublin, Ireland, 1941, 1943.

Ludlow, Victor L. *Isaiah: Prophet, Seer, and Poet*. Salt Lake City, 1981.

Tvedtnes, John A. "Isaiah Variants in the Book of Mormon." In *Isaiah and the Prophets*, ed. M. Nyman. Provo, Utah, 1984.

Young, Edward J. *Introduction to the Old Testament*. Grand Rapids, Mich., 1949.

ADDITIONAL SOURCES

Brewster, Hoyt W. *Isaiah Plain and Simple: The Message of Isaiah in the Book of Mormon*. Salt Lake City: Deseret Book, 1995.

Parry, Donald W., and John W. Welch, eds. *Isaiah in the Book of Mormon*. Provo, Utah: FARMS, 1998.

VICTOR L. LUDLOW

Texts in the Book of Mormon

The Isaiah texts quoted in the Book of Mormon are unique. They are the only extant Isaiah texts that have no "original" language source with which the translation can be textually compared. These English texts date to the translation and initial publication of the Book of Mormon (1829).

These Isaiah texts were quoted and paraphrased by many Book of Mormon prophets who had a copy of Isaiah on the PLATES of brass. Attempts to determine the authenticity of those Book of Mormon Isaiah texts by comparing them with Hebrew, Greek, and Latin texts of Isaiah hold interest, but such efforts are moot because the ancient texts behind the Book of Mormon Isaiah translation are not available for study. However, much can be learned by comparing the numerous ancient versions and translations of Isaiah with the Book of Mormon Isaiah texts. Such comparisons result in granting the Book of Mormon Isaiah full recensional status.

The Isaiah materials in the Book of Mormon exhibit many similarities to those in the King James translation of the Bible, which would seem to indicate that both share a Hebrew Masoretic origin. However, many other peculiarities in the Book of Mormon texts point to an origin related to texts similar to those from which the Greek Septuagint and the Latin Vulgate were derived. These peculiar readings are significant enough that they preclude relegating the Book of Mormon Isaiah texts to being a mere copy of the King James Version. The Isaiah texts found in English translation in the Book of Mormon possess a distinctive character that indicates a unique textual origin. The important question is not, "Are the Book of Mormon Isaiah texts authentic?" Rather, the issue is, "Do the Book of Mormon Isaiah texts provide clear evidence of variant texts besides those normally acknowledged?" Should they not be considered as valid as, say, the Dead Sea Isaiah texts?

One of the major criticisms of the Book of Mormon Isaiah texts is that they contain parts

Isaiah Passages in the Book of Mormon
Listed by Book of Mormon Reference*

Direct Quotations

1 Nephi 20:1–21:26	Isaiah 48:1–49:26
2 Nephi 6:6–7	Isaiah 49:22–23
2 Nephi 6:16–8:25	Isaiah 49:24–52:2
2 Nephi 9:50	Isaiah 55:1
2 Nephi 12:1–24:32	Isaiah 2:1–14:32
2 Nephi 26:18	Isaiah 29:5
2 Nephi 27:2–5	Isaiah 29:6–10
2 Nephi 27:25–35	Isaiah 29:13–24
2 Nephi 30:9	Isaiah 11:4
2 Nephi 30:11–15	Isaiah 11:5–9
Mosiah 12:21–24	Isaiah 52:7–10
Mosiah 14:1–12	Isaiah 53:1–12
Mosiah 15:6	Isaiah 53:7
Mosiah 15:29–31	Isaiah 52:8–10
3 Nephi 16:18–20	Isaiah 52:8–10
3 Nephi 20:32	Isaiah 52:8
3 Nephi 20:34–35	Isaiah 52:9–10
3 Nephi 20:36–38	Isaiah 52:1–3
3 Nephi 20:39–40	Isaiah 52:6–7
3 Nephi 20:41–45	Isaiah 52:11–15
3 Nephi 21:8	Isaiah 52:15
3 Nephi 22:1–17	Isaiah 54:1–17

Paraphrases

1 Nephi 10:8	Isaiah 40:3
1 Nephi 13:37	Isaiah 52:7
1 Nephi 14:7	Isaiah 29:14
1 Nephi 17:36	Isaiah 45:18
1 Nephi 22:6	Isaiah 49:22–23
1 Nephi 22:8	Isaiah 29:14
1 Nephi 22:8	Isaiah 49:22–23
1 Nephi 22:10	Isaiah 52:10
1 Nephi 22:11	Isaiah 52:10
2 Nephi 6:15	Isaiah 29:6
2 Nephi 9:51	Isaiah 55:2
2 Nephi 25:17	Isaiah 11:11
2 Nephi 25:17	Isaiah 29:14
2 Nephi 26:15–16	Isaiah 29:3–4
2 Nephi 26:17	Isaiah 29:11
2 Nephi 26:25	Isaiah 55:1
2 Nephi 27:6–9	Isaiah 29:4
2 Nephi 27:15–19	Isaiah 29:11–12
2 Nephi 27:25	Isaiah 29:13
2 Nephi 28:9	Isaiah 29:15
2 Nephi 28:14	Isaiah 29:13
2 Nephi 28:16	Isaiah 29:21
2 Nephi 28:30	Isaiah 28:10
2 Nephi 28:30	Isaiah 28:13
2 Nephi 29:1	Isaiah 11:11
2 Nephi 29:1	Isaiah 29:14
2 Nephi 29:2	Isaiah 5:26
2 Nephi 29:2	Isaiah 49:22
2 Nephi 29:3	Isaiah 5:26
Mosiah 15:10	Isaiah 53:10
Mosiah 15:14	Isaiah 52:7
Mosiah 15:15–18	Isaiah 52:7
Helaman 12:16	Isaiah 51:10
Helaman 12:16	Isaiah 44:27
3 Nephi 21:29	Isaiah 52:12
Moroni 10:31	Isaiah 52:1–2
Moroni 10:31	Isaiah 54:2

*From John W. Welch and J. Gregory Welch, *Charting the Book of Mormon: Visual Aids for Personal Study and Teaching* (Provo, Utah: FARMS, 1999), chart 97.

of what have come to be termed "First Isaiah" and "Deutero-Isaiah" by Bible scholars. It is evident that the Book of Mormon Isaiah texts provide evidence contravening modern theories of multiple authorship of Isaiah's book (*see* ISAIAH: AUTHORSHIP); for if the origins of the Isaiah material in the Book of Mormon are accepted as stated by its authors, then by 600 B.C. the book of Isaiah was essentially as it is today. The chief value of textual criticism, in this case, is to help identify special themes and language patterns, that is, to provide a better understanding of the message, not a determination of authorship. The most viable and certainly the most productive option for determining the origin of the Book of Mormon Isaiah texts is therefore an internal examination.

The Book of Mormon indicates that in "the first year of the reign of Zedekiah, king of Judah" (1 Ne. 1:4) the prophet NEPHI$_1$ and his brothers retrieved from Jerusalem a "record" written by their ancestors on plates of brass (1 Ne. 3–4), which they carried with them to the Western Hemisphere. Included in the record were prophecies of Isaiah (1 Ne. 19:22–23; cf. 5:13). All of the Isaiah texts in the Book of Mormon are quotations from that record, except perhaps those cited by the risen Jesus (cf. 1 Ne. 16, 21–22). Whether quoting directly or paraphrasing, Book of Mormon prophets were trying to do two things: "persuade [people] to believe in the Lord their Redeemer" (1 Ne. 19:23) and reveal the plans of God for his people, as noted by the prophet Isaiah (e.g., 2 Ne. 25:7; Hel. 8:18–20; 3 Ne. 23:1–2). These features give a singular quality to the Isaiah texts of the Book of Mormon, because it preserves almost exclusively the texts pertaining to salvation and saving principles and ignores Isaiah's historical material. The concerns of Book of Mormon prophets were doctrinal, and passages were utilized to expound their testimonies. Moreover, the passages that concern salvation from the later chapters of Isaiah are presented to show that Jesus was the promised Messiah (cf. Mosiah 13:33–15:31, which cites Isa. 53; 52:7, 8–10). While nineteenth-century biblical scholarship held that the concept of a "saving Messiah" arose after the Babylonian exile (587–538 B.C.) and therefore the later chapters of Isaiah are to be dated to the end of the sixth century or later, the Book of Mormon texts obviously undermine that theory.

Minor changes in the Book of Mormon Isaiah texts have been made since the publication of the work in 1830. These changes in recent editions have attempted to correct early errors in printing and to bring the Isaiah texts of the present edition into "conformity with prepublication manuscripts and early editions edited by the Prophet Joseph Smith" ("A Brief Explanation about the Book of Mormon," 1981 edition of the Book of Mormon). None of these changes has been substantive.

BIBLIOGRAPHY

Eissfeldt, Otto. *The Old Testament: An Introduction*, pp. 303–46. New York, 1965.

Nibley, Hugh W. *Since Cumorah*, pp. 111–34. In CWHN 7.

Sperry, Sidney B. *Answers to Book of Mormon Questions*. Salt Lake City, 1967.

Tvedtnes, John A. "The Isaiah Variants in the Book of Mormon." *FARMS* Paper. Provo, Utah, 1981.

LEGRANDE DAVIES

ISHMAEL

Little is known of the Book of Mormon Ishmael. An Ephraimite from Jerusalem (cf. *JD* 23:184), he cooperated in fulfilling God's command (brought to him from the wilderness by Lehi's sons) that he, his wife, five daughters, two sons, and their households travel into the wilderness to join the exodus of the prophet LEHI from Jerusalem about 600 B.C. (1 Ne. 7:2–5).

While en route to Lehi's camp, a division arose in which four of Ishmael's children collaborated with LAMAN and Lemuel, the older sons of Lehi, against the others of their party. A reprimand by NEPHI₁, the fourth son of Lehi, provoked them to bind him and threaten to leave him to die. Their hearts were softened toward him only when other members of Ishmael's family pleaded for Nephi's safety (1 Ne. 7:6–21).

After joining with Lehi in the valley of Lemuel, Nephi, his brothers, and ZORAM married the daughters of Ishmael (1 Ne. 16:7). As the journey continued Ishmael died and "was buried in the place which was called Nahom" (16:34). Ishmael's death and the combination of other adversities caused such grieving among his children that they again complained against Lehi and Nephi, repenting only after the voice of the Lord chastened them (16:34–39).

CHRISTINE PURVES BAKER

J

JACOB, SON OF LEHI

Jacob was the fifth son of LEHI and Sariah and the elder of the two sons born during the days of his parents' wilderness tribulation. His birth apparently occurred soon after the family left Jerusalem (c. 599 B.C.). Jacob's life demonstrated him to be a spiritual leader: He was a defender of the faith, keeper of the sacred records, visionary, doctrinal teacher, expressive writer, and plainspoken servant of Christ.

From birth, Jacob was a child of affliction. As Lehi's firstborn in the wilderness, he never knew the family's earlier life in Jerusalem or indeed any period of sustained family harmony. Rather, he grew up knowing only the hardships of a nomadic life, coupled with deepening dissensions between his two oldest brothers and the rest of the family—conflicts that would erupt into open violence before Jacob was forty years old (2 Ne. 5:34). This bitter family strife, which nearly killed his parents from grief on the sea voyage from the Near East to the Western Hemisphere, deeply distressed young Jacob as well. Nephi records that Jacob and his younger brother,

Joseph, "grieved because of the afflictions of their mother" while on the ship (1 Ne. 18:19). Lehi told young Jacob in a farewell blessing, "Thou hast suffered afflictions and much sorrow, because of the rudeness of thy brethren" (2 Ne. 2:1). Nevertheless, Lehi assured him that God "shall consecrate thine afflictions for thy gain" (2 Ne. 2:2).

Long affliction seems to have rendered Jacob all the more spiritually sensitive, and he became one of the most profound doctrinal teachers in the Book of Mormon. Near the time of his death, he summarized the harsh, melancholic conditions of his life in words of haunting beauty and deep humanity: "Our lives passed away like as it were unto us a dream, we being a lonesome and a solemn people, wanderers, cast out from Jerusalem, born in tribulation, in a wilderness, and hated of our brethren, which caused wars and contentions; wherefore, we did mourn out our days" (Jacob 7:26).

Lehi blessed Jacob to spend his days in the service of God and to live safely with NEPHI₁ (2 Ne. 2:3). From his youth to his death, Jacob indeed labored in the Lord's service (2 Ne. 5:26; Jacob 1:18), working closely with Nephi for many years. Nephi consecrated him a priest and a teacher (Jacob 1:18; 2 Ne. 5:26; 6:2), recorded one of his sermons (2 Ne. 6–10), and gave him a stewardship over the records on the small PLATES and other sacred objects (Jacob 1:2). This latter fact had notable consequences for the Book of Mormon, for all subsequent authors of the small plates were direct descendants of Jacob (*see* BOOK OF MORMON: BOOK OF ENOS; BOOK OF JAROM; BOOK OF OMNI).

Jacob was a powerful personal witness of the anticipated Redeemer, which was his most prominent theme. Nephi noted that "Jacob, also has seen him [the premortal Christ] as I have seen him" (2 Ne. 11:3), and Lehi indicated that it was in his youth that Jacob had beheld the glory of the Lord (2 Ne. 2:4). So firm was Jacob's faith in Christ that Sherem, an ANTICHRIST, could not shake him by subtle argument, for, declared Jacob, "I truly had seen angels, and they had ministered unto me. And also, I had heard the voice of the Lord speaking unto me in very word, from time to time" (Jacob 7:5; cf. 7:12). Jacob was the first Nephite prophet to reveal that the Savior would be called Christ, having received that information from an angel (2 Ne. 10:3). He characterized his ministry as persuading his people to come unto Christ (Jacob 1:7). Likewise, he explained that he wrote on the plates so that future generations "may know that we knew of Christ, and we had a hope of his glory many hundred years before his coming" (Jacob 4:1–4). (Note: "Christ" is a Greek-English title, equivalent to Hebrew "Messiah," and it means "anointed," that is, divinely appointed as the Savior of mankind.)

A second prominent theme in the book of Jacob is the scattering and subsequent gathering of Israel. Jacob spoke often and longingly of the Lord's promises to scattered Israel. In his first sermon in the Book of Mormon, Jacob quoted and commented extensively on Isaiah

50 about Israel's restoration (2 Ne. 6–8), assuring his people that "the Lord remembereth all them who have been broken off, wherefore he remembereth us also" (2 Ne. 10:22). Likewise, Jacob quoted the words of a prophet named ZENOS, in which God's love for the scattered branches of Israel was depicted through an allegory of the olive trees. "How merciful is our God unto us," exclaimed Jacob as he explained the allegory to his people, "for he remembereth the house of Israel, both roots and branches" (Jacob 6:4).

Jacob employed a unique style, the distinctive features of which are conspicuous in an exhortation in which he condemned the pride, materialism, and unchastity of his people. He began his sermon by confessing his "anxiety" over his people and over his painful duty to rebuke them for their sins (Jacob 2:3). In like fashion, Jacob prefaced his two other discourses by alluding to his "anxiety" (2 Ne. 6:3; Jacob 4:18). No other Book of Mormon prophet so begins a sermon; indeed, half the references to "anxiety" in the Book of Mormon occur in his writing.

Jacob's stylistic stamp is also evident in other features throughout his writings, which are replete with a vivid, intimate vocabulary either unique to him or disproportionally present. Two-thirds of the uses of "grieve" and "tender" (or their derivatives) are attributable to Jacob. Likewise, he is the only Book of Mormon author to use "delicate," "contempt," "lonesome," "sobbings," "dread," and "daggers." He deploys this last term in a metaphor about spiritual anguish: "daggers placed to pierce their souls and wound their delicate minds" (Jacob 2:9). Similarly, Jacob alone uses "wound" in reference to emotions, and never uses it (as do many others) to describe a physical injury. Jacob uses "pierce" or its variants four of nine instances in the Book of Mormon, and he alone uses it in a spiritual sense.

Such stylistic evidence suggests that Jacob lived close to his feelings and was gifted in expressing them. Moreover, the complex consistency of his style, linking as it does widely separated passages from two different books (2 Nephi and Jacob), bears out the portrait of the man that emerges from the narrative. Story, style, and subject matter all reveal Jacob, Lehi's child of tribulation, to have become a sensitive and effective poet-prophet, preacher, writer, and powerful witness of Jesus Christ.

BIBLIOGRAPHY

Matthews, Robert J. "Jacob: Prophet, Theologian, Historian." In *The Book of Mormon: Jacob through Words of Mormon, To Learn With Joy*, ed. M. Nyman and C. Tate, Jr., pp. 33–53. Provo, Utah, 1990.

Tanner, John S. "Literary Reflections on Jacob and His Descendants." In *The Book of Mormon: Jacob through Words of Mormon, To Learn With Joy*, ed. M. Nyman and C. Tate, Jr., pp. 251–69.

Warner, C. Terry. "Jacob." *Ensign* 6 (Oct. 1976): 24–30.

JOHN S. TANNER

JAREDITES

The Jaredites are a people described in the book of Ether (*see* BOOK OF MORMON: BOOK OF ETHER) whose name derives from their first leader, Jared. The Jaredites date to the time of the great tower mentioned in the Old Testament (Gen. 11:1–9), which was built in or around Mesopotamia. Led by God, the Jaredites left their homeland for a new land somewhere in the Americas, and there they established a kingdom. They grew to be a numerous population with kings and prophets, and, like the NEPHITES after them, were eventually annihilated by internecine war evidently sometime between 600 and 300 B.C. Their story was recorded by their last prophet, Ether. Around A.D. 400, the last Nephite survivor, MORONI$_2$, abridged the record of Ether and appended his summary to the account of the Nephites that had been prepared by his father, MORMON. Although the record is brief, it hints at an epic genre rooted in the ancient Near East.

The Jaredite origin in the Old World probably dates to the third millennium B.C., which due to the scarcity of historical material presents obstacles to the use of comparative literature or archaeology. Parallels with the ancient Near East can only be described in general forms, and no artifacts or writings identifiable as Jaredite have ever been found outside the Book of Mormon. But while parallels may be nebulous, certain Jaredite terms and names refer to practices, objects, or places in the ancient Near East. Several types, and a few specifics, may be analyzed in order to better understand the Jaredites and their civilization.

The principal theme of the Jaredite story is familiar in the genre of the ancient Near East. God calls a man to lead his people to a new and a promised land. Once settled in the land, the people alternate between stages of good and evil, relying on their king for guidance. When the king is good, the people tend to be good and follow God; when the king is evil, so too are the people. While parallels to the literature of the ancient Near East, especially the Old Testament, are apparent, the Jaredite narrative is unique in that the first leader, Jared, was not the one who received the call from God, but his brother (*see* BROTHER OF JARED). The roles of the two men differ, as do the roles of king and prophet in the Old Testament. From the earliest days after arriving in America, the Jaredites had a monarchical government apparently patterned after Bronze Age Mesopotamian society.

The story of the Jaredites has an epic flavor. Stories of heroes, kings, and princes who perform great deeds dominate the book of Ether. The heroes are great warriors who win decisive battles. Accounts dealing with cycles of life and death, good and evil, prosperity and hardship are the types of things that were done and written about in the epics in the book of Ether and the epics of the ancient Near East (CWHN 5:283–443).

The book of Ether begins with a genealogy spanning at least thirty generations, from the final prophet and historian Ether back to Jared. The list is reminiscent of genealogies in Old Testament or king lists common to antiquity. The thirty listed by name are:

Name	Number
Jared	1
Orihah	2
Kib	3
Shule	4
Omer	5
Emer	6
Coriantum	7
Com	8
Heth	9
Shez	10
Riplakish	11
Morianton	12
Kim	13
Levi	14
Corom	15
Kish	16
Lib	17
Hearthom	18
Heth	19
Aaron	20
Amnigaddah	21
Coriantum	22
Com	23
Shiblon(m)	24
Seth	25
Ahah	26
Ethem	27
Moron	28
Coriantor	29
Ether	30

Except for the lengthy accounts concerning the first and the last of these figures, all information about the people in this lineage is found in Ether, chapters 7–11. This dynasty endured for many centuries, always passing directly from father to son, except possibly in the case of Morianton, who was "a descendant of Riplakish," following him by an interval of "many years" (Ether 10:9).

The Jaredites crossed the sea to the New World in eight "barges" in 344 days, driven by currents and winds. Their route is unknown. Perhaps coincidentally, the North Pacific current takes about the same time to cross from Japan to Mexico (Sorenson, p. 111). The question of ancient long-distance sea travel has been much debated, but extensive indications have been found of pre-Columbian transoceanic voyaging (Sorenson and Raish). The Bering land bridge "is no longer recognized as the only scientifically acceptable theory to explain the means and timing of human entry into the New World" (Dixon, p. 27).

The design of the Jaredite barges is unclear. They were built according to instructions given by God. Ether described them as being "light upon the water" like a fowl (Ether 2:16). They were "tight like unto a dish; and the ends thereof were peaked." To allow light and air inside they had some sort of a "hole in the top, and also in the bottom" (Ether 2:17, 20). Ether also compared the barges with Noah's ark (Ether 6:7). Thus it may be relevant that Utnapishtim, the Sumerian Noah in the *Epic of Gilgamesh*, similarly is said to have built his boat with a ceiling and water plugs, and to have waterproofed the entire inside with bitumen. Utnapishtim's story also recounts the raging winds that slammed water into the mountains and people, vividly paralleling the Jaredites' experience of being driven by a furious wind (Ether 6:6).

Stones were made to shine by the touch of God's finger to light these barges. Shining stones are not unique to the book of Ether. One reference to a shining stone in Noah's ark appears in the Jerusalem Talmud, stating that a stone in the ark shone brighter in the night than in the day so that Noah could distinguish the times of day (*Pesachim* I, 1; discussed in CWHN 6:337–38, 349). Shining stones were also said to be present in the Syrian temple of the goddess Aphek (see CWHN 5:373) and are mentioned several times in the pseudepigraphic *Pseudo-Philo* (e.g., 25:12).

Little original detail remains about the culture of the Jaredite people. Some of them were obviously literate. While their royalty was strictly hereditary, sons sometimes deposed their fathers or were rivals to their brothers. Kings held their opponents in captivity for long periods, entered into SECRET COMBINATIONS, and waged battles. The record indicates that some of these kings were "anointed" (e.g., Ether 6:27; 9:4; 10:10), sat upon beautiful thrones (Ether 10:6), and had concubines (Ether 10:5–6). Their economy was basically agrarian. They were settled people, the ruling lines living most of their long history in a single land called Moron, somewhere near and north of what would later be called the Nephite "narrow neck of land." In some eras, the Jaredites built many cities and buildings (Ether 9:23; 10:5–12, 20). One of their kings "saw the Son of Righteousness" (Ether 9:22). They once fought off a plague of poisonous snakes that came upon the land as a curse (Ether 10:19). At times they mined several ores (e.g., gold, silver, iron, copper) and made metal weapons and tools (Ether 7:9; 10:23–25; *see* ECONOMY AND TECHNOLOGY). "Elephants" were useful to them (Ether 9:19). This may refer to the mastodon or mammoth, but it is not possible to date the final disappearance of these animals in the New World. A section in the book of Ether talks of the hunt (10:19–21), a common pattern known in the Near East of the king who is also hunter. In this passage, the Jaredite king Lib designated the land to the south as a hunting preserve. An early Mesopotamian example of a royal hunter is Nimrod, who comes from about the same period as Jared. Other Jaredite parallels are of interest. The dance of Jared's daughter for the life of Omer (Ether 8:10) has been compared with similar incidents from ancient lore (CWHN 5:213).

The theophany of the brother of Jared, in which he sees the finger of the Lord, parallels the story of MOSES. The brother of Jared goes up a mountain to pray (Ether 3:1; cf. Ex. 3:1–3); sees the finger of the Lord (Ether 3:6; cf. Ex. 31:18); fears the Lord (also meaning "held in awe"; Ether 3:6; cf. Ex. 3:6); sees the whole spirit body of the Lord (Ether 3:13, 16–18; cf. Ex. 33:11); learns the name of the Lord (Ether 3:14; cf. Ex. 3:14); and, finally, receives a symbol of power and authority (Ether 3:23; cf. Ex. 4:1–5). The unique aspect of the story of the brother of Jared is his extended revelation concerning the nature of God, who appeared to him in a spirit body "like unto flesh and blood" (Ether 3:6).

Some Jaredite prophets were apparently similar to the prophets in biblical Israel. They condemned idolatry and wickedness, and foretold the annihilation of the society and destruction of the people unless they repented. Although some prophets received the protection of the government, most were rejected by the people, and, like Ether, were forced to hide for fear of their lives. Ether's prophecies looked beyond the despair of the final destruction of his people toward the future destiny of the Jaredite land. He foresaw it as the place of "the New Jerusalem, which should come down out of heaven, and the holy sanctuary of the Lord" (Ether 13:3).

The final battle reported by Ether took place at the hill Ramah, the same place where

Mormon later buried the sacred Nephite records (Ether 15:11). The war involved two vast armies, and hostilities continued several days until all the soldiers and one of the kings were slain. An exhausted Coriantumr culminated his victory over Shiz by decapitating him. Near Eastern examples of decapitation of enemies are evident in early art and literature, as on the Narmer palette; and decapitation of captured kings is represented in ancient Mesoamerica (Warren, pp. 230–33). Coriantumr was later discovered by the people of Zarahemla (Mulekites), with whom he lived for "nine moons" (Omni 1:21). Ether's plates (historical records), together with the decayed remains from the final Jaredite battle were later found by a group of lost Nephites who were searching for the city of Zarahemla (Mosiah 8:8–11).

Ether writes of the annihilation of his people, but this was not necessarily an extermination of the entire population. One may assume that many of the commoners were not in the two armies and thus survived after these wars. The Jaredite people were crushed and dispersed, but probably not exterminated, since explicit features of Jaredite culture (especially personal names) were later evident in the Nephite culture (CWHN 5:237–41; Sorenson, p. 119).

The similarity between the Jaredite and Nephite histories is striking. But the similarity may be chiefly one of literary convention, which Moroni used to compare the two peoples. Other than possessing similar epic tales of people who were led across the sea to build kingdoms that eventually fell, the underlying cultures were probably quite different; for example, the Jaredite laws and government predate the LAW OF MOSES, and thus their system of justice was different from that of the Israelites and Nephites.

The message drawn by Moroni from the histories of the Jaredites and the Nephites is, however, the same: God revealed himself to both peoples. He gave both a land of promise, where their prosperity was conditioned on righteousness. Both met their demise because of wickedness and secret combinations, and both endings are included in the Book of Mormon to teach this hard-learned lesson. Concerning this, Moroni states: "The Lord worketh not in secret combinations, neither doth he will that man should shed blood, but in all things hath forbidden it, from the beginning of man" (Ether 8:19).

BIBLIOGRAPHY

Hugh Nibley provides material on the Jaredites in *The World of the Jaredites* and *There Were Jaredites*, in Vol. 5 of CWHN; see also CWHN 6:329–58; reviewed and updated by D. Honey, "Ecological Nomadism Versus Epic Heroism in Ether," *Review of Books on the Book of Mormon* 2 (1990): 143–63.

On the epic genre, see H. Munro Chadwick, *The Growth of Literature*, 3 vols. (Cambridge, England, 1932–1940), especially Vol. 1; Samuel Noah Kramer, "New Light on the Early History of the Ancient Near East," *American Journal of Archaeology* 52 (1948): 156–64; David M. Knipe, "Epics," in *Encyclopedia of Religion*, Vol. 5, pp. 127–32, and T. G. Panches, "Heroes and Hero-Gods (Babylonian)," in James Hastings, ed., *Encyclopedia of Religion and Ethics*, Vol. 6, pp. 642–46 (New York, 1951).

Concerning kingship in the ancient Near East, see Henri Frankfort, *Kingship and the Gods* (Chicago, 1948). An English translation of the story of Noah's lighted stones may be found in Louis Ginzberg, ed., *The Legends of the Jews*, Vol. 1, pp. 162–63 (Philadelphia, 1937).

On possible ancient connections between the Old World and the New, see John L. Sorenson and Martin H. Raish, *Pre-Columbian Contact with the Americas across the Oceans: An Annotated Bibliography* (Provo, Utah, 1990). See also Cyrus H. Gordon, *Before Columbus: Links between the Old World and Ancient America* (New York, 1971); Carroll L. Riley, et al., eds., *Man across the Sea: Problems of Pre-Columbian Contacts* (Austin, 1971), especially the chapter by Sorenson. See also E. James Dixon, "The Origins of the First Americans," *Archaeology* 38, no. 2 (1985): 22–27; Thor Heyerdahl, *Early Man and the Ocean* (Garden City, N.Y., 1979); and Bruce W. Warren, "Secret Combinations, Warfare, and Captive Sacrifice in Mesoamerica and the Book of Mormon," in S. Ricks and W. Hamblin, eds., *Warfare in the Book of Mormon*, pp. 225–36 (Salt Lake City, 1990).

John L. Sorenson, *An Ancient American Setting for the Book of Mormon* (Salt Lake City, 1985), guides the reader through the archaeology of Mesoamerica and proposes possible Jaredite locations in areas occupied at comparable times, during the early and middle preclassic periods in Mexico, which include the Olmec civilization.

ADDITIONAL SOURCE

Sorenson, John L. "New Discoveries in Mexico on the Jaredite Period." *Insights: An Ancient Window*, March 1991, 2.

MORGAN W. TANNER

JESUS CHRIST

Jesus Christ is the central figure in the doctrine of The Church of Jesus Christ of Latter-day Saints. The Prophet Joseph SMITH explained that "the fundamental principles of our religion are the testimony of the Apostles and Prophets, concerning Jesus Christ, that He died, was buried, and rose again the third day, and ascended into heaven; and all other things which pertain to our religion are only appendages to it" (*TPJS*, p. 121). Latter-day Saints believe that complete salvation is possible only through the life, death, resurrection, doctrines, and ordinances of Jesus Christ and in no other way.

Christ's relationship to mankind is defined in terms of his divine roles in the three phases of existence—premortal, mortal, and postmortal.

PREMORTAL JESUS. In the premortal life, Jesus Christ, whose main title was Jehovah, was the firstborn spirit child of God the Father and thus the eldest brother and preeminent above all other spirit children of God. In that first estate, he came to be more intelligent than all other spirits, one "like unto God" (Abr. 3:19, 24), and served as the representative of the Father in the creation of "worlds without number" (Heb. 1:1–3; D&C 76:24; Moses 1:33; 7:30). LDS leaders have declared that all revelation since the FALL OF ADAM has been by, and through, Jehovah (Jesus Christ) and that whenever the Father has appeared unto man, it has been to introduce and bear record of the Son (JST John 1:19; DS 1:27). He was known to Adam, and the patriarchs from Adam to Noah worshiped him in humble reverence. He was the Almighty God of Abraham, Isaac, and Jacob, the God-Lawgiver on Sinai, the Holy One of Israel. Scriptural records affirm that all the prophets from the beginning spoke or wrote of the time when Jehovah would come to earth in the form of man, in the role of a messiah. Peter said, "to him give all the prophets witness" (Acts 2:25–31; 10:43). Jacob taught that "none of the prophets have written, nor prophesied, save they have spoken concerning this Christ" (Jacob 7:11; cf. Mosiah 3:5–10; 13:33; 3 Ne. 20:24).

MORTAL JESUS. Jehovah was born into this life in Bethlehem of Judea and grew up as Jesus of Nazareth. He came in condescension—

leaving his station as the Lord Omnipotent to undertake a mission of pain and humiliation, having everlasting consequences for mankind (see 1 Ne. 11; Mosiah 3:5–10; *see also* CONDESCENSION OF GOD). His life was one of moral perfection—he was sinless and completely submissive to the will of the Father (John 5:30; 2 Cor. 5:21; Heb. 4:15; 1 Pet. 2:22; Mosiah 15:2). Jesus is the model and exemplar of all who seek to acquire the divine nature. As taught by Joseph Smith, the Savior "suffered greater sufferings, and was exposed to more powerful contradictions than any man can be." Through all of this, "he kept the law of God, and remained without sin" (*Lectures on Faith*, Lecture 5, paragraph 2). The risen Lord asked the Nephites, "What manner of men ought ye to be? Verily I say unto you, even as I am" (3 Ne. 27:27; cf. 12:48).

Jesus was more, however, than sinlessness, goodness, and love. He was more than a model and teacher, more than the embodiment of compassion. He was able to accomplish his unique ministry—a ministry of reconciliation and salvation—because of who and what he was. President Ezra Taft Benson stated, "The Church of Jesus Christ of Latter-day Saints proclaims that Jesus Christ is the Son of God in the most literal sense. The body in which He performed His mission in the flesh was fathered by that same Holy Being we worship as God, our Eternal Father. Jesus was not the son of Joseph, nor was He begotten by the Holy Ghost. He is the Son of the Eternal Father!" (Benson, p. 4). From Mary, a mortal woman, Jesus inherited mortality, including the capacity to die. From his exalted Father he inherited immortality, the capacity to live forever. The Savior's dual nature—man and God—enabled him to make an infinite atonement, an accomplishment that no other person, no matter how capable or gifted, could do (cf. Alma 34:9–12). First, he

was able, in Gethsemane, in some majestic but incomprehensible manner, to assume the burdens and effects of the sins of all mankind and, in doing so, to engage suffering and anguish beyond what a mere mortal could endure (2 Ne. 9:21; Mosiah 3:7; D&C 18:11; 19:16; Taylor, p. 148). Second, he was able to submit to physical death, to willingly lay down his life and then take up his body again in the RESURRECTION (John 5:26; 10:17, 18; 2 Ne. 2:8).

POSTMORTAL JESUS. Latter-day Saints believe that between his death on the cross at Calvary and his resurrection, Jesus' spirit entered the spirit world, a postmortal place of the disembodied, those awaiting and preparing for the reunion of their bodies and spirits. Peter taught that Christ went into this realm to preach to the spirits in prison (1 Pet. 3:18–20; 4:6). A modern revelation explains that Jesus did not go himself among the wicked and disobedient who had rejected the truth. Rather, he ministered to the righteous in paradise and organized and empowered them to teach those spirits who remained in darkness under the bondage of sin and ignorance (see D&C 138:29–32). Thus, the Messiah's mission to "preach good tidings unto the meek," to "bind up the brokenhearted, to proclaim liberty to the captives, and the opening of the prison to them that are bound" (Isa. 61:1; Luke 4:18–19) extended after death into the life beyond.

Jesus broke "the bands of death"; he was the "firstfruits of them that slept" (1 Cor. 15:20; Alma 11:40–41). He rose from the tomb with an immortal, glorified body and initiated the first resurrection or the resurrection of the just, the raising of the righteous dead who had lived from the days of Adam to the time of Christ (Matt. 27:52–53; Mosiah 15:21–25; Hel. 14:25–26; 3 Ne. 23:7–13). Jesus Christ will come again to earth in power and glory. The first resurrection, begun at the time of Christ's resurrection, will resume as the righteous dead from the meridian of time to his second coming return with him in resurrected and immortal glory. This second advent will also signal the beginning of the Millennium, a thousand years of earthly peace during which Satan will be bound and have no power over the hearts of those who remain on earth (Rev. 20:1–2; 1 Ne. 22:26). Joseph Smith taught that "Christ and the resurrected Saints will reign over the earth during the thousand years. They will not probably dwell upon the earth [constantly], but will visit it when they please, or when it is necessary to govern it" (*TPJS*, p. 268). During this era, Jesus will reveal himself, and, in the words of Isaiah, "the earth shall be full of the knowledge of the Lord, as the waters cover the sea" (Isa. 11:9; Heb. 2:14).

Jesus Christ is the God of the whole earth and invites all nations and people to come unto him. His mortal ministry, as described in the New Testament, was primarily among the Jews. Following his death and resurrection he appeared to his "other sheep," groups of scattered Israelites. First, as described in the Book of Mormon, he ministered to the NEPHITES in America. He taught them his gospel and authorized them to officiate in his name. He then visited the lost tribes, the ten northern tribes of Israel, which were scattered at the time of the Assyrian captivity in 721 B.C. (John 10:16; 3 Ne. 15:12–16; 17:4). In addition to the appearances recorded in the Bible and the Book of Mormon, which are ancient scriptural witnesses of the Redeemer, Joseph Smith testified that Jesus Christ, in company with his Eternal Father, appeared to him near Palmyra, New York, in the spring of 1820 to open the dispensations of the fulness of times (JS—H 1:1–20). On subsequent occasions the risen Savior has visited and revealed himself

to his latter-day prophets and continues to direct his latter-day Church and kingdom.

Latter-day Saints center their worship in, and direct their prayers to, God the Eternal Father. This, as with all things—sermons, testimonies, prayers, and sacraments or ordinances—they do in the name of Jesus Christ (2 Ne. 25:16; Jacob 4:4–5; 3 Ne. 18:19; D&C 20:29; Moses 5:8). The Saints also worship Christ the Son as they acknowledge him as the source of truth and redemption, as the light and life of the world, as the way to the Father (John 14:6; 2 Ne. 25:29; 3 Ne. 11:11). They look to him for deliverance and seek to be like him (see D&C 93:12–20; McConkie, 1978, pp. 568–69). In emphasizing the transforming power of Christ's example, President David O. McKay observed that "no man can sincerely resolve to apply to his daily life the teachings of Jesus of Nazareth without sensing a change in his own nature" (*IE* 65 [June 1962]: 405).

Jesus Christ brought to pass the bodily resurrection of all who have lived or who will yet live upon the earth (1 Cor. 15:21–22; Alma 11:40–42). Because he overcame the world, all men and women may—by exercising faith in him, trusting in his merits, and receiving his grace—repent of their sins and know the peace of personal purity and spiritual wholeness (John 14:27; Phil. 4:7; 2 Ne. 2:8; 25:23; Enos 1:1–8; Mosiah 4:1–3). Those who have learned to rely on the Lord and lean upon his tender mercies "sing the song of redeeming love" (Alma 5:26). NEPHI₁, the Book of Mormon prophet-leader, exulted, "I glory in my Jesus, for he hath redeemed my soul from hell" (2 Ne. 33:6). "We talk of Christ, we rejoice in Christ, we preach of Christ, we prophesy of Christ, . . . that our children may know to what source they may look for a remission of their sins" (2 Ne. 25:26). A latter-day apostle has written:

I believe in Christ;
He stands supreme!
From him I'll gain my fondest dream;
And while I strive through grief and pain,
His voice is heard: Ye shall obtain.
I believe in Christ; so come what may,
With him I'll stand in that great day
When on this earth he comes again
To rule among the sons of men.
(Bruce R. McConkie. "I Believe in Christ."
In *Hymns of the Church of Jesus Christ of
Latter-day Saints*, no. 134. Salt Lake City:
Deseret Book, 1985.)

BIBLIOGRAPHY

Benson, Ezra Taft. *Come unto Christ*. Salt Lake City, 1983.

Dahl, Larry E., and Charles D. Tate, Jr., eds. *The Lectures on Faith in Historical Perspective*. Provo, Utah, 1990.

McConkie, Bruce R. *The Promised Messiah*. Salt Lake City, 1978.

———. *The Mortal Messiah*, 4 vols. Salt Lake City, 1979–1981.

———. *The Millennial Messiah*. Salt Lake City, 1982.

Talmage, James E. *Jesus the Christ*. Salt Lake City, 1972.

Taylor, John. *The Mediation and Atonement of Our Lord and Savior Jesus Christ*. Salt Lake City, 1882.

ROBERT L. MILLET

JESUS CHRIST, FATHERHOOD AND SONSHIP OF

Latter-day Saint scriptures refer to Jesus Christ as both the Father and the Son. Most notably in the Book of Mormon, Christ introduced himself to the BROTHER OF JARED saying, "I am the Father and the Son" (Ether 3:14); NEPHI₁ referred to the Lamb of God as "the Eternal Father" (1 Ne. 11:21, 1830 ed.), and the prophet ABINADI said that the Messiah would be "the Father . . . and the Son" (Mosiah 15:3). Such usage has been explained in several ways consistent with the fundamental LDS understanding of the Godhead as three distinct beings.

There is no lack of clarity about Christ's sonship. Jesus is the Son of God in at least three ways. First, he is the firstborn spirit child of God the Father and thereby the elder brother of the spirits of all men and women as God the Father, known also by the exalted name-title Elohim, is the father of the spirits of all mankind (Num. 16:22; Heb. 12:9; John 20:17). Thus, when Christ is called the Firstborn (e.g., Rom. 8:29; Col. 1:15; D&C 93:21), Latter-day Saints accept this as a possible reference to Christ's spiritual birth. Second, he is the literal physical son of God, the Only Begotten in the Flesh (e.g., John 1:14; 3:16; 2 Ne. 25:12; Jacob 4:11; D&C 29:42; 93:11; Moses 1:6; 2:26). Third, spiritually he is also a son by virtue of his submission unto the will of the Father (Heb. 5:8).

Jesus Christ is also known by the title of Father. The meaning of scriptures using this nomenclature is not always immediately clear, primarily owing to the fact that Christ and his Father are virtually inseparable in purpose, testimony, glory, and power. In most cases, however, the scriptural usage can be explained in several ways:

Christ is sometimes called Father because of his role as Creator from the beginning. Before his mortal birth, and acting under the direction of the Father, Jesus was Jehovah, the Lord Omnipotent, through whom God created worlds without number (Moses 1:33; 7:30; John 1:1–3; Heb. 1:2). Because of his creative role, Christ-Jehovah is called "the Father of heaven and earth, the Creator of all things from the beginning" in the Book of Mormon (Mosiah 3:8; see also 2 Ne. 25:16; Alma 11:39; 3 Ne. 9:15). Jesus' role as Creator is similarly attested in the Bible (e.g., John 1:3; Eph. 3:9; Col. 1:16) and the Doctrine and Covenants (e.g., D&C 38:1–3; 45:1; 76:24; 93:9).

Jesus Christ is also known as Father through the spiritual rebirth of mankind (*see* BORN OF GOD). As the foreordained Redeemer, he became the "author of eternal salvation unto all them that obey him" (Heb. 5:9). He is the Savior. No person will come unto the Father except through him and by his name (John 14:6; Acts 4:12; Mosiah 3:17). Those who accept the gospel of Jesus Christ and receive its saving covenantal ordinances, living worthy of its sanctifying and enlightening powers, are "born again" unto Christ and become known as the children of Christ, "his sons and his daughters," his "seed" (Mosiah 5:5–8; 15:10–13; 27:25–26; Alma 5:14). Christ thus becomes the Father of their salvation, the Father of life in the Spirit, the Father of the new birth. In a related sense, he is also the Father of all mankind in that the RESURRECTION of the entire human family comes through him (Sperry, p. 35).

Furthermore, Jesus is called Father because of the authority God gave him to act for the Father. He explained in Jerusalem: "I can of mine own self do nothing . . . I am come in my Father's name" (John 5:30, 43). An LDS leader has clarified this: "All revelation since the fall has come through Jesus Christ, who is the Jehovah of the Old Testament. . . . The Father has never dealt with man directly and personally since the fall, and he has never appeared except to introduce and bear record of the Son" (*DS* 1:27). Latter-day Saints understand this to mean that, except when introducing the Son, God always acts and speaks to mankind through Jesus Christ. Accordingly, the Father has placed his name upon the Son, authorized and empowered him to speak even in the first person for him, as though he were the Father. An example of this is when the Lord Jehovah (who would later come to earth as Jesus of Nazareth) spoke to Moses: "Moses, my son; . . . thou art in the similitude of mine Only Begotten; and mine Only Begotten is and shall be the Savior" (Moses 1:6). Sometimes the Savior has spoken both as the Father (Elohim) and as the Son (Jesus) in the same revelation (e.g., D&C 29:1, 42; 49:5, 28).

In addition, Christ is Father in that he literally inherited attributes and powers from his Father (Elohim). From Mary, his mother, Jesus inherited mortality, the capacity to die. From God, his Father, Jesus inherited immortality, the capacity to live forever: "As the Father hath life in himself; so hath he given to the Son to have life in himself" (John 5:26; cf. Hel. 5:11). Christ is "the Father, because he was conceived by the power of God" (Mosiah 15:3). "This is a matter of his Eternal Parent investing him with power from on high so that he becomes the Father because he exercises the power of that Eternal Being" (McConkie, p. 371).

Christ is also Father in that he spiritually received all that the Father has. "I am in the Father, and the Father in me, and the Father and I are one—The Father because he gave me of his fulness, and the Son because I was in the world" (D&C 93:3–4).

Other explanations are likewise possible. All persons have multiple roles in life. A man can be a father, son, and brother; a woman can be a mother, daughter, and sister. These titles describe roles or functions at a given time, as well as relationships to others. For Latter-day Saints, this is so with the Christ. He has many names and titles. He ministers as both the Father and the Son. After explaining that the God of Abraham, Isaac, and

Jacob would come to earth, take a body, and minister as both Father and Son, Abinadi summarized: "And they are one God, yea, the very Eternal Father of heaven and earth" (Mosiah 15:4; see also Mosiah 7:26–27; D&C 93:14). The Father and the Son, the Spirit and the flesh, the God and the man—these titles, roles, and attributes are blended wondrously in one being, Jesus Christ, in whom "dwelleth all the fulness of the Godhead bodily" (Col. 2:9).

BIBLIOGRAPHY

"'The Father and the Son': A Doctrinal Exposition of the First Presidency and the Twelve," June 30, 1916. In *MFP* 5:26–34. Salt Lake City, 1971.

McConkie, Bruce R. *The Promised Messiah*, chaps. 4, 9, 20. Salt Lake City, 1978.

Smith, Joseph Fielding. *DS* 1:26–34. Salt Lake City, 1954.

Sperry, Sidney B. *Answers to Book of Mormon Questions*, pp. 31–38. Salt Lake City, 1967.

ROBERT L. MILLET

JESUS CHRIST, FORTY-DAY MINISTRY AND OTHER POST-RESURRECTION APPEARANCES OF

After his RESURRECTION, Jesus spent much of the next forty days with his disciples, "speaking of the things pertaining to the kingdom of God" (Acts 1:3) and opening "their understanding, that they might understand the scriptures," namely, what is "in the law of Moses, and in the prophets, and in the psalms, concerning [him]" (Luke 24:44–45). As part of Jesus' ministry, these forty days are important to Latter-day Saints. In addition, a major section of the Book of Mormon is devoted to his post-resurrection ministry in the Western Hemisphere.

The New Testament mentions the forty-day ministry but provides only limited detail. For example, during this time Jesus appeared to the Twelve with Thomas present (John 20:26–29), spoke of "things pertaining to the kingdom of God" (Acts 1:3), "and many other signs truly did Jesus in the presence of his disciples, which are not written in this book" (John 20:30). Paul mentions that on one occasion Jesus "was seen of above five hundred brethren at once" (1 Cor. 15:6). Finally, before his ascension Jesus commanded the apostles to go "into all the world, and preach the gospel to every creature" (Mark 16:15–16; cf. Matt. 28:18–20; Luke 24:47–48; John 21:15–17; Acts 1:4–5).

Over forty accounts outside scripture claim to tell what Jesus said and did during his forty-day ministry. Latter-day Saints believe that some of these accounts, like the apocrypha, contain things "therein that are true," but in addition contain "many things . . . that are not true" (D&C 91).

These accounts report the following: Jesus teaches the apostles the gospel they should preach to the world. He tells of a premortal life and the creation of the world, adding that this life is a probationary state of choosing between good and evil, and that those who choose good might return to the glory of God. He foretells events of the last days, including the return of Elijah. He also tells the disciples that the primitive church will be perverted after one generation, and teaches them to prepare for tribulation. These apocryphal accounts state that Christ's resurrection gives his followers hope for their own resurrection in glory. Besides salvation for the living, salvation of the dead is a major theme, as are the ordinances: BAPTISM, the SACRAMENT or eucharist, ordination of the apostles to authority, their being blessed one by one, and an initiation or endowment (cf. Luke 24:49; usually called "mysteries"), with an emphasis on garments, marriage, and prayer circles. These accounts, usually called secret (Greek, *apokryphon*; Coptic, *hep*), are often connected somehow to the temple, or compared to the mount of transfiguration. Sometimes the apostles are said to ascend to heaven where they see marvelous things. Whether everything in such accounts is true or not, the actions of the apostles after the post-resurrection visits of Jesus contrast sharply with those before.

Many people dismiss accounts outside the New Testament with the labels apocrypha, pseudepigrapha, fiction, or myth. Some ascribe them to psychological hallucinations that the trauma of Jesus' death brought on the disciples. Others discard such traditions because sects later branded as "heresies" championed them. Most ignore them. Latter-day Saints generally tend to give thoughtful consideration to them, primarily because of the long, detailed account in the Book of Mormon of Christ's post-resurrection ministry among the Nephites and Lamanites "who [had been] spared" (3 Ne. 10:12; 11–28).

Many elements found in the Old World forty-day literature also appear in 3 Nephi in the Book of Mormon. This account tells how Jesus was announced by his Father to some of the surviving Nephites and Lamanites, and how he descended from heaven to the temple at Bountiful to minister to the multitude there for three days. The people "did see with their eyes and did feel with their hands, and did know of a surety and did bear record" that Jesus had risen from the dead (3 Ne. 11:13–17). Jesus chose twelve disciples, gave them authority to perform ordinances, and commanded them to teach all the people (3 Ne. 11:18–41; 18:36–39; 19:4–13; Moro. 2). He declared his doctrine, forbidding disputation about it: "The Father commandeth all men, everywhere, to repent and believe in me. And whoso believeth in me, and is baptized, the same shall be saved" (3 Ne. 11:32–33). Jesus' teachings, including

a version of the SERMON ON THE MOUNT very similar to the one contained in the New Testament, comprise "the law and the commandments" for the people (3 Ne. 12:19). Jesus healed their sick, blessed their children, and prayed for the multitude (3 Ne. 17:2–25; 19:5–36). Many were transfigured when angels descended to minister to them (3 Ne. 17:22–25; 19:14–16). Jesus instituted the ordinances of baptism and the sacrament of bread and wine (3 Ne. 11:22–29; 18:1–14, 26–35; 19:10–13; 20:3–9), and taught the multitude how to live their lives free from sin (3 Ne. 18:12–25). He also taught that sin prevents participation in the ordinances, but no one is forbidden to attend the synagogue or to repent and come to him (3 Ne. 18:25–33). He described the future in terms of covenants made with the house of Israel, quoting Old Testament prophecies of Moses (Deut. 18:15–19 = 3 Ne. 20:36–38; Gen. 12:3; 22:18 = 3 Ne. 20:25, 27), ISAIAH (Isa. 52:1–3, 6–8, 9–10, 11–15 = 3 Ne. 20:36–40, 32, 34–35, 41–45; Isa. 52:8–10 = 3 Ne. 16:18–20; Isa. 52:12, 15 = 3 Ne. 21:29, 8; Isa. 54 = 3 Ne. 22), Micah (Micah 4:12–13; 5:8–15 = 3 Ne. 20:18–19, 16–17; 21:12–18), and Habakkuk (Hab. 1:5 = 3 Ne. 21:9), that the remnants of Israel will be gathered when the prophecies of Isaiah begin to be fulfilled and when the remnants begin to believe in Christ, the Book of Mormon itself being a sign of the beginning of these events (3 Ne. 16:4–20; 20:10–23:6; 26:3–5). After inspecting their records, Jesus gave them additional prophecies that they had not had (Mal. 3–4 = 3 Ne. 24–25), and "did expound all things" to their understanding (3 Ne. 20:10–26:11).

Even more sacred things said and done by Jesus during his three-day visit to the Western Hemisphere were not included in the present record (3 Ne. 26:6–12). His post-resurrection ministries to the people of Nephi and to the Old World disciples were only two of several he performed and of which records were made (3 Ne. 15:11–16:3; cf. D&C 88:51–61; *TPJS*, p. 191). Latter-day Saints hope to prepare themselves to receive the fuller accounts that are yet to come (2 Ne. 29:11–14; D&C 25:9; 101:32–35; 121:26–33; A of F 9).

BIBLIOGRAPHY

Brown, S. Kent, and C. Wilfred Griggs. "The Forty-Day Ministry of Christ." *Ensign* 5 (Aug. 1975): 6–11, also in *Studies in Scripture*, ed. K. Jackson, Vol. 6, pp. 12–23. Salt Lake City, 1987.

Nibley, Hugh W. "Evangelium Quadraginta Dierum." *Vigiliae Christianae* 20 (1966): 1–24, reprinted in CWHN 4:10–44.

For comparisons with the Book of Mormon, see H. Nibley, "Christ among the Ruins," *Ensign* 13 (June 1983): 14–19, in CWHN 8:407–34; and *Since Cumorah*, CWHN 7. Specialized studies include H. Nibley, "The Early Christian Prayer Circle," *BYU Studies* 19 (1978): 41–78, in CWHN 4:45–99.

For the primary sources, see the references in the preceding works; English translations of many are found in Edgar Hennecke and Wilhelm Schneemelcher, *New Testament Apocrypha*, 2 vols., Philadelphia, 1965, and James M. Robinson, *The Nag Hammadi Library*, San Francisco, 1978, rev. ed. 1988.

JOHN GEE

JESUS CHRIST, PROPHECIES ABOUT

Prophecies concerning the birth, mortal ministry, and post-Resurrection ministry of Jesus Christ permeate the Bible. Moreover, the latter-day scriptures used by members of The Church of Jesus Christ of Latter-day Saints—the Book of Mormon, which bears the modern subtitle "Another Testament of Jesus Christ," the Doctrine and Covenants, and the Pearl of Great Price—contain numerous prophetic utterances about the Messiah that in general are clearer than those in the Bible. For Latter-day Saints, these four volumes of scripture constitute the principal sources for the prophecies about Jesus' life and mission. This article reviews the prophecies concerning Jesus most often referred to by Latter-day Saints.

The New Testament teaches that the divinity of Jesus Christ was recognized by some during his own lifetime, as well as by God's ancient prophets. For example, Andrew announced to his brother Simon Peter that he had found the Messiah (John 1:41). The Book of Mormon prophets ABINADI and NEPHI₂, son of HELAMAN₂, taught that all of God's prophets, including Moses and Abraham, "have testified of the coming of Christ" (Mosiah 13:33; Hel. 8:16–22; cf. Jacob 4:4).

The scriptures are rich in prophetic detail concerning the birth of Jesus. Isaiah declared, "Behold, a virgin shall conceive, and bear a son, and shall call his name Immanuel" (Isa. 7:14), a passage that Matthew cited as having reference to Jesus (Matt. 1:22–23). Micah poetically pronounced, "Beth-lehem Ephratah, though thou be little among the thousands of Judah, yet out of thee shall he come forth unto me that is to be ruler in Israel; whose goings forth have been from of old, from everlasting" (Micah 5:2). Among Book of Mormon people, NEPHI₁ foretold that "even six hundred years from the time that my father [Lehi] left Jerusalem," the Savior would be raised up (1 Ne. 10:4; 19:8). SAMUEL THE LAMANITE (c. 6 B.C.) told a doubting generation of the signs to be given in the Western Hemisphere that would accompany the birth of Christ (Hel. 14:2–8). These included the appearance of a new star and two days and one night without darkness (Hel. 14:4–5).

Some prophecies of the Messiah's birth were fulfilled when the angel of the Lord announced to shepherds near Bethlehem: "Unto you is born this day in the city of David a Saviour, which is Christ the Lord" (Luke 2:11). On the other side of the world, the day before his birth, the Lord announced to his prophet Nephi$_3$ that he should be of "good cheer; for behold, the time is at hand, and on this night shall the sign be given, and on the morrow come I into the world, to show unto the world that I will fulfil all that which I have caused to be spoken by the mouth of my holy prophets" (3 Ne. 1:13).

Latter-day Saints believe that the mission of Jesus Christ has been known since earliest times. The angel of the Lord declared to Adam that the Son was "the Only Begotten of the Father from the beginning," and that Adam would "be redeemed, and all mankind, even as many as will," if they "repent and call upon God in the name of the Son forevermore" (Moses 5:8–9). The message that Jesus Christ is the Advocate, the Redeemer, and the Intercessor, and that "There is no other way nor means whereby man can be saved, only through the atoning blood of Jesus Christ" (Hel. 5:9), has been repeated by God's representatives in all ages (see Moses 5:14–15; Isa. 53:4–5; Acts 4:12; 2 Ne. 2:9–10; 9:6–7; Mosiah 4:8; 5:8; Alma 11:40; D&C 45:3).

Events of Jesus' mortal life and ministry are found in numerous prophecies. In the Joseph Smith Translation of the Bible (JST), an insightful passage states "that Jesus grew up with his brethren, and waxed strong, and waited upon the Lord for the time of his ministry to come . . . [and] needed not that any man should teach him" (JST Matt. 3:24–25). Nephi$_1$ saw in a vision, and King BENJAMIN learned from an angel, that the Savior would perform healings, cast out devils, and raise the dead (1 Ne. 11:31; Mosiah 3:5–6). According to New Testament writers, Jesus' triumphal ride into Jerusalem on a beast of bur-

den was foreknown by Zechariah (Zech. 9:9; Matt. 21:5; John 12:14–15), as was his betrayal for thirty pieces of silver (Zech. 11:12–13; Matt. 27:9–10). From the angel, King Benjamin learned that blood would come "from every pore, so great shall be his [Jesus'] anguish for the wickedness and the abominations of his people" (Mosiah 3:7). Christ's rejection by his own people was prophesied both by himself and by others (e.g., Ps. 69:8; Mosiah 15:5; 3 Ne. 9:16; John 1:11).

Many years before the event, prophets such as Enoch and Nephi$_1$ saw the Lord lifted up on the cross (Moses 7:47, 55; 1 Ne. 11:33). Isaiah prophesied that the suffering servant would make "his grave with the wicked, and with the rich in his death" (Isa. 53:9). The Book of Mormon prophet Abinadi (c. 150 B.C.) associated that passage in Isaiah with Jesus (Mosiah 15), and its fulfillment was recorded by Luke (23:32–33). Matthew tells of the physical disturbances that occurred at the moment Jesus gave up his life (Matt. 27:50–54), events that ZENOS saw in a vision hundreds of years earlier (1 Ne. 19:10–12).

Christ foretold his own death and resurrection when he answered a demand for a sign: "Destroy this temple [physical body], and in three days I will raise it up" (John 2:19). Jesus' eventual victory over death was known by the ancients, for God told Enoch that "righteousness will I send down out of heaven; and truth will I send forth out of the earth, to bear testimony of mine Only Begotten; his resurrection from the dead; yea, and also the resurrection of all men" (Moses 7:62). Later, inspired men in the Americas learned of this event. Nephi$_1$, JACOB, Benjamin, and Samuel proclaimed the time when Christ "layeth down his life according to the flesh, and taketh it again by the power of the Spirit, that he may bring to pass the resurrection of the dead, being the first that should rise"

(2 Ne. 2:8; cf. 1 Ne. 10:11; Mosiah 3:10; Hel. 14:15–17).

Jesus Christ's ministry to the spirit prison (1 Pet. 3:18–19) was anticipated by Isaiah when he recorded that "after many days shall [the prisoners gathered in the pit] be visited" (Isa. 24:22). Section 138 of the Doctrine and Covenants records a vision of this event, received by a modern prophet, President Joseph F. Smith, when he saw "the hosts of the dead, both small and great . . . awaiting the advent of the Son of God into the spirit world, to declare their redemption from the bands of death" (D&C 138:11, 16).

The righteous of earlier ages have looked forward to the second coming of Jesus Christ. Jesus told his disciples to "watch therefore, for ye know neither the day nor the hour wherein the Son of man cometh" (Matt. 25:13; cf. D&C 49:6–7), and indicated that he would come "as a thief" in the night (1 Thess. 5:2; Rev. 3:3; 16:15). He revealed to Joseph Smith that a universal revelation would be given so that "all flesh shall see me together" (D&C 101:23; cf. Isa. 40:5). Isaiah foresaw events of the second coming (Isa. 63–66), as did Daniel, Micah, Zechariah, and Malachi (Dan. 7:13; Micah 1:3; Zech. 12:10; 13:6; Mal. 3:12). When the resurrected Lord appeared among the Nephites, he spoke about his eventual triumphant return to earth, quoting Malachi, chapters 3 and 4 (3 Ne. 24–25).

The Prophet Joseph Smith clarified and added to prophecies of the events surrounding Jesus' second coming, including the restoration of the gospel (D&C 133:36–37), the resurrection of the dead (D&C 88:95–102), the beginning of the Millennium (D&C 43:30–31), and the binding of Satan for a thousand years (D&C 88:110; D&C 45:55). Both ancient and modern prophets foretold that, at the end of a thousand years of peace, Satan would be loosed and the final battle between good and evil would be waged (Rev. 20:7–8; D&C

43:31). John the Revelator and the ancient prophet Ether, who both saw in vision all of these events, beheld the renewal of the earth and the establishment of the New Jerusalem (Rev. 21; Ether 13:1–10). This city will have "no need of the sun, neither of the moon, to shine in it: for the glory of God did lighten it, and the Lamb is the light thereof" (Rev. 21:23).

BIBLIOGRAPHY

Jackson, Kent P. "The Beginnings of Christianity in the Book of Mormon." In *The Book of Mormon: The Keystone Scripture*, ed. P. Chessman. Provo, Utah, 1988.

Matthews, Robert J. "The Doctrine of the Atonement—The Revelation of the Gospel to Adam." In *Studies in Scripture*, ed. R. Millet and K. Jackson, Vol. 2, pp. 111–29. Salt Lake City, 1985.

———. *A Bible! A Bible!* Salt Lake City, 1990.

McConkie, Bruce R. *The Promised Messiah*. Salt Lake City, 1978.

———. *The Millennial Messiah*. Salt Lake City, 1982.

ADDITIONAL SOURCE

Draper, Richard D. "The Mortal Ministry of the Savior Understood by the Book of Mormon Prophets." *Journal of Book of Mormon Studies* 2/1 (Spring 1993): 80–92.

GARY LEE WALKER

JESUS CHRIST, TAKING THE NAME OF, UPON ONESELF

It is a doctrine of The Church of Jesus Christ of Latter-day Saints that the only way to obtain salvation is to take the name of Jesus Christ upon oneself. This is categorically stated in several latter-day revelations. Although not specifically stated in the Bible, the concept is implied in Paul's declaration to "put on Christ" (Gal. 3:27; Rom. 13:14); Peter's statement that Jesus Christ is the only name given "among men, whereby we must be saved" (Acts 4:12; Ex. 15:2; 1 Sam. 2:1; Ps. 27:1); and the Lord's instruction to Moses to "put my name upon the children of Israel" (Num. 6:27; cf. Jer. 15:16). The taking of the name of Christ upon oneself in this dispensation begins with being baptized into his Church and keeping the commandments.

The Lord declared to the Prophet Joseph SMITH that all persons desiring a place in the kingdom of the Father must take upon themselves the name of Christ (D&C 18:24–25, 27). Amulek, in the Book of Mormon, counseled the wayward Zoramites to "take upon you the name of Christ" (Alma 34:38). The resurrected Jesus promised, "Whoso taketh upon him my name, and endureth to the end, the same shall be saved at the last day" (3 Ne. 27:5–6; cf. Mosiah 25:23; 26:18). Abraham was told by the Lord, "I will take thee, to put upon thee my name" (Abr. 1:18).

Sacred covenant making is associated with taking the name of Jesus upon oneself. King BENJAMIN said, "There is no other name given whereby salvation cometh; therefore, I would that ye should take upon you the name of Christ, all you that have entered into the covenant with God that ye should be obedient unto the end of your lives" (Mosiah 5:8; cf. 18:8–12; Alma 46:15). The covenants of BAPTISM (D&C 20:37; cf. 2 Ne. 31:13) and of the Lord's Supper (D&C 20:77; Moro. 4:3) require taking the name of Jesus Christ upon oneself. Bruce R. McConkie, a latter-day apostle, stated, "We have taken upon ourselves his name in the waters of baptism. We renew the covenant therein made when we partake of the sacrament [Lord's Supper]. If we have been born again, we have become the sons and daughters of the Lord Jesus Christ" (McConkie, p. 393).

Dallin H. Oaks, also an apostle, further explained that "we take upon us the name of Christ when we are baptized in his name, when we belong to his Church and profess our belief in him, and when we do the work of his kingdom. There are other meanings as well, deeper meanings that the more mature members of the Church should understand and ponder" (Oaks, p. 80). The "deeper meanings" are identified as inheriting the fulness of God's glory and obtaining exaltation in the celestial kingdom (Oaks, pp. 81–83).

BIBLIOGRAPHY

McConkie, Bruce R. "Jesus Christ and Him Crucified." In *BYU Devotional Speeches of the Year*, pp. 391–405. Provo, Utah, 1976.

Oaks, Dallin H. "Taking upon Us the Name of Jesus Christ." *Ensign* 15 (May 1985): 80–83.

PAUL R. WARNER

JESUS CHRIST IN THE SCRIPTURES

[*This entry consists here of the articles:*

Jesus Christ in the Bible
Jesus Christ in the Book of Mormon

Jesus Christ is the central focus in all scriptures accepted by Latter-day Saints. Jesus Christ in the Bible *details how Jesus is seen as the central figure—both in prophecy and in its fulfillment—in the Old and New Testaments. The article* Jesus Christ in the Book of Mormon *treats the pivotal prophetic interest in Christ manifested in the Book of Mormon, including his post-resurrection appearance to people in the Western Hemisphere.*]

Jesus Christ in the Bible
Latter-day Saints view Jesus Christ as the central figure of the entire Bible. The Old and New Testaments are divinely inspired records that reveal the mission of Jesus as Creator, God of Israel, Messiah, Son of God, Re-

deemer, and eternal King. The Bible contains history, doctrinal teachings, and prophecy of future events, with Jesus Christ as the main subject in every category.

The Old Testament contains an account of the Creation, and of the dealings of God with the human family from Adam to about 400 B.C. The promise of a messiah is a generally pervading theme. The New Testament chronicles principal events in the earth life of Jesus the Messiah from his birth through death, resurrection, and ascension into heaven, with a promise that he will return to earth to judge the world and then reign as king. Latter-day Saints identify Jesus as Jehovah, the Creator, the God of Adam, of Abraham, of Moses, and of Israel. Jesus is Jehovah come to earth as the promised Messiah (see JESUS CHRIST). Hence, the dealings of God with the human family throughout the Old Testament and New Testament periods form a record of the premortal and the mortal Jesus Christ.

THE HISTORICAL JESUS. Latter-day Saints take the biblical message about Jesus literally. The historical Jesus is the Jesus of the Bible: the Only Begotten Son of God in the flesh, born of the Virgin Mary in Bethlehem, baptized by John the Baptist. He performed a variety of miracles, was a teacher of the gospel who occasionally spoke in parables, and "went about doing good" (Acts 10:38). He chose twelve apostles, organized a church, gathered many followers, and was rejected by the Jewish rulers. His attitudes toward Samaritans, women, political leaders (e.g., Herod, Caesar), ritual law, and prayer were rather revolutionary for his day. He suffered at Gethsemane, bled at every pore, was crucified, died, was resurrected from the dead, and subsequently ascended into heaven from the Mount of Olives. Latter-day Saints consider both the historical portion of the record of the life of Jesus, and the prophetic portion,

to be accurate. The promises that this same Jesus will come again in glory, in person to judge the world, then reign on the earth as King of Kings, are future realities that are taken literally.

PORTRAYAL OF JESUS THROUGH CEREMONY. Throughout the Bible, the mission of Jesus Christ is portrayed in ceremonies that are types and symbols of actual events. To the Old Testament prophets, animal sacrifices prefigured and typified the coming of Jesus to shed his blood and sacrifice his life for the sins of mankind. Because lambs were frequently offered, Jesus is spoken of in the New Testament as the Lamb of God (John 1:29, 36; cf. 1 Ne. 11:21).

For the animal sacrifice to symbolize Jesus' sacrifice, it had to be from among the firstlings of the flock (meaning the first male born to its mother) without blemish, offered without a bone being broken, and its blood had to be shed. Each of these points had a counterpart in Jesus' life on earth. Even details of the Passover service, requiring the blood of the lamb to be placed on the door post so that the angel of death might pass over that house (Ex. 12:3–24, 46), prefigured the mission and saving power of Jesus, the Lamb of God, who was crucified at the time of the annual Passover celebration. Paul, understanding this symbolism, exclaims, "For even Christ our passover is sacrificed for us" (1 Cor. 5:7).

The LAW OF MOSES is identified by Paul as "our schoolmaster to bring us unto Christ" (Gal. 3:24). To do that, it foreshadowed and typified Christ. When he worked out the Atonement, Christ fulfilled all the law; therefore the law had an end in him, and was replaced by the fulness of the gospel (3 Ne. 9:17; cf. Matt. 5:17–18; Heb. 10:1). LDS understanding of the role of the law of Moses and of other Old Testament ordinances is clearly spoken by the Book of Mormon prophet Nephi about 600 B.C.:

> Behold, my soul delighteth in proving unto my people the truth of the coming of Christ; for, for this end hath the law of Moses been given; and all things which have been given of God from the beginning of the world, unto man, are the typifying of him. (2 Ne. 11:4; cf. Jacob 4:5)

When Jesus ate the Passover meal with the Twelve at the Last Supper, he gave them bread representing his flesh, which would be broken, and wine representing his blood, which would be shed. Believers were commanded to partake of this symbolic ceremony often: "This do in remembrance of me" (Luke 22:17–20; cf. 3 Ne. 18:3–13; 20:8–9).

OLD TESTAMENT FORESHADOWINGS. The writers of the four Gospels saw things in the Old Testament that foreshadowed the actual events in Jesus' life. Matthew (1:23) cites Isaiah 7:14: "A virgin shall conceive, and bear a son, and shall call his name Immanuel," a name meaning "God with us." He likewise cites Hosea 11:1, "I . . . called my son out of Egypt" (Matt. 2:15).

John (13:8–11) notes that the betrayal of Jesus by a friend was spoken of in earlier scripture (Ps. 41:9). John (19:24) also cites the dealing of the soldiers for Jesus' robe as a fulfillment of Psalm 22:18, and the sponge with vinegar pressed to Jesus' lips (John 19:28–30) as having been alluded to in Psalm 69:21. John (19:33–36) also notes that Jesus' legs were not broken on the cross, in harmony with Exodus 12:46.

Isaiah prophesied that in Israel a son would be born of the lineage of David, who would be called the "mighty God," the "Prince of Peace" (Isa. 9:6–7). The Messiah's mission as redeemer, suffering for the sins of mankind, is portrayed in Isaiah 53 and 61.

THE GOD OF ISRAEL IS JESUS OF NAZA-RETH. Revelation to the Prophet Joseph SMITH shows that, beginning with Adam, there have been several gospel dispensations on the earth. The prophets in each of these dispensations knew of Christ, taught his gospel (including the ceremonies and ordinances), and held the holy priesthood, which was called "the Holy Priesthood, after the Order of the Son of God" (D&C 107:3; cf. Alma 13:1–16). These ancient prophets not only knew of the future coming of Jesus as the Messiah, but they also knew that the God whom they worshiped, Jehovah, would come to earth and become that Messiah (cf. Mosiah 13:33–35). As noted earlier, in Isaiah 7:14 the name Immanuel identifies Jesus as God. New Testament passages illustrate this concept.

Jesus directed his listeners to search the scriptures, for "they are they which testify of me" (John 5:39). He told the Jewish rulers that Moses "wrote of me" (John 5:45–46; cf. John 1:45; 1 Cor. 10:1–4). Later he informed them that "Abraham rejoiced to see my day: and he saw it, and was glad" (John 8:56). When asked how he and Abraham could have known each other when their lives on earth were separated by so much time, Jesus replied, "Before Abraham was, I am" (John 8:58). The Greek term here translated "I am" is identical with the Septuagint phrase in Exodus 3:14 that identifies Jehovah as "I AM."

That Jesus' audience understood that he had plainly told them he was none other than Jehovah, also known as I AM, the God of Abraham and of Moses, is evident, for "then took they up stones to cast at him" (John 8:59) because they supposed that he had blasphemed. A further demonstration that they understood Jesus' assertion that he was God come to earth is shown later when they "took up stones again to stone him," and Jesus asked: "For which of [my] works do ye stone me?" Their reply was "for blasphemy; and because that thou, being a man, makest thyself God" (John 10:31–33).

After his resurrection Jesus went through the passages of the Old Testament with his disciples, "beginning at Moses and all the prophets," expounded to them "in all the scriptures the things concerning himself" (Luke 24:27), and showed them "in the law of Moses, and in the prophets, and in the psalms" the prophecies pertaining to his mission (Luke 24:44; see JESUS CHRIST, PROPHECIES ABOUT).

Peter wrote that the ancient prophets "searched diligently" and had the "Spirit of Christ," which "testified beforehand the sufferings of Christ," and that these prophets did "minister [in their day] the things, which are now reported" about Jesus Christ (1 Pet. 1:10–12). And Paul declared that in all his teachings about Jesus, he had said "none other things than those which the prophets and Moses did say should come" (Acts 26:22).

Extensive prophecies that Jesus will come again to the earth as Judge and King are recorded in Matthew (16:27; 24:1–51) and Joseph Smith—Matthew (1:1–55). Latter-day Saints believe that just as Old Testament foreshadowing and prophecies of Christ were fulfilled in his first coming, so will prophecies of his second coming be literally fulfilled.

CLARIFICATIONS FROM LATTER-DAY REVELATION. The foregoing items from the Bible, coupled with confirmatory and illuminating statements in latter-day revelation, lead members of the Church to see both the Old and the New Testaments as reliable records about the premortal, mortal, postmortal, and future millennial mission of Jesus Christ. Latter-day Saints fully accept the biblical message about Jesus Christ, and, in addition, because of other sacred scriptures that strengthen and supplement the biblical re-

port, they appreciate the mission of Jesus in a wider sense than is possible from the Bible alone. For example, Jesus spoke to Jewish hearers about "other sheep," not of the Jews, whom he would visit and who would "hear my voice" (John 10:16). Many have supposed that these were the Gentiles. However, in the Book of Mormon the resurrected Jesus specifically identifies these other sheep as a branch of the house of Israel on the American continent whom he was visiting, personally showing them his body and vocally teaching them his gospel (3 Ne. 15:13–24). The Book of Mormon thus explains a passage about the Savior beyond what the Bible offers, and also enlarges the concept of Jesus' ministry.

Latter-day revelation also provides a deeper appreciation for events that occurred on the Mount of Transfiguration than is available in the Bible alone. That which the New Testament offers is accepted as historically correct, but incomplete. One learns from latter-day revelation that on the mount, Jesus, Moses, and Elijah gave the keys of the priesthood to Peter, James, and John in fulfillment of the Savior's promise in Matthew 16:19 (TPJS, p. 158). The three apostles also saw a vision of the future glorification of the earth (D&C 63:20–21). These points are lacking in the biblical account. Moses and Elijah (called Elias) "appeared in glory, and spake of [Jesus'] decease which he should accomplish at Jerusalem" (Luke 9:30–31), which shows that they knew him and knew of his mission.

Jesus' ministry is also clarified in other instances in latter-day revelation. John 3:23 suggests that Jesus personally performed baptisms in water, but this is largely negated by John 4:2, which states that it was in fact not Jesus, but his disciples, who performed the baptisms. Through the Joseph Smith Translation of the Bible, the text of John 4:2–3 is clarified to assert that Jesus did indeed perform water baptisms, but not as many as did his disciples. Topics discussed in the latter work include Jesus at the temple at age twelve; his precocious childhood; his temptations in the wilderness; his parables; his ability to redeem little children; and his compassion for people.

BIBLIOGRAPHY

Matthews, Robert J. "A Greater Portrayal of the Master." *Ensign* 13 (Mar. 1983): 6–13.

McConkie, Bruce R. *Doctrinal New Testament Commentary,* 3 vols. Salt Lake City, 1965, 1970, 1973.

———. *The Promised Messiah; The Mortal Messiah; The Millennial Messiah,* 6 vols. Salt Lake City, 1978, 1979, 1980, 1981, 1982.

Talmage, James E. *Jesus the Christ.* Salt Lake City, 1963.

ROBERT J. MATTHEWS

Jesus Christ in the Book of Mormon

The main purpose of the Book of Mormon is to convince all people "that Jesus is the Christ, the Eternal God, manifesting himself unto all nations" (title page). Through the spiritual experiences of its writers, many of whom were prophets and eyewitnesses of Christ's glory, the Book of Mormon communicates clear, personal knowledge that Jesus Christ lives. It explains his mission from the Creation to the Final Judgment, and expresses his pure and atoning love for all mankind.

The Book of Mormon is an intimate scripture. It exhorts each reader to "come unto Christ, and lay hold upon every good gift," mindful that "every good gift cometh of Christ" (Moro. 10:18, 30).

The book is singularly focused. In the words of Nephi$_1$, "We talk of Christ, we re-joice in Christ, we preach of Christ, we prophesy of Christ" (2 Ne. 25:26). Only by Jesus' sacrifice can the repentant "answer the ends of the law" (2 Ne. 2:7). "There is no other head whereby ye can be made free. There is no other name given whereby salvation cometh" (Mosiah 5:8).

All Book of Mormon prophets proclaimed the same word of Jesus Christ (Jacob 4:5). In visions, public speeches, and personal statements they typically declared (1) that Jesus is the Son of God, the Creator, the Lord God Omnipotent, the Father of heaven and earth, and the Holy One of Israel, (2) who would come and did come down to earth to live as a mortal born of Mary, a virgin, (3) to heal the sick, cast out devils, and suffer temptation, (4) to take upon himself the sins of the world and redeem his people, (5) to be put to death by crucifixion and rise from the dead, (6) to bring to pass the resurrection of all mankind, and (7) to judge all people in the last day according to their works (1 Ne. 11–14; Mosiah 3:5–27; Alma 33:22).

The personality and attributes of Jesus are expressed in the Book of Mormon (see Black, pp. 49–64). He is a person who invites, comforts, answers, exhorts, loves, cries, is troubled over the sins of mankind, and is filled with joy. He welcomes all who will come unto him. He patiently pleads with the Father on behalf of all who have become saints through his atoning blood. He is a true and merciful friend. He visits those who believe in him. He heals those who weep at the thought of being separated from him. With hands still bearing the wounds of his death, he touches, is touched, and gives power. He remembers all his covenants and keeps all his promises. He is all-powerful, judging the world and vanquishing the wicked. He is "the light, and the life, and the truth of the world" (Ether 4:12).

The Sacrament in the New World, by Minerva K. Teichert (c. 1952, oil on masonite, 36" x 48"). After his resurrection, Jesus Christ ministered to a group of people in the Americas. The Book of Mormon records that he taught them, blessed them, and instituted the sacrament among them as a remembrance of the body which he had shown them (3 Ne. 18:1–11). © Courtesy Museum of Art, Brigham Young University. All rights reserved.

Book of Mormon prophets who taught extensively of Christ before his birth include the BROTHER OF JARED (Ether 3); LEHI (1 Ne. 10; 2 Ne. 2); NEPHI₁ (1 Ne. 11, 19; 2 Ne. 25, 31–33); JACOB (2 Ne. 9); ABINADI (Mosiah 13–16); BENJAMIN (Mosiah 3–5); ALMA₂ (Alma 5, 7, 12–13, 33, 36, 42); AMULEK (Alma 34); SAMUEL THE LAMANITE (Hel. 14); and NEPHI₃ (3 Ne. 1). The apex of the Nephite record is the appearance of the resurrected Lord Jesus Christ to a congregation of 2,500 men, women, and children who had gathered at their temple in the land Bountiful. For three days, Jesus personally ministered among them (3 Ne. 11–28; *see* BOOK OF MORMON: THIRD NEPHI). The Book of Mormon ends with testimonies of Jesus by MORMON (Morm. 7; Moro. 7) and his son MORONI₂ (Ether 4; Moro. 10). Some 101 appellations for Jesus are found in the 3,925 references to Christ in the Book of Mormon's 6,607 verses (Black, pp. 16–30).

In addition to his visitations in 3 Nephi, Jesus appeared to Lehi (1 Ne. 1:9), Nephi₁, Jacob (2 Ne. 11:2–3), King Lamoni (Alma 19:13), Mormon (Morm. 1:15), Moroni₂ (Ether 12:39), and the brother of Jared (Ether 3:14). Each bore personal testimony of Jesus Christ. Many others heard his voice.

From visions and revelations received before he left Jerusalem about 600 B.C., Lehi knew the tender mercies of the promised Messiah. To him the Messiah would be the Redeemer who would restore the fallen, lost, and displaced. In one vision, Lehi read a heavenly book that "manifested plainly of the coming of a Messiah, and also the redemption of the world" (1 Ne. 1:19). This knowledge focused all subsequent Nephite preaching and interpretation on the mission of the Savior. It was also revealed to Lehi that in six hundred years "a prophet would the Lord God raise up among the Jews—even a Messiah, or, in other words, a Savior of the world" (1 Ne. 10:4), the same pleading and merciful servant of whom other prophets had written, including ZENOS in his allegory of the Lord's olive tree representing Israel (Jacob 5). Being "grafted in" to that tree was interpreted by Lehi as "com[ing] to the knowledge of the true Messiah" (1 Ne. 10:14).

From the prophecies of ISAIAH as well as from his own visions, Lehi knew that a prophet would prepare the way of the Lord before his coming (1 Ne. 10:8; cf. Isa. 40:3) and that "after he had baptized the Messiah with water, he should behold and bear record that he had baptized the Lamb of God, who should take away the sins of the world" (1 Ne. 10:10). Furthermore, Isaiah spoke of the Lord's servant being "despised and rejected . . . wounded for our transgressions, . . . bruised for our iniquities, . . . brought as a lamb to the slaughter" (Isa. 53:3–7); and Lehi prophesied that the Jews would slay the Messiah, adding that the Redeemer would rise from the dead (1 Ne. 10:11).

Nephi₁ asked the Lord for a greater understanding of his father's visions, especially for a clearer understanding of the TREE OF LIFE. He acquired a love for the CONDESCENSION OF GOD that would bring the Son of God down to dwell in the flesh, born of a beautiful virgin. Christ's goodness stands in sharp contrast with his rejection and crucifixion (1 Ne. 11:13–33; 19:10; cf. Deut. 21:22). Nephi₁ (who himself knew what it meant to be persecuted for righteousness' sake) referred more than sixty times to the divine offering of this sacrificial Lamb of God (1 Ne. 11:21). As ruler and teacher of his people, Nephi emphasized that they should follow the rule of Christ, the only true Savior who would ever come, the sole source of their life and law, and the only one in whom all things would be fulfilled (2 Ne. 25:16–18, 25–27).

In connection with his calling as a priest and teacher, Jacob, the brother of Nephi₁, expounded on the atonement of Christ. He told how Christ would suffer and die for all mankind so that they might become subject to him through his "infinite atonement," which overcomes the Fall and brings resurrection and incorruptibility (2 Ne. 9:5–14).

Certain terms such as "Messiah" (anointed) and "Lamb of God" were used often by Lehi, Nephi₁ and Jacob as designations for Christ before it was revealed by an angel that the Messiah's "name shall be Jesus Christ, the Son of God" (2 Ne. 25:19; cf. 2 Ne. 10:3; Mosiah 3:8). The name Jesus, like Joshua, derives from the Hebrew root *yasha'*, meaning "to deliver, rescue, or save"; and *christos* is the Greek equivalent of the Hebrew *mashiyach*, meaning "anointed" or "Messiah." Thus, the Nephites used the intimate yet freely spoken

name of the mortal Jesus as their name for God, while the ineffable YHWH (see JESUS CHRIST) appears only twice in the book (2 Ne. 22:2; Moro. 10:34).

Some, such as Sherem, whose cultural roots lay in the monotheistic world of Jerusalem, resisted the worship of the Messiah, alleging that this violated the law of Moses (Ex. 20:3; Jacob 7:7; *see* ANTICHRISTS). Nephi had previously declared that the Father, Son, and Holy Ghost were "one God" (2 Ne. 31:21), but Nephite challengers continued to attack the proposition that Jesus was God, to deny that his atonement could be efficacious in advance of its occurrence, and to argue that there could not be many Gods who were still one God (e.g., Mosiah 17:8; Alma 11:28). Abinadi and others gave inspired explanations (Mosiah 14–16; *see* JESUS CHRIST, FATHERHOOD AND SONSHIP OF), but until the resurrected Jesus appeared, announced by and praying to the Father, such issues were not firmly put to rest.

About 124 B.C., King BENJAMIN received from an angel a succinct declaration of the atoning mission of Christ (Mosiah 3:2–27). It places central attention on the atoning blood of Christ and corroborates that Jesus would sweat blood from every pore in anguish for his people (Mosiah 3:7; see also Luke 22:43–44; D&C 19:18; Irenaeus, *Against Heresies* 3.22.2). Christ's blood will atone for the sins of all those who repent or have ignorantly sinned (see Mosiah 3:11, 15, 16, 18). When Benjamin's people passionately cried out in unison for God to "apply the atoning blood of Christ that we may receive forgiveness of our sins" (Mosiah 4:2), Benjamin gave them the name of Christ by covenant, the only name "whereby salvation cometh" (Mosiah 5:7–8).

Alma₂, the judicial and religious defender

of the freedom of belief (c. 100–73 B.C.), taught faith in Jesus Christ as the master of personal CONVERSION. Alma had tasted the transforming joy that came when he called upon the name of Jesus Christ for mercy (Alma 36:18), and in his subsequent sermons he described how the "image of God" might be "engraven upon your countenances" (Alma 5:19), and how the word of God is to be planted in each convert's soul, where, if nourished, it will spring up as an everlasting tree of life (Alma 32:40; 33:22–23; for a similar image, see the early Christian *Odes of Solomon* 11:18).

About 30 B.C. a group of Lamanites were converted to Christ when God's light shone and his voice spoke out of an enveloping cloud of darkness (Hel. 5:33–43). Twenty-five years later, a prophet named Samuel the Lamanite foretold that more significant signs of light would appear at the time of Jesus' birth and that massive destruction and darkness would be seen at his death (Hel. 14:2–27). Five years after Samuel, Nephi₃ heard the voice of Jesus declaring that he would come into the world "on the morrow," (3 Ne. 1:13) and the signs of Jesus' birth were seen; thirty-three years and four days after that, all the land heard the voice of Christ speaking through the thick darkness on the Western Hemisphere that accompanied his crucifixion and death (3 Ne. 9).

Within that same year, they saw the resurrected Jesus Christ come down out of heaven (3 Ne. 11:8). The resurrected Christ appeared to a congregation of righteous Nephites at their temple and allowed them to feel the wounds in his hands and feet, and thrust their hands into his side (3 Ne. 11:15). They heard the voice of the Father saying, "Behold my Beloved Son, in whom I am well pleased, in whom I have glorified my name—hear ye him" (3 Ne. 11:7).

For three days, Jesus was with these people. He called and ordained twelve disciples, and taught his gospel of faith, repentance, baptism, and the gift of the Holy Ghost. As the one who had given and fulfilled the law of Moses, he gave the people commandments of obedience, sacrifice of a broken heart, brotherly love and reconciliation, faithfulness to one's spouse, chastity, integrity, charity, and consecration. He taught them to fast and pray, in secret and in their families. He healed their sick, and in the presence of angels and witnesses he blessed the parents and their children. They entered into a sacred covenant with him, and he promised that if they would do his will and keep his commandments they would always have his spirit to be with them (*see* SACRAMENT), would personally know the Lord and would be welcomed into his presence at the last day (3 Ne. 14:21–23; see Welch, pp. 34–83).

As revealed in the Book of Mormon, Jesus wants all people to become like him and their Father in Heaven. Jesus said, "Therefore, what manner of men ought ye to be? Verily I say unto you, even as I am" (3 Ne. 27:27). He invited all, saying, "I would that ye should be perfect even as I, or your Father who is in heaven is perfect" (3 Ne. 12:48). His constant and loving purpose was to make that possible.

BIBLIOGRAPHY

Black, Susan E. *Finding Christ through the Book of Mormon*. Salt Lake City, 1987.

Charlesworth, James H. "Messianism in the Pseudepigrapha and the Book of Mormon." In *Reflections on Mormonism*, ed. Truman G. Madsen, pp. 99–137. Provo, Utah, 1978.

Roberts, B. H. "Christ in the Book of Mormon." *IE* 27 (1924): 188–92.

Scharffs, Stephen. "Unique Insights on Christ

from the Book of Mormon." *Ensign* 18 (Dec. 1988): 8–13.

Welch, John W. *Illuminating the Sermon at the Temple and Sermon on the Mount: An Approach to 3 Nephi 11–18 and Matthew 5–7.* Provo, Utah: FARMS, 1999.

ADDITIONAL SOURCES

Holland, Jeffrey R. *Christ and the New Covenant: The Messianic Message of the Book of Mormon.* Salt Lake City: Deseret Book, 1997.

Oaks, Dallin H. "Another Testament of Jesus Christ." Provo, Utah: FARMS video transcript, 1994.

JOHN W. WELCH

JOSEPH OF EGYPT

[*This entry consists of three articles:*

    Joseph, Son of Jacob
    Writings of Joseph
    Seed of Joseph

Latter-day Saint scripture portrays a broader interest in Joseph of Egypt than the Bible does. The article Joseph, Son of Jacob *deals with the resulting wide sweep of LDS interests in Joseph, including the promises of the Lord about the latter-day importance of Joseph's posterity and his ancestral relationship to the Prophet Joseph Smith. The article* Writings of Joseph *treats specifically the matter of the writings of Joseph preserved in LDS scripture. The article* Seed of Joseph *focuses on the ancestral connection between Book of Mormon peoples and Joseph, son of Jacob.*]

Joseph, Son of Jacob

The Book of Mormon prophet NEPHI₁ said of Joseph, son of Jacob, "He truly prophesied concerning all his seed. And the prophecies which he wrote, there are not many greater" (2 Ne. 4:2). Latter-day Saints hold Joseph to be

a progenitor of a branch of the house of Israel, including certain Book of Mormon PEOPLES about whom he prophesied. Additionally, he is honored as an ancestor of the Prophet Joseph SMITH and many Church members and as one who prophesied concerning the restoration of the gospel of Jesus Christ through Joseph Smith.

The current Bible text preserves little scripture attributed to Joseph of Egypt. However, some writings of Joseph were recorded on the PLATES of brass, a scriptural record brought to the Western Hemisphere from Jerusalem by the prophet LEHI, and known among the Book of Mormon people. Another prophecy, restored by Joseph Smith, is now found in the Joseph Smith Translation (JST) Genesis 50. In this text, the ancient Joseph prophesied the bondage of his father's family in Egypt and their eventual deliverance by Moses, and specifically names him and his brother, Aaron. Moses was to deliver Israel from Egypt, have power over the Red Sea, receive commandments from God, and be assisted by Aaron as his spokesman (JST Gen. 50:24, 29, 34–35).

The same source indicates that the Lord visited Joseph, promising him a righteous posterity, a branch of which would be separated from their kindred and taken to a distant country (JST Gen. 50:25–26). According to the Bible, Jacob had already prophesied that Joseph's branches—Ephraim and Manasseh—would inherit the "utmost bound of the everlasting hills" (Gen. 49:26). Moses described the new land of their inheritance as containing riches of both heaven and earth (Deut. 33:13–15). The Book of Mormon records the partial fulfillment of these prophecies with the exodus of the families of Lehi, a descendant of Manasseh (Alma 10:3), and Ishmael, a descendant of Ephraim (*JD* 23:184), to the western continents. The Book of Mormon is called "the stick of Ephraim" in modern revelation (D&C 27:5) and both "the stick of Ephraim" and "the stick of Joseph" (Ezek. 37:15–28, esp. verses 16 and 19).

Notwithstanding Israel's anticipated deliverance from Egypt under the leadership of Moses, Joseph of Egypt also foresaw that the Israelites would eventually be scattered. Still he was assured that they would be remembered by the Lord and that he would bring their descendants out of "bondage" in the last days. A "choice seer" was to be raised up, a descendant of Joseph, who would bear his name and whose father would also bear the same name. The prophecy stated that this latter-day Joseph would be highly esteemed by Joseph's descendants and would bring them knowledge of their progenitors. Moreover, he would be like both Joseph and Moses. As the ancient Joseph gathered his father's family in Egypt and supplied them with bread during famine, so the latter-day Joseph would gather their descendants from the ends of the earth to feast upon the words of everlasting life. Like Moses, he would bring forth the word of God (the Book of Mormon and other revelations), which would testify of, and sustain, other words of God that had already gone forth (the Bible), thereby confounding false doctrines and laying contentions to rest. As Moses would liberate Israel from Egyptian bondage, the "choice seer" of the last days would liberate them from the bondage of false traditions; as Moses would reveal a new covenant and prepare Israel to enter the promised land, so his latter-day counterpart would reveal a new and everlasting covenant and prepare modern Israel, the Church, for the day of Christ's millennial reign (JST Gen. 50:24–38; cf. 2 Ne. 3; JST Gen. 48:11).

When Joseph Smith's father, Joseph Smith, Sr., acting in his office of patriarch, gave his son a patriarchal blessing, he further illuminated what was known to the ancient Joseph.

> I bless thee with the blessings of thy fathers Abraham, Isaac and Jacob; and . . . thy father Joseph, the son of Jacob. Behold, he looked after his posterity in the last days, when they should be scattered and driven by the Gentiles, and wept before the Lord; he sought diligently to know from whence the Son should come who should bring forth the word of the Lord, by which they might be enlightened, and brought back to the true fold, and his eyes beheld thee, my son; . . . and he said, As my blessings are to extend to the utmost bounds of the everlasting hills; as my father's blessing prevailed, over the blessings of his progenitors, and as my branches are to run over the wall, and my seed are to inherit the choice land whereon the Zion of God shall stand in the last days, from among my seed, scattered with the Gentiles, shall a choice Seer arise, whose bowels shall be a fountain of truth, whose loins shall be girded with the girdle of righteousness, whose hands shall be lifted with acceptance before the God of Jacob to turn away his anger from his anointed, whose heart shall meditate great wisdom, whose intelligence shall circumscribe and comprehend the deep things of God, and whose mouth shall utter the law of the just . . . and he shall feed upon the heritage of Jacob his father. (*Utah Genealogical and Historical Magazine* 23 [Oct. 1932]: 175)

A blessing pronounced by Joseph Smith on Oliver COWDERY (Dec. 18, 1833) notes that Joseph of Egypt had seen Oliver in vision and knew of his scribal role in the translation of the Book of Mormon. Oliver was also told that Joseph of Egypt knew that Oliver would be present when the Aaronic Priesthood, or lesser priesthood, was restored and again when the Melchizedek Priesthood, or higher priesthood, was restored by messengers who received it from Jesus during his earthly ministry (Joseph F. Smith, *IE* 7 [Oct. 1904]: 943). With the restoration of these priesthoods in 1829 and the publication of the Book of Mormon in 1830, the stage was set for fulfilling Moses' promise that the posterity of Ephraim and Manasseh would "push" or gather scattered Israel from the four quarters of the earth (cf. Deut. 33:17).

BIBLIOGRAPHY

Horton, George A., Jr. "Joseph: A Legacy of Greatness." In *Studies in Scripture*, ed. K. Jackson and R. Millet, Vol. 3, pp. 63–92. Salt Lake City, 1985.

McConkie, Joseph Fielding. *His Name Shall Be Joseph*. Salt Lake City, 1980.

JOSEPH FIELDING MCCONKIE

Writings of Joseph

Certain prophecies of Joseph of Egypt were preserved on brass plates carried by NEPHI₁ from Jerusalem to the Americas in approximately 590 B.C. The Book of Mormon makes available some of these prophecies. Although it is not known when Joseph's prophetic texts were recorded, they are doubtless very ancient. By contrast, the *History of Joseph, Prayer of Joseph, Testament of Joseph,* and *Joseph and Asenath* are considered to be Hellenistic Jewish writings, dating between 200 B.C. and A.D. 200, and are of unknown authorship (see Charlesworth). Joseph SMITH noted "writings of Joseph" on papyri that he owned (*HC* 2:236).

According to Alma 46:24, Jacob the patriarch saw that part of Joseph's coat would be preserved, symbolizing a remnant of Joseph's seed (cf. CWHN 6:211–21). In addition, two similar though not identical texts from Joseph are preserved in 2 Nephi 3 and JST Genesis

50. Both prophesy that Moses will arise, that writings from "the fruit of the loins of Judah, shall grow together" with writings of Joseph's descendants, and that a seer named Joseph—whose father would also be named Joseph—would appear in the last days (2 Ne. 3:6–17; JST Gen. 50:24–35; for similar expectations in pseudepigraphic texts, see McConkie). Associates of Joseph Smith saw him as the predicted seer, as did Joseph Smith himself. For instance, President John Taylor affirmed:

> God called [Joseph Smith] to occupy the position that he did. How long ago? Thousands of years ago . . . Prophets prophesied about his coming, that a man should arise whose name should be Joseph, and that his father's name should be Joseph, and also that he should be a descendant of that Joseph who was sold into Egypt. (*JD* 26:106)

BIBLIOGRAPHY

Charlesworth, James H. *The Old Testament Pseudepigrapha*, 2 vols. Garden City, New York, 1983–1985.

McConkie, Joseph F. "Joseph Smith as Found in Ancient Manuscripts." In *Isaiah and the Prophets*, ed. M. Nyman. Provo, Utah, 1984.

JAMES R. CLARK

Seed of Joseph

The Book of Mormon teaches that Joseph, son of Jacob, "obtained a promise of the Lord" that his seed would become a "righteous branch unto the house of Israel" (2 Ne. 3:5) and that a latter-day descendant also named Joseph would have a role in bringing Joseph's seed and all the house of Israel "unto salvation" (2 Ne. 3:15).

While many of Joseph's posterity were among the ten tribes of Israel taken into captivity about 722 B.C. (2 Kgs. 17:5–6), a few descendants had settled in Jerusalem some 200 years earlier (cf. 2 Chr. 15:9–10). From those came the Book of Mormon leaders LEHI and ISHMAEL, who, about 600 B.C., led their families to the Western Hemisphere. Their descendants were later called "a remnant of the seed of [Joseph]" (Alma 46:23–24). Lehi reported that Joseph's prophecies concerning his seed included the following: (1) they would become a righteous people; (2) the Messiah would manifest himself to them; (3) a latter-day seer like Moses, raised up by God from Joseph's seed, would himself be called Joseph (2 Ne. 3:1–25); and (4) the righteous seed of the ancient Joseph who accept the gospel will help in building the New Jerusalem and will participate in events of the last days (3 Ne. 20:10–28; 21:2–26).

BIBLIOGRAPHY

Ludlow, Daniel H. *A Companion to Your Study of the Book of Mormon.* Salt Lake City, 1976.

Pratt, Orson. "The Blessings of Joseph." *JD* 14:7–11.

LIESEL C. MCBRIDE

JUDGMENT

All humankind shall stand before Jesus, "and he shall separate them one from another, as a shepherd divideth his sheep from the goats" (Matt. 25:32). The verb "separate" reflects the Lord's determination of exact boundaries between good and evil, since he "cannot look upon sin with the least degree of allowance" (D&C 1:31). The Greek New Testament word for judgment *(krino)* means to separate or to decide, and refers not only to God's decisions but to those made by man as well (Matt. 7:1–2).

AMULEK warned that this life is the time to prepare to meet God (Alma 34:32). Mortal-

ity requires basic decisions of a moral and spiritual character, in which individuals are free to choose for themselves yet are accountable to God for their choices. In turn, God will render a perfect and just decision to determine blessings or punishments. In the judgment there will be a perfect restoration of joy for righteous living and of misery for evil (Alma 41:3–5). After death is not the time to repent: "Ye cannot say, when ye are brought to that awful crisis, that I will repent, that I will return to my God; . . . for that same spirit which doth possess your bodies at the time that ye go out of this life . . . will have power to possess your body in that eternal world" (Alma 34:34).

Judgment applies to "the whole human family" (Morm. 3:20; cf. John 5:25–29; *TPJS*, p. 149). Every soul will come before the bar of God through the power of the atonement and the RESURRECTION (Jacob 6:9). Indeed, as Christ was lifted up on the cross, he will raise all men before him in judgment (3 Ne. 27:14–15; *TPJS*, p. 62). Christ has been given the responsibility for judgment. He taught, "The Father judgeth no man, but hath committed all judgment unto the Son" (John 5:22). Others have been given some role in judgment, such as the twelve apostles in Palestine and the twelve disciples among the Nephites as described in the Book of Mormon (Morm. 3:18–19). Individuals will also judge themselves either by having a perfect knowledge of their joy and righteousness or by having a perfect knowledge of their guilt and unrighteousness (2 Ne. 9:14, 46). All have the assurance, however, that final judgment is in the hands of Christ (2 Ne. 9:41).

Three sets of records will be used in judgment: the records kept in heaven, the records kept on earth (D&C 128:6–7), and the records embedded in the consciousness of each individual (*MD*, p. 97; cf. Alma 11:43). Individuals are judged according to their works, thoughts, words, and the desires of their hearts (Alma 12:14; D&C 137:9).

There can be no pretense or hypocrisy in the manner in which people accept and live the gospel (2 Ne. 31:13). The Lord will judge members of the Church as to whether they have sought to deny themselves all ungodliness (Moro. 10:32) and whether they have served others with their whole soul (D&C 4:2–3). Other criteria for judgment include their concern for the needs of others, both spiritual and physical, and the use they make of the light and talents that they have been given (D&C 82:2–3). To merit God's approval, everyone must live and serve according to his will (Matt. 7:21–23) and do all things the Lord commands (Abr. 3:25). Yet, since "all have sinned, and come short of the glory of God" (Rom. 3:23), except Jesus only, all are dependent on the Atonement and on repentance to escape the demands of justice (*see* JUSTICE AND MERCY).

Judgment is an expression of the love of God for his children and is exercised mercifully. Mercy takes into account the variety and differing circumstances of human life. For instance, many of God's expectations are relative to the opportunity that individuals have had to know the gospel. Nevertheless, mercy cannot rob justice, and those who rebel openly against God merit punishment (Alma 42:25; Mosiah 2:38–39; 2 Pet. 2:9). Although the Lord's "arms of mercy are extended [to all]" (Alma 5:33), only those who repent have claim on mercy through the Son (Alma 12:33–34). God's judgment reflects the truth that he is "a perfect, just God, and a merciful God also" (Alma 42:15). Eventually all persons will acknowledge that God's judgment is just: "every nation, kindred, tongue, and people shall see eye to eye and shall confess before God that his judgments are just" (Mosiah 16:1).

The principle of judgment was operative

in the premortal estate, is continuously operative during mortal life, and will continue in the spirit world and beyond, through resurrection and final judgment. In the premortal state Satan and "a third part" of God's children were denied the opportunity of mortality because they rebelled against God (Abr. 3:24–28; D&C 29:36–38). In mortal life nations and peoples have been destroyed or scattered when they have become ripened in iniquity and the judgments of God have thereby come upon them (1 Ne. 17:37).

Judgment during mortality is a continuous process to assess people's worthiness to participate in the saving ordinances of the gospel and to serve in the Church. This is done by means of interviews with local Church leaders. Priesthood leaders are called upon to judge the deeds of members who transgress God's commandments to determine their standing in the Church. Judgment also occurs at death as individuals are received into the spirit world either in happiness or in misery (Alma 40:9–14).

In LDS doctrine, individual destiny after the final judgment is not limited to either heaven or hell. Although the wicked will be thrust into hell (D&C 76:106); nevertheless, all humankind (except those who deny the Holy Ghost and become sons of perdition) will be redeemed when Christ perfects his work (D&C 76:107). Thus, nearly everyone who has lived on the earth will eventually inherit a degree of glory, it being that amount of heavenly bliss and glory that they have the capacity and the qualifications to receive.

Concerning those who die without an opportunity to hear the gospel, the Lord revealed to Joseph SMITH that "all who have died without a knowledge of this gospel, who would have received it if they had been permitted to tarry, shall be heirs of the celestial kingdom of God; Also all that shall die henceforth without a knowledge of it, who would have received it with all their hearts, shall be heirs of that kingdom" (D&C 137:7–8). Little children who die also receive the full blessings of salvation (Moro. 8:11, 22). All mankind will be taught the gospel, either on earth or in the spirit world. All necessary ordinances will be performed on the earth vicariously by living proxies in the temple for those who did not have the opportunity to receive the gospel while in this life, so that they may accept or reject the gospel in the spirit world and be judged on the same basis as those who receive the gospel on earth and remain faithful (1 Pet. 4:6). Such doctrine is not only just; it is also a merciful expression of the pure love of Christ (*TPJS*, p. 218; Moro. 7:44–47).

BIBLIOGRAPHY

McConkie, Bruce R. *MD*, pp. 398–99, 400–408. Salt Lake City, 1966.

Smith, Joseph Fielding, comp. *TPJS*, pp. 216–23. Salt Lake City, 1938.

DEAN JARMAN

JUSTICE AND MERCY

Justice and mercy are attributes of deity. They are also eternal principles. The "justice of God" (Alma 41:2; 42:14) is a principle so fundamental that without it, "God would cease to be God" (Alma 42:13). Of equivalent significance is God's mercy, which, broadly, is the ultimate source of all of the blessings of the human race and, specifically, is the principle that allows mankind's redemption. The competing demands of justice's claim for punishment and mercy's claim for forgiveness are reconciled by the unifying power of the atonement of Jesus Christ.

On one hand, justice rewards righteousness. "And when we obtain any blessing from God, it is by obedience to that law upon which it is predicated" (D&C 130:21, see also D&C 82:10). On the other, justice requires penalties as a consequence of disobedience to the laws of God, for "I the Lord cannot look upon sin with the least degree of allowance" (D&C 1:31). Just as obedience to divine law leads to blessings, justice affixes a punishment to each violation of the Lord's commandments (Alma 42:17–18, 22), and men and women will be "punished for their own sins" (A of F 2). Each person will thus be judged according to his or her works (Rom. 2:5–6; 3 Ne. 27:14; Alma 41:2–6), although the degree of accountability varies according to the extent of each person's knowledge and culpability (2 Ne. 9:25; Mosiah 3:11). Yet the principle of mercy allows the atonement of Jesus Christ to pay the demands of justice on a repentant transgressor's behalf in a way that reconciles the principles of mercy and justice.

Not just any person may invoke mercy on behalf of another: "Now there is not any man that can sacrifice his own blood which will atone for the sins of another. . . . therefore there can be nothing which is short of an infinite atonement which will suffice for the sins of the world" (Alma 34:11–12). Jesus Christ alone can achieve such an infinite atonement "once for all" (Hebrews 10:10) because of his nature as the actual son of God in the flesh and because he was himself without sin.

Mercy is not extended arbitrarily. To protect individuals from the undeserved effects of sins for which they are not responsible, the Atonement unconditionally paid the penalty for the transgression of Adam and Eve in the Garden of Eden. It pays similarly for sins committed in ignorance (Mosiah 3:11; see also Moses 6:54). However, the Atonement removes the penalty for personal sins for which one is accountable only on the condition of individual repentance.

In this way, the concepts of justice, mercy,

and the Atonement retain both a specific integrity and a logically consistent relationship: "The plan of mercy could not be brought about except an atonement should be made; therefore God himself atoneth for the sins of the world, to bring about the plan of mercy, to appease the demands of justice, that God might be a perfect, just God, and a merciful God also. . . . But there is a law given, and a punishment affixed, and a repentance granted; which repentance mercy claimeth; otherwise, justice claimeth the creature. . . . For behold, justice exerciseth all his demands, and also mercy claimeth all which is her own; and thus, none but the truly penitent are saved" (Alma 42:13, 15, 22, 24).

Mercy is thus rehabilitative, not retributive or arbitrary. The Lord asks repentance from a transgressor, not to compensate the Savior for paying the debt of justice, but to induce the transgressor to undertake a meaningful process of personal development toward a Christlike nature.

At the same time, mercy depends ultimately on the Lord's extension of unmerited grace. Even though conditioned on repentance for personal sins, mercy is never fully "earned" by its recipients. Repentance is a necessary, but not a sufficient, condition of salvation and exaltation. "For we know that it is by grace that we are saved, after all we can do" (2 Ne. 25:23). The unearned nature of mercy is demonstrated by the Atonement's having unconditionally compensated for the disabilities imposed on mankind by the FALL OF ADAM. Adam and Eve and their posterity were utterly powerless to overcome the physical and spiritual deaths that were introduced by the Fall. Moreover, transgressors do not "pay" fully for their sins through the process of repentance. Even though repentance requires restitution to the extent of one's ability, most forms of restitution are beyond any person's ability to achieve. No matter how com-

plete our repentance, it would all be to no avail without a mediator willing and able to pay our debt to justice, on condition of our repentance. Thus, even with sincere and complete repentance, all are utterly dependent on Jesus Christ.

Through the atonement of Jesus Christ, justice and mercy are interdependent and interactive, demonstrating that God cannot be just without being merciful, nor merciful without being just.

BIBLIOGRAPHY

Hafen, Bruce C. "Justice, Mercy, and Rehabilitation." In *The Broken Heart*, pp. 143–54. Salt Lake City, 1989.

Oaks, Dallin H. "The Atonement and the Principles of Justice and Mercy." Unpublished manuscript, from May 1, 1985, General Authority training meeting.

Roberts, B. H. *The Atonement*. Salt Lake City, 1911.

Taylor, John. *Mediation and Atonement*. Salt Lake City, 1882.

BRUCE C. HAFEN

L

LAMAN

Laman was the eldest of six sons of LEHI and Sariah. Lehi was the patriarchal head and prophet at the beginning of the Book of Mormon, and Laman opposed his father and his younger brother NEPHI₁. Unlike the family conflicts in the book of Genesis between Esau and Jacob and between Joseph and his jealous brothers, the hostilities between Laman and Nephi were never quieted or reconciled.

Laman's opposition to the things of God arose from a combination of conflicting spiritual values and a common reaction against the favor he perceived going to a younger brother. The record of Nephi portrays Laman as strong-willed, hard-hearted, impulsive, violent, judgmental, and lacking in faith. Though Laman followed his father in their journeyings, he never shared in the spiritual calling that inspired Lehi.

In his rebelliousness, Laman charged that Lehi was a visionary and foolish man (1 Ne. 2:11). Still Lehi continued to exhort him "with all the feeling of a tender parent," even though he feared from what he had seen in a vision that Laman and Lemuel would refuse to come into God's presence (1 Ne. 8:36–37).

Laman objected to leaving Jerusalem and the family's lands, possessions, and security, and to traveling to a new land (1 Ne. 2:11). Throughout their journey he complained of the hardships and was resentful that God had selected Nephi to become "a ruler and a teacher" ahead of him (1 Ne. 2:21–22; 16:36–38). Laman and Lemuel beat Nephi with a rod (1 Ne. 3:28), attempted to leave him tied up in the wilderness to die (1 Ne. 7:16), bound him on board ship, and treated him harshly (1 Ne. 18:11). On various occasions, Laman was rebuked by an angel, chastened by the voice of the Lord, or "shocked" by divine power (1 Ne. 17:53). Still, he longed for the popular life of Jerusalem even though Lehi had prophesied the city would be destroyed.

Laman was supported in his stance by his wife and children, by Lemuel (the next eldest son) and his family, and by some of the sons of ISHMAEL and their families. Before he died, Lehi left his first blessing with Laman and Lemuel on the condition that they would "hearken unto the voice of Nephi" (2 Ne. 1:28–29), but they so opposed Nephi that he was instructed by God to lead the faithful to settle a new land away from Laman and Lemuel in order to preserve their lives and religious beliefs.

Laman and his followers became the LAMANITES, persistent enemies of the NE-PHITES. Stemming from these early personal conflicts, the Lamanites insisted for many generations that Nephi had deprived them of their rights. Thus, the Lamanites taught their children "that they should hate [the Nephites] . . . and do all they could to destroy them" (Mosiah 10:17). When Laman's descendants were converted to faith in Christ, however, they were exemplary in righteousness; and Book of Mormon prophets foretold a noteworthy future for them in the latter days.

BIBLIOGRAPHY

Matthews, Robert J. *Who's Who in the Book of Mormon*. Salt Lake City, 1976.

McConkie, Joseph F., and Robert L. Millet. *Doctrinal Commentary on the Book of Mormon*, Vol. 1. Salt Lake City, 1987.

ALAN K. PARRISH

LAMANITES

The name Lamanite refers to an Israelite people spoken of in the Book of Mormon, who were descendants of LEHI and Ishmael, both of whom were descendants of JOSEPH OF EGYPT (1 Ne. 5:14). They were part of the prophet Lehi's colony, which was commanded of the Lord to leave Jerusalem and go to a new promised land (in the Western Hemisphere). The Lamanite peoples in the Book of Mormon during the first 600 years of their history are all linked in some way to LAMAN and Lemuel, Lehi's oldest sons. At times the name refers to "the people of Laman"; at other times it can identify unbelievers and ignore ancestral lines, depending on contextual specifics regarding peoples, time, and place.

LAMANITES IN THE BOOK OF MORMON. After the death of the prophet Lehi (c. 582 B.C.), the colony divided into two main groups, Lamanites and NEPHITES, (2 Ne. 5), each taking the name from their leader. These patronyms later evolved into royal titles (Mosiah 24:3; cf. Jacob 1:11). The Book of Mormon, though a Nephite record, focuses on both Lamanites and Nephites, by means of complex contrasts between the two groups. In the text, other peoples are generally subsumed under one of these two main divisions:

> Now the people which were not Lamanites were Nephites; nevertheless, they were called Nephites, Jacobites, Josephites, Zoramites, Lamanites, Lemuelites, and Ishmaelites. But I, Jacob, shall not hereafter distinguish them by these names, but I shall call them Lamanites that seek to destroy the people of Nephi, and those who are friendly to Nephi I shall call Nephites, or the people of Nephi, according to the reigns of the kings. (Jacob 1:13–14; see also Morm. 1:8–9)

In the beginning, political and religious disagreements arose between the Lamanites and the Nephites. Subsequently, an increasing cultural differentiation of the Lamanite people from the Nephites seems to have resulted from their different responses to Lehi's religious teachings. Social change quickly took place along many lines. Consequently, the name Lamanite can refer to descendants of Laman and his party; to an incipient nationality based upon an ideology, with its own lineage history and religious beliefs (Mosiah 10:12–17); or to one or more cultures.

The Book of Mormon describes several Lamanite cultures and lifestyles, including hunting-gathering (2 Ne. 5:24), commerce (Mosiah 24:7), sedentary herding (Alma 17), a city-state pattern of governance, and nomadism (Alma 22:28). The politicized nature of early Lamanite society is reflected in the way in which dissenters from Nephite society sought refuge among Lamanites, were accepted, and came to identify themselves with them, much as some Lamanites moved in the opposite direction.

Early in the sixth century of Lamanite history (c. 94–80 B.C.), large-scale Lamanite conversions further divided the Lamanite peoples as many embraced the messianic faith in Jesus Christ taught by Nephite missionaries (Alma 17–26). The Lamanite king Lamoni, a vassal; his father, the suzerain king; and many of their subjects accepted the prophesied Christ and rejected their former lifestyles. They took upon themselves a covenant of pacifism, burying their weapons and renouncing warfare, and moved into Nephite territory for their safety (Alma 27:21–26; 43:11–12). This pattern of Lamanite conversion lasted for at least eighty-four years and through several generations (cf. Alma 24:5–6, 15–19, 20–24; 26:31–34; 44:20; Hel. 5:51; 15:9). This major division of Lamanite society had significant political impact: the identity of some of these converts remained Lamanite, but distinct from those who rejected the religion; others chose to be numbered among the Nephites (3 Ne. 2:12, 14–16); and the unconverted Lamanites were strengthened by numerous dissenters from Nephite subgroups (Alma 43:13), some of whom chose explicitly to retain their former identities (3 Ne. 6:3).

After the destructions that occurred at the time of Christ's crucifixion and the subsequent conversions (3 Ne. 11–28), a new society was established in which ethnic as well as economic differences were overcome, and there were no "Lamanites, nor any manner of -ites; but they were in one, the children of Christ" (4 Ne. 1:17). This situation persisted until almost the end of the second century A.D., when those who rejected the Christian church, regardless of their ancestry, "had revolted from the church and taken upon them the name of Lamanites; therefore there began to be Lamanites again in the land" (4 Ne. 1:20). Divisions increased, so that by A.D. 231 "there arose a people who were called the Nephites, and they were true believers in Christ; and among them there were those who were called by the Lamanites—Jacobites, and Josephites, and Zoramites. . . . and . . . they who rejected the gospel were called Lamanites, and Lemuelites, and Ishmaelites" (4 Ne. 1:36–45).

It had been prophesied that eventually only Lamanite peoples and those who joined them would remain of the original groups (Alma 45:13–14). After the final battles between Lamanites and Nephites, only those who accepted Lamanite rule survived in Book of Mormon lands (Morm. 6:15).

LAMANITES IN EARLY LDS HISTORY. At the beginning of LDS Church history, one reason the Book of Mormon was published was so that it could be taken to the Lamanites (D&C 19:26–27). Within six months of the Church's organization, missionaries were sent to people thought to have Lamanite ancestry (D&C 28:8; 32:2).

[See also Peoples of the Book of Mormon; Native Americans.]

BIBLIOGRAPHY

"The Church and Descendants of Book of Mormon Peoples." *Ensign* 5 (Dec. 1975); the entire issue is devoted to this topic.

De Hoyos, Arturo. *The Old and the Modern Lamanite*. Provo, Utah, 1970.

Sorenson, John L. *An Ancient American Setting for the Book of Mormon*. Salt Lake City, 1985.

Tyler, S. Lyman. *Modern Results of the Lamanite Dispersion: The Indians of the Americas*. Provo, Utah, 1965.

Widtsoe, John A., and Franklin S. Harris, Jr. *Seven Claims of the Book of Mormon*. Independence, Mo., 1935.

ADDITIONAL SOURCE

Bushman, Richard L. "The Lamanite View of Book of Mormon History." In *By Study and Also by Faith: Essays in Honor of Hugh W. Nibley*, edited by John M. Lundquist and Stephen D. Ricks, 2:52–72. Salt Lake City and Provo, Utah: Deseret Book and FARMS, 1990.

GORDON C. THOMASSON

LANGUAGE

The language of the Book of Mormon exhibits features typical of a translation from an ancient Near Eastern text as well as the stamp of nineteenth-century English and the style of the King James Version (KJV) of the Bible. That the language of the Book of Mormon should resemble that of the KJV seems only natural, since in the time of the Prophet Joseph SMITH, the KJV was the most widely read book in America and formed the standard of religious language for most English-speaking people (see CWHN 8:212–18). Furthermore, the Book of Mormon shares certain affinities with the KJV: both include works of ancient prophets of Israel as well as accounts of part of the ministry of Jesus Christ, both are translations into English, and both are to become "one" in God's hand as collections of his word to his children (Ezek. 37:16–17; 1 Ne. 13:41; D&C 42:12).

LANGUAGES USED BY THE NEPHITES. Statements in the Book of Mormon have spawned differing views about the language in which the book was originally written. In approximately 600 B.C., NEPHI₁—the first Book of Mormon author and one who had spent his youth in Jerusalem—wrote, "I make a record [the small plates of Nephi] in the language of my father, which consists of the learning of the Jews and the language of the Egyptians" (1 Ne. 1:2). One thousand years later, MORONI₂, the last Nephite prophet, noted concerning the PLATES of Mormon that "we have written this record . . . in the characters which are called among us the reformed Egyptian, being handed down and altered by us, according to our manner of speech. And if our plates [metal leaves] had been sufficiently large we should have written in Hebrew; but the Hebrew hath been altered by us also. . . . But the Lord knoweth . . . that none other people knoweth our language" (Morm. 9:32–34). In light of these two passages, it is evident that Nephite record keepers knew Hebrew and something of Egyptian. It is unknown whether Nephi, Mormon, or Moroni wrote Hebrew in modified Egyptian characters or inscribed their plates in both the Egyptian language and Egyptian characters or whether Nephi wrote in one language and Mormon and Moroni, who lived some nine hundred years later, in another. The mention of "characters" called "reformed Egyptian" tends to support the hypothesis of Hebrew in Egyptian script. Although Nephi's observation (1 Ne. 1:2) is troublesome for that view, the statement is ambiguous and inconclusive for both views.

Nephite authors seem to have patterned their writing after the plates of brass, a record containing biblical texts composed before 600 B.C. that was in the possession of descendants of JOSEPH OF EGYPT (1 Ne. 5:11–16). At least portions of this record were written in Egyptian, since knowledge of "the language of the Egyptians" enabled LEHI, father of Nephi, to "read these engravings" (Mosiah 1:2–4). But whether it was the Egyptian language or Hebrew written in Egyptian script is again not clear. Egyptian was widely used in Lehi's day, but because poetic writings are skewed in translation, because prophetic writings were generally esteemed as sacred, and because Hebrew was the language of the Israelites in the seventh century B.C., it would have been unusual for the writings of Isaiah and Jeremiah—substantially preserved on the brass plates (1 Ne. 5:13; 19:23)—to have been translated from Hebrew into a foreign tongue at this early date. Thus, Hebrew portions written in Hebrew script, Egyptian portions in Egyptian script, and Hebrew portions in Egyptian script are all possibilities. If the brass plates came into being while the Israelites were still in Egypt, then earlier portions (e.g., prophecies of Joseph in Egypt) were possibly written in Egyptian and later portions (e.g., words of Jeremiah) in Hebrew.

Concerning Book of Mormon composition, Mormon 9:33 indicates that limited space on the GOLD PLATES dictated using Egyptian characters rather than Hebrew. In Lehi's day, both Hebrew and Egyptian were written with consonants only. Unlike Hebrew, Egyptian had biconsonantal and even triconsonantal signs. Employing such characters—particularly in modified form—would save space.

Written characters were handed down and altered according to Nephite speech (Morm. 9:32). This observation suggests that at least later generations of Nephites used Egyptian characters to write their contemporary spoken language, an altered form of Hebrew. It is extremely unlikely that a people isolated from simultaneous contact with the two languages could have maintained a conversational distinction between, and fluency in the two languages over a thousand-year period. Thus, if Egyptian characters were altered as the living language changed, then the Nephites were probably using such characters to write their spoken language, which was largely Hebrew.

Though some of Lehi's group that left Jerusalem may have spoken Egyptian, a reading knowledge of the script on the brass plates would have allowed them to "read these engravings" (Mosiah 1:4). But the possibility that Lehi's colony could maintain spoken Egyptian as a second language through a thousand years without merging it with Hebrew or losing it is beyond probability. Therefore, the fact that the Nephites had "altered" the Egyptian characters according to their "manner of speech" underscores the probability that they were writing Hebrew with Egyptian characters. In addition, Moroni's language (c. A.D. 400) was probably different enough from that of Lehi (c. 600 B.C.) that reading Lehi's language may have required as much study in Moroni's day as Old English requires of modern English-speaking people.

LANGUAGE AMONG NATIVE AMERICANS. Because Moroni's time represents a near midpoint between Lehi and the present, a consideration of the near end of the continuum could be helpful. The vague picture presented by statements in the text might be brought into focus by examining American Indian languages. The time depth from Latin to modern Romance languages is only slightly less than that from Lehi to the present. Similarities among Romance languages are plentiful and obvious, while language similarities between Native American languages and Hebrew or Egyptian are generally viewed as neither plentiful nor obvious.

Though some professionals have alluded to similarities, no study has yet convinced scholars of Near Eastern links with any pre-Columbian American language.

One study, however, holds promise for demonstrating links to the Uto-Aztecan language family (Stubbs, 1988). Though other language groups offer suggestive leads, Uto-Aztecan yields more than seven hundred similarities to Hebrew, in phonological, morphological, and semantic patterns consistent with modern linguistic methods. While a handful of Egyptian words are identifiable, they are minimal compared to Hebrew correspondents.

HEBRAISMS IN THE BOOK OF MORMON. Many typical Hebrew language patterns have been identified in the Book of Mormon, though several are also characteristic of other Near Eastern languages. For example, the cognate accusative, literarily redundant in English, is used in Hebrew for emphasis: "They feared a fear" (Ps. 14:5, Hebrew text). Similar structures appear in the Book of Mormon: "to fear exceedingly, with fear" (Alma 18:5), another possible translation of the same cognate accusative (cf. 1 Ne. 3:2; 8:2; Enos 1:13).

Hebrew employs prepositional phrases as adverbs more often than individual adverbs, a feature typical of Book of Mormon language: "in haste" (3 Ne. 21:29) instead of "hastily" and "with gladness" (2 Ne. 28:28) instead of "gladly."

Tvedtnes has noted a possible example of Hebrew agreement: "This people *is* a free people" (Alma 30:24; emphasis added). In English, "people" is usually considered grammatically plural, but in Hebrew it is often singular. While this phrase in Alma may have been verbless, it may also have contained the third-person singular pronoun /hu/ placed between the two noun phrases or at the end as an anaphoric demonstrative functioning as

a copula verb. Uto-Aztecan Indian languages also have the word /hu/, which is a third-person singular pronoun in some languages but a "be" verb in others.

Possession in English is shown in two constructs—"the man's house" and "the house of the man"—but only the latter construct is employed in Hebrew. The lack of apostrophe possession in the Book of Mormon is consistent with a translation from the Hebrew construct. Further, the "of" construct is common for adjectival relationships in Hebrew. Correspondingly, the Book of Mormon consistently employs phrases such as "plates of brass" (1 Ne. 3:12) instead of "brass plates" and "walls of stone" (Alma 48:8) rather than "stone walls."

Sentence structures and clause-combining mechanisms in Hebrew differ from those in English. Long strings of subordinate clauses and verbal expressions, such as those in Helaman 1:16–17 and Mosiah 2:20–21 and 7:21–22, are acceptable in Hebrew, though unorthodox and discouraged in English: "Ye all are witnesses . . . that Zeniff, who was made king, . . . he being over-zealous, . . . therefore being deceived by . . . king Laman, who having entered into a treaty, . . . and having yielded up [various cities], . . . and the land round about—and all this he did, for the sole purpose of bringing this people . . . into bondage" (Mosiah 7:21–22).

Frequent phrases such as "from before" and "by the hand of" represent rather literal translations from Hebrew. For example, "he fled from before them" (Mosiah 17:4), instead of the more typically English "he fled from them," portrays the common Hebrew compound preposition /millifne/.

While many words and names found in the Book of Mormon have exact equivalents in the Hebrew Bible, certain others exhibit Semitic characteristics, though their spelling does not always match known Hebrew forms. For example, "Rabbanah" as "great king" (Alma 18:13) may have affinities with the Hebrew root /rbb/, meaning "to be great or many." "Rameumptom" (Alma 31:21), meaning "holy stand," contains consonantal patterns suggesting the stems /rmm/ramah/, "to be high," and /tmm/tam/tom/, "to be complete, perfect, holy." The /p/ between the /m/ and /t/ is a linguistically natural outgrowth of a bilabial /m/ in cluster with a stop /t/, such as the /p/ in /assumption/ from /assume + tion/, and the /b/ in Spanish /hombre/ from Latin /homere/.

Claims that Joseph Smith composed the Book of Mormon by merely imitating King James English, using biblical names and inventing others, typically exhibit insensitivities about its linguistic character. Names such as "Alma" have been thought peculiar inventions. However, the discovery of the name "Alma" in a Jewish text (second century A.D.), the seven hundred observed similarities between Hebrew and Uto-Aztecan, literary patterns such as chiasmus, and numerous other features noted in studies since 1830 combine to make the fabrication of the book an overwhelming challenge for anyone in Joseph Smith's day.

[See also Authorship of the Book of Mormon; Literature, Book of Mormon as; Names in the Book of Mormon; Near Eastern Background of the Book of Mormon; Translation of the Book of Mormon by Joseph Smith.]

BIBLIOGRAPHY

Hoskisson, Paul Y. "Ancient Near Eastern Background of the Book of Mormon." *FARMS Reprint.* Provo, Utah, 1982.

Nibley, Hugh W. *Lehi in the Desert and the World of the Jaredites.* CWHN 5.

———. *An Approach to the Book of Mormon.* CWHN 6.

Sperry, Sidney B. "The Book of Mormon as Translation English." *IE* 38 (Mar. 1935): 141, 187–88.

———. "Hebrew Idioms in the Book of Mormon." *IE* 57 (Oct. 1954): 703, 728–29.

———. *Book of Mormon Compendium.* Salt Lake City, 1968.

Stubbs, Brian D. "A Creolized Base in Uto-Aztecan." *FARMS Paper.* Provo, Utah, 1988.

Tvedtnes, John A. "Hebraisms in the Book of Mormon: A Preliminary Survey." *BYU Studies* 11 (Autumn 1970): 50–60.

BRIAN D. STUBBS

LAW OF MOSES

Distinctive views concerning the law of Moses and its relationship to Christ and to the attainment of individual salvation are set forth in the Book of Mormon and Doctrine and Covenants. The Church of Jesus Christ of Latter-day Saints teaches that this law was given by God to Moses, that it formed part of a peculiar covenant of obedience and favor between God and his people, that it symbolized and foreshadowed things to come, and that it was fulfilled in the atonement of Jesus Christ.

The law of Moses is best understood in a broad sense. It consists of "judgments," "statutes," "ordinances," and "commandments." The Book of Mormon refers to it also as including various "performances," "sacrifices," and "burnt offerings." Nowhere in scripture is its full breadth, depth, diversity, and definition made explicit. On such matters, information can be drawn from the Pentateuch itself (the Torah) and from biblical scholarship, but one can only conjecture as to what these terms meant to Book of Mormon writers.

A narrow definition would confine the law of Moses to a body of prohibitions and commands set forth in separate, unrelated literary units within the first five books of the Bible. This view makes it difficult to speak of "biblical law," since these provisions are not drawn together as a unity by the Torah itself. The scattered codes and series include the Covenant Code (Ex. 20:23–23:19), Deuteronomic Law (Deut. 12–26), the Holiness Code (Lev. 17–26), purity laws (Lev. 11–15), festival rituals (Deut. 16), regulations pertaining to sacrifices (Num. 28–29), and the Ten Commandments (Ex. 20:2–17; Deut. 5:6–21). While some biblical scholars conclude that "these were once independent units, subsisting in their own right, each having its own purpose and sphere of validity, and having been transmitted individually for its own sake in the first place" (Noth, p. 7), Latter-day Saints generally accept at face value statements in the Bible that attribute authorship to Moses, but the Church has taken no official stand concerning the collection and transmission of these legal texts in the Pentateuch. Scribes and copyists evidently made a few changes after the time of Moses (e.g., compare Moses 1–5 with Gen. 1–6).

Compounding the question of what was meant by the term "law of Moses" in the Book of Mormon is the fact that the "five books of Moses" that the Nephites possessed predated Ezra's redaction and canonization of the Pentateuch (444 B.C.). Quoted passages (e.g., Mosiah 13:12–24), however, indicate that the Nephite laws were substantially similar to the biblical texts that Jews and Christians have today.

As early as the third century A.D., the Jewish view held that the commandments numbered 613. Rabbi Simlai reportedly stated that "613 commandments were revealed to Moses at Sinai, 365 being prohibitions equal in number to the solar days, and 248 being mandates corresponding in number to the limbs [sic] of the human body" (Encyclopedia Judaica 5:760, quoting Talmud Bavli, Makkot 23b). About a third of these commandments have long been obsolete, such as those relating to the tabernacle and the conquest of Canaan. Others were directed to special classes, such as the Nazarites, judges, the king, or the high priest, or to circumstances that would rarely occur. Excluding these, about a hundred apply to the whole people and range from the spiritually sublime to the mundane. Examples of eternally relevant commandments of the law of Moses are the Ten Commandments and those relating to loving God, worshiping God, loving one's neighbor, loving the stranger, giving charity to the poor, dealing honestly, not seeking revenge, and not bearing a grudge. Other commandments cover a kaleidoscope of daily matters, including valuing houses and fields, laws of inheritance, paying wages, agriculture, animal husbandry, and forbidden foods. Jewish scholars classify these as commandments vis-à-vis God and commandments vis-à-vis fellow human beings (Mishnah Yoma 8:9).

Two other definitions should be mentioned. One identifies the law of Moses as coextensive with the Pentateuch. Around the time of Christ, New Testament writers sometimes called the Pentateuch "the law" (Luke 24:44; Gal. 4:21), even though the word "torah" has broader meaning (i.e., "teachings") and the Pentateuch contains poetry and narratives in addition to commandments, and some passages speak to all persons and nations (Gen. 9:1–7). The other defines the law as theologically synonymous with the doctrinal belief, whether mistaken or not, that salvation is dependent upon the keeping of commandments, thus distinguishing the law from grace, which for many Christians eliminates the task of sorting out which Mosaic laws are still in force.

Agreeing in some respects and departing in others from traditional Jewish or Christian views, the main lines of LDS belief about the law of Moses are as follows:

1. Jesus Christ was Jehovah, the God of the Old Testament who gave the law to Moses (3 Ne. 15:5; *TPJS*, p. 276). Jesus, speaking after his atonement and resurrection, stated, "The law is fulfilled that was given unto Moses. Behold, I am he that gave the law, and I am he who covenanted with my people Israel" (3 Ne. 15:4–9).

2. The entire law was in several senses fulfilled, completed, superseded, and enlivened by Jesus Christ. Jesus said, "In me it hath *all* been fulfilled" (3 Ne. 12:17–18). Its "great and eternal gospel truths" (*MD*, p. 398) are applicable through Jesus Christ in all dispensations as he continues to reveal his will to prophets "like unto Moses" (2 Ne. 3:9–11).

3. Latter-day Saints believe that the law of Moses was issued to the Israelites as a preparatory gospel to be a schoolmaster to bring them to Christ and the fulness of his gospel (Gal. 3:24; cf. Jacob 4:5; Alma 34:14). The authority to act in the name of God is embodied in two priesthoods, the Melchizedek or higher, which embraces all divinely delegated authority and extends to the fulness of the law of the gospel, and the Aaronic or lesser, which extends only to lesser things, such as the law of carnal commandments and baptism (D&C 84:26–27). While Moses and his predecessors had the higher priesthood and the fulness of the gospel of Christ, both of which were to be given to the children of Israel, "they hardened their hearts and could not endure [God's] presence; therefore, the Lord in his wrath . . . took Moses out of their midst, and the Holy Priesthood also; and the lesser priesthood continued" (D&C 84:23–24; see Heb. 3:16–19; Mosiah 3:14; *TPJS*, p. 60).

4. Book of Mormon people brought the law of Moses with them from Jerusalem. Even though they endeavored to observe it strictly until the coming of Christ (e.g., 2 Ne.

5:10; Alma 30:3), they believed in Christ and knew that salvation did not come by the law alone but by Christ (2 Ne. 25:23–24), and understood that the law would be superseded by the Messiah (Mosiah 13:27–28; 2 Ne. 25:23–25).

5. For Latter-day Saints, all things are given of God to man as types and shadows of the redeeming and atoning acts of Christ (2 Ne. 11:4; Mosiah 13:31). Thus, the law of Moses typified various aspects of the atonement of Christ.

6. Covenant making, promises, and obedience to commandments are part of the fulness of the gospel of Christ: "Through the Atonement of Christ, all mankind may be saved, by obedience to the laws and ordinances of the Gospel" (A of F 3). Both for Latter-day Saints and regarding Jewish observance of the law of Moses, GRACE, FAITH, and works are all essential to salvation: "It is by grace that we are saved, after all we can do" (2 Ne. 25:23). No mortal's obedience to law will ever be perfect. By law alone, no one will be saved. The grace of God makes up the deficit. The Church does not subscribe to a doctrine of free-standing grace unrelated to instructions and expectations required of man. It does have commandments relating to diet, modesty, and chastity, as well as many ordinances, such as BAPTISM, laying on of hands, and washing and anointing. If man were perfect, salvation could come on that account; walking in the way of the Lord would be perfectly observed. Since man is mortal and imperfect, God in his love makes known the way his children should walk, and extends grace "after all [they] can do."

BIBLIOGRAPHY

Daube, David. *Studies in Biblical Law*. New York, 1969.

Falk, Ze'ev. *Hebrew Law in Biblical Times*. Jerusalem, 1964.

Jackson, Kent P. "The Law of Moses and the Atonement of Christ." In *Studies in Scripture*, Vol. 3, pp. 153–72. Salt Lake City, 1985.

Noth, Martin. *The Laws in the Pentateuch and Other Studies*. Edinburgh, 1966.

Patrick, Dale. *Old Testament Law*. Atlanta, 1985.

DOUGLAS H. PARKER

ZE'EV W. FALK

LEHI

The patriarch and prophet Lehi led his family from Jerusalem to the western hemisphere about 600 B.C. and was the progenitor of two major Book of Mormon peoples, the NEPHITES and the LAMANITES. His visions and prophecies were concerned chiefly with the pending destruction of Jerusalem, the mortal ministry of the coming Messiah—including the time of his coming and the prophet who would precede him—and future events among his own descendants in the promised land. His words provided spiritual guidance to both lines of his posterity during their mutual history (1 Ne. 1, 8, 10; 2 Ne. 1–3). Several of his prophecies concerning his posterity remain to be fulfilled. Although Lehi wrote much, only portions were preserved in the present Book of Mormon from the records of two of his sons NEPHI₁ and JACOB (cf. 1 Ne. 1:16–17; 19:1; Jacob 2:23–34; 3:5; see Brown).

At the time of his first known vision, Lehi lived near Jerusalem, was familiar with "the learning of the Jews," and possessed "gold and silver, and all manner of riches" (1 Ne. 1:2; 3:16). He knew the Egyptian language and was familiar with desert nomadic life. Some scholars have suggested that Lehi was a merchant or smith with ties to Egypt (CWHN 5:34–42; 6:58–92).

His life was dramatically changed when he beheld a "pillar of fire" and "saw and heard much" while praying about the predicted fall of Jerusalem (1 Ne. 1:6). In a vision he saw God and a radiant being—accompanied by twelve others—who gave him a book in which he read of the impending destruction of the city and of "the coming of a Messiah, and also the redemption of the world" (1 Ne. 1:19). Like the speeches of his contemporary Jeremiah, Lehi's warnings to the people of Jerusalem roused strong opposition. Surrounded by growing hatred, he was warned by God that the people sought his life; therefore, he was to flee with his family, consisting of his wife, Sariah, his sons LAMAN, Lemuel, Sam, and Nephi, and his daughters (1 Ne. 1:8–2:5).

Sariah once accused her husband of being a "visionary man" in a hard test of her faith (1 Ne. 5:2). The phrase aptly characterizes Lehi, for he dreamed dreams and saw visions through which God guided his family to the promised land. After fleeing Jerusalem, at divine behest Lehi twice sent his sons back: once to obtain written records (containing the holy scriptures, a record of the Jews from the beginning, the law, prophecies, and genealogical records) needed to preserve the family's history, language and religion; and a second time to invite ISHMAEL and his family—including marriageable daughters—to join the exodus (chaps. 3–4, 7).

Through revelation, Lehi instructed his sons where game could be hunted in the wilderness (1 Ne. 16:30–31). In this he was assisted by a curious compasslike object (*see* LIAHONA) that operated according to the faith, diligence, and heed they gave it (16:10, 28–29).

One of Lehi's grandest visions was of the tree of life (1 Ne. 8). In a highly symbolic setting, Lehi saw the prospects for his family members measured against the PLAN OF SALVATION. Nephi had the same vision opened to him and gave details and interpretation to what his father had seen (1 Ne. 11–14). Lehi first saw a man dressed in white who led him through a "dark and dreary waste" (1 Ne. 8:5–7). After traveling many hours, he prayed for divine help, and found himself in a large field where there grew a tree whose fruit was white and desirable (symbolic of God's love). When he urged his family to come and partake, all did so except Laman and Lemuel. Lehi also saw a path, alongside which ran an iron rod (representing God's word) leading to the tree and extending along the bank of a river. Many people pressing forward to reach the path became lost in a mist of darkness (temptations); some reached the tree and partook, only to become ashamed and fall away; others, following the rod of iron, reached the tree and enjoyed the fruit. On the other side of the river Lehi saw a large building (the PRIDE of the world) whose inhabitants ridiculed those eating the fruit. LDS scholars have pointed out that the features of Lehi's dream are quite at home in the desert in which Lehi was traveling (CWHN 6:253–64; cf. Griggs; Welch).

Lehi's prophecies concerned the future redemption of Israel. He spoke of the destruction of Jerusalem (587 B.C.), the taking of the Jews to Babylon, and their subsequent return to Jerusalem. He foretold the mission of John the Baptist and the Messiah's coming, death, and RESURRECTION. Finally, Lehi compared Israel's eventual scattering to "an olive-tree, whose branches should be broken off and . . . scattered upon all the face of the earth" (1 Ne. 10:12; cf. ALLEGORY OF ZENOS).

In the wilderness Sariah bore two sons, Jacob and Joseph (1 Ne. 18:7). Apparently the

journey was so difficult that she and Lehi aged substantially. During the transoceanic voyage, their grief—caused by the rebellion of their two eldest sons—brought them close to death (18:17–18).

In the New World, Lehi gathered his family before his death to give them final teachings and blessings (2 Ne. 1–4). He taught them that he had received a great promise regarding his descendants and the land they now possessed. This promise was conditioned upon their righteousness: "Inasmuch as ye shall keep my commandments ye shall prosper in the land; but inasmuch as ye will not keep my commandments ye shall be cut off from my presence" (2 Ne. 1:20; cf. Abr. 2:6).

Lehi addressed his son Jacob about the plan of salvation (2 Ne. 2). Instead of using imagery, he explained it plainly and logically. He taught that while all know good from evil, many have fallen short. However, the Messiah has paid the debt if men and women will accept his help with a contrite spirit. He further explained that a fundamental opposition in all things exists so that people must choose. He reasoned that, as freedom of choice allowed Adam and Eve to fall, so it permits each to choose between "liberty and eternal life, through the great Mediator of all men, or to choose captivity and death, according to the captivity and power of the devil" (2 Ne. 2:27).

Before giving his final blessings to others in the family (2 Ne. 4:3–11), Lehi spoke to Joseph, his youngest (2 Ne. 3), mentioning two other Josephs: JOSEPH who was sold into Egypt, and another, of whom the first Joseph had prophesied—Joseph SMITH. He then set forth Joseph Smith's mission of bringing forth the Book of Mormon, prophesying that a "cry from the dust" would summon Lehi's seed

(2 Ne. 3:19–25), and he promised the sons and daughters of Laman and Lemuel, "in the end thy seed shall be blessed" (2 Ne. 4:9).

After Lehi's death, family dissentions forced Nephi and others who believed the revelations of God to separate from the group led by the two oldest brothers, causing a rupture in the colony. While Lehi lived, his family stayed together, a demonstration of his leadership abilities.

[*See also* Book of Mormon: First Book of Nephi.]

BIBLIOGRAPHY

Brown, S. Kent. "Lehi's Personal Record: Quest for a Missing Source." *BYU Studies* 24 (Winter 1984): 19–42.

Griggs, C. Wilfred. "The Book of Mormon as an Ancient Book." *BYU Studies* 22 (Summer 1982): 259–78.

Nibley, Hugh W. *Lehi in the Desert, An Approach to the Book of Mormon*, and *Since Cumorah*. In CWHN vols. 5–7.

Welch, John W. "The Narrative of Zosimus and the Book of Mormon." *BYU Studies* 22 (Summer 1982): 311–32.

ADDITIONAL SOURCES

Brown, S. Kent. *From Jerusalem to Zarahemla: Literary and Historical Studies of the Book of Mormon*. Provo, Utah: BYU Religious Studies Center, 1998.

Sorenson, John L. "The Composition of Lehi's Family." In *By Study and Also by Faith: Essays in Honor of Hugh W. Nibley*, edited by John M. Lundquist and Stephen D. Ricks, 2:174–96. Salt Lake City and Provo, Utah: Deseret Book and FARMS, 1990.

S. KENT BROWN

TERRENCE L. SZINK

LIAHONA

The Liahona was a compass or director "prepared . . . by the hand of the Lord" for the Book of Mormon prophet LEHI as he and his family traveled in the wilderness (2 Ne. 5:12). It was shown to the Prophet Joseph SMITH and the Three Witnesses in 1829 along with the Book of Mormon plates (D&C 17:1). The Liahona was also understood as a symbol for the words of Christ: "For just as surely as this [Liahona] did bring our fathers, by following its course, to the promised land, shall the words of Christ, if we follow their course, carry us . . . into a far better land of promise" (Alma 37:45).

Described as a ball made of fine brass and "of curious workmanship," it had two spindles, one pointing the direction Lehi's family should travel (1 Ne. 16:10). The term "Liahona" appears only once in the Book of Mormon (Alma 37:38). It was usually referred to as "the ball" (1 Ne. 16:16, 26–27; etc.), "compass" (1 Ne. 18:12; Alma 37:43–44; etc.), or "director" (Mosiah 1:16; cf. D&C 17:1).

Lehi found the Liahona, provided by the Lord (Alma 37:38), outside of his tent door while camping in the wilderness after leaving Jerusalem (1 Ne. 16:10). As his party traveled through the Arabian desert and across the ocean to the promised land, one of the spindles pointed the direction to travel. Moreover, the Liahona was a medium through which God communicated with Lehi's family. Written messages occasionally appeared on it, giving them specific directions (1 Ne. 16:26–29).

The instrument worked according to the faith and obedience of Lehi's family. When they lacked faith or disobeyed, it ceased to function. Passed down from generation to generation along with the sacred records, it was stored with the GOLD PLATES.

Lehi and His People Discover the Liahona, by Arnold Friberg (1951; oil on canvas, 43" x 61"), in the South Visitors' Center, Temple Square, Salt Lake City. While traveling in the wilderness south of Jerusalem, the Book of Mormon prophet Lehi and his family found the Liahona, a compass or director prepared by the Lord. © by Intellectual Reserve, Inc. Used by permission.

Liahona is the title of an international Spanish-language magazine published by the Church.

BIBLIOGRAPHY

Nibley, Hugh W. *Since Cumorah.* 2nd ed. CWHN 7:251–63. Salt Lake City, 1988.

DOUGLAS KENT LUDLOW

LITERATURE, BOOK OF MORMON AS

Although understated as literature in its clear and plain language, the Book of Mormon exhibits a wide variety of literary forms, including intricate Hebraic poetry, memorable narratives, rhetorically effective sermons, diverse letters, allegory, figurative language, imagery, symbolic types, and wisdom literature. In recent years these aspects of Joseph Smith's 1829 English translation have been increasingly appreciated, especially when compared with biblical and other ancient forms of literature.

There are many reasons to study the Book of Mormon as literature. Rather than being "formless" as claimed by one critic (Bernard DeVoto, *American Mercury* 19 [1930]: 5), the Book of Mormon is both coherent and polished (although not obtrusively so). It tells "a densely compact and rapidly moving story that interweaves dozens of plots with an inexhaustible fertility of invention and an uncanny consistency that is never caught in a slip or contradiction" (CWHN 7:138).

Despite its small working vocabulary of about 2,225 root words in English, the book distills much human experience and contact with the divine. It presents its themes artfully through simple yet profound imagery, direct yet complex discourses, and straightforward yet intricate structures. To read the Book of

Mormon as literature is to discover how such literary devices are used to convey the messages of its content. Attention to form, diction, figurative language, and rhetorical techniques increases sensitivity to the structure of the text and appreciation of the work of the various authors. The stated purpose of the Book of Mormon is to show the LAMANITES, a remnant of the House of Israel, the covenants made with their fathers, and to convince Jew and Gentile that Jesus is the Christ (*see* Book of Mormon title page). MORMON selected materials and literarily shaped the book to present these messages in a stirring and memorable way.

While the discipline of identifying and evaluating literary features in the Book of Mormon is very young and does not supplant a spiritual reading of the text, those analyzing the book from this perspective find it a work of immediacy that shows as well as tells as great literature usually does. It no longer fits Mark Twain's definition of a classic essentially as a book everyone talks about but no one reads; rather, it is a work that "wears you out before you wear it out" (J. Welch, "Study, Faith, and the Book of Mormon," *BYU 1987–88 Devotional and Fireside Speeches*, p. 148 [Provo, Ut., 1988]). It is increasingly seen as a unique work that beautifully and compellingly reveals and speaks to the essential human condition.

POETRY. Found embedded in the narrative of the Book of Mormon, poetry provides the best examples of the essential connection between form and content in the Book of Mormon. When many inspired words of the Lord, angels, and prophets are analyzed according to ancient verse forms, their meaning can be more readily perceived. These forms include lineforms, symmetry, parallelism, and chiastic patterns, as defined by Adele Berlin (*The Dynamics of Biblical Parallelism* [Bloomington, 1985]) and Wilford Watson (*Classical Hebrew Poetry* [Sheffield, 1984]). Book of Mormon texts shift smoothly from narrative to poetry, as in this intensifying passage:

> But behold, the Spirit hath said this much unto me, saying: Cry unto this people, saying—
>> Repent ye, and prepare the way of the Lord, and walk in his paths, which are straight; for behold, the kingdom of heaven is at hand, and the Son of God cometh upon the face of the earth. (Alma 7:9)

The style of the Book of Mormon has been criticized by some as being verbose and redundant, but in most cases these repetitions are orderly and effective. For example, parallelisms, which abound in the Book of Mormon, serve many functions. They add emphasis to twice-repeated concepts and give definition to sharply drawn contrasts. A typical synonymous parallelism is in 2 Nephi 9:52:

> *Pray* unto him continually *by day,*
> and *give thanks* unto his holy name
> *by night.*

Nephi's discourse aimed at his obstinate brothers includes a sharply antithetical parallelism:

> Ye are *swift* to do *iniquity*
> But *slow* to *remember* the Lord your God.
> (1 Ne. 17:45)

Several fine examples of chiasmus (an a–b–b–a pattern) are also found in the Book of Mormon. In the Psalm of Nephi (2 Ne. 4:15–35), the initial appeals to the *soul* and *heart* are accompanied by negations, while the subsequent mirror uses of *heart* and *soul* are conjoined with strong affirmations, making the contrasts literarily effective and climactic:

> Awake, my *soul*! No longer droop in sin.
>> Rejoice, O my *heart*, and give place no more for the enemy of my soul.
>>> Do not anger again because of mine enemies.
>>> Do not slacken my strength because

of mine afflictions.

Rejoice, O my *heart*, and cry unto the
Lord, and say:

O Lord, I will praise thee forever;
yea, my *soul* will rejoice in thee, my God,
and the rock of my salvation. (2 Ne.
4:28–30)

Other precise examples of extended chiasmus (a–b–c—c–b–a) are readily discernible in Mosiah 5:10–12 and Alma 36:1–30 and 41:13–15. This literary form in Alma 36 effectively focuses attention on the central passage of the chapter (Alma 36:17–18); in Alma 41, it fittingly conveys the very notion of restorative justice expressed in the passage (cf. Lev. 24:13–23, which likewise uses chiasmus to convey a similar notion of justice).

Another figure known as *a fortiori* is used to communicate an exaggerated sense of multitude, as in Alma 60:22, where a "number parallelism" is chiastically enclosed by a twice-repeated phrase:

Yea, will ye sit in idleness
  while ye are surrounded with *thousands*
  of those,
    yea, and *tens of thousands*,
who do also sit in idleness?

Scores of Book of Mormon passages can be analyzed as poetry. They range from Lehi's brief desert poems (1 Ne. 2:9–10, a form Hugh Nibley identifies as an Arabic *qasida*) [CWHN 6:270–75] to extensive sermons of Jacob, Abinadi, and the risen Jesus (2 Ne. 6–10; Mosiah 12–16; and 3 Ne. 27).

NARRATIVE TEXTS. In the Book of Mormon, narrative texts are often given vitality by vigorous conflict and impassioned dialogue or personal narration. Nephi relates his heroic actions in obtaining the brass plates from Laban; Jacob resists the false accusations of Sherem, upon whom the judgment of the Lord falls; Ammon fights off plunderers at the waters of Sebus and wins the confidence of king Lamoni; Amulek is confronted by the smooth-tongued lawyer Zeezrom; Alma₂ and Amulek are preserved while their accusers are crushed by collapsing prison walls; Captain Moroni₁ engages in a showdown with the Lamanite chieftain Zerahemnah; Amalickiah rises to power through treachery and malevolence; a later prophet named NEPHI₂ reveals to an unbelieving crowd the murder of their chief judge by the judge's own brother; and the last two Jaredite kings fight to the mutual destruction of their people.

Seen as a whole, the Book of Mormon is an epic account of the history of the NEPHITE nation. Extensive in scope with an eponymic hero, it presents action involving long and arduous journeys and heroic deeds, with supernatural beings taking an active part. Encapsulated within this one-thousand-year account of the establishment, development, and destruction of the Nephites is the concentrated epic of the rise and fall of the Jaredites who preceded them in type and time. (For its epic milieu, see CWHN 5:285–394.) The climax of the book is the dramatic account of the visit of the resurrected Jesus to an assemblage of righteous Nephites.

SERMONS AND SPEECHES. Prophetic discourse is a dominant literary form in the Book of Mormon. Speeches such as king BENJAMIN's address (Mosiah 1–6), Alma₂'s challenge to the people of Zarahemla (Alma 5), and Mormon's teachings on faith, hope and charity (Moro. 7) are crafted artistically and have great rhetorical effectiveness in conveying their religious purposes. The public oration of SAMUEL THE LAMANITE (Hel. 13–15) is a classic prophetic judgment speech. Taking rhetorical criticism as a guide, one can see how Benjamin's ritual address first aims to persuade the audience to reaffirm a present point of view and then turns to deliberative rhetoric—"which aims at effecting a decision about future action, often the very immediate future" (Kennedy, *New Testament*

Interpretation through Rhetorical Criticism [1984], p. 36). King Benjamin's speech is also chiastic as a whole and in several of its parts (Welch, pp. 202–5).

LETTERS. The eight epistles in the Book of Mormon are conversational in tone, revealing the diverse personalities of their writers. These letters are from Captain Moroni₁ (Alma 54:5–14, 60:1–36), Ammoron (Alma 54:16–24), Helaman₁ (Alma 56:2–58:41), Pahoran (Alma 61:2–21), Giddianhi (3 Ne. 3:2–10), and Mormon (Moro. 8:2–30, 9:1–26).

ALLEGORY, METAPHOR, IMAGERY, AND TYPOLOGY. These forms are also prevalent in the Book of Mormon. ZENOS's allegory of the olive tree (Jacob 5) vividly incorporates dozens of horticultural details as it depicts the history of God's dealings with Israel. A striking simile curse, with Near Eastern parallels, appears in Abinadi's prophetic denunciation: The life of king Noah shall be "as a garment in a furnace of fire, . . . as a stalk, even as a dry stalk of the field, which is run over by the beasts and trodden under foot" (Mosiah 12:10–11).

An effective extended metaphor is Alma's comparison of the word of God to a seed planted in one's heart and then growing into a fruitful TREE OF LIFE (Alma 32:28–43). In developing this metaphor, Alma uses a striking example of synesthesia: As the word enlightens their minds, his listeners can know it is real—"ye have *tasted* this *light*" (Alma 32:35).

Iteration of archetypes such as tree, river, darkness, and fire graphically confirms Lehi's understanding "that there is an opposition in all things" (2 Ne. 2:11) and that opposition will be beneficial to the righteous.

A figural interpretation of God-given words and God-directed persons or events is insisted on, although not always developed, in the Book of Mormon. "All things which have been given of God from the beginning of the world, unto man, are the typifying of [Christ]" (2 Ne. 11:4); all performances and ordinances of the law of Moses "were types of things to come" (Mosiah 13:31); and the LIAHONA, or compass, was seen as a type: "For just as surely as this director did bring our fathers, by following its course, to the promised land, shall the words of Christ, if we follow their course, carry us beyond this vale of sorrow into a far better land of promise" (Alma 37:45). In its largest typological structure, the Book of Mormon fits well the seven phases of revelation posited by Northrop Frye: creation, revolution or exodus, law, wisdom, prophecy, gospel, and apocalypse (*The Great Code: The Bible and Literature* [New York, 1982]).

WISDOM LITERATURE. Transmitted sayings of the wise are scattered throughout the Book of Mormon, especially in counsel given by fathers to their sons. Alma counsels, "O, remember, my son, and learn wisdom in thy youth; yea, learn in thy youth to keep the commandments of God" (Alma 37:35; see also 38:9–15). Benjamin says, "I tell you these things that ye may learn wisdom; that ye may learn that when ye are in the service of your fellow beings ye are only in the service of your God" (Mosiah 2:17). A memorable aphorism is given by Lehi: "Adam fell that men might be; and men are, that they might have joy" (2 Ne. 2:25). Pithy sayings such as "fools mock, but they shall mourn" (Ether 12:26) and "wickedness never was happiness" (Alma 41:10) are often repeated by Latter-day Saints.

APOCALYPTIC LITERATURE. The vision in 1 Nephi 11–15 (sixth century B.C.) is comparable in form with early apocalyptic literature. It contains a vision, is delivered in dialogue form, has an other-worldly mediator or escort, includes a commandment to write, treats the disposition of the recipient, prophesies persecution, foretells the judgment of the wicked and of the world, contains cosmic transformations, and has an other-worldly place as its spatial axis. Later Jewish developments of complex angelology, mystic numerology, and symbolism are absent.

STYLE AND TONE. Book of Mormon writers show an intense concern for style and tone. Alma desires to be able to "speak with the trump of God, with a voice to shake the earth," yet realizes that "I am a man, and do sin in my wish; for I ought to be content with the things which the Lord hath allotted unto me" (Alma 29:1–3). Moroni₂ expresses a feeling of inadequacy in writing: "Lord, the Gentiles will mock at these things, because of our weakness in writing . . . Thou hast also made our words powerful and great, even that we cannot write them; wherefore, when we write we behold our weakness, and stumble because of the placing of our words" (Ether 12:23–25; cf. 2 Ne. 33:1). Moroni's written words, however, are not weak. In cadences of ascending strength he boldly declares:

> O ye pollutions, ye hypocrites, ye teachers, who sell yourselves for that which will canker, why have ye polluted the holy church of God? Why are ye ashamed to take upon you the name of Christ? . . . Who will despise the works of the Lord? Who will despise the children of Christ? Behold, all ye who are despisers of the works of the Lord, for ye shall wonder and perish. (Morm. 8:38, 9:26)

The styles employed by the different writers in the Book of Mormon vary from the unadorned to the sublime. The tones range from Moroni's strident condemnations to Jesus' humblest pleading: "Behold, mine arm of mercy is extended towards you, and whosoever will come, him will I receive" (3 Ne. 9:14).

A model for communication is Jesus, who,

Moroni reports, "told me in plain humility, even as a man telleth another in mine own language, concerning these things; And only a few have I written, because of my weakness in writing" (Ether 12:39–40). Two concepts in this report are repeated throughout the Book of Mormon—plain speech and inability to write about some things. "I have spoken plainly unto you," Nephi says, "that ye cannot misunderstand" (2 Ne. 25:28). "My soul delighteth in plainness" he continues, "for after this manner doth the Lord God work among the children of men" (2 Ne. 31:3). Yet Nephi also delights in the words of Isaiah, which "are not plain unto you" although "they are plain unto all those that are filled with the spirit of prophecy" (2 Ne. 25:4). Containing both plain and veiled language, the Book of Mormon is a spiritually and literarily powerful book which is direct yet complex, simple yet profound.

BIBLIOGRAPHY

England, Eugene. "A Second Witness for the Logos: The Book of Mormon and Contemporary Literary Criticism." In *By Study and Also By Faith*, 2 Vols., ed. J. Lundquist and S. Ricks, 2:91–125. Salt Lake City, 1990.

Jorgensen, Bruce W., Richard Dilworth Rust, and George S. Tate. Essays on typology in *Literature of Belief*, ed. Neal E. Lambert. Provo, 1981.

Nichols, Robert E., Jr. "Beowulf and Nephi: A Literary View of the Book of Mormon." *Dialogue* 4 (Autumn 1969): 40–47.

Parry, Donald W. "Hebrew Literary Patterns in the Book of Mormon." *Ensign* 19 (Oct. 1989): 58–61.

Rust, Richard Dilworth. "Book of Mormon Poetry." *New Era* (Mar. 1983): 46–50.

Welch, John W. "Chiasmus in the Book of Mormon." In *Chiasmus in Antiquity*, ed. J. Welch, pp. 198–210. Hildesheim, 1981.

ADDITIONAL SOURCES

Pinnock, Hugh W. *Finding Biblical Hebrew and Other Ancient Literary Forms in the Book of Mormon.* Provo, Utah: FARMS, 1999.

Rust, Richard Dilworth. *Feasting on the Word: The Literary Testimony of the Book of Mormon.* Salt Lake City and Provo, Utah: Deseret Book and FARMS, 1997.

RICHARD DILWORTH RUST

DONALD W. PARRY

Manuscript, Lost 116 Pages

The first 116 pages of the original manuscript of Joseph SMITH's translation of the Book of Mormon from the plates of Mormon are commonly known as "the 116 pages" or the "lost manuscript." These foolscap-size pages were handwritten in Harmony, Pennsylvania, between April and June 14, 1828. Although principally transcribed by Martin HARRIS from dictation by Joseph Smith, some of the pages may also have been transcribed by Joseph's wife, Emma Smith, or her brother, Reuben Hale.

The pages contained materials "from the Book of Lehi, which was an account abridged from the plates of Lehi, by the hand of Mormon," as Joseph explained in the preface to the first edition of the Book of Mormon (see also *HC* 1:56). LEHI's record is mentioned in 1 Nephi 1:16–17 and, today, is partially preserved through NEPHI's abridgment of it primarily in 1 Nephi 1–10.

In June 1828 Martin Harris asked Joseph Smith repeatedly to allow him to show the 116 pages to family members to allay their skepticism and criticism of the translation. After prayerful inquiry of the Lord, Joseph Smith twice emphatically denied these requests. As Joseph's 1832 and 1839 histories indicate, a third request received divine permission for Harris to take the 116 manuscript pages to Palmyra, New York. The Prophet required Harris to solemnly covenant that he would show them only to his brother, his parents, his wife, and her sister.

Harris's failure to return to Harmony as promised caused Joseph great anxiety and necessitated a strenuous journey to Manchester. There, a reluctant Harris reported that someone had stolen the manuscript from his home after he had broken his covenant and indiscriminately showed it to persons outside his family. Grief-stricken, Joseph Smith readily shared responsibility for the loss. The most widespread rumor was that Harris's wife, irritated at having earlier been denied a glimpse of the ancient PLATES had removed the manuscript translation from Martin's unlocked bureau and burned it. Not long afterward, she and Martin separated.

In consequence of this loss and of having

Emma Hale Smith, wife of Joseph Smith, was the seventh of nine children. She was a tall, attractive young woman, dark-complexioned, with brown eyes and black hair. Used by permission, Utah State Historical Society. Photo no. 13561.

wearied the Lord with the requests to let Harris take the pages, Joseph temporarily lost custody of the plates and the URIM AND THUMMIM to the angel MORONI (D&C 3). Lucy Mack Smith notes also that two-thirds of Harris's crop was oddly destroyed by a dense fog, which she interpreted as a sign of God's displeasure (Smith, p. 132). Following much humble and painful affliction of soul, Joseph Smith again received the plates as well as the Urim and Thummim and his gifts were restored.

Joseph Smith was forbidden by the Lord to retranslate that part of the record previously translated because those who had stolen the manuscript planned to publish it in an altered form to discredit his ability to translate accurately (D&C 10:9–13). Instead, he was to translate the Small Plates of Nephi (1 Nephi–Omni) down to that which he had translated (D&C 10:41). Those plates covered approximately the same period as had the lost manuscript, or four centuries from Lehi to BENJAMIN. Mormon had been so impressed with the choice prophecies and sayings contained in the small plates that he had included them with his own abridgment of Nephite writings when told to by the Spirit for "a wise purpose" known only to the Lord (W of M 1:7).

The loss of the 116 pages taught Joseph Smith and his associates several lessons: that one should be satisfied with the first answers of the Lord, that keeping one's covenants is a serious matter, that God forgives the repentant in spite of human weakness, and that through his caring foresight and wisdom the Lord fulfills his purposes.

BIBLIOGRAPHY

Bushman, Richard L. *Joseph Smith and the Beginnings of Mormonism*, pp. 89–94. Urbana, Ill., 1984.

Jessee, Dean C., ed. *The Papers of Joseph Smith*, Vol. 1, pp. 9–10, 286–88. Salt Lake City, 1989.

Smith, Lucy Mack. *History of Joseph Smith*, pp. 124–32. Salt Lake City, 1958.

WILLIAM J. CRITCHLOW III

MANUSCRIPTS OF THE BOOK OF MORMON

The printed versions of the Book of Mormon derive from two manuscripts. The first, called the original manuscript (O), was written by at least three scribes as Joseph SMITH translated and dictated. The most important scribe was Oliver COWDERY. This manuscript was begun no later than April 1829 and finished in June 1829.

A page from the original Book of Mormon manuscript, covering 1 Nephi 4:38–5:14. It shows how fluent Joseph Smith's dictation was. He did not revise the text as he dictated. Oliver Cowdery, one of his scribes, stated, "Day after day I continued, uninterrupted, to write from his mouth . . . a voice dictated by the inspiration of heaven." © by Intellectual Reserve, Inc. Used by permission.

A copy of the original was then made by Oliver Cowdery and two other scribes. This copy is called the printer's manuscript (P) since it was the one normally used to set the type for the first (1830) edition of the Book of Mormon. It was begun in July 1829 and finished early in 1830.

The printer's manuscript is not an exact copy of the original manuscript. There are on the average three changes per original manuscript page. These changes appear to be natural scribal errors; there is little or no evidence of conscious editing. Most of the changes are minor, and about one in five produce a discernible difference in meaning. Because they were all relatively minor, most of the errors thus introduced into the text have remained in the printed editions of the Book of Mormon and have not been detected and corrected except by reference to the original manuscript. About twenty of these errors were corrected in the 1981 edition.

The compositor for the 1830 edition added punctuation, paragraphing, and other printing marks to about one-third of the pages of the printer's manuscript. These same marks appear on one fragment of the original, indicating that it was used at least once in typesetting the 1830 edition.

In preparation for the second (1837) edition, hundreds of grammatical changes and a few textual emendations were made in P. After the publication of this edition, P was retained by Oliver Cowdery. After his death in 1850, his brother-in-law, David WHITMER, kept P until his death in 1888. In 1903 Whitmer's grandson sold P to the Reorganized Church of Jesus Christ of Latter Day Saints, which owns it today. It is wholly extant except for two lines at the bottom of the first leaf.

The original manuscript was not consulted for the editing of the 1837 edition.

However, in producing the 1840 edition, Joseph Smith used O to restore some of its original readings. In October 1841, Joseph Smith placed O in the cornerstone of the Nauvoo House. Over forty years later, Lewis Bidamon, Emma Smith's second husband, opened the cornerstone and found that water seepage had destroyed most of O. The surviving pages were handed out to various individuals during the 1880s.

Today approximately 25 percent of the text of O survives: 1 Nephi 2 through 2 Nephi 1, with gaps; Alma 22 through Helaman 3, with gaps; and a few other fragments. All but one of the authentic pages and fragments of O are housed in the archives of the LDS Historical Department; one half of a sheet (from 1 Nephi 14) is owned by the University of Utah.

BIBLIOGRAPHY

Heater, Shirley R. "Gold Plates, Foolscap, & Printer's Ink, Part I: Manuscripts of the Book of Mormon." *Zarahemla Record* 35–36 (1987): 3–15.

Jessee, Dean C. "The Original Book of Mormon Manuscript." *BYU Studies* 10 (1970): 259–78.

ROYAL SKOUSEN

MELCHIZEDEK

[*This entry consists here of the article* LDS Sources, *a discussion of what is known of Melchizedek from Church scripture and revelation.*]

LDS Sources

As a king and high priest of the Most High God (Gen. 14:18), Melchizedek holds a place of great honor and respect among Latter-day Saints. An example of righteousness and the namesake of the higher priesthood, he represents the scriptural ideal of one who obtains the power of God through FAITH, RE-

This mosaic shows Melchizedek standing behind an altar symbolically receiving the sacrifices of Abel and Abraham. Saint Apollonaire in Classe, Ravenna, Italy (sixth century A.D.). Courtesy John W. Welch.

PENTANCE, and sacred ordinances, for the purpose of inspiring and blessing his fellow beings.

Melchizedek was evidently a prince by birth, for he became king of Salem (later Jerusalem—Gen. 14:18; Ps. 76:2), where he reigned "under his father" (Alma 13:18). "Melchizedek was a man of faith, who wrought righteousness; and when a child he feared God, and stopped the mouths of lions, and quenched the violence of fire" (JST Gen. 14:26). Yet the people among whom he lived "waxed strong in iniquity and abomination; yea, they had all gone astray; they were full of all manner of wickedness" (Alma 13:17).

Though living among a wicked people, Melchizedek "exercised mighty faith, and received the office of the high priesthood according to the holy order of God" (Alma 13:18). This priesthood was after the order of the covenant that God had made with Enoch

(JST Gen. 14:27), and Melchizedek ruled both as king and priest over his people.

As high priest, some of his functions were keeping "the storehouse of God" where the "tithes for the poor" were held (JST Gen. 14:37–38), giving blessings to individuals such as Abraham (JST Gen. 14:18, 25, 37), preaching repentance (Alma 13:18; cf. 5:49), and administering ordinances "after this manner, that thereby the people might look forward on the Son of God . . . for a remission of their sins, that they might enter into the rest of the Lord" (Alma 13:16; JST Gen. 14:17). With extraordinary goodness and power, Melchizedek diligently administered in the office of high priest and "did preach repentance unto his people. And behold, they did repent; and Melchizedek did establish peace in the land in his days" (Alma 13:18). Consequently, Melchizedek became known as "the Prince of peace" (JST Gen. 14:33; Heb. 7:1–2; Alma 13:18). "His people wrought righteousness, and obtained heaven" (JST Gen. 14:34). His Hebrew name means "King of Righteousness."

For ALMA₂ and several biblical authors, the order of the priesthood to which Melchizedek was ordained was of prime importance. It was this "order," coupled with faith, that gave Melchizedek the power and knowledge that influenced his people to repent and become worthy to be with God. This order was "after the order of the Son of God; which order came, not by man, nor the will of man; neither by father nor mother; neither by beginning of days nor end of years; but of God" (JST Gen. 14:28; JST Heb. 7:3; Ps. 110:4). It was given to Melchizedek "through the lineage of his fathers, even till Noah," and from Melchizedek to Abraham (D&C 84:14). Those ordained to this order were to "have power, by faith," and, according to "the will of the Son of God," to work miracles. Ultimately, those in this order were

"to stand in the presence of God" (JST Gen. 14:30–31). This was accomplished by participating in the ordinances of this order (Alma 13:16; D&C 84:20–22). The result was that "men having this faith, coming up unto this order of God, were translated and taken up into heaven" (JST Gen. 14:32). Accordingly, the Prophet Joseph SMITH taught that the priesthood held by Melchizedek had "the power of 'endless lives'" (TPJS, p. 322).

So righteous and faithful was Melchizedek in the execution of his high priestly duties that he became a prototype of Jesus Christ (Heb. 7:15). The Book of Mormon prophet Alma said of him, "Now, there were many [high priests] before him, and also there were many afterwards, but none were greater" (Alma 13:19). The Doctrine and Covenants states that Melchizedek was "such a great high priest" that the higher priesthood was called after his name. "Before his day it was called *the Holy Priesthood, after the Order of the Son of God*. But out of respect or reverence to the name of the Supreme Being, to avoid the too-frequent repetition of his name, they, the church, in the ancient days, called that priesthood after Melchizedek, or the Melchizedek Priesthood" (D&C 107:2–4; italics in original).

It was asserted by some early LDS leaders that Melchizedek was Shem, son of Noah (see, e.g., T&S 5:746). Though Shem is also identified as a great high priest (D&C 138:41), it would appear from the Doctrine and Covenants 84:14 that the two might not be the same individual (MD, p. 475), and Jewish sources equating Melchizedek and Shem are late and tendentious.

BIBLIOGRAPHY

Madsen, Ann N. "Melchizedek, the Man and the Tradition." Master's thesis, Brigham Young University, 1975.

Welch, John W. "The Melchizedek Material in Alma 13:13–19." In *By Study and Also by Faith*, ed. J. Lundquist and S. Ricks, Vol. 2, pp. 238–72. Salt Lake City, 1990.

Widtsoe, John A. "Who Was Melchizedek?" *Evidences and Reconciliations*, pp. 231–33. Salt Lake City, 1960.

BRUCE SATTERFIELD

MORMON

Mormon was a prophet, an author, and the last NEPHITE military commander (c. A.D. 310–385). The Book of Mormon bears his name because he was the major abridger-writer of the GOLD PLATES from which it was translated. He was prepared by the experiences of his youth to become a prophet: he was taught "the learning of [his] people," was a "sober child" and "quick to observe," and in his fifteenth year was "visited of the Lord" (Morm. 1:2, 15). At sixteen he became the general of all the Nephite armies and largely succeeded in preserving his people from destruction until A.D. 385, when virtually all of them but his son MORONI$_2$ were destroyed in battles with the LAMANITES (6:8–15; 8:1–3). As keeper of the Nephite records, Mormon abridged the large PLATES of Nephi, bound with them the small plates of Nephi, and added his own short history (W of M 1:1–5; Morm. 1:1). Before his death, he hid the records entrusted to him in the hill CUMORAH, "save it were these few plates which I gave unto my son Moroni" (Morm. 6:6). The Prophet Joseph SMITH received and translated Mormon's abridgment, the small plates of Nephi, and a few other documents, and published them in 1830 as the Book of Mormon.

First and foremost, Mormon was a prophet to his people, urging them to "re-

pent, and be baptized in the name of Jesus, and lay hold upon the gospel of Christ" (Morm. 7:8). He taught that they were "a remnant of the seed of Jacob" (7:10) and could have the blessings of Israel if they would live for them. He also underscored the supporting relationship of the Bible and the Book of Mormon: "For behold, this [record, the Book of Mormon] is written for the intent that ye may believe that [record, the Bible]; and if ye believe that ye will believe this also" (7:9).

Mormon's son Moroni$_2$ finished the record, including one of Mormon's addresses and two of Mormon's epistles in his own book of Moroni. Mormon's talk on faith, hope, and CHARITY (Moro. 7) teaches that charity, the greatest of those three virtues, is "the pure love of Christ, and it endureth forever; and whoso is found possessed of it at the last day, it shall be well with him" (7:47). One of Mormon's letters (Moro. 8) condemns INFANT BAPTISM as a practice that denies the Atonement of Jesus Christ, stating "it is solemn mockery before God, that ye should baptize little children" (8:9). Rather, little children need not repent, but "are alive in Christ, even from the foundation of the world" (8:12). In the other epistle (Moro. 9) Mormon notes that the destruction of the Nephites is just retribution for their wickedness, which is so bad that he "cannot recommend them unto God lest he should smite me" (9:21).

As abridger of Nephite records, Mormon had access to a veritable library of engraved documents and was commanded to make an abridgment of the large plates of Nephi so that Lamanites, Jews, and gentiles of the latter days could know of the Lord's covenants and what he had done for their ancestors and could thereby be convinced that Jesus is the Christ (*see* BOOK OF MORMON: TITLE PAGE). While making his abridgment, Mormon often noted that he could not include even a hundredth part of the source records (e.g., Hel. 3:14). He regularly sought opportunity to draw spiritual lessons from the course of events experienced by his people. The phrase "and thus we see" frequently introduces one of Mormon's interpretive observations (cf. Hel. 3:27–30). One of the most significant passages from his hand appears in Helaman 12 wherein he offers compelling views about the often vain and fickle character of human nature, especially in response to material prosperity.

As an author, Mormon expressed his feelings, sorrowing at living in a wicked society (Morm. 2:19), and confessing that he had loved and prayed for his people (3:12), but was at last without hope (5:2). He measured civility by how women and children fared (4:14, 21), seeking to unite them with husbands and fathers even when facing certain doom (6:2, 7). When the last Nephites fell, he penned a poignant lament in their memory (6:16–22).

As general of the Nephite armies (Morm. 2–6), Mormon helped to preserve his people from destruction by the Lamanites for some fifty-eight years, but then began to lose them first to sin and then to death (Morm. 2:11–15). Even so, he taught survivors that they would be spared if they would repent and obey the gospel of JESUS CHRIST, "but it was in vain; and they did not realize that it was the Lord that had spared them, and granted unto them a chance for repentance" (3:3). At one time the Nephites became so vicious and hardened that Mormon refused to lead them into battle (3:11). But he could not bear to watch them perish, and although he had no hope that they could survive, he relented (5:1–2) and led them into their last battle from which only he, his son Moroni₂, and a few others survived (8:2–3). Moroni₂ lived to complete his father's record (8:1).

BIBLIOGRAPHY

Holland, Jeffrey R. "Mormon: The Man and the Book." *Ensign* 8 (Mar. 1978): 15–18; (Apr. 1978): 57–59.

ADDITIONAL SOURCE

Mackay, Thomas W. "Mormon's Philosophy of History: Helaman 12 in the Perspective of Mormon's Editing Procedure." In *The Book of Mormon: Helaman through 3 Nephi 8, According to Thy Word*, edited by Monte S. Nyman and Charles D. Tate, Jr., 129–46. Provo, Utah: BYU Religious Studies Center, 1992.

PHYLLIS ANN ROUNDY

MORONI, ANGEL

The angel Moroni is the heavenly messenger who first visited the Prophet Joseph SMITH in 1823. As a mortal named MORONI₂, he had completed the compilation and writing of the Book of Mormon. He ministered to Joseph Smith as a resurrected being, in keeping with his responsibility for the Book of Mormon, inasmuch as "the keys of the record of the stick of Ephraim" had been committed to him by the Lord (D&C 27:5). Pursuant to this responsibility he first appeared to Joseph Smith on the night of September 21–22, 1823 (JS—H 1:29–49; D&C 128:20), and thereafter counseled with him in several reappearances until the book was published in 1830. During that time, he instructed Joseph Smith, testified to the Three Witnesses of the Book of Mormon, and otherwise assisted in the work of restoring the gospel.

Because of the angel Moroni's role in restoring the everlasting gospel to be preached to all the world (cf. Rev. 14:6–7; D&C 133:31–39), the Church placed a statue depicting him as a herald of the Restoration atop the Salt Lake Temple, and later on

The Angel Moroni, by Cyrus Dallin (1891; cast bronze, gilded 12'), on the Salt Lake Temple in Salt Lake City. Moroni, a Book of Mormon prophet, returned to earth as a resurrected being and prepared Joseph Smith to receive and translate the gold plates. A symbol of the restoration of the gospel through divine messengers, such statues stand on the top of several LDS temples. © by Intellectual Reserve, Inc. Used by permission.

the hill CUMORAH near Palmyra, New York, where anciently he had buried the Book of Mormon plates. Copies of the statue have also been placed atop several other LDS temples.

[*See also* Moroni, Visitations of.]

BIBLIOGRAPHY

Peterson, H. Donl. *Moroni: Ancient Prophet, Modern Messenger.* Bountiful, Utah, 1983.

JOSEPH B. ROMNEY

MORONI, VISITATIONS OF

From 1823 to 1829, the angel Moroni₂ appeared at least twenty times to Joseph SMITH and others. Those appearances opened the

way for the translation and publication of the Book of Mormon and laid the foundation of many of the Church's most characteristic teachings. As a resurrected messenger of God, Moroni told Joseph Smith about the Nephite record on gold plates and taught him concerning the gathering of Israel, the forthcoming visit of Elijah, the imminence of the second coming of Jesus Christ, and the judgments to be poured out on the world prior to that event.

Of Moroni's first appearance on the night of September 21, 1823, Joseph Smith recorded:

> After I had retired to my bed for the night, I betook myself to prayer and supplication to Almighty God for forgiveness of all my sins and follies, and also for a manifestation to me, that I might know of my state and standing before him. . . . While I was thus in the act of calling upon God, I discovered a light appearing in my room, which continued to increase until the room was lighter than at noonday, when immediately a personage appeared at my bedside, standing in the air. . . . He had on a loose robe of most exquisite whiteness. It was a whiteness beyond anything earthly I had ever seen. . . . His hands were naked, and his arms also, a little above the wrist; so, also, were his feet naked, as were his legs, a little above the ankles. His head and neck were also bare. . . . His whole person was glorious beyond description, and his countenance truly like lightning. (JS—H 1:29–32)

The angel introduced himself as Moroni, and as he told about the Nephite record, its contents, and the interpreters buried with it, Joseph saw in vision their location in the hill CUMORAH. Moroni warned Joseph not to show the plates or the interpreters to anyone except those whom the Lord designated. Moroni also quoted certain prophecies from the

Bible, including Malachi 3–4, Isaiah 11, and Acts 3:22–23.

After the angel left, Joseph lay contemplating this experience, and Moroni returned a second time and repeated verbatim everything he had said in his first visit, adding more detail about the coming judgments, and then returned a third time to repeat his instructions and to warn Joseph that he must put all thoughts of worldly wealth aside and concentrate solely on the translation of the record and the establishment of the kingdom of God.

As Moroni left the third time, Joseph said he heard the cock crow, the visitations having occupied the entire night. He arose and went into the fields with his father and his older brother Alvin, but felt tired and feeble. His father, noticing his son's condition, told him to return to the house. As Joseph was climbing over a fence, he fell to the ground unconscious.

The next thing he remembered seeing was Moroni standing over him, repeating his instructions of the night before, adding that Joseph should now tell his father about the visitations. Joseph did so, and his father, assured that the vision came from God, told Joseph to follow the angel's instructions (JS—H 1:46–50).

Joseph Smith then went to the hill and found the place shown him the night before in vision. He uncovered the plates and was about to remove them when Moroni appeared again, counseling Joseph that the time was not yet right. Instead, he instructed Joseph to return to this spot at the same time the following year and that he should continue to do so until the time had come for obtaining the plates (JS—H 1:51–54).

It is reported that during those years Joseph Smith also received visits from Mormon, Nephi, and other "angels of God unfolding the majesty and glory of the events

Joseph Smith Visited by Moroni in the Field, by Gary E. Smith (1980s, oil on canvas, 36" x 42"). After seeing the angel Moroni three times the night before in his bedroom, Joseph Smith was so exhausted that he fell while attempting to cross a fence. Again the angel appeared, commanding Joseph to tell his father about the vision. Courtesy Blaine T. Hudson.

that should transpire in the last days" (*HC* 4:537; cf. *JD* 17:374; Petersen, p. 131). Joseph shared with his family some of his experiences. His mother, Lucy Mack Smith, recalled, "From this time forth, Joseph continued to receive instructions from the Lord, and we continued to get the children together every evening for the purpose of listening while he gave us a relation of the same. . . . He would describe the ancient inhabitants of this continent, their dress, mode of traveling, and the animals upon which they rode; their cities, their buildings, with every particular; their mode of warfare; and also their religious worship. This he would do with as much ease, seemingly, as if he had spent his whole life among them" (pp. 82–83).

Moroni temporarily reclaimed the plates and the interpreters after Martin HARRIS had

Joseph Receives the Plates, by Max Rezler (1973, Brazil, inlaid wood, 24" x 21"). This work by LDS Brazilian artist Max Rezler portrays the occasion when the angel Moroni, on September 22, 1827, delivered to Joseph Smith the plates containing the Book of Mormon record. Courtesy Museum of Church History and Art. © by Intellectual Reserve, Inc. Used by permission.

lost the first 116 manuscript pages of the translation. Later, when Joseph Smith moved from Harmony, Pennsylvania, to Fayette, New York, in June 1829, Moroni returned them to him there (Smith, pp. 149–50). Still later, Moroni showed the plates to the Three Witnesses (*HC* 1:54–55), took them after the translation had been completed (JS—H 1:60), and once more returned them briefly to Joseph to show to the Eight Witnesses (*see* WITNESSES OF THE BOOK OF MORMON).

In addition to Joseph and the Three Witnesses, Mary Whitmer also saw the angel and talked with him. Mary Whitmer said she was shown the gold plates when she conversed with Moroni (Peterson, pp. 114, 116). Other sources indicate that Moroni appeared also to W. W. Phelps, Heber C. Kimball, John Taylor, and Oliver Granger (Peterson, pp. 151–52).

BIBLIOGRAPHY

Backman, Milton V., Jr. *Eyewitness Accounts of the Restoration*, rev. ed. Salt Lake City, 1986.

Cheesman, Paul R. *The Keystone of Mormonism*, rev. ed. Provo, Utah, 1988.

Peterson, H. Donl. *Moroni: Ancient Prophet, Modern Messenger*. Bountiful, Utah, 1983.

Smith, Lucy Mack. *History of Joseph Smith*. Preston Nibley, ed. Salt Lake City, 1958.

ELDIN RICKS

MORONI₁

The first Moroni mentioned in the Book of Mormon (died c. 56 B.C.) was twenty-five years old when he was appointed captain of the NEPHITE armies (Alma 43:16–17). He upheld the liberty of the Nephites against threats posed by invading armies and by "kingmen" who tried to reestablish a monarchy by force after failing to win popular support. Moroni rallied his people for a seven-year struggle by raising "the title of liberty," a banner on which he wrote his reasons for defense, and by having his people covenant to defend their freedom and obey God's commandments (Alma 46:12–13, 20).

Despite many battles, Moroni did not become bloodthirsty. He operated within legal authority, and when he gained advantage over enemies, he offered them freedom if they would lay down their weapons and take an oath not to war again. He introduced new armor and fortifications and sought the direction of a prophet about what his armies should do (Alma 43:23; *see also* WARFARE IN THE BOOK OF MORMON). Five hundred years later, MORMON, the chief editor and compiler of the Book of Mormon, wrote, "If all men had been . . . like unto Moroni, behold, the very powers of hell would have been shaken

The Title of Liberty, maker unknown, Cuna Indian from Panama (mola–cloth appliqué, reverse embroidery and embroidery, 13"x 15"). In rallying his people to defensive battle, Captain Moroni rent his coat and wrote upon it: "In memory of our God, our religion, and freedom, and our peace, our wives, and our children—and he fastened it upon the end of a pole . . . and he called it the title of liberty" (Alma 46:12–13). © by Intellectual Reserve, Inc. Used by permission.

forever" (Alma 48:17). Mormon even named his son, MORONI₂, after him.

BIBLIOGRAPHY

England, Eugene. "Moroni and His Captains." *Ensign* 7 (Sept. 1977): 29–36.

MELVIN J. THORNE

MORONI₂

Moroni₂ is the last prophet and author of the last book in the Book of Mormon. His life spanned the latter part of the fourth century and the early fifth century. He led ten thousand troops in the last battle against the LAMANITES, serving under his father MORMON, who was commander-in-chief. Prior to the final war, Mormon had abridged the PLATES of Nephi that covered a thousand years of his people's history. He commanded Moroni to conclude the Nephite record by writing "the sad tale of the destruction of

[their] people" (Morm. 8:3) and to preserve all the sacred writings (Moro. 9:24).

After Moroni wrote the required postscript to his father's record and prophesied its future discovery (Morm. 8–9), he added an abridgment of ancient Jaredite engravings, a record of a nation that had inhabited the Western Hemisphere for approximately 1,700 years prior to the Nephites' arrival, or perhaps overlapping their arrival (the Book of Ether). "According to the will of the Lord," he then added ten concluding chapters on ordinances, principles, and church practices that he called the Book of Moroni (Moro. 1:4).

Moroni spoke with prophetic assurance of conditions in the last days because "Jesus Christ hath shown you unto me, and I know your doing" (Morm. 8:35). With fervor, he proclaimed Christ to be a God of miracles who is the same in all ages unless unbelief causes miracles to cease. He spoke with confidence of the divinity and teachings of Jesus Christ because "I have seen Jesus, and . . . he hath talked with me face to face, . . . even as a man telleth another in mine own language, concerning these things" (Ether 12:39).

Moroni also recorded prophecies of the BROTHER OF JARED, a Jaredite prophet, who helped lead his colony to the New World. These prophecies are "sealed" to come forth at a future day (Ether 4:1–7).

Moroni's last entry in the Book of Mormon was likely written about A.D. 421, thirty-six years after the final battle. He then finished writing the title page of the Book of Mormon and finally buried the Book of Mormon plates to preserve them for a future generation.

Fourteen hundred years later this same Moroni, then a resurrected being "sent from the presence of God," appeared to Joseph Smith, a seventeen-year-old youth, on the night of September 21, 1823, and told him of the sacred records deposited in a stone box in a nearby hill (the hill Cumorah) in what is now Ontario County, New York, within a few miles of Joseph's home in Manchester Township. Moroni appeared to Joseph more than twenty times during the next six years, tutoring him for his calling as a prophet and giving counsel and information concerning the acquisition, translation, and guardianship of the Book of Mormon plates (Joseph Smith—History 1:27–54).

Moroni is frequently identified with the Church because portrayals of him blowing a trumpet, handling the gold plates, or instructing Joseph Smith are commonly displayed—for instance on LDS temple spires, on covers of several printings of the Book of Mormon, and in paintings. A depiction of Moroni with a trumpet is the official emblem on grave markers of American Mormon servicemen.

Moroni is commonly portrayed with a trumpet because of an interpretation of a prophecy of John the Revelator wherein he saw an angel heralding the return of the everlasting gospel to the earth in the last days:

> And I saw another angel fly in the midst of heaven, having the everlasting gospel to preach unto them that dwell on the earth, and to every nation, and kindred, and tongue, and people, Saying with a loud voice, Fear God, and give glory to him; for the hour of his judgment is come: and worship him that made heaven, and earth, and the sea, and the fountains of waters. (Rev. 14:6–7)

BIBLIOGRAPHY

Peterson, H. Donl. *Moroni: Ancient Prophet, Modern Messenger*. Bountiful, Utah, 1983.

H. DONL PETERSON

The Angel Moroni, by Millard F. Malin (1953, cast aluminum, gilded). This statue of Moroni, shown with sculptor, shows the angel carrying the gold plates from which the Book of Mormon was translated and, with trumpet in hand, proclaiming the gospel (see Rev. 14:6). It now stands on top of the Los Angeles Temple. © by Intellectual Reserve, Inc. Used by permission.

MOSIAH₁

The first Mosiah mentioned in the Book of Mormon, a king, saved those NEPHITES who "would hearken unto the voice of the Lord" by leading them away from their ancestral home, the land of Nephi, where they were threatened by LAMANITES about 200 B.C. (Omni 1:12). After they had wandered for an unknown period, Mosiah and his group "discovered a people, who were called the people of Zarahemla" (Omni 1:13–14; *see also* PEOPLES OF THE BOOK OF MORMON; MULEK). He taught them his language—their language having deteriorated because they lacked written records—and was chosen ruler over both groups (Omni 1:17–19). "By the gift and power of God" he interpreted "engravings" on a stone that the people of Zarahemla had discovered, telling of yet another and earlier migration (Omni 1:20–22; *see also* JAREDITES). Mosiah ruled for about four decades and was succeeded as king by his son BENJAMIN.

BIBLIOGRAPHY

Ludlow, Victor L. "Scribes and Scriptures." In *Studies in Scripture*, ed. K. Jackson, Vol. 7, pp. 196–204. Salt Lake City, 1987.

MELVIN J. THORNE

MOSIAH₂

Mosiah₂ (c. 153–91 B.C.) ruled as a Nephite king during almost thirty-three years of Book of Mormon history. His reign was marked by an innovative separation of religious and civic functions and a popular political reform, reflecting the increased pluralism of Nephite society during this historical period.

Mosiah's people consisted of two groups, Nephites and Mulekites, who had voluntarily united under his grandfather, MOSIAH₁. They appear, to some extent, to have retained their separate identities (Mosiah 25:4). The Mulekites were the more numerous group, but the Nephite leaders were able to rule effectively, relying on covenant and commitment rather than force. The people entered into a sacred covenant by which they were promised deliverance and prosperity if they would keep their king's commandments, "or the commandments of God," which he would give them (Mosiah 2:31)—a commitment they honored during all of Mosiah's reign.

Mosiah learned the languages and regard for the sacred records of his ancestors from his father, BENJAMIN, and was a wise and patient man who knew the laws and prophecies contained in the Nephite records (Mosiah 1:2–3). Mosiah became king (c. 124 B.C.) three years before his aged father's death. The coronation, described in detail in Mosiah 1–6, exhibits several features similar to ancient Near Eastern coronations. The account of the coronation also provides valuable information about the religious and political patterns of the time (*see* BENJAMIN). Mosiah was in his thirtieth year when he began to reign. He walked "in the ways of the Lord," and like his father, he provided for his own temporal needs so that he would not become a burden to his people (Mosiah 6:6–7).

Challenges soon arose for Mosiah. Limhi's people arrived in Zarahemla and had to be assimilated into Nephite society. They brought with them the twenty-four PLATES of Ether, which Mosiah, being a seer, translated (Mosiah 28:10–19). This Jaredite record revealed an ominous lesson, for wickedness, oppression, and violence had led to the extinction of a people. In contrast, Mosiah promoted righteousness, equality, and harmony in his kingdom. When another group led by ALMA₁ arrived in Zarahemla, Mosiah authorized Alma to organize churches and gave him control over them, including the power to admit members to, or expel members from, that covenant community. The creation of this subgroup comprised of seven churches in Nephite society (Mosiah 25:23) allowed Alma's followers to live as they wished, but it also appears to have sowed seeds of civic tension.

At this time, an opposition group formed. Under a strident leader named Nehor, it rejected Alma's teachings and advocated the creation of a publicly supported priesthood. Mosiah's sons, Ammon, Aaron, Omner, and Himni, together with ALMA₂ and a rising generation that had been too young at the time of Mosiah's coronation to understand the words of King Benjamin (Mosiah 26:1), joined these dissenters. They engaged in systematic religious persecution of the church, wreaking havoc among the Nephite community and with Mosiah's family and reputation. Mosiah dealt with the problem by prohibiting acts of religious persecution (Mosiah 27:2). He also sought divine help through fervent prayer and fasting to reform his sons. Angelic intervention (Mosiah 27:10–32) led to the spiritual transformation of these rebellious souls. Deeming it better soon thereafter to proclaim the gospel than to rule over the kingdom, none of his four sons would accept the Nephite throne.

Under these circumstances and near the end of his life, Mosiah effected a political reform that abolished Nephite kingship. His final speech in 91 B.C. justified righteous monarchs such as his father and himself, but warned against the overriding threats posed by wicked rulers (Mosiah 29:13–21).

In place of kingship, Mosiah created a unique system of judges subject to the voice of the people. From what is known about this legal reform, it appears that each judge was chosen by popular voice, "that every man should have an equal chance"; higher judges judged the lower judges, and a selected body of lower judges judged the higher judges (Mosiah 29:25–29, 38). This law set new precedents by providing that judges should be paid; it also established an Egyptian-style system of measures for exchanging various grains and precious metals (Alma 11:1, 4–19), prohibited all forms of slavery (Alma 27:9), imposed a severe punishment on those who would not pay their debts (Alma 11:2), and granted liberty of belief (Mosiah 29:39; Alma 30:11). The people accepted the law of Mosiah and selected their judges, including Alma₂ as

the first chief judge. The equity and justice of this prophet-king won for him the love of his people:

> And they did wax strong in love towards Mosiah; yea, they did esteem him more than any other man; for they did not look upon him as a tyrant who was seeking for gain, . . . for he had not exacted riches of them, neither had he delighted in the shedding of blood; but he had established peace in the land, and he had granted unto his people that they should be delivered from all manner of bondage; therefore they did esteem him, yea, exceedingly, beyond measure. (Mosiah 29:40)

BIBLIOGRAPHY

"The Coronation of Kings." *FARMS Update*. Provo, Utah, July 1989.

"The Law of Mosiah." *FARMS Update*. Provo, Utah, March 1987.

ADDITIONAL SOURCE

Nyman, Monte S., and Charles D. Tate, Jr., eds. *The Book of Mormon: Mosiah, Salvation Only through Christ*. Provo, Utah: BYU Religious Studies Center, 1991.

PAUL RYTTING

MULEK

Mulek, a Book of Mormon person, son of Zedekiah, escaped the sack of Jerusalem (587 B.C.) and went with others to a place in the Western Hemisphere that they called the land of Mulek (Hel. 6:10). Later a region was named for Zarahemla, a descendant of Mulek (Mosiah 25:2). These people were eventually discovered by Nephite refugees from LAMANITE predations in the south. Mulek is important because he established one of the Book of

Mormon PEOPLES and because Bible students have assumed that Nebuchadnezzar executed all of Zedekiah's sons, an observation unsupported by ancient evidence and refuted by the Book of Mormon account of Mulek's survival.

According to the Book of Mormon, the Nephites and "Mulekites" formed a coalition, making Mosiah₂ king over both groups. The Nephites discovered in Mulek's descendants an additional witness concerning the destruction of Jerusalem. The Mulekites were elated to have access to Nephite records, since their own language and traditions had been distorted in the absence of historical documents. The Mulekites lived thenceforth among the Nephites, enjoying separate-but-equal status and ultimately outnumbering the descendants of Nephi (Mosiah 25:1–4, 13).

Ancient Near Eastern sources affirm that during the Babylonian destruction of Jerusalem, Mulek's father, Zedekiah, who was deserted by all who escaped, was captured with members of his family and a few courtiers. Nebuchadnezzar slew Zedekiah's sons and courtiers, put his eyes out, and deported him to Babylon (Josephus, *Antiquities*, 10.8.2). But his daughters, and presumably his wives, stayed at Mizpah until Gedeliah, a former minister with Babylonizing tendencies in Zedekiah's cabinet, was murdered by Ishmael, who then tried to deport the Mizpah colony. When pursued, Ishmael abandoned his captives and fled with eight men to Ammon. The people of Mizpah, including Zedekiah's women, headed for Egypt, fearful of Chaldean reprisals (2 Kgs. 25; Jer. 41–43).

Mulek might have been away when the city fell; perhaps he eluded his captors at Jericho; the women could have hidden him (as Jehosheba hid her nephew Joash of the royal line earlier [see 2 Kgs. 11:2–4]); he may even have been unborn, although he probably avoided captivity some other way. But nothing in the Bible or other known sources precludes the possibility of his escape from Jerusalem.

Concerning Mulek's existence, the Bible offers important evidence. Mulek is a nickname derived from *melek* (Hebrew, king), a diminutive term of endearment meaning "little king." Its longer form occurs in the Bible as *Malkiyahu* (in English, Malchiah), meaning "Jehovah is king." Malchiah is identified as "the son of Hammelech" in Jeremiah 38:6. But Hammelech is a translator's error, since *ben-hammelek* means "son of the king" and is not a proper name—a fact confirmed by the Septuagint (LXX Jer. 45:6). A fictive paternity thus obscures the lineage of Malchiah as the actual son of Zedekiah. It is also known that names ending in *-yahu* (in English, *-iah*) were common during the late First Temple period, that Zedekiah indeed had a son named Malkiyahu (Aharoni, p. 22), and that the familial forms of *yahu*-names were shorter than their "full" forms. The study of a seal owned by Jeremiah's scribe shows that his full name was Berekyahu (in English, Berechiah), although the biblical text uses only the shorter Baruch (Avigad). This is consistent with viewing the hypocoristic Mulek as the diminutive of Malkiyahu, since *a* is often assimilated to *o* or *u* in the vocalic structure of most Semitic languages. It is therefore possible that the Mulek of the Book of Mormon is "Malchiah, son of the king" mentioned in Jeremiah 38:6.

BIBLIOGRAPHY

Aharoni, Yohanan. "Three Hebrew Ostraca from Arad." *Bulletin of the American Schools of Oriental Research* 197 (Feb. 1970): 16–42.

Avigad, Nahman. "Jerahmeel & Baruch." *Biblical Archeologist* 42:2 (Spring 1979): 114–18.

"New Information about Mulek, Son of the King." *FARMS Update*. Provo, Utah, 1984.

Rainey, Anson. "The Prince and the Pauper." *Ugarit-Forschungen* 7 (1975): 427–32.

ADDITIONAL SOURCE

Sorenson, John L. "The Mulekites." *BYU Studies* 30/3 (1990): 6–22.

H. CURTIS WRIGHT

N

NAMES IN THE BOOK OF MORMON

The Book of Mormon contains 337 proper names and 21 gentilics (or analogous forms) based on proper names. Included in this count are names that normally would not be called proper, such as kinds of animals, if they appear as transliterations in the English text and not as translations. Conversely, proper names that appear only in translation are not included, such as Bountiful and Desolation. Of these 337 proper names, 188 are unique to the Book of Mormon, while 149 are common to the Book of Mormon and the Bible. If the textual passages common to the Book of Mormon and the Bible are excluded, 53 names occur in both books.

It would seem convenient to divide the Book of Mormon collection or listing of names (onomasticon) into three groups because it mentions (1) JAREDITES, (2) the community founded by LEHI (which might be termed "Lehites"), and (3) the people referred to as the people of Zarahemla (who might be called "Mulekites"), each of which con-

tributed to the history of the Book of Mormon and therefore to the list of proper names (*see* PEOPLES OF THE BOOK OF MORMON). While this grouping can be made with some degree of accuracy for Jaredite names, it is not easy to maintain the distinction between Lehite and Mulekite, because a portion of the Lehites united with the Mulekites sometime before 130 B.C.; practically nothing is known about Mulekite names before that time. For the present, Lehite and Mulekite names must be treated together. Given this grouping of the Book of Mormon onomasticon, 142 of the 188 unique Book of Mormon names are Lehite-Mulekite, 41 are Jaredite, and 5 are common to both groups.

Much preliminary work remains to be done on the Book of Mormon onomasticon. The transliteration system of the English text must be clarified: does the j of the text indicate only the Nephite phoneme /y/ or can it also represent /h/ in the name "Job," as it does once in the King James Version? A reliable critical analysis of the text is needed: what is the range of possible spellings of

Cumorah that might indicate phonemic values? Linguistic phenomena beg explanation: there are no exclusively Book of Mormon names that begin with /b/; but several begin with /p/. Q, and x do not occur in any Book of Mormon name. V, w, and y do not occur in any exclusively Book of Mormon name. D, f, and u do not begin any exclusively Book of Mormon name.

The Lehite-Mulekite names often show greatest affinity with Semitic languages (CWHN 6:281–94). For instance, Abish and Abinadi resemble *ab*, father, names in Hebrew; Alma appears in a Bar Kokhba letter (c. A.D. 130) found in the Judean desert; Mulek could be a diminutive of West Semitic *mlk*, king; Omni and Limhi appear to have the same morphology as Old Testament Omri and Zimri; Jershon is remarkably close to a noun form of the Hebrew root yrš (see below). Some Lehite-Mulekite names more closely resemble Egyptian: Ammon, Korihor, Pahoran and Paanchi (CWHN 5:25–34). Jaredite names exhibit no consistently obvious linguistic affinity.

Like proper names in most languages, the proper names of the Book of Mormon probably had semantic meanings for Book of Mormon peoples. Such meanings are evident from several instances wherein the Book of Mormon provides a translation for a proper name. For example, Irreantum means "many waters" (1 Ne. 17:5), and Rabbanah is interpreted as "powerful or great king" (Alma 18:13). The single greatest impediment to understanding the semantic possibilities for the Book of Mormon proper names remains the lack of the original Nephite text. The transliterations of the English text allow only educated conjectures and approximations about the nature of the names and their possible semantic range. In addition, such postulations,

if to be of any value, must be based on a knowledge of the possible linguistic origins of the names, such as Iron Age Hebrew and Egyptian for Lehite and Mulekite names.

The proper names of the Book of Mormon can provide information about the text and the language(s) used to compose it. When studied with apposite methodology, these names testify to the ancient origin of the Book of Mormon. For example, Jershon is the toponym for a land given by the Nephites to a group of Lamanites as an inheritance; based on the usual correspondence in the King James Version of j for the Hebrew phoneme /y/, Book of Mormon Jershon could correspond to the Hebrew root yrš meaning "to inherit," thus providing an appropriate play on words in Alma 27:22: "and this land Jershon is the land which we will give unto our brethren for an inheritance." Similarly, one Book of Mormon name used for a man that might have seemed awkward, Alma, now is known from two second-century A.D. Hebrew documents of the Bar Kokhba period (Yadin, p. 176) and thus speaks for a strong and continuing Hebrew presence among Book of Mormon peoples.

BIBLIOGRAPHY

Hoskisson, Paul Y. "An Introduction to the Relevance of and a Methodology for a Study of the Proper Names of the Book of Mormon." In *By Study and Also By Faith*, ed. J. Lundquist and S. Ricks, Vol. 2, pp. 126–35. Salt Lake City, 1990.

Tvedtnes, John A. "A Phonemic Analysis of Nephite and Jaredite Proper Names." *FARMS Paper*. Provo, Utah, 1977.

Yadin, Y. *Bar Kokhba*, p. 176. Jerusalem, 1971.

PAUL Y. HOSKISSON

NATIVE AMERICANS

LDS BELIEFS. The Book of Mormon, published in 1830, addresses a major message to Native Americans. Its title page states that one reason it was written was so that Native Americans today might know "what great things the Lord hath done for their fathers."

The Book of Mormon tells that a small band of Israelites under LEHI migrated from Jerusalem to the Western Hemisphere about 600 B.C. Upon Lehi's death his family divided into two opposing factions, one under Lehi's oldest son, LAMAN (see LAMANITES), and the other under a younger son, NEPHI₁ (see NEPHITES).

During the thousand-year history narrated in the Book of Mormon, Lehi's descendants went through several phases of splitting, warring, accommodating, merging, and splitting again. At first, just as God had prohibited the Israelites from intermarrying with the Canaanites in the ancient promised land (Ex. 34:16; Deut. 7:3), the Nephites were forbidden to marry the Lamanites with their dark skin (2 Ne. 5:23; Alma 3:8–9). But as large Lamanite populations accepted the gospel of Jesus Christ and were numbered among the Nephites in the first century B.C., skin color ceased to be a distinguishing characteristic. After the visitations of the resurrected Christ, there were no distinctions among any kind of "ites" for some two hundred years. But then unbelievers arose and called themselves Lamanites to distinguish themselves from the Nephites or believers (4 Ne. 1:20).

The concluding chapters of the Book of Mormon describe a calamitous war. About A.D. 231, old enmities reemerged and two hostile populations formed (4 Ne. 1:35–39), eventually resulting in the annihilation of the Nephites. The Lamanites, from whom many present-day Native Americans descend, remained to inhabit the American continent. Peoples of other extractions also migrated there.

The Book of Mormon contains many promises and prophecies about the future directed to these survivors. For example, Lehi's grandson Enos prayed earnestly to God on behalf of his kinsmen, the Lamanites. He was promised by the Lord that Nephite records would be kept so that they could be "brought forth at some future day unto the Lamanites, that, perhaps, they might be brought unto salvation" (Enos 1:13).

The role of Native Americans in the events of the last days is noted by several Book of Mormon prophets. Nephi₁ prophesied that in the last days the Lamanites would accept the gospel and become a "pure and a delightsome people" (2 Ne. 30:6). Likewise, it was revealed to the Prophet Joseph SMITH that the Lamanites will at some future time "blossom as the rose" (D&C 49:24).

After Jesus' resurrection in Jerusalem, he appeared to the more righteous Lamanites and Nephites left after massive destruction and prophesied that their seed eventually "shall dwindle in unbelief because of iniquity" (3 Ne. 21:5). He also stated that if any people "will repent and hearken unto my words, and harden not their hearts, I will establish my church among them, and they shall come in unto the covenant and be numbered among this the remnant of Jacob [the descendants of the Book of Mormon peoples], unto whom I have given this land for their inheritance"; together with others of the house of Israel, they will build the New Jerusalem (3 Ne. 21:22–23). The Book of Mormon teaches that the descendants of Lehi are heirs to the blessings of Abraham and will receive the blessings promised to the house of Israel.

THE LAMANITE MISSION (1830–1831).

Doctrine and a commandment from the Lord motivated the Latter-day Saints to introduce the Book of Mormon to the Native Americans and teach them of their heritage and the gospel of Jesus Christ. Just a few months after the organization of the Church, four elders were called to preach to Native Americans living on the frontier west of the Missouri River.

The missionaries visited the Cattaraugus in New York, the Wyandots in Ohio, and the Shawnees and Delawares in the unorganized territories (now Kansas). Members of these tribes were receptive to the story of the Restoration. Unfortunately, federal Indian agents worrying about Indian unrest feared that the missionaries were inciting the tribes to resist the government and ordered the missionaries to leave, alleging that they were "disturbers of the peace" (Arrington and Bitton, p. 146). LDS pro–Native American beliefs continued to be a factor in the tensions between Latter-day Saints and their neighbors in Ohio, Missouri, and Illinois, which eventually led to persecution and expulsion of the Latter-day Saints from Missouri in 1838–1839 and from Illinois in 1846.

RELATIONS IN THE GREAT BASIN. When the Latter-day Saints arrived in the Great Salt Lake Valley in 1847, they found several Native American tribal groups there and in adjacent valleys. The Church members soon had to weigh their need to put the limited arable land into production for the establishment of Zion against their obligation to accommodate their Native American neighbors and bring them the unique message in the Book of Mormon.

Brigham Young taught that kindness and fairness were the best means to coexist with Native Americans and, like many other white Americans at the time, he hoped eventually to assimilate the Indians entirely into the mainstream culture. He admonished settlers to extend friendship, trade fairly, teach white man's ways, and generously share what they had. Individuals and Church groups gave, where possible, from their limited supplies of food, clothing, and livestock. But the rapid expansion of LDS settlers along the Wasatch Range, their preoccupation with building Zion, and the spread of European diseases unfortunately contravened many of these conciliatory efforts.

A dominating factor leading to resentment and hostility was the extremely limited availability of life-sustaining resources in the Great Basin, which in the main was marginal desert and mountain terrain dotted with small valley oases of green. Although Native Americans had learned to survive, it was an extremely delicate balance that was destroyed by the arrival of the Latter-day Saints in 1847. The tribal chiefs who initially welcomed the Mormons soon found themselves and their people being dispossessed by what appeared to them to be a never-ending horde, and in time they responded by raiding LDS-owned stock and fields, which resources were all that remained in the oases which once supported plants and wildlife that were the staples of the Native American diet. The Latter-day Saints, like others invading the western frontier, concerned with survival in the wilderness, responded at times with force.

An important factor in the conflict was the vast cultural gap between the two peoples. Native Americans in the Great Basin concentrated on scratching for survival in a barren land. Their uncanny survival skills could have been used by the Mormons in 1848, when drought and pestilence nearly destroyed the pioneers' first crops and famine seriously threatened their survival.

The Utes, Shoshones, and other tribal groups in the basin had little interest in being farmers or cowherders, or living in stuffy sod or log houses. They preferred their hunter-gatherer way of life under the open sky and often resisted, sometimes even scoffed at, the acculturation proffered them. Nor did they have a concept of land ownership or the accumulation of property. They shared both the land and its bounty—a phenomenon that European Americans have never fully understood. The culture gap all but precluded any significant acculturation or accommodation.

Within a few years, LDS settlers inhabited most of the arable land in Utah. Native Americans, therefore, had few options: They could leave, they could give up their own culture and assimilate with the Mormons, they could beg, they could take what bounty they could get and pay the consequences, or they could fight. Conflict was inevitable. Conflict mixed with accommodation prevailed in Utah for many years. Violent clashes occurred between Mormons and Native Americans in 1849, 1850 (Chief Sowiette), 1853 (Chief Walkara), 1860, and 1865–1868 (Chief Black Hawk)—all for the same primary reasons and along similar lines. Conflict subsided, and finally disappeared, only when most of the surviving Native Americans were forced onto reservations by the United States government.

Still, the LDS hand of fellowship was continually extended. Leonard Arrington accurately comments that "the most prominent theme in Brigham's Indian policy in the 1850s was patience and forbearance. . . . He continued to emphasize always being ready, using all possible means to conciliate the Indians, and acting only on the defensive" (Arrington, p. 217). Farms for the Native Americans were established as early as 1851, both to raise crops for their use and to teach them how to farm; but most of the "Indian farms" failed owing to a lack of commitment on both sides as well as to insufficient funding. LDS emissaries (such as Jacob Hamblin, Dudley Leavitt, and Dimmick Huntington) continued, however, to serve Native American needs, and missionaries continued to approach them in Utah and in bordering states. Small numbers of Utes, Shoshones, Paiutes, Gosiutes, and Navajos assimilated into the mainstream culture, and some of that number became Latter-day Saints. But overall, reciprocal contact and accommodation were minimal. By the turn of the century, contact was almost nil because most Native Americans lived on reservations far removed from LDS communities. Their contact with whites was mainly limited to government soldiers and agency officials and to non-Mormon Christian missionaries.

RELATIONS IN RECENT TIMES. Beginning in the 1940s, the Church reemphasized reaching out to Native Americans. The Navajo-Zuni Mission, later named the Southwest Indian Mission, was created in 1943. It was followed by the Northern Indian Mission, headquartered in South Dakota. Eventually, missionaries were placed on many Indian reservations. The missionaries not only proselytize, but also assist Native Americans with their farming, ranching, and community development. Other Lamanite missions, including several in Central and South America and in Polynesia, have also been opened. Large numbers of North American Indians have migrated off reservations, and today over half of all Indians live in cities. In response, some formerly all-Indian missions have merged with those serving members of all racial and ethnic groups living in a given geographical area.

An Indian seminary program was initiated to teach the gospel to Native American children on reservations, in their own languages if necessary. Initially, Native American children of all ages were taught the principles of the gospel in schools adjacent to federal public schools on reservations and in remote Indian communities. The Indian seminary program has now been integrated within the regular seminary system, and Indian children in the ninth through twelfth grades attend seminary, just as non-Indian children do.

The Indian Student Placement Services (ISPS) seeks to improve the educational attainment of Native American children by placing member Indian children with LDS families during the school year. Foster families, selected because of their emotional, financial, and spiritual stability, pay all expenses of the Indian child, who lives with a foster family during the nine-month school year and spends the summer on the reservation with his or her natural family. Generally, the children enter the program at a fairly young age and return year after year to the same foster family until they graduate from high school.

From a small beginning in 1954, the program peaked in 1970 with an enrollment of nearly 5,000 students. The development of more adequate schools on reservations has since then reduced the need for the program and the number of participants has declined. In 1990, about 500 students participated. More than 70,000 Native American youngsters have participated in ISPS, and evaluations have shown that participation significantly increased their educational attainment.

In the 1950s, Elder Spencer W. Kimball, then an apostle, encouraged Brigham Young University to take an active interest in Native American education and to help solve economic and social problems. Scholarships were established, and a program to help Indian students adjust to university life was inaugurated. During the 1970s more than 500 Indian students, representing seventy-one tribes, were enrolled each year. But enrollment has declined, so a new program for Indian students is being developed that will increase the recruiting of Native American students to BYU and raise the percentage who receive a college degree. The Native American Educational Outreach Program at BYU presents educational seminars to tribal leaders and Indian youth across North America. It also offers scholarships. American Indian Services, another outreach program originally affiliated with BYU, provides adult education and technical and financial assistance to Indian communities. In 1989, American Indian Services was transferred from BYU to the Lehi Foundation, which continues this activity.

In 1975, George P. Lee, a full-blooded Navajo and an early ISPS participant, was appointed as a General Authority. He was the first Indian to achieve this status and served faithfully for more than ten years. Elder Lee became convinced that the Church was neglecting its mission to the Lamanites, and when he voiced strong disapproval of Church leaders, he was excommunicated in 1989.

The Church has always had a strong commitment to preaching the gospel to Native Americans and assisting individuals, families, communities, and tribes to improve their education, health, and religious well-being. Programs vary from time to time as conditions and needs change, but the underlying beliefs and goodwill of Latter-day Saints toward these people remain firm and vibrant.

BIBLIOGRAPHY

Arrington, Leonard J. *Brigham Young: American Moses*. New York, 1985.

Arrington, Leonard J., and Davis Bitton. *The Mormon Experience: A History of the Latter-day Saints*. New York, 1979.

Chadwick, Bruce A., Stan L. Albrecht, and Howard M. Bahr. "Evaluation of an Indian Student Placement Program." *Social Casework* 67, no. 9 (1986): 515–24.

Walker, Ronald W. "Toward a Reconstruction of Mormon and Indian Relations, 1847–1877." *BYU Studies* 29 (Fall 1989): 23–42.

BRUCE A. CHADWICK

THOMAS GARROW

NEAR EASTERN BACKGROUND OF THE BOOK OF MORMON

According to the Book of Mormon, the JARED-ITES, the NEPHITES, and the "Mulekites" (*see* MULEK) migrated to the Western Hemisphere from the Near East in antiquity, a claim that has been challenged. While Book of Mormon students readily admit that no direct, concrete evidence currently exists substantiating the links with the ancient Near East that are noted in the book, evidence can be adduced—largely external and circumstantial—that commands respect for the claims of the Book of Mormon concerning its ancient Near Eastern background (CWHN 8:65–72). A few examples will indicate the nature and strength of these ties, particularly because such details were not available to Joseph Smith, the translator of the Book of Mormon, from any sources that existed in the early nineteenth century (*see* TRANSLATION OF THE BOOK OF MORMON BY JOSEPH SMITH).

1. LEHI (c. 600 B.C.) was a righteous, wellborn, and prosperous man of the tribe of Manasseh who lived in or near Jerusalem. He traveled much, had a rich estate in the country, and had an eye for fine metalwork. His family was strongly influenced by the contemporary Egyptian culture. At a time of mounting tensions in Jerusalem (the officials were holding secret meetings by night), he fa-

vored the religious reform party of Jeremiah, while members of his family were torn by divided loyalties. One of many prophets of doom in the land, "a visionary man," he was forced to flee with his family, fearing pursuit by the troops of one Laban, a high military official of the city. Important records which Lehi needed were kept in the house of Laban (1 Ne. 1–5; CWHN 6:46–131; 8:534–35). This closely parallels the situation in Lachish at the time, as described in contemporary records discovered in 1934–1935 (H. Torczyner, *The Lachish Letters*, 2 vols., Oxford, 1938; cf. CWHN 8:380–406). The Bar Kokhba letters, discovered in 1965–1966, recount the manner in which the wealthy escaped from Jerusalem under like circumstances in both earlier and later centuries (Y. Yadin, *Bar Kokhba*, Chs. 10 and 16, Jerusalem, 1971; cf. CWHN 8:274–88).

2. Lehi's flight recalls the later retreat of the Desert Sectaries of the Dead Sea, both parties being bent on "keeping the commandments of the Lord" (cf. 1 Ne. 4:33–37; *Battle Scroll* [1QM] x.7–8). Among the Desert Sectaries, all volunteers were sworn in by covenant (*Battle Scroll* [1QM] vii. 5–6). In the case of NEPHI$_1$, son of Lehi, he is charged with having "taken it upon him to be our ruler and our teacher. . . . He says that the Lord has talked with him . . . [to] lead us away into some strange wilderness" (1 Ne. 16:37–38). Later in the New World, Nephi, then MOSIAH$_1$ and then ALMA$_1$ (c. 150 B.C.) led out more devotees, for example, the last-named, to a place of trees by "the waters of Mormon" (2 Ne. 5:1–10; Omni 1:12–13; Mosiah 18). The organization and practices instigated by Alma are like those in the Old World communities: swearing in, baptism, one priest to fifty members, traveling teachers or inspectors, a special day for assembly, all labor and share alike, called "the children of God," all defer to one preeminent Teacher, and so on

(Mosiah 18; 25). Parallels with the Dead Sea Scroll communities are striking, even to the rival Dead Sea colonies led by the False Teacher (CWHN 6:135–44, 157–67, 183–93; 7:264–70; 8:289–327).

3. "And my father dwelt in a tent" (1 Ne. 2:15). Mentioned fourteen times in 1 Nephi, the sheikh's tent is the center of everything. When Lehi's sons returned from Jerusalem safely after fleeing Laban's men and hiding in caves, "they did rejoice . . . and did offer sacrifices . . . [on] an altar of stones . . . and gave thanks" (1 Ne. 2:7; 5:9). Taking "seeds of every kind" for a protracted settlement, "keeping to the more fertile parts of the wilderness," they hunt along the way, mak-

Canaanite horned altar or incense burner from Megiddo in ancient Palestine (c. 1900 B.C.) in the Rockefeller Museum, Jerusalem. This distinctive style of altar was also used by the Israelites (see Lev. 4:7; 1 Kgs. 1:50; 2:28). Courtesy LaMar C. Berrett photo archive.

ing "not much fire," living on raw meat, guided at times by a "Liahona"—a brass ball "of curious workmanship" with two divination arrows that show the way. One long camping was "at a place we call Shazer" (cf. Arabic *shajer*, trees or place of trees); and they buried Ishmael at Nahom, where his daughters mourned and chided Lehi (1 Ne. 16; cf. Arabic *Nahm*, a moaning or sighing together, a chiding). Lehi vividly describes a *sayl*, a flash flood of "filthy water" out of a wadi or stream bed that can sweep one's camp away (1 Ne. 8:13, 32; 12:16), a common event in the area where he was traveling. At their first "river of water" Lehi recited a formal "*qasida*," an old form of desert poetry, to his sons Laman and Lemuel, urging them to be like the stream and the valley in keeping God's commands (1 Ne. 2). He describes the terror of those who in "a mist of darkness . . . did lose their way, wandered off and were lost." He sees "a great and spacious building," appearing to stand high "in the air . . . filled with people, . . . and their manner of dress was exceeding fine" (1 Ne. 8; cf. the "skyscrapers" of southern Arabia, e.g., the town of Shibam). The building fell in all its pride like the fabled Castle of Ghumdan. Other desert imagery abounds (CWHN 5:43–92).

4. Among lengthier connected accounts, MORONI₁ (c. 75 B.C.), leading an uprising against an oppressor, "went forth among the people, waving the rent part of his garment" to show the writing on it (Alma 46:19–20). The legendary Persian hero Kawe did the same thing with his garment. The men of Moroni "came running, . . . rending their garments . . . as a covenant [saying] . . . may [God] cast us at the feet of our enemies . . . to be trodden underfoot" (Alma 46:21–22). Both the rending of and the treading on the garments were ancient practices (CWHN

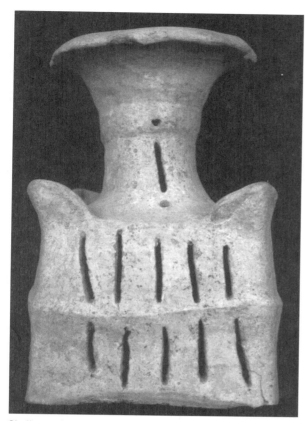

Similar to the horn altar from Israel is this four-cornered altar or incense burner from Oaxaca, Mexico, dating to the Monte Alban 1 period (c. 500–100 B.C.). Specimen in Museo-Frissell, Oaxaca, Mexico. Courtesy Gayle C. Palmer.

6:216–18; 7:198–202; 8:92–95). The inscription on the banner, "in memory of our God, our religion, . . . and our peace, our wives, and our children" (Alma 46:12), is similar to the banners and trumpets of the armies in the Dead Sea *Battle Scroll* ([1QM] iii.1–iv.2). Before the battle Moroni goes before the army and dedicates the land southward as Desolation, and the rest he named "a chosen land, and the land of liberty" (Alma 46:17). In the *Battle Scroll* ([1QM] vii.8ff.) the high priest similarly goes before the army and dedicates the land of the enemy to destruction and that of Israel to salvation (CWHN 6:213–16). Moroni compares his torn garment-banner to the coat of Joseph, half of which was preserved and half decayed: "Let us remember the

words of Jacob, before his death . . . as this remnant of [the coat] hath been preserved, so shall a remnant of [Joseph] be preserved." So Jacob had both "sorrow . . . [and] joy" at the same time (Alma 46:24–25). An almost identical story is told by the tenth century savant Tha'labi, the collector of traditions from Jewish refugees in Persia (CWHN 6:209–21; 8:249, 280–81).

5. There is a detailed description of a coronation in the Book of Mormon which is paralleled only in ancient nonbiblical sources, notably Nathan ha-Babli's description of the coronation of the Prince of the Captivity. The Book of Mormon version in Mosiah 2–6 (c. 125 B.C.) is a classic account of the well-documented ancient "Year Rite": (a) The people gather at the temple, (b) bringing firstfruits and offerings (Mosiah 2:3–4); (c) they camp by families, all tent doors facing the temple; (d) a special tower is erected, (e) from which the king addresses the people, (f) unfolding unto them "the mysteries" (the real ruler is God, etc.); (g) all accept the covenant in a great acclamation; (h) it is the universal birthday, all are reborn; (i) they receive a new name, are duly sealed, and registered in a national census; (j) there is stirring choral music (cf. Mosiah 2:28; 5:2–5); (k) they feast by families (cf. Mosiah 2:5) and return to their homes (CWHN 6:295–310). This "patternism" has been recognized only since the 1930s.

6. The literary evidence of old world ties with the Book of Mormon is centered on Egyptian influences, requiring special treatment. The opening colophon to Nephi's autobiography in the Book of Mormon is characteristic: "I, Nephi . . . I make it with mine own hand" (1 Ne. 1:1, 3). The characters of the original Book of Mormon writing most closely resemble Meroitic, a "reformed Egyptian" known from an Egyptian colony established on the upper Nile River in the same

period (*see* ANTHON TRANSCRIPT; LANGUAGE). Proper names in the Book of Mormon include Ammon (the most common name in both 26th Dynasty Egypt [664–525 B.C.] and the Book of Mormon); Alma, which has long been derided for its usage as a man's name (now found in the Bar Kokhba letters as "Alma, son of Judah"); Aha, a Nephite general (cf. Egyptian *aha*, "warrior"); Paankhi (an important royal name of the Egyptian Late Period [525–332 B.C.]); Hermounts, a country of wild beasts (cf. Egyptian Hermonthis, god of wild places); Laman and Lemuel, "pendant names" commonly given to eldest sons (cf. Qabil and Habil, Harut and Marut); Lehi, a proper name (found on an ancient potsherd in Ebion Gezer about 1938); Manti, a form of the Egyptian god Month; Korihor (cf. Egyptian Herhor, Horihor); and Giddianhi (cf. Egyptian Djhwti-ankhi, "Thoth is my life"), etc. (CWHN 5:25–34; 6:281–94; 7:149–52, 168–72; 8:281–82; *see* NAMES IN THE BOOK OF MORMON).

7. The authenticity of the GOLD PLATES on which the Book of Mormon was inscribed has often been questioned until the finding of the Darius Plates in 1938. Many other examples of sacred and historical writing on metal plates have been found since (C. Wright in *By Study and Also by Faith*, 2:273–334, ed. J. Lundquist and S. Ricks, Salt Lake City, 1990). The brass (bronze) plates recall the Copper Scroll of the Dead Sea Scrolls, the metal being used to preserve particularly valuable information, namely the hiding-places of treasures—scrolls, money, sacred utensils—concealed from the enemy. The Nephites were commanded, "They shall hide up their treasures . . . when they shall flee before their enemies;" but if such treasures are used for private purposes thereafter, "because they will not hide them up unto [God], cursed be they

This gold plate of Darius proclaims his majesty and the vast extent of his Persian empire. It was buried in a neatly made stone box in 516–515 B.C. at Persepolis. This gold plate and its duplicate silver tablet were discovered in 1933. Similarly, the Nephites of the sixth century B.C. kept two sets of records on gold plates, one of which was buried in a stone box in A.D. 421. Courtesy Millie F. Cheesman.

and also their treasures" (Hel. 13:19–20; CWHN 5:105–7; 6:21–28; 7:56–57, 220–21, 272–74).

8. In sharp contrast to other cultures in the book, the JAREDITES carried on the warring ways of the steppes of Asia "upon this north country" (Ether 1, 3–6). Issuing forth from the well-known dispersion center of the great migrations in western Asia, they accepted all volunteers in a mass migration (Ether 1:41–42). Moving across central Asia they crossed shallow seas in barges (Ether 2:5–6). Such great inland seas were left over from the last ice age (CWHN 5:183–85, 194–96). Reaching the "great sea" (possibly the Pacific), they built ships with covered decks and peaked ends, "like unto the ark of Noah" (Ether 6:7), closely resembling the prehistoric "magur boats" of Mesopotamia. The eight ships were lit by shining stones, as was Noah's Ark according to the Palestinian Tal-

mud, the stones mentioned in the Talmud and elsewhere being produced by a peculiar process described in ancient legends. Such arrangements were necessary because of "the furious wind . . . [that] did never cease to blow" (Ether 6:5, 8). In this connection, there are many ancient accounts of the "wind-flood"—tremendous winds sustained over a period of time—that followed the Flood and destroyed the Tower (CWHN 5:359–79; 6:329–34; 7:208–10).

9. The society of the Book of Ether is that of the "Epic Milieu" or "Heroic Age," a product of world upheaval and forced migrations (cf. descriptions in H. M. Chadwick, *The Growth of Literature*, 3 vols., Cambridge, 1932–1940). On the boundless plains loyalty must be secured by oaths, which are broken as individuals seek ever more power and gain. Kings' sons or brothers rebel to form new armies and empires, sometimes putting the king and his family under lifelong house arrest, while "drawing off" followers by gifts and lands in feudal fashion. Regal splendor is built on prison labor; there are plots and counterplots, feuds, and vendettas. War is played like a chess game with times and places set for battle and challenges by trumpet and messenger, all culminating in the personal duel of the rulers, winner take all. This makes for wars of extermination and total social breakdown with "every man with his band fighting for that which he desired" (Ether 7–15; CWHN 5:231–37, 285–307).

10. Elements of the archaic matriarchy were brought from the Old World by Book of Mormon peoples (Ether 8:9–10). For instance, a Jaredite queen plots to put a young successor on the throne by treachery or a duel, and then supplants him with another, remaining in charge like the ancient perennial Great Mother in a royal court (cf. CWHN 5:210–13).

The mother-goddess apparently turns up also among the Nephites in a cult-place (Siron), where the harlot Isabel and her associates were visited by crowds of devotees (Alma 39:3–4, 11); Isabel was the name of the great hierodule of the Phoenicians (CWHN 8:542).

BIBLIOGRAPHY

Nibley, Hugh W. CWHN, Vols. 5–8. Salt Lake City, 1988–1989.

HUGH W. NIBLEY

NEPHI₁

The first of several leaders named Nephi in the Book of Mormon, Nephi₁ was an influential prophet and the founder of the NEPHITE people. He was apparently well-educated, faithful and obedient to God, courageous, and bold. An inspired prophet, he had visions of Jesus Christ and of the world's future; he also interpreted the prophecies of others, such as his father, LEHI, and Isaiah. He authored the first two books in the Book of Mormon, which provide virtually all known information about him. He was a skilled craftsman and leader, and succeeded Lehi as leader of the family (ahead of his three older brothers). Above all, he trusted in God: "My voice shall forever ascend up unto thee, my rock and mine everlasting God" (2 Ne. 4:35).

HISTORY. Nephi was born c. 615 B.C. His father, the prophet Lehi, led his family group out of Jerusalem just after 600 B.C., through the Arabian desert, and across the ocean to the Western Hemisphere. While in the wilderness, Nephi saw a vision that was to shape many of his basic views; it is partially reported in 1 Nephi 11–14. In the promised land, he was designated by his father to succeed him as leader of the family (2 Ne.

1:28–29), but his older brothers LAMAN and Lemuel rebelled and half the group associated with them. Nephi was inspired to flee with all who believed in the warnings and revelations of God (2 Ne. 5:6) and set up a new city, the city of Nephi.

Nephi established his people on sound political, legal, economic, and religious bases. They acclaimed him king, although he resisted this action initially. He taught them to be industrious and to provide for their needs, and he prepared them with training and weapons for defense against their enemies. He followed the law of Moses, built a temple like the temple of Solomon (though without "so many precious things"), and anointed his younger brothers Jacob and Joseph as priests and teachers to instruct the people and lead them in spiritual matters (2 Ne. 5:10, 16, 26). Before he died, he appointed a new king (called the "second Nephi"; Jacob 1:11) and appointed his brother Jacob as the caretaker of religious records (Jacob 1:1–4, 18).

VISIONS. Because of the great visions and revelations he received, Nephi shared a role with his father as a founding prophet. At a young age he was inspired by the Holy Spirit and believed his father's words. He heard the voice of the Lord telling him that he would become a ruler and teacher over his brothers (1 Ne. 2:22). He witnessed the vision of the TREE OF LIFE shown earlier to his father (1 Ne. 8), which showed him the future birth, baptism, and ministry of Jesus Christ, as well as the future rise and demise of his own people. He was shown also the future establishment of the Gentiles in the Western Hemisphere and the restoration of the gospel in their midst (1 Ne. 11–14). Because of these revelations, Nephi was able to teach his people the gospel or "doctrine of Christ"—the means by which they could come unto Christ and be saved (2 Ne. 30:5; 31:2–32:6). His carefully formulated teaching of this doctrine provided a

model that other Nephite prophets invoked repeatedly (see GOSPEL).

Because the Nephites had received the fulness of the gospel of Jesus Christ, their strict observance of the LAW OF MOSES was oriented toward its ultimate fulfillment in Jesus, and Nephi explained to his people that they should observe the law of Moses as a means of keeping Christ's future atonement always in their minds (2 Ne. 25:29–30). The law itself had become "dead" to those who were "made alive in Christ" and who knew that Jesus was the one to whom they could look directly "for a remission of their sins" (2 Ne. 25:25–27).

RECORD KEEPING AND LITERACY. Nephi founded the extensive Nephite tradition of record keeping (see PLATES AND RECORDS IN THE BOOK OF MORMON). He was inspired to keep two separate accounts, both of which were continued for hundreds of years. The official record kept by the kings, known as the large plates of Nephi, began with the book of Lehi and contained the historical chronicles of the Nephites for one thousand years. The GOLD PLATES given to Joseph Smith contained Mormon's abridged version of Nephi's large plates and provided most of the text for the Book of Mormon (from the book of Mosiah to the book of Mormon). However, thirty years after leaving Jerusalem, Nephi was instructed by God to compose a second record focusing on spiritual matters. Known as the small plates of Nephi, this record contains Nephi's retrospective account of the founding events and subsequent prophecies of a line of prophets and priests that descended from Jacob down to about 200 B.C. The opening books in today's printed Book of Mormon, 1 Nephi through Omni, come from this record. Nephi's revelations and inspired teachings shaped the religious understanding of his followers, the Nephites.

When Nephi began writing his small

plates, he was a mature prophet-king. The record reveals his concern with helping his people and their descendants to understand the future atonement of Jesus Christ and the legitimacy of his own calling as their ruler and teacher. In composing this record, Nephi used his father's record and his own earlier and more comprehensive record, both unavailable today.

The exceptional literacy of the later Nephite leaders may have been due to the fact that Nephi was a man of letters. The text suggests that he was probably fluent in both Hebrew and Egyptian and states that he had been "taught somewhat in all the learning" of the Jews and of his father (1 Ne. 1:1–3).

Nephi displayed literary learning in the way he organized his writings and in the variety of literary forms and devices he employed, including those of narrative, rhetoric, and poetry, including a psalm. The techniques, stories, prophecies, and teachings of Nephi provided models and substance for his successors (see LITERATURE, BOOK OF MORMON AS). He loved the writings of Isaiah and quoted them extensively (e.g., 1 Ne. 20–21; 2 Ne. 12–24), often providing interpretations.

THE MAN AND HIS MESSAGES. Nephi constructed the book of 1 Nephi on a tightly balanced and interrelated set of founding stories and revelations, all designed to show "that the tender mercies of the Lord are over all those whom he hath chosen, because of their faith, to make them mighty even unto the power of deliverance" (1 Ne. 1:20). Nephi supports this thesis in 1 Nephi with stories of how God has intervened in human affairs to deliver his faithful followers, and Nephi in particular, from their enemies. But these are only types and shadows. Nephi's true proof is set forth in 2 Nephi, where he says that the atonement of Jesus Christ makes available to all who have faith in Christ a liberation from sin and spiritual redemption from hell and

the devil, their greatest enemy. All men and women who follow the example of Christ and enter into his way through repentance and baptism will be blessed with a baptism of fire and the Holy Ghost—which brings a remission of sin and individual guidance—so that they might endure to the end in faith and receive eternal life (2 Ne. 31).

Into a more spiritual account on his small plates, Nephi also wove a vivid defense of his own political primacy by using allusions to Moses and JOSEPH OF EGYPT (Reynolds, 1987). In defending his ruling position as a younger son, Nephi tells how the two oldest sons rejected their father and the Lord and how he (Nephi) was selected and blessed by the Lord and his father. He relates how, with the help of the Lord, he acquired the brass plates (1 Ne. 3–4), persuaded Ishmael and his family to join Lehi's group (1 Ne. 7), prevented starvation in the wilderness (1 Ne. 16), and constructed a ship and sailed it successfully across the ocean (1 Ne. 17–18). In these exploits, Nephi was consistently opposed and threatened, even with death, by Laman and Lemuel; but in each crisis, he was miraculously delivered by the power of the Lord and blessed to complete his task.

Though he was unable to bridge the gulf between himself and his brothers, Nephi's writings reveal that he was a man with an impressive range of human sensitivities, and he yearned for their welfare. He developed his enormous faith in his father and in the Lord at a young age and never faltered. Consequently, he obeyed without murmuring. He pondered his father's prophecies and repeatedly asked the Lord for personal understanding and direction. He had a deep love and sense of responsibility for his people: "I pray continually for them by day, and mine eyes water my pillow by night, because of them" (2 Ne. 33:3). He also had charity for all other people. Nephi gloried in plainness and in truth, and he knew that his words were harsh against unrepentant sinners (2 Ne. 33:5–9). He anguished deeply because of temptations and his own sins, and particularly because of his feelings of anger against his enemies (2 Ne. 4:26–29). His spiritual strength and depth were grounded in the knowledge that Jesus Christ had heard his pleas and had redeemed his soul from hell (2 Ne. 33:6).

BIBLIOGRAPHY

Bergin, Allen E. "Nephi, A Universal Man." *Ensign* 6 (Sept. 1976): 65–70.

Cannon, George Q. *The Life of Nephi.* Salt Lake City, 1883; repr. 1957.

Reynolds, Noel B. "Nephi's Outline." *BYU Studies* 20 (Winter 1980): 131–49.

———. "The Political Dimension in Nephi's Small Plates." *BYU Studies* 27 (Fall 1987): 15–37.

Sondrup, Steven P. "The Psalm of Nephi: A Lyric Reading." *BYU Studies* 21 (Summer 1981): 357–72.

Turner, Rodney. "The Prophet Nephi." In *The Book of Mormon: First Nephi, the Doctrinal Foundation,* ed. M. Nyman and C. Tate, Jr., pp. 79–97. Provo, Utah, 1988.

ADDITIONAL SOURCE

Welch, John W. "Legal Perspectives on the Slaying of Laban." *Journal of Book of Mormon Studies* 1 (Fall 1992): 119–41.

NOEL B. REYNOLDS

NEPHI₂

Nephi₂ succeeded his father HELAMAN₃ in 39 B.C. as the Nephite chief judge, evidently at a young age. Because of wickedness among the Nephites, he resigned the judgment seat in 30 B.C. and went with his younger brother Lehi to preach the gospel of Jesus Christ among the Lamanites. Although imprisoned and threatened with death, they were preserved by the power of God and converted thousands of Lamanites (Hel. 5).

Nephi returned thereafter to Zarahemla, boldly condemned the corrupt Nephite leaders, miraculously revealed the identity of a murderer, and exercised the power of God to invoke a famine on the Nephites. Although the Nephites repented occasionally, their conversion and the peace that followed did not last. When time was about to expire on the prophecy of SAMUEL THE LAMANITE regarding the birth of Christ, Nephi passed the records to his son Nephi₃ and left, never to be heard of again (3 Ne. 1:3; 2:9).

BIBLIOGRAPHY

Welch, John W. "Longevity of Book of Mormon People and the Age of Man." *Journal of the Collegium Aesculapium* 3 (1985): 34–42.

MELVIN J. THORNE

NEPHI₃

Nephi₃ was the eldest son of Nephi₂. He was given responsibility for all the Nephite records in 1 B.C. (3 Ne. 1:2). Because of his great faith and his concern for his people, he was told by the voice of Jesus the day before Jesus' birth that the Savior would be born "on the morrow" (3 Ne. 1:13). Later, he consolidated, led, and defended the righteous, moving them to the land Bountiful. He survived the destructions occurring in the Western Hemisphere at the Savior's death (3 Ne. 8–9) and was the first to whom the resurrected Christ gave the power to baptize (3 Ne. 11:18–21). He served as the leading disciple in the Church spoken of in this part of the Book of Mormon and saw his people enjoy years of peace and righteousness.

BIBLIOGRAPHY

Arnold, Marilyn. "The Nephi We Tend to Forget." *Ensign* 8 (Jan. 1978): 68–71.

MELVIN J. THORNE

NEPHI₄

Nephi₄ was the son of NEPHI₃. Nephi₄ kept the Nephite records during the extraordinarily blessed era that followed the appearance of Jesus Christ to the Nephites. He saw his people live in love, unity (having all things in common), righteousness, and obedience because the love of God abounded in their hearts. A type of united order or law of consecration was practiced by them during this time. His people experienced the rebuilding of cities, prosperity, miracles, peace, and happiness. Little else is known about his life. He died sometime after A.D. 110 (see 4 Ne. 1:1–19).

MELVIN J. THORNE

NEPHITES

[*The Nephites are the primary group who kept the record known as the Book of Mormon. This complex population was initially descended from Lehi through four of his sons (Sam, Nephi₁, Jacob, and Joseph) and their friend Zoram, although the descendants of other people also joined themselves to the Nephites from time to time (see* Peoples of the Book of Mormon). *The Nephites were distinguished by their belief in the gospel of Jesus Christ, as taught by Lehi and Nephi, as opposed to the lack of faith of the Lamanites, often their enemies but also descendants of Lehi.*

For an account of Nephite life, see Economy and Technology. *Political and legal practices among the Nephites are described in* Government and Legal History in the Book of Mormon. *The traditions of record keeping among the Nephites are summarized in* Plates and Records in the Book of Mormon. *Nephite religious belief and culture are detailed in* Religious Teachings and Practices in the Book of Mormon. *Nephite women and their contributions are reported in* Women in the Book of Mormon.]

NEUM

Neum was an ancient Israelite prophet whose words were contained on the PLATES of brass, a record carried to the Western Hemisphere from Jerusalem about 600 B.C. by the Book of Mormon prophet LEHI and his colony. Neum's work is not preserved in the Hebrew Bible or other known sources. Concerning the time of his writing, it is only definite that he predated Lehi's departure.

Neum is mentioned only once in the Book of Mormon. In writing to his future readers, NEPHI₁ cited him along with other prophets who foretold aspects of the mortal mission of JESUS CHRIST. According to Neum's words, the God of Abraham, Isaac, and Jacob (Jesus Christ) would be crucified (1 Ne. 19:10). This confirmed what Nephi himself had seen previously in a vision (1 Ne. 11:32–33).

KENT P. JACKSON

OPPOSITION

Opposition and agency are eternal and interrelated principles in the theology of The Church of Jesus Christ of Latter-day Saints. Agency is man's innate power to choose between alternative commitments and finally between whole ways of life. Opposition is the framework within which these choices and their consequences are possible.

In his account of the FALL OF ADAM, LEHI teaches that the philosophy of opposites is at the heart of the plan of redemption. Had Adam and Eve continued in a state of premortal innocence, they would have experienced "no joy, for they knew no misery; doing no good, for they knew no sin" (2 Ne. 2:23). Hence, Lehi concludes, "it must needs be, that there is an opposition in all things . . . [otherwise] righteousness could not be brought to pass, neither wickedness, neither holiness nor misery, neither good nor bad" (2 Ne. 2:11).

Latter-day Saints understand that contrast and opposition were manifest in premortal life as well as on earth (Abr. 3:23–28;

Moses 6:56) and that the distinction between good and evil is eternal. Prior to earth life the spirits of all men had opportunities to choose God and demonstrate love for him by obeying his LAW (Matt. 22:37) or to yield to satanic proposals for rebellion and coercion (2 Ne. 2:11–15; cf. Luke 16:13; 2 Ne. 10:16). Different, indeed opposite, consequences followed these choices (Abr. 3:26).

Scripture relates the principle of opposition to crucial states of human experience. Among them are life and death, knowledge and ignorance, light and darkness, growth and atrophy.

LIFE AND DEATH. As a consequence of Adam and Eve's partaking of the fruit of the tree of knowledge of good and evil, they and all their posterity became subject to physical death and to the afflictions and degeneration of the mortal body (2 Ne. 9:6–7). They also became subject to spiritual death, which means spiritual separation from God because of sin. However, through Christ, provision had already been made for their redemption (2 Ne. 2:26), the overcoming of both deaths, and the return to the presence of God. In the span of eternity, the worst form of death is subjection to Satan and thereby exclusion from the presence of God (2 Ne. 2:29). Christ came to bring life, abundant life, everlasting life with God (John 10:28; 17:3; D&C 132:23–24).

KNOWLEDGE AND IGNORANCE. Opposition was, and is, a prerequisite of authentic knowledge, "for if they never should have bitter they could not know the sweet" (D&C 29:39; cf. 2 Ne. 2:15). Such knowledge is participative. Because "it is impossible for a man to be saved in ignorance" (D&C 131:6), the Prophet Joseph SMITH taught, "A man is saved no faster than he gets [such] knowledge" (TPJS, p. 217; cf. 357). One may aspire to all truth (D&C 93:28), but not without confronting the heights and depths of mortal experience, either vicariously or actually.

LIGHT AND DARKNESS. Latter-day Saints find a parallel between light and darkness, the concept of the "two ways," and the idea of the warring "sons of darkness" and "sons of light" apparent in the Dead Sea Scrolls. Jesus teaches that "if therefore the light that is in thee be darkness, how great is that darkness!" (Matt. 6:23) and that "he who sins against the greater light shall receive the greater condemnation" (D&C 82:3). Finally, the sons and daughters of God are to reach the point where "there shall be no darkness in [them]" (D&C 88:67).

GROWTH AND ATROPHY. The principle of opposition also implies that people cannot be tested and strengthened unless there are genuine alternatives (Abr. 3:23–25) and resistances. Life is a predicament in which there are real risks, real gains, real losses. From such tests emerge responsibility, judgment, and soul growth. Latter-day Saints believe that this encounter with choice and conditions for progression will continue forever. It follows that in the gospel framework, once one is committed, there is no such thing as neutrality or standing still. Joseph Smith taught, "If we are not drawing towards God in principle, we are going from Him" (TPJS, p. 216).

One may err in religion by attempting to reconcile the irreconcilable; so one may assume opposition when there is none. In some forms of Judaism and Christianity, for example, the view prevails that the flesh and the spirit are opposed and antithetical. Paul is often cited in this connection. But a close reading of Paul and other writers shows that "flesh" most often applies to man bound by sin, and "spirit" to one regenerated through Christ. Thus, it is not the flesh, but the vices of the flesh that are to be avoided. And it is not the earth, but worldliness (wickedness) that is to be transcended (JST Rom. 7:5–27). Similarly, Latter-day Saints do not finally pit faith against reason, or the spirit against the senses, or the life of contemplation against the life of activity and service. Only when these are distorted are they opposed, for when the self is united under Christ, they are reconciled.

In the plan of redemption, opposition is not obliterated but overcome: evil by good, death by life, ignorance by knowledge, darkness by light, weakness by strength.

BIBLIOGRAPHY

Roberts, B. H. The Gospel. Liverpool, 1888.

———. Comprehensive History of the Church. Vol. 2, pp. 403–6. Salt Lake City, 1930.

KAY P. EDWARDS

P

PALMYRA/MANCHESTER, NEW YORK

The Palmyra/Manchester area of New York is significant to the LDS Church because the Joseph Smith, Sr., family settled there in 1816, and the hill CUMORAH, from which came the gold plates of the Book of Mormon, is nearby. Many events in early Church history occurred in the vicinity, including Joseph Smith's first vision, and also the visits of the ANGEL MORONI leading to the translation and publication of the Book of Mormon in Palmyra. A number of persons, including Martin HARRIS, Oliver COWDERY, and E. B. Grandin, prominent in the early scenes of the Church, also lived in the vicinity. Four revelations now published in the Doctrine and Covenants were received in the area (see D&C 2, 19, 22, 23).

The Joseph Smith, Sr., family arrived in the village of Palmyra, New York, in 1816 from their home in Norwich, Vermont. By the fall of 1817 they made a down payment on a 100-acre farm two miles south of the village in the adjoining township of Farmington (which became Manchester in 1822). During the winter of 1817–1818, they began the construction of a log house, which was completed by the fall of 1818 (Enders, p. 16). A 1982 archaeological dig revealed the exact location of the log cabin on the southern edge of Palmyra township (Berge, pp. 24–26).

In the early spring of 1820, Joseph Smith, Jr., sought the Lord in prayer and experienced the First Vision, in a grove of trees near the home, and three years later, on the evening of September 21–22, 1823, the angel Moroni visited him in the log cabin and gave him instructions about the coming forth of the Book of Mormon. The hill Cumorah where Joseph first viewed the gold plates and received annual visits from Moroni is about three miles to the southeast, on the Canandaigua Road.

From 1822 to 1826 the Smiths built a frame house in Manchester; and in January 1827 Joseph and his new bride, Emma Hale Smith, came to that home to work on the farm. Attempts to steal the gold plates required their being concealed both under the hearthstone of the house and in the cooper's shop.

Church history sites near Palmyra, N.Y., 1820–1831.

The Book of Mormon was printed by Egbert B. Grandin in his Palmyra Bookstore, with Martin Harris's mortgaged farm guaranteeing that the printing costs would be met. With the organization of the Church on April 6, 1830, at Fayette, the Manchester/Palmyra area was identified as one of three branches.

The Church still has interest in the area, maintaining visitors' centers in the Grandin printing shop and bookstore; at the Smith farm and Sacred Grove; and also at the hill

Cumorah, where an appropriate monument and building have been erected, and where an annual pageant is held. A portion of the Martin Harris farm is also owned by the Church. Members of the Smith family and others prominent in the early history of the Church are buried in the cemeteries of the area.

BIBLIOGRAPHY

Berge, Dale L. "Archaeological Work at the Smith Log House." *Ensign* 15 (Aug. 1985): 24–26.

Enders, Donald L. "'A Snug Log House': A Historical Look at the Joseph Smith, Sr., Family Home in Palmyra, New York." *Ensign* 15 (Aug. 1985): 14–23.

Porter, Larry C. "A Study of the Origins of The Church of Jesus Christ of Latter-day Saints in

In such a grove of towering beeches, maples, and other trees, about one-fourth mile west of the Smith family home near Palmyra, New York, fourteen-year-old Joseph Smith saw God the Father and Jesus Christ in the spring of 1820. Photograph by George E. Anderson, 1907. © by Intellectual Reserve, Inc. Used by permission.

the States of New York and Pennsylvania, 1816–1831." Ph.D. diss., Brigham Young University, 1971.

LARRY C. PORTER

PEOPLES OF THE BOOK OF MORMON

At least fifteen distinct groups of people are mentioned in the Book of Mormon. Four (NEPHITES, LAMANITES, JAREDITES, and the people of Zarahemla [Mulekites]) played a primary role; five were of secondary concern; and six more were tertiary elements.

NEPHITES. The core of this group were direct descendants of NEPHI₁, the son of founding father LEHI. Political leadership within the Nephite wing of the colony was "conferred upon none but those who were descendants of Nephi" (Mosiah 25:13). Not only the early kings and judges but even the last military commander of the Nephites, MORMON, qualified in this regard (he explicitly notes that he was "a pure descendant of Lehi" [3 Ne. 5:20] and "a descendant of Nephi" [Morm. 1:5]).

In a broader sense, "Nephites" was a label given all those governed by a Nephite ruler, as in Jacob 1:13: "The people which were not Lamanites were Nephites; nevertheless, they were called [when specified according to descent] Nephites, Jacobites, Josephites, Zoramites, Lamanites, Lemuelites, and Ishmaelites." It is interesting to note that groups without direct ancestral connections could come under the Nephite sociopolitical umbrella. Thus, "all the people of Zarahemla were numbered with the Nephites" (Mosiah 25:13). This process of political amalgamation had kinship overtones in many instances, as when a body of converted Lamanites "took upon themselves the name of Nephi, that they might be called the children of Nephi and be numbered among those who were

called Nephites" (Mosiah 25:12). The odd phrase "the people of the Nephites" in such places as Alma 54:14 and Helaman 1:1 suggests a social structure where possibly varied populations ("the people") were controlled by an elite ("the Nephites").

Being a Nephite could also entail a set of religious beliefs and practices (Alma 48:9–10; 4 Ne. 1:36–37) as well as participation in a cultural tradition (Enos 1:21; Hel. 3:16). Most Nephites seem to have been physically distinguishable from the Lamanites (Jacob 3:5; Alma 55:4, 8; 3 Ne. 2:15).

The sociocultural and political unity implied by the use of the general title "Nephites" is belied by the historical record, which documents a long series of "dissensions" within and from Nephite rule, with large numbers periodically leaving to join the Lamanites (Alma 31:8; 43:13; Hel. 1:15).

The Book of Mormon—a religiously oriented lineage history—is primarily a record of events kept by and centrally involving the Nephites. Since the account was written from the perspective of this people (actually, of its leaders), all other groups are understood and represented from the point of view of Nephite elites. There are only fragments in the Nephite record that indicate directly the perspectives of other groups, or even of Nephite commoners.

LAMANITES. This name, too, was applied in several ways. Direct descendants of Laman, Lehi's eldest son, constituted the backbone of the Lamanites, broadly speaking (Jacob 1:13–14; 4 Ne. 1:38–39). The "Lemuelites" and "Ishmaelites," who allied themselves with the descendants of Laman in belief and behavior, were also called Lamanites (Jacob 1:13–14). So were "all the dissenters of [from] the Nephites" (Alma 47:35). This terminology was used in the Nephite record, although one cannot be sure that all dissenters applied the term to themselves. However, at least one such dissenter, Ammoron, a Zoramite, bragged, "I am a bold Lamanite" (Alma 54:24).

Rulers in the Lamanite system appear to have had more difficulty than Nephite rulers in binding component social groups into a common polity (Alma 17:27–35; 20:4, 7, 9, 14–15; 47:1–3). They seem to have depended more on charisma or compulsion than on shared tradition, ideals, or an apparatus of officials. Whether a rule existed that Lamanite kings be descendants of Laman is unclear. Early in the second century B.C. two successive Lamanite kings were called Laman (Mosiah 7:21; 24:3); since this designation was being interpreted across a cultural boundary by a record keeper of Nephite culture, it is possible that "Laman" was really a title of office, in the same manner that Nephite kings bore the title "Nephi" (Jacob 1:9–11). Later, however, Lamoni, a local Lamanite ruler, is described as "a descendant of Ishmael," not of Laman (Alma 17:21), and his father, king over the entire land of Nephi (originally a homeland of the Nephites, but taken and occupied by the Lamanites throughout much of the remainder of Book of Mormon history), would have had the same ancestry. Evidently, if there was a rule that Laman's descendants inherit the throne, it was inconsistently applied. Moreover, Amalickiah and his brother, both Nephite dissenters, gained the Lamanite throne and claimed legitimacy (Alma 47:35; 52:3).

Repeatedly, the Lamanites are said to have been far more numerous than the Nephites (Jarom 1:6; Mosiah 25:3; Hel. 4:25), a fact that might appear to be inconsistent with the early Nephite characterization of them as savage hunters, which normally require much more land per person than farmers require (Enos 1:20; Jarom 1:6). The expression "people of the Lamanites" (Alma 23:9–12) may indicate that Lamanite elites dominated a disparate peasantry.

The few direct glimpses that Nephite history allows of the Lamanites indicate a level well beyond "savage" culture, though short of the "civilization" claimed for the Nephites. Perhaps their sophistication was due somewhat to the influence of Nephite dissenters among them (see Mosiah 24:3–7). Apparently some Lamanites proved apt learners from this source; moreover, those converted to the prophetic religion taught by Nephite missionaries are usually described as exemplary (Alma 23:5–7; 56; Hel. 6:1).

The People of Zarahemla (Mulekites). In the third century B.C., when the Nephite leader Mosiah₁ and his company moved from the land of Nephi down to the Sidon river, "they discovered a people, who were called the people of Zarahemla" (Omni 1:13–14) because their ruler bore that name. These people were descendants of a party that fled the Babylonian conquest of Jerusalem in 586 B.C., among whom was a son of the Jewish king Zedekiah, MULEK. Hence Latter-day Saints often refer to the descendants of this group of people as Mulekites, although the Book of Mormon never uses the term. When discovered by the Nephites around 200 B.C., this people were "exceedingly numerous," although culturally degenerate due to illiteracy and warfare (Omni 1:16–17). The Nephite account says the combined population welcomed Mosiah as king.

Mosiah found that the people of Zarahemla had discovered the last known survivor of the Jaredites shortly before his death. By that means, or through survivors not mentioned, elements of Jaredite culture seem to have been brought to the Nephites by the people of Zarahemla (CWHN 5:238–47). The fact that the people of Zarahemla spoke a language unintelligible to the Nephites further hints at an ethnic makeup more diverse than the brief text suggests, which assumes a solely Jewish origin.

The Mulekites are little referred to later, probably because they were amalgamated thoroughly into eclectic Nephite society (Mosiah 25:13). However, as late as 51 B.C., a Lamanite affiliate who was a descendant of king Zarahemla attacked and gained brief control over the Nephite capital (Hel. 1:15–34).

JAREDITES. This earliest people referred to in the Book of Mormon originated in Mesopotamia at the "great tower" referred to in Genesis 11. From there a group of probably eight families journeyed to America under divine guidance.

The existing record is a summary by MORONI₂, last custodian of the Nephite records, of a history written on gold plates by Ether, the final Jaredite prophet, around the middle of the first millennium B.C. Shaped by the editorial hands of Ether, Moroni₂, and MOSIAH₂ (Mosiah 28:11–17), and by the demand for brevity, the account gives but a skeletal narrative covering more than two millennia of Jaredite history. Most of it concerns just one of the eight lineages, Jared's, the ruling line to which Ether belonged, hence the name Jaredites (see PLATES AND RECORDS IN THE BOOK OF MORMON).

Eventually a flourishing cultural tradition developed (Ether 10:21–27), although maintaining a viable population seems to have been a struggle at times (Ether 9:30–34; 11:6–7). By the end, millions were reported victims of wars of extermination witnessed by the prophet Ether (Ether 15:2). A single survivor, Coriantumr, the last king, was encountered by the people of Zarahemla sometime before 200 B.C., although it is plausible that several remote groups also could have survived to meld unnoticed by historians into the successor Mulekite and Lamanite populations.

SECONDARY GROUPS. The same seven lineage groups are mentioned among Lehi's descendants near the beginning of the Nephite record and again 900 years later (Jacob 1:13; Morm. 1:8). Each was named after a first-generation ancestor and presumably consisted of his descendants. Among the Nephites there were four: Nephites proper, Jacobites, Josephites, and Zoramites. Within the Lamanite faction, Laman's own descendants were joined by the Lemuelites and Ishmaelites. These divisions disappeared after the appearance of Christ at Bountiful (there were neither "Lamanites, nor any manner of -ites" [4 Ne. 1:17]), but that descent was not forgotten, for the old lineages later reappeared (4 Ne. 1:20, 36–37). What might have happened was that some public functions which the groups had filled were taken over for several generations by the Christian church, which they all had joined. Based on analogy to social systems in related lands, it is possible that membership in these seven groups governed marriage selection and property inheritance, and perhaps residence (Alma 31:3). The Lemuelites evidently had their own city (Alma 23:12–13), and descent determined where the Nephites and the people of Zarahemla sat during Mosiah₂'s politico-religious assembly (Mosiah 25:4; cf. 25:21–23). Such functions may also have been filled by groups other than the seven lineages.

The seven lineage groups may be referred to as "tribes," as in 3 Nephi 7:2–4. Immediately before the natural disasters that signaled the crucifixion of Jesus Christ, Nephite social unity collapsed, and they "did separate one from another into tribes, every man according to his family and his kindred and friends; . . . therefore their tribes became exceedingly great" (3 Ne. 7:2–4).

The **Jacobites** are always listed first of the three secondary peoples among the Nephites. They were descendants of Nephi's younger brother, Jacob. Nothing is said of them as a group except that they were counted as

Nephites politically and culturally. Since Jacob himself was chief priest under the kingship of his brother Nephi, and since he and his descendants maintained the religious records begun by Nephi, it is possible that the Jacobites as a lineage group bore some special priestly responsibilities.

The **Josephites** are implied to have been descendants of Joseph, Nephi's youngest brother. The text is silent on any distinctive characteristics.

The **Zoramites** descended from Zoram, Laban's servant who agreed under duress to join the party of Lehi following the slaying of Laban in Jerusalem (1 Ne. 4:31–37). Both early and late in the account (Jacob 1:13 and 4 Ne. 1:36), the Zoramites are listed in alignment with Nephi's descendants, although around 75 B.C. at least some of them dissented for a time and joined the Lamanite alliance (Alma 43:4). As they were then "appoint[ed] . . . chief captains" over the Lamanite armies (Alma 48:5), they may earlier have played a formal military role among the Nephites. A reason for their split with the Nephites was evidently recollection of what had happened to their founding ancestor: Ammoron, dissenter from the Nephites and king of the Lamanites in the first century B.C., recalled: "I am . . . a descendant of Zoram, whom your fathers pressed and brought out of Jerusalem" (Alma 54:23).

During their dissidence, their worship, characterized as idolatrous yet directed to a god of spirit, was conducted in "synagogues" from which the wealthy drove out the poor (Alma 31:1, 9–11; 32:5). Their practices departed from both Nephite ways and the LAW OF MOSES (Alma 31:9–12). Shortly after the signs marking the birth of Christ and almost eight years after the earliest mention of their separation from the Nephites, these Zoramites were still dissident and were luring naive Nephites to join the Gadianton robbers by means of "lyings" and "flattering words" (3 Ne. 1:29). Yet two centuries later they were back in the Nephite fold (4 Ne. 1:36).

The list of secondary peoples among the Lamanites starts with the **Lemuelites**. Presumably they were the posterity of Lehi's second eldest son, Lemuel. Nothing is said of the group as a separate entity other than routine listings among the Nephites' enemies (Jacob 1:13–14; Morm. 1:8–9), although a "city of Lemuel" is mentioned in Alma 23:12.

The **Ishmaelites** were descendants of the father-in-law of Nephi and his brothers (1 Ne. 7:2–5). Why Ishmael's sons (1 Ne. 7:6) did not found separate lineages of their own is nowhere indicated. As with the other secondary groups, there is little to go on in characterizing the Ishmaelites. At one time they occupied a particular land of Ishmael within the greater land of Nephi, where one of their number, Lamoni, ruled (Alma 17:21).

Somehow, by the days of Ammon and his fellow missionaries (first century B.C.), the Ishmaelites had gained the throne over the entire land of Nephi as well as kingship over some component kingdoms. (Alma 20:9 has the grand king implying that Lamoni's brothers, too, were rulers.) Yet the king recited the familiar Lamanite litany of complaint about how in the first generation Nephi had "robbed our fathers" of the right to rule (Alma 20:13). Evidently he was a culturally loyal Lamanite even though of a minor lineage.

The final information known about both Ishmaelites and Lemuelites is their presence in the combined armies fighting against the Nephites in Mormon's day (Morm. 1:8). Presumably their contingents were involved in the final slaughter of the Nephites at CUMORAH.

TERTIARY GROUPS. Six other groups qualify as peoples, even though they did not exhibit the staying power of the seven lineages.

The earliest described are the **people of Zeniff** (Zeniffites). Zeniff, a Nephite, about half a century after Mosiah had first discovered the people and land of Zarahemla, led a group out of Zarahemla who were anxious to resettle "the land of Nephi, or . . . the land of our fathers' first inheritance" (Mosiah 9:1). Welcomed at first by the Lamanites there, in time they found themselves forced to pay a high tax to their overlords. A long section on them in the book of Mosiah (Mosiah 9–24) relates their dramatic temporal and spiritual experiences over three generations until they were able to escape back to Zarahemla. There they became Nephites again, although perhaps they retained some residential and religious autonomy as one of the "seven churches" (Mosiah 25:23).

Two groups splintered off from the people of Zeniff. The **people of Alma₁** were religious refugees who believed in the words of the prophet Abinadi and fled from oppression and wickedness under king Noah, the second Zeniffite king (Mosiah 18, 23–24). Numbering in the hundreds, they maintained independent social and political status for less than twenty-five years before escaping from Lamanite control and returning to Nephite territory, where they established the "church of God" in Zarahemla (Mosiah 25:18) but soon disappeared from the record as an identifiable group.

The second Zeniffite fragment started when the priests of king Noah, headed by Amulon, fled into the wilderness to avoid execution by their rebellious subjects. In the course of their escape, they kidnaped Lamanite women and took them as wives, thus founding the **Amulonites** in a land where they established their own version of Nephite culture (Mosiah 24:1). In time, they

adopted the religious order of Nehor (see below), usurped political and military leadership, and "stirred up" the Lamanites to attack the Nephites (Alma 21:4; 24:1–2; 25:1–5). They and the Amalekites (see below) helped the Lamanites construct a city named Jerusalem in the land of Nephi. Judging from brief statements by the Nephites (Mosiah 12–13; Alma 21:5–10), both Amulonites and Amalekites saw themselves as defenders of a belief system based on the Old Testament, which no doubt explains the naming of their city.

One of the earliest groups of Nephite dissenters was the **Amlicites**. Ambitious Amlici, a disciple of Nehor, likely claiming noble birth (Alma 51:8), gathered a large body of followers and challenged the innovative Nephite system of rule by judges instituted by Mosiah₂; Amlici wished to be king. When his aim was defeated by "the voice of the people," he plotted an attack coordinated with the Lamanites that nearly succeeded in capturing Zarahemla, the Nephite capital. Loyal forces under ALMA₂ finally succeeded in destroying or scattering the enemy (Alma 2:1–31). Amlici was slain, but the fate of his forces is unclear. Likely, elements of them went with the defeated Lamanite army to the land of Nephi. The name Amlicite is not used thereafter.

Another group of Nephite dissenters, the **Amalekites**, lived in the land of Nephi (Alma 21:2–3; 43:13). Their origin is never explained. However, based on the names and dates, it is possible that they constituted the Amlicite remnant previously mentioned, their new name possibly arising by "lamanitization" of the original. They were better armed than common Lamanites (Alma 43:20) and, like some Zoramites, were made military leaders within the Lamanite army because of their "more wicked and murderous disposition"

(Alma 43:6). From the record of the Nephite missionaries, we learn that they believed in a god (Alma 22:7). Many of them, like the Amlicites, belonged to the religious order of Nehor and built sanctuaries or synagogues where they worshipped (Alma 21:4, 6). Like the Amulonites, they adamantly resisted accepting Nephite orthodox religion (Alma 23:14). Instead, they believed that God would save all people. From their first mention to the last, only about fifteen years elapsed.

During a fourteen-year mission in the land of Nephi, the Nephite missionaries Ammon and his brothers gained many Lamanite converts (Alma 17–26). A Lamanite king, Lamoni, who was among these converts, gave the Lamanite converts the name **Anti-Nephi-Lehies**. These people were singularly distinguished by their firm commitment to the gospel of Jesus Christ, including, most prominently, the Savior's injunctions to love one's enemies and not to resist evil (3 Ne. 12:39, 44; Matt. 5:39, 44). Ammon maintained that in Christlike love this people exceeded the Nephites (Alma 26:33). After their conversion, the Book of Mormon says, they "had no more desire to do evil" (Alma 19:33) and "did not fight against God any more, neither against any of their brethren" (Alma 23:7). Having previously shed human blood, they covenanted as a people never again to take human life (Alma 24:6) and even buried all their weapons (Alma 24:17). They would not defend themselves when attacked by Lamanites, and 1,005 of them were killed (Alma 24:22). Ammon urged the vulnerable Anti-Nephi-Lehies to flee to Nephite territory. Among the Nephites they became known as the **people of Ammon** (or **Ammonites**; see Alma 56:57). They ended up in a separate locale within the Nephite domain, the land of Jershon (Alma 27:26). Later, they moved en masse to the land of Melek (Alma 35:13), where they were joined from time to time by other Lamanite refugees.

Some years later, desiring to assist the Nephite armies in defending the land but not wishing to break their covenant (Alma 53:13), the people of Ammon sent 2,000 of their willing sons to be soldiers, since their sons had not taken the covenant of nonviolence that they had. These "two thousand stripling soldiers" (Alma 53:22) became known as the sons of Helaman, their Nephite leader, and had much success in battle (Alma 56:56). Although they were all wounded, none were ever killed, a remarkable blessing ascribed "to the miraculous power of God, because of their exceeding faith" (Alma 57:26; cf. 56:47).

According to Helaman 3:11, a generation later some of the people of Ammon migrated into "the land northward." This is the last mention of them in the Book of Mormon.

OTHER GROUPS. Among the other groups mentioned in the Book of Mormon are the widespread secret combinations or "robbers." Yet these groups do not qualify as "peoples" but as associations, which individuals could join or leave on their own volition.

Another group, the "order of Nehor," was a cult centered around the ideas that priests should be paid and that God would redeem all people. They were not really a "people" in the technical sense—the term implies a biological continuity that a cult lacks.

The inhabitants of separate cities were also sometimes called peoples. Local beliefs and customs no doubt distinguished them from each other, but insufficient detail prohibits describing units of this scale.

BIBLIOGRAPHY

Nibley, Hugh W. *Lehi in the Desert; The World of the Jaredites; There Were Jaredites.* CWHN 5. Salt Lake City, 1988.

Sorenson, John L. *An Ancient American Setting for the Book of Mormon*. Salt Lake City, 1985.

Welch, John W. "Lehi's Last Will and Testament: A Legal Approach." In *The Book of Mormon: Second Nephi, The Doctrinal Structure*, ed. M. Nyman and C. Tate, Jr., pp. 61–82. Provo, Utah, 1989.

ADDITIONAL SOURCES

Carter, George F. "Movement of People and Ideas across the Pacific." *The Cornerstone of Book of Mormon Archaeology* 1/4 (October 1990): 45–59; reprinted from *Plants and the Migrations of Pacific Peoples: A Symposium*, edited by Jacques Barrau, 7–22. Honolulu: Bishop Museum, 1963.

Sorenson, John L., and Martin A. Raish. *Pre-Columbian Contact with the Americas across the Oceans: An Annotated Bibliography*. 2 vols. Provo, Utah: Research Press, 1990.

Tvedtnes, John A. "Book of Mormon Tribal Affiliation and Military Caste." In *Warfare in the Book of Mormon*, edited by Stephen D. Ricks and William J. Hamblin. Salt Lake City and Provo, Utah: Deseret Book and FARMS, 1990.

JOHN L. SORENSON

PLAN OF SALVATION, PLAN OF REDEMPTION

Latter-day Saints believe that eons ago, God, in his infinite wisdom and never-ending mercy, formulated a plan whereby his children could experience a physical existence, including mortality, and then return to live in his presence in eternal felicity and glory. This plan, alternately called "the plan of salvation" (Jarom 1:2; Alma 42:5; Moses 6:62), "the plan of redemption" (Jacob 6:8; Alma 12:25; 42:11), and the "great plan of happiness" (Alma 42:8), provided both the way and the means for everyone to receive salvation and gain

eternal life. Eternal life is God's greatest gift to his children (D&C 6:13), and the plan of salvation is his way of making it available to them. Although the term "plan of salvation" is used repeatedly in latter-day scripture, it does not occur in the Bible, though the doctrines pertaining to it are discoverable in its pages.

The Father is the author of the plan of salvation; JESUS CHRIST is its chief advocate; the Holy Spirit helps carry it out, communicating God's will to men and helping them live properly.

THE PREMORTAL EXISTENCE. Latter-day Saints believe that all humans are spirit children of heavenly parents, and they dwelt with them prior to birth on this earth (Heb. 12:9; cf. Jer. 1:5; Eph. 1:4). In that premortal life, or first estate, those spirit children could not progress fully. They needed a physical body in order to have a fulness of joy (D&C 93:33–34), and the spirits also needed to be placed in an environment where, by the exercise of agency, they could prove their willingness to keep God's commandments (Abr. 3:25). On the other hand, if they succumbed to temptation, they would be shut out from God's presence, for "no unclean thing can dwell with God" (1 Ne. 10:21; Eph. 5:5). To bring those who yielded to temptation back into God's presence, a plan of redemption had to be set in place, and this required a redeemer.

A Council in Heaven was held of all the spirits, and two individuals volunteered to serve as the redeemer. One was Lucifer, a son of the morning (Isa. 14:12; D&C 76:26), who said he would "redeem all mankind, that one soul shall not be lost," but they would have no choice in the matter. Their agency would be destroyed (Moses 4:1–3). Such a proposal was out of harmony with the plan of the Father, for the agency of mankind is an absolute prerequisite to progress. Jehovah, the premortal Jesus Christ, had first stepped forward and volunteered to give his life as payment for all sins. He set no plan or conditions of his own, but said, "Father, thy will be done, and the glory be thine forever" (Moses 4:2). He was selected by the Father.

When Lucifer would not accept the Father's choice, a war in heaven ensued, and he was cast out for rebellion (Moses 4:3; D&C 76:25), along with those who followed him, numbering about a third of the spirits (Rev. 12:4, 7–9; D&C 29:36–38). After Satan's expulsion, the Father's plan was carried forward. Three events ordained and instituted by God before the creation of the Earth constitute the foundation stones upon which the plan of salvation rests. These are the creation, the FALL OF ADAM, and the atonement of Jesus Christ. "These three divine events—the three pillars of eternity—are inseparably woven together into one grand tapestry known as the eternal plan of salvation" (McConkie, p. 81).

THE CREATION. One of the purposes for creating this earth was for God's spirit children to obtain physical bodies and learn to walk by FAITH. Earth life is the second estate. The scriptures teach that by the power of his Only Begotten Son, the Father has created "worlds without number" (Moses 1:33; cf. John 1:3; Heb. 1:2), but the Lord has revealed to us detailed information only about this world (Moses 1:40).

Ecclesiastes states that "whatsoever God doeth, it shall be for ever" (Eccl. 3:14). God does not work for temporal ends (D&C 29:34–35). The scriptures specify that when God created the earth, it was in a paradisiacal and deathless state. If Adam and Eve had not transgressed and fallen, "all things which were created must have remained in the same state in which they were after they were cre-

ated; and they must have remained for ever, and had no end" (2 Ne. 2:22; cf. Moses 3:9; DS, pp. 75–77).

THE FALL. An earth in a deathless and paradisiacal state did not fulfill conditions needed for the progression of God's children. The Book of Mormon gives some reasons why the Fall was part of the foreordained plan of God. Agency is of paramount importance in the proving process. Critical to agency are choices or alternatives. LEHI taught that there "must needs be . . . an opposition in all things" (2 Ne. 2:11). But in the state in which Adam and Eve found themselves, there was no such opposition. They had physical bodies, but were in a state of innocence. There was no death, sin, sorrow, or pain. Furthermore, in that state they would have had no children (2 Ne. 2:22–23). It appears that a major reason Lucifer and his followers had access to those on earth is the necessity that everyone be enticed by both good and evil (2 Ne. 2:16).

Eve was beguiled by Satan to partake of the forbidden fruit, exercised her agency and did so. Adam also chose to partake, realizing that if he did not, Eve and he would be separated and the command to multiply and replenish the earth would be thwarted. Therefore, "Adam fell that men might be" (2 Ne. 2:25). "With the eating of the 'forbidden fruit,' Adam and Eve became mortal, sin entered, blood formed in their bodies, and death became a part of life. . . . After Adam fell, the whole creation fell and became mortal. Adam's fall brought both physical and spiritual death into the world upon all mankind" (Bible Dictionary, p. 670; DS 1:77; Hel. 14:16–17). Later, both Adam and Eve rejoiced in the opportunities that had come to them because of the Fall (Moses 5:10–11).

The Fall was part of God's plan for

mankind and came as no surprise. "All things have been done in the wisdom of him who knoweth all things" (2 Ne. 2:24). Latter-day Saints affirm that Adam and Eve were actual beings, the first parents, and that the Fall was a literal event both in time and place. Elder Joseph Fielding Smith explained, "If Adam did not fall, there was no Christ, because the atonement of Jesus Christ is based on the fall of Adam" (DS 1:120). Elder James E. Talmage wrote, "It has become a common practice with mankind to heap reproaches on the progenitors of the family, and to picture the supposedly blessed state in which we would be living but for the fall; whereas our first parents are entitled to our deepest gratitude for their legacy to posterity" (AF, p. 70).

THE ATONEMENT. The Atonement is the crowning phase of the plan of salvation, without which all else would have been without purpose and all would have been lost. Atonement literally means "at-one-ment" and carries the idea of reconciliation, or the reuniting, of the human family with Heavenly Father. Understanding reconciliation necessitates an examination of the operation of the laws of JUS-TICE AND MERCY.

God's perfect love, patience, long-suffering, and care for humanity's eternal welfare are the manifestations of his mercy. God is also just and so "cannot look upon sin with the least degree of allowance" (Alma 45:16). Perfect justice requires that every violation of God's law be punished and every act of obedience to the law be rewarded or blessed (D&C 130:20–21). Mercy and justice are basic to God's nature, and neither can be ignored. If the demands of justice were the only consideration and mercy ignored, no one could come back into God's presence, for "all have sinned, and come short of the glory of God" (Rom. 3:23). If God were to excuse sin, then

mercy would rob justice. Such cannot be. "What, do ye suppose that mercy can rob justice? I say unto you, Nay; not one whit. If so, God would cease to be God" (Alma 42:25).

In the atonement of Jesus Christ, justice and mercy are combined to bring about the plan of redemption. As the Only Begotten Son of a divine Father and a mortal mother, Jesus was subject to the effects of the fall of Adam (mortality, temptation, pain, etc.), but had the power to live a perfect, sinless life (Heb. 4:15; D&C 45:4) and to lay down his life and take it up again (John 5:26; 10:17). In LDS doctrine, the miraculous conception and virgin birth of Jesus Christ are accepted as literally true and absolutely essential to the working of the plan of salvation. Because of his sinless life, justice had no claim on him. Because of his infinite, divine power, he could pay the price of sin for all of God's children and satisfy justice in their behalf (D&C 45:3–5). His was not a human sacrifice, but an infinite, eternal sacrifice (Alma 34:14). He atoned not only for the fall of Adam but also for the individual sins of every person. He extends forgiveness to everyone upon the condition of repentance.

In Gethsemane, Christ took upon himself the burden of the sins of the world and suffered for them in a way that is incomprehensible to mortals. "He suffereth the pains of all men, yea, the pains of every living creature, both men, women, and children, who belong to the family of Adam" (2 Ne. 9:21). This incomprehensible agony was so intense that it caused Jesus, "even God, the greatest of all, to tremble because of pain, and to bleed at every pore, and to suffer both body and spirit" (D&C 19:18; Mosiah 3:7; cf. Luke 22:42). Because he had power over death, Jesus endured (JC, p. 613). The shame, suffering, trials, scourging, and crucifixion were such that a mortal, finite being cannot fathom the price required before the Redeemer could say, "It is finished!" (John 19:30). God's great plan of redemption was implemented, and justice was not robbed by mercy, but rather was *paid* in full by the atoning blood of Jesus Christ. This payment for everyone's sins is called the grace of Jesus Christ. Without it, all stand condemned to eternal damnation. Hence, NEPHI₁ declared, "It is by grace that we are saved, after all we can do" (2 Ne. 25:23). Paul also taught the doctrine of salvation by grace (Eph. 2:8–9)—that is, without Christ's atonement, nothing any mortal could do would suffice.

Some aspects of Christ's atonement are unconditional. All mortal beings will be resurrected and brought back into the presence of God for the judgment regardless of the kind of lives they have lived (1 Cor. 15:22; 2 Ne. 9:12–15; Hel. 14:16–17), thus redeeming all humankind from both the mortal and spiritual deaths occasioned by the fall of Adam. Another unconditional aspect of Christ's mercy applies to young children who are not capable of understanding the difference between good and evil and therefore are not accountable. They cannot sin or be tempted of Satan (D&C 29:47; Moro. 8:8). "They are all alive in [Christ] because of his mercy" (Moro. 8:19; cf. D&C 29:46). LDS doctrine states that all children who die before the age of accountability (age eight) are saved in the celestial kingdom (D&C 137:10). Mercy extends also to those who through mental handicaps do not reach the mental age of eight, the level of accountability (D&C 29:50).

However, for those who are mentally accountable, part of their estrangement from God is the direct result of their own sins, in addition to Adam's transgression. Unless something is done in their behalf, they will not be allowed to return to the presence of God after their judgment, for no unclean thing can enter there (1 Ne. 10:21). The Lord

has set in place certain principles and ordinances called the gospel, which must be followed to have Christ's full atoning power applied to one's own sins: (1) FAITH IN JESUS CHRIST, (2) REPENTANCE, (3) BAPTISM by immersion for the remission of sins by one having authority, and (4) the gift of the Holy Ghost by the laying on of hands. Paul and others emphasized that humans are saved by GRACE and not by their own works (Eph. 2:8). This is true because no mortals can work perfectly enough to save themselves. No mortals have, or can have, the power to overcome the effects of the fall of Adam, or even their own sins. Everyone must depend on the atoning blood of the Savior for salvation. With equal clarity and firmness, the Savior and his servants have taught that how people live is a condition for bringing the power of the Atonement to bear in their own lives. "Not every one that saith unto me, Lord, Lord, shall enter into the kingdom of heaven; but he that doeth the will of [the] Father" (Matt. 7:21). "The hearers of the law are [not] just before God, but the doers of the law shall be justified" (Rom. 1:18; 2:13). "They which do [the works of the flesh] shall not inherit the kingdom of God" (Gal. 5:21). "Behold, [Christ] offereth himself a sacrifice for sin, to answer the ends of the law, unto all those who have a broken heart and a contrite spirit; and unto none else can the ends of the law be answered" (2 Ne. 2:7).

THE SPIRIT WORLD AND THE THREE DEGREES OF GLORY. When mortals complete their sojourn on earth and pass through the portal called death, they enter the postmortal spirit world. As part of the plan of salvation, the Lord set a time between death and the RESURRECTION when men and women can continue their progression and further learn principles of perfection before they are brought to the final judgment (Alma 40:6–21). Jesus Christ went to the postmortal spirit world while his body lay in the tomb to preach the gospel to them (1 Pet. 3:19–20; 4:6; D&C 138:11–37) so that those spirits in the postmortal spirit world could hear and accept or reject the gospel. Since baptism, the gift of the Holy Ghost, temple endowment, and sealing are earthly ordinances, Latter-day Saints perform the ordinances vicariously for the dead in their temples. Because individuals differ so widely in their obedience to God's commandments, LDS theology rejects the traditional Christian concepts of the single option of heaven or hell in explaining the final destiny of souls. Through a vision given to the Prophet Joseph Smith (D&C 76), the Lord has shown, as he also revealed to Paul, that there are several degrees of glory in mankind's eternal reward (D&C 76; cf. 1 Cor. 15:40–42).

The plan of salvation was created by the Father, brought into reality by the atoning sacrifice of his Beloved Son, and facilitated by the gifts of the Holy Ghost. It embraces the Creation, the Fall, and the Atonement, including the Resurrection, and sweeps across all time from the premortal existence to the final state of immortality and eternal life.

BIBLIOGRAPHY

McConkie, Bruce R. *A New Witness for the Articles of Faith*, pp. 81–104, 144–59. Salt Lake City, 1985.

Packer, Boyd K. *Our Father's Plan*. Salt Lake City, 1984.

Taylor, John. *The Mediation and Atonement of Our Lord and Savior Jesus Christ*. Salt Lake City, 1882.

ADDITIONAL SOURCE

Millet, Robert L. "The Regeneration of Fallen Man." In *Nurturing Faith through the Book of Mormon*, 119–48. Salt Lake City: Deseret Book, 1995.

GERALD N. LUND

PLATES AND RECORDS IN THE BOOK OF MORMON

The Book of Mormon is a complex text with a complicated history. It is primarily an abridgment of several earlier records by its chief editor and namesake, MORMON. All these records are referred to as "plates" because they were engraved on thin sheets of metal. Various source documents were used by Mormon in his compilation, leading to abrupt transitions and chronological disjunctions that can confuse readers. However, when one is aware of the history of the text, these are consistent and make good sense. The various plates and records referred to in the Book of Mormon and used in making it are (1) the plates of brass; (2) the record of LEHI; (3) the large plates of NEPHI$_1$; (4) the small plates of Nephi; (5) the plates of Mormon; and (6) the twenty-four gold plates of Ether.

THE GOLD PLATES. The gold plates that the Prophet Joseph SMITH received and translated were the plates of Mormon on which Mormon and his son MORONI$_2$ made their abridgment. Mormon, a prophet and military leader who lived at the end of the NEPHITE era (c. A.D. 385), was the penultimate custodian of the records of earlier Nephite prophets and rulers. In particular, he had the large plates of Nephi, which were the official Nephite chronicle and which he was commanded to continue (Morm. 1:4). He later made his own plates of Mormon, on which he compiled an abridgment of the large plates of Nephi (W of M 1:3–5; 3 Ne. 5:9–10), which covered 985 years of Nephite history, from Lehi's day to his. The large plates drew on still earlier records and the writings of various prophets and frequently included various source materials such as letters, blessings, discourses, and memoirs.

After Mormon had completed his abridgment through the reign of King BENJAMIN (c. 130 B.C.), he discovered the small plates of Nephi, a separate history of the same time period focusing on the spiritual events of those years and quoting extensively from the plates of brass. Inspired to add the small plates of Nephi to his own record, Mormon inserted a brief explanation for the double account of early Nephite history (W of M 1:2–9).

Mormon continued his abridgment, selecting from the large plates, paraphrasing, and often adding his own comments, extending the account down to his time. Anticipating death, he passed the plates to his son Moroni. Over the next few decades, Moroni wandered alone, making additions to his father's record, including two chapters now included in a book previously abridged by his father (Morm. 7–8) and an account of the JAREDITES that he had abridged from the twenty-four gold plates of Ether. He also copied an extensive vision of the last days that had been recorded by an early Jaredite prophet, the BROTHER OF JARED, and which Moroni was commanded to seal (Ether 4:4–5). He also added brief notes on church rituals (Moro. 1–6), a sermon and two letters from his father (Moro. 7–9), and an exhortation to future readers (Moro. 10). Finally, Moroni took this somewhat heterogeneous collection of records—the plates of Mormon, the small plates of Nephi, his abridgment of the plates of Ether, and the sealed portion containing the vision of the Brother of Jared—and buried them in the earth. About 1,400 years later, in 1823, Moroni, now resurrected, appeared to the Prophet Joseph Smith and revealed the location of these records. The plates of Mormon, which, except for the sealed portion, were subsequently translated by Joseph Smith, are known today as the gold plates.

The present English Book of Mormon, however, is not simply a translation of all those gold plates. Joseph Smith and Martin HARRIS began by translating the plates of Mormon, and when they had reached the reign of King Benjamin, they had 116 pages of translation. Harris borrowed these pages to show to his wife, then lost them, and they were never recovered (see MANUSCRIPT, LOST 116 PAGES). Joseph was commanded not to retranslate this material (D&C 10:30–46), but instead to substitute a translation of the parallel small plates of Nephi, which includes the books of 1 Nephi, 2 Nephi, Jacob, Enos, Jarom, and Omni. Thus, the present Book of Mormon contains only the second account of early Nephite history.

The translation continues from the rest of the plates of Mormon, which were abridged from the large plates of Nephi, and includes the six books of Mosiah, Alma, Helaman, 3 Nephi, 4 Nephi, and Mormon (the last two chapters of which were written by Moroni). Next follow Moroni's abridgment of Jaredite history (the book of Ether) and his closing notes (the book of Moroni). Joseph Smith was commanded not to translate the sealed vision of the Brother of Jared, which apparently made up a substantial portion of the gold plates (Ludlow, p. 320). Although Joseph Smith translated only from the gold plates, he and his associates saw many other records (*JD* 19:38; *Millennial Star* 40 [1878]: 771–72).

THE PLATES OF BRASS. It is now known that many ancients of the Mediterranean area wrote on metal plates. "Where the record was one of real importance, plates of copper, bronze, or even more precious metal were used instead of the usual wooden, lead, or clay tablets" (CWHN 5:119; see also H. C. Wright, in *Journal of Library History* 16 [1981]: 48–70). Such a metal record was in the possession of one Laban, a leader in Jerusalem in

600 b.c. How Laban obtained these plates and where they originally came from are not known. Several theories have been advanced, including the possibility that the plates of brass originated in the days of JOSEPH OF EGYPT (Ludlow, p. 56). The Book of Mormon indicates that Laban and his father had inherited and preserved the record because they were descendants of this Joseph (1 Ne. 5:16).

The Book of Mormon does tell how the prophet Lehi came to possess the plates of brass. After fleeing Jerusalem, Lehi was commanded by God to send his sons back to the city to obtain the plates from Laban. When he received them, Lehi found that they contained the five books of Moses, a record of the Jews from the beginning down to the reign of Zedekiah, the prophecies of the holy prophets for that same time period (including some of Jeremiah's prophecies), and a genealogy of Lehi's fathers (1 Ne. 3–5).

Nephi and succeeding spiritual leaders highly valued the plates of brass. They were passed down by major prophets from Nephi to Mormon, and since they were written in an adapted form of Egyptian (see LANGUAGE), their keepers were taught to read that language (Mosiah 1:2–4). The plates of brass were the basic scriptures of the Nephite nation, and for centuries their prophets read them, quoted them in sermons, and excerpted material from them to enrich their own writings. For example, when the prophet ABINADI cited the Ten Commandments in a disputation with the priests of Noah, his knowledge of the Ten Commandments was due, at least indirectly, to the plates of brass (Mosiah 12–13). As MOSIAH$_2$ stated, "For it were not possible that our father, Lehi, could have remembered all these things, to have taught them to his children, except it were for the help of these plates" (Mosiah 1:4).

Book of Mormon records, particularly the small plates of Nephi, occasionally quote at length from the plates of brass, and these quotations include twenty-one complete chapters from Isaiah. Although the translation of these quotations generally follows the wording of the King James Version of the Bible, there are many significant differences, which may indicate the existence of older textual sources (Tvedtnes, pp. 165–77). It is also evident from the scriptural quotations in the Book of Mormon that the plates of brass contained a more extensive record of the writings of Hebrew prophets than does the present Old Testament. For example, the Book of Mormon includes prophecies of Joseph of Egypt that are not found in the Bible, as well as writings of ZENOS, ZENOCK, NEUM, and EZIAS, prophets who are not specifically named in the Old Testament.

THE RECORD OF LEHI. Unfortunately, Mormon's abridgment of the record of Lehi was the material translated in the 116 manuscript pages that were lost, and consequently it is not available in the present Book of Mormon. Lehi wrote an account of his life and spiritual experiences that was included in the large plates of Nephi (1 Ne. 19:1). Mormon abridged this record in his plates, and Joseph Smith translated it, but since it was lost by Martin Harris, very little is now known about it except what can be inferred from references in other texts (Brown, pp. 25–32; see also the preface to the first edition [1830] of the Book of Mormon). When Nephi and JACOB cite the words of Lehi, they seem to be quoting from this now-lost text, and at least the first eight chapters of 1 Nephi (part of the small plates) appear to be based on the record of Lehi. Other passages in the small plates may also have been derived from that record.

THE LARGE PLATES OF NEPHI. Nephi began

the large plates soon after his arrival in the New World. They were the official continuous chronicle of the Nephites from the time they left Jerusalem (c. 600 B.C.) until they were destroyed (A.D. 385). Apparently the large plates were divided into books, each named for its primary author. These plates "contained a 'full account of the history of [Nephi's] people' (1 Ne. 9:2, 4; 2 Ne. 4:14; Jacob 1:2–3), the genealogy of Lehi (1 Ne. 19:2) and the 'more part' of the teachings of the resurrected Jesus Christ to the Nephite nation (3 Ne. 26:7)" (Ludlow, p. 57). Begun as basically a secular history, they later became a combined record, mingling a thousand years of Nephite history and religious experiences.

The large plates emphasize the covenants made with the house of Israel and quote messianic prophecies of Old World prophets not found in the Old Testament. This information was excerpted from the plates of brass that Lehi's colony brought with it from Jerusalem. They also record wars and contentions, correspondence between military leaders, and information on various missionary journeys. The interventions and miraculous power of God permeate this history. The recorded sermons of King Benjamin, Abinadi, and ALMA$_2$ are indicative of these individuals' deep understanding of the gospel of Jesus Christ and of their faith in his prophesied coming. These plates feature an account of the post-Resurrection ministry and teachings of Christ to the people of the western world (3 Ne. 11–28).

The large plates of Nephi were passed down from king to king until they came into the possession of Mosiah$_2$. He added such records as those of Zeniff and ALMA$_1$ to the large plates and then gave them to Alma$_2$. The plates subsequently passed through a line of prophets until Ammaron's day in the early fourth century A.D. Ammaron chose Mormon, then only a child, to continue the

record when he was mature. Mormon recorded the events of his day on the large plates and then used them as the source for his abridgment, which was later buried in the hill CUMORAH. Joseph Smith did not receive the large plates, but the Book of Mormon suggests that they may yet be published to the world (3 Ne. 26:6–10).

THE SMALL PLATES OF NEPHI. Approximately twenty years after beginning the large plates, Nephi was commanded to make another set of plates. This second set was to be reserved for an account of the ministry of his people (1 Ne. 9; 2 Ne. 5:28–33). They were to contain the things considered most precious—"preaching which was sacred, or revelation which was great, or prophesying" (Jacob 1:2–4).

The small plates were kept for over four centuries, not quite half the time covered by the large plates, by nine writers: Nephi, Jacob, Enos, Jarom, Omni, Amaron, Chemish, Abinadom, and Amaleki. All of these authors were the sons or brothers of their predecessors. Though these plates include the writings of many over a long time period, 80 percent of the text was written by Nephi, the first writer, and an additional 12 percent by his brother Jacob.

Mormon included the small plates with his record when he delivered the plates of Mormon to his son Moroni because their witness of Christ pleased him and because he was impressed by the Spirit of the Lord to include them "for a wise purpose" (W of M 1:3–7). However, since the small plates covered the historical period already recorded in his abridgment of the record of Lehi (namely, from Lehi down to the reign of King Benjamin) and since the book of Mosiah began with the end of King Benjamin's reign, Mormon found it necessary to write a brief explanation to show how the small plates of Nephi connect with the book of Mosiah. He entitled this explanation "Words of Mormon."

While the writers of the small plates recognized the need to provide a historical narrative, their main purpose was to talk of Christ, to preach of Christ, and to prophesy of Christ (2 Ne. 25:26). Because Nephi was concerned with teaching his people the covenants and promises made to ancient Israel, he extracted these teachings from earlier prophets as recorded on the plates of brass. He quoted extensively from the prophet Isaiah (2 Ne. 12–24; cf. Isa. 2–14) and then wrote a commentary on it, predicting the future of Jews, Lamanites, and Gentiles and prophesying much that would happen in the latter days (2 Ne. 25–30).

Jacob continued his brother's approach by recording his own sermons and a long quotation from and explanation of a prophecy of Zenos. The writings of later authors in the small plates are much briefer and less concerned with spiritual matters.

Amaleki noted in his writings that the small plates were full and turned them over to King Benjamin (Omni 1:25, 30), who then possessed both the large and the small plates of Nephi, as well as the plates of brass. All these sets of plates were handed down from generation to generation until they were entrusted to Mormon.

THE PLATES OF MORMON. After Mormon received the plates, he made a new set on which he engraved his abridgment of the large plates of Nephi (3 Ne. 5:10–11). It is this abridgment plus some additions by Mormon's son Moroni that constitute the gold plates given to Joseph Smith. He described them as follows:

> These records were engraven on plates which had the appearance of gold, each plate was six inches wide and eight inches long and not quite so thick as common tin.

They were filled with engravings, in Egyptian characters and bound together in a volume, as the leaves of a book with three rings running through the whole. The volume was something near six inches in thickness, a part of which was sealed. The characters on the unsealed part were small, and beautifully engraved. (Jessee, p. 214)

The descriptions reported by other witnesses add details which suggest that the plates were composed of a gold alloy (possibly tumbaga) and that they weighed about fifty pounds (Putnam, pp. 788–89, 829–31). Each plate was as thick as parchment or thick paper.

Most of the time, Mormon relied on the large plates of Nephi for his information. Much of the historical narrative in the Book of Mormon appears to be his paraphrase of earlier records, but occasionally first-person documents are worked into the text. For example, in Mosiah 9 and 10 the narrative suddenly includes a first-person account of Zeniff (apparently an earlier document that Mormon simply copied), and then in chapter 11 Mormon's paraphrase resumes. In addition, many sermons, blessings, and letters appear to be reproduced intact.

Nevertheless, some passages can definitely be ascribed to Mormon: the abridgment of his contributions to the large plates (Morm. 1–7), his sermon and letters recorded by Moroni (Moro. 7–9), and the explanatory comments that he inserted into his narrative. In some of these interpolations he identifies himself (W of M; 3 Ne. 5:8–26; 26:6–12; 28:24; 4 Ne. 1:23), but it seems likely that the frequent "thus we see" comments are also Mormon attempting to stress matters of particular spiritual importance to his readers (e.g., Alma 24:19, 27; 50:19–23; Hel. 3:27–30; 12:1–2).

THE TWENTY-FOUR GOLD PLATES OF ETHER. These twenty-four gold plates were a record of ancient Jaredites, inhabitants of the Americas before the Nephites. This particular people left the Tower of Babel at the time of the confusion of tongues. Their prophet-leaders were led to the ocean, where they constructed eight peculiar barges. These were driven by the wind across the waters to America, where the Jaredites became a large and powerful nation. After many centuries, wickedness and wars led to a final war of annihilation. During that final war, Ether, a prophet of God, wrote their history and spiritual experiences on twenty-four gold plates, perhaps relying on earlier Jaredite records (see J. Welch, "Preliminary Comments on the Sources behind the Book of Ether," in *FARMS Manuscript Collection*, pp. 3–7. Provo, Utah, 1986).

After witnessing the destruction of his people, Ether hid the twenty-four gold plates. Many years later (c. 121 B.C.) they were discovered by a small Nephite exploring party and given to Mosiah₂, a prophet-king, who translated them into the Nephite language through the use of SEER STONES (Mosiah 8:8–9; 28:11–16). Much later (c. A.D. 400) Moroni abridged this history of the Jaredites as his father Mormon had intended, concentrating on spiritual matters and adding inspired commentaries. Moroni included this abridgment, now known as the book of Ether, with what he and his father had already written. (The twenty-four gold plates of Ether were not among the plates received by Joseph Smith.)

CHARACTERISTICS OF MORMON'S EDITING. The Book of Mormon is quite complicated. The foregoing summary of the plates and other records from which the book was derived is drawn from a number of scattered but consistent comments included in the present text. The narrative itself is often complex. For instance, in Mosiah 1–25, Mormon narrates the stories of three separate groups

and subgroups of people—principally the people of Mosiah, of Limhi, and of Alma—with their respective histories and interactions with each other and with the Lamanites (*see* PEOPLES OF THE BOOK OF MORMON). The story might have been quite confusing, as it jumps from one people to another, and back and forth in time, but Mormon has kept it remarkably clear. Alma 17–26 is a lengthy flashback recounting the histories of several missionaries on the occasion of their reunion with old friends, and Alma 43–63 narrates the history of a war with the Lamanites, keeping straight the events that happened on two fronts.

Mormon's account might have been much more complex. He emphasizes that he is presenting less than one hundredth of the material available to him (e.g., W of M 1:5; 3 Ne. 26:6–7). Furthermore, his source materials give a lineage history of one family, Lehi and his descendants, and do not encompass all events in the ancient western world (Sorenson, 1985, pp. 50–56). Mormon further simplifies his record by continuing Jacob's practice of lumping diverse peoples into two major groups:

> Now the people which were not Lamanites were Nephites; nevertheless, they were called Nephites, Jacobites, Josephites, Zoramites, Lamanites, Lemuelites, and Ishmaelites. But I, Jacob, shall not hereafter distinguish them by these names, but I shall call them Lamanites that seek to destroy the people of Nephi, and those who are friendly to Nephi I shall call Nephites, or the people of Nephi, according to the reigns of the kings. (Jacob 1:13–14; see also Morm. 1:8–9)

The vast editing project that produced the Book of Mormon would require clear guidelines for selecting materials for inclusion. Mormon is quite explicit about the purpose of his abridgment. Like Nephi, he is writing a history to lead people to Christ, and he is writing specifically for the people of later times (2 Ne. 25:23; Morm. 7). The plates of Mormon were created to come forth in the latter days. Mormon is interested in pointing out the principles that will be of most use to such people, and his careful editing and his "thus" and "thus we see" passages are all directed at making the moral lessons easier to identify and understand.

Finally, Mormon took his job as record keeper and abridger very seriously. He was commanded by God to make his record (title page to the Book of Mormon; 3 Ne. 26:12). Also, Nephite society had a strong tradition of the importance of written records, and this was one of the criteria by which they distinguished themselves from the more numerous Mulekites (Omni 1:14–19). Furthermore, the various plates seem to have been handed down from one prophet or king to another as sacred relics and symbols of authority (Mosiah 28:20; 3 Ne. 1:2). In addition, the Nephites had a ceremonial record exchange when different branches of the family were reunited (Mosiah 8:1–5; 22:14). Most important, the Nephites knew that they would be held responsible for and would be judged by what was written in the records, just as all people will be (2 Ne. 25:21–22; 33:10–15; Morm. 8:12).

BIBLIOGRAPHY

Brown, S. Kent. "Lehi's Personal Record: Quest for a Missing Source." *BYU Studies* 24 (Winter 1984): 19–42.

Doxey, Roy W. "What is the Approximate Weight of the Gold Plates from Which the Book of Mormon Was Translated?" In *A Sure Foundation: Answers to Difficult Gospel Questions*, pp. 50–52. Salt Lake City, 1988.

Jessee, Dean C. *PWJS*. Salt Lake City, 1984.

Ludlow, Daniel H. *A Companion to Your Study of the Book of Mormon*. Salt Lake City, 1976.

Putnam, Read H. "Were the Golden Plates Made of Tumbaga?" *IE* 69 (Sept. 1966): 788–89, 828.

Sorenson, John L. "The 'Brass Plates' and Biblical Scholarship." *Dialogue* 10 (Autumn 1977): 31–39.

———. *An Ancient American Setting for the Book of Mormon*. Salt Lake City, 1985.

Sperry, Sidney B. *Our Book of Mormon*. Salt Lake City, 1950.

Tvedtnes, John A. "Isaiah Variants in the Book of Mormon." In *Isaiah and the Prophets*, ed. M. Nyman, pp. 165–77. Provo, Utah, 1984.

ADDITIONAL SOURCES

Eggington, William. "'Our Weakness in Writing': Oral and Literate Cultures in the Book of Mormon." Provo, Utah: FARMS, 1992.

Reynolds, Noel B. "The Brass Plates Version of Genesis." In *By Study and Also by Faith: Essays in Honor of Hugh W. Nibley*, edited by John M. Lundquist and Stephen D. Ricks, 2:136–73. Salt Lake City and Provo, Utah: Deseret Book and FARMS, 1990.

Sorenson, John L. "The Book of Mormon as a Mesoamerican Record." In *Book of Mormon Authorship Revisited*, edited by Noel B. Reynolds, 391–521. Provo, Utah: FARMS, 1997.

GRANT R. HARDY

ROBERT E. PARSONS

PLATES, METAL

[*The Book of Mormon mentions several records, most of which were inscribed on metal plates. The text of the Book of Mormon was inscribed on metal plates; see* Plates and Records in the Book of Mormon; Book of Mormon: The Words of Mormon; *and* Gold Plates. *In addition, the scriptural record possessed by the Book of Mormon colony that fled Jerusalem and came to the Americas under the leadership of the prophet Lehi was engraved on plates of brass; see* Book of Mormon: Overview. *This colony continued to prepare metal plates, which were then used to inscribe records both sacred and secular; see* Economy and Technology. *It is also known that a prophet named Ether inscribed on metal leaves the record of his people, the earliest Book of Mormon group to migrate to the Western Hemisphere; see* Book of Mormon: Book of Ether *and* Jaredites. *The final set of plates abridged by Mormon were seen by the* Witnesses of the Book of Mormon. *For information about the major writers or abridgers of these plates, see* Mormon; Moroni₂; Mosiah₂; *and* Nephi₁.]

PRIDE

In an address drawing together Book of Mormon and other scriptural teachings regarding pride, President Ezra Taft Benson called it "the universal sin, the great vice" (1989, p. 6). He characterized its central feature as "enmity—enmity toward God and enmity toward our fellowmen" and defined "enmity" as "hatred toward, hostility to, or a state of opposition." He observed that "pride is essentially competitive in nature," arising when individuals pit their will against God's or their intellects, opinions, works, wealth, and talents against those of other people (p. 4). He warned that "pride is a damning sin in the true sense of that word," for "it limits or stops progression" and "adversely affects all our relationships" (p. 6).

The scriptures abound with admonitions against pride. "Pride goeth before destruction" (Prov. 16:18). Pride felled Lucifer (cf. Moses 4:1–3; 2 Ne. 24:12–15; D&C 29:36; 76:28) and destroyed the city of Sodom (Ezek. 16:49–50). In the closing chapters of the Book of Mormon, the prophet Mormon wrote, "Be-

hold, the pride of this nation, or the people of the Nephites, hath proven their destruction" (Moro. 8:27). Three times in the Doctrine and Covenants the Lord uses the phrase "beware of pride," including warnings to Oliver COWDERY, the second elder of the Church, and to Emma Smith, the wife of Joseph Smith (D&C 23:1; 25:14; 38:39). The Lord has said that when he cleanses the earth by fire, the proud shall burn as stubble (3 Ne. 25:1; D&C 29:9; Mal. 4:1).

While most consider pride a sin of the rich, gifted, or learned looking down on others, President Benson warned that it is also common among those looking up—"fault-finding, gossiping . . . living beyond our means, envying, coveting, withholding gratitude . . . and being unforgiving and jealous" (1989, p. 5).

God has commanded the Saints to "seek to bring forth and establish the cause of Zion" (D&C 6:6). When Zion is established, its people will be "of one heart and one mind" and will dwell together in righteousness (Moses 7:18). But "pride is the great stumbling block to Zion" (Benson, 1989, p. 7). Pride leads people to diminish others in the attempt to elevate themselves, resulting in selfishness and contention.

The proud love "the praise of men more than the praise of God" (John 12:42–43) and fear the judgment of men more than that of God (cf. D&C 3:6–7; 30:1–2; 60:2). They do not receive counsel or correction easily but justify and rationalize their frailties and failures, making it difficult for them to repent and receive the blessings of the Atonement. They have difficulty rejoicing in their blessings, because they are constantly comparing them to see whether they have more or less than someone else. Consequently, they are often ungrateful.

The antidote for pride is humility, "a broken heart and a contrite spirit" (3 Ne. 9:20, 12:19). Men can choose to do those things that will foster the growth of humility: they can choose to confess and forsake their sins, forgive others, receive counsel and chastisement, esteem others as themselves, render service, love God, and submit to his will (Benson, 1989, p. 7). By yielding "to the enticings of the Holy Spirit," the prideful individual can become "a saint through the atonement of Christ" and become "as a child, submissive, meek, humble" (Mosiah 3:19; cf. Alma 13:28).

BIBLIOGRAPHY

Benson, Ezra Taft. "Cleansing the Inner Vessel." *Ensign* 16 (May 1986): 4–7.

———. "Beware of Pride." *Ensign* 19 (May 1989): 4–7.

Burton, Theodore M. "A Disease Called Pride." *Ensign* 1 (Mar. 1971): 26–29.

REED A. BENSON

PROMISED LAND, CONCEPT OF A

In the Book of Mormon, the prophet LEHI spoke of a particular promised land as "choice above all other lands; a land which the Lord God hath covenanted with me should be a land for the inheritance of my seed" (2 Ne. 1:5). Because the earth belongs to the Lord (Ps. 24:1), those who inherit a promised land must covenant to "serve the God of the land," who will then keep them "free from bondage, and from captivity" (Ether 2:12); otherwise they will "be swept off" (Ether 2:10; cf. Deut. 27–28).

From the beginning, the Lord has reserved choice lands for righteous followers. They include the Garden of Eden for Adam and Eve (Gen. 2:9), a "land of promise" for Enos (Moses 6:17), and Zion for Enoch and

his people (Moses 7:19). Notably, God received up Zion's inhabitants (Moses 7:69), who will return to earth to the New Jerusalem during the last days (Moses 7:62–64; Rev. 21:2). Moreover, God gave the land of Canaan "unto [Abraham's] seed . . . for an everlasting possession" if "they hearken to [God's] voice" (Abr. 2:6). This promise was partially fulfilled when Moses led the Israelites out of Egypt to Canaan.

The Book of Mormon PEOPLES, including the family of Lehi and the JAREDITES, were given a promised land in the hemisphere now called the Americas, on condition of keeping God's commandments (1 Ne. 2:20; Ether 1:42–43). The prophet MORONI$_2$ warned future inhabitants of this land: "Behold, this is a choice land, and whatsoever nation shall possess it shall be free . . . if they will but serve the God of the land, who is Jesus Christ" (Ether 2:12). This admonition applies to all lands that the Lord has promised to any of his peoples.

Latter-day Zion, a "promised land" for members of The Church of Jesus Christ of Latter-day Saints, includes the city New Jerusalem that will be built in the Americas (A of F 10) and, in another sense, the stakes of the Church in all the world. Members also believe that the New Jerusalem is where the "lost ten tribes" will first come (D&C 133:24–26).

Through the Prophet Joseph SMITH, the Lord promised in 1831 to lead the Saints to a "land of promise" (D&C 38:18; cf. Ex. 3:8). Because of persecution by enemies and sin among Church members, Joseph Smith was unsuccessful in establishing a permanent community (D&C 101:1–8). After his death, the Saints migrated to the Rocky Mountains, "a land of peace" (D&C 136:16), and still anticipate fulfillment of the Lord's promises to open the way for building New Jerusalem in the designated place (D&C 42:9; 57:1–5; 101:9–22).

BIBLIOGRAPHY

Davies, William D. "Israel, the Mormons, and the Land." In *Reflections on Mormonism*, ed. Truman G. Madsen, pp. 79–87. Provo, Utah, 1978.

CLARISSA KATHERINE COLE

PROPHECY IN THE BOOK OF MORMON

The Book of Mormon reports prophecies made during a thousand-year period concerning the future of the NEPHITES and LAMANITES, the earthly ministry of Jesus Christ, his visit to the Western Hemisphere, the future restoration of the gospel to the gentiles, and related events of the last days. While this record includes the fulfillment of some prophecies, Latter-day Saints see fulfillment of other prophecies in the restoration of the gospel through the Prophet Joseph SMITH and expect yet others to be fulfilled in the future.

Messianic prophecies include the number of years until Jesus' birth (1 Ne. 10:4; Hel. 14:2), conditions surrounding his birth (1 Ne. 11:13–21), his mother's identity (Mosiah 3:8), the manner and location of his baptism by John the Baptist (1 Ne. 10:7–10), his miracles and teachings (1 Ne. 11:28–31), and his atonement, resurrection, and second coming. Prophets foretold details concerning Christ's crucifixion and his atoning sacrifice, one stating that "blood cometh from every pore, so great shall be his anguish for the wickedness and the abominations of his people" (Mosiah 3:7). Furthermore, he would rise on the third day (2 Ne. 25:13) and appear to many (Alma 16:20). SAMUEL THE LAMANITE prophesied specific signs of Christ's birth and death to be experienced among Book of Mormon PEOPLES (Hel. 14).

During his visit to the Americas, the risen Jesus attested to the authenticity of these prophecies by stating that "the scriptures concerning my coming are fulfilled" (3 Ne. 9:16). Later, he reminded NEPHI₃ of a prophecy of his resurrection, the fulfillment of which had not been recorded. The details were promptly added to Nephite records (3 Ne. 23:6–13; cf. Hel. 14:25).

The Book of Mormon relates the fulfillment of other prophecies foretelling events among Book of Mormon peoples. Besides many Messianic prophecies, examples include ALMA₂ prophesying that the Nephites, dwindling in unbelief, would eventually become extinct (Alma 45:9–14; Morm. 6:11–15) and ABINADI forecasting the destiny of his captors and their descendants (Mosiah 11:20–25; 17:15–18). Other prophecies anticipated more immediate events. For example, on the eve of Jesus' birth, when lives of believers were threatened by unbelievers, Nephi₃ received divine assurance that "on the morrow" the signs of Christ's birth would be seen (3 Ne. 1:9–15).

Book of Mormon prophets also forecast events of the latter days. They foretold the European exploration of America (1 Ne. 13:12–15), the American Revolution (1 Ne. 13:16–19), and the gathering of Israel (1 Ne. 22; 3 Ne. 20–22). They warned of deceptive practices among religionists, including priestcraft, secret combinations, and neglect of the poor. They foretold the impact of the Book of Mormon on latter-day people and the destruction of the wicked. The prophecies of MORONI₂ included admonitions addressed to those who would live in the last days: "Behold, I speak unto you as if ye were present, . . . behold, Jesus Christ hath shown you unto me, and I know your doing" (Morm. 8:35).

Under inspiration, prophets in the Book of Mormon frequently quoted previous prophets in support of their teachings. They warned that in rejecting the living prophet's witness, their hearers were rejecting the testimonies of such revered prophets as Isaiah, Moses, and ZENOS (Hel. 8:11–20).

Prophesying falsely was viewed as a crime among the Nephites (W of M 1:15–16). Agreement with past prophets was a test of a prophet's authenticity. For instance, during a debate, JACOB exposed Sherem as a false prophet by showing that his testimony contradicted previous prophecy. Jacob then demonstrated that his own teachings agreed with former prophets, thus sealing Sherem's conviction as a false prophet (Jacob 7:9–12).

Prophecy sometimes came in dreams or visions after pondering and prayer. Lehi and NEPHI₁ were caught up in the Spirit (1 Ne. 1:7–8, 11:1). King BENJAMIN and Samuel the Lamanite were visited by angels (Mosiah 3:2; Hel. 13:7). Prophecy was delivered variously, as in a psalm by Nephi₁ (2 Ne. 4:20–35), in Zenos' allegory (Jacob 5), or in Jacob's chastisements (2 Ne. 9:30–38).

Besides their service to God, as his messengers, prophets served as religious leaders (ALMA₁), kings (Benjamin; MOSIAH₂), military leaders (Helaman₁), and historians (Nephi₃). They were also social and moral critics of their society. Jacob denounced wickedness among his people not only because of its effects on that generation but also for wounds inflicted on the next (Jacob 2–3). Samuel the Lamanite foretold dire future consequences of the Nephites' lifestyle, criticizing their state of degradation (Hel. 13).

The presence of prophets and of contemporary prophecies were important to the Book of Mormon people. MORMON testified, "I also know that as many things as have been prophesied concerning us . . . have been fulfilled, and as many as go beyond this day must surely come to pass" (W of M 1:4).

BIBLIOGRAPHY

Nibley, Hugh W. *The Prophetic Book of Mormon*. In CWHN 8. Salt Lake City, 1989.

Parsons, Robert E. "The Prophecies of the Prophets." In *First Nephi, the Doctrinal Foundation*, ed. M. Nyman and C. Tate, Jr. Provo, Utah, 1988.

CAMILLE FRONK

R

RECORD KEEPING

The keeping of records is done in response to a direct commandment from the Lord and is considered a sacred trust and obligation. "The matter of record keeping is one of the most important duties devolving on the Church," said Elder Joseph Fielding Smith (p. 96). Indeed, the very day the LDS Church was organized, the Prophet Joseph SMITH received a revelation: "Behold, there shall be a record kept among you" (D&C 21:1). This requirement apparently has been the same in every dispensation. The Pearl of Great Price states that a book of remembrance was first kept in the Adamic language, and Adam's children were taught to read and write, "having a language which was pure and undefiled"; therefore, it was given unto many "to write by the spirit of inspiration" (Moses 6:5–6). Enoch, seventh in descent from Adam and the father of Methuselah, also kept a record and commented upon the divine prototype of it: "For a book of remembrance we have written among us, according to the pattern given by the finger of God" (Moses 6:46). Abraham continued the practice, affirming that "records of the fathers" had come into his hands and stating, "I shall endeavor to write some of these things upon this record, for the benefit of my posterity that shall come after me" (Abr. 1:31). Such records are of three types: (1) accounts of God's dealings with his children (the scriptures, for example); (2) records of religious ordinances; and (3) histories of nations and peoples, including personal histories.

SCRIPTURES. Prophets have been commanded to write scripture. For example, Moses in his time received a great revelation concerning the creation of heaven and earth with the divine imperative, "Write the words which I speak" (Moses 2:1). Those words are largely preserved in Genesis in the Bible. During Jeremiah's difficult mission a king desecrated a scroll containing some of God's revelations and the word of the Lord came to Jeremiah saying, "Take thee again another roll, and write in it all the former words that were in the first roll" (Jer. 36:27–32). Jeremiah and his scribe did so, and those words are in the book of Jeremiah.

Near the time of Jeremiah's vicissitudes, the Book of Mormon prophet LEHI took his family and fled from Jerusalem into the wilderness in 600 B.C. He was commanded by the Lord to send his sons back to Jerusalem to obtain certain plates of brass that had been kept by his forebears. The plates were engraved with the genealogy of Lehi's family, the five books of Moses, and writings of the prophets down to Jeremiah (1 Ne. 5:11–14). LAMAN and NEPHI₁, two of the sons of Lehi, tried to get Laban, the keeper of the plates, to give them the plates or to exchange them for certain other treasures, but Laban refused and sought to kill Lehi's sons. Eventually Laban himself was condemned of the Lord and slain (see SWORD OF LABAN), for "it is better that one man should perish than that a nation should dwindle and perish in unbelief" (1 Ne. 4:12–13). Thus the plates were procured and preserved, and they provided the cultural and spiritual foundation of the Nephite civilization in their promised land in the Western world (Mosiah 1:3–5; *DS* 2:198).

After his resurrection at Jerusalem, Jesus Christ appeared to the Nephites and personally emphasized the importance of record keeping. He provided them some of the revelations given to Malachi. The Lord then commanded NEPHI₃ (the record keeper at the time of Jesus' advent and a descendent of the first Nephi) to bring out the records kept by the Nephites. He examined them and reminded Nephi that Samuel, a Lamanite prophet, had testified that he (Christ) should arise from the dead and prophesied that at Christ's resurrection others would also arise and appear to many. Jesus then inquired, "How be it that ye have not written this thing . . . ? And it came to pass that Jesus commanded that it should be written; therefore it was written according as he commanded" (3 Ne. 23:11, 13).

RELIGIOUS ORDINANCES. Just as the doctrines and commandments from God must be recorded, so also must the responses and actions of the children of God be written. Prophetic scriptures warn that God's children will be judged out of sacred records kept both on earth and in heaven. Those responsible for keeping the records on earth are charged to make them as accurate as possible. Ordinances such as baptisms, confirmations, ordinations to the priesthood, patriarchal blessings, endowments, and sealings—all should be precisely recorded. Financial records of donations are especially carefully preserved, such as the tithing record. Earthly and spiritual conduct is to be measured by the things written (Mal. 3:16–18; Rev. 20:12). The Prophet Joseph Smith affirmed, "Our acts are recorded, and at a future day they will be laid before us, and if we should fail to judge right and injure our fellow-beings, they may there, perhaps, condemn us; there they are of great consequence, and to me the consequence appears to be of force, beyond anything which I am able to express" (*TPJS*, p. 69).

To qualify for eternal blessings, each person must come unto God through Christ, make commitments and covenants through certain ordinances, and have them properly recorded. Those who have died without hearing the gospel of Jesus Christ must have the ordinances of salvation and exaltation performed in their behalf, and record keeping is vital for all such ordinances performed in the Church. Vicarious ordinances can be performed only for individuals properly identified through dependable records. The Church sponsors programs to locate and microfilm family records worldwide and make them available to members and others in their genealogical research and family history work. Many members are involved in such research and in vicarious service in the temples of the Church in behalf of the dead. It is all done in the faith that whatsoever is done by proper authority, in the name of the Lord, truly and faithfully, and with accurate records kept, is established on earth and in heaven, and cannot be annulled, according to the decrees of the great Jehovah (cf. D&C 128:9).

HISTORIES. Church members are counseled to include personal histories among the records they keep. All such records are valuable in the preservation and transmission of culture within each family, and they often have an impact broader than anticipated by those who write them. Nephi₁, who wrote a history of his people as commanded by God, did anticipate its benefit to others, saying, "I write the things of my soul. . . . For my soul delighteth in the scriptures, and my heart pondereth them, and writeth them for the learning and the profit of my children" (2 Ne. 4:15).

President Spencer W. Kimball offered this challenge: "Get a notebook . . . a journal that will last through all time, and maybe the angels may quote from it for eternity. Begin today and write in it your goings and comings, your deepest thoughts, your achievements and your failures, your associations and your triumphs, your impressions and your testimonies" (1975, p. 5). Parents may not see, in the present moment, the potential value of what they write in a personal journal, nor can they predict the response of their descendants to it, but anyone who holds the journal of an ancestor can testify of the joy in possessing it. Minimally, parents should record accurately special events such as dates of birth, marriages, ordinations, and deaths. While it is not necessary to write everything that occurs each day, things of a spiritual nature and other happenings that arouse poignant feelings should be recorded. One parent recounted with regret, "I remembered [a] . . . spiritual experience I had had years earlier, just before my baptism. I hadn't written that in my journal, . . . and now I couldn't remember enough details of the story to retell it. I wanted to share that event with my son—and because I hadn't recorded it, I could not" (Espinosa, p. 24). President Kimball promised: "As our posterity read of our life's experiences, they, too, will come to know and love us. And in the glorious day when our families are together in the eternities, we will already be acquainted" (1980, p. 61).

Record keeping has resulted in the creation of sacred scriptures of incalculable value; records of ordinances done and covenants made will have eternal significance; and the histories of nations and individuals have helped throughout the ages in the developments of civilization.

BIBLIOGRAPHY

Espinosa, Luis V. "The Voice Spoke Spanish." *Ensign* 7 (Jan. 1977): 24.

"Eternal Implications of the Gospel: Life Everlasting, Family Records, Temple Blessings." *Ensign* 7 (Jan. 1977): 2–75.

Kimball, Spencer W. "The Angels May Quote from It." *New Era* 5 (Oct. 1975): 4–5.

———. "President Kimball Speaks Out on Personal Journals." *Ensign* 10 (Dec. 1980): 61.

Smith, Joseph Fielding. *Church History and Modern Revelation*, pp. 96–97, 99. Salt Lake City, 1946.

BEVERLY J. NORTON

RELIGIOUS TEACHINGS AND PRACTICES IN THE BOOK OF MORMON

Most of the Book of Mormon is about a group of Israelites who were guided by prophets, had the doctrines and ordinances of the gospel of Jesus Christ, but lived the law of Moses until the coming of Christ. After his resurrection, Jesus appeared to some of them, and organized his church, and for four generations they lived in peace and happiness. Many details about the religious teachings and practices of these people are found in the Book of Mormon. Latter-day Saints believe that these Christian teachings are applicable in the world today, both because the eternal doctrine of God is as binding on one generation as on the next and because the contents of the Book of Mormon were selected and preserved by prophets with the modern world in mind. These teachings are also found in the revelations that established contemporary LDS practices and ordinances.

In 3 Nephi and Moroni, documents recorded by firsthand witnesses preserve many words of the resurrected Jesus and give the basic doctrines, covenants, and ordinances of his church. Some of the main points follow:

1. Jesus defined his doctrine. Ye must "repent, and believe in me . . . and be baptized in my name, and become as a little child. . . . This is my doctrine" (3 Ne. 11:32, 38–39). The promise is given that God will visit such people "with fire and with the Holy Ghost" (3 Ne. 11:35).

2. Jesus instructed the people to be baptized by immersion, and gave the words of the BAPTISMAL PRAYER (3 Ne. 11:26–27). Only those who were "accountable and capable of committing sin" were baptized (Moro. 8:9–15; cf. 6:3).

3. Jesus ordained twelve disciples and gave them authority to baptize (3 Ne. 11:21–22). Moroni 2:2 preserves the words that Jesus spoke when he laid his hands on these disciples and gave them power to give the Holy Ghost (3 Ne. 18:36–37). The words the disciples used in subsequent ordinations of priests and teachers are found in Moroni 3:1–4.

4. The SACRAMENT PRAYERS are recorded in Moroni 4–5. The words of these prayers derive from the first-person expressions that Jesus spoke when he administered the sacrament in 3 Nephi 18:6–11.

5. The Nephite church met together often "to fast and to pray, and to speak one with another concerning the welfare of their souls. And . . . to partake of bread and wine, in remembrance of the Lord Jesus" (Moro. 6:5–6).

6. These Christians regularly renewed their covenant to keep the commandments Jesus had given them: for instance, to have no contention, anger, or derision; to offer a sacrifice of a broken heart and contrite spirit; to keep the law of chastity in thought and in deed; to love their enemies; to give sustenance to the poor; to do secret acts of charity; to pray alone and with others; to serve only God, not the things of the world; and to strive to become perfected like God and Jesus (3 Ne. 11–14; see SERMON ON THE MOUNT). They were promised that Jesus' spirit would continue with them and that they would be raised up at the last day.

7. This church was led by Nephi₃, one of the twelve disciples chosen by Jesus and sent out to preach the things they had heard him say and had seen him do (3 Ne. 27:1). The people were admonished to "give heed unto the words of these twelve" (3 Ne. 12:1).

8. At the Lord's instruction, the church was called by the name of Jesus Christ, and members called on the Father in the name of Christ in all things (3 Ne. 27:8–9).

9. The disciples healed the sick and worked miracles in the name of Jesus (4 Ne. 1:5).

10. They followed Jesus' examples in prayer, reverencing and praising God, asking for forgiveness, and praying that the will of God would be done (3 Ne. 13:9–13; 19:16–35). The people were commanded to "pray in [their] families" (3 Ne. 18:21).

11. They had "all things common among them, every man dealing justly, one with another. . . . Therefore there were not rich and poor" (3 Ne. 26:19; 4 Ne. 1:3).

12. As Jesus had instructed, his followers were strict in keeping iniquity out of their communities and synagogues, with "three witnesses of the church" being required to excommunicate offenders; nevertheless, all were helped, and those who sincerely repented were forgiven (3 Ne. 18:28–32; Moro. 6:7–8).

During the centuries before Christ, Nephite prophets had taught the fulness of the gospel and prepared the people for the coming of Jesus Christ. With respect to the points mentioned above, compare the following antecedents in Nephite history. Some can be traced back into ancient Israel; others were introduced at various times through inspiration or revelation:

1. The doctrine of Christ—faith in the Lord Jesus Christ, repentance, baptism, and the purging of sin by the fire of the Holy Ghost—was taught in the Book of Mormon as early as the time of Nephi$_1$ (2 Ne. 31). Nephite prophets frequently spoke about the "plan of redemption" or, as Alma called it, "the great plan of happiness" (Alma 42:8). They looked forward to the coming of God himself to earth to redeem mankind from their lost and fallen state. They knew that he would atone for the transgression of Adam and for all the sins of those who would "not procrastinate the day of [their] repentance" (Alma 34:33), and that all mankind would be physically resurrected and then judged according to the JUSTICE AND MERCY of God (Alma 40–42).

2. Covenantal baptisms were performed from the beginning of the record, notably by Alma$_1$ at the waters of Mormon (Mosiah 18). His baptismal prayer sought sanctification of the heart as the covenantor promised to serve

God "even until death" so that he or she might be granted eternal life through the redemption of Christ (Mosiah 18:12–13). Alma's group remained intact even after they took up residence among other Nephites, and those Nephites who submitted to baptism "after the manner he [had baptized] his brethren in the waters of Mormon" belonged to this church (Mosiah 25:18).

3. Centuries before the time of Christ, Nephite priests and teachers were consecrated (2 Ne. 5:26), appointed (Mosiah 6:3; Alma 45:22–23), or ordained by the laying-on of hands (Alma 6:1; cf. Num. 27:23). They watched over the church, stirred the people to remember their covenants (Mosiah 6:3), preached the law and the coming of the Son of God (Alma 16:18–19), and offered their firstlings in "sacrifice and burnt offerings according to the law of Moses" (Mosiah 2:3; cf. Deut. 15:19–23), which they understood to be a type of Christ (2 Ne. 11:4). Nephites and Lamanites had temples, the first one being built "after the manner of the temple of Solomon" (2 Ne. 5:16). The altar was a place of worship where the people assembled, "watching and praying continually, that they might be delivered from Satan, and from death, and from destruction" (Alma 15:17). Nephite priests also taught in synagogues, or gathering places, and ideally no one was excluded (2 Ne. 26:26; Alma 32:2–12). Because they held the Melchizedek Priesthood (Alma 13:6–19), they could function in the ordinances of the Aaronic Priesthood even though they were not Levites. Nephite priests were ordained in a manner that looked "forward on the Son of God, [the ordination] being a type of his order" (Alma 13:16).

4. The covenantal language used by King BENJAMIN (c. 124 B.C.) was similar to the language of the Nephite sacrament prayers. Benjamin's people witnessed that they were

willing to keep God's commandments, took upon them the name of Christ, and promised to "remember to retain the name written always in [their] hearts" (Mosiah 5:5–12; cf. Num. 6:27).

5. The Nephites gathered to fast and pray for spiritual blessings (Mosiah 27:22; Hel. 3:35). In addition, like their Israelite ancestors, they fasted in connection with mourning for the dead (Hel. 9:10; cf. 2 Sam. 3:35).

6. Covenant renewals were a long-standing part of the law of Moses, pursuant to which all men, women, and children were required to gather around the temple at appointed times to hear and recommit themselves to keep the law of God (Deut. 31:10–13; cf. Mosiah 2:5). Nephite religious law at the time of Alma$_2$ prohibited sorcery, idol worship, idleness, babbling, envy, strife, wearing costly apparel, pride, lying, deceit, malice, reviling, stealing, robbing, whoredom, adultery, murder, and all manner of wickedness (Alma 1:32; 16:18). In addition, Nephi$_2$ counseled against oppressing the poor, withholding food from the hungry, sacrilege, denying the spirit of prophecy, and deserting to the Lamanites (Hel. 4:12).

7. The righteous Nephites were accustomed to being led by prophets, inspired kings, high priests, and chief judges. These leaders kept the sacred records that were frequently cited in Nephite religious observances. The institutions of Nephite prophecy varied from time to time: some prophets were also kings; subsidiary prophets worked under King Benjamin (W of M 1:17–18); others, like ABINADI, were lone voices crying repentance. Their surviving messages, however, were constant and accurate: they preached the gospel and the coming of Christ, and they knew that when he came he would ordain twelve authorized leaders both in the East (1 Ne. 1:10; 11:29) and in the West (1 Ne. 12:7–10).

8. The name of Jesus Christ was revealed to the early Nephite prophets (2 Ne. 10:3; 25:19), and thereafter the Nephites prayed and acted in the name of Jesus Christ (2 Ne. 32:9; Jacob 4:6). Alma$_1$ called his followers "the church of Christ" (Mosiah 18:17).

9. Like the Israelite prophets, the Nephite prophets performed miracles in the name of the Lord. As had Elijah (1 Kgs. 17), for example, Nephi$_2$ closed the heavens and caused a famine (Hel. 11:4), and Nephi$_3$ raised the dead and healed the sick (3 Ne. 7:19–22).

10. The Nephites watched and prayed continually (Alma 15:17). They were counseled to pray three times a day—morning, noon, and night—for mercy, for deliverance from the power of the devil, for prosperity, and for the welfare of their families (Alma 34:18–25; cf. Ps. 55:17). They taught that effective prayer had to be coupled with charitable actions (Alma 34:26–29), which are necessary to retain a remission of sin (Mosiah 4:26).

11. Regarding wealth and possessions, many early Book of Mormon prophets condemned the evils of seeking power and riches. The cycle leading from prosperity to pride, wickedness, and then catastrophe was often repeated, echoing formulas characteristic of Deuteronomy. The righteous Nephites covenanted to give liberally to the poor and to bear one another's burdens.

12. Typically, those who entered into the required covenant became "numbered" among the Nephites. If they transgressed, their names were "blotted out," presumably being removed from a roster (Mosiah 5:11; 6:1). Detailed procedures for excommunicating transgressors were established by Alma$_1$, who was given authority by King MOSIAH$_2$ to

judge members of the church. Forgiveness was to be extended "as often as [the] people repent" (Mosiah 26:29–30).

Teachings and practices such as these specifically prepared the way for the personal coming of Jesus Christ after his resurrection. Despite years of preparation, the immediate reaction of some of the Nephite multitude to the initial words of the resurrected Christ was still to wonder "what he would concerning the law of Moses" (3 Ne. 15:2). Even though the prophets had long explained the limited function of the law, it remained a sacred and integral part of their lives until it was fulfilled by Jesus (e.g., 2 Ne. 25:24–25; Alma 30:3; 3 Ne. 1:24). When Jesus spoke, it became evident how old things "had become new" (3 Ne. 15:2).

The diversity of religious experience in the Book of Mormon is further seen in the great number of religious communities it mentions in varying situations. Outside of orthodox Nephite circles (whose own success varied from time to time), there were an extravagant royal cult of King Noah and his temple priests (Mosiah 11); a false, rivaling church in Zarahemla formed by Nehor (Alma 1); centers of worship among the Lamanites (Alma 23:2); the wicked and agnostic Korihor (Alma 30); an astounding aristocratic and apostate prayerstand (an elevated platform for a single worshipper) of the Zoramites (Alma 31:13–14); and secret combinations or societies with staunch oath-swearing adherents intent on murder and gain (3 Ne. 3:9). Frequent efforts were made by Nephite missionaries, such as Alma$_2$, Ammon, and Nephi$_2$, to convert people from these groups to the gospel of Jesus Christ and to organize them into righteous churches and communities. On occasion, the converts became more righteous than all their contemporaries. Even

among the righteous, there were varying degrees of comprehension and knowledge, for the mysteries of God were imparted by God and his prophets according to the diligence of the hearers (Alma 12:9–11).

Many doctrinal points and practical insights fill the pages of the Book of Mormon. A few of them are the following: Alma$_2$ explains that by his suffering Jesus came to "know according to the flesh how to succor his people" (Alma 7:12). Alma$_2$ describes how faith may be nurtured into knowledge (Alma 32). Benjamin identifies sin as "rebellion against God" (Mosiah 2:36–37) and presents a hopeful outlook for all who will "yield to the enticings of the Holy Spirit, and [put] off the natural man" (Mosiah 3:19). Alma$_2$ depicts the condition of spirits after death as they return to God, "who gave them life" (Alma 40:11). Jacob speaks poignantly of the nakedness of the unrepentant, who will stand filthy before the judgment of God (2 Ne. 9:14). Benjamin extols the "blessed and happy state" of the righteous who taste the love and goodness of God (Mosiah 2:41; 4:11). And Lehi states the purpose of existence: "Men are, that they might have joy" (2 Ne. 2:25). The Book of Mormon teaches the one pathway to eternal happiness by numerous inspiring images, instructions, and examples.

Many Book of Mormon prophetic teachings have already been fulfilled (e.g., 1 Ne. 13; 2 Ne. 3; Hel. 14), but several still look to the future. One reason some people were puzzled when Jesus declared he had fulfilled the law and the prophets was that many prophecies of Isaiah, Nephi$_1$, and others remained open—in particular, the Nephites had not yet been reunited with a redeemed people of Israel. Jesus explained: "I do not destroy that which hath been spoken concerning things which are to come" (3 Ne. 15:7). Yet to be fulfilled in the prophetic view of the Book of Mormon are promises that the branches of scattered Israel will be gathered in Christ and will combine their records into one (2 Ne. 29:13–14), that the remnants of Lehi's descendants will be greatly strengthened in the Lord (2 Ne. 30:3–6; 3 Ne. 21:7–13), and that a great division will occur: a New Jerusalem will be built in the Western Hemisphere by the righteous (3 Ne. 21:23; Ether 13:1–9), while the wicked will be destroyed (2 Ne. 30:10). "Then," Jesus said, "shall the power of heaven come down among them; and I also will be in the midst" (3 Ne. 21:25).

[*See also* Jesus Christ in the Book of Mormon.]

BIBLIOGRAPHY

Most Latter-day Saint doctrinal writings refer to the Book of Mormon on particular topics, but no comprehensive analysis of Nephite religious experience as such has been written.

In general, see Sidney B. Sperry, *Book of Mormon Compendium*. Salt Lake City, 1968; and Rodney Turner, "The Three Nephite Churches of Christ," in *The Keystone Scripture*, ed. P. Cheesman, pp. 100–126. Provo, Utah, 1988.

For a cultural anthropologist's approach to Nephite religious institutions and practices, see John L. Sorenson, *An Ancient American Setting for the Book of Mormon*. Salt Lake City, 1985.

ADDITIONAL SOURCE

Welch, John W. "The Temple in the Book of Mormon: The Temples at the Cities of Nephi, Zarahemla, and Bountiful." In *Temples of the Ancient World: Ritual and Symbolism,* edited by Donald W. Parry, 297–387. Salt Lake City and Provo, Utah: Deseret Book and FARMS, 1994.

JOHN W. WELCH

REMISSION OF SINS

"Remission of sins" is the scriptural phrase that describes the primary purpose of BAPTISM: to obtain God's forgiveness for breaking his commandments and receive a newness of life. It is fundamental among the first principles and ordinances of the gospel: FAITH in the Lord JESUS CHRIST, REPENTANCE, BAPTISM by immersion for the remission of sins, and laying on of hands for the gift of the Holy Ghost. To grant pardon of sins is one manifestation of God's mercy, made possible by the atonement. It is the blessing sought by those who fervently prayed, "O have mercy, and apply the atoning blood of Christ that we may receive forgiveness of our sins, and our hearts may be purified" (Mosiah 4:2). Having one's sins remitted is a vital part of the developmental process that results in godhood and lies at the heart of the religious experience of a Latter-day Saint.

Baptism for the remission of sins is one of the most prominent themes of the scriptures, being both a requirement and a blessing associated with accepting Christ as the divine Redeemer and Savior of the world and joining his Church. According to LDS scriptures and teachings, the principles and ordinances of the gospel, including baptism for the remission of sins, were taught and practiced by all the prophets from Adam and Enoch (Moses 6:52–60, 64–68; 7:10–11) to the present time. The doctrine was taught before the earthly ministry of Jesus by BENJAMIN (Mosiah 4:3–4) and John the Baptist (Mark 1:3–4). It was articulated by Christ himself to the twelve apostles in Jerusalem (Matt. 28:16–20; John 20:21–23) and to the Nephites (3 Ne. 12:2), preached by Peter following Christ's ascension (Acts 2:37–38), and commanded of the Church as part of the restoration (D&C 49:11–14; 84:64). Authority to administer the ordinance of baptism by immersion for the remission of sins is held by bearers of the Aaronic Priesthood (D&C 13; 107:20) as well as by those who hold the Melchizedek Priesthood (D&C 20:38–45).

God commands all but little children and the mentally incompetent to submit to the first principles and ordinances (Moro. 8:11; D&C 29:46–50; 68:27), not as acts of compliance with his sovereignty, but because uncleanliness (sinfulness) is incompatible with godliness. There is no alternative path to exaltation (1 Ne. 15:33; 3 Ne. 27:19; Moses 6:57). Thus, those who do not receive a remission of sins through baptism are not BORN OF GOD and exclude themselves from his kingdom (Alma 7:14–16; D&C 84:74). Remission includes the pardoning of sins by God, who releases sinners with the promise that "their sins and their iniquities will I remember no more" (Heb. 8:12). Remission also includes the repentant person's recognition of God's communication of that forgiveness. Such a realization is accompanied by peace of conscience and feelings of inexpressible joy (Mosiah 4:1–3, 20). Having been "washed [by] the blood of Christ" (Alma 24:13; 3 Ne. 27:19), one is granted relief from the unhappiness that accompanies wickedness (Alma 41:10; 36:12–21) and increases in love for God, knowing that forgiveness is made possible only by the Savior's atoning sacrifice (D&C 27:2; 2 Ne. 9:21–27).

Remission of sins is an achievement made possible through the Atonement and earned through genuine changes in spirit and a discontinuation of behavior known to be wrong. Enos described the process as a "wrestle . . . before God" (Enos 1:2). The essential experience is to recognize one's unworthiness, taste of Christ's love, stand steadfast in faith toward him (Mosiah 4:11), and with contrite heart acknowledge that he was crucified for the sins of the world (D&C 21:9; 3 Ne. 9:20–22). Thus committed to Christ and engaged in repentance, one keeps the commandments by submitting to baptism and receiving the gift of the Holy Ghost. The initial sense of repentance and forgiveness that leads one to the ordinances (3 Ne. 7:25; D&C 20:37) is amplified and confirmed through the baptism of fire administered by the Comforter (2 Ne. 31:17; D&C 19:31). This series of experiences forms the basis for a spiritual testimony of the truthfulness of the GOSPEL OF JESUS CHRIST and a lifelong commitment to Christian living and Church service.

Remission of sins can be lost through recurrent transgression, for "unto that soul who sinneth shall the former sins return, saith the Lord your God" (D&C 82:7). Benjamin therefore enjoins the forgiven to retain their state by righteous living: "For the sake of retaining a remission of your sins from day to day, that ye may walk guiltless before God . . . ye should impart of your substance to the poor, every man according to that which he hath, such as feeding the hungry, clothing the naked, visiting the sick and administering to their relief, both spiritually and temporally, according to their wants" (Mosiah 4:26).

BIBLIOGRAPHY

Kimball, Spencer W. *The Miracle of Forgiveness.* Salt Lake City, 1969.

WILLIAM S. BRADSHAW

REPENTANCE

Repentance is the process by which humans set aside or overcome sins by changing hearts, attitudes, and actions that are out of harmony with God's teachings, thereby conforming their lives more completely to his will. In the words of one latter-day prophet, repentance is "to change one's mind in regard to past or intended actions or conduct" (McKay, p. 14). Paul observes that "all have sinned, and come short of the glory of God" (Rom. 3:23). For this reason, the Lord "gave commandment that all men must repent" (2 Ne. 2:21; Moses 6:57). This means that repentance is required of every soul who has not reached perfection.

Repentance has been central to God's dealings with his children since they were first placed on the earth. Old Testament prophets constantly called the children of Israel individually and collectively to repent and *turn* to God and righteous living from rebellion, apostasy, and sin. In New Testament times, the work of Jesus Christ on earth may be described as a ministry of repentance—that is, of calling on God's children to return to their God by changing their thinking and behavior and becoming more godlike. The Savior taught, "Be ye therefore perfect, even as your Father which is in heaven is perfect" (Matt. 5:48). Christ's apostles were called primarily to preach FAITH in Christ and to declare repentance to all the world (Mark 6:12). In modern times, few topics occur in the Lord's revelations as pervasively as this one. He has given latter-day prophets and all messengers of his gospel repeated instructions to declare "nothing but repentance unto this generation" (D&C 6:9). The Prophet Joseph Smith identified repentance and faith in Jesus Christ as the two fundamental principles of the gospel (A of F 4). And the gospel itself has been called "a gospel of repentance" (D&C 13; 84:27).

In modern as in earlier times, the term "repentance" literally means a turning from sin and a reversing of one's attitudes and behavior. Its purposes are to develop the divine nature within all mortal souls by freeing them from wrong or harmful thoughts and actions and to assist them in becoming more Christlike by replacing the "natural man" (1 Cor. 2:14) with the "new man" in Christ (Eph. 4:20–24).

This process is not only necessary in preparing humans to return and live with God, but it enlarges their capacity to love their fellow beings. Those who have reconciled themselves with God have the spiritual understanding, desire, and power to become reconciled with their fellow beings. God has commanded all humans to forgive each other: "I, the Lord, will forgive whom I will forgive, but of you it is required to forgive all men" (D&C 64:10). As God shows his love by forgiving ("I will forgive their iniquity, and I will remember their sin no more"; Jer. 31:34), his children, as they forgive others, also reflect this love.

True repentance, while seldom easy, is essential to personal happiness, emotional and spiritual growth, and eternal salvation. It is the only efficacious way for mortals to free themselves of the permanent effects of sin and the inevitable attendant burden of guilt. To achieve it, several specific changes must occur. One must first recognize that an attitude or action is out of harmony with God's teachings and feel genuine sorrow or remorse for it. Paul calls this "godly sorrow" (2 Cor. 7:10). Other scriptures describe this state of mind as "a broken heart and a contrite spirit" (Ps. 51:17; 2 Ne. 2:7; 3 Ne. 9:20). This recognition must produce an inward change of attitude. The prophet Joel exhorted Israel to "rend your heart, and not your garments" (Joel 2:12–13), thereby bringing the inner transformation necessary to begin the process of repentance.

Some form of confession is also necessary in repentance. In some cases, the transgressor may need to confess to the person or persons wronged or injured and ask forgiveness; in other cases, it may be necessary to confess sins to a Church leader authorized to receive such confessions; in still other cases, a confession to God alone may be sufficient; and sometimes all three forms of confession may be necessary.

In addition, repentance requires restitution to others who have suffered because of the sin. Whenever possible, this should be done by making good any physical or material losses or injury. Even when this is not possible, repentance requires other, equally significant actions, such as apologies; increased acts of kindness and service toward offended persons; intensified commitment to, and activity in, the Lord's work; or all of these in concert.

Finally, for repentance to be complete, one must abandon the sinful behavior. A change of heart begins the process; a visible outward change of direction, reflected in new patterns of behavior, must complete it (Mosiah 5:2). Failure to alter outward actions means that the sinner has not repented, and the weight of the former sin returns (D&C 82:7; cf. Matt. 18:32–34).

One purpose of repentance is to bless people by affording through forgiveness the one and only way of relieving the suffering that attends sin: "For behold, I, God, have suffered these things for all, that they might not suffer if they would repent; But if they would not repent they must suffer even as I" (D&C 19:16–17).

The Lord has repeatedly promised that all who repent completely shall find forgiveness of their sins, which in turn brings great joy. The parables of the lost sheep and the lost coin exemplify the joy in heaven over one sinner who repents (Luke 15:4–10); the parable

of the prodigal son (or lost son) illustrates the joy in heaven and similar joy in the circle of family and friends and within the repentant son himself over his return from sin (Luke 15:11–32).

Though repentance is indispensable to eternal salvation and to earthly happiness, it is not sufficient by itself to reunite a person with God. Complete repentance first requires faith in the Lord Jesus Christ, which in turn generates strong motivation and power to repent. Both are necessary for, and thus must precede, BAPTISM, the reception of the gift of the Holy Ghost, and membership in the Lord's kingdom. After awakening faith in Christ in the hearts of his listeners on the day of Pentecost, Peter exhorted them to "repent, and be baptized every one of you in the name of Jesus Christ for the remission of sins, and ye shall receive the gift of the Holy Ghost" (Acts 2:38). Only with the requisite repentance, symbolized by a broken heart and a contrite spirit and the abandonment of former sinful deeds and thought patterns, is one prepared to be baptized, receive the Holy Ghost, and have all previous sins remitted. Through baptism, a repentant person enters the kingdom of God by making covenants to remember Christ always and keep his commandments. The REMISSION OF SINS comes "by fire and by the Holy Ghost" (2 Ne. 31:17; D&C 20:37).

Since repentance is an ongoing process in the mortal effort to become Christlike, the need for it never diminishes. It requires active, daily application as humans recognize and strive to overcome sin and error and in this way endure to the end. For this reason, the Lord has instituted a means whereby each person who has repented and entered into the baptismal covenant may renew it by partaking of the SACRAMENT in remembrance of him. This time of self-examination allows one to reflect on the promises made at baptism, which were to take Christ's name upon oneself, to remember him always, and to keep his commandments. Thus, the process of repentance is kept alive by this frequent period of reflection as the participant partakes of symbols of Christ's body and blood in remembrance of his sacrifice to atone for human sin.

Scriptures inform us that "this life is the time for men to prepare to meet God" and that so-called deathbed repentance is usually not effective:

> Ye cannot say, when ye are brought to that awful crisis, that I will repent, that I will return to my God. Nay, ye cannot say this; for that same spirit which doth possess your bodies at the time that ye go out of this life, that same spirit will have power to possess your body in that eternal world. . . . If ye have procrastinated the day of your repentance even until death, behold, ye have become subjected to the spirit of the devil. (Alma 34:32–35)

To return to God's presence, mortals must strive during this life to attain Christlike qualities, which can only be gained by turning from sin. To defer such efforts blocks the exercise of faith essential to repentance, prevents the operation of the Holy Ghost, and retards the development of the personal qualities reflected in the "broken heart and contrite spirit" necessary to live in God's presence.

Repentance is one of the most powerful redemptive principles of the restored gospel of Jesus Christ. Without it, there would be no eternal progression, no possibility of becoming Christlike, no relief from the burden of guilt that every human incurs in a lifetime. With it, there is the glorious promise uttered by Isaiah that even for grievous sins there might be forgiveness: "Though your sins be as scarlet, they shall be as white as snow; though they be red like crimson, they shall be as wool" (Isa. 1:18).

BIBLIOGRAPHY

Gillum, Gary P. "Repentance Also Means Rethinking." In *By Study and Also by Faith*, ed. J. Lundquist and S. Ricks, Vol. 2, pp. 406–37. Salt Lake City, 1990.

Kimball, Spencer W. *The Miracle of Forgiveness*. Salt Lake City, 1969.

———. *The Teachings of Spencer W. Kimball*, ed. Edward L. Kimball, pp. 80–114. Salt Lake City, 1982.

McKay, David O. *Gospel Ideals*, pp. 12–14. Salt Lake City, 1953.

JAMES K. LYON

RESURRECTION

Resurrection is the reunion of the spirit with an immortal physical body. The body laid in the grave is mortal; the resurrected physical body is immortal. The whole of man, the united spirit and body, is defined in modern scripture as the "soul" of man. Resurrection from the dead constitutes the redemption of the soul (D&C 88:15–16).

Although the idea of resurrection is not extensively delineated in the Old Testament, there are some definite allusions to it (e.g., 1 Sam. 2:6; Job 14:14; 19:26; Isa. 26:19; Dan. 12:2). And in the New Testament, the resurrection of Jesus Christ, as the prototype of all resurrections, is an essential and central message: "I am the resurrection, and the life" (John 11:25).

The evidence of Christ's resurrection is measurably strengthened for Latter-day Saints by other records of post-Resurrection visitations of the Christ (*see* JESUS CHRIST, FORTY-DAY MINISTRY AND OTHER POST-RESUR-

RECTION APPEARANCES OF). For example, in the 3 Nephi account in the Book of Mormon, an entire multitude saw, heard, and touched him as he appeared in transcendent resurrected glory. This is accepted by Latter-day Saints as an ancient sacred text. The tendency of some recent scholarship outside the Church to radically separate the "Jesus of history" and the "Christ of faith" and to ascribe the resurrection faith to later interpreters is challenged by these later documents and by modern revelation.

Ancient witnesses, including Paul, came to their assurance of the reality of the Resurrection by beholding the risen Christ. From like witnesses, Latter-day Saints accept the record that at the resurrection of Christ "the graves were opened," in both the Old World and the new, and "many bodies of the saints which slept arose" (Matt. 27:52; 3 Ne. 23:9–10). In the current dispensation, resurrected beings, including John the Baptist, Peter, James, and MORONI₂ appeared and ministered to Joseph SMITH and Oliver COWDERY.

In the theology of Judaism and some Christian denominations resurrection has often been spiritualized—that is, redefined as a symbol for immortality of some aspect of man such as the active intellect, or of the soul considered to be an immaterial entity. In contrast, scientific naturalism tends to reject both the concept of the soul and of bodily resurrection. Latter-day Saints share few of the assumptions that underlie these dogmas. In LDS understanding, the spirit of each individual is not immaterial, but consists of pure, refined matter: "It existed before the body, can exist in the body; and will exist separate from the body, when the body will be mouldering in the dust; and will in the resurrection, be again united with it" (*TPJS*, p. 207). Identity and personality persist with the

spirit, and after the resurrection the spirit will dwell forever in a physical body.

Platonism and gnosticism hold that embodiment is imprisonment, descent, or association with what is intrinsically evil. In contrast, the scriptures teach that the physical body is a step upward in the progression and perfection of all. The body is sacred, a temple (1 Cor. 3:16; D&C 93:35). Redemption is not escape from the flesh but its dedication and transformation. Joseph Smith taught, "We came into this earth that we might have a body and present it pure before God in the celestial kingdom" (*TPJS*, p. 181). On the other hand, if defiled, distorted, and abused, the body may be an instrument of degradation, an enemy of genuine spirituality.

In contrast to the view that the subtle powers of intellect or soul must finally transcend the body or anything corporeal, the Prophet Joseph Smith taught that all beings "who have tabernacles (bodies), have power over those who have not" (*TPJS*, p. 190; 2 Ne. 9:8). At minimum, this is taken to mean that intellectual and spiritual powers are enhanced by association with the flesh. It follows that a long absence of the spirit from the body in the realm of disembodied spirits awaiting resurrection will be viewed not as a beatific or blessed condition, but instead as a bondage (D&C 45:17; 138:50). Moreover, "spirit and element [the spirit body and the physical body], inseparably connected, [can] receive a fulness of joy; And when separated, man cannot receive a fulness of joy" (D&C 93:33, 34).

In contrast to the view that the body when buried or cremated has no identifiable residue, Joseph Smith taught that "there is no fundamental principle belonging to a human system that ever goes into another in this world or the world to come" (*HC* 5:339).

Chemical disintegration is not final destruction. The resurrected body is tangible, but when the flesh is quickened by the Spirit there will be "spirit in their [veins] and not blood" (*WJS*, p. 270; see also *TPJS*, p. 367).

Resurrection is as universal as death. All must die and all must be resurrected. It is a free gift to everyone. It is not the result of the exercise of faith or accumulated good works. The Book of Mormon prophet Amulek declares, "Now, this restoration shall come to all, both old and young, both bond and free, both male and female, both the wicked and the righteous" (Alma 11:44; cf. *TPJS*, pp. 199–200, 294–97, 310–11, 319–21, 324–26).

Not all will be resurrected at the same moment, "but every man in his own order: Christ the firstfruits; afterward they that are Christ's at his coming" (1 Cor. 15:23). "Behold, there is a time appointed that all shall come forth from the dead," Alma writes, to stand embodied before God to be judged of their thoughts, words, and deeds (Alma 40:4).

"All men will come from the grave as they lie down, whether old or young" (*TPJS*, p. 199). And he who quickeneth all things shall "change our vile body, that it may be fashioned like unto his glorious body" (Philip. 3:21). "The body will come forth as it is laid to rest, for there is no growth nor development in the grave. As it is laid down, so will it arise, and changes to perfection will come by the law of restitution. But the spirit will continue to expand and develop, and the body, after the resurrection will develop to the full stature of man" (Joseph F. Smith, *IE* 7 [June 1904]: 623–24).

The resurrected body will be suited to the conditions and glory to which the person is assigned in the day of judgment. "Some dwell in higher glory than others" (*TPJS*, p. 367). The Doctrine and Covenants teaches that "your glory shall be that glory by which your bodies are quickened" (D&C 88:28), and

three glories are designated (D&C 76). Paul (1 Cor. 15:40) also mentioned three glories of resurrected bodies: one like the sun (celestial), another as the moon (terrestrial), and the third as the stars. In a revelation to Joseph Smith, the glory of the stars was identified as telestial (D&C 76). The lights of these glories differ, as do the sun, the moon, and the stars as perceived from earth. "So also is the resurrection of the dead" (1 Cor. 15:40–42).

In a general sense, the Resurrection may be divided into the resurrection of the just, also called the first resurrection, and the resurrection of the unjust, or the last resurrection. The first resurrection commenced with the resurrection of Christ and with those who immediately thereafter came forth from their graves. In much larger numbers, it will precede the thousand-year millennial reign, inaugurated by the "second coming" of the Savior (D&C 45:44–45; cf. 1 Thes. 4:16–17). At that time, some will be brought forth to meet him, as he descends in glory. This first resurrection will continue in proper order through the Millennium. The righteous who live on earth and die during the Millennium will experience immediate resurrection. Their transformation will take place in the "twinkling of an eye" (D&C 63:51). The first resurrection includes the celestial and terrestrial glories.

The final resurrection, or resurrection of the unjust, will occur at the end of the Millennium. In the words of the apocalypse, "the rest of the dead lived not again until the thousand years were finished" (Rev. 20:5). This last resurrection will include those destined for the telestial glory and perdition.

Of his visionary glimpses of the Resurrection, the Prophet Joseph Smith remarked, "The same glorious spirit gives them the likeness of glory and bloom; the old man with his silvery hairs will glory in bloom and beauty. No man can describe it to you—no man can write it" (*TPJS*, p. 368). Referring to the doctrine of the Resurrection as "principles of consolation," he pled, "Let these truths sink down in our hearts that, we may even here, begin to enjoy that which shall be in full hereafter." He added, "All your losses will be made up to you in the resurrection, provided you continue faithful. By the vision of the Almighty I have seen it" (*TPJS*, p. 296).

The hope of a glorious resurrection undergirds the radiance that characterized the faith of New Testament Saints as well as those who have since kept that faith alive in the world, including the Saints of the latter days.

BIBLIOGRAPHY

Ballard, Melvin J. "The Resurrection." In *Melvin Ballard: . . . Crusader for Righteousness,* ed. Melvin R. Ballard. Salt Lake City, 1966.

Nickelsburg, George W. *Resurrection, Immortality, and Eternal Life in Intertestamental Judaism.* Cambridge, Mass., 1972.

Smith, Joseph F. *Gospel Doctrine.*

Talmage, James E. *AF.*

ADDITIONAL SOURCE

Matthews, Robert J. "The Doctrine of the Resurrection as Taught in the Book of Mormon." *BYU Studies* 30/3 (1990): 41–56.

DOUGLAS L. CALLISTER

RIGDON, SIDNEY

Sidney Rigdon (1793–1876) was one of Joseph SMITH's closest friends and advisers. He was also a renowned early convert to the Church, its most persuasive orator in the first decade, and First Counselor in the First Presidency from 1832 to 1844. Following the Prophet Joseph Smith's martyrdom, Rigdon became one of the Church's best-known apostates.

Rigdon was born February 19, 1793, on a farm in St. Clair Township, near Pittsburgh, Pennsylvania, the fourth child and youngest son of William and Nancy Briant Rigdon. In 1817, while supporting his widowed mother on the family farm, Rigdon experienced Christian conversion and a year later qualified himself to become a licensed preacher with the Regular Baptists. He moved to eastern Ohio to preach under the tutelage of Adamson Bentley, a popular Baptist minister, and in June 1820 he married Phebe Brooks, Bentley's sister-in-law. After ordination as a Baptist minister, Rigdon became pastor of the First Baptist Church in Pittsburgh in 1821. Famed for his dynamic preaching, Rigdon attracted listeners until his congregation became one of the largest in the city. One of his critics, William Hayden, described him as being of "medium height, rotund in form; of countenance, while speaking, open and winning, with a little cast of melancholy. His action was graceful, his language copious, fluent in utterance, with articulation clear and musical" (quoted in Chase, p. 24).

Throughout his early ministry, Rigdon kept looking for the pure New Testament church that practiced laying on of hands for the gift of the Holy Ghost and healing the sick. Drawn to Alexander Campbell and Walter Scott, fellow ministers with similar views, Rigdon associated with leading members of the Mahoning Baptist Association, the forerunner of the restorationist Disciples of Christ movement. In 1826 he became the pastor of a Grand River Association congregation in Mentor, Ohio. In 1830, however, Rigdon broke with Campbell and Scott, who went on to form the Disciples of Christ, while Rigdon established a communal "family" near Kirtland.

In late October 1830 four Mormon missionaries visited Rigdon in Ohio. One was Parley P. Pratt, whom Rigdon had converted to the reformed Baptists a year earlier. Pratt told Rigdon about the Book of Mormon and the restoration of the gospel through Joseph

Smith. After two weeks of earnest investigation, Rigdon announced that he believed the new church to be the true apostolic church restored to the earth. In mid-November 1830 he was baptized and ordained an elder. More than a hundred members of his Kirtland congregation and common stock community followed him into the Church.

Rigdon, along with Edward Partridge, a young hatter who was interested in Mormonism, left almost immediately for Fayette, New York, to meet Joseph Smith. After their arrival, a revelation to Joseph commended Rigdon for his previous service, but called him to "a greater work," including that of scribe to the Prophet on his "new translation" of the Bible then under way (D&C 35:3). In December 1830, Smith, with Rigdon's help, worked on the manuscript that eventually became the seventh and eighth chapters of the Book of Moses in the Pearl of Great Price.

Rigdon's report of the harvest of souls in the Mentor-Kirtland area in Ohio may have encouraged Joseph to ask for guidance on moving the headquarters of the Church; in December 1830 a revelation commanded them to leave New York for Ohio (D&C 37; cf. 38). On February 1, 1831, Joseph and Sidney arrived in Kirtland, where they renewed their work on the inspired translation of the Bible.

In the summer of 1831, Joseph, Sidney, and other leaders journeyed to Independence, Missouri, which a revelation identified as the location of the latter-day Zion and the New Jerusalem. Sidney was instructed to dedicate the land of Zion for the gathering of the Saints and to write a description of the country for publication (D&C 58:50). Upon their return to Ohio, Joseph and Sidney resumed the translation of the scriptures, and on February 16, 1832, they jointly received the vision of the degrees of glory that is now Doc-

trine and Covenants section 76. In March 1832 they were brutally attacked by a mob and tarred and feathered. Sidney received head injuries that occasionally affected his emotional stability for the rest of his life. His friend Newel K. Whitney said that thereafter he was "either in the bottom of the cellar or up in the garrett window" (Chase, p. 115).

In March 1833 Sidney Rigdon and Frederick G. Williams were formally set apart as counselors to Joseph Smith in the First Presidency. Sidney had already been called as a counselor to Joseph a year earlier, before there was a First Presidency. In 1833 Rigdon was also called to be a "spokesman" for the Church and for Joseph Smith. Rigdon was promised that he would be "mighty in expounding all scriptures" (D&C 100:11). At this same time, Joseph said of him, "Brother Sidney is a man whom I love, but he is not capable of that pure and steadfast love for those who are his benefactors that should characterize a President of the Church of Christ. This, with some other little things, such as selfishness and independence of mind . . . are his faults. But notwithstanding these things, he is a very great and good man; a man of great power of words, and can gain the friendship of his hearers very quickly. He is a man whom God will uphold, if he will continue faithful to his calling" (HC 1:443).

In 1834 Rigdon assisted in recruiting volunteers for Zion's Camp and, while Joseph was away on that undertaking, had charge of affairs in Kirtland, including the construction of the temple. He was a leading teacher at the Kirtland school and helped arrange the revelations for publication in the 1835 edition of the Doctrine and Covenants. Under the Prophet's direction, Sidney helped compose and deliver many of the doctrinally rich Lectures on Faith. He often preached long, extravagant biblically based sermons, notably one at the dedication of the Kirtland Temple. In the persecution that followed the failure of the Kirtland Safety Society, Rigdon, along with Joseph Smith and other Saints, fled for their lives to Far West, Missouri, in 1838. There Rigdon delivered two famous volatile speeches, the Salt Sermon and the Independence Day oration, both of which stirred up fears and controversy in Missouri and contributed to the Extermination Order and the Battle of Far West. With Joseph and Hyrum Smith, Rigdon was taken prisoner and locked up in Liberty Jail, but was released early because of severe apoplectic seizures.

Rigdon took an active part in the founding of Nauvoo and in 1839 accompanied Joseph Smith to Washington, D.C., to present the grievances of the Saints to the federal government. He was elected to the Nauvoo City Council and served also as city attorney, postmaster, and professor of Church history in the embryonic university projected for the city. Despite his many appointments, however, he was nearly silent during this time and often sick. He was accused of being associated with John C. Bennett and other enemies of the Church in their seditious plans to displace Joseph Smith, but this he always denied. He did not endorse the principle of plural marriage, although he never came out in open opposition to it. Joseph Smith eventually lost confidence in Rigdon and in 1843 wished to reject him as a counselor, but because of the intercession of Hyrum Smith, retained him in office.

Early in 1844, when Joseph Smith became a candidate for president of the United States, Rigdon was nominated as his running mate and he established residence in Pittsburgh to carry on the campaign. He was there when news arrived of Joseph Smith's murder. He hastened to Nauvoo to offer himself as a "guardian of the Church," promising to act as such until Joseph Smith was resurrected from the dead. His claims were duly considered, but at a memorable meeting in Nauvoo on August 8, 1844, Church members rejected him as guardian. The Twelve Apostles were sustained as the head of the Church. When he undertook to establish a rival leadership, Rigdon was excommunicated in September 1844 and left with a few disciples for Pennsylvania, where they organized a Church of Christ. Acting erratically, he lost most of his followers in less than two years. In 1863, he made another effort, founding the Church of Jesus Christ of the Children of Zion, which continued into the 1880s. From 1847 to his death in 1876, Rigdon resided in Friendship, New York, usually in a state of emotional imbalance and unhappiness.

In 1834, in *Mormonism Unvailed*, Eber D. Howe attacked the authenticity of the Book of Mormon by adopting Philastus Hurlbut's argument that Sidney Rigdon purloined the "Manuscript Story" of Solomon Spaulding (*see* SPAULDING MANUSCRIPT), plagiarized it to compose the Book of Mormon, and gave it to Joseph Smith to publish under his name. During his lifetime Rigdon and members of his family consistently denied any connection with Spaulding, and after the discovery in 1885 of one of Spaulding's manuscripts, the story was discredited.

BIBLIOGRAPHY

Backman, Milton V., Jr. *The Heavens Resound: A History of the Latter-day Saints in Ohio, 1830–1838*. Salt Lake City, 1983.

Chase, Daryl. "Sidney Rigdon—Early Mormon." Master's thesis, University of Chicago, 1931.

McKiernan, F. Mark. *The Voice of One Crying in the*

Wilderness: Sidney Rigdon, Religious Reformer 1793–1876. Lawrence, Kan., 1971.

BRUCE A. VAN ORDEN

RIGHTEOUSNESS

Righteousness comprises a broad group of concepts and traits. As with the biblical Hebrew *sedek* and the Greek *dikaiosunē*, the English word "righteousness" describes the ideal of religious life, with Godlike behavior as the norm. Righteousness is right conduct before God and among mankind in all respects. The scriptures give the following perspectives:

Righteousness is ultimately synonymous with holiness or godliness. Christ himself is known as "the Righteous" (Moses 7:45, 47) and as "the Son of Righteousness" (3 Ne. 25:2). His "ways are righteousness forever" (2 Ne. 1:19).

The state of righteousness is available to mankind through the redemption of Christ as one is BORN OF GOD: "Marvel not that all mankind, yea, men and women . . . must be born again; yea, born of God, changed from their carnal and fallen state, to a state of righteousness, being redeemed of God, becoming his sons and daughters" (Mosiah 27:25).

The terms "righteous" and "righteousness" also apply to mortals who, though beset with weaknesses and frailties, are seeking to come unto Christ. In this sense, righteousness is not synonymous with perfection. It is a condition in which a person is moving toward the Lord, yearning for godliness, continuously repenting of sins, and striving honestly to know and love God and to follow the principles and ordinances of the gospel. Saints of God are urged to do "the works of righteousness" (D&C 59:23) and to "bring to pass much righteousness" (D&C 58:27).

Inherent in the meaning of righteousness is the concept of justification. It is impossible for finite mortals to live in perfect obedience to God's laws or to atone infinitely for their sins. "For all have sinned," Paul wrote, "and come short of the glory of God" (Rom. 3:23). Christ's atonement mercifully reconciles the demands of justice (*see* JUSTICE AND MERCY), making it possible for repentant mortals to become "right" with God—"at one" with him.

When Saul of Tarsus saw the resurrected Christ on the road to Damascus, "he trembling and astonished said, Lord, what wilt thou have me to do?" (Acts 9:6). From that moment on, he sought to know the will of God and live accordingly. But he also lamented over mortal weaknesses: "For I know that in me, that is, in my flesh, dwelleth no good thing . . . only in Christ" (JST, Rom. 7:19). "There is none righteous, no, not one" (Rom. 3:10). Like all apostles and prophets, however, Paul also taught the glorious message that through the grace of Christ mortals can "put off . . . the old man"—their fallen and sinful selves—and "put on the new man, which after God is created in righteousness and true holiness" (Eph. 4:22, 24).

The scriptures abound in similar exhortations to flee wickedness, accept the Lord's grace, and come unto Christ in righteousness. "O wretched man that I am!" exclaimed Nephi. "Yea, my heart sorroweth because of my flesh; my soul grieveth because of mine iniquities." But recognizing the Savior as "the rock of [his] righteousness," Nephi cried: "O Lord, wilt thou redeem my soul? . . . Wilt thou make me that I may shake at the appearance of sin? . . . Wilt thou encircle me around in the robe of thy righteousness!" (2 Ne. 4:17–35).

Righteousness begins in the heart—the "broken heart." It begins when individuals see themselves where they really are: in a fallen state, as "unworthy creatures" who are unable to pull themselves out of their own sins. As they confront the monumental gulf between "the greatness of God, and [their] own nothingness," their hearts break and they "humble [themselves] even in the depths of humility, calling on the name of the Lord daily, and standing steadfastly in the faith" (Mosiah 4:11).

Righteous souls then seek to become right with the Lord, by asking sincerely for forgiveness. As the Lord blesses such with his grace, they desire to respond with even greater faithfulness, love, and obedience. Although they may not reach perfect righteousness in mortality, their lives are beyond reproach—"as becometh saints" (Eph. 5:3).

Scriptures provide a wealth of insight into the attitudes, behaviors, and beliefs that form the basis of a righteous life (e.g., 2 Pet. 1:4–8; D&C 4:5–6). Notably, in the SERMON ON THE MOUNT (Matt. 5–7; cf. 3 Ne. 12–14), Jesus revealed the meaning of righteousness—a pattern that he exemplified by his own life:

Those who seek righteousness become humble, poor in spirit. They reverence the Lord, acknowledging that "all things which are good cometh of God" (Moroni 7:12).

They mourn for their sins—and their "godly sorrow worketh repentance" (2 Cor. 7:10). They also compassionately "mourn with those that mourn; yea, and comfort those that stand in need of comfort" (Mosiah 18:9).

The righteous strive to be meek—kind and long-suffering, generous, sacrificing, patient, filled with love for their enemies, not "puffed up," and "not easily provoked" (1 Cor. 13:4–5).

Hungering and thirsting after righteousness, they continually seek the Lord through sincere prayer, fasting, scripture study, Sabbath worship, and service in the holy temples.

They seek to be merciful—to forgive as they would be forgiven, to judge as they would be judged, to love as they would be loved, to serve as they would be served (D&C 38:24–25).

They seek to be pure in heart—thinking no evil, envying not, and rejoicing not in iniquity but in the truth (1 Cor. 13:4–6). They are honest in their covenants with God and in their dealings with their fellowmen. They are chaste and also virtuous.

Seekers of righteousness are peacemakers. They avoid contention, anger, and evil-speaking. They promote goodwill, brotherhood, and sisterhood; they seek to establish God's will and his kingdom on earth as it is in heaven.

When persecuted for righteousness' sake or when reviled or maligned for their allegiance to the Lord, they bear all things and endure all things (1 Cor. 13:7).

Such scriptural descriptions of righteousness are not to be reduced to lists that individuals self-righteously check off. They are constant reminders on the journey toward God, who has promised a Comforter—the Holy Ghost—to give guidance and direction on that path (John 14:26).

The Lord delights "to honor those who serve [him] in righteousness" (D&C 76:5). At the last day, "the righteous, the saints of the Holy One of Israel, they who have believed in the Holy One of Israel, they who have endured the crosses of the world, and despised the shame of it, they shall inherit the kingdom of God, which was prepared for them from the foundation of the world, and their joy shall be full forever" (2 Ne. 9:18).

BIBLIOGRAPHY

Benson, Ezra T. "A Mighty Change of Heart." *Ensign* 19 (Oct. 1989): 2–5.

McConkie, Bruce R. "The Dead Who Die in the Lord." *Ensign* 6 (Nov. 1976): 106–8.

Scoresby, A. Lynn. "Journey toward Righteousness." *Ensign* 10 (Jan. 1980): 52–57.

MARVIN K. GARDNER

S

Sacrament Prayers

The sacrament prayers, which were revealed by the Lord to the Prophet Joseph SMITH, are among the few set prayers in the Church, and the only ones members are commanded to offer "often" (D&C 20:75). They are offered regularly during the administration of the ordinance of the sacrament in sacrament meeting, occupying a central place in the religious lives of Latter-day Saints. They originate in ancient practice and, with one exception (the current use of water instead of wine), preserve the wording of NEPHITE sacramental prayers:

O God, the Eternal Father, we ask thee in the name of thy Son, Jesus Christ, to bless and sanctify this bread to the souls of all those who partake of it; that they may eat in remembrance of the body of thy Son, and witness unto thee, O God, the Eternal Father, that they are willing to take upon them the name of thy Son, and always remember him, and keep his commandments which he hath given them, that they may always have his Spirit to be with them. Amen. (Moroni 4:3)

O God, the Eternal Father, we ask thee, in the name of thy Son, Jesus Christ, to bless and sanctify this wine to the souls of all those who drink of it, that they may do it in remembrance of the blood of thy Son, which was shed for them; that they may witness unto thee, O God, the Eternal Father, that they do always remember him, that they may have his Spirit to be with them. Amen. (Moroni 5:2)

The prayers, in turn, formalize language used by the resurrected Savior when he visited the Americas (3 Ne. 18:5–11; cf. D&C 20:75–79). Subsequent to a revelation in August 1830 (D&C 27) water has been used instead of wine.

No such exact wording of the prayers is included in the New Testament. However, one scholar has detected parallels between Latter-day Saint sacrament prayers and ancient eucharistic formulas (Barker, pp. 53–56). The Joseph Smith Translation of the Bible (JST) confirms that key elements of the sacrament prayers were part of the original Last Supper: Jesus included covenantal obligations similar to those in the prayers (JST Matt. 26:25) and made clear that his action introduced a formal "ordinance" that they were to repeat often (JST Mark 14:24). Further, in the JST, Jesus does not say, "This is my body," and "This is my blood"—metaphors whose interpretation has historically divided Christians on the matter of "transubstantiation." He said instead, "This is in remembrance of my body," and "This is in remembrance of my blood" (JST Matt. 26:22, 24; cf. JST Mark 14:21, 23).

The sacrament prayers invite personal introspection, repentance, and rededication, yet they are also communal, binding individuals into congregations who jointly and publicly attest to their willingness to remember Christ. This shared commitment to become like Christ, repeated weekly, defines the supreme aspiration of Latter-day Saint life.

BIBLIOGRAPHY

Barker, James L. *The Protestors of Christendom.* Independence, Mo., 1946.

Tanner, John S. "Reflections on the Sacrament Prayers." *Ensign* 16 (Apr. 1986): 7–11.

Welch, John W. "The Nephite Sacrament Prayers." *FARMS Update.* Provo, Utah, 1986.

ADDITIONAL SOURCE

Anderson, Richard Lloyd. "Religious Validity: The Sacrament Covenant in Third Nephi." In *By Study and Also by Faith: Essays in Honor of Hugh W. Nibley,* edited by John M. Lundquist and Stephen D. Ricks, 2:1–51. Salt Lake City and Provo, Utah: Deseret Book and FARMS, 1990.

JOHN S. TANNER

SAMUEL THE LAMANITE

Samuel the LAMANITE was the only Book of Mormon prophet identified as a Lamanite. Apart from his sermon at Zarahemla (Hel. 13–15), no other record of his life or ministry is preserved. Noted chiefly for his prophecies about the birth of Jesus Christ, his prophetic words, which were later examined, commended, and updated by the risen Jesus (3 Ne. 23:9–13), were recorded by persons who accepted him as a true prophet and even faced losing their lives for believing his message (3 Ne. 1:9).

Approximately five years before Jesus' birth, Samuel began to preach repentance in Zarahemla. After the incensed Nephite inhabitants expelled him, the voice of the Lord directed him to return. Climbing to the top of the city wall, he delivered his message unharmed, even though certain citizens sought his life (Hel. 16:2). Thereafter, he fled and "was never heard of more among the Nephites" (Hel. 16:8).

Samuel prophesied that Jesus would be born in no more than five years' time, with two heavenly signs indicating his birth. First, "one day and a night and a day" of continual light would occur (Hel. 14:4; cf. Zech. 14:7). Second, among celestial wonders, a new star would arise (Hel. 14:5–6). Then speaking of mankind's need of the atonement and RESURRECTION, he prophesied signs of Jesus' death: three days of darkness among the Nephites would signal his crucifixion, accompanied by storms and earthquakes (14:14–27).

Samuel framed these prophecies by pronouncing judgments of God upon his hearers. He spoke of a final devastation—four hundred years distant—that would end Nephite civilization because of its rebellion against God. This desolation would come through "the sword and with famine and with pestilence" (13:9; cf. Morm. 1:19). He spoke of curses from God on the land (13:17–20, 23, 30, 35–36), on property (13:18–19, 21, 31), and on the people themselves (13:19, 21, 32, 38). Such afflictions would arise because the Nephites would knowingly reject true prophets while accepting false ones, clamor for wealth, and refuse to acknowledge the blessings of God (13:19–34). Samuel reiterated the judgments of God against the Nephites (15:1–3, 17) and then emphasized the divine promises extended to the Lamanites—including assurances for "the latter times" of "restoration" (15:4–16).

ADDITIONAL SOURCE

Brown, S. Kent. "The Prophetic Laments of Samuel the Lamanite." In *From Jerusalem to Zarahemla: Literary and Historical Studies of the Book of Mormon,* 128–45. Provo, Utah: BYU Religious Studies Center, 1998.

S. MICHAEL WILCOX

SCRIPTURE, INTERPRETATION WITHIN SCRIPTURE

The key to interpreting scriptural passages often lies in the body of scripture itself. For example, some passages from the Old Testament receive commentary and interpretation in the New Testament. Jesus Christ frequently taught from the Old Testament, not only giving interpretation—as in David's need to eat the temple shew bread (1 Sam. 21:1–6) as justification for his disciples plucking wheat on the Sabbath (Mark 2:23–26)—but also often emphasizing that the scriptures testify of himself as Messiah (Luke 4:18–21; John 5:39). The additional scriptures that Latter-day Saints accept—the BOOK OF MORMON, the Doctrine and Covenants, and the Pearl of Great Price—also cite and interpret the Bible. In fact, many of the clearest explications of doctrine arise from modern revelations or restored scripture.

In the Pearl of Great Price, the book of Moses and the book of Abraham augment the Old Testament Genesis account of the Creation (Moses 2–3; Abr. 4–5), affirm human

agency (Moses 3:17; 7:32), clarify the fall of Adam (Moses 4; Abr. 5), and explain the resulting need for a redeemer (Moses 6:59; cf. 4:1–2; 5:7–8). In addition, these two books add information on the claims of Satan and the choosing of Christ in the premortal world (Moses 4:1–4; Abr. 3:27–28) where all the spirits of mankind lived before their advent on the earth.

In Joseph Smith—Matthew, the Prophet Joseph Smith received clarification of the Savior's discussion in Matthew 24 of the events to precede the fall of Jerusalem and those to precede Jesus' latter-day coming. According to the Joseph Smith—History, MORONI₂ quoted Malachi 4:6 to Joseph Smith differently from the Old Testament version, suggesting that the phrase "the fathers" refers to the patriarchs, especially Abraham, with whom God made covenants pertaining to Abraham's posterity, who would bear priesthood ordinances to the world for the exaltation of the human family (JS—H 1:36–39; D&C 27:9–10).

The Book of Mormon clarifies many of the writings of Old Testament prophets. The prophet NEPHI₁ quoted Isaiah 48–49 (1 Ne. 20–21) and then gave a plain commentary on the major points of those chapters in 1 Nephi 22, emphasizing that the NEPHITES were a remnant of scattered Israel, who would eventually be gathered with the aid of the gentiles. In another example, about 148 B.C. the Nephite prophet ABINADI identified the "suffering servant" of Isaiah 53 as Jesus Christ (Mosiah 15:2–5) and enlarged on Isaiah's discussion of the Messiah's atonement (Mosiah 14–15).

The Book of Mormon also illuminates the SERMON ON THE MOUNT (Matt. 5–7). In a similar sermon given in the Western Hemisphere (3 Ne. 12–14), the resurrected Jesus said, "Blessed are the poor in spirit *who come unto* me" (3 Ne. 12:3; italics added). Such added words, plus the context of Jesus' address, indicate that one must come to the Savior through BAPTISM and righteousness to receive the blessings promised in the BEATITUDES.

The Doctrine and Covenants offers explication on several obscure points in the book of Revelation that pertain to events of the Last Days, such as the gathering of Israel and their receiving priesthood ordinances (D&C 77:8–9, 11). Elucidation of biblical passages that focus on latter-day signs to precede Jesus' second coming are found especially in Doctrine and Covenants 45 and 86. While pondering 1 Peter 3:18–20, President Joseph F. Smith received a vision of the redemption of the dead (now D&C 138) that clarified and enlarged the Savior's redemptive work in the spirit world following his crucifixion.

Much modern revelation came to the Prophet Joseph Smith in response to questions arising from his work on the Joseph Smith Translation of the Bible (JST). For example, while meditating on the resurrection to life or damnation mentioned in John 5:29, Joseph Smith and Sidney Rigdon received the revelation on the degrees of glory in the resurrection (D&C 76). Joseph Smith recorded several instances in which, while pondering a passage of scripture (e.g., James 1:5, an invitation to ask the Lord for wisdom), he prayed and received additional scripture from the Lord that made the first more plain or confirmed its reality (JS—H 1:11–20). While translating from the Book of Mormon PLATES, Joseph Smith and Oliver COWDERY prayed after reading about baptism. In answer, John the Baptist came with authority and instructions on baptism (JS—H 1:68–72). After their baptisms, the Prophet described their being filled with the Holy Ghost: "Our minds being now enlightened, we began to have the scriptures laid open to our understandings, and the true meaning and intention of their more mysteri-

ous passages revealed unto us in a manner which we never could attain to previously, nor ever before had thought of" (JS—H 1:74).

Nephi observed that having the spirit of prophecy is essential to grasping the correct understanding of scripture. He mentioned in particular Isaiah, "for because the words of Isaiah are not plain unto you, nevertheless they are plain unto all those that are filled with the spirit of prophecy" (2 Ne. 25:4). In chapters 25–30, Nephi provided prophetic insight into the teachings of Isaiah.

Modern revelation and restored scripture offer indispensable interpretations of the Bible, helping Latter-day Saints to understand the Bible more fully. Jesus rebuked those who had taken away the "key of knowledge" or the means whereby the biblical scriptures could be understood (JST Luke 11:53), thereby causing confusion in the interpretation of scripture. The Lord said, "Because that ye have a Bible ye need not suppose that it contains all my words; neither need ye suppose that I have not caused more to be written. . . . I shall speak unto the Jews and they shall write it; and I shall also speak unto the Nephites and they shall write it; and I shall also speak unto the other tribes of the house of Israel . . . and they shall write it. . . . And my word also shall be gathered in one" (2 Ne 29:10, 12, 14; cf. Ezek 37:16–20). Latter-day Saints interpret the Bible in the light of restored scripture and modern revelation because these have reestablished the lost key of knowledge.

BIBLIOGRAPHY

Gileadi, Avraham. "Isaiah: Four Latter-day Keys to an Ancient Book." In *Isaiah and the Prophets*, ed. M. Nyman. Provo, Utah, 1984.

McConkie, Bruce R. "The Bible, a Sealed Book." In *Supplement to a Symposium on the New Testament*, Church Educational System, pp. 1–7. Salt Lake City, 1984.

Rust, Richard Dilworth. "'All Things Which Have Been Given of God . . . Are the Typifying of Him': Typology in the Book of Mormon." In *Literature of Belief*, ed. N. Lambert. Provo, Utah, 1981.

M. CATHERINE THOMAS

SECRET COMBINATIONS

In latter-day scriptures, secret combinations are groups of conspirators who plot and initiate works of darkness for evil and selfish purposes. Secret combinations have existed since the days of Cain (Moses 5:51). Satan is their author (2 Ne. 26:22), power and gain are their motives (Ether 8:15, 25), and conspiracy is their method of operation (Hel. 6:22–24). Secret combinations may be brotherhoods, groups, societies, or governments. They operate in secrecy to perform evil acts for the purpose of gaining power over the minds and actions of people.

As the enemies of honest men and women governed by the rule of law, such secret combinations seek to subvert public virtue and legally constituted authority. They defile, defraud, murder, deceive, and destroy the elements of good government, religious or secular. Their goal is to seize power and to rule over all the people (3 Ne. 6:27–30), which results in the destruction of human freedom and agency and the paralysis of peaceful and just communities.

Secret combinations and their practices have a scriptural and historic tradition that extends from the days of Cain's secret covenant with Satan to modern times. Members of these Satanic combinations are bound by secret oaths and covenants. The devil proclaims, initiates, and sustains these combinations and their conspiratorial practices (Moses 5:29–33, 47–52).

In the Book of Mormon, several secret combinations challenged governments ruled by the "voice of the people" or by righteous kings. They were a continuing threat to the Jaredites, who succumbed eventually to their power. Later, they were a threat to the Nephite and Lamanite nations when the Gadianton combinations, over a period of many years, challenged the constituted authorities and eventually seized power. The concerted effort of the whole populace later defeated the Gadiantons, but others rose in their place. The Book of Mormon details the tactics and strategies of the Gadiantons, mentions a variety of countermeasures, and shows that a secret combination was responsible for the final downfall of the Nephites (Hel. 2:13–14; Ether 8:21; *see also* BOOK OF MORMON: HELAMAN and BOOK OF MORMON: 3 NEPHI).

In the contemporary world, secret combinations take various forms and operate at different levels of society. They are expressed in organized crime and in religious, economic, and political conspiracies. The Lord has warned that secret combinations will be present in modern society (D&C 38:29; Ether 8:20–25). They threaten freedom everywhere. However, Latter-day Saints believe that secret combinations and their practices can be overcome, but only through righteous living and full support of honest government.

Secret combinations are often referred to in latter-day scripture, particularly in the book of Moses and the Book of Mormon. In the Doctrine and Covenants, this term describes those who have conspired against the Saints (D&C 42:64). It does not appear in the Bible, but the equivalent "conspiracy" is used at least ten times.

BIBLIOGRAPHY

Hillam, Ray C. "The Gadianton Robbers and Protracted War." *BYU Studies* 15 (Winter 1975): 215–24.

Meservy, Keith H. "'Gadiantonism' and the

Destruction of Jerusalem." In *The Pearl of Great Price: Revelations from God*, ed. H. D. Peterson and C. Tate, Jr., pp. 171–95. Provo, Utah, 1989.

Peterson, Daniel C. "The Gadianton Robbers as Guerrilla Warriors." In *Warfare in the Book of Mormon*, ed. S. Ricks and W. Hamblin, pp. 146–73. Salt Lake City, 1990.

"Secret Combinations." FARMS Update (Oct. 1989).

RAY C. HILLAM

SEER STONES

Joseph SMITH wrote that in 1823 an angel told him about "two stones in silver bows . . . fastened to a breastplate . . . the possession and use of [which] constituted 'seers' in ancient or former times" (JS—H 1:35). Joseph used these and other seer stones that he found in various ways (occasionally referred to by the biblical term URIM AND THUMMIM) for several purposes, primarily in translating the Book of Mormon and receiving revelations (see *HC* 1:21–23, 33, 36, 45, 49; 3:28; 5:xxxii; *CHC* 6:230–31).

Historical sources suggest that effective use of the instruments required Joseph to be at peace with God and his fellowmen, to exercise faith in God, and to exert mental effort (*CHC* 1:128–33). Otherwise, little is said authoritatively about their operation. Occasionally, people have been deceived by trying to use stones to receive revelation, the best-known latter-day example in the Church being Hiram Page (D&C 28:11–12).

While useful in translating and receiving revelation, seer stones are not essential to those processes. Elder Orson Pratt reported that Joseph Smith told him that the Lord gave him the Urim and Thummim when he was inexperienced as a translator but that he later pro-

gressed to the point that he no longer needed the instrument ("'Two Days' Meeting at Brigham City," *Millennial Star* 36 [1874]: 498–99).

RICHARD E. TURLEY, JR.

SERMON ON THE MOUNT

The Sermon on the Mount (Matt. 5–7) is for Latter-day Saints, as well as for all other Christians, a key source for the teachings of Jesus and of Christian behavior ethics. The fact that parallel accounts appear in the BOOK OF MORMON (3 Ne. 12–14) and the Joseph Smith Translation of the Bible (JST Matt. 5–7) offers both the opportunity for a better understanding of the Sermon and the obligation to refute notions of mere plagiarism by the Prophet Joseph SMITH. A careful comparison of the texts reveals significant differences that are attributable primarily to the specific setting of the Book of Mormon sermon.

In the Book of Mormon account, the resurrected Jesus appeared to the more righteous survivors of a fierce storm and major earthquake in the Western Hemisphere who had gathered at the temple in the land called Bountiful. The setting includes the performance of ordinances, for the people prepared for baptism, first that of water by twelve men whom Jesus had ordained, followed by that of fire from the Lord himself (3 Ne. 12:1–2). The sermon at the temple thus provides the assembled multitude with an understanding of their duties and obligations. It also introduces them to the fulness of the gospel that Jesus established among them because he had fulfilled the law "that was given unto Moses" (3 Ne. 15:4–10) under which they had lived. Obedience to Jesus' gospel gave the Book of Mormon people two hundred years of peace and harmony as it became established throughout their lands (4 Ne. 1:17–23). Since Jesus himself observes that he had given a similar sermon in Palestine before he ascended to his Father (3 Ne. 15:1), Latter-day Saints have no doubt that the Sermon on the Mount reflects a unified presentation that the Savior possibly gave on several occasions (JST Matt. 7:1–2, 9, 11) and not merely a collection brought together by Matthew or his sources. As in many speaking situations, a speaker can repeat the basic message with appropriate alterations to fit the specific audience.

SETTING OF THE SERMONS. While much of the text in 3 Nephi 12–14 is identical to Matthew 5–7, there are numerous and significant differences. Most of the differences stem from the specific setting of the Book of Mormon sermon. First, the risen Jesus opened his Book of Mormon sermon with three additional BEATITUDES that underscore its purpose as an address to believers: "Blessed are ye if ye shall give heed unto the words of these twelve whom I have chosen; . . . blessed are ye if ye shall believe in me and be baptized; . . . more blessed are they who shall believe in your words . . . and be baptized . . . [and] receive a remission of their sins" (3 Ne. 12:1–2). Further, the Book of Mormon account is post-Resurrection, and the emphasis is on the fact that the Lord has completely fulfilled his mission of salvation. Thus, Jesus can summarize the series of antitheses recorded in 3 Nephi 12:21–45: "Those things which were of old time, which were under the law, in me are all fulfilled" (3 Ne. 12:46). Furthermore, rather than instructing the people "Be ye therefore perfect, even as your Father which is in heaven is perfect" (Matt. 5:48), Jesus in meaningfully modified words told them, "I would that ye should be perfect even as I, or your Father who is in heaven is perfect" (3 Ne. 12:48).

In place of the open-ended "one jot or one tittle shall in no wise pass from the law, till all be fulfilled" (Matt. 5:18), the Book of Mormon passage replaced the phrase "till all be fulfilled" with "but in me it hath all been fulfilled" (3 Ne. 12:18).

Other changes reflect both the Book of Mormon setting and the absence of antipharisaic statements that figure prominently in Matthew's account. Two examples of the former are the replacement of the "farthing" (Matt. 5:26) with the "senine" (3 Ne. 12:26), which was the smallest Nephite measure of gold (Alma 11:3, 15–19), and the lack of reference to the swearing "by Jerusalem . . . the city of the great King" (Matt. 5:35). Similarly, the sermon at the temple in Bountiful does not mention surpassing the righteousness of the scribes and Pharisees, as in Matthew 5:20, or that of the publicans who are loved by their friends (Matt. 5:46–47). In place of the references to the scribes and Pharisees (Matt. 5:20), the Lord told the Nephites: "Except ye shall keep my commandments, which I have commanded you at this time, ye shall in no case enter into the kingdom of heaven" (3 Ne. 12:20). Also, the Book of Mormon account does not contain the references to self-mutilation found in Matthew 5:29–30, or the qualifying phrase "without a cause" in Matthew 5:22 (cf. 3 Ne. 12:22).

CLARIFICATIONS. A further type of difference consists of additions to the Sermon on the Mount text that often provide sensible clarifications. Several examples are found in the Beatitudes. The Book of Mormon version noted that it is "the poor in spirit *who come unto me*" who inherit the kingdom of heaven (3 Ne. 12:3; Matt. 5:3; emphasis added). At the end of 3 Nephi 12:6 (cf. Matt. 5:6), one finds "blessed are all they who do hunger and thirst after righteousness, for they shall be filled *with the Holy Ghost"* (emphasis added). While these might seem to be small changes, they nonetheless enhance understanding of Jesus' meaning.

For Latter-day Saints, the message of the Sermon on the Mount centers on its normative value. As a covenant-making people, they take upon themselves the obligation to emulate the Savior in their personal lives and to work toward the ultimate goal of becoming like him. Although the demands are substantial, they are provided an incentive to strive to become like their divine model (cf. 2 Ne. 31:7–10, 16; 3 Ne. 27:27). The simple words and teachings that Jesus gave to his followers in Palestine and to the Book of Mormon survivors are still applicable to his Saints today.

BIBLIOGRAPHY

Stendahl, Krister. "The Sermon on the Mount and Third Nephi." In *Reflections on Mormonism*, ed. Truman G. Madsen, pp. 139–54. Provo, Utah, 1978.

Thomas, M. Catherine. "The Sermon on the Mount: The Sacrifice of the Human Heart." In *Studies in Scripture*, ed. K. Jackson and R. Millet, Vol. 5, pp. 236–50. Salt Lake City, 1986.

Welch, John W. *The Sermon at the Temple and the Sermon on the Mount*. Salt Lake City, 1990.

ADDITIONAL SOURCE

Welch, John W. *Illuminating the Sermon at the Temple and Sermon on the Mount: An Approach to 3 Nephi 11–18 and Matthew 5–7*. Provo, Utah: FARMS, 1999.

ROBERT TIMOTHY UPDEGRAFF

SMITH, JOSEPH

[*This entry*, The Prophet, *is a biography of Joseph Smith. See also* Visions of Joseph Smith.]

An early oil painting of the Prophet Joseph Smith (1805–1844). People who knew Joseph Smith personally commented that no picture could do him justice, for when he spoke compassion and power were evident, sometimes to the point that his countenance became visibly radiant. Artist unknown. Courtesy Library-Archives, Reorganized Church of Jesus Christ of Latter Day Saints.

The Prophet

Joseph Smith, Jr. (1805–1844), often referred to as the Prophet Joseph Smith, was the founding prophet of The Church of Jesus Christ of Latter-day Saints. Latter-day Saints call him "the Prophet" because, in the tradition of Old and New Testament prophets, he depended on revelation from God for his teachings, not on his own learning. They accept his revelations, many of them published as the Doctrine and Covenants and as the Pearl of Great Price, as scripture to accompany the Bible. As a young man, Joseph Smith also translated a sacred record from ancient America known as the BOOK OF MORMON. These revelations and records restored to the earth the pure gospel of Christ. Joseph

Smith's role in history was to found the Church of Jesus Christ based on this restored gospel in preparation for the second coming of Christ.

Little in his background pointed toward this momentous life. Joseph Smith's ancestors were ordinary New England farm people. His Smith ancestors emigrated from England to America in the seventeenth century and settled in Topsfield, Massachusetts, where they attained local distinction. His grandfather Asael Smith, unable at the time to pay the debts on the family farm, sold the farm, liquidated the debts, and migrated in 1791 to Tunbridge, Vermont, where he purchased enough land to provide for his sons. Joseph Smith's Mack ancestors, from Scotland, settled in Lyme, Connecticut, prospered for a while, and then fell on hard times. Joseph's grandfather Solomon Mack attempted various enterprises in New England and New York, with little financial success. One of the Mack sons moved to Tunbridge, and through him Lucy Mack met Joseph Smith, Sr., one of Asael's sons. The pair married in 1796. They had eleven children, nine of whom lived to adulthood. Joseph Smith, Jr., born December 23, 1805, in Sharon, Vermont, was the third son to live and the fourth child.

Young Joseph had little formal schooling. His parents lost their Tunbridge farm in 1803 through a failed business venture and for the next fourteen years moved from one tenant farm to another. In 1816 they migrated to Palmyra, New York, just north of the Finger Lakes, where in 1817 they purchased a farm in Farmington (later Manchester), the township immediately south of Palmyra. Clearing land and wresting a living from the soil left little time for school. "As it required the exertions of all that were able to render any assistance for the support of the Family," Joseph wrote in 1832, "we were deprived of the bennifit of an education suffice it to say I was

mearly instructid in reading writing and the ground rules of Arithmatic which constuted my whole literary acquirements" (Jessee, 1989, 1:5). His mother described him as "much less inclined to the perusal of books than any of the rest of the children, but far more given to meditation and deep study" (Smith, p. 84). His knowledge of the Bible and his biblical style of writing suggest that much of his early education came from that source.

One subject he pondered was religion. His parents had been reared under the influence of New England Congregationalism but, dissatisfied with the preachers around them, they were not regular churchgoers. Both parents had deep religious experiences and an intense longing for salvation, without having a satisfactory way to worship. A few years after settling in Palmyra, Lucy Smith and three of the children joined the Presbyterians; Joseph, Sr., and the others stayed home, Joseph, Jr., among them. Young Joseph was deeply perplexed about which church to join, and the preaching of the revival ministers in the area intensified his uncertainty.

In the spring of 1820, when he was just fourteen, Joseph turned directly to God for guidance. The answer was astonishing. As he prayed in the woods near his house, the Father and the Son appeared to him. Assuring him that his sins were forgiven, the Lord told him that none of the churches were right and that he should join none. Latter-day Saints call this Joseph Smith's first vision, the initial event in the restoration of the gospel. At the time, it made little impression on the people around Joseph Smith. He told a minister about the vision and was rebuffed. Believing the Bible sufficient, ministers were skeptical of direct revelation. The scorn upset Joseph, who had only tried to report his actual experience, and alienated him still further from the churches.

After three years with no further revelations,

Joseph wondered if he still was in favor with God and prayed again for direction and forgiveness. The vision he received on September 21, 1823, set the course of his life for the next seven years. An angel appeared and instructed him about a sacred record of an ancient people. This angel, MORONI₂, told Joseph that he was to obtain the record, written on GOLD PLATES, and translate it. He also told him that God's covenant with ancient Israel was about to be fulfilled, that preparation for the second coming of Christ was about to commence, and that the gospel was to be preached to all nations to prepare a people for Christ's millennial reign. In a vision Joseph saw the hill near his home where the plates were buried. When he went the next day to get the plates, the angel stopped him. He was told that he must wait four years to obtain the plates and that, until then, he was to return each year for instructions. On September 22, 1827, he obtained the plates from which he translated the Book of Mormon (*see* MORONI, VISITATIONS OF).

The discovery of gold plates in a hillside resonated strangely with other experiences of the Smith family. Like many other New Englanders, they were familiar with searches for lost treasure by supernatural means. Joseph Smith's father was reputed to be one of these treasure-seekers, and Joseph Smith himself had found a stone, called a SEER STONE, which reportedly enabled him to find lost objects. Treasure-seekers wanted to employ him to help with their searches. One, a man named Josiah Stowell (sometimes spelled Stoal), hired Joseph and his father in 1825 to dig for a supposed Spanish treasure near Harmony, Pennsylvania. The effort came to nothing, and the Smiths returned home, but the neighbors continued to think of the Smiths as part of the treasure-seeking company. Joseph Smith had to learn, in his four years of waiting, to appreciate the plates solely for their re-

ligious worth and not for their monetary value. The angel forbade Joseph to remove the plates on his first viewing because thoughts of their commercial worth had crossed his mind. Joseph had to learn to focus on the religious purpose of the plates and put aside considerations of their value as gold.

While working in Harmony in 1825, Joseph Smith met Emma Hale at the Hale home where he and his father boarded. He continued seeing her through the next year while working at other jobs in the area, and on January 18, 1827, they married. She was tall, straight, slender, and dark-haired; he stood over six feet tall with broad chest and shoulders, light brown hair, and blue eyes. After the wedding they went to live with the Smith family in Manchester, close to the hill Cumorah where the plates still lay buried.

On September 22, 1827, Joseph Smith went to the hill for the fifth time. This time the angel permitted him to take the plates, with strict instructions to show them to no one. Designing people tried strenuously to get the plates, however, and he was not left in peace to begin translation. Eventually he and Emma were compelled to move, for their safety, to Harmony, near Emma's family.

For the next three years, Joseph's work depended on the support of a few loyal friends who came to his aid and helped buffer him from troublesome inquirers. His open manner inspired confidence, and his candor in simply narrating what had happened to him disarmed skepticism. His brother later wrote that Joseph's youth, his lack of education, and his "whole character and disposition" convinced the family that he was incapable of "giving utterance to anything but the truth" (*William Smith on Mormonism*, Lamoni, Iowa, 1883, pp. 9–10). By the time the translation was completed and the

Book of Mormon published, three or four dozen people believed in his mission and divine gifts.

Martin HARRIS, a prosperous Palmyra farmer, was one of these friends. He helped Joseph move to Harmony and then moved there himself to help with the translation. To enable him to translate, Joseph received with the plates a special instrument called interpreters or URIM AND THUMMIM. As he dictated, Martin Harris wrote (*see* TRANSLATION OF THE BOOK OF MORMON BY JOSEPH SMITH). In the spring of 1828, after three months of work, Martin Harris took the 116 pages of the translation home to show his wife, and they were lost or stolen. This interrupted the translation and left Joseph desolate. Soon after, he received a scathing rebuke in a revelation (D&C 3). About this time, Joseph and Emma's firstborn son died on the day of his birth, June 15, 1828, wrenching Joseph's feelings even further.

Translation resumed in the fall of 1828, continuing intermittently until the spring of 1829. Then Oliver COWDERY, a schoolteacher who learned of the plates from Joseph's parents, believed in Joseph and agreed to take dictation. From April to June 1829 they labored together. When the two friends prayed on May 15 for an understanding of baptism, a messenger who announced himself as John the Baptist appeared, conferred priesthood authority upon them, and instructed them to baptize each other. Oliver later wrote: "These were days never to be forgotten—to sit under the sound of a voice dictated by the inspiration of heaven, awakened the utmost gratitude of this bosom!" (JS—H 1:71n).

Oliver was not the only additional witness to the revelations. When opposition began to build in Harmony, Oliver and Joseph moved in June 1829 to Fayette, New York, to the family home of Oliver's friend David WHITMER. Here again Joseph received needed support from people who believed in him. Once the translation was completed, Joseph was told that others would be allowed to see the plates, which until that time only he had viewed. The angel Moroni appeared to Martin Harris, Oliver Cowdery, and David Whitmer and showed them the gold plates while a voice from heaven declared that the translation was done by the power of God and was true (*see* WITNESSES OF THE BOOK OF MORMON). Joseph's mother reported that Joseph came into the house after this revelation and threw himself down beside her, exclaiming that at last someone else had seen the plates. "Now they know for themselves, that I do not go about to deceive" (Smith, p. 139). His words suggest the pressure he felt in being the only witness of his remarkable experiences.

In March 1830 the Book of Mormon was published, ending one phase of Joseph's life but not his divine mission. Revelations in 1829 instructed him to organize a church. On April 6, 1830, at the Whitmers' house in Fayette, New York, the Church of Christ was organized with Joseph Smith and Oliver Cowdery as first and second elders.

Leadership of the Church set Joseph Smith's life on a new course. Up to this time he had been a young man with a divine gift and a mission to translate the Book of Mormon; now, without any previous organizational experience, he was responsible for organizing a church and leading a people. He had to rely on revelation. Over the next six years, he received many revelations, 90 of which fill 190 pages in the Doctrine and Covenants. They range from instructions on mundane details of administration to exalted depictions of life hereafter. Typically, when problems had to be solved, whether administrative or doctrinal, the Prophet sought divine guidance and by virtue of this help led the Church.

The course the revelations laid out for the new Church was extraordinarily challenging. The Prophet received instructions for ventures reaching halfway across the continent and involving a reorganization of society. At the core of the instruction was the establishment of Zion. Book of Mormon teachings of Christ made reference to a New Jerusalem, a city of Zion that would be established in America (3 Ne. 20:22). Later revelations outlined the nature of the new order. The central concept was the gathering of the pure and honest from among the nations into communities where they could learn to live in unity and love under divine direction, and where temples could be built to administer the sacred ordinances of salvation.

In September–October 1830, missionaries were called to teach Native Americans who resided near the western boundary of Missouri. These missionaries were told that the city of Zion would be located somewhere in that region. Later revelations called for a gathering to Missouri to organize Zion, and a new economic order designed to enable the Saints to live together in unity. Joseph and other leading figures in the Church journeyed to Jackson County, Missouri, in the summer of 1831, and there learned by revelation that the city was to be constructed and a temple built near Independence, Missouri. The gathering was to commence immediately.

When it is remembered that Joseph Smith was not yet twenty-six, and five years earlier was an uneducated farmer notable only for his spiritual gifts, the daring of these plans is hard to comprehend. The magnitude of his conceptions never troubled him. "I intend to lay a foundation that will revolutionize the whole world," he later remarked (HC 6:365). He acted in the certainty that the directions

were from God and that the Church would triumph against all odds.

In the spring of 1831 virtually all Latter-day Saints left New York for Ohio. Joseph and Emma settled in Kirtland, Ohio, near a body of new converts, and for the next six years this was Church headquarters. The other focal point of Church life until 1838 was Missouri, first Independence, the site of the future city of Zion, then northern Missouri. As Latter-day Saints migrated to Missouri, tensions with old settlers increased. In Jackson County, in 1831–1833, and again in Caldwell County, in 1836–1838, efforts to establish Zion aroused violent opposition to what non-Mormons perceived as a threat to their way of life.

Joseph Smith also made efforts to realize his vision of Zion during the seven years that the Latter-day Saints were in Ohio. He organized the first stakes and set up the presiding priesthood structure of the Church. The Prophet established a bank, a newspaper, and a printing office; he supervised the building of the Church's first temple, and initiated extensive missionary work in the United States, Canada, and England. His revelations, including a law of health, tutored the Saints in the conduct of daily life. He made a translation of the Bible. He introduced a school system to prepare the Saints for leadership and missionary roles and was himself a student of Hebrew in the school. The high point of the Kirtland years was the dedication of the temple. Although Joseph Smith had received priesthood authority several years earlier, in 1836, in the Kirtland Temple, he received important additional keys of authority from Moses, Elias, and Elijah pertaining to the gathering of Israel and the eternal sealing of families.

Opposition had beset the Prophet from the time he first told people about his visions. In 1832 he was tarred, feathered, and beaten by a mob who broke into the house where he was staying at Hiram, Ohio, an intrusion that led to the death of a child. At Kirtland, dissent arose within the Church over the nature of the new society and the Prophet's involvement in economics and politics; some accused him of attempting to control their private lives and labeled him a fallen prophet. By early 1838, opposition, especially among Ohio leadership, grew to the point that the Prophet and loyal members moved to Missouri.

Joseph Smith arrived with his family at Far West, Caldwell County, Missouri, in March 1838, where he sought once again to establish a gathering place for the Saints and to build a temple. But, as before, the influx of outsiders with differing social, religious, and economic practices was unacceptable to the old settlers. Opposition flared into violence at Gallatin, Daviess County, on August 6, 1838, when enemies of the Church tried to prevent Latter-day Saints from voting. The ensuing fight produced injuries on both sides. A subsequent misunderstanding with a local justice of the peace led to charges against the Prophet. As rumors spread, citizens of several counties, then militias, mobilized to expel the Latter-day Saints.

The crisis came to a head on October 31, 1838, when Joseph Smith and several others, expecting to discuss ways to defuse the volatile situation, were arrested—it was the beginning of five months of confinement. A November court of inquiry at Richmond, Ray County, accused the Prophet and others with acts of treason connected with the conflict and committed them to Liberty Jail to await trial. Meanwhile, the Saints were driven from the state.

Harsh imprisonment made worse by forced separation from his family and the Church left Joseph time to reflect on the meaning of human suffering. His writings from prison contain some of the most sublime

passages of his ministry. Excerpts from his letters were added to the collection of his revelations. Acknowledging all that he had experienced, one of the revelations reminded him that however great his sufferings, they did not exceed the Savior's: "The Son of Man hath descended below them all. Art thou greater than he?" (D&C 122:8).

The following April, while being taken under guard to Boone County, Missouri, for a change in venue, the Prophet and his fellow prisoners were allowed to escape. Within a month of rejoining family and friends at Quincy, Illinois, Joseph Smith had authorized the purchase of land on the Mississippi River near Commerce, Hancock County, Illinois, and had moved his family into a two-room log cabin. During the summer of 1839, the Saints began settling their new gathering place, which they named Nauvoo.

Like many areas along the river bottoms, Nauvoo was at first poorly drained and disease-infested. During a malaria epidemic, the Prophet gave up his home to the sick and lived in a tent. Witnesses reported miraculous healing under his administration. "There was many sick among the saints on both sides of the river and Joseph went through the midst of them taking them by the hand and in a loud voice commanding them in the name of Jesus Christ to arise from their beds and be made whole" (Wilford Woodruff Diary, July 22, 1839, Ms., LDS Church Archives). Deaths were so frequent that a mass funeral was held.

Late in 1839 the Prophet traveled to Washington, D.C., to seek redress from the federal government for losses sustained by his people in Missouri. While there he obtained interviews with President Martin Van Buren and prominent congressmen, but came away frustrated and without relief.

Nauvoo was soon incorporated under the state-authorized Nauvoo charter. Within the

The Joseph Smith homestead in Nauvoo. The Prophet and his family lived here from 1839 to 1843. About 1856 the Prophet's son Joseph Smith III added the larger part of the building to the west. © by Intellectual Reserve, Inc. Used by permission. Note: Photo differs from that in the *Encyclopedia*.

next few years the city grew to rival Chicago as the largest in Illinois. Joseph served on the city council and eventually became mayor. As mayor he also served as presiding judge of the municipal court and as registrar of deeds. With the rank of lieutenant general, he led the Nauvoo Legion, or municipal militia. He was also proprietor of a merchandise store and became editor and publisher of the newspaper *Times and Seasons*.

The relative security of Nauvoo provided Joseph Smith with an opportunity to move forward the work of the kingdom with renewed vigor. He sent the Quorum of the Twelve Apostles to Great Britain, where they expanded missionary work and launched an emigration program that provided a stream of immigrants into the new place of gathering. At Nauvoo the Prophet organized the first wards, the basic geographical units of the Church. He expanded the ecclesiastical authority of the Twelve to include jurisdiction within stakes, placing them for the first time in a position of universal authority over the Church under the First Presidency. He supervised the building of the Nauvoo Temple

and established the Female Relief Society of Nauvoo.

The Prophet faced a dilemma as he began to restore long-lost divine principles. Prompted by forebodings that his remaining time was short, he wished to hasten his efforts, but because many did not understand his mission and opposed him, he had to move slowly. "I could explain a hundred fold more than I ever have of the glories of the kingdoms manifested to me . . . were the people prepared to receive them," he wrote in 1843 (*HC* 5:402). To resolve this dilemma, the Prophet presented some principles privately to a small number of faithful members, intending to plant the seeds before he died. As early as 1841, he introduced plural marriage, a necessary part of the restoration of the ancient order of things, to members of the Twelve and a few others. Although he had understood the principle since 1831 and apparently had married one plural wife several years earlier, he married his first recorded plural wife, Louisa Beaman, in 1841. During his remaining years, he married at least twenty-seven others.

In May 1842 the Prophet introduced the full endowment, religious ordinances subsequently observed in all LDS temples, to a small group in the upper room of his Nauvoo store. A year later he performed the first sealings of married couples for time and eternity. In addition, he taught the Saints important doctrines pertaining to the nature of God and man. In March 1844 he organized the council of fifty, the political arm of the kingdom of God. By the time of his death three months later, he had completed all that he felt was essential for the continuation of the kingdom. By then he had transferred to the Twelve the keys of authority, confident that the program he had initiated would now continue regardless of what befell him.

Teaching these principles privately to a small circle enabled Joseph Smith to fulfill his mission but complicated the situation at Nauvoo and unleashed forces that eventually led to his death. Some Saints had difficulty in accepting these unusual teachings. Upon being taught plural marriage, Brigham Young said it was the first time in his life that he had desired the grave. Joseph's wife Emma at one point became "very bitter and full of resentment" ["Statement of William Clayton," *Woman's Exponent* 15 (June 1, 1886): 2]. As knowledge of the private teachings leaked into the community, speculation and distorted rumors proliferated.

While the Prophet pursued his objectives, forces outside the Church organized against him. Missouri authorities tried three times to extradite him from Illinois, resulting in lengthy periods of legal harassment. Because of the loss of property in earlier persecutions, he was unable to pay his debts and had to fend off creditors. When Illinois political leaders turned against the Latter-day Saints and no national leaders would champion their cause, the Prophet declared his candidacy for president of the United States, gaining a platform from which to discuss the rights of his people.

By April 1844, dissenters openly challenged Joseph Smith's leadership by organizing a reform church and publishing a newspaper, the *Nauvoo Expositor*, for the purpose of denouncing him. Perceiving the *Expositor* as a threat to the peace of the community, the Nauvoo city council, with Joseph Smith presiding as mayor, authorized him to order the destruction of the press—an act that ignited the opposition. On June 12 the Prophet was charged with riot for destruction of the press. After a flurry of legal maneuvers, Joseph submitted to arrest at nearby Carthage, the county seat, under the governor's pledge of

protection. Joseph had premonitions of danger, and the vocal threats of hotheads in adjoining towns gave substance to his fears. On June 27, 1844, while in Carthage Jail awaiting a hearing, Joseph Smith and his brother Hyrum were killed when a mob with blackened faces stormed the jail. The next day the brothers' bodies were returned to Nauvoo, where ten thousand Latter-day Saints gathered to mourn the loss of their Prophet.

Despite the adversity that dogged him from youth until death, Joseph Smith was not the somber, forbidding person his contemporaries generally envisioned in the personality of a prophet. An English convert wrote that Joseph was "no saintish long-faced fellow, but quite the reverse" [John Needham to Thomas Ward, July 7, 1843, *Latter-Day Saints' Millennial Star* 4 (Oct. 1843): 89]. It was not uncommon to see him involved in sports activities with the young and vigorous men of a community. He is known to have wrestled, pulled sticks, engaged in snowball fights, played ball, slid on the ice with his children, played marbles, shot at a mark, and fished. Tall and well built, Joseph Smith did not hesitate to use his strength. Once in his youth he thrashed a man for wife-beating. In 1839, as he was en route to Washington, D.C., by stagecoach, the horses bolted while the driver was away. Opening the door of the speeding coach, the Prophet climbed up its side into the driver's seat, where he secured the reins and stopped the horses.

Joseph was also deeply spiritual. His mother said of him that in his youth he "seemed to reflect more deeply than common persons of his age upon everything of a religious nature" (Lucy Smith, "Biographical Sketches of Joseph Smith," preliminary manuscript, p. 46, LDS Church Archives). When he was just twelve, as he later wrote, his mind became "seriously imprest with regard to the all important concerns for the wellfare of my immortal Soul" (*PJS* 1:5). Years after he began receiving revelations, he continued to seek spiritual comfort. In 1832 while on a journey, he wrote of visiting a grove "which is Just back of the town almost every day where I can be Secluded from the eyes of any mortal and there give vent to all the feelings of my heart in meaditation and prayr" (*PWJS*, p. 238). Clearly he spoke from the heart in declaring that "the things of God are of deep import: and time, and experience, and careful and ponderous and solemn thoughts can only find them out" (*HC* 3:295).

Joseph Smith deeply loved his family, and his personal writings are filled with prayerful outpourings of tenderness and concern. "O Lord bless my little children with health and long life to do good in this generation for Christs sake Amen" (*PWJS*, p. 28). His family consisted of eleven children, including adopted twins. Of these, four sons and a daughter died in infancy or early childhood; five were living when their father was killed, and a sixth, a son, was born four months after his death. Occasional glimpses into his family life show him sliding on the ice with his son Frederick, taking his children on a pleasure ride in a carriage or sleigh, and attending the circus.

He was also a loyal friend and cared deeply about others. He repeatedly extended a forgiving hand to prodigals, some of whom had caused him pain and misery. "I feel myself bound to be a friend to all . . . wether they are just or unjust; they have a degree of my compassion & sympathy" (*PWJS*, p. 548). One observer noted that the Prophet would never go to bed if he knew there was a sick person who needed assistance. He taught that "love is one of the leading characteristics of Deity, and ought to be manifested by those who aspire to be the sons of God. A man filled with the love of God, is not content with blessing his family alone but ranges through the world, anxious to bless the whole of the human family" (*PWJS*, p. 481). One Church member who stayed at the Smith home and witnessed the Prophet's "earnest and humble devotions . . . nourishing, soothing, and comforting his family, neighbours, and friends," found observation of his private life a greater witness of Joseph Smith's divine calling than observing his public actions (*JD* 7:176–77).

Joseph Smith spent his life bringing forth a new dispensation of religious knowledge at great personal cost. He noted that "the envy and wrath of man" had been his common lot and that "deep water" was what he was "wont to swim in" (*D&C* 127:2). A little more than a year before his death he told an audience in Nauvoo, "If I had not actually got into this work and been called of God, I would back out. But I cannot back out: I have no doubt of the truth" (*HC* 5:336). He lived in the hope of bringing that truth to life in a society of Saints, and died the victim of enemies who did not understand his vision.

BIBLIOGRAPHY

Anderson, Richard L. *Joseph Smith's New England Heritage*. Salt Lake City, 1971.

Brodie, Fawn M. *No Man Knows My History*. New York, 1946.

Bushman, Richard L. *Joseph Smith and the Beginnings of Mormonism*. Urbana, Ill., 1984.

Ehat, Andrew F., and Lyndon W. Cook. *The Words of Joseph Smith: The Contemporary Accounts of the Nauvoo Discourses of the Prophet Joseph*. Provo, Utah, 1980.

Gibbons, Francis M. *Joseph Smith: Martyr, Prophet of God*. Salt Lake City, 1982.

Hill, Donna. *Joseph Smith, The First Mormon*. Garden City, New York, 1977.

Jessee, Dean C., ed. *PWJS*. Salt Lake City, 1984.

———. *The Papers of Joseph Smith*. Salt Lake City, 1989.

Millet, Robert L., ed., *Joseph Smith: Selected Sermons and Writings*. New York, 1989.

Porter, Larry C., and Susan Easton Black, eds. *The Prophet Joseph: Essays on the Life and Mission of Joseph Smith.* Salt Lake City, 1988.

Smith, Lucy. *Biographical Sketches of Joseph Smith the Prophet.* Liverpool, 1853.

RICHARD L. BUSHMAN

DEAN C. JESSEE

SPAULDING MANUSCRIPT

The Spaulding Manuscript is a fictional story about a group of Romans who, while sailing to England early in the fourth century A.D., were blown off course and landed in eastern North America. One of them kept a record of their experiences among eastern and midwestern American Indian tribes. The 175-page manuscript was first published as a 115-page monograph in 1885, some seventy years after the death of its author, Solomon Spaulding (sometimes spelled Spalding). The only known manuscript was lost from 1839 until its discovery in Honolulu, Hawaii, in 1884. It was promptly published by both the Latter-day Saints and Reorganized Latter Day Saint churches to refute the theory of some critics that it had served as an original source document for the Book of Mormon, supposedly supplied to Joseph Smith by Sidney Rigdon.

Spaulding was born in Ashford, Connecticut, on February 21, 1761. He served in the American Revolution, later graduated from Dartmouth College, and became a clergyman. He subsequently lost his faith in the Bible, left the ministry, and worked unsuc-

cessfully at a variety of occupations in New York, Ohio, and Pennsylvania until his death near Pittsburgh in 1816. About 1812 he wrote *Manuscript Found*, which he attempted to publish to relieve pressing debts.

There are similarities in the explanation for the origins of both *Manuscript Found* and the Book of Mormon. The introduction to the Spaulding work claims that its author was walking near Conneaut, Ohio (about 150 miles west of the place in New York where Joseph Smith obtained the gold plates), when he discovered an inscribed, flat stone. This he raised with a lever, uncovering a cave in which lay a stone box containing twenty-eight rolls of parchment. The writing was in Latin. The story is primarily a secular one, having virtually no religious content. A character in the novel possessed a seerstone, similar to objects used by Joseph Smith. However, none of the many names found in either volume matches any of those in the other, nor is there the remotest similarity in literary styles.

The first to assert that a direct connection existed between the Book of Mormon and *Manuscript Found* was Doctor Philastus Hurlbut, who was excommunicated from the Church in June 1833. Desiring to discredit his former coreligionists, Hurlbut set out in the ensuing months to refute Joseph Smith's claims for the origins of the Book of Mormon. He interviewed members of Spaulding's family, who swore that there were precise similarities between Spaulding's work and the Book of Mormon. He also located the neglected manuscript, but must have been disappointed to discover that it had no demonstrable connection with the Book of Mormon.

In 1834, Hurlbut was involved with Eber D. Howe in preparing a significant anti-Mormon publication, *Mormonism Unvailed*. Its final chapter dealt with the Spaulding theory of the origin of the Book of Mormon. Howe admitted in the book that the only document known to have been authored by Spaulding had been found, but he asserted that this was not *Manuscript Found*. The title penciled on the brown paper cover was *Manuscript Story—Conneaut Creek*. Howe speculated that Spaulding must have composed another manuscript that served as the source of the Book of Mormon, but no additional writings of Spaulding have ever surfaced. By the 1840s, the so-called Spaulding theory had become the main anti-Mormon explanation for the Book of Mormon.

Spaulding's manuscript, lost for forty-five years, was among items shipped from the office of the Ohio *Painesville Telegraph*, owned by Eber D. Howe, when that office was purchased in 1839 by L. L. Rice, who subsequently moved to Honolulu. Rice discovered the manuscript in 1884 while searching his collection for abolitionist materials for his friend James H. Fairchild, president of Oberlin College. Believers in the Book of Mormon felt vindicated by this discovery, and they published Spaulding's work to show the world it was not the source for the Book of Mormon.

Since 1946, no serious student of Mormonism has given the Spaulding Manuscript theory much credibility. In that year, Fawn Brodie published *No Man Knows My History*. This biography of Joseph Smith, hostile to his prophetic claims, dismissed the idea of any connection between Spaulding and Smith or their writings. Rigdon first met Joseph Smith in December 1830 after the Book of Mormon was published.

Nevertheless, some have continued to promote the Spaulding theory (e.g., see Holley). In 1977, graphologists claimed to have detected similarities between the handwriting of Spaulding and of one of the scribes who transcribed some of the Book of Mormon from Joseph Smith's dictation. After considerable media attention and further scrutiny, anti-Mormon spokespersons acknowledged that they had been too hasty. The handwriting evidence did not support a connection between Solomon Spaulding and Joseph Smith.

BIBLIOGRAPHY

Bush, Lester E., Jr. "The Spaulding Theory Then and Now." *Dialogue* 4 (Autumn 1977): 40–69.

Bushman, Richard L. *Joseph Smith and the Beginnings of Mormonism*. Urbana, Ill., 1985.

Fairchild, James H. "Manuscript of Solomon Spaulding and the Book of Mormon." *Bibliotheca Sacra*, pp. 173–74. Cleveland, Ohio, 1885.

Holley, Vernal. "Book of Mormon Authorship: A Closer Look." Ogden, Utah, 1983; this booklet is reviewed by A. Norwood, *Review of Books on the Book of Mormon* 1 (1989): 80–88.

LANCE D. CHASE

STUDIES OF THE BOOK OF MORMON

Since the publication of the BOOK OF MORMON in 1830, a substantial amount of material analyzing, defending, and attacking it has been published. Studies of this complex record have taken various approaches, for the book itself invites close scrutiny and rewards patient and reflective research.

For most Latter-day Saints the primary purpose of scripture study is not to prove to themselves the truth of scriptural records—which they already accept—but to gain wisdom and understanding about the teachings of these sacred writings and to apply in daily life gospel principles learned there. Because of the origins of the Book of Mormon, however, many people have also explored the secondary features of this document: its vocabulary, style, factual assertions, main themes, and subtle nuances.

Book of Mormon research has generally followed many of the same forms as biblical research. In both fields, writings range from expository texts to doctrinal, historical, geographical, textual, literary, and comparative commentaries. But there are also several salient differences. For example, unlike the authors of the Bible, the prophets, compilers, and abridgers of the Book of Mormon frequently state explicitly the dates when they worked, their purposes in writing, and the sources from which they drew, thus clarifying many compositional and interpretive issues; furthermore, academic and archaeological studies of the Book of Mormon are more limited than in biblical research because the earliest extant text is Joseph SMITH's 1829 English translation and the precise locations of Book of Mormon settlements are unknown. Nevertheless, a significant number of internal and comparative analyses have been pursued. The works of the following individuals are most notable.

ALEXANDER CAMPBELL. The founder of the Disciples of Christ and a colleague of Sidney Rigdon before Rigdon converted to Mormonism, Alexander Campbell (1788–1866) composed a response to the Book of Mormon that he published on February 7, 1831, in his paper the *Millennial Harbinger* (reprinted as a pamphlet called *Delusions*). In it, Campbell challenged the idea that the Book of Mormon had been written by multiple ancient prophets and attacked the character of Joseph Smith. He said that the book was solely the product of Joseph Smith, written by him alone and "certainly conceived in one cranium" (p. 13). Campbell claimed that the book simply represents the reflections of Joseph Smith on the social, political, and religious controversies of his day: "infant baptism, ordination, the trinity, regeneration, repentance, justification, the fall of man, the atonement, transubstantiation, fasting, penance, church government, religious experience, the call to the ministry, the general resurrection, eternal punishment, who may baptize, and even the question of freemasonry, republican government, and the rights of man" (p. 13). He also asserted that the Book of Mormon misunderstands Israelite and Jewish history (portraying the Nephites as Christians hundreds of years before the birth of Christ) and is written in abysmal English grammar. Campbell characterized Joseph Smith as a "knave" who was "ignorant" and "impudent" (p. 11). *Delusions* is significant among Book of Mormon studies because in many ways it set the agenda for most subsequent critiques of the Book of Mormon (e.g., that the book derives from, or responds to, various trends in early-nineteenth-century upstate New York). Subsequently, however, Campbell changed his position, adopting the Spaulding-Rigdon theory, according to which Sidney Rigdon purloined a copy of a manuscript by Solomon Spaulding, developed from it what became the Book of Mormon, which he passed on to Joseph Smith in the late 1820s, and later pretended to have met Joseph for the first time in 1830 (*see* SPAULDING MANUSCRIPT).

ORSON PRATT. In *Divine Authenticity of the Book of Mormon* (1850–1851), a series of six pamphlets, Orson Pratt (1811–1881), a member of the Quorum of the Twelve Apostles, drew together early Latter-day Saint thinking about the Book of Mormon. He argued on logical grounds for the divine authenticity of the Book of Mormon, confronted criticisms of it, and presented evidence in favor of its truth, relying heavily on biblical and historical evidences. He did not discuss the contents of the Book of Mormon directly, but addressed ideas of other churches that hindered their acceptance, or even serious consideration, of the Book of Mormon.

The first three pamphlets discussed the nature of revelation, giving evidence to support Pratt's claim that continued communication from God is both necessary and scriptural. The final three pamphlets reported on many witnesses who received heavenly visions substantiating Joseph Smith's claims (*see* WITNESSES OF THE BOOK OF MORMON), and asserted that the divinity of the Book of Mormon is confirmed by many miracles, similar to those recorded in the Bible, experienced by Latter-day Saints. Finally, he appealed to prophetic evidence for the Book of Mormon, taken from Daniel and Isaiah. In an 1872 discourse, Pratt proposed a geography for the Book of Mormon that has greatly influenced LDS thinking (*see* GEOGRAPHY).

GEORGE REYNOLDS AND JANNE M. SJODAHL. During the nineteenth century, most defenses of, and attacks on, the Book of Mormon were based primarily on reason, on examinations of the environment contemporary with the book, or on the Bible. But George Reynolds (1842–1909) and Janne M. Sjodahl (1853–1939), in their seven-volume Commentary on the Book of Mormon (reissued 1955–1961), investigated the plausibility of the claims of the Book of Mormon by examining external evidences of a historical, cultural, linguistic, or religious nature from the Old World and the New. Although their examples and explanations are often not heavily documented and were sometimes mistaken, this work was the first major effort to study the cultural and historical contexts of the Book of Mormon (i.e., to place the book in a historical context by adducing relevant materials from the ancient world).

George Reynolds (1842–1909) held many Church positions in England before coming to America in 1865. He served as secretary to the First Presidency until the end of his life and was called as one of the First Seven Presidents of the Seventy in 1890. He was the first to write extensive commentaries on the Book of Mormon. His Book of Mormon concordance required twenty-one years to produce. © by Intellectual Reserve, Inc. Used by permission.

Whereas in *The Story of the Book of Mormon*, an earlier work, Reynolds had agreed with Orson Pratt on Book of Mormon geography, in their *Commentary* he and Sjodahl placed geography at a low level of priority and were interested primarily in establishing an internally consistent map of all Book of Mormon sites, without attempting to identify those sites with modern locations (Reynolds, pp. 19, 49, 301–330; Reynolds and Sjodahl, Vol. 1, pp. ix–xi). Reynolds eventually authored nearly three hundred articles and several Book of Mormon resource works. Sjodahl published *An Introduction to the Study of the Book of Mormon*, featuring a wide variety of cultural and linguistic theories.

B. H. ROBERTS. Among the most influential Latter-day Saint writers of his time, B. H. Roberts (1857–1933) wrote widely on a variety of Church-related topics, including the Book of Mormon. Like Reynolds and Sjodahl, he was interested not only in the theological implications of the Book of Mormon but also in its historical, geographical, and cultural setting (1909, Vol. 2, pp. 143–44, 162, 347–458; Vol. 3, pp. 3–92). Roberts was not afraid to ask difficult—and, for him, sometimes unanswerable—questions about the Book of Mormon, but affirmed his faith in the Book of Mormon to the end of his life (1985, pp. 61–148; J. Welch, *Ensign* 16 [Mar. 1986]: 58–62).

FRANCIS KIRKHAM. In his two-volume study *A New Witness for Christ in America* (1942), Francis Kirkham (1877–1972) examined the 1820s' historical evidence relating to the coming forth of the Book of Mormon. Kirkham showed that the testimonies of Joseph Smith and his friends are consistent and coherent, while those of his enemies are frequently inconsistent and contradictory. He carefully documented how alternative explanations for the origin of the Book of Mormon sometimes changed or were abandoned. While favoring the traditional view of Book of Mormon origins, Kirkham allowed all to speak for themselves with little commentary. He liberally presented the primary materials, published and unpublished, from libraries and archives across the United States. His use of the widest available range of primary sources set a new standard in the study of the origins of the Book of Mormon.

Kirkham's second volume of *A New Witness for Christ in America* (1951) examined the alternative explanations of Book of Mormon origins. Regarding the assertion that Joseph Smith wrote the book personally, Kirkham presented statements of some who knew Jo-

seph well, with views representing both sides of the issue of whether he was capable of writing such a book. Kirkham also gave extensive evidence to show that the Spaulding hypothesis was fraught with difficulties. The theory provides only the most circumstantial and dubious evidence for Rigdon's theft of the manuscript and for his passing it on to Joseph Smith with no one else's knowledge. Even though the Spaulding hypothesis has fallen into disfavor as an explanation of the Book of Mormon during the past several decades, it is still occasionally revived.

HUGH W. NIBLEY. In his considerable

Hugh W. Nibley (1910–   ), noted linguist and historian of religion, was one of the first to detect and explore numerous cultural similarities between ancient Near Eastern literatures and Book of Mormon texts. His candid wit and wide-ranging insights emphasize the relevance of the Book of Mormon to modern world circumstances. Photographer: Mark A. Philbrick (1989). Courtesy FARMS.

corpus of writings on the Book of Mormon, written over a period of some forty years, Hugh W. Nibley (b. 1910) has taken several approaches, mainly historical contextualization based on the internal claims of the Book of Mormon as a document of people who come from the ancient Near East, but also testing the book for authenticity on the basis of internal evidence alone, and seeing the fateful collapse of mighty civilizations as an ominous warning to people today.

In *Lehi in the Desert* (1949–1952), after reviewing the great American archaeologist William F. Albright's criteria for determining the historical plausibility of ancient accounts, Nibley asks these questions about the story of Lehi: "Does it correctly reflect 'the cultural horizon and religious and social ideas and practices of the time'? Does it have authentic historical and geographical background? Is the *mise-en-scène* mythical, highly imaginative, or extravagantly improbable? Is its local color correct, and are its proper names convincing?" (CWHN 5:4). The proper approach to the Book of Mormon, according to Nibley, is simply to give the book the benefit of the doubt, granting that it is what it claims to be (a historically authentic ancient document of a people who originated in ancient Israel) and then testing the internal evidence of the book itself (names, cultural and religious ideas) against what can be known about the ancient Near East. When this is done, a picture emerges that is strikingly consistent with what can be determined about the ancient Near East. Most of Nibley's examples come from the Arabs, Egyptians, and Israelites.

With wit and erudition, Nibley argues against alternative explanations of the Book of Mormon. For example, in discussing Thomas O'Dea's environmentalist assertion that the book is obviously an American work, Nibley calls for greater specificity and uniqueness of the American sentiments that allegedly permeate the work (CWHN 8:185–86). With skillful parry and thrust, Nibley proceeds in his studies on the Book of Mormon, sometimes defending points in the book, sometimes taking the offensive against those who attack it, always enriching the reader's understanding of its setting. As a teacher, lecturer, and writer, Nibley has been widely influential on subsequent studies of the Book of Mormon.

JOHN L. SORENSON. Devoting his attention to Mesoamerica in an effort to understand better the geographical, anthropological, and cultural setting of Book of Mormon PEOPLES, John L. Sorenson (b. 1924) examines the text of the Book of Mormon. He carefully analyzes the Mesoamerican evidence, particularly the geography, climatic conditions, modes of life and warfare, and archaeological remains in *An Ancient American Setting for the Book of Mormon*, in order to create a plausible, coherent matrix for understanding the book. With regard to Book of Mormon geography, Sorenson concludes that the events recorded in the Book of Mormon occurred in a fairly restricted area of southern Mexico and Guatemala:

> The narrow neck of land is the Isthmus of Tehuantepec. The east sea is the Gulf of Mexico or its component, the Gulf of Campeche. The west sea is the Pacific Ocean to the west of Mexico and Guatemala. The land southward comprises that portion of Mexico east and south of the Isthmus of Tehuantepec. . . . The land northward consists of part of Mexico west and north of the Isthmus of Tehuantepec. . . . The final battleground where both Jaredite and Nephite peoples met their end was around the Tuxtla Mountains of south-central Veracruz. (pp. 46–47)

An Ancient American Setting for the Book of

Mormon has placed the study of the ancient American background of the Book of Mormon on a scholarly footing as no previous work (*see* GEOGRAPHY).

CURRENT DIRECTIONS IN BOOK OF MORMON STUDIES. Much of the scholarly work on the Book of Mormon has been devoted to a fuller understanding of its theological riches or concerned with applying the Book of Mormon principle to "liken all scriptures unto us" (1 Ne. 19:23). Some of the recent publications of the Religious Studies Center at Brigham Young University have focused on various theological aspects of the Book of Mormon and on seeking life applications from the book (e.g., essays by various authors in Cheesman, in McConkie and Millet, and in Nyman and Tate).

Following the lead of Nibley, Sorenson, and others, several recent studies on the Book of Mormon have been concerned with enhancing an understanding of its Old World background and American setting. The research and publications of the Foundation for Ancient Research and Mormon Studies (FARMS), the Society for Early Historic Archaeology (SEHA), and the Archaeological Research Institute have been particularly concerned with the historical and geographic context of the Book of Mormon.

In certain circles, one of the major focuses in current Book of Mormon studies is concerned with its historicity. Whereas in the past, positions on the Book of Mormon divided themselves roughly between those who accepted it as an inspired and historically authentic ancient document and those who rejected it in both these regards, several different lines of approach have developed.

According to one view—a position that has existed since even before its first publication—the Book of Mormon is a conscious fabrication of Joseph Smith. Those holding to this view see the book as reflecting no inspiration and having no historical value, although they may see some religious value in it as a statement of Joseph Smith's religious feelings. The assumption underlying this view may be either a doctrinaire rejection of divine intervention in human affairs or a specific rejection of Joseph Smith's claims to experience with the divine. Those maintaining this position may accept either the Spaulding theory or, more commonly, various environmentalist explanations for the contents of the book (*see* VIEW OF THE HEBREWS). One environmentalist explanation that has attracted some interest in the recent past among both believers and nonbelievers is based on the purported "magic worldview" that suffused the environment in which Joseph Smith grew up. However, this position has been heavily criticized and has not been widely received.

Another view of the Book of Mormon accepts its inspiration but rejects its historical authenticity, seeing it as in some sense inspired but not the product of antiquity, coming rather from the pen of Joseph Smith.

A third position accepts parts of the Book of Mormon as ancient, but views other parts of the book as inspired expansions on the text. This view has suffered because a concession that any part of the book is authentically ancient (and beyond the powers of Joseph Smith to have established through research) seems an admission that the Book of Mormon is what it claims to be and what has traditionally been claimed for it: that it is ancient.

While these views have been articulated by some members in the LDS community, the majority of LDS students of the Book of Mormon accept the traditional view of its divine authenticity and study it as both an ancient document and a tract for modern days, thereby enhancing their appreciation of, and benefit from, the book.

BIBLIOGRAPHY

For bibliographies, see annual issues of the *Review of Books on the Book of Mormon* and John W. Welch, Gary P. Gillum, and DeeAnn Hofer, *Comprehensive Bibliography of the Book of Mormon*, FARMS Report, Provo, Utah, 1982. For essays on Pratt, Reynolds, Roberts, Kirkham, Sperry, and Nibley, see articles in the *Ensign*, 1984–1986.

Bush, Lester E., Jr. "The Spalding Theory Then and Now." *Dialogue* 10 (Autumn 1977): 40–69.

Cheesman, Paul R., ed. *The Book of Mormon: The Keystone Scripture.* Provo, Utah, 1988.

Clark, John. "A Key for Evaluating Nephite Geographies" (review of F. Richard Hauck, *Deciphering the Geography of the Book of Mormon*). *Review of Books on the Book of Mormon* 1 (1989): 20–70.

Kirkham, Francis W. *A New Witness for Christ in America*, rev. ed., 2 vols. Salt Lake City, 1959–1960.

McConkie, Joseph Fielding, Robert L. Millet, and Brent L. Top. *Doctrinal Commentary on the Book of Mormon*, 4 vols. Salt Lake City, 1987–1992.

Nibley, Hugh W. *Lehi in the Desert/The World of the Jaredites/There Were Jaredites; An Approach to the Book of Mormon; Since Cumorah;* and *The Prophetic Book of Mormon.* In CWHN 5–8.

Nyman, Monte S., and Charles D. Tate, Jr., eds. *The Book of Mormon: First Nephi, The Doctrinal Foundation; Second Nephi, The Doctrinal Structure; Jacob through Words of Mormon, to Learn with Joy.* Provo, Utah, 1988–1990.

Reynolds, George. *The Story of the Book of Mormon.* Salt Lake City, 1888.

———, and Janne M. Sjodahl. *Commentary on the Book of Mormon*, 5th ed., 7 vols. Salt Lake City, 1972.

Reynolds, Noel B., ed. *Book of Mormon Authorship: New Light on Ancient Origins.* Provo, Utah, 1982.

Ricks, Stephen D., and William J. Hamblin, eds. *Warfare in the Book of Mormon.* Salt Lake City, 1990.

Roberts, B. H. *New Witnesses for God*, Vols. 2–3. Salt Lake City, 1909.

———. *Studies of the Book of Mormon*, ed. B. Madsen. Urbana, Ill., 1985.

Sjodahl, Janne M. *An Introduction to the Study of the Book of Mormon.* Salt Lake City, 1927.

Sorenson, John L. *An Ancient American Setting for the Book of Mormon.* Salt Lake City, 1985.

Sperry, Sidney B. *Book of Mormon Compendium.* Salt Lake City, 1968.

ADDITIONAL SOURCE

Parry, Donald W., Jeanette W. Miller, and Sandra A. Thorne, eds. *A Comprehensive Annotated Book of Mormon Bibliography.* Provo, Utah: Research Press, 1996.

STEPHEN D. RICKS

SWORD OF LABAN

Laban, a Book of Mormon contemporary of NEPHI₁ in Jerusalem (c. 600 B.C.), possessed a unique sword. "The hilt thereof was of pure gold, and the workmanship thereof was exceedingly fine, and . . . the blade thereof was of the most precious steel" (1 Ne. 4:9). Nephi was "constrained by the Spirit" to kill Laban (1 Ne. 4:10). Among other things he had opposed the Lord's imperative to relinquish the plates and had "sought to take away" Nephi's life (1 Ne. 4:11). Using Laban's "own sword," Nephi slew him (1 Ne. 4:18), retained the sword, and brought it to the Western Hemisphere.

Nephi made many swords "after the

The gold-hilted daggar (left) with a blade of rare nonmeteoric iron, from the tomb of Tutankhamun (d. 1325 B.C.), is reminiscent of another treasure, the sword of Laban (c. 600 B.C.), described in the Book of Mormon: "the hilt thereof was of pure gold, and the workmanship thereof was exceedingly fine, and I saw that the blade thereof was the most precious steel" (1 Ne. 4:9). Courtesy the Egyptian Government.

manner" of the sword of Laban (2 Ne. 5:14) and used the sword in "defence" of his people (Jacob 1:10), as did King BENJAMIN (W of M 1:13). Benjamin later delivered the sword to his son MOSIAH₂ (Mosiah 1:16). The sword of Laban seems to have been preserved as a sacred object among the Nephites, as was Goliath's sword in ancient Israel (1 Sam. 21:9).

In June 1829 the three WITNESSES to the Book of Mormon plates were promised a view of the sword (D&C 17:1). According to David WHITMER's report, that promise was fulfilled "in the latter part of the month" (Andrew Jenson, *Historical Record*, nos. 3–5, May 1882, Vol. VI, Salt Lake City, p. 208).

President Brigham Young also reported that the Prophet Joseph SMITH and Oliver COWDERY saw the sword of Laban when they entered a cave in the hill CUMORAH with a large room containing many PLATES. "The first time they went there the sword of Laban hung upon the wall; but when they went again it had been taken down and laid upon the table across the gold plates; it was unsheathed, and on it was written these words: 'This sword will never be sheathed again until The Kingdoms of this world become the Kingdom of our God and his Christ'" (JD 19:38).

BIBLIOGRAPHY

Millard, Alan R. "King Og's Bed." *Bible Review*, VI, no. 2 (Apr. 1990): 19. Contains a description of a sword or dagger discovered in Pharaoh Tutankhamen's tomb in 1922 that is remarkably similar to the sword of Laban.

ADDITIONAL SOURCES

Holbrook, Brett L. "The Sword of Laban as a Symbol of Divine Authority and Kingship." *Journal of Book of Mormon Studies* 2/1 (Spring 1993): 39–72.

Rolph, Daniel N. "Prophets, Kings, and Swords: The Sword of Laban and Its Possible Pre-Laban Origin." *Journal of Book of Mormon Studies* 2/1 (Spring 1993): 73–79.

REED A. BENSON

T

THREE NEPHITES

LDS stories of the Three Nephites comprise one of the most striking religious legend cycles in the United States. Bearing some resemblance to stories of the prophet Elijah in Jewish lore, or of the Christian saints in the Catholic tradition, Three Nephite accounts are nevertheless distinctly Mormon. Part of a much larger body of LDS traditional narratives, these stories are not official doctrine and are not published in official literature. They are based on the Book of Mormon account of Christ's granting to three Nephite disciples, during his visit to the New World following his death and resurrection, the same wish he had earlier granted to John the Beloved—to tarry in the flesh in order to bring souls to him until his second coming (see John 21:22; 3 Ne. 28:4–9). The Book of Mormon account states: "And they [the Three Nephites] are as the angels of God, and . . . can show themselves unto whatsoever man it seemeth them good. Therefore, great and marvelous works shall be wrought by them, before the great and coming day [of judg-

ment]" (3 Ne. 28:30–31; *see also* BOOK OF MORMON: THIRD NEPHI).

As the newly founded Church grew in numbers, an ever-increasing body of stories began circulating among the people, telling of kindly old men, usually thought to be these ancient Nephite disciples, who had appeared to individuals in physical or spiritual distress, helped them solve their problems, and then suddenly disappeared.

Because they span a century and a half of LDS history, these narratives mirror well the changing physical and social environments in which Latter-day Saints have met their tests of faith. For example, in pre–World War II agrarian society, the stories told of Nephites' guiding pioneer trains to water holes, saving a rancher from a blizzard, providing herbal remedies for illnesses, plowing a farmer's field so that he could attend to Church duties, or delivering food to starving missionaries. In the contemporary world, the stories tell of Nephites' leading LDS genealogists to difficult library resources, pulling a young man from a lake after a canoeing accident and administering artificial respiration, stopping to fix a widow's furnace, guiding motorists lost in blizzards, comforting a woman who has lost her husband and daughter in an airplane crash, and pulling missionaries from a flaming freeway crash.

Even though the settings of the newer stories have moved from pioneer villages with a country road winding past to urban settings with freeways sounding noisily in the background, some circumstances have remained constant. In the stories, the Three Nephites continue to bless people and, in telling these stories, Latter-day Saints continue to testify to the validity of Church teachings and to encourage obedience to them. The stories continue to provide the faithful with a sense of security in an unsure world, persuading them that just as God helped righteous pioneers overcome a hostile physical world, so will he help the faithful endure the evils of urban society. Taken as a whole, then, the stories continue to provide understanding of the hearts and minds of Latter-day Saints and of the beliefs that move them to action.

BIBLIOGRAPHY

Lee, Hector. *The Three Nephites: The Substance and Significance of the Legend in Folklore.* University of New Mexico Publication in Language and Literature, no. 2. Albuquerque, N.M., 1949.

Wilson, William A. "Freeways, Parking Lots, and Ice Cream Stands: The Three Nephites in Contemporary Society." *Dialogue* 21 (Fall 1988): 13–26.

WILLIAM A. WILSON

TRANSLATION OF THE BOOK OF MORMON BY JOSEPH SMITH

By its own terms, the Book of Mormon is a translation of an ancient book; yet Joseph SMITH knew no ancient languages at the time he dictated this text to his scribes. He and several of his close associates testified that the translation was accomplished "by the gift and power of God" (*HC* 1:315; see also D&C 1:29; 20:8).

Little is known about the translation process itself. Few details can be gleaned from comments made by Joseph's scribes and close associates. Only Joseph Smith knew the actual process, and he declined to describe it in public. At a Church conference in 1831, Hyrum Smith invited the Prophet to explain more fully how the Book of Mormon came forth. Joseph Smith responded that "it was not intended to tell the world all the particulars of the coming forth of the Book of Mormon; and . . . it was not expedient for him to relate these things" (*HC* 1:220).

Much is known, however, about when and where the work of translation occurred. The events are documented by several independent firsthand witnesses. Joseph Smith first obtained the GOLD PLATES at the hill CUMORAH in New York, in the early morning hours of September 22, 1827. To avoid local harassment and mobs, he moved to Harmony, Pennsylvania, in December 1827. There he copied and translated some of the characters from the plates, with his wife Emma and her brother Reuben Hale acting as scribes. In 1856, Emma recalled that Joseph dictated the translation to her word for word, spelled out the proper names, and would correct her scribal errors even though he could not see what she had written. At one point while translating, Joseph was surprised to learn that Jerusalem had walls around it (E. C. Briggs, "Interview with David Whitmer," *Saints' Herald* 31 [June 21, 1884]: 396–97). Emma was once asked in a later interview if Joseph had read from any books or notes while dictating. She answered, "He had neither," and when pressed, added: "If he had anything of the kind he could not have concealed it from me" (*Saints' Herald* 26 [Oct. 1, 1879]: 290).

Martin HARRIS came to Harmony in February 1828, and shortly afterward took a transcript and translation of some of the characters to New York City, where he showed them to Professor Charles Anthon at Columbia College (*see* ANTHON TRANSCRIPT). He returned fully satisfied that Joseph was telling the truth, and from April 12 to June 14, 1828, Harris acted as scribe while Joseph Smith translated the book of Lehi.

On June 15, 1828, Joseph and Emma's first son was born but died a few hours later. About July 15, Joseph learned that Martin Harris had lost the 116 pages they had translated (*see* MANUSCRIPT, LOST 116 PAGES), and subsequently the angel MORONI took the plates and the interpreters temporarily from Joseph, who was chastened but reassured by the Lord that the work would go forth (D&C 3:15–16).

On September 22, 1828, the plates and translation tools were returned to Joseph Smith, and during that winter he translated "a few more pages" (D&C 5:30). The work progressed slowly until April 5, 1829, when Oliver COWDERY, a school teacher who had seen the Lord and the plates in a vision (*PWJS*, p. 8), arrived in Harmony and offered his scribal services to Joseph. Virtually all of the English text of the Book of Mormon was then translated between April 7 and the last week of June, less than sixty working days.

The dictation flowed smoothly. From the surviving portions of the Original Manuscript it appears that Joseph dictated about a dozen words at a time. Oliver would read those words back for verification, and then they would go on. Emma later added that after a meal or a night's rest, Joseph would begin, without prompting, where he had previously left off (*The Saints' Herald* 26 [Oct. 1, 1879]: 290). No time was taken for research, internal cross-checking, or editorial rewriting. In 1834 Oliver wrote: "These were days never to be forgotten—to sit under the sound of a voice dictated by the inspiration of heaven, awakened the utmost gratitude of this bosom! Day after day I continued, uninterrupted, to write from his mouth as he translated" (*Messenger and Advocate* 1 [Oct. 1834]: 14).

During April, May, and June 1829, many events occurred in concert with the translation of the Book of Mormon. By May 15, the account of Christ's ministry in 3 Nephi had been translated. That text explicitly mentions the necessity of being baptized by proper authority, and this injunction inspired Joseph Smith and Oliver Cowdery to pray, leading to the restoration of the Aaronic Priesthood on May 15 (JS—H 1:68–74) and of the Melchizedek Priesthood soon afterward. Time was also required for trips to Colesville, New York, for supplies (thirty miles away); to earn money to purchase paper; to obtain a federal copyright on June 11, 1829; to baptize Samuel and Hyrum Smith; to preach to several interested people; and, during the first week of June, to move by buckboard over 100 miles to the Peter Whitmer farm in Fayette, New York, where about 150 final pages were translated, with some of the Whitmers also acting as scribes. The work was completed before the end of June, at which time the Three and the Eight Witnesses were allowed to see the plates (*see* WITNESSES OF THE BOOK OF MORMON).

Most evidence supports the idea that Joseph and Oliver began their work in April 1829 with the speech of BENJAMIN (Mosiah 1–6), translated to the end of the book of Moroni in May, then translated the Title Page, and finally translated the small plates of

Reconstructed log home at the site of Peter Whitmer, Sr., home in Fayette, New York. Here the Book of Mormon translation was completed, the testimony of the Three Witnesses was signed (June 1829), and the Church was organized on April 6, 1830. Twenty revelations in the Doctrine and Covenants were received here. Courtesy LaMar C. Berrett photo archive. Note: Photo differs from that in the *Encyclopedia*.

Nephi (1 Nephi–Omni) and the Words of Mormon before the end of June (Welch and Rathbone). The text of the Title Page, "the last leaf" of the plates of Mormon (*HC* 1:71), was used as the book's description on the copyright form filed on June 11, 1829.

Many factors, including divine sources of knowledge and Joseph's own spiritual efforts and personal vocabulary, apparently played their roles in producing the English text of the Book of Mormon. Some accounts emphasize the divine factor. Years later, David WHITMER indicated that words would appear to Joseph on something resembling a piece of parchment and that he would read the words off to his scribe (*An Address to All Believers in Christ*, 1887, p. 12). Other accounts indicate that human effort was also involved. When Oliver Cowdery attempted to translate in April 1829, he was told by the Lord: "You must study it out in your mind; then you must ask me if it be right" (D&C 9:8). According to David Whitmer, Joseph could only translate when he was humble and faithful. One morning something had gone wrong about the

house; Joseph could not translate a single syllable until he went into an orchard, prayed, and then he and Emma made amends (*CHC* 1:131). Joseph's ability to translate apparently increased as the work progressed.

Most reports state that throughout the project Joseph used the "Nephite interpreters" or, for convenience, he would use a SEER STONE (see *CHC* 1:128–30). Both instruments were sometimes called by others the URIM AND THUMMIM. In 1830, Oliver Cowdery is reported to have testified in court that these tools enabled Joseph "to read in English, the reformed Egyptian characters, which were engraved on the plates" (Benton, *Evangelical Magazine and Gospel Advocate* 2 [Apr. 9, 1831]: 15). In an 1891 interview, William Smith indicated that when his brother Joseph used the "interpreters" (which were like a silver bow twisted into the shape of a figure eight with two stones between the rims of the bow connected by a rod to a breastplate), his hands were left free to hold the plates. Other late reports mention a variety of further details, but they cannot be historically confirmed or denied.

Regarding the nature of the English translation, its language is unambiguous and straightforward. Joseph once commented that the book was "translated into our own language" (*TPJS*, p. 17; cf. D&C 1:24). In several chapters, for good and useful reasons, this meant that the language would follow the King James idiom of the day (*see* CWHN 8:212–16; Welch, 1990, pp. 134–63). It also assured that the manuscript would contain human misspellings and grammatical oddities, implying that if it had been translated in another decade its phraseology and vocabulary might have been slightly different.

At the same time, circumstantial evidence in the English text suggests that the transla-

The original manuscript for Helaman 1:15–16 shows how the name "Coriantumr" was first written by Oliver Cowdery phonetically but was then crossed out and spelled correctly on the same line as the translation progressed. Witnesses stated that Joseph Smith spelled the proper names that he translated. © by Intellectual Reserve, Inc. Used by permission.

tion was quite precise. For example, the independent and identical translations of 1 Nephi 1:8 and of Alma 36:22 (precisely quoting twenty-one of Lehi's words in 1 Nephi 1:8) typify the internal accuracy manifested in this long and complex record. Moreover, sev-

eral formulaic terms, Hebraisms, stylistic indications of multiple authorship, varieties of parallelism and extended chiasmus (see AUTHORSHIP OF THE BOOK OF MORMON; LITERATURE, BOOK OF MORMON AS), as well as certain Semitic proper names and some textual variants, not at all evident from the King James Bible, corroborate the claim that the translation was faithful to a consistent underlying text.

Naturally, it is rarely possible to translate exactly the same range of meanings, word for word, from one language into another, and thus opinions have varied about the nature of the correspondence of the ancient text to the English translation. David Whitmer is quoted as saying that "frequently one character would make two lines of manuscript while others made but a word or two words" (*Deseret News*, Nov. 10, 1881). Nevertheless, the linguistic relationship between the English translation and the characters on the plates cannot be determined without consulting the Nephite original, which was returned to the angel Moroni in 1829 (*see* MORONI, VISITATIONS OF).

BIBLIOGRAPHY

Roberts, B. H. "Translation of the Book of Mormon." *IE* 9 (Apr. 1906): 706–13.

Ricks, Stephen D. "Joseph Smith's Means and Methods of Translating the Book of Mormon." *FARMS Paper*. Provo, Utah, 1984.

Welch, John W. "How Long Did It Take Joseph Smith to Translate the Book of Mormon?" *Ensign* 18 (Jan. 1988): 46.

Welch, John W., and Tim Rathbone. "The Translation of the Book of Mormon: Basic Historical Information." *FARMS Paper*. Provo, Utah, 1986.

ADDITIONAL SOURCES

Porter, Larry C. "The Book of Mormon: Historical Setting for Its Translation and Publication." In *Joseph Smith: The Prophet, The Man*, edited by Susan Easton Black and Charles D. Tate, Jr., 49–64. Provo, Utah: BYU Religious Studies Center, 1993.

Skousen, Royal. "Translating the Book of Mormon: Evidence from the Original Manuscript." In *Book of Mormon Authorship Revisited*, edited by Noel B. Reynolds, 61–93. Provo, Utah: FARMS, 1997.

Welch, John W. *Illuminating the Sermon at the Temple and Sermon on the Mount: An Approach to 3 Nephi 11–18 and Matthew 5–7*, 179–210. Provo, Utah: FARMS, 1999.

JOHN W. WELCH

TIM RATHBONE

TRANSLATIONS OF THE BOOK OF MORMON

After the Prophet Joseph SMITH's original translation of the Book of Mormon from the gold plates into English in 1829 and the return of those plates to the angel Moroni, no translations from English into other languages appeared until the 1850s. During the late nineteenth and early twentieth centuries, the Church produced translations of the Book of Mormon irregularly, often in groups of languages, and at widely separated intervals. However, in the 1970s and later, translations from the English text of the Book of Mormon became systematic and frequent.

Making the Book of Mormon and other standard works available in many languages is foreshadowed by the divine injunction "that every man shall hear the fulness of the gospel in his own tongue, and in his own language" (D&C). As missions were opened on the continent of Europe in 1850 and 1851, Church leaders in many of the newly opened missions mounted simultaneous translation efforts. The Danish edition (1851), produced by Erastus Snow for the Scandinavian Mission from a Danish translation by Peter Olsen Hansen, was the first printed. At the same time, John Taylor supervised translations into French by Curtis E. Bolton and German by

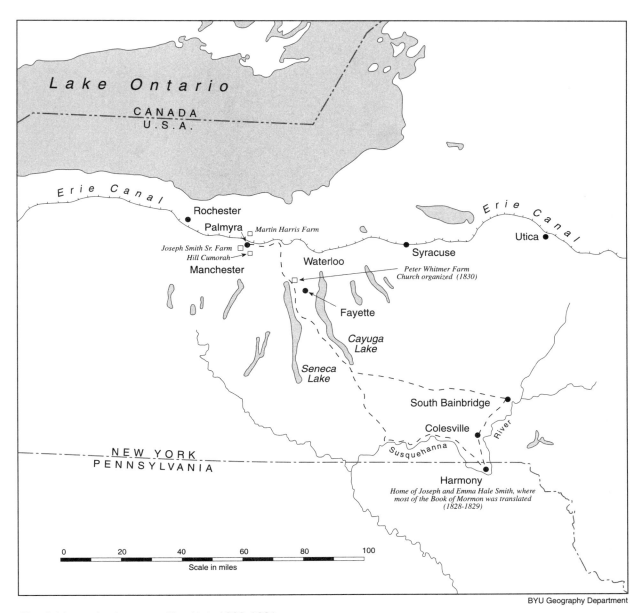

Church history sites in western New York, 1820–1831.

George P. Dykes, while Lorenzo Snow was working on the Italian edition and John Davis on a Welsh one. All of these appeared in 1852, and culminated with George Q. Cannon's translation of the Book of Mormon into Hawaiian in 1855. No further translations were published for twenty years.

In 1875 Meliton G. Trejo and Daniel W. Jones produced the first translation of selec-

tions from the Book of Mormon into Spanish. This ninety-six-page document, comprising only the books of 1 and 2 Nephi, Omni, 3 Nephi, and Mormon, was the first partial translation and one of only two partial printings of the Book of Mormon in book form at the time. (The other was the publication of 1 Nephi–Words of Mormon in the Deseret Alphabet.) Trejo and James Z. Stewart completed a translation of the entire book into Spanish in 1886. The remainder of the nineteenth century produced three further translations: Swedish (1878), Maori (1889), and Dutch (1890). Sixteen more, including the first in Asian languages and several in South Pacific tongues, appeared between 1903 and 1977.

In 1971, in support of an expanding missionary program, the Church organized a Translation Services Department to direct a systematic program of scripture translation. They began with the production of a large number of translations of *Selections from the Book of Mormon*, designed to place selected chapters in the hands of missionaries, general readers, and members as quickly as possible and to train translators. The *Selections*, chosen and approved by the First Presidency and the Quorum of the Twelve Apostles, were the same in all these languages, and consisted of the following:

Book	Chapters
1 Nephi	1–7, 16–18
2 Nephi	1–4; 5:1–20; 9, 29, 31–33
Enos	all
Mosiah	2–5, 17, 18
Alma	5, 11, 12, 32, 34, 39–42
Helaman	13–16
3 Nephi	1, 8, 11–30
4 Nephi	all
Mormon	1, 4, 6–9
Moroni	all

This *Selections* volume is being progressively replaced by full translations. As of 1990, the entire Book of Mormon was available in 36 languages (including English), while *Selections* was available in 44 additional languages.

Retranslations of early editions began in 1952 with the second translation into Spanish. Subsequently, the Japanese, Italian, and German editions were retranslated; other retranslations appeared as *Selections* from 1980 on. With the issuance of the 1981 English edition of the Book of Mormon (*see* EDITIONS 1830–1981), the Church Translation Department began systematically reviewing all existing translations, setting priorities for retranslation, and producing new editions more in conformity with the English format.

BIBLIOGRAPHY

"Book of Mormon Editions, Translated and Published." *Deseret News 1989–90 Church Almanac*. Salt Lake City, 1988.

The Millennial Star, Vols. 13–14 (1850–1851).

HUGH G. STOCKS

TREE OF LIFE

Four images of the Tree of Life are significant for Latter-day Saints: in the Garden of Eden; in LEHI's vision (1 Ne. 8); in the parable of ALMA₂ comparing the word to a seed that can grow to be "a tree springing up unto everlasting life" (Alma 32:28–43); and in the so-called Tree of Life Stone from pre-Hispanic Mexico.

From earliest times, people in many cultures have venerated trees because they are majestic and, compared to a person's life span, seemingly immortal. Groves were among the first places used for sacred rites, and many cultures envisioned the heavens supported by the branches of a giant tree whose roots led to the underworld and whose sturdy trunk formed the link between the two realms. The most important attribute ascribed to the Tree of Life by those for whom such a symbol existed was its ability to provide immortality to those who ate its fruit. The Tree of Life was present in the Garden of Eden (Gen. 2:9) and is a standard symbol in ancient temples, as well as in temples of The Church of Jesus Christ of Latter-day Saints. It will be present at the end and its fruit available to eat for "him that overcometh" (Rev. 2:7).

Lehi's vision conveys an unforgettable message of the need to "give heed to the word of God and remember to keep his commandments always in all things" (1 Ne. 15:25). In his vision, Lehi saw by a fountain of living waters a tree "whose fruit was desirable to make one happy" (1 Ne. 8:10). The tree represented "the love of God" (1 Ne. 11:25). A path led to the tree, and great numbers of people walked the path, but many became lost in a mist of darkness. A "rod of iron" ran along the path, and only those in the multitude who pressed "their way forward, continually holding fast to the rod" (1 Ne. 8:30), reached the tree and partook of the desired fruit.

Alma used the Tree of Life image to teach about the acquisition of faith in the word of God, which he compared to a seed. When planted in one's heart and nourished with much care, it would grow in the believer to yield the same sweet and pure fruit described by Lehi. By diligence and patience, one can "feast upon [this] fruit even until ye are filled, that ye hunger not, neither shall ye thirst" (Alma 32:42). Other ancient texts also describe the faithful as trees in God's paradise (Ps. 1:3; Odes of Solomon 11).

Interest was generated among Latter-day Saints in the 1950s by the discovery of a pre-Columbian sculpture that bore a complex Tree of Life scene similar to those found in the ancient Near East. Izapa Stela 5, carved sometime between 100 B.C. and A.D. 100, portrays a large tree in full leaf, laden with fruit, and surrounded by several persons and objects, including water. Some investigators are convinced that the scene is a depiction of Lehi's

Izapa Stela 5, discovered in 1935 in southwestern Mexico near the Guatemalan border. This preclassic Mayan monument (c. 300 B.C. to A.D. 50) and parts of its imagery have been linked by some archaeologists to Lehi's dream (1 Ne. 8). Standing behind the stone with a native boy are (left to right) Ernest L. Wilkinson (president of Brigham Young University), Thomas S. Ferguson, Mark E. Peterson, Marion G. Romney, and one other person. Courtesy Rare Books and Manuscripts, Brigham Young University.

vision; others are less certain, since the scene also contains items that are difficult to understand, such as triangles and U-shaped elements. The elaborate clothing and headdresses worn by the people, the various objects they hold, and an array of other elements make this carving, which is one of the most complex from this period in Mexico, exceptionally difficult to interpret.

Another intricate Tree of Life carving discovered in Mexico is the beautiful sarcophagus lid from the tomb in the Temple of the Inscriptions at Palenque. Once thought to depict a deity, it is now thought to portray a king named Pacal (meaning "shield") at the moment of his death. As he falls to the earth (represented by the monster face), the sacred ceiba tree rises toward the heavens, topped

This sarcophagus cover from the tomb of King Pacal in the Mayan Temple of Inscriptions, Palenque (c. A.D. 683), shows a ceiba tree emerging from the center of the reclining ruler as he is about to be reborn as a god. Similar imagery may be seen in Alma 32:41–42, which speaks of the tree of God's goodness taking root in the believer and growing up to eternal life. Courtesy Merle Greene Robertson.

BIBLIOGRAPHY

Christensen, Ross, ed. *The Tree of Life in Ancient America*. Provo, Utah, 1968; on Izapa Stela 5 research up to 1965.

James, E. O. *The Tree of Life: An Archaeological Study*. Leiden, 1966.

Norman, V. Garth. *Izapa Sculpture*. Provo, Utah, 1973; for the most complete description of Izapa Stela 5.

Robertson, Merle G. *The Sculpture of Palenque*, Vol. 1, fig. 99. Princeton, 1983.

ADDITIONAL SOURCES

Brewer, Stewart W. "The History of an Idea: The Scene on Stela 5 from Izapa, Mexico, as a Representation of Lehi's Vision of the Tree of Life." *Journal of Book of Mormon Studies* 8/1 (1999): 12–21.

Clark, John E. "A New Artistic Rendering of Izapa Stela 5: A Step toward Improved Interpretation." *Journal of Book of Mormon Studies* 8/1 (1999): 22–33.

Oman, Richard G. "Lehi's Vision of the Tree of Life: A Cross-Cultural Perspective in Contemporary Latter-day Saint Art." *BYU Studies* 32 (Fall 1992): 5–34.

MARTIN RAISH

by the divine serpent-bird, and flanked by two oval cartouches emblematic of the sun.

Whether or not such artworks are related to the Book of Mormon, the remains of cultures from the Near East (CWHN 6:254–55; 7:189–92) and Mesoamerica show that the Tree of Life was a significant image in many areas of the world.

U

URIM AND THUMMIM

The Urim and Thummim is mentioned in the Bible and, with added details about its use and significance, in latter-day scriptures. It is an instrument prepared by God through which revelation may be received. Abraham learned about the universe through the Urim and Thummim (Abr. 3:1–4). The Prophet Joseph Smith "through the medium of the Urim and Thummim . . . translated the [Book of Mormon] by the gift and power of God" (*HC* 4:537; D&C 10:1; JS—H 1:62). Servants of God who are allowed to use the Urim and Thummim have been known as seers (Mosiah 8:13), among whom were Abraham, Moses, the BROTHER OF JARED, MOSIAH₂, ALMA₁, HELAMAN₁, MORONI₂, and Joseph SMITH.

In antiquity at least two different Urim and Thummim existed, and possibly three. Chronologically, the brother of Jared received the first known one (D&C 17:1). This same set came into the hands of Mosiah₂ and other Book of Mormon prophets, subsequently being deposited with the GOLD PLATES (JS—H 1:35). The fate of the second set, given to

Abraham (Abr. 3:1), remains unknown. Unless Abraham's Urim and Thummim had been passed down, Moses received a third set mentioned first in Exodus 28:30. The Urim noted in 1 Samuel 28:6, probably an abbreviated form of Urim and Thummim, was most likely the one possessed by Moses (cf. Num. 27:18–21). What happened to this one is also unknown, though certainly by postexilic times the Urim and Thummim were no longer extant (Ezra 2:63; Neh. 7:65).

Joseph Smith described the Urim and Thummim as "two transparent stones set in the rim of a [silver] bow fastened to a breast plate" (*HC* 4:537; JS—H 1:35). Biblical evidence allows no conclusive description, except that it was placed in a breastplate over the heart (Ex. 28:30; Lev. 8:8).

Urim and Thummim is the transliteration of two Hebrew words meaning, respectively, "light(s)" and "wholeness(es)" or "perfection(s)." While it is usually assumed that the *-im* ending on both words represents the Hebrew masculine plural suffix, other explanations are possible.

The Urim and Thummim to be used

during and after the Millennium will have a functional similarity to the Urim and Thummim mentioned above. God's dwelling place is called a Urim and Thummim; and the white stone of Revelation 2:17 is to become a Urim and Thummim for inheritors of the celestial kingdom (D&C 130:8–10).

PAUL Y. HOSKISSON

V

View of the Hebrews

Ethan Smith's *View of the Hebrews* (Poultney, Vt., 1823; second enlarged edition, 1825) combines scriptural citations and reports from various observers among American Indians and Jews to support the claim that the Indians were the descendants of the Lost Ten Tribes of Israel. It is one of several books reflecting the popular fascination at the time of Joseph Smith with the question of Indian origins. While some have claimed it to be a source for the Book of Mormon, no direct connections between this book and the Book of Mormon have been demonstrated.

The full title of the 1825 edition is *View of the Hebrews; or the Tribes of Israel in America. Exhibiting the Destruction of Jerusalem; the Certain Restoration of Judah and Israel; the Present State of Judah and Israel; and an Address of the Prophet Isaiah to the United States Relative to Their Restoration*. The author, Ethan Smith (no relation to Joseph Smith), was pastor of the Congregational church in Poultney, Vermont.

The first chapter deals with the destruction of Jerusalem in A.D. 70 by the Romans, as referred to in scriptural prophecy and historical sources. The second chapter tells of the literal expulsion of the Ten Tribes of Israel in 721 B.C. and the establishment of the kingdom of Judah; it also maintains that their restoration will be literal, and it quotes heavily from Isaiah. The third chapter summarizes the outcast condition of Israel in 1823; it also argues that the natives of America are "the descendants of Israel" and propounds that all pre-Columbian Americans had one origin, that their language appears originally to have been Hebrew, that they had an ark of the covenant, that they practiced circumcision, that they acknowledged one and only one God, that their tribal structure was similar to Hebrew organization, that they had cities of refuge, and that they manifest a variety of Hebraic traits of prophetic character and tradition. These claims are supported by citations from James Adair and Alexander von Humboldt. The fourth chapter emphasizes the restoration of Israel, quoting from Isaiah and using Isaiah chapter 18 to create an "Address" to the United States to save Israel. In conclusion, Ethan Smith pleads that the "suppliants of God in the West" be faithful and helpful in bringing scattered Israel "to the place of the name of the Lord of hosts, the Mount Zion."

Alleged relationships of *View of the Hebrews* to the Book of Mormon have attracted interest periodically through the years. Ethan Smith's book was published in the adjoining county west of Windsor County, where Joseph Smith was born and lived from 1805 to 1811. Nevertheless, there is no evidence that Joseph Smith ever knew anything about this book. Detractors have pointed to several "parallels" between the two books, but others point to numerous "unparallels"; as two of many examples, the Book of Mormon never mentions an ark of the covenant or cities of refuge.

I. Woodbridge Riley in 1902 was the first author to suggest a relationship between *View of the Hebrews* and the Book of Mormon (*The Founder of Mormonism*, New York, 1902, pp. 124–26). In 1921, LDS Church authorities were asked to reply to questions posed by a Mr. Couch of Washington, D.C., regarding Native American origins, linguistics, technology, and archaeology. B. H. Roberts, a member of the First Quorum of Seventy, undertook a study of Couch's issues; he received some assistance from a committee of other General Authorities. Roberts's first report, in December 1921, was a 141-page paper entitled "Book of Mormon Difficulties." However, he was not satisfied with that work and later delved more deeply into other critical questions about Book of Mormon origins, which led him to a major analysis of *View of the Hebrews*.

Around March–May 1922, Roberts wrote a 291-page document, "A Book of Mormon Study," and an eighteen-point summary entitled "A Parallel." In the "Study" Roberts looked candidly at the possibility that Joseph Smith could have been acquainted with Ethan Smith's book and could have used it as a source of the structure and some ideas in the Book of Mormon. He cited some twenty-six similarities between the two books. In all his writings, Roberts did not draw any conclusions that Joseph Smith used Ethan Smith's work to write the Book of Mormon, but rather posed questions that believers in the Book of Mormon should be aware of and continue to find answers for. Roberts's faith in the Book of Mormon as divinely revealed scripture was unshaken by his studies.

Roberts's papers were published in 1985. This again stirred an interest in the relationship of *View of the Hebrews* and the Book of Mormon, especially since the editorial "Introduction" concluded that "the record is mixed" as to whether Roberts kept his faith in the authenticity of the Book of Mormon after making his studies (B. D. Madsen, p. 29). Subsequent research, however, strongly indicates that Roberts remained committed to the full claims of the origin and doctrine of the Book of Mormon to the end of his life (Welch, pp. 59–60), and substantial evidence favors the position that there is little in common between the ideas and statements in *View of the Hebrews* and the Book of Mormon.

BIBLIOGRAPHY

Madsen, Brigham D., ed. *B. H. Roberts: Studies of the Book of Mormon.* Urbana, Ill., 1985.

Madsen, Truman G., comp. *B. H. Roberts: His Final Decade.* Provo, Utah, 1985.

Welch, John W. "B. H. Roberts: Seeker After Truth." *Ensign* 16 (Mar. 1986): 56–62.

RICHARD C. ROBERTS

VISIONS OF JOSEPH SMITH

Ancient prophets were typically called through a revelatory process—visions and/or revelations: "If there be a prophet among you, I the Lord will make myself known unto him in a vision, and will speak unto him in a dream" (Num. 12:6). The prophet Joel anticipated that visions would increase in the last days, saying, "Old men shall dream dreams, [and] young men shall see visions" (Joel 2:28–32).

The Prophet Joseph Smith had his first vision at the age of fourteen while praying in a grove of trees in western New York. The appearance of the Lord to him, like that to Saul of Tarsus, was attended by a shining light from heaven (Acts 9:3). The Lord spoke face-to-face with Joseph and called him to service. This was the first of a series of visions Joseph SMITH received, many of which were shared with other persons. Blessed like John on the isle of Patmos and Paul who spoke of the third heavens, the Prophet Joseph Smith affirmed, "Could you gaze into heaven five minutes, you would know more than you would by reading all that ever was written on the subject" (*TPJS*, p. 324; cf. *HC* 6:50). He also declared that "the best way to obtain truth and wisdom is not to ask it from books, but to go to God in prayer, and obtain divine teaching" (*TPJS*, p. 191).

President John Taylor said that Joseph Smith had contact with prophets from every dispensation:

> Because he [Joseph] stood at the head of the dispensation of the fulness of times, which comprehends all the various dispensations that have existed upon the earth, and that as the Gods in the eternal worlds and the Priesthood that officiated in time and eternity had declared that it was time for the issuing forth of all these

things, they all combined together to impart to him the keys of their several missions. (*JD* 18:326)

A new dispensation requires the conferral of priesthood and keys, in accordance with the law of witnesses: "In the mouth of two or three witnesses shall every word be established" (2 Cor. 13:1). During the restoration sequence when priesthood and keys were conferred by angelic ministrants, the Prophet was accompanied by one or more witnesses. Oliver COWDERY was a principal figure in the fulfillment of this law of witnesses (*see* WITNESSES, LAW OF); others were David WHITMER, Martin HARRIS, and Sidney Rigdon. Distinguishing dreams from visions and associating visions and visitations, Joseph said, "An open vision will manifest that which is more important" (*TPJS*, p. 161). Crucial visions received by the Prophet Joseph Smith are the source of many cardinal doctrines and teachings of the Latter-day Saints.

THE FIRST VISION. Lucy Mack Smith recalled that as the Joseph Smith, Sr., family worked their Manchester, New York, farm in the period of 1820, "there was a great revival in religion, which extended to all denominations of Christians in the surrounding country." Lucy and three of the children joined the Western Presbyterian Church in Palmyra, but Joseph remained "unchurched." He later wrote, "It was impossible . . . to come to any certain conclusion who was right and who was wrong" (JS—H 1:8). In answer to a biblical prompting that "if any of you lack wisdom, let him ask of God" (James 1:5), Joseph retired to the woods and uttered what he termed his first vocal prayer. His prayer of faith was answered. Joseph recorded, "I saw two Personages, whose brightness and glory defy all description, standing above me in the air. One of them spake unto me, calling me by name and said, pointing to the other—*This is My Beloved Son. Hear Him!"* Responding to his inquiry concerning which church he should join, the Lord instructed Joseph to join none of them, saying that he must continue as he was "until further directed" (JS—H 1:17–19, 26). When Joseph left the grove, he possessed the knowledge that God and his Son were actual personages, that the Godhead was composed of separate individuals, and that God hears and answers prayers. He also knew that he must not affiliate with the existing denominations (Backman, 1971, pp. 206–208). This vision set in motion a train of visitations by angelic ministrants directing the young prophet in the process of restoring the gospel of Jesus Christ.

VISITATIONS OF MORONI. The Prophet continued to pursue his common vocations until September 21, 1823, while "suffering severe persecution at the hands of all classes of men," in part as a result of his claims concerning his first vision (JS—H 1:27). As he prayed that evening that he might know his standing before God, an angel appeared at his bedside, saying that he had been sent from the presence of God and that his name was Moroni. He explained "that God had a work for [Joseph] to do; and that [his] name should be had for good and evil among all nations" (JS—H l:33). He instructed Joseph concerning a book that was written on gold plates, giving an account of the former inhabitants of the continent. The fulness of the everlasting gospel was contained in the record as delivered by the Savior to these people. Joseph was also shown a vision of a nearby hill and the place where the plates containing this record were deposited.

The next day, Joseph went to the hill, subsequently known by his followers as Cumorah, removed a stone covering, and viewed the contents of the box beneath, the plates, the URIM AND THUMMIM, and a breastplate. The angel reappeared and informed him that the time for the removal of the plates had not arrived and that he was to meet him for further instruction at that same site over a succession of four years (JS—H 1:53–59). A further vision was opened to Joseph's view, and he saw the "prince of darkness, surrounded by his innumerable train of associates." The heavenly messenger said, "All this is shown, the good and the evil, the holy and impure, the glory of God and the power of darkness, that you may know hereafter the two powers and never be influenced or overcome by that wicked one" (*Messenger and Advocate* 2:198).

From 1824 to 1827, Joseph returned to the hill each year as specified. On September 22, 1827, he met the angel and received final instructions regarding the record. Moroni gave the record to the Prophet to translate. Joseph said, "The same heavenly messenger delivered them up to me with this charge: that I should be responsible for them; that if I should let them go carelessly, or through any neglect of mine, I should be cut off; but that if I would use all my endeavors to preserve them, until he, the messenger, should call for them, they should be protected" (JS—H 1:59). The messenger did not limit his instruction solely to these annual meetings, but made contact with Joseph on numerous occasions (Peterson, pp. 119–20). In all, the angel Moroni visited Joseph Smith at least twenty times (*see* MORONI, VISITATIONS OF). Joseph informed associates that other Book of Mormon prophets also visited him, including Nephi, son of Lehi (Cheesman, pp. 38–60). Lucy Mack Smith recalled that her son Joseph was enabled from this tutoring to describe "with much ease" the ancient inhabitants of America, "their dress, mode of traveling, and the animals upon which they rode; their cities, their buildings, with every particular; their mode of warfare; and also their religious worship" (p. 83).

JOHN THE BAPTIST. While translating the Book of Mormon at Harmony, Pennsylvania, on May 15, 1829, Joseph Smith and Oliver COWDERY became concerned about baptism for the remission of sins as described in 3 Nephi 11. They went into the woods to pray for enlightenment. Both record that a messenger from heaven, identifying himself as John the Baptist, laid hands on them and ordained them to the Aaronic Priesthood, saying, "Upon you my fellow servants, in the name of Messiah, I confer the Priesthood of Aaron, which holds the keys of the ministering of angels, and of the gospel of repentance, and of baptism by immersion for the remission of sins; and this shall never be taken again from the earth until the sons of Levi do offer again an offering unto the Lord in righteousness" (JS—H 1:69; D&C 13; cf. *TPJS*, pp. 172–73).

PETER, JAMES, AND JOHN. John the Baptist also informed Joseph and Oliver that "this Aaronic Priesthood had not the power of laying on hands for the gift of the Holy Ghost, but that this should be conferred on us hereafter." John stated "that he acted under the direction of Peter, James and John, who held the keys of the Priesthood of Melchizedek, which Priesthood, he said, would in due time be conferred on us" (JS—H 1:70, 72).

This restoration occurred during the latter part of May or early June 1829, someplace between Harmony and Colesville on the Susquehanna River. Of this visitation, Joseph Smith later testified, "The Priesthood is everlasting. The Savior, Moses, & Elias—gave the Keys to Peter, James & John on the Mount when they were transfigured before him. . . .

How have we come at the priesthood in the last days? It came down, down in regular succession. Peter, James & John had it given to them & they gave it up [to us]" (*WJS*, p. 9).

THREE WITNESSES OF THE BOOK OF MORMON. By revelation Oliver Cowdery, David Whitmer, and Martin Harris were selected to be witnesses of the plates and the authentic translation of the Book of Mormon (2 Ne. 11:3; 27:12; Ether 5:2–4; D&C 5:11–18; D&C 17). During the latter part of June 1829, in company with Joseph Smith, these three men went into the woods adjacent to the Whitmer home in Fayette, New York, and knelt in prayer. When the promised revelation was not immediately received, Martin Harris stated that he felt he might be the cause of their failure. After Martin Harris withdrew, the others knelt in prayer again. David Whitmer described the visitation of Moroni:

> The angel stood before us. He was dressed in white, and spoke and called me by name and said "Blessed is he that keepeth His commandments. . . ." A table was set before us and on it the Records of the Nephites, from which the Book of Mormon was translated, the breast plates [and also the Urim and Thummim], the Ball of Directors [Liahona], the Sword of Laban and other plates. While we were viewing them the voice of God spoke out of heaven saying that the Book was true and the translation correct. (Quoted in "Letter from Elder W. H. Kelley," *Saints' Herald* 29 [Mar. 1, 1882]: 68)

Afterward, Joseph found Martin Harris, and together they experienced a similar manifestation. The Three Witnesses later endorsed a statement describing their experience that has been appended to all copies of the Book of Mormon. They swore that they had seen the angel and the plates and that "we also know that they have been translated by the gift and power of God, for his voice hath declared it unto us" (*see* WITNESSES OF THE BOOK OF MORMON). Subsequently, eight others were privileged to see and handle the plates, but without the presence of the angel or having heard the voice of God.

VISION OF GLORIES. While preparing the text of his translation of the Bible, Joseph Smith, with Sidney Rigdon, moved to the John Johnson home in Hiram, Ohio, on September 12, 1831. As the two men worked on the Gospel of John, it became apparent to them that many important points concerning the salvation of individuals had been lost from the Bible. Joseph wrote, "It appeared self-evident from what truths were left, that if God rewarded every one according to the deeds done in the body the term 'Heaven,' as intended for the Saints' eternal home must include more kingdoms than one" (*HC* 1:245). On February 16, 1832, in an upper room of the Johnson home, while he and Sidney Rigdon were examining the passage from John 5:29, they saw a multifaceted vision (D&C 76), commencing with a vision of the Father and the Son in the highest glory. This scene was followed by a series of visions, including Perdition and the sons of Perdition and then the celestial, terrestrial, and telestial kingdoms of glory. One witness, Philo Dibble, present in the room recalled that the two men sat motionless for about an hour. One would say, "What do I see," and describe it, and the other would say, "I see the same" (*Juvenile Instructor* 27 [May 15, 1892]: 303–4).

It is apparent that the Prophet Joseph Smith did not impart all that he saw in vision, for he later said, "I could explain a hundred fold more than I ever have of the glories of the kingdoms manifested to me in the vision, were I permitted, and were the people prepared to receive them" (*TPJS*, p. 305).

KIRTLAND TEMPLE VISIONS. From January 21 to May 1, 1836, many of the Saints in Kirt-

land experienced an outpouring of the Spirit, a "Pentecostal season." On January 21, the Prophet assembled with others in the west schoolroom on the third story of the Kirtland Temple. Here Joseph beheld a vision of the celestial kingdom of God (D&C 137). He beheld the Father and the Son and several ancient worthies, including Adam, Abraham, and his own mother and father (both still living), and his brother Alvin, who had died in 1823 (verse 5). As Joseph marveled over Alvin's station in the celestial kingdom, the voice of the Lord declared, "All who have died without a knowledge of this gospel, who would have received it if they had been permitted to tarry, shall be heirs of the celestial kingdom of God" (verse 7). He was also instructed concerning the destiny of little children. The Prophet recorded, "I also beheld that all children who die before they arrive at the years of accountability are saved in the celestial kingdom of heaven" (verse 10).

During the dedication of the Kirtland Temple on March 27, 1836, many testified of the presence of angels. The Prophet specifically identified the ancient apostles Peter and John as present among them (Backman, *The Heavens Resound*, 1983, pp. 299–300; cf. *JD* 9:376).

One week later, on April 3, 1836, Joseph Smith and Oliver Cowdery had retired to the Melchizedek Priesthood pulpits on the west side of the first floor of the temple. The curtains were dropped around the pulpit area as the men prayed. "The veil was taken from our minds, and the eyes of our understanding were opened" (D&C 110:1). The Lord stood before them on the breastwork of the pulpit. "His eyes were as a flame of fire; the hair of his head was white like the pure snow; his countenance shone above the brightness of the sun; and his voice was as the sound of the rushing of great waters, even the voice of Jehovah" (D&C 110:3). The Savior accepted the newly completed structure and promised that his name and glory would be present and that thousands of persons would receive an outpouring of blessings because of the temple and the endowment received by his servants in that house (D&C 110:6–9).

Following the Savior's appearance, three other messengers presented themselves. Each bestowed specific priesthood keys on the two leaders. Moses came and "committed [to them] the keys of the gathering of Israel" (verse 11). As Moses departed, Elias, possessing the keys of "the gospel of Abraham," appeared and administered the keys of this dispensation, saying "that in us and our seed all generations after us should be blessed" (verse 12). Further priesthood keys were restored by Elijah, who declared, "Behold, the time has fully come, which was spoken of by the mouth of Malachi—testifying that he [Elijah] should be sent . . . To turn the hearts of the fathers to the children, and the children to the fathers" (verses 14–15).

OTHER HEAVENLY MANIFESTATIONS. A variety of accounts affirm that other persons also witnessed such appearances not only in association with the Kirtland Temple but in an earlier period during meetings in the log schoolhouse on the Isaac Morley farm and in the School of the Prophets, held in the Newel K. Whitney store (K. Anderson, pp. 107–113, 169–77; Backman, *The Heavens Resound*, 1983, pp. 240, 264–68, 284–309).

The visions discussed herein are but a few of the myriad manifestations that gave the Prophet direction. Joseph mentions having seen others in vision, including Michael, Gabriel, and Raphael, but does not detail their association (D&C 128:20–21). President John Taylor identified yet others who ministered to the Prophet, notably Adam, Seth, Enoch, Noah, Abraham, Isaac, and Jacob (*JD* 17:374; 18:325–26; 21:65, 94, 161; 23:48).

One writer has commented, "He had visions of the past as well as of the future. As a seer, he knew things about the past that are not part of our own scripture, but which he spoke of in discourse" (Madsen, p. 44). "I saw Adam in the valley of Adam-ondi-Ahman" (*TPJS*, p. 158). To Joseph Knight, Sr., the Prophet commented on the vistas opened to him through the Urim and Thummim, which he found deposited with the gold plates. Knight explained, "He seemed to think more of the glasses or Urim and Thummim . . . says he, 'I can see anything; they are marvelous'" (Jessee, 1976, p. 33). Accordingly, after reading Foxe's *Book of the Martyrs*, Joseph remarked that he had "seen those martyrs, and they were honest, devoted followers of Christ, according to the light they possessed, and they will be saved" (Stevenson, p. 6). He saw in vision marchers in Zion's Camp who had perished from cholera in Clay County, Missouri. He related their condition, observing to the survivors, "Brethren, I have seen those men who died of the cholera in our camp; and the Lord knows, if I get a mansion as bright as theirs, I ask no more" (*HC* 2:181n). The organizations of the Quorum of the Twelve Apostles and the First Quorum of the Seventy were made known to him "by vision and by the Holy Spirit," and he established those priesthood offices in February 1835 (*HC* 2:182). In an earlier vision, he "saw the Twelve Apostles of the Lamb, who are now upon the earth, who hold the keys of this last ministry, in foreign lands, standing together in a circle, much fatigued, with their clothes tattered and feet swollen, with their eyes cast downward, and Jesus standing in their midst, and they did not behold Him. The Savior looked upon them and wept" (*HC* 2:381). He saw a vision enabling him to designate the "central place" in Independence, Missouri (*TPJS*, p. 79). Of a vision of the resurrection of the dead, he explained, "So plain was the vision, that I actually saw men, before they had ascended from the tomb, as though they were getting up slowly" (*TPJS*, pp. 295–96). He also saw the Kirtland and Nauvoo temples in vision before their construction and gave detailed instructions to the architects, describing the windows and their illumination (*JD* 13:357; 14:273; *HC* 6:196–97). He foresaw the struggles of the Saints in crossing the plains, their establishment in the Rocky Mountains, and the future condition of the Saints (*HC* 5:85n–86n).

He remarked late in his life, "It is my meditation all the day & more than my meat & drink to know how I shall make the saints of God to comprehend the visions that roll like an overflowing surge, before my mind" (*WJS*, p. 196).

BIBLIOGRAPHY

Anderson, Karl Ricks. *Joseph Smith's Kirtland*. Salt Lake City, 1989.

Anderson, Richard Lloyd. *Investigating the Book of Mormon Witnesses*. Salt Lake City, 1981.

Andrus, Hyrum. *Joseph Smith, the Man and the Seer*. Salt Lake City, 1960.

Backman, Milton V., Jr. *Joseph Smith's First Vision*. Salt Lake City, 1971.

———. *Eyewitness Accounts of the Restoration*. Orem, Utah, 1983.

———. *The Heavens Resound*. Salt Lake City, 1983.

Bushman, Richard L. *Joseph Smith and the Beginnings of Mormonism*. Urbana, Ill., 1984.

Cheesman, Paul R. *The Keystone of Mormonism*. Provo, Utah, 1988.

Ehat, Andrew F., and Lyndon W. Cook. *The Words of Joseph Smith*. Salt Lake City, 1980.

Jessee, Dean C. "Joseph Knight's Recollection of Early Mormon History." *BYU Studies* 17 (Autumn 1976): 29–39.

———. *The Papers of Joseph Smith*, Vol. l. Salt Lake City, 1989.

Ludlow, Daniel H. *A Companion to Your Study of the Doctrine and Covenants*, Vol. 1. Salt Lake City, 1978.

Madsen, Truman G. *Joseph Smith the Prophet*. Salt Lake City, 1989.

Peterson, H. Donl. *Moroni, Ancient Prophet, Modern Messenger*. Bountiful, Utah, 1983.

Porter, Larry C. "Dating the Restoration of the Melchizedek Priesthood." *Ensign* 9 (June 1979): 4–10.

———. "The Priesthood Restored." In *Studies in Scripture*, ed. R. Millet and K. Jackson, Vol. 2, pp. 389–409. Salt Lake City, 1985.

Smith, Lucy Mack. *History of Joseph Smith*, ed. Preston Nibley. Salt Lake City, 1958.

Sperry, Sidney B. *Doctrine and Covenants Compendium*. Salt Lake City, 1960.

Stevenson, Edward. *Reminiscences of Joseph, the Prophet*. Salt Lake City, 1893.

ADDITIONAL SOURCE

Baugh, Alexander L. "Parting the Veil: The Visions of Joseph Smith." *BYU Studies* 38/1 (1999): 22–69.

LARRY C. PORTER

"VOICE FROM THE DUST"

For Latter-day Saints, the phrase "voice from the dust" speaks of the coming forth of the BOOK OF MORMON (cf. 2 Ne. 25:18; 26:16), which was translated from metal PLATES buried in the ground for fourteen centuries. As early as Joseph SMITH, LDS leaders have consistently indicated that this phrase applies to the Book of Mormon (*PJS*, p. 307; Hinckley, p. 10). This distinctive phrase and others like it usually appear in a context that speaks of the need for repentance and of an accompanying voice of warning that will "whisper out of the dust" (Isa. 29:4).

Latter-day Saints believe prophets foresaw that in the latter days a book, a companion to the Bible, would come forth as another testament of Jesus Christ (Ezek. 37:15–19; 2 Ne. 29:1–14). This other testament is the Book of Mormon. The Lord foretold the coming forth of such a record to Enoch: "And righteousness will I send down out of heaven; and truth will I send forth out of the earth, to bear testimony of mine Only Begotten" (Moses 7:62; cf. Ps. 85:11; *TPJS*, p. 98). According to the Book of Mormon, JOSEPH OF EGYPT also prophesied that one of his descendants would write words from the Lord that "shall cry from the dust; yea, even repentance unto their brethren, even after many generations have gone by them" (2 Ne. 3:18–20; cf. 33:13; Morm. 8:16, 23, 26; Moro. 10:27).

BIBLIOGRAPHY

Hinckley, Gordon B. *Faith: The Essence of True Religion*. Salt Lake City, 1989.

WILLIAM SHEFFIELD

W

WARFARE IN THE BOOK OF MORMON

Much of the Book of Mormon deals with military conflict. In diverse, informative, and morally instructive accounts, the Book of Mormon reports a wide variety of military customs, technologies, and tactics similar to those found in many premodern societies (before A.D. 1600–1700), especially some distinctive Israelite beliefs and conventions as adapted to the region of Mesoamerica.

The Book of Mormon teaches that war is a result of iniquity. Wars and destructions were brought upon the Nephites because of the contentions, murderings, idolatry, whoredoms, and abominations "which were among themselves," while those who were "faithful in keeping the commandments of the Lord were delivered at all times" from captivity, death, or unbelief (Alma 50:21–22).

The Book of Mormon implicitly condemns wars of aggression. Until their final calamity, all Nephite military objectives were strictly defensive. It was a mandatory, sacred obligation of all able-bodied Nephite men to defend their families, country, and religious freedoms (Alma 43:47; 46:12), but only as God commanded them.

WARFARE. In the Book of Mormon, aside from the Ammonite converts who swore an oath against bloodshed and a remarkable period of peace following the visitation of Christ, armed conflict at different levels of intensity was a nearly constant phenomenon. Several prophets and heroes of the Book of Mormon were military men who fought in defense of their people, reflecting the grim realities of warfare in ancient history.

Religion and warfare were closely connected in the Book of Mormon. Certain elements of the Israelite patterns of "holy war" were continued in the Book of Mormon, such as the important ancient idea that success in war was due fundamentally to the will of God and the righteousness of the people (Alma 2:28; 44:4–5; 50:21; 56:47; 57:36; -58:33; Morm. 2:26). Nephite armies consulted prophets before going to battle (Alma 16:5; 43:23–24; 3 Ne. 3:19) and entered into covenants with God before battle. On one occasion, the Nephite soldiers swore a solemn oath, covenanting to obey God's commandments and to fight valiantly for the cause of righteousness, casting their garments on the ground at the feet of their leader and inviting God to cast themselves likewise at the feet of their enemies if they should violate their oath (Alma 46:22; cf. 53:17). A purity code for warriors may be seen in the account of the stripling warriors of Helaman (Alma 56–58).

As was the case in all premodern situations, warfare in the Book of Mormon was closely bound to the natural environment and ecology: weather, altitude, terrain, food supply, seasonality, and agricultural cycles. Geography determined some of the strategy and tactics in Book of Mormon warfare (Sorenson, 1985, pp. 239–76). The favorable times for campaigns in the Book of Mormon appear to have been between the eleventh and the fourth months, which has been compared with the fact that military action often took place during the cool and dry post-harvest months from November through April in Mesoamerica (see Alma 16:1; 49:1; 52:1; 56:27; Ricks and Hamblin, pp. 445–77).

Animals, either used as beasts of burden or ridden into battle, evidently were not widely available or practical in the Nephite world: No animal is ever mentioned as being used for military purposes in the Book of Mormon.

Technologically, Nephite soldiers fought, in one way or other, with missile or melee weapons in face-to-face, hand-to-hand encounters, frequently wearing armor. They used metallurgy for making weapons and armor, and engineering for building fortifications. In the Book of Mormon, Nephi taught his people to make swords modeled after the sword of Laban (2 Ne. 5:14–15). Innovations described include a proliferation of fortifications (once thought absent in ancient America) and Nephite armor in the first century B.C. (Alma 43:19; 48), soon copied by the Lamanites (Alma 49:24). It has been pointed out that the weapons (swords, scimitars, bows, and arrows) and armor (breastplates, shields, armshields, bucklers, and headplates) mentioned in the Book of Mormon are comparable to those found in Mesoamerica; coats of mail, helmets, battle chariots, cavalry, and sophisticated siege engines are absent from the Book of Mormon and Mesoamerica, despite their importance in biblical descriptions (Ricks and Hamblin, pp. 329–424).

The ability to recruit, equip, train, supply, and move large groups of soldiers represented a major undertaking for these societies, often pressing them beyond their limits and thereby ultimately contributing to their collapse. As the story of MORONI[1] and Pahoran illustrates, warfare exerted terrible social and economic pressure on Nephite society (Alma 58–61). Nephite army sizes coincided with general demographic growth: Armies numbered in the thousands in the first century B.C. and in the tens of thousands in the fourth century A.D.

It appears that Book of Mormon military organization was aristocratic and dominated by a highly trained hereditary elite. Thus, for example, military leaders such as Moroni[1], his son Moronihah, and MORMON each became the chief captain at a young age (Alma 43:17; 62:39; Morm. 2:1).

Book of Mormon armies were organized on a decimal system of hundreds, thousands, and ten thousands, as they typically were in ancient Israel and many other ancient military organizations.

The book of Alma chronicles the grim realities, strain, and pain of war, vividly and realistically (CWHN 7:291–333). Preparations for war were complex; provisioning, marching, and countermarching are frequently mentioned. Manpower was recruited from the ordinary ranks of the citizenry; soldiers had to be equipped and organized into units for marching and tactics and mobilized at central locations.

Some battles were fought at prearranged times and places, as when Mormon met the Lamanites at Cumorah (Morm. 6:2; cf. 3 Ne. 3:8). But much was typified by guerrilla warfare or surprise attacks: The Gadianton robbers typically raided towns, avoided open conflict, made terrorizing demands, and secretly assassinated government officials.

Actual battlefield operations usually represented only a small portion of a campaign. Scouts and spies reconnoitered for food, trails, and the location of enemy troops. Battle plans were generally made shortly before the enemy was encountered and frequently took the form of a council, as Moroni held in Alma 52:19.

When actual fighting began, controlling the army undoubtedly proved difficult. Soldiers generally fought in units distinguished by banners held by an officer. Moroni's banner, or "title of liberty," apparently served such functions (Alma 43:26, 30; 46:19–21, 36).

As far as one can determine, attacks typically began with an exchange of missiles to wound and demoralize the enemy; then hand-to-hand combat ensued. The battle described in Alma 49 offers a good description of archery duels preceding hand-to-hand melees. When panic began to spread in the ranks, complete collapse could be sudden and devastating. The death of the king or commander typically led to immediate defeat or surrender, as happened in Alma 49:25. The death of one Lamanite king during the night before the New Year proved particularly demoralizing (Alma 52:1–2). Most casualties occurred during the flight and pursuit after the disintegration of the main units; there are sev-

eral examples in the Book of Mormon of the rout, flight, and destruction of an army (e.g., Alma 52:28; 62:31).

Laws and customary behavior also regulated military relations and diplomacy. Military oaths were taken very seriously. Oaths of loyalty from troops and oaths of surrender from prisoners are mentioned frequently in the Book of Mormon, and treaties were concluded principally with oaths of nonaggression (Alma 44:6–10, 20; 50:36; 62:16; 3 Ne. 5:4–5). Legally, robbers or brigands were considered to be military targets, not common offenders (Hel. 11:28). Further elements of martial law in the Book of Mormon included the suspension of normal judicial processes and transferral of legal authority to commanding military officers (Alma 46:34), restrictions on travel, warnings before the commencement of hostilities (3 Ne. 3; cf. Deut. 20:10–13), the extraordinary granting of military exemption on condition that those exempted supply provisions and support (Alma 27:24; cf. Deut. 20:8; Babylonian Talmud, *Sotah* 43a–44a), and requirements of humanitarian treatment for captives and women.

WARS. Eighty-five instances of armed conflict can be identified in the Book of Mormon (Ricks and Hamblin, pp. 463–74). Some were brief skirmishes; others, prolonged campaigns. Some were civil wars; others, intersectional. Causes of war varied, and alliances shifted accordingly. The main wars include the following:

In the early tribal conflicts (c. 550–200 B.C.), social, religious, and cultural conflicts led to repeated Lamanite aggression after the Nephites separated from the Lamanites. The Nephites did not flourish under these circumstances, and to escape further attacks they eventually left the land of Nephi, moving northward to Zarahemla.

King Laman's son (c. 160–150 B.C.), envious

of Nephite prosperity and angry at them for taking the records (especially the plates of brass, Mosiah 10:16), attacked both the people of Zeniff (Nephites who had returned to the land of Nephi) and the people of BENJAMIN (Nephites and Mulekites in the land of Zarahemla). As a result of these campaigns, Zeniff became a tributary to the Lamanites; Benjamin's victory more firmly united the land of Zarahemla under his rule (W of M; Mosiah 9–10).

The war of Amlici (87 B.C.) was a civil war in Zarahemla, sparked by the shift of government from a kingship to judgeship and by the execution of Nehor. Amlici, a follower of Nehor, militated in favor of returning to a kingship. This civil war was the first recorded time Nephite dissenters allied themselves with Lamanites; it resulted in an unstable peace (Alma 2–3).

The sudden destruction of Ammonihah (81 B.C.), a center of the recalcitrant followers of Nehor, was triggered by Lamanite anger toward certain Nephites who had caused some Lamanites to kill other Lamanites (Alma 16; 24–25).

The Ammonite move (77 B.C.) from Lamanite territory to the land of Jershon to join the Nephites led to a major Lamanite invasion of Nephite lands (Alma 28).

Three years later, many Zoramite poor were converted by the Nephites and moved from Antionum (the Zoramite capital) to Jershon (the land given to the Ammonites with guarantees of protection by the Nephites). The loss of these workers ignited the Zoramite attack allied with Lamanites and others against the Nephites (Alma 43–44). New forms of armor introduced by the Nephites figured prominently in this war.

During this turbulent decade, a politically ambitious man named Amalickiah, with Lamanite allies, sought to reestablish a kingship in Zarahemla after the disappearance of ALMA₂. Amalickiah was defeated (72 B.C.), but he swore to return and kill Moroni₁ (Alma 46–50). A seven-year campaign ensued (67–61 B.C.), fought in two arenas, one southwest of Zarahemla and the other in the seaboard north of Zarahemla. Outlying towns fell, and the capital city was plagued with civil strife. At length, a costly victory was won by the Nephites (Alma 51–62).

In the short war of Tubaloth (51 B.C.), Ammoron's son Tubaloth and Coriantumr (a descendant of King Zarahemla) captured but could not hold the land of Zarahemla during the political chaos that followed the rebellion of Paanchi after the death of the chief judge Pahoran (Hel. 1). In the aftermath, the Gadianton robbers rose to power, and some Nephites began migrating to the north.

The war of Moronihah (38, 35–30 B.C.) followed the appointment of NEPHI₂ as chief judge (Hel. 4). Nephite dissenters, together with Lamanites, occupied half of the Nephite lands, and Nephi₂ resigned the judgment seat.

The wars of Gadianton and Kishkumen (26–19 B.C.) began with the assassinations of two consecutive chief judges, Cezoram and his son; greed and struggles for power brought on conflicts with the Gadianton robbers around Zarahemla. Lamanites joined with Nephites against these robbers until a famine, called down from heaven by the prophet Nephi₂, brought a temporary Nephite victory (Hel. 6–11).

Giddianhi and Zemnarihah (A.D. 13–22) led menacing campaigns against the few righteous Nephites and Lamanites who remained and joined forces at this time (3 Ne. 2–4). Low on supplies, the Gadianton robbers became more open and aggressive; they claimed rights to Nephite lands and government. The coalition of Nephites and Lamanites eventually defeated the robbers.

The final Nephite wars (A.D. 322, 327–328, 346–350) began after heavy population growth and infestation of robbers led to a border dispute, and the Nephites were driven to a narrow neck of land. The Nephites fortified the city of Shem and managed to win a ten-year peace treaty (Morm. 1–2), but the Nephites eventually counterattacked in the south. Gross wickedness existed on both sides (Morm. 6; Moro. 9), until at a prearranged battleground the Nephites met the Lamanites and were annihilated (c. A.D. 385).

Many chapters in the Book of Mormon deal with war, and for several reasons.

1.   The inevitability of war was a fundamental concern in virtually all ancient civilizations. Disposable economic resources were often largely devoted to maintaining a military force; conquest was a major factor in the transformation and development of Book of Mormon societies, as it was in the growth of most world civilizations.

2.   The Book of Mormon is a religious record, and for the people of the Book of Mormon, as in nearly all ancient cultures, warfare was fundamentally sacral. It was carried out in a complex mixture of religious ritual and ideology.

3.   Mormon, the compiler and abridger of the Book of Mormon, was himself a military commander. Many political and religious rulers in the Book of Mormon were closely associated with, if not the same as, their military commanders or elites.

4.   Important religious messages are conveyed through these accounts. Wars in Nephite history verify the words of their prophets such as ABINADI and SAMUEL THE LAMANITE (Morm. 1:19). Wars were instruments of God's judgment (Morm. 4:5) and of God's deliverance (Alma 56:46–56). Ultimately they stand as a compelling witness to warn people today against falling victim to the same fate that the Nephites and Jaredites finally brought upon themselves (Morm. 9:31; Ether 2:11–12).

BIBLIOGRAPHY

de Vaux, Roland. *Ancient Israel*. New York, 1965.

Hillam, Ray. "The Gadianton Robbers and Protracted War." *BYU Studies* 15 (1975): 215–24.

Ricks, Stephen D., and William J. Hamblin, eds. *Warfare in the Book of Mormon*. Salt Lake City, 1990. (Further bibliography is listed on pp. 22–24.)

Sorenson, John L. *An Ancient American Setting for the Book of Mormon*, pp. 239–76. Salt Lake City, 1985.

WILLIAM J. HAMBLIN

WEALTH, ATTITUDES TOWARD

Latter-day Saints view wealth as a blessing and also as a test. The Lord has repeatedly promised his people, "Inasmuch as ye shall keep the commandments of God ye shall prosper in the land" (Alma 36:30). But wealth can lead to pride and inequality: "Wo unto the rich, who are rich as to the things of the world. For because they are rich they despise the poor, and they persecute the meek, and their hearts are upon their treasures" (2 Ne. 9:30). Therefore, attitudes toward wealth and the use of material abundance reveal a person's priorities: "Before ye seek for riches, seek ye for the kingdom of God. And after ye have obtained a hope in Christ ye shall obtain riches, if ye seek them; and ye will seek them for the intent to do good" (Jacob 2:18–19). To those who will inherit the celestial kingdom, God has promised the riches of eternity.

LDS beliefs about the nature and purpose of life influence Church members' attitudes toward wealth. Thus, the concept of wealth has both materialistic and spiritual dimensions: wealth is an accumulation of worldly possessions; it is also an acquisition of knowledge or talents. Since matter and spirit are of the same order, material wealth can become refined and sanctified by the influence of God's spirit as it is consecrated to his purposes. Latter-day Saints are encouraged to increase in all honorable forms of wealth, knowledge, and obedience, which increase the "wealth" or worth of the human soul and to "lay up . . . treasures in heaven" (Matt. 6:20; D&C 18:10; 130:19).

The world and its resources belong to the Creator. Material blessings may be delivered from heaven if the recipient conforms to the Christian ideals of integrity, honesty, and charity. All people are of divine origin and have come to earth to know good and evil and to be tested to see if they will choose the good. By the grace of God and by their diligent labors consistent with divine law, both the earth and mankind can be perfected and glorified.

If the earth's resources are not wisely and carefully husbanded, however, wealth can become a curse. It is the "love of money," not money itself, that is identified as the root of all evil (1 Tim. 6:10). President Brigham Young warned that wealth and perishable things "are liable to decoy the minds of [the] saints" (CWHN 9:333). Wealth may result in misuse and un-Christian conduct, immoral exploitation, or dishonesty. Greed and harmful self-indulgence are sins, and the pursuit of materialistic goals at the expense of other Christian duties is to be avoided. People with materialistic wealth draw special warnings regarding responsibility toward the poor; riches can canker the soul and make entrance into heaven exceedingly difficult (Matt. 19:24; D&C 56:16).

Thus, the accumulation and utilization of wealth confront the human family with some of its major challenges in determining the righteousness of goals and the correctness of behavior. "In many respects the real test of a man is his attitude toward his earthly possessions" (F. Richards, p. 46). The prosperity that results from honest and intelligent work is not necessarily repugnant to the spiritual quality of life; but the Church consistently warns of the risks of "selfishness and personal aggrandizement" that lurk in accumulating wealth (S. Richards, CR [Apr. 1928]: 31).

Personal reflection, prayer, and inspiration are needed in deciding how to use one's wealth. Fairness, justice, mercy, and social responsibility are individual requirements; improper behavior is not to be excused by the behavior of others, reflected in market forces or windfall accumulations. The responsibility of each human being is to think and act in ways that ennoble the divine nature. President N. Eldon Tanner outlined five principles that epitomize the Church's counsel on personal economic affairs: pay an honest tithing, live on less than you earn, distinguish between needs and wants, develop and live within a budget, and be honest in all financial affairs (Ensign 9 [Nov. 1979]: 81–82).

While not taking vows of poverty, Latter-day Saints covenant to use their wealth, time, talents, and knowledge to build up the kingdom of God on earth (D&C 42:30; 105:5). Providing for a family is a sacred requirement (1 Tim. 5:8). The mission of the Church in many countries of the world requires considerable resources to sustain Church members in seeking the spiritual growth and perfection of themselves and others. Ignorance, disease, and poverty can be overcome only with the assistance of material assets that result from the wise use of human talent and the resources abundant in nature. Thus the Church and its members seek to obtain the material resources that are needed to build the kingdom of God.

The principles taught in the standard works concerning the accumulation and use of wealth are sufficiently broad to permit an ongoing dialogue among Church members about what is pleasing in the sight of the Lord. Some emphasize that man must work and that the fruits of his labor are his due and right (D&C 31:5). Others point out that although man must work, God makes life and its abundance possible, and thus everything rightly belongs to him (Mosiah 2:21–25) and comes to man "in the form of trust property" to be used for God's purposes (S. Richards, *CR* [Apr. 1923]: 151). Some suggest that there are no limits on the profits one may gather provided the pursuit is legal and the ultimate utilization is appropriate. Others see business and legal standards of secular society as falling short: "Except your righteousness shall exceed the righteousness of the scribes and Pharisees, ye shall in no case enter into the kingdom of heaven. . . . Ye cannot serve God and mammon" (Matt. 5:20; 6:24). Having taught correct principles in the scriptures and through his priesthood leaders, the Lord leaves it to Church members to govern themselves through individual righteousness, with knowledge that all will be held personally accountable for the choices they make.

BIBLIOGRAPHY

Johnson, Richard E. "Socioeconomic Inequality: The Haves and the Have Nots." *BYU Today* 44 (Sept. 1990): 46–58.

Nibley, Hugh W. *Approaching Zion,* Vol. 9 in CWHN. Salt Lake City, 1989.

Richards, Franklin D. "The Law of Abundance." *Ensign* 1 (June 1971): 45–47.

R. THAYNE ROBSON

WHITMER, DAVID

David Whitmer (1805–1888) was one of the Three Witnesses to the Book of Mormon whose testimony has been printed in all published copies of the book (*see* WITNESSES OF THE BOOK OF MORMON). Although Whitmer was excommunicated from the Church in 1838, he never repudiated his testimony of the Book of Mormon, reaffirming it thereafter on at least seventy recorded occasions.

David Whitmer was born to Peter Whitmer, Sr., and Mary Musselman Whitmer near Harrisburg, Pennsylvania, on January 7, 1805. In 1809 the family moved to Fayette, New

David Whitmer (1805–1888), the most interviewed of the Three Witnesses to the Book of Mormon. An individualist who was doggedly unwavering in his testimony of the spiritual manifestations received in June 1829, he was known as an honest, conscientious, and guileless man. Courtesy Library-Archives, Reorganized Church of Jesus Christ of Latter Day Saints.

York, where they worked a large farm. He learned about the Book of Mormon from Oliver COWDERY, who was scribe for Joseph SMITH during the translation. When persecution grew severe in Harmony, Pennsylvania, where the two were working, Whitmer invited Joseph, Oliver, and Joseph's wife, Emma, to his family's house in Fayette. The translation of the Book of Mormon was completed there in June 1829.

In the same month, Joseph Smith told David Whitmer that he, along with Cowdery and Martin HARRIS, another supporter of the work, were to be witnesses of the Book of Mormon. In answer to their prayers, an angel appeared to them near the Whitmer house and showed them the gold plates from which the Book of Mormon was translated. An account of this experience comprises the Testimony of the Three Witnesses in the Book of Mormon. David's brothers, Christian, Jacob, John, and Peter, Jr., were four of the Eight Witnesses to whom Joseph Smith showed the plates without an angelic visitation and whose testimony also appears in the book.

In 1829, David, John, and Peter, Jr., received revelations through Joseph Smith calling them to missionary work (D&C 14:6; 15:6; 16:6). In April 1830 the Church was organized in Peter Whitmer, Sr.'s, house. However, David's close association with Joseph Smith did not prevent occasional chastisement. A revelation in 1830 warned Whitmer, "Your mind has been on the things of the earth more than on the things of me, your Maker, and the ministry whereunto you have been called; and you have not given heed unto my Spirit, and to those who were set over you, but have been persuaded by those whom I have not commanded" (D&C 30:2). In view of Whitmer's later separation from the Church, this statement seems prophetic.

When the Church moved from New York in 1831, the Whitmers went with the Saints to Kirtland, Ohio, and then to Jackson County, Missouri, which had been designated as Zion, a gathering place for the Saints. By July 1832, the Whitmers had settled along the Big Blue River in Kaw Township (now Kansas City). To their great disappointment, the hopes for Zion were short-lived. The differences between the Latter-day Saints and the local settlers erupted into open conflict. On one occasion, a mob threatened to kill Whitmer and other Church leaders if they did not admit that the Book of Mormon was a fraud. Whitmer absolutely refused.

Driven from Jackson County, the Whitmers settled in adjacent Clay County, Missouri, along with other Latter-day Saint refugees. As their numbers grew, a stake was organized and Whitmer became the stake president in July 1834, making him the leading figure in Church administration in the area. By October 1834, David and John Whitmer had moved back to Kirtland, Ohio, to prepare for the spiritual blessing promised to the Saints when the Kirtland Temple was completed. In February 1835, in accord with an earlier commission received by revelation, David Whitmer with Oliver Cowdery and Martin Harris selected the twelve men who constituted the first Quorum of Twelve Apostles in the Church (D&C 18:37–38). Whitmer was also a member of the committee that drafted rules for the regulation of the temple. On the day of its dedication, March 27, 1836, he testified of an outpouring of the Spirit from on high, as the Lord had promised (*HC* 2:427).

In spite of all their great contributions to the work, by 1838 David and the remainder of the Whitmers had left the Church (Christian and Peter, Jr., had previously died in Clay County). The year 1837 was a time of disillusion and financial trial for the Saints in Kirtland. To help shore up the local economy, Joseph Smith and other leaders organized a banking society. When it failed, many members who lost their savings were embittered. Brigham Young said it was a time when the "knees of many of the strongest men in the Church faltered" (Elden Jay Watson, ed., *Manuscript History of Brigham Young, 1801–1844*, Salt Lake City, 1968, p. 16). Even earlier, in February 1837, some dissenters wanted to depose Joseph Smith and replace him with David Whitmer. Whitmer, a proud and stubborn man, was still smarting from conflicts over his leadership in Missouri. In the disciplinary council that excommunicated Whitmer, on April 13, 1838, one of the main charges brought against him was "possessing the same spirit with the Dissenters" (Donald Q. Cannon and Lyndon W. Cook, eds., *Far West Record, Minutes of The Church of Jesus Christ of Latter-day Saints, 1830–1844*, Salt Lake City, 1983, p. 177).

After Whitmer left the Church, he moved to Richmond, Missouri, and opened a livery stable, which he ran until 1888. A respected citizen in the community, he served on fair boards, was a member of the city council, and was elected mayor. Over his lifetime, hundreds of visitors inquired about and heard his testimony of the Book of Mormon.

A year before his death Whitmer wrote a pamphlet, *An Address to All Believers in Christ* (1887), apparently to justify his separation from the Church. In the pamphlet, he again gave witness to the truth of the Book of Mormon, but claimed that Joseph Smith drifted into errors after completing the translation. Whitmer rejected many later developments in the Church, such as the offices of high priest and prophet, seer, and revelator; the Doctrine and Covenants; and the doctrines of gathering and of plural marriage.

Shortly before his death, Whitmer re-peated once more, for the *Richmond Conservator*, what he had written in the *Address*: "I have never at any time denied that testimony or any part thereof, which has so long since been published with that Book, as one of the three witnesses. Those who know me best, well know that I have always adhered to that testimony." He died in Richmond, Missouri, on January 25, 1888, bearing testimony again on his deathbed of the authenticity of the Book of Mormon.

BIBLIOGRAPHY

Anderson, Richard Lloyd. *Investigating the Book of Mormon Witnesses*. Salt Lake City, 1981.

Cook, Lyndon W., and Matthew K. Cook, eds. *David Whitmer Interviews: A Restoration Witness*. Orem, Utah, 1991.

Nibley, Preston, comp. *The Witnesses of the Book of Mormon*. Salt Lake City, 1973.

Perkins, Keith W. "True to the Book of Mormon: The Whitmers." *Ensign* 19 (Feb. 1989): 34–42.

KEITH W. PERKINS

WITNESSES OF THE BOOK OF MORMON

Beginning with the first edition of 1830, the Book of Mormon has generally contained two sets of testimonies—the "Testimony of Three Witnesses" and the "Testimony of Eight Witnesses." When Joseph SMITH first obtained the GOLD PLATES, he was told to show them to no one. As translation progressed, he and those assisting him learned, both in the pages of the Book and by additional revelation, that three special witnesses would know, by the power of God, "that these things are true" and that several besides himself would see the plates and testify to their existence (Ether 5:2–4; 2 Ne. 27:12–13; D&C 5:11–13). The

Joseph Smith and the Eight Witnesses, by Harold T. (Dale) Kilbourn (1984), illustrates Joseph Smith allowing the Eight Witnesses to touch the gold plates from which the Book of Mormon was translated. "We did handle with our hands; and we also saw the engravings thereon, all of which has the appearance of ancient work, and of curious workmanship. And this we bear record with words of soberness." © by Intellectual Reserve, Inc. Used by permission.

testimonies of the witnesses affirm that these things occurred.

The witnesses were men known for truthfulness and sobriety. Though each of the Three Witnesses was eventually excommunicated from the Church (two returned), none ever denied or retracted his published testimony. Each reaffirmed at every opportunity the veracity of his testimony and the reality of what he had seen and experienced.

A June 1829 revelation confirmed that Oliver COWDERY, David WHITMER, and Martin HARRIS would be the Three Witnesses (D&C 17). Soon thereafter, they, with Joseph Smith, retired to the woods near Fayette, New York, and prayed for the promised divine manifestation. The "Testimony of Three Witnesses" summarizes the supernatural event that followed, when an angel appeared and showed them the plates and engravings and they heard the Lord declare that the Book

of Mormon was "translated by the gift and power of God." They said that the same divine voice "commanded us that we should bear record of it."

Joseph Smith's mother later recounted Joseph's great relief at no longer being the sole witness of the divine experiences of the restoration (*see* WITNESSES, LAW OF). That others had also seen an angel and "will have to testify to the truth of what I have said for now they know for themselves" relieved him of a great burden (Lucy Smith Preliminary Manuscript, Church Archives).

Soon afterward, at the Smith farm in New York, eight others were allowed to view and handle the plates: Christian Whitmer, Jacob Whitmer, Peter Whitmer, Jr., John Whitmer, Hiram Page, Joseph Smith, Sr., Hyrum Smith, and Samuel H. Smith. Their signed "Testimony of Eight Witnesses" reports that Joseph Smith showed these eight men the metal plates, which they "hefted" while turning the individual "leaves" and examining the engravings of "curious workmanship." In 1829 the word *curious* carried the meaning of the Latin word for "careful," suggesting that the plates were wrought "with care and art." Five of these Eight Witnesses remained solidly with the Church; John Whitmer was excommunicated in 1838, and his brother Jacob Whitmer and brother-in-law Hiram Page then became inactive.

Most of these eleven witnesses were members of the large Smith and Whitmer families—families who had assisted in guarding and in translating the ancient record. Not surprisingly, other family members reported indirect contact with the plates and the translation. Young William Smith once helped his brother Joseph carry the plates wrapped in a work frock. Joseph's wife Emma SMITH felt the pliable plates as she dusted around the cloth-covered record on her husband's translating table. Burdened with daily chores and caring for her family and visitors working on the translation, Mother Whitmer (Peter Whitmer, Sr.'s, wife) was shown the plates by a heavenly messenger to assure her that the work was of God.

Martin Harris, a prosperous farmer of Palmyra, New York, who had long sought a religion fulfilling biblical prophecy, assisted with the translation previous to his experience as a witness. In 1828 he spent two months transcribing as Joseph Smith dictated the first major segment of Book of Mormon translation—116 handwritten pages. After Martin lost these pages, he wrote no more for the Prophet, but he later financed the publication of the book.

Oliver Cowdery was the main scribe for the Book of Mormon. A schoolteacher, he learned of the gold plates and the translation while boarding with Joseph Smith's parents near Palmyra, New York. In early April 1829, Oliver walked from the Smith home to Harmony, Pennsylvania, where Joseph Smith was translating. On the way Oliver visited his friend David Whitmer, who also developed an intense interest in the new scripture. When persecution increased in Harmony, David came as requested and moved Joseph and Oliver to his family farm near Fayette (more than 100 miles away), about June 1.

Joseph Smith later recalled the insistent pleading of Harris, Whitmer, and Cowdery after they learned that three would be permitted to see the plates. The June 1829 revelation confirmed that they would be the Three Witnesses—and that they would then testify both from firsthand knowledge and "by the power of God" to the end "that my servant Joseph Smith, Jun., may not be destroyed" (D&C 17:3–4). Of the perhaps 200 recorded interviews with the Three Witnesses, a significant percentage stress the spiritual intensity

of the witnesses as they described the angel and the plates. By themselves, the Prophet's reputation and claims were vulnerable, but the testimony of additional reputable, solemn witnesses who shared a divine experience added credibility.

Lucy Smith's autobiography records the overwhelming gratitude of the Three Witnesses as they returned to the Whitmer house after sharing this experience. Joseph Smith's own history gives the fullest details of the event: repeated prayers followed by a vision given simultaneously to the Prophet, Cowdery, and Whitmer, and soon after a nearly identical vision experienced by the Prophet with Harris. According to Joseph, the intense glory of God enveloped the natural surroundings, and in this divine light the angel appeared, carefully displayed the plates, specifically counseled David Whitmer—the only one of the three who did not eventually return to the Church—to endure to the end, and the voice of God declared the book divine (HC 1:54–56).

By early 1838, disagreements on Church policies brought disaffection and excommunication for each of the Three Witnesses, and they separated; Cowdery died in 1850, Harris in 1875, and Whitmer in 1888. Throughout their lives, each witness freely answered questions about his firsthand experience with the angel and the plates. Obviously not relying on Joseph Smith's account, which was not written until the months following their excommunication, each spoke spontaneously and independently; yet the details harmonized with each other and with Joseph Smith's history.

The alienation of the witnesses from the Church stemmed largely from conflicts regarding authority. After receiving revelation, the Three Witnesses felt they shared equally with Joseph Smith in foundational experiences, and their certainty about a past vision contributed to their inflexibility concerning future revelations. They sided with the Prophet's critics who reacted negatively to the failure of the Kirtland Safety Society, and they opposed Joseph Smith's vigorous doctrinal and administrative leadership. After their excommunication, each felt deep rejection, resulting, predictably, in their harsh criticisms of Church leadership. Even in these circumstances, each of the Three Witnesses continued to maintain vigorously the authenticity of their published testimony. None expressed any doubt as to what they had testified. Both Oliver Cowdery and Martin Harris returned to the Church at the end of their lives; David Whitmer retained religious independence but to the end aggressively defended the Book of Mormon.

Skeptics have discounted the "Testimony of Three Witnesses" on the ground of collusion or deception. Yet each of the three was a respected and independent member of non-Mormon society, active in his community. Their lives, fully documented, clearly demonstrate their honesty and intelligence. David Whitmer repeatedly reacted against charges of possible "delusion." To one skeptic, he responded: "Of course we were in the spirit when we had the view . . . but we were in the body also, and everything was as natural to us, as it is at any time" (Anderson, p. 87). Perhaps their later alienation makes them even more credible as witnesses, for no collusion could have withstood their years of separation from the Church and from each other.

The testimonies of the Three and Eight Witnesses balance the supernatural and the natural, the one stressing the angel and heavenly voice, the other the existence of a tangible record on gold plates. To the end of their lives, each of the Three said he had seen the plates, and each of the Eight insisted that he had handled them. Most of the Eight and all

of the Three Witnesses reiterated their Book of Mormon testimonies just before death. Together with Joseph Smith they fulfill Nephi's prophecy: "They shall testify to the truth of the book and the things therein" (2 Ne. 27:12).

BIBLIOGRAPHY

Contributions of the Three Witnesses to the translation of the Book of Mormon are detailed in Lucy Mack Smith, *Biographical Sketches of Joseph Smith the Prophet and His Progenitors for Many Generations* (Liverpool, 1853 [reprinted Salt Lake City, 1902 under the title *History of the Prophet Joseph by His Mother Lucy Mack Smith*]). Joseph Smith's recollections of the events of June 1829 are found in Dean C. Jessee, ed., *The Papers of Joseph Smith*, Vol. 1 (Salt Lake City, 1989) (see transcriptions of the 1839 draft and 1839 manuscript history). See also Joseph Smith's published *History of the Church*.

For the Witnesses' testimonies, and their lives outside the Church, see Richard Lloyd Anderson, *Investigating the Book of Mormon Witnesses* (corr. ed.; Salt Lake City, 1989). Primary documents concerning their testimonies appear in Preston Nibley, *Witnesses of the Book of Mormon* (Salt Lake City, 1953). For life sketches, see Andrew Jenson, *Latter-day Saints Biographical Encyclopedia*, Vol. 1 (Salt Lake City, 1901). Profiles for most of the Witnesses are also in Lyndon Cook, *Revelations of the Prophet Joseph Smith* (Salt Lake City, 1985).

RICHARD LLOYD ANDERSON

WITNESSES, LAW OF

The scriptural law of witnesses requires that in the mouth of two or three individuals shall every word be established (Deut. 19:15; 2 Cor. 13:1; 1 Tim. 5:19). This law applies in divine as well as human relations, for members of the Godhead bear witness of one another (John 5:31–37; 3 Ne. 11:32), and books of holy writ give multiple witness to the work of God in the earth (2 Ne. 29:8–13). The law of witnesses is prominent in the history and practice of The Church of Jesus Christ of Latter-day Saints.

A witness gives personal verification of, or attests to the reality of, an event. To "witness" in the scriptural sense is much the same as in the legal sense: to give personal testimony based on firsthand evidence or experience. To bear false witness is a very serious offense (Deut. 5:20; 19:16–21). When prophets have an experience with the Lord, often he commands them to "bear record" of him and of the truths that have been revealed (1 Ne. 10:10; 11:7; D&C 58:59; 112:4; 138:60). In legal affairs, testimony is usually related to what a person knows by the physical senses. In spiritual matters there is additional knowledge or information received through the Holy Spirit.

The Bible illustrates that God often works with mankind through two or more witnesses (Num. 35:30; Deut. 17:6; 19:15; Matt. 18:15–16). Likewise, latter-day scripture teaches the need for witnesses (D&C 6:28; 42:80–81; 128:3). One person's word alone, even though it may be true, may not be sufficient to establish and bind the hearer to the truth. Witnesses provide the means of establishing faith in the minds of people, for faith comes by hearing the word of God through the power of human testimony accompanied by the Holy Ghost (Rom. 10:17; *TPJS*, p. 148; *Lectures on Faith*, 2). In the BOOK OF MORMON, the prophet NEPHI₁ combined his brother Jacob's testimony with Isaiah's testimony to reinforce and verify his own witness of the divine sonship of the Redeemer (2 Ne. 11:2–3). Likewise, Alma₂ called upon the words of ZENOS, ZENOCK, and Moses to corroborate his own testimony of the Son of God (Alma 33:2–23).

When the keys of the priesthood were restored to the Prophet Joseph SMITH and often when visions were received, the Prophet was accompanied by a witness. This is the case with the restoration of the Aaronic Priesthood, the Melchizedek Priesthood, the keys given in the Kirtland Temple (Ohio), and the vision of the degrees of glory (D&C 13; 76; 110). Subsequent to the translation of the Book of Mormon and prior to its publication, three men on one occasion, and eight men on a separate occasion, in addition to Joseph Smith, became witnesses of the Book of Mormon PLATES (*see* WITNESSES OF THE BOOK OF MORMON). The Prophet Joseph was likewise accompanied in his martyr's death by his brother Hyrum, a second martyr or witness, making their testimony valid forever (D&C 135:3; 136:39). The meaning of the Greek word *martyr* is "witness."

The scriptures also indicate other ways in which the law of witnesses applies:

THE DIVINITY OF JESUS CHRIST. John the Baptist testified of the divinity of Jesus (John 1:15; 3:26; 5:32–39), the Father testified of Christ (Matt. 3:17; 17:5; John 8:18), and Christ himself bore record of his own divinity as the Son of God (Matt. 26:63–64; John 11:4; 13:31). The theme of John 5–8 illustrates the principle of witnesses. When Jesus spoke in his own behalf, some Jews, referring to the law of witnesses, said, "Thou bearest record of thyself; thy record is not true" (John 8:13). Jesus had earlier explained that both John the Baptist and the Father in Heaven had borne record of him (John 5:31–39; 8:18) and his testimony was therefore valid and binding. He declared that his works testified that he was the Son of God (John 5:31–38). Peter also bore testimony that Jesus was the Son of God, a fact he had learned by revelation (Matt. 16:16).

JESUS' RESURRECTION FROM THE DEAD. Witnesses to the RESURRECTION of Christ included groups of women, two disciples on the road to Emmaus, and the apostles (Matt.

28; Luke 24; Acts 4:33; 5:32). Paul records that there were in Galilee over 500 witnesses to Jesus' resurrected body (1 Cor. 15:6). The Book of Mormon reports that about 2,500 people in America witnessed the resurrected body of Jesus Christ by seeing and touching it, and did "bear record" of it (3 Ne. 11:14–16; 17:25).

AUTHENTICATION OF RITES AND CEREMONIES. In the Church, witnesses are officially present for all baptisms and marriages. Witnesses also confirm proxy baptisms, endowments, marriages, and sealings in the temples on behalf of the dead (D&C 127:6). Missionaries travel in pairs as witnesses for one another (Mark 6:7; Luke 10:1; D&C 42:6; 52:10; 61:35; 62:5).

ON JUDGMENT DAY. In the final judgment that God will render to all mankind, the fact of the gospel having been taught on the earth by multiple witnesses will be important. Nephi$_1$ has written, "Wherefore, by the words of three, God hath said, I will establish my word. Nevertheless, God sendeth more witnesses, and he proveth all his words" (2 Ne. 11:3; cf. 27:14).

In a very fundamental way, the Bible and the Book of Mormon are witnesses to each other. Each record establishes the truth found in the other, and the Doctrine and Covenants establishes the truth of them both (1 Ne. 13:20–40; 2 Ne. 3:12; 29:8–14; Morm. 7:8–9; D&C 17:6; 20:11–12; 42:12). The written testimony of two nations, the Jews and the Nephites, is a witness to the world that there is a God (2 Ne. 29:8).

BIBLIOGRAPHY

McConkie, Bruce R. *A New Witness for the Articles of Faith*, pp. 446–47. Salt Lake City, 1985.

Trites, Allison A. *The New Testament Concept of Witness*. Cambridge, 1977.

Van Orden, Bruce A. "The Law of Witnesses in 2 Nephi." In *The Book of Mormon: Second Nephi,*

The Doctrinal Structure, ed. M. Nyman and C. Tate, Jr., pp. 307–21. Provo, Utah, 1989.

ROBERT L. MARROTT

WOMEN IN THE BOOK OF MORMON

Some general conclusions about Book of Mormon women can be drawn from the book's fragmentary material about marriage, family, and religious organization. Six women are mentioned by name: Sariah, Isabel, Abish, Eve, Sarah, and Mary. Since no women are mentioned as religious or military leaders and only a few as political leaders, it appears that males held virtually all leadership positions in this society. Also, since the Book of Mormon was written primarily to remind future readers of the goodness of God and to persuade them to believe in Christ, it contains no law books and little intellectual or social history discussing the meshing of familial and religious practices. It is reasonable to assume, however, that these people began with many customs similar to their ancestral Semitic cultures and that their practices changed somewhat over the years.

In Nephite society, marriage and childbearing were expected, carrying religious significance and responsibilities (1 Ne. 7:1; Mosiah 4:14–15; 4 Ne. 1:11). Marriages may have been arranged within ethnic groups (1 Ne. 16:7; Alma 17:24) and were restricted outside certain groups (Alma 3:8). Polygamy and concubinage were prohibited and scorned; monogamy was expected, except as the Lord might command otherwise to "raise up seed" unto himself (Jacob 2:27–30).

Husbands and wives were expected to be faithful and loyal to each other (Jacob 3:7). One case shows that a wife was valued, even if unable to conceive. The righteous Jaredite king Coriantum remained with his barren wife until her death at age 102. He then married a young maid and fathered sons and daughters (Ether 9:23–24). It was, likewise, a sign of great wickedness that the priests of king Noah deserted their families. While in hiding, they abducted twenty-four Lamanite women for wives. When Lamanite kinsmen discovered and sought to kill the priests several years later, however, these women faithfully pleaded for the lives of their husbands (Mosiah 23:33).

Men were expected to support their wives and children, as well as the widows and children of men killed in war (Mosiah 21:17). Men were to pray for their households (Alma 34:21), and many took up arms to defend their families.

Both parents were concerned about their offspring (1 Ne. 5:1–7; 8:37). LEHI blessed and counseled his granddaughters and grandsons (2 Ne. 4:3–9). Children were taught to honor their mother and father. HELAMAN₁ and his 2,000 young warriors credited their Ammonite mothers with instilling in them the faith that "if they did not doubt, God would deliver them" (Alma 56:47).

In religious life, women participated in assemblies at the temple (Jacob 2:7; Mosiah 2:5–8), in teaching their children about God (Alma 56:46–47), and in offering sacrifice (1 Ne. 5:9). Evidently they were not excluded from, or segregated during, worship (2 Ne. 26:28–33); nor is there any indication that they were considered ritually unclean during menstruation. The gospel taught by the NEPHITES and Christ in the Book of Mormon is addressed to all, regardless of gender, age, or descent (2 Ne. 26:33; Mosiah 27:25; Alma 11:44; 32:23; 3 Ne. 17:25). BAPTISM was offered to all men and women who believed (Mosiah 18:16). Women demonstrated profound faith and were tested by great sacrifice. In Ammonihah, women were burned to death with their children for refusing to renounce their faith in Christ (Alma 14:7–11). Apparently the

LIAHONA responded to the collective faith and diligence of the entire group, men and women (1 Ne. 16:28).

During the years in the wilderness, the Lehite women toiled and were strong, but little is known about their activities, other than pregnancy and childbirth. Spinning is the only work specifically attributed to women (Mosiah 10:5; Hel. 6:13). Women's dancing is associated with leisure and sometimes with wickedness (1 Ne. 18:9; Mosiah 20:1; Ether 8:10–11). Harlots provided immoral sexual activity in return for sustenance (Mosiah 11:14).

Politically, women had rights of succession to the Lamanite throne, for when Amalickiah murdered a Lamanite king, rule passed to the queen, whom Amalickiah then married to gain the throne (Alma 47:32–35). In extreme crises women took up arms in war alongside their men (Alma 54:12; 55:17; Ether 15:15).

Assignment of tasks in the family or in the whole economy—trade, planting and harvesting crops, and tending animals—is not apparent. Cycles of colonization, agriculture, urbanization, war, destruction, and renewal, as well as differing belief systems, certainly affected family and work patterns.

The Book of Mormon women Sariah, Abish, and Isabel can be viewed not only as historical figures but also as archetypal figures of, respectively, the righteous mother, the godly servant, and the attractive but sexually impure outsider.

Sariah was the faithful mother of the Nephite and Lamanite nations. She left a comfortable home near Jerusalem with Lehi and their family to suffer the rigors of desert and ocean travel, bearing two more sons, JACOB and JOSEPH, late in life while in the wilderness (1 Ne. 18:7, 17–19). She complained against Lehi when she thought their sons were dead, but affirmed his calling and

Widow of King Lehonti, Minerva K. Teichert (1935, oil on canvas, 36" x 48"). After assassinating the Lamanite king Lehonti, the treacherous Amalickiah married the queen, legitimating his accession to the throne (Alma 47:18–35). The paintings of Minerva Teichert are particularly sensitive to the extensive but understated importance of women in the Book of Mormon. © Courtesy Museum of Art, Brigham Young University. All rights reserved.

the power of God when they returned unharmed (1 Ne. 5:2–8). With Lehi she gave sacrifice in thanksgiving. She was the mother of six sons and at least two daughters (2 Ne. 5:6).

Abish, a Lamanite convert of surpassing faith, servant to the queen of king Lamoni, recognized that the power of God had overcome the king, queen, and Ammon when they fell to the ground unconscious; she gathered people to witness the event and then raised the queen with her touch when the confusion of the crowd led to contention. Many believed the testimonies of the revived queen, who then raised the king, who also testified of Jesus (Alma 19:16–36).

Isabel, according to ALMA₂ (Alma 39:3–4), was a harlot who stole the hearts of many, including that of Alma's son Corianton, who for a time forsook the ministry to go after her (Alma 39:3).

The other three named women are biblical figures: Eve (e.g., 2 Ne. 2:15–20; cf. several

references to "our first parents," e.g., 2 Ne. 9:9); Sarah (2 Ne. 8:2); and Mary, the mother of Jesus (e.g., Mosiah 3:8). Eve is mentioned in the context of an explication of the doctrine of the FALL OF ADAM as the precursor of the salvation of mankind. Sarah is recognized as the faithful mother of nations. Mary is called "a virgin, most beautiful and fair above all other virgins" (1 Ne. 11:15).

Other women are known in the Book of Mormon only by their individual deeds: the wife of NEPHI₁ a daughter of Ishmael, tried to soften wicked hearts with her tears (1 Ne. 7:19; 18:19); Ishmael's wife and three of their daughters supported Nephi (1 Ne. 7:6); a maidservant fled from Morianton's camp, after being severely beaten by him, to warn MORONI₁ of the plans of her rebel master (Alma 50:30–31); a daughter of Jared originated a plot to regain the kingdom for her father through enticement, violence, and deceit (Ether 8–9); two Lamanite queens were converted by the sons of Mosiah₂ (Alma 19:29–30; 22:19–24). Perhaps, as in some Semitic cultures today, the formal or more polite way of referring to a woman was not by her given name, but by describing her position in the family, such as "the daughter of Jared." Others so designated include Ishmael's wife, Ishmael's daughters, Ishmael's eldest daughter and wife of Zoram, Lehi's daughters and Nephi's sisters, Lamoni's daughter; and Coriantumr's unrepentant daughters.

The behavior and treatment of women were seen as an index of social and spiritual health. Many references to women concern their suffering during war, captivity, and hardship. Nephi and his brothers measure the difficulty of their travels in terms of the suffering of their wives, though Nephi emphasizes that the women were made strong like the men, while his brothers describe their wives' sufferings as being worse than death (1 Ne. 17:1, 20). Jacob sharply contrasts male infidelity with the tenderness of the women (Jacob 2–3); immorality is described as precipitating the collapse of both family and society. The inhumanity and depravity of dying civilizations are also described in terms of the suffering of women: Lamanites fed to women and children the flesh of their dead husbands and fathers (Moro. 9:8); Nephite women were sacrificed to idols (Morm. 4:15, 21); Nephites raped captured Lamanite women, tortured them to death, and then ate their flesh as a token of their bravery (Moro. 9:9–10).

Much of the imagery involving women in the Book of Mormon parallels that in the Bible. For example, Christ compares his gathering of the repentant to a mother hen gathering her chicks under her wing. As in Proverbs 3:13–20, wisdom is female (Mosiah 8:20), as is mercy (Alma 42:24). Sometimes female imagery is applied to the Lord, as when the mother nursing her child is the image used of the Lord comforting and remembering his covenant children (1 Ne. 21:15).

In a sense, the woman is the image of God's people. The biblical imagery of God as husband and his people as wife is continued in the Book of Mormon, mostly from the writings of Isaiah. Decadent Israel is described as devoid of honorable men, in that they valued women as decorative sex objects (2 Ne. 13:16–26; Isa. 3:16–26). When God's people become unfaithful to him, they are called "the whore of all the earth" (2 Ne. 10:16). When he calls his people to repentance, the Lord asks rhetorically, "Have I put thee away . . . ? Where is the bill of your mother's divorcement?" (2 Ne. 7:1; Isa. 50:1). The images of a mother too weak to nurse her child and a pregnant woman so near term she is unable to flee destruction are used to motivate the Nephites to repent (Hel. 15:1–2); the woman whose children are lost is the image of desolation (1 Ne. 21:20–21). Those who accept "marriage" with the Lord are to experience joy as abundant as that of a barren woman who becomes a mother of many children, and the Lord consoles his people by saying, "For thy maker, thy husband, the Lord of Hosts is his name; . . . For a small moment have I forsaken thee, but with great mercies will I gather thee" (3 Ne. 22:1, 5–8; Isa. 54:1, 5–8).

BIBLIOGRAPHY

Spencer, Majorie Meads. "My Book of Mormon Sisters." *Ensign* 7 (Sept. 1977): 66–71.

ADDITIONAL SOURCE

Bennion, Francine. "Women and the Book of Mormon." In *Women of Wisdom and Knowledge*, 169–78. Salt Lake City: Deseret Book, 1990.

DONNA LEE BOWEN
CAMILLE S. WILLIAMS

Z

ZENOCK

Zenock was a preexilic Israelite prophet whose words were found on the PLATES of brass, a record carried from Jerusalem to the new promised land in the Western Hemisphere by the Book of Mormon prophet LEHI c. 600 B.C. Zenock is not known from the Hebrew Bible or other sources and is noted in only five passages in the Book of Mormon. It is possible that he was of the lineage of JOSEPH OF EGYPT and an ancestor of the NEPHITES (3 Ne. 10:16).

Each reference to Zenock refers to his teaching of either the coming or redemptive mission of Jesus Christ. NEPHI₁, son of Lehi, in teaching from the words of previous prophets, stated that the God of Abraham, Isaac, and Jacob (Jesus Christ) would be "lifted up, according to the words of Zenock" (1 Ne. 19:10), referring to his crucifixion. Alma 33:16 contains the only direct quotation of Zenock's words, citing him as one of many Israelite prophets who foretold the mission of the Son of God (Alma 33:14–17; cf. 34:7) and quoting him on the mercies that God grants

because of his Son. ALMA₂ noted, however, that because the people "would not understand" Zenock's words, they "stoned him to death" (Alma 33:17). NEPHI₂ cited Zenock and others who testified of the coming of the Son of God (Hel. 8:20). In the last reference to his work, MORMON wrote that ZENOS and Zenock foretold the destruction that preceded the coming of Christ to the remnant of their posterity (3 Ne. 10:14–16).

KENT P. JACKSON

ZENOS

Zenos is one of four Israelite prophets of Old Testament times cited in the BOOK OF MORMON whose writings appeared on the PLATES of brass but who are not mentioned in the Old Testament (see also ZENOCK; NEUM; and EZIAS). Zenos is quoted or mentioned by NEPHI₁ (1 Ne. 19:10–17), JACOB (Jacob 5:1–77; 6:1), ALMA₂ (Alma 33:3–11, 13, 15), Amulek (Alma 34:7), NEPHI₂ (Hel. 8:19–20), and MORMON (3 Ne. 10:14–17).

Although specific dates and details of

Zenos' life and ministry are not known, the Book of Mormon provides considerable information about him from his teachings and related facts. Evidently he lived sometime between 1600 and 600 B.C. because he was apparently a descendant of JOSEPH OF EGYPT and his writings were on the plates of brass taken from Jerusalem to the Americas by Nephi₁ about 600 B.C. He may also have been a progenitor of the Book of Mormon prophet LEHI (cf. 3 Ne. 10:16). Zenos spent time "in the wilderness" (Alma 33:4), but also preached "in the midst" of the "congregations" of God (Alma 33:9). Some of his enemies became reconciled to him through the power of God, but others were visited "with speedy destruction" (Alma 33:4, 10). Finally, he was slain because of his bold testimony of the coming of the "Son of God" (Hel. 8:13–19).

A major theme in the teachings of Zenos was the destiny of the house of Israel. His allegory or parable comparing the house of Israel to a tame olive tree and the Gentiles to a wild olive tree constitutes the longest single chapter in the Book of Mormon, Jacob chapter 5 (*see* BOOK OF MORMON: BOOK OF JACOB). The allegory refers to major events in the scattering and gathering of the house of Israel (*see* ALLEGORY OF ZENOS).

The second-longest quotation from Zenos in the Book of Mormon is his hymn of thanksgiving and praise recorded in Alma 33:3–11, which emphasizes prayer, worship, and the mercies of God. A careful comparison of the style and contents of this hymn with *Hymn* H (or 8) and *Hymn* J (or 10) of the *Thanksgiving Hymns* of the Dead Sea Scrolls, noting certain striking similarities, suggests that the three may have been written by the same person. Further, the life situations of the author (or authors) are very similar (CWHN 7:276–83). Some LDS scholars anticipate that

other evidences of Zenos' writings may appear as additional ancient manuscripts come to light.

Book of Mormon prophets frequently quoted Zenos because of his plain and powerful testimony of the future life, mission, atonement, death, and resurrection of the Son of God. Alma₂ recorded part of Zenos' prayer to God, recounting that "it is because of thy Son that thou hast been thus merciful unto me, therefore I will cry unto thee in all mine afflictions, for in thee is my joy; for thou hast turned thy judgments away from me, because of thy Son" (Alma 33:11). Nephi₁ recalled Zenos' knowledge that after the Son of God was crucified, he would "be buried in a sepulchre" for three days, and a sign of darkness should be "given of his death unto those who should inhabit the isles of the sea, more especially given unto those who are of the house of Israel" (1 Ne. 19:10). AMULEK quoted Zenos' words to show "that redemption cometh through the Son of God" (Alma 34:7). Mormon included Zenos as one of the prophets who spoke of events associated with "the coming of Christ" (3 Ne. 10:15), as did Nephi₂, who stated, "Yea, behold, the prophet Zenos did testify boldly; for the which he was slain" (Hel. 8:19).

Elder Bruce R. McConkie of the Quorum of the Twelve Apostles summarized some of the teachings of Zenos and evaluated his contributions as follows:

> It was Zenos who wrote of the visit of the Lord God to Israel after his resurrection; of the joy and salvation that would come to the righteous among them; of the desolations and destructions that awaited the wicked among them; of the fires, and tempests, and earthquakes that would occur in the Americas; of the scourging and crucifying of the God of Israel by those in Jerusalem; of the scattering of the Jews among all nations; and of their gathering

again in the last days "from the four quarters of the earth" (1 Ne. 19:11–17). I do not think I overstate the matter when I say that next to Isaiah himself—who is the prototype, pattern, and model for all the prophets—there was not a greater prophet in all Israel than Zenos. (p. 17)

BIBLIOGRAPHY

McConkie, Bruce R. "The Doctrinal Restoration." In *The Joseph Smith Translation, The Restoration of Plain and Precious Things*, ed M. Nyman and R. Millet. Provo, Utah, 1985.

Nibley, Hugh W. "Prophets in the Wilderness." CWHN 7:264–90.

DANIEL H. LUDLOW

ZORAM

Three men named Zoram are noted in the Book of Mormon. The first Zoram was the servant of Laban, a Jewish commander in Jerusalem about 600 B.C. (1 Ne. 4:31). This Zoram gave the disguised NEPHI₁ the plates of brass thinking he was Laban. Offered freedom if he would become part of Nephi's group in the wilderness, Zoram accepted Nephi's offer and made an oath to stay with them from that time on (1 Ne. 4:20–38). He married one of the daughters of Ishmael (1 Ne. 16:7), was a true friend to Nephi, was blessed by Nephi's father Lehi (2 Ne. 1:30–32), and went with Nephi when the Nephite colony separated after Lehi's death (2 Ne. 5:5–6). His descendants were called Zoramites.

A second Zoram was the chief captain over the armies of the Nephites in 81 B.C. He consulted with Alma₂, the high priest over the church, regarding his military actions (Alma 16:5–8).

The third Zoram was the leader of a group called Zoramites who separated themselves from the Nephites about 24 B.C. and apostatized from the established church. These Zoramites killed Korihor, the antichrist (Alma 30:59). Alma₂ led a missionary contingent among them to try to reclaim them from their apostasy and to prevent them from entering into an alliance with the Lamanites. While several of their poor were reconverted, the majority continued in their wicked ways (Alma 31:35), eventually joining the Lamanites and becoming antagonists to the Nephites. Some Zoramites served as Lamanite military commanders and even as kings (Alma 43:4–44; 48:5; 3 Ne. 1:29).

BIBLIOGRAPHY

Nibley, Hugh W. CWHN 6:127–30; 8:543–44.

MONTE S. NYMAN

INDEX OF PASSAGES

1:1–8, pp. 60, 135
1:3–4, p. 44
1:13, pp. 164, 195
1:13–16, p. 44
1:20, p. 214
1:21, pp. 85, 86, 213
1:25, p. 65
1:27, p. 44

Jarom

1, p. 85
1:2, p. 219
1:5, p. 107
1:6, p. 214
1:8, pp. 85, 87

Omni

1, p. 24
1:12, pp. 24, 188
1:12–13, pp. 86, 199
1:12–15, p. 35
1:13–14, pp. 188, 214
1:14, p. 44
1:14–19, p. 229
1:16–17, p. 214
1:17–18, p. 88
1:17–19, p. 188
1:19, p. 24
1:20–22, p. 189
1:21, pp. 99, 132
1:22, p. 98
1:25, p. 227
1:27–30, p. 86
1:30, p. 227

Words of Mormon

1, pp. 1, 306
1:1–5, p. 182
1:2–9, p. 224
1:3, p. 45
1:3–5, p. 223
1:3–7, p. 226
1:4, p. 233
1:4–7, p. 45
1:5, pp. 81, 228
1:7, p. 178
1:13, p. 24
1:15–16, p. 233
1:16–17, p. 1
1:17, p. 24
1:17–18, p. 240

1:18, p. 24
1:25, p. 24

Mosiah

1–6, pp. 45, 173, 283
1–25, p. 228
1–29, p. 1
1:2, p. 118
1:2–3, pp. 24, 189
1:2–4, pp. 163, 225
1:3–5, p. 236
1:4, pp. 163, 225
1:16, pp. 170, 279
2–5, p. 15
2–6, p. 24
2:3, p. 239
2:3–4, p. 201
2:5, pp. 201, 240
2:5–8, p. 317
2:13, p. 108
2:17, p. 174
2:20–21, p. 164
2:21–25, p. 309
2:28, p. 201
2:31, pp. 24, 189
2:36–37, pp. 83, 241
2:38, p. 1
2:38–39, p. 155
2:41, p. 241
3–5, p. 148
3:2, p. 233
3:2–27, p. 149
3:5, pp. 24, 70
3:5–6, p. 141
3:5–7, p. 70
3:5–10, pp. 133, 134
3:5–27, p. 147
3:7, pp. 24, 134, 141, 149, 221, 232
3:8, pp. 24, 137, 149, 318
3:10, pp. 24, 142
3:11, pp. 149, 156
3:13, p. 24
3:14, p. 167
3:15, p. 149
3:16, pp. 64, 149
3:17, pp. 101, 137
3:18, pp. 64, 149
3:18–19, p. 25
3:19, pp. 60, 94, 112, 231, 241
3:20, p. 1
3:24, p. 36

3:24–25, p. 1
4–5, p. 72
4:1–3, pp. 135, 243
4:2, pp. 149, 242
4:3–4, p. 242
4:8, p. 141
4:11, pp. 241, 243, 253
4:12, p. 112
4:14–15, p. 316
4:20, p. 243
4:26, pp. 240, 243
5:2, pp. 60, 245
5:2–5, p. 201
5:5–8, p. 137
5:5–12, p. 240
5:7, p. 60
5:7–8, p. 149
5:8, pp. 141, 143, 147
5:10–12, p. 173
5:11, p. 240
6:1, p. 240
6:3, p. 239
6:4, p. 65
6:6–7, p. 189
7:1–6, p. 24
7:1–8:21, p. 45
7:19–22, p. 46
7:21, p. 214
7:21–22, p. 164
7:26–27, p. 138
7:26–28, p. 3
7:33, p. 46
8:1–5, p. 229
8:3, p. 24
8:8, p. 99
8:8–9, p. 228
8:8–11, p. 132
8:9, p. 46
8:13, p. 291
8:20, p. 319
9, p. 86
9–10, p. 306
9–22, p. 45
9–24, p. 217
9:1, p. 217
9:9, p. 86
9:12, p. 85
10:5, p. 317
10:12–17, p. 160
10:16, p. 306
10:17, p. 160

PEARL OF GREAT PRICE

Moses

THE FOUNDATION FOR ANCIENT RESEARCH AND MORMON STUDIES

The Foundation for Ancient Research and Mormon Studies (FARMS) encourages and supports research and publication about the Book of Mormon: Another Testament of Jesus Christ and other ancient scriptures.

FARMS is a nonprofit, tax-exempt educational foundation affiliated with Brigham Young University. Its main research interests in the scriptures include ancient history, language, literature, culture, geography, politics, religion, and law. Although research on such subjects is of secondary importance when compared with the spiritual and eternal messages of the scriptures, solid scholarly research can supply certain kinds of useful information, even if only tentatively, concerning many significant and interesting questions about the ancient backgrounds, origins, composition, and meanings of scripture.

The work of the Foundation rests on the premise that the Book of Mormon and other scriptures were written by prophets of God. Belief in this premise—in the divinity of scripture—is a matter of faith. Religious truths require divine witness to establish the faith of the believer. While scholarly research cannot replace that witness, such studies may reinforce and encourage individual testimonies by fostering understanding and appreciation of the scriptures. It is hoped that this information will help people to "come unto Christ" (Jacob 1:7) and to understand and take more seriously these ancient witnesses of the atonement of Jesus Christ, the Son of God.

The Foundation works to make interim and final reports about its research available widely, promptly, and economically, both in scholarly and in popular formats. FARMS publishes information about the Book of Mormon and other ancient scripture in the *Insights* newsletter, books and research papers, *FARMS Review of Books, Journal of Book of Mormon Studies,* reprints of published scholarly papers, and videos and audiotapes. FARMS also supports the preparation of the Collected Works of Hugh Nibley.

To facilitate the sharing of information, FARMS sponsors lectures, seminars, symposia, firesides, and radio and television broadcasts in which research findings are communicated to working scholars and to anyone interested in faithful, reliable information about the scriptures. Through Research Press, a publishing arm of the Foundation, FARMS publishes materials addressed primarily to working scholars.

For more information about the Foundation and its activities, contact the FARMS office at 1-800-327-6715 or (801) 373-5111. You can also visit the FARMS website at http://farms@byu.edu.